Microsoft® Official Academic Course

Configuring Advanced Windows Server® 2012 R2 Services Exam 70-412

Patrick Regan

WILEY

VP & PUBLISHER	Don Fowley
EXECUTIVE EDITOR	John Kane
EXECUTIVE MARKETING MANAGER	Chris Ruel
MICROSOFT PRODUCT MANAGER	Natasha Chornesky of Microsoft Learning
EDITORIAL PROGRAM ASSISTANT	Jessy Lentz
TECHNICAL EDITOR	Brian Svidergol
ASSOCIATE MARKETING MANAGER	Debbie Martin
ASSOCIATE PRODUCTION MANAGER	Joyce Poh
COVER DESIGNER	Thomas Nery
SENIOR PRODUCT DESIGNER	Thomas Kulesa
CONTENT EDITOR	Wendy Ashenberg

This book was set in Garamond by Aptara, Inc.

ISBN 978-1-118-88299-3

The inside back cover will contain printing identification and country of origin if omitted from this page. In addition, if the ISBN on the back cover differs from the ISBN on this page, the one on the back cover is correct.

Printed in the United States of America

10 9 8 7 6 5

This page left intentionally blank.

Preface

Welcome to the Microsoft Official Academic Course (MOAC) program for becoming a Microsoft Certified Solutions Associate for Windows Server 2012 R2. MOAC represents the collaboration between Microsoft Learning and John Wiley & Sons, Inc. Microsoft and Wiley teamed up to produce a series of textbooks that deliver compelling and innovative teaching solutions to instructors and superior learning experiences for students. Infused and informed by in-depth knowledge from the creators of Windows Server 2012 R2, and crafted by a publisher known worldwide for the pedagogical quality of its products, these textbooks maximize skills transfer in minimum time. Students are challenged to reach their potential by using their new technical skills as highly productive members of the workforce.

Because this knowledgebase comes directly from Microsoft, architect of Windows Server 2012 R2 and creator of the Microsoft Certified Solutions Associate exams, you are sure to receive the topical coverage that is most relevant to students' personal and professional success. Microsoft's direct participation not only assures you that MOAC textbook content is accurate and current; it also means that students will receive the best instruction possible to enable their success on certification exams and in the workplace.

■ The Microsoft Official Academic Course Program

The Microsoft Official Academic Course series is a complete program for instructors and institutions to prepare and deliver great courses on Microsoft software technologies. With MOAC, we recognize that because of the rapid pace of change in the technology and curriculum developed by Microsoft, there is an ongoing set of needs beyond classroom instruction tools for an instructor to be ready to teach the course. The MOAC program endeavors to provide solutions for all these needs in a systematic manner in order to ensure a successful and rewarding course experience for both instructor and student—including technical and curriculum training for instructor readiness with new software releases; the software itself for student use at home for building hands-on skills, assessment, and validation of skill development; and a great set of tools for delivering instruction in the classroom and lab. All are important to the smooth delivery of an interesting course on Microsoft software, and all are provided with the MOAC program. We think about the model below as a gauge for ensuring that we completely support you in your goal of teaching a great course. As you evaluate your instructional materials options, you may wish to use the model for comparison purposes with available products.

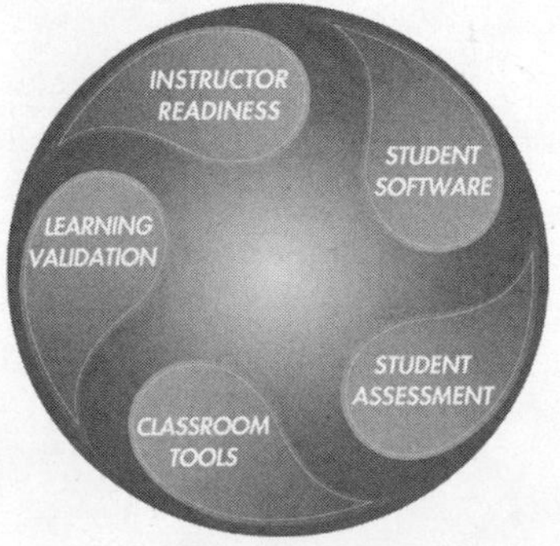

Illustrated Book Tour

■ Textbook Organization

This textbook is organized in twenty-one lessons, with each lesson corresponding to a particular exam objective for the 70-412 Configuring Advanced Windows Server 2012 Services exam. This MOAC textbook covers all the learning objectives for the 70-412 certification exam, which is the third of three exams needed in order to obtain a Microsoft Certified Solutions Associate (MCSA) certification. The exam objectives are highlighted throughout the textbook.

■ Pedagogical Features

Many pedagogical features have been developed specifically for Microsoft Official Academic Course programs.

Presenting the extensive procedural information and technical concepts woven throughout the textbook raises challenges for the student and instructor alike. The Illustrated Book Tour that follows provides a guide to the rich features contributing to Microsoft Official Academic Course program's pedagogical plan. Following is a list of key features in each lesson designed to prepare students for success on the certification exams and in the workplace:

- Each lesson begins with an overview of the skills covered in the lesson. More than a standard list of learning objectives, the overview correlates skills to the certification exam objective.
- Illustrations: Screen images provide visual feedback as students work through the exercises. The images reinforce key concepts, provide visual clues about the steps, and allow students to check their progress.
- Key Terms: Important technical vocabulary is listed at the beginning of the lesson. When these terms are used later in the lesson, they appear in bold italic type and are defined.
- Engaging point-of-use reader aids, located throughout the lessons, tell students why this topic is relevant (*The Bottom Line*), provide students with helpful hints (*Take Note*), or show cross-references to where content is covered in greater detail (*X Ref*). Reader aids also provide additional relevant or background information that adds value to the lesson.
- Certification Ready features throughout the text signal students where a specific certification objective is covered. They provide students with a chance to check their understanding of that particular exam objective and, if necessary, review the section of the lesson where it is covered.
- Using Windows PowerShell: ***Windows PowerShell*** is a Windows command-line shell that can be utilized with many Windows Server 2012 functions. The Using Windows PowerShell sidebar provides Windows PowerShell-based alternatives to graphical user interface (GUI) functions or procedures. These sidebars begin with a brief description of what the Windows PowerShell commands can do, and they contain any parameters needed to perform the task at hand. When needed, explanations are provided for the functions of individual parameters.

- Knowledge Assessments provide lesson-ending activities that test students' comprehension and retention of the material taught, presented using some of the question types that they'll see on the certification exam.
- An important supplement to this textbook is the accompanying lab work. Labs are available via a Lab Manual, and also by MOAC Labs Online. MOAC Labs Online provides students with the ability to work on the actual software simply by connecting through their Internet Explorer web browser. Either way, the labs use real-world scenarios to help students learn workplace skills associated with administering a Windows Server 2012 R2 infrastructure in an enterprise environment.

Lesson Features

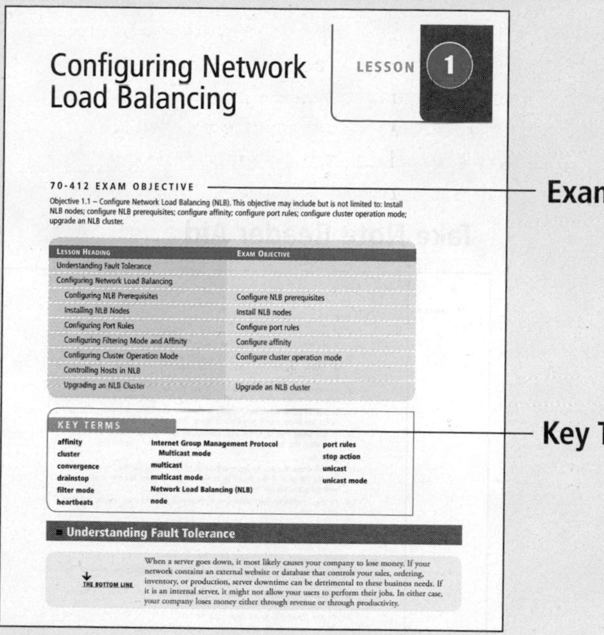

Configuring Network Load Balancing

LESSON 1

70-412 EXAM OBJECTIVE

Objective 1.1 – Configure Network Load Balancing (NLB). This objective may include but is not limited to: Install NLB nodes; configure NLB prerequisites; configure affinity; configure port rules; configure cluster operation mode; upgrade an NLB cluster.

Lesson Heading	Exam Objective
Understanding Fault Tolerance	
Configuring Network Load Balancing	
Configuring NLB Prerequisites	Configure NLB prerequisites
Installing NLB Nodes	Install NLB nodes
Configuring Port Rules	Configure port rules
Configuring Filtering Mode and Affinity	Configure affinity
Configuring Cluster Operation Mode	Configure cluster operation mode
Controlling Hosts in NLB	
Upgrading an NLB Cluster	Upgrade an NLB cluster

KEY TERMS

affinity	**Internet Group Management Protocol Multicast mode**	**port rules**
cluster	**multicast**	**stop action**
convergence	**multicast mode**	**unicast**
drainstop	**Network Load Balancing (NLB)**	**unicast mode**
filter mode	**node**	
heartbeats		

Understanding Fault Tolerance

THE BOTTOM LINE

When a server goes down, it most likely causes your company to lose money. If your network contains an external website or database that controls your sales, ordering, inventory, or production, server downtime can be detrimental to these business needs. If it is an internal server, it might not allow your users to perform their jobs. In either case, your company loses money either through revenue or through productivity.

Exam Objective

Key Terms

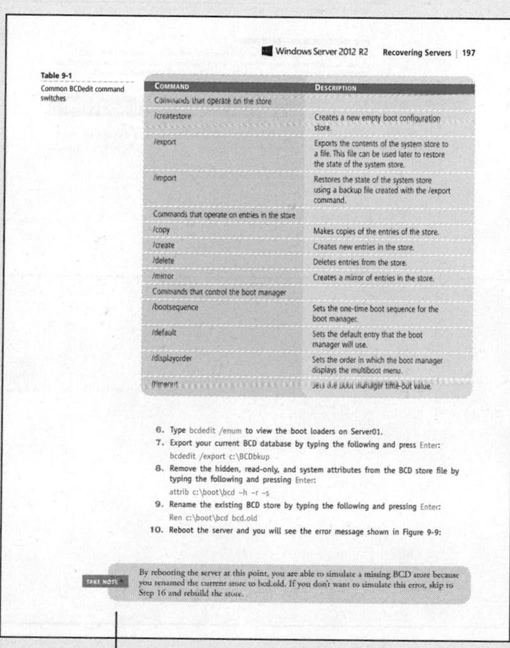

Windows Server 2012 R2 Recovering Servers | 197

Table 9-1
Common BCDedit command switches

Command	Description
Commands that operate on the store	
/createstore	Creates a new empty boot configuration store.
/export	Exports the contents of the system store to a file. This file can be used later to restore the state of the system store.
/import	Restores the state of the system store using a backup file created with the /export command.
Commands that operate on entries in the store	
/copy	Makes copies of the entries of the store.
/create	Creates new entries in the store.
/delete	Deletes entries from the store.
/mirror	Creates a mirror of entries in the store.
Commands that control the boot manager	
/bootsequence	Sets the one-time boot sequence for the boot manager.
/default	Sets the default entry that the boot manager will use.
/displayorder	Sets the order in which the boot manager displays the multiboot menu.
/timeout	Sets the boot manager time-out value.

6. Type bcdedit /enum to view the boot loaders on Server01.
7. Export your current BCD database by typing the following and press Enter:
   bcdedit /export c:\BCDbkup
8. Remove the hidden, read-only, and system attributes from the BCD store file by typing the following and pressing Enter:
   attrib c:\boot\bcd -h -r -s
9. Rename the existing BCD store by typing the following and pressing Enter:
   Ren c:\boot\bcd bcd.old
10. Reboot the server and you will see the error message shown in Figure 9-9:

TAKE NOTE* By rebooting the server at this point, you are able to simulate a missing BCD store because you renamed the current store to bcd.old. If you don't want to simulate this error, skip to Step 16 and rebuild the store.

Easy-to-Read Tables

Bottom Line Reader Aid

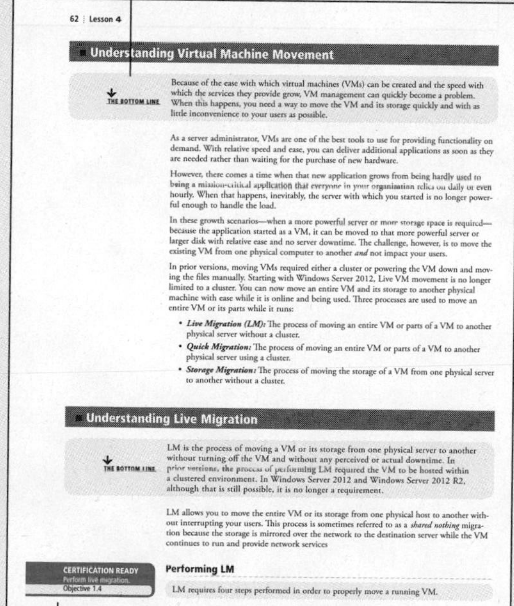

62 | Lesson 4

Understanding Virtual Machine Movement

THE BOTTOM LINE

Because of the ease with which virtual machines (VMs) can be created and the speed with which the services they provide grow, VM management can quickly become a problem. When this happens, you need a way to move the VM and its storage quickly and with as little inconvenience to your users as possible.

As a server administrator, VMs are one of the best tools to use for providing functionality on demand. With relative speed and ease, you can deliver additional applications as soon as they are needed rather than waiting for the purchase of new hardware.

However, there comes a time when that new application grows from being hardly used to being a mission-critical application that everyone in your organization relies on daily or even hourly. When that happens, inevitably, the server with which you started is no longer powerful enough to handle the load.

In these growth scenarios—when a more powerful server or more storage space is required—because the application started as a VM, it can be moved to that more powerful server or larger disk with relative ease and no server downtime. The challenge, however, is to move the existing VM from one physical computer to another *and* not impact your users.

In prior versions, moving VMs required either a cluster or powering the VM down and moving the files manually. Starting with Windows Server 2012, Live VM movement is no longer limited to a cluster. You can now move an entire VM and its storage to another physical machine with ease while it is online and being used. Three processes are used to move an entire VM or its parts while it runs:

- ***Live Migration (LM):*** The process of moving an entire VM or parts of a VM to another physical server without a cluster.
- ***Quick Migration:*** The process of moving an entire VM or parts of a VM to another physical server using a cluster.
- ***Storage Migration:*** The process of moving the storage of a VM from one physical server to another without a cluster.

Understanding Live Migration

THE BOTTOM LINE

LM is the process of moving a VM or its storage from one physical server to another without turning off the VM and without any perceived or actual downtime. In prior versions, the process of performing LM required the VM to be hosted within a clustered environment. In Windows Server 2012 and Windows Server 2012 R2, although that is still possible, it is no longer a requirement.

LM allows you to move the entire VM or its storage from one physical host to another without interrupting your users. This process is sometimes referred to as a *shared nothing* migration because the storage is mirrored over the network to the destination server while the VM continues to run and provide network services

CERTIFICATION READY
Perform live migration.
Objective 1.4

Performing LM

LM requires four steps performed in order to properly move a running VM.

Certification Ready Alert

78 | Lesson 4

- Enable a gigabit or greater network connection between the source computer and the VM host.
- Use dynamic virtual hard disks (VHDs) to conserve disk space on the destination host.
- For an online P2V conversion, ensure that all applications running on the source computer have VSS-aware writers or are stopped.
- For an offline P2V, ensure that any and all NIC and storage drivers are available on the VMM server.

CONVERTING PHYSICAL COMPUTERS TO VMS

With SCVMM, P2V conversions can be done either online or offline. You can perform an online P2V conversion if you cannot take the physical machine offline. This is the default action. Should you choose to do this, ensure that all critical applications running on the source computer have Volume Shadow Copy Service (VSS)-aware writers or that the applications have been stopped.

In an online P2V conversion, SCVMM creates a copy of the source NTFS volumes and data of VSS-aware applications. SCVMM uses the VSS to:

- Verify that data is reliably backed up while the source computer continues to service user requests.
- Create a VHD based on the read-only snapshot created.

An offline P2V conversion is the only way to ensure a consistent conversion. Also, it is the only way to migrate FAT volumes and domain controllers.

SCVMM restarts the source computer into Windows PE. Then it clones the volume(s) as a VHD and restarts the source computer.

MORE INFORMATION
Additional information on online versus offline conversion can be obtained from Microsoft's TechNet website.

More Information Reader Aid

P2V ANOTHER WAY—DISK2VHD

The Disk2vhd tool from the Microsoft Sysinternals website is another tool that will allow a physical machine to be converted to the older VHD format. Should you wish to convert the VHD to the VHDX format; a simple Windows PowerShell script will do the job.

Converting a Virtual Machine to Virtual Machine (V2V) Using SCVMM

THE BOTTOM LINE: In Hyper-V, there are no native functions that permit the conversion of a VM from another vendor to a native Hyper-V VM.

There are three formats which SCVMM can convert

- Citrix XenServer
- VMware ESX
- The Open Virtualization Format (OVF)

Take Note Reader Aid

74 | Lesson 4

7. If you selected the *Register* option, you are presented with the *Completing Import Wizard* box. Verify that your selections are correct, and then click Finish.
8. If you selected the *Restore* option, you are presented with the *Choose Folders for Virtual Machine Files* box. Select the Store the virtual machine in a different location checkbox.
9. In the *Virtual machine configuration folder* box, specify the path of the folder or browse to it and select the folder where you wish to place the current configuration.
10. In the *Snapshot store* box, specify the path of the folder or browse to it and select the folder where you wish to place the current configuration.
11. In the *Smart Paging Folder* box, specify the path of the folder or browse to it and select the folder where you wish to place the Smart Paging files.
12. Click Next.
13. On the *Chose Folders to Store Virtual Hard Disks* page, in the *Location:* box, specify the path of the folder or browse to it and select the folder where you wish to place the VM hard disk, and then click Next.
14. On the *Completing Move Wizard*, verify that your selections are correct, and then click Finish.

IMPORT A VIRTUAL MACHINE

GET READY. To import a VM, perform the following steps:

1. Open *Hyper-V Manager* and in the navigation pane, select the name of the source server.
2. In the *Actions s* section of *Hyper-V Manager*, click Import Virtual Machine. The *Import Virtual Machine Wizard* opens.
3. On the *Before You Begin* page, click Next.
4. On the *Locate Folder* page, specify the path of the folder or browse to it and select the folder of the exported VM, and then click Next.
5. On the *Select Virtual Machine* page, select the name of the VM to import, and then click Next.
6. On the *Choose Import Type* page, select Copy the virtual machine (create a new unique ID), and then click Next.

TAKE NOTE: When importing a VM multiple times, remember that the actual name of the VM will be the same as the exported VM in Hyper-V Manager. The VM name can be changed in Hyper-V Manager, but the file names should remain the same.

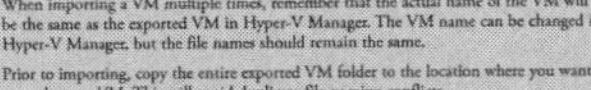

Prior to importing, copy the entire exported VM folder to the location where you want to store the new VM. This will avoid duplicate file naming conflicts.

7. In the *Choose Folders for Virtual Machine Files* box (see Figure 4-4), if you want to move the files from their current location, select the Store the virtual machine in a different location checkbox. Then, choose one of the following:
   - In the *Virtual machine configuration folder* box, specify the path of the folder or browse to it and select the folder where you wish to place the current configuration.
   - In the *Snapshot store* box, specify the path of the folder or browse to it and select the folder where you wish to place the current configuration.

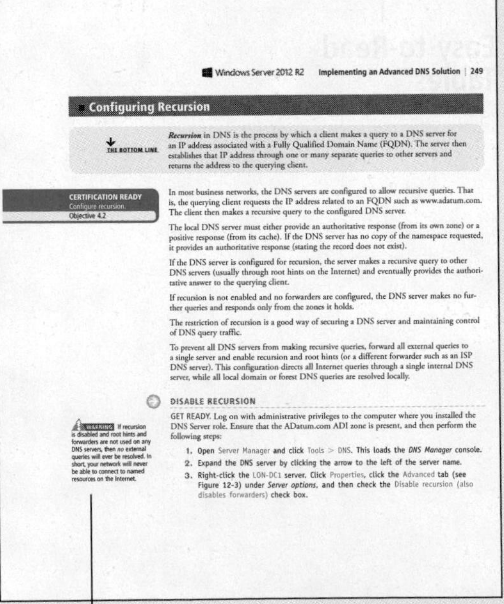

Windows Server 2012 R2 Implementing an Advanced DNS Solution | 249

Configuring Recursion

THE BOTTOM LINE: *Recursion* in DNS is the process by which a client makes a query to a DNS server for an IP address associated with a Fully Qualified Domain Name (FQDN). The server then establishes that IP address through one or many separate queries to other servers and returns the address to the querying client.

CERTIFICATION READY
Configure recursion.
Objective 4.2

In most business networks, the DNS servers are configured to allow recursive queries. That is, the querying client requests the IP address related to an FQDN such as www.adatum.com. The client then makes a recursive query to the configured DNS server.

The local DNS server must either provide an authoritative response (from its own zone) or a positive response (from its cache). If the DNS server has no copy of the namespace requested, it provides an authoritative response (stating the record does not exist).

If the DNS server is configured for recursion, the server makes a recursive query to other DNS servers (usually through root hints on the Internet) and eventually provides the authoritative answer to the querying client.

If recursion is not enabled and no forwarders are configured, the DNS server makes no further queries and responds only from the zones it holds.

The restriction of recursion is a good way of securing a DNS server and maintaining control of DNS query traffic.

To prevent all DNS servers from making recursive queries, forward all external queries to a single server and enable recursion and root hints (or a different forwarder such as an ISP DNS server). This configuration directs all Internet queries through a single internal DNS server, while all local domain or forest DNS queries are resolved locally.

DISABLE RECURSION

WARNING: If recursion is disabled and root hints and forwarders are not used on any DNS servers, then no external queries will ever be resolved. In short, your network will never be able to connect to named resources on the Internet.

GET READY. Log on with administrative privileges to the computer where you installed the DNS Server role. Ensure that the ADatum.com ADI zone is present, and then perform the following steps:

1. Open Server Manager and click Tools > DNS. This loads the *DNS Manager* console.
2. Expand the DNS server by clicking the arrow to the left of the server name.
3. Right-click the LON-DC1 server. Click Properties, click the Advanced tab (see Figure 12-3) under *Server options*, and then check the Disable recursion (also disables forwarders) check box.

Warning Reader Aid

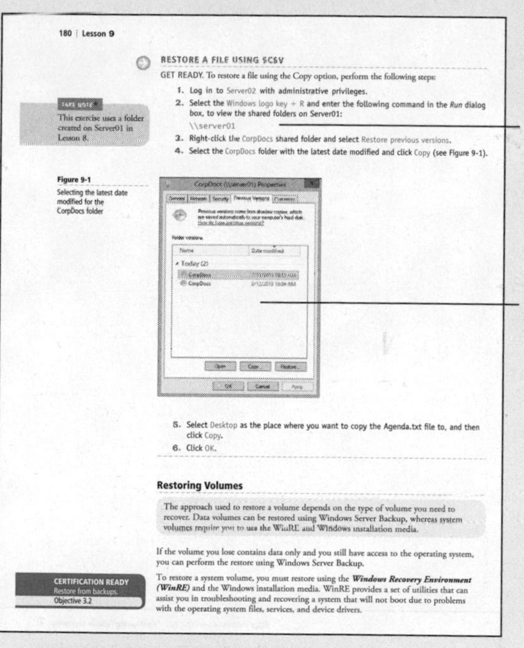

180 | Lesson 9

RESTORE A FILE USING SCSV

GET READY. To restore a file using the Copy option, perform the following steps:

TAKE NOTE* This exercise uses a folder created on Server01 in Lesson 8.

1. Log in to Server02 with administrative privileges.
2. Select the Windows logo key + R and enter the following command in the *Run* dialog box, to view the shared folders on Server01:

```
\\server01
```

3. Right-click the CorpDocs shared folder and select Restore previous versions.
4. Select the CorpDocs folder with the latest date modified and click Copy (see Figure 9-1).

Figure 9-1
Selecting the latest date modified for the CorpDocs folder

5. Select Desktop as the place where you want to copy the Agenda.txt file to, and then click Copy.
6. Click OK.

Restoring Volumes

The approach used to restore a volume depends on the type of volume you need to recover. Data volumes can be restored using Windows Server Backup, whereas system volumes require you to use the WinRE and Windows installation media.

If the volume you lose contains data only and you still have access to the operating system, you can perform the restore using Windows Server Backup.

CERTIFICATION READY
Restore from backups.
Objective 3.2

To restore a system volume, you must restore using the ***Windows Recovery Environment (WinRE)*** and the Windows installation media. WinRE provides a set of utilities that can assist you in troubleshooting and recovering a system that will not boot due to problems with the operating system files, services, and device drivers.

Step-by-Step Exercises

Screen Images

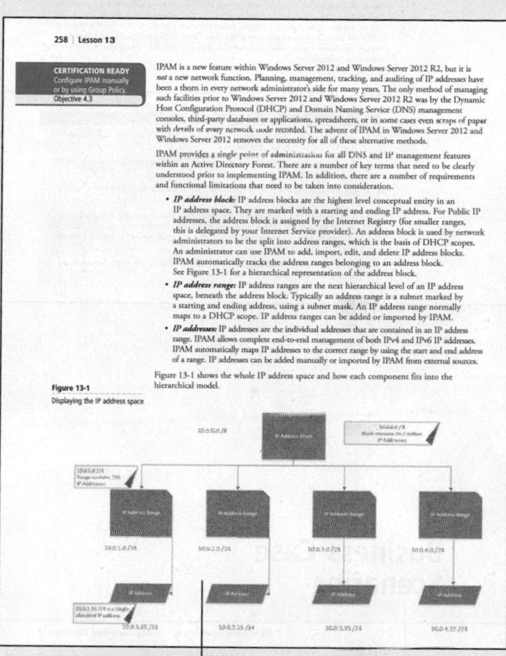

258 | Lesson 13

CERTIFICATION READY
Configure IPAM manually or by using Group Policy.
Objective 4.3

IPAM is a new feature within Windows Server 2012 and Windows Server 2012 R2, but it is *not* a new network function. Planning, management, tracking, and auditing of IP addresses have been a thorn in every network administrator's side for many years. The only method of managing such facilities prior to Windows Server 2012 and Windows Server 2012 R2 was by the Dynamic Host Configuration Protocol (DHCP) and Domain Naming Service (DNS) management consoles, third-party databases or applications, spreadsheets, or in some cases even scraps of paper with details of every network node recorded. The advent of IPAM in Windows Server 2012 and Windows Server 2012 removes the necessity for all of these alternative methods.

IPAM provides a single point of administration for all DNS and IP management features within an Active Directory Forest. There are a number of key terms that need to be clearly understood prior to implementing IPAM. In addition, there are a number of requirements and functional limitations that need to be taken into consideration.

- ***IP address block:*** IP address blocks are the highest level conceptual entity in an IP address space. They are marked with a starting and ending IP address. For Public IP addresses, the address block is assigned by the Internet Registry (for smaller ranges, this is delegated by your Internet Service provider). An address block is used by network administrators to be the split into address ranges, which is the basis of DHCP scopes. An administrator can use IPAM to add, import, edit, and delete IP address blocks. IPAM automatically tracks the address ranges belonging to an address block. See Figure 13-1 for a hierarchical representation of the address block.
- ***IP address range:*** IP address ranges are the next hierarchical level of an IP address space, beneath the address block. Typically an address range is a subnet marked by a starting and ending address, using a subnet mask. An IP address range normally maps to a DHCP scope. IP address ranges can be added or imported by IPAM.
- ***IP addresses:*** IP addresses are the individual addresses that are contained in an IP address range. IPAM allows complete end-to-end management of both IPv4 and IPv6 IP addresses. IPAM automatically maps IP addresses to the correct range by using the start and end address of a range. IP addresses can be added manually or imported by IPAM from external sources.

Figure 13-1 shows the whole IP address space and how each component fits into the hierarchical model.

Figure 13-1
Displaying the IP address space

Informative Diagrams

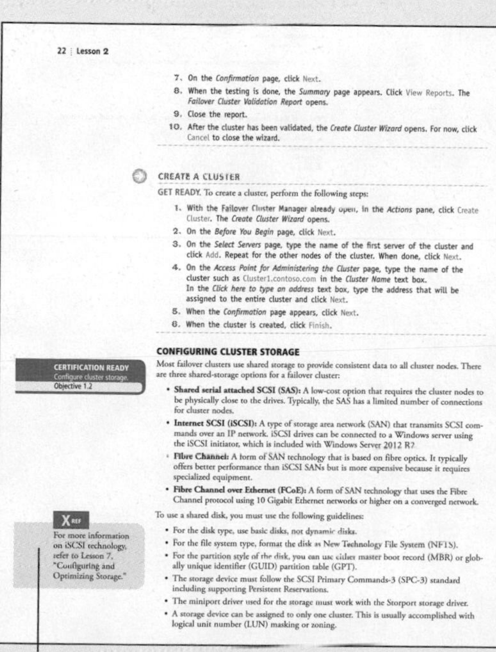

22 | Lesson 2

7. On the *Confirmation* page, click Next.
8. When the testing is done, the *Summary* page appears. Click View Reports. The *Failover Cluster Validation Report* opens.
9. Close the report.
10. After the cluster has been validated, the *Create Cluster Wizard* opens. For now, click Cancel to close the wizard.

CREATE A CLUSTER

GET READY. To create a cluster, perform the following steps:

1. With the Failover Cluster Manager already open, in the *Actions* pane, click Create Cluster. The *Create Cluster Wizard* opens.
2. On the *Before You Begin* page, click Next.
3. On the *Select Servers* page, type the name of the first server of the cluster and click Add. Repeat for the other nodes of the cluster. When done, click Next.
4. On the *Access Point for Administering the Cluster* page, type the name of the cluster such as Cluster1.contoso.com in the *Cluster Name* text box.
   In the *Click here to type an address* text box, type the address that will be assigned to the entire cluster and click Next.
5. When the *Confirmation* page appears, click Next.
6. When the cluster is created, click Finish.

CONFIGURING CLUSTER STORAGE

CERTIFICATION READY
Configure cluster storage.
Objective 1.2

Most failover clusters use shared storage to provide consistent data to all cluster nodes. There are three shared-storage options for a failover cluster:

- **Shared serial attached SCSI (SAS):** A low-cost option that requires the cluster nodes to be physically close to the drives. Typically, the SAS has a limited number of connections for cluster nodes.
- **Internet SCSI (iSCSI):** A type of storage area network (SAN) that transmits SCSI commands over an IP network. iSCSI drives can be connected to a Windows server using the iSCSI initiator, which is included with Windows Server 2012 R2.
- **Fibre Channel:** A form of SAN technology that is based on fibre optics. It typically offers better performance than iSCSI SANs but is more expensive because it requires specialized equipment.
- **Fibre Channel over Ethernet (FCoE):** A form of SAN technology that uses the Fibre Channel protocol using 10 Gigabit Ethernet networks or higher on a converged network.

X REF
For more information on iSCSI technology, refer to Lesson 7, "Configuring and Optimizing Storage."

To use a shared disk, you must use the following guidelines:

- For the disk type, use basic disks, not dynamic disks.
- For the file system type, format the disk as New Technology File System (NTFS).
- For the partition style of the disk, you can use either master boot record (MBR) or globally unique identifier (GUID) partition table (GPT).
- The storage device must follow the SCSI Primary Commands-3 (SPC-3) standard including supporting Persistent Reservations.
- The miniport driver used for the storage must work with the Storport storage driver.
- A storage device can be assigned to only one cluster. This is usually accomplished with logical unit number (LUN) masking or zoning.

X Ref Reader Aid

40 | Lesson 2

replicates the configuration to the witness disk. Therefore, be sure to back up the System State, Cluster folders, and the witness disk.

You still have to back up the individual applications running the server and the associated data such as SQL databases, Exchange databases, or shared files. To back up application data, you can install backup software on the cluster node that owns the disk resource, or you can run the backup against the clustered resource over the network. If you use CSV volumes, you can run backup from any node that is attached to the CSV volume.

To restore the cluster, you can perform one of the two types of restores:

- ***Non-authoritative restore:*** A type of restore that restores the information that was performed when originally backed up but is overwritten by current information stored on other cluster nodes.
- ***Authoritative restore:*** A type of restore that restores the information that was performed when originally backed up but is marked as the current and authoritative configuration, which will then overwrite the configuration on the other nodes.

If you have a single cluster node that has failed, you can perform the non-authoritative restore. After fixing or replacing the failed node, perform a non-authoritative restore including the system state. When you restart the node, the restored node will join the cluster and automatically receive the latest cluster configuration from the other nodes or the witness disk.

Alternatively, you can remove a node and add a new node to the cluster. The new node will automatically receive the cluster information.

If an administrator accidently removed clustered resources or modified other cluster settings and you need to restore the cluster back to a specific point in time before the changes were made, you will perform an authoritative restore. To perform an authoritative restore, you will need to stop the cluster restores on all nodes. You then perform a system state recovery on a single node. After the restore, restart the cluster service so that the cluster service will mark the current configuration as the most recent configuration. As you bring the remaining cluster nodes online and start the cluster service, the other nodes will receive the restored configuration.

SKILL SUMMARY

Skill Summary

IN THIS LESSON YOU LEARNED:

- A failover cluster is a set of independent computers that work together to increase the availability of services and applications.
- The clustered servers (called nodes) are connected through a network connection (physical or virtual) and by software.
- Failover clustering is best suited for stateful applications that are derived from a single set of data.
- A cluster resource is the most basic and smallest configurable unit that can provide a service to clients, or is important component that makes up the cluster. It can be a network application server or hardware device, such as a storage device, that is defined and managed by the cluster server.
- Cluster storage is a storage system that is shared between cluster nodes and usually connects using Fibre Channel or iSCSI.

Windows Server 2012 R2 Configuring Failover Clustering | 41

- Initially installing a failover cluster is a three-step process: install the Failover Clustering feature, validate the cluster configuration, and create the cluster.
- Before you add storage to a cluster, be sure that all nodes can see the storage device and that the storage device has been initialized, partitioned, and formatted, and that the same drive letter is assigned to the storage device on all nodes.
- Traditionally, a single node controls a LUN on the shared storage. However, starting with Windows Server 2008 R2, Windows can use a Cluster Shared Volume (CSV), which allows multiple nodes to share a single LUN concurrently.
- A quorum is used with a failover cluster to determine the number of failures that the cluster can sustain. If a quorum (the majority of the votes) is not reached, the cluster will stop running.
- With Windows Server 2012 R2, you can deploy clustered storage spaces by using Storage Spaces and Failover Clustering to provide a resilient, highly available, and cost efficient solution.
- Windows Server 2012 R2 introduced Active Directory-detached cluster, which allows you to deploy a failover cluster without any dependencies in Active Directory Domain Services (AD DS) for network names.
- The Failover Cluster Manager manages and monitors the cluster and its nodes.
- Cluster-Aware Updating (CAU) lets administrators update cluster nodes automatically, with little or no downtime, particularly if you use Hyper-V with live migration.
- You can back up the cluster configuration and restore using Windows Server Backup or a non-Microsoft Backup tool.

Knowledge Assessment

Knowledge Assessment

Multiple Choice

Select the correct answer for each of the following questions.

1. Which type of clustering is used for back-end databases?
   a. Network Load Balancing (NLB) cluster
   b. failover cluster
   c. aggregated cluster
   d. power cluster
2. What is the maximum number of nodes you can have in a single cluster?
   a. 2
   b. 8
   c. 32
   d. 64
3. Which of the following can networks can you use in a Windows failover cluster? (Choose all that apply.)
   a. public-and-private
   b. private
   c. public
   d. central

Business Case Scenarios

Windows Server 2012 R2 Configuring Failover Clustering | 45

2. Identify the basic steps necessary to upgrade a cluster to Windows Server 2012 R2 by placing the number of the step in the appropriate space.
   _______ Create a one-node failover cluster
   _______ Evict the node from a cluster
   _______ Remove the last node from the cluster and install Windows Server 2012 R2
   _______ Perform a clean installation of Windows Server 2012 R2
   _______ Add second node to new cluster
   _______ Remove resources from one node
   _______ Migrate the clustered services and applications from the old cluster node to that failover cluster

Business Case Scenarios

Scenario 2-1: Configuring a Redundant Server

You work for the Contoso Corporation. You have a server that acts as a file server for clients. You must make sure that the server is up at all times. What would you recommend?

Scenario 2-2: Upgrading a Cluster to Windows Server 2012 R2

You work for the Contoso Corporation. You have a cluster used as a file server that is running Windows Server 2008 R2. You do not have any other free servers. How would you upgrade the cluster to Windows Server 2012 R2?

Conventions and Features Used in This Book

This book uses particular fonts, symbols, and heading conventions to highlight important information or to call your attention to special steps. For more information about the features in each lesson, refer to the Illustrated Book Tour section.

CONVENTION	MEANING
THE BOTTOM LINE	This feature provides a brief summary of the material to be covered in the section that follows.
CERTIFICATION READY	This feature signals the point in the text where a specific certification objective is covered. It provides you with a chance to check your understanding of that particular exam objective and, if necessary, review the section of the lesson where it is covered.
TAKE NOTE* MORE INFORMATION	Reader aids appear in shaded boxes found in your text. *Take Note* and *More Information* provide helpful hints related to particular tasks or topics.
USING WINDOWS POWERSHELL	The Using Windows PowerShell sidebar provides Windows PowerShell-based alternatives to graphical user interface (GUI) functions or procedures.
WARNING	*Warning* points out instances when error or misuse could cause damage to the computer or network.
X REF	These *X Ref* notes provide pointers to information discussed elsewhere in the textbook or describe interesting features of Windows Server that are not directly addressed in the current topic or exercise.
A ***shared printer*** can be used by many individuals on a network.	Key terms appear in bold italic.
`[cd\windows\system32\ServerMigrationTools]`	Commands that are to be typed are shown in a special font.
Click Install Now.	Any button on the screen you are supposed to click on or select will appear in blue.

Instructor Support Program

The Microsoft Official Academic Course programs are accompanied by a rich array of resources that incorporate the extensive textbook visuals to form a pedagogically cohesive package. These resources provide all the materials instructors need to deploy and deliver their courses. Resource information available at www.wiley.com/college/microsoft includes:

- **Instructor's Guide.** The Instructor's Guide contains solutions to all the textbook exercises as well as chapter summaries and lecture notes. The Instructor's Guide and Syllabi for various term lengths are available from the Instructor's Book Companion site.
- **Test Bank.** The Test Bank contains hundreds of questions organized by lesson in multiple-choice, best answer, build a list, and essay formats and is available to download from the Instructor's Book Companion site. A complete answer key is provided.
- **PowerPoint Presentations.** A complete set of PowerPoint presentations is available on the Instructor's Book Companion site to enhance classroom presentations. Tailored to the text's topical coverage, these presentations are designed to convey key Windows Server 2012 R2 concepts addressed in the text.
- **Available Textbook Figures.** All figures from the text are on the Instructor's Book Companion site. By using these visuals in class discussions, you can help focus students' attention on key elements of Windows Server and help them understand how to use it effectively in the workplace.
- **MOAC Labs Online.** MOAC Labs Online is a cloud-based environment that enables students to conduct exercises using real Microsoft products. These are not simulations but instead are live virtual machines where faculty and students can perform any activities they would on a local virtual machine. MOAC Labs Online relieves the need for local setup, configuration, and most troubleshooting tasks. This represents an opportunity to lower costs, eliminate the hassle of lab setup, and support and improve student access and portability. Contact your Wiley rep about including MOAC Labs Online with your course offering.
- **Lab Answer Keys.** Answer keys for review questions found in the lab manuals and MOAC Labs Online are available on the Instructor's Book Companion site.
- **Lab Worksheets.** The review questions found in the lab manuals and MOAC Labs Online are gathered in Microsoft Word documents for students to use. These are available on the Instructor's Book Companion site.

This page left intentionally blank.

Student Support Program

Book Companion Website (www.wiley.com/college/microsoft)

The students' book companion site for the MOAC series includes any resources, exercise files, and web links that will be used in conjunction with this course.

■ Microsoft Certification

Microsoft Certification has many benefits and enables you to keep your skills relevant, applicable, and competitive. In addition, Microsoft Certification is an industry standard that is recognized worldwide—which helps open doors to potential job opportunities. After you earn your Microsoft Certification, you have access to a number of benefits, which can be found on the Microsoft Certified Professional member site.

Microsoft Learning has reinvented the Microsoft Certification Program by building cloud-related skills validation into the industry's most recognized certification program. Microsoft Certified Solutions Expert (MCSE) and Microsoft Certified Solutions Developer (MCSD) are Microsoft's flagship certifications for professionals who want to lead their IT organization's journey to the cloud. These certifications recognize IT professionals with broad and deep skill sets across Microsoft solutions. The Microsoft Certified Solutions Associate (MCSA) is the certification for aspiring IT professionals and is also the prerequisite certification necessary to earn an MCSE. These new certifications integrate cloud-related and on-premise skills validation in order to support organizations and recognize individuals who have the skills required to be productive using Microsoft technologies.

On-premise or in the cloud, Microsoft training and certification empowers technology professionals to expand their skills and gain knowledge directly from the source. Securing these essential skills will allow you to grow your career and make yourself indispensable as the industry shifts to the cloud. Cloud computing ultimately enables IT to focus on more mission-critical activities, raising the bar of required expertise for IT professionals and developers. These reinvented certifications test on a deeper set of skills that map to real-world business context. Rather than testing only on a feature of a technology, Microsoft Certifications now validate more advanced skills and a deeper understanding of the platform.

Microsoft Certified Solutions Associate (MCSA)

The Microsoft Certified Solutions Associate (MCSA) certification is for students preparing to get their first jobs in Microsoft technology. Whether in the cloud or on-premise, this certification validates the core platform skills needed in an IT environment. The MCSA certifications are a requirement to achieve Microsoft's flagship

Microsoft Certified Solutions Expert (MCSE) and Microsoft Certified Solutions Developer (MCSD) certifications.

The MCSA Windows Server 2012 certification shows that you have the primary set of Windows Server skills that are relevant across multiple solution areas in a business environment. The MCSA Windows Server 2012 certification is a prerequisite for earning the MCSE Server Infrastructure certification, the MCSE Desktop Infrastructure certification, or the MCSE Private Cloud certification.

Exam 70-412, Configuring Advanced Windows Server 2012 Services, is part three of a series of three exams that validate the skills and knowledge necessary to administer a Windows Server 2012 R2 Infrastructure in an enterprise environment. This exam will validate the advanced configuring tasks necessary to deploy, manage, and maintain a Windows Server 2012 R2 infrastructure, such as fault tolerance, certificate services, and identity federation. This exam along with the other two exams will collectively validate the skills and knowledge necessary for implementing, managing, maintaining, and provisioning services and infrastructure in a Windows Server 2012 R2 environment.

If you are a student new to IT who may not yet be ready for MCSA, the Microsoft Technology Associate (MTA) certification is an optional starting point that may be available through your school.

You can learn more about the MCSA certification at the Microsoft Training & Certification website.

Preparing to Take an Exam

Unless you are a very experienced user, you will need to use test preparation materials to prepare to complete the test correctly and within the time allowed. The Microsoft Official Academic Course series is designed to prepare you with a strong knowledge of all exam topics, and with some additional review and practice on your own, you should feel confident in your ability to pass the appropriate exam.

After you decide which exam to take, review the list of objectives for the exam. You can easily identify tasks that are included in the objective list by locating the exam objective overview at the start of each lesson and the Certification Ready sidebars in the margin of the lessons in this book.

To register for the 70-412 exam, visit the Microsoft Training & Certifications Registration webpage for directions on how to register. Keep in mind these important items about the testing procedure:

- **What to expect.** Microsoft Certification testing labs typically have multiple workstations, which may or may not be occupied by other candidates. Test center administrators strive to provide a quiet and comfortable environment for all test takers.
- **Plan to arrive early.** It is recommended that you arrive at the test center at least 30 minutes before the test is scheduled to begin.
- **Bring your identification.** To take your exam, you must bring the identification (ID) that was specified when you registered for the exam. If you are unclear about which forms of ID are required, contact the exam sponsor identified in your registration information. Although requirements vary, you typically must show two valid forms of ID, one with a photo, both with your signature.

- **Leave personal items at home.** The only item allowed into the testing area is your identification, so leave any backpacks, laptops, briefcases, and other personal items at home. If you have items that cannot be left behind (such as purses), the testing center might have small lockers available for use.
- **Nondisclosure agreement.** At the testing center, Microsoft requires that you accept the terms of a nondisclosure agreement (NDA) and complete a brief demographic survey before taking your certification exam.

About the Author

Patrick Regan has been a PC technician, network administrator/engineer, design architect, and security analyst for the past 23 years since graduating with a bachelor's degree in physics from the University of Akron. He has taught many computer and network classes at Sacramento local colleges (Heald Colleges and MTI Colleges) and participated in and led many projects (Heald Colleges, Intel Corporation, Miles Consulting Corporation, and Pacific Coast Companies). For his teaching accomplishments, he received the Teacher of the Year award from Heald Colleges and he has received several recognition awards from Intel. Previously, he worked as a product support engineer for the Intel Corporation Customer Service, a senior network engineer for Virtual Alert supporting the BioTerrorism Readiness suite and as a senior design architect/engineer and training coordinator for Miles Consulting Corporation (MCC), a premiere Microsoft Gold partner and consulting firm. He is currently a senior network engineer and consultant supporting a large enterprise network at Pacific Coast Companies, which is also a Microsoft Gold Partner and consulting firm. As a senior system administrator, he supports approximately 120 servers and 1,500 users spread over 5 subsidiaries and 70 sites. He has designed, implemented, and managed systems running Exchange Server 2010, SharePoint 2010, and SQL Server 2008 R2. To manage the servers and client computers, Pat and his team use group policies, SCOM, SCCM, and Symantec server.

He has earned several certifications, including Microsoft's MCSE, MCSA, and MCT; CompTIA's A+, Network+, Server+, Linux+, and Security+; Cisco's CCNA; and Novell's CNE and CWNP Certified Wireless Network Administrator (CWNA). Over the past several years, he has written several textbooks for Prentice Hall, including Troubleshooting the PC, Networking with Windows 2000 and 2003, Linux, Local Area Networks, Wide Area Networks, and the Acing Series (Acing the A+, Acing the Network+, Acing the Security+, and Acing the Linux+). For Que Publishing he has written several Exam Cram books for Windows Server 2008 certification tracks. For Wiley Publishing, he has written books on SharePoint 2010, Windows 7, and Window Server 2012.

Acknowledgements

We thank the MOAC faculty and instructors who have assisted us in building the Microsoft Official Academic Course courseware. These elite educators have acted as our sounding board on key pedagogical and design decisions leading to the development of the MOAC courseware for future Information Technology workers. They have provided invaluable advice in the service of quality instructional materials, and we truly appreciate their dedication to technology education.

Brian Bridson, Baker College of Flint

David Chaulk, Baker College Online

Ron Handlon, Remington College – Tampa Campus

Katherine James, Seneca College of Applied Arts & Technology

Wen Liu, ITT Educational Services

Zeshan Sattar, Pearson in Practice

Jared Spencer, Westwood College Online

David Vallerga, MTI College

Bonny Willy, Ivy Tech State College

We also thank Microsoft Learning's Tim Sneath, Keith Loeber, Natasha Chornesky, Wendy Johnson, Brian Swan, Briana Roberts, Jim Clark, Anne Hamilton, Shelby Grieve, Erika Cravens, Paul Schmitt, Jim Cochran, Julia Stasio, and Heidi Johnson for their encouragement and support in making the Microsoft Official Academic Course programs the finest academic materials for mastering the newest Microsoft technologies for both students and instructors.

Brief Contents

Contents

Configuring Network Load Balancing

LESSON 1

70-412 EXAM OBJECTIVE

Objective 1.1 – Configure Network Load Balancing (NLB). This objective may include but is not limited to: Install NLB nodes; configure NLB prerequisites; configure affinity; configure port rules; configure cluster operation mode; upgrade an NLB cluster.

LESSON HEADING	EXAM OBJECTIVE
Understanding Fault Tolerance	
Configuring Network Load Balancing	
Configuring NLB Prerequisites	Configure NLB prerequisites
Installing NLB Nodes	Install NLB nodes
Configuring Port Rules	Configure port rules
Configuring Filtering Mode and Affinity	Configure affinity
Configuring Cluster Operation Mode	Configure cluster operation mode
Controlling Hosts in NLB	
Upgrading an NLB Cluster	Upgrade an NLB cluster

KEY TERMS

affinity
cluster
convergence
drainstop
filter mode
heartbeats
Internet Group Management Protocol Multicast mode
multicast
multicast mode
Network Load Balancing (NLB)
node
port rules
stop action
unicast
unicast mode

■ Understanding Fault Tolerance

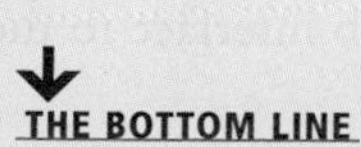

When a server goes down, it most likely causes your company to lose money. If your network contains an external website or database that controls your sales, ordering, inventory, or production, server downtime can be detrimental to these business needs. If it is an internal server, it might not allow your users to perform their jobs. In either case, your company loses money either through revenue or through productivity.

As a server administrator, you need to minimize downtime by identifying potential failures and taking steps to avoid those failures and to reduce their effects. High availability is a combination of technology, protocols, and redundant hardware that ensures a certain degree of operational continuity during a given measurement period while resisting disaster and failure. Generally, the term *downtime* is used to refer to periods when a system is unavailable. Availability is usually expressed as a percentage of uptime in a given year as shown in Table 1-1.

Table 1-1

Availability Guidelines

AVAILABILITY %	DOWNTIME PER YEAR	DOWNTIME PER MONTH
99%	3.65 days	7.20 hours
99.9% ("three nines")	8.76 hours	43.8 minutes
99.99% ("four nines")	52.6 minutes	4.32 minutes
99.999% ("five nines")	5.26 minutes	25.9 seconds
99.9999% ("six nines")	31.5 seconds	2.59 seconds

When designing servers and the services they provide, they are often assigned service level agreements (SLA), which state the level of availability those servers or services must maintain. Of course, to have a server design that can support five or six nines is much more expensive than supporting an availability of 99%.

If there is miscommunication about service-level expectations between the customer and the IT department, poor business decisions, unsuitable investment, levels, and customer dissatisfaction is likely to occur. Therefore, you need to express availability requirements clearly so that there are no misunderstandings about the implications.

To make a server more fault tolerant, you should first look at what components are the most likely to fail and implement technology to make a system less likely to fail. Some of the components that are made redundant within a system are usually the following:

- **Disks:** Use some form of RAID and hot spares.
- **Power supplies:** Use redundant power supplies.
- **Network cards:** Use redundant network cards.

Although you can make these components fault tolerant, the entire server still won't be fault tolerant. Instead, you can use a cluster to provide server redundancy.

A ***cluster*** is a group of linked computers that work together as one computer. Based on the technology used, clusters can provide fault tolerance (often referred to as *availability*), load balancing, or both. If the system fails, including the processor, memory, or motherboard, a cluster that provides fault tolerance can still service requests.

The two most popular forms of clusters are failover clusters and load-balancing clusters. Common uses of clusters include:

- A load-balancing cluster for the front end that provides the web interface to the back-end servers.
- A failover cluster for back-end servers such as a database (such as SQL Server) or mail server (such as Exchange Server).

Configuring Network Load Balancing

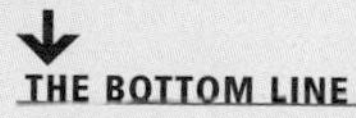

THE BOTTOM LINE

Network Load Balancing (NLB) transparently distributes traffic across multiple servers by using virtual IP addresses and a shared name. With NLB, you gain fault tolerance and enhanced performance. It is often used with mission-critical web servers but can also be found with other types of servers.

A cluster has two or more servers, known as nodes. Each ***node*** runs a separate copy of the desired service application such as a web server, an FTP server, or a Secure Shell (SSH) / Remote Desktop Server. NLB is a scalable, high availability feature found in Windows Server 2012 and Windows Server 2012 R2. It is considered scalable because you add additional servers to meet increasing demand.

Windows Sever 2012 NLB clusters can have between 2 and 32 nodes. When you create an NLB cluster, you create a virtual network address and adapter that is assigned to the entire cluster. As network requests are sent to the virtual network address, the requests are distributed across the nodes in the cluster. Based on your needs, you can configure the cluster to even out the requests or you can configure one node to be preferred over another node.

All hosts in the NLB cluster receive the incoming traffic. However, only one node in the cluster accepts the traffic and the other nodes drop the traffic. The node that accepts the traffic is determined by the configuration of port rules and affinity settings, which is configured later in this lesson.

If a node fails, the node will no longer be able to accept requests. However, no service is lost because the other nodes are available to accept the request. When the node comes back online, it will start accepting requests and the traffic will be distributed among the nodes.

NLB can detect the failure of cluster nodes by sending packets known as ***heartbeats***. NLB cluster heartbeats are transmitted every second between nodes in the cluster. If a node misses five consecutive heartbeats, the node is automatically removed from the NLB cluster.

When a node is added or removed from a cluster, a process known as ***convergence*** occurs, in which the cluster determines its current configuration by building a membership of nodes and mapping clients requests based on the available nodes. Convergence can occur only if each node is configured with the same port rules.

Configuring NLB Prerequisites

Although editions of Windows Server 2012 R2 support NLB and NLB supports running different editions of Windows Server 2012 R2, it is best practice to use computers with similar hardware specifications that run the same version and edition of the Windows Server 2012 R2 operating system. However, if you are mixing Windows Server 2012 and Windows Server 2012 R2, you will need to manage the cluster from Windows Server 2012 R2 or administrative tools for Windows Server 2012 R2.

CERTIFICATION READY
Configure NLB prerequisites.
Objective 1.1

To support NLB, your systems must use the following requirements:

- All hosts in the cluster must reside on the same subnet.
- Within each cluster, all network adapters must be either multicast or unicast. You cannot have some nodes configured as multicast while other nodes are configured as unicast within a single cluster. We discuss multicast and unicast configuration later in the lesson.
- If unicast mode is used, the network adapter that is used to handle client-to-cluster traffic must support changing its media access control (MAC) address.
- The IP addresses assigned to the nodes must be static.

Although hosts can span multiple geographical areas, to achieve convergence successfully, the latency between nodes cannot exceed 250 milliseconds. If you need geographical dispersed NLB clusters, you should deploy an NLB cluster at each site and then use Domain Name System (DNS) round-robin to distribute traffic between sites.

Installing NLB Nodes

To install and configure an NLB node, you must first install NLB. Unlike most of the Windows components installed in the 70-410 and 70-411 exam, the NLB is a feature, and not a role. It is used to enhance other roles such as web services or Remote Desktop Services. After NLB is installed on each machine, you then have to create the cluster and add each host to the cluster.

CERTIFICATION READY
Install NLB nodes.
Objective 1.1

To add the NLB feature to a computer running Windows Server 2012 or Windows Server 2012 R2, you use Server Manager. After the NLB feature is installed, you can then use the NLB Manager to configure the NLB cluster. Because an NLB is made of multiple computers, you need to install NLB on each server that will be part of the cluster.

INSTALL THE NETWORK LOAD BALANCING FEATURE

GET READY. To install the Network Load Balancing feature, perform the following steps:

1. On the task bar, click the Server Manager button to open the *Server Manager*.
2. At the top of *Server Manager*, click Manage and click Add Roles and Features. The *Add Roles and Feature Wizard* opens.
3. On the *Before you begin* page, click Next.
4. Select Role-based or feature-based installation and then click Next.
5. On the *Select destination server* page, click Next.
6. On the *Select server roles* page, click Next.
7. On the *Select features* page, click to select the Network Loading Balancing and click Next.
8. When it asks you to add features required for NLB, click Add Features.
9. On the *Select features* page, click Next.
10. On the *Confirm installation selections* page, click Install.
11. When the installation is complete, click Close.

USING WINDOWS POWERSHELL

To install the NLB cluster and the NLB tools using Windows PowerShell, you can use the following command:

```
Add-WindowsFeature NLB,RSAT-NLB
```

To configure the NLB cluster, you must configure three types of the parameters:

- **Host parameters:** Defines what each node can do in an NLB cluster.
- **Cluster parameters:** Configures the NLB cluster as a whole.
- **Port rules:** Controls which ports the NLB cluster services and how requests are balanced across all servers.

CREATE A WINDOWS SERVER 2012 OR WINDOWS SERVER 2012 R2 NLB CLUSTER

GET READY. To install the Remote Access Role, perform the following steps:

1. On the task bar, click the Server Manager button to open the *Server Manager*.
2. Click Tools > Network Load Balancing Manager. The *Network Load Balancing Manager* opens as shown in Figure 1-1.

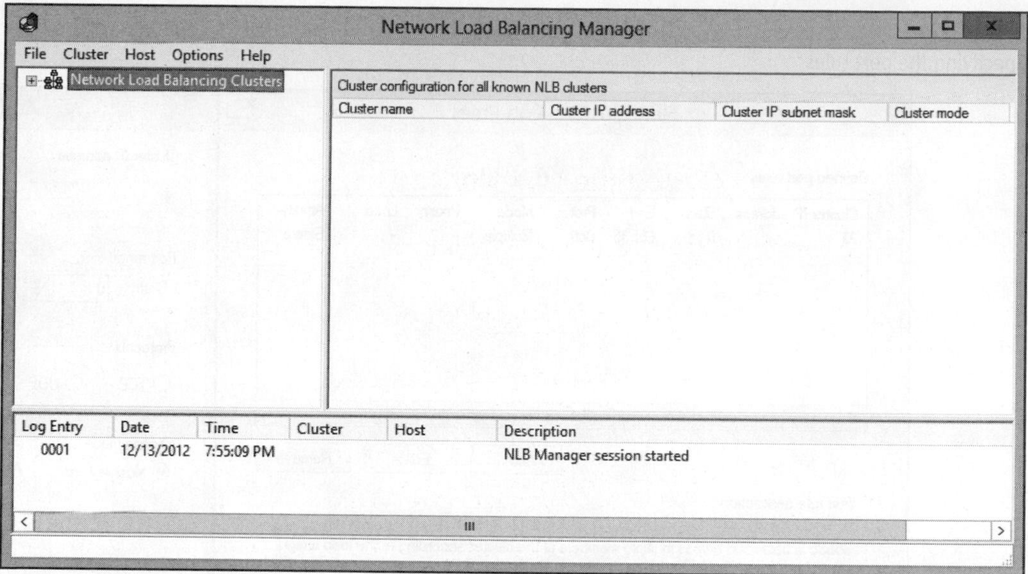

Figure 1-1

Opening the *Network Load Balancing Manager*

3. Right-click Network Load Balancing Clusters and click New Cluster. The *New Cluster: Connect* Wizard opens.
4. In the *Host* text box, type the name of the current server and click Connect.
5. The interface hosts the virtual IP address and receives the client traffic to load balance. Select an interface that you want to use for the cluster and click Next.
6. On the *Host parameters* page, you select a value in the *Priority (unique host identifier)* drop-down list. The parameter specifies a unique ID for each host. The host with the lowest priority handles all the cluster's network traffic not covered by a port rule.
7. In the *Dedicated IP addresses* section, verify that the dedicated IP address from the chosen interface is visible in the list and click Next.
8. On the *New Cluster: Cluster IP Addresses* page, click Add to enter the cluster IP address shared by every host in the cluster. NLB adds this IP address to each selected interface of all hosts chosen to be part of the cluster. Click Next.
9. On the *New Cluster: Cluster Parameters* page, type the full Internet name for the cluster. Then in the *Cluster operation mode* section, specify Unicast, Multicast, or IGMP multicast. Click Next.
10. On the *New Cluster: Port Rules* page, click Edit to open the *Add/Edit Port Rule* dialog box, as shown in Figure 1-2. Port rules define which incoming TCP/IP requests are balanced among the hosts in the NLB cluster. You can specify the cluster IP addresses or use the All option. In the *Port range* area, specify a range corresponding to the service you want to provide in the NLB cluster. For web access, use port 80 or 443. For Remote Desktop Services, use 3389.
11. In the *Filtering mode* area, select Multiple host if you want multiple hosts in the cluster to handle network traffic for the port rule. If you want a single host to handle the network traffic for the port rule, choose Single host.
12. If you choose *Multiple host*, you can select None, Single, or Network. If you want multiple connections from the same client IP address to be handled by different cluster hosts, select None. If you want NLB to direct multiple requests from the same client IP address to the same cluster host, select Single (which is the default). If you want NLB to direct multiple requests from the local subnet to the same cluster host, click Network. Click OK to close the *Add/Edit Port Rule* dialog box.

Figure 1-2
Specifying the port rules

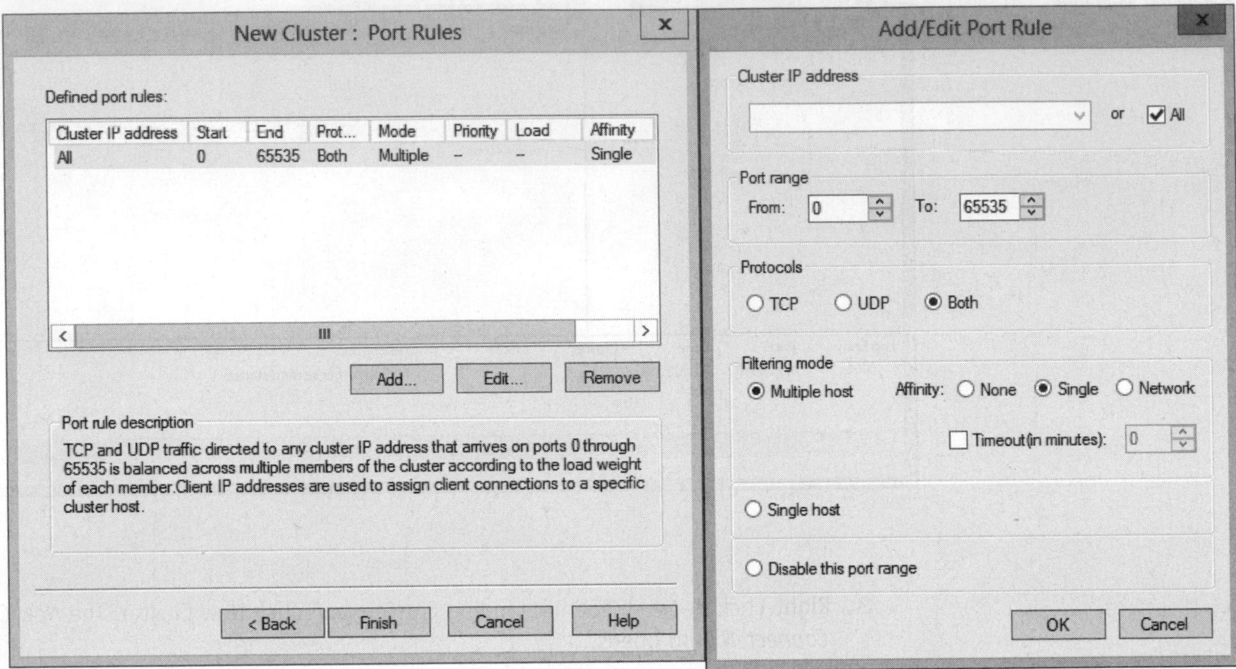

13. After you define the port rules, click Finish.

To add additional hosts to the cluster, right-click the cluster in Network Load Balancing Manager and click *Add Host to Cluster*. You then select an interface for the cluster, configure the unique priority, and define port rules. After a host is added, convergence will occur (as shown in Figure 1-3). When convergence is complete, the host will participate in the cluster.

Figure 1-3
Showing a server (Server02) converging

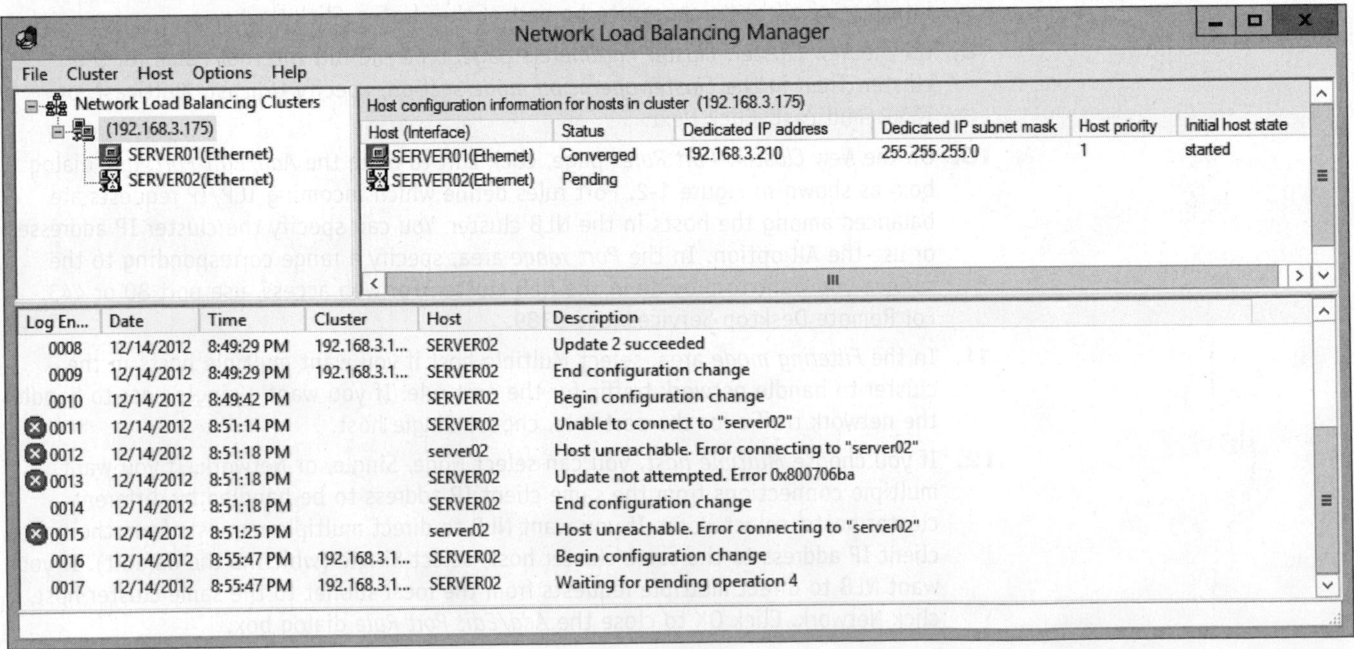

USING WINDOWS POWERSHELL

You can configure and manage Networking Loading Balancing using the following cmdlets:

- `Add-NlbClusterNode`: Adds a new node to the NLB cluster.
- `Add-NlbClusterNodeDip`: Adds a dedicated IP address to an NLB cluster.
- `Add-NlbClusterPortRule`: Adds a new port rule to an NLB cluster.
- `Add-NlbClusterVip`: Adds a virtual IP address to an NLB cluster.
- `Disable-NlbClusterPortRule`: Disables a port rule on an NLB cluster or on a specific host in the cluster.
- `Enable-NlbClusterPortRule`: Enables a port rule on an NLB cluster or on a specific node in the cluster.
- `Get-NlbCluster`: Retrieves information about the NLB cluster object that is queried by the caller.
- `Get-NlbClusterDriverInfo`: Retrieves information about the NLB driver on the local machine.
- `Get-NlbClusterNode`: Retrieves information about the NLB cluster object that is queried by the caller.
- `Get-NlbClusterNodeDip`: Retrieves the dedicated IP address that is queried by the caller.
- `Get-NlbClusterNodeNetworkInterface`: Retrieves information about interfaces, including information about the NLB driver, on a host.
- `Get-NlbClusterPortRule`: Retrieves the port rule objects that are queried by the caller.
- `Get-NlbClusterVip`: Retrieves virtual IP addresses that are queried by the caller.
- `New-NlbCluster`: Creates an NLB cluster on the specified interface that is defined by the node and network adapter name.
- `New-NlbClusterIpv6Address`: Generates IPv6 addresses to create cluster virtual IP addresses or node dedicated IP addresses.
- `Remove-NlbCluster`: Deletes an NLB cluster.
- `Remove-NlbClusterNode`: Removes a node from the NLB cluster.
- `Remove-NlbClusterNodeDip`: Removes a dedicated IP address from an NLB cluster.
- `Remove-NlbClusterPortRule`: Removes a port rule from an NLB cluster.
- `Remove-NlbClusterVip`: Removes a virtual IP address from an NLB cluster.
- `Resume-NlbCluster`: Resumes all nodes in an NLB cluster.
- `Resume-NlbClusterNode`: Resumes the node in an NLB cluster that was suspended.
- `Set-NlbCluster`: Edits the configuration of an NLB cluster.
- `Set-NlbClusterNode`: Edits the NLB cluster node settings.
- `Set-NlbClusterNodeDip`: Edits the dedicated IP address of an NLB cluster.
- `Set-NlbClusterPortRule`: Edits the port rules for an NLB cluster.
- `Set-NlbClusterPortRuleNodeHandlingPriority`: Sets the host priority of a port rule for a specific NLB node.
- `Set-NlbClusterPortRuleNodeWeight`: Sets the load weight of a port rule for a specific NLB node.
- `Set-NlbClusterVip`: Edits the virtual IP address of an NLB cluster.
- `Start-NlbCluster`: Starts all nodes in an NLB cluster.
- `Start-NlbClusterNode`: Starts an NLB cluster node.
- `Stop-NlbCluster`: Stops all nodes of an NLB cluster.
- `Stop-NlbClusterNode`: Stops a node in an NLB cluster.
- `Suspend-NlbCluster`: Suspends all nodes of an NLB cluster.
- `Suspend-NlbClusterNode`: Suspends a specific node in an NLB cluster.

EXAMPLES FOLLOW:

To view or get information about nodes in a cluster, you use the following command:

```
Get-NlbClusterNode
```

To add a Server02 to the cluster on Server01, you use the following command:

```
Get-NlbCluster Server01 | Add-NlbClusterNode -NewNodeName Server02
-NewNodeInterface vlan-1
```

(continued)

To change or set the primary IP address of the cluster, you use the following command:

```
Get-NlbCluster | Set-NlbCluster -ClusterPrimaryIP 172.24.100.100
```

To stop a node in the NLB cluster, you use the following command:

```
Stop-NlbClusterNode Server02
```

For more information about NLB Windows PowerShell commands, visit technet.microsoft.com.

Configuring Port Rules

Often after a cluster is created, you will need to further configure NLB. Most of these options are similar to the configuration that you performed while first creating the cluster. One of the items that you configured previously was the ***port rules***, which specify how NLB directs traffic based on the port and protocol.

CERTIFICATION READY
Configure port rules.
Objective 1.1

With port rules, you can configure how requests to specific IP addresses and ports are directed by the NLB cluster. For example, you can load balance web traffic using TCP port 80 across all nodes in an NLB cluster, while directing all requests to TCP port 3389 to a specific host.

When you configure the port rules, you configure the following:

- The virtual IP address that the rule should apply to.
- The TCP or UDP port range that this rule should apply to.
- The protocols that this rule should apply to, including TCP, UDP, or both.
- The filtering mode that specifies how the cluster handles traffic, which is described by the port range and the protocols. Filtering mode is discussed in the next section.

To modify the port rules (including the filter mode and affinity), right-click the cluster in Network Load Balancing Manager and click *Properties*. When you click the *Port Rules* tab, select the defined port rule and click *Edit* to open the Add/Edit Port Rule dialog box.

Configuring Filtering Mode and Affinity

Affinity determines how the servers are going to balance the load. You use affinity settings when you use multiple hosts filter mode.

CERTIFICATION READY
Configure affinity.
Objective 1.1

When you configure port rules, you first select the filter mode. The ***filter mode*** specifies which hosts can respond to requests. The filter mode includes the following:

- **Multiple hosts:** Permits all cluster hosts to actively respond to client requests. NLB nodes respond according to the weight assigned to each node. Because this allows the customizing of the affinity and load balancing, it is the most common mode used. Multiple host filtering increases availability and scalability, because you can increase capacity by adding nodes, and the cluster continues to function in the event of node failure.
- **Single host:** Allows only one cluster host (the host with the highest priority) in the cluster to actively respond to client requests. If the host fails, the host with the next highest priority takes over for the failed host. It is usually used to configure one host as the primary server and other hosts as backup servers. Single host rules increase availability, but do not increase scalability.
- **Disable:** Prevents the cluster from responding to a specific type of client traffic.

If you choose the multiple host filtering mode, you can then configure the affinity. When you configure affinity, you can choose one of the three options:

- **None:** Any cluster node responds to any client request, even if the client is reconnecting after an interruption. This option is suitable for stateless application, where the server that is servicing the request does not have to remember the previous events to complete the request. As a result, the client can jump from one server to another within the cluster without problem.
- **Single:** A single cluster node handles all requests from a single client. This option is useful for stateful applications where the status of a process or transaction is maintained through the entire connection including when using SSL and e-commerce shopping cart applications.
- **Class C:** A single node responds to all requests from a class C network (a network with a subnet of 255.255.255.0), often found when used with multiple proxy servers. This type of server is often used with cookie-based affinity or when a common database or session state server is used.

Each node in a cluster must have identical port rules. The only exception is the load weight when in multiple-hosts filter mode and handling priority in single-host filter mode. If the port rules are not identical, the cluster will not converge.

To modify the port rules for an individual host, right-click the host in the left pane and click *Host Properties*. Then, click the *Port Rules* and click *Edit* to open the Add/Edit Port Rule dialog box (as shown in Figure 1-4). To specify a different load weight while in multiple host, click to deselect the *Equal* option and then specify the load weight. If you are in Single host, specify the handling priority.

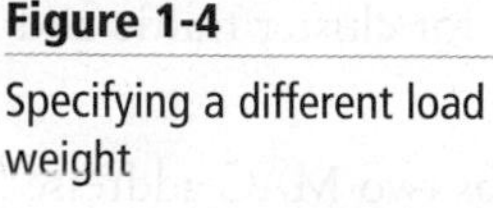

Figure 1-4

Specifying a different load weight

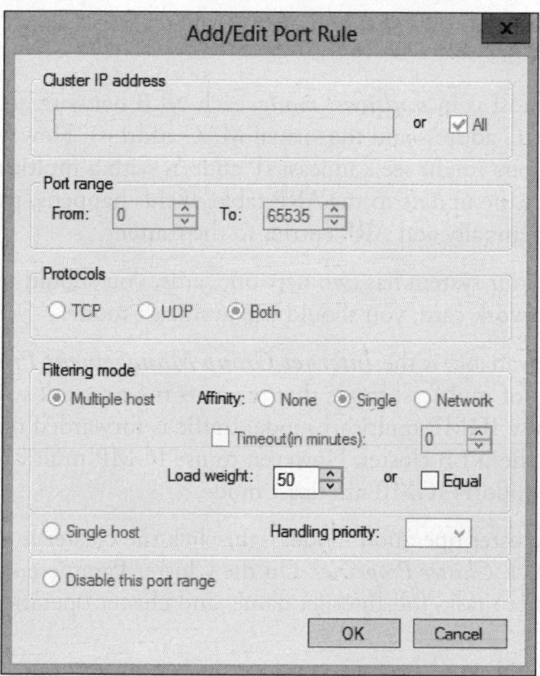

When creating port rules, the number and type of rules must be the same for each host in the cluster. If a host attempts to join the cluster with a different number of rules than the other hosts, it is not accepted as part of the cluster, and the rest of the cluster continues to handle the traffic as before.

Configuring Cluster Operation Mode

On the Cluster Parameters tab, you configure the virtual IP address, subnet mask, and DNS name that the cluster will use. You also can configure the cluster operation mode, which specifies whether a multicast MAC address should be used for cluster operations.

CERTIFICATION READY
Configure cluster operation mode.
Objective 1.1

When a host communicates with another host, the host uses unicast or multicast packets. When communicating using ***unicast***, each packet is sent to a single network destination identified by a unique address. In other words, a host sends packets to a single computer.

With ***multicast***, packets are sent to multiple computers simultaneously in a single transmission from the source. In other words, when a host sends packets using multicasting, a single set of packets is sent to all computers at once. Copies are automatically created on routers, when the packet needs to go to different subnets. If you have five hosts on the same subnet, and two hosts on another subnet, one set of packets is sent from the source host. When the packets get to a router where the packets need to be sent through two different pathways, the packets are copied and sent to the two separate subnets. When the first set of packets gets sent to the subnet with five hosts, only one set of packets gets sent to all five hosts. The second set of packets gets sent to the subnet with two hosts, and only one set of packets gets sent to the two hosts.

When you configure an NLB cluster to use ***unicast mode***, NLB replaces the network card's original MAC address and all cluster hosts use the same unicast MAC address. When you use unicast mode with a single network adapter on each node, the computer can communicate only with other computers within the same subnet. If you perform management tasks on the computer, you need to perform these tasks on a computer that is on the same TCP/IP subnet as the node, or you have to use a second network adapter and address. Lastly, if you use unicast mode, you can use separate virtual local area networks (VLANs) for cluster traffic and management traffic.

When an NLB host is in ***multicast mode***, each NLB network adapter has two MAC addresses (the original MAC address and the virtual MAC address). However, when using multicast mode, some routers might see a unicast IP address with a multicast MAC address as an invalid packet and reject the update to the ARP table. If this happens, the network administrators might need to manually add ARP entries to the router.

In summary, if your system has two network cards, you should use unicast. If a server has only a single network card, you should use multicast mode.

Another mode available is the ***Internet Group Management Protocol Multicast mode***, which is a special form of multicast mode that prevents the network switch from flooding with traffic. When you use IGMP multicast mode, traffic is forwarded only through the switch ports that are part of the NLB cluster. However, to use IGMP multicast mode, you need switch hardware that supports IGMP multicast mode.

To modify the cluster operation mode, right-click the cluster in the Network Load Balancing Manager and click *Cluster Properties*. On the Cluster Parameters, you can modify the cluster IP address, subnet mask, full Internet name, and cluster operation mode.

Controlling Hosts in NLB

As an administrator, you can manually add or remove nodes from an NLB cluster by using the Network Load Balancing Manager. You can also suspend and resume a cluster node and perform a drainstop.

To remove a node, you can perform a stop or a drainstop action. The ***stop action*** terminates all existing connections to the cluster node and stops the NLB service. The ***drainstop*** action blocks all new connections without terminating existing sessions. Therefore, to perform maintenance on an NLB node, which needs to be temporarily removed from the NLB cluster, you should choose drainstop so that connections are not prematurely stopped before the requests are completed. To control the host, you right-click the node, click *Control Host*, and select the appropriate option (Start, Stop, Drainstop, Suspend, or Resume).

Upgrading an NLB Cluster

There are two ways to upgrade a Windows Server 2008 R2 with SP1 or Windows Server 2012 NLB cluster to Windows Server 2012 R2. It includes upgrading all the hosts at one time or upgrading each host, one at a time.

CERTIFICATION READY
Upgrade an NLB cluster.
Objective 1.1

The quickest upgrade path is to take the entire cluster offline and perform a rolling upgrade. Of course, if you use this method, the cluster is not available. If you require no down-time, you can upgrade each individual cluster host, one at a time. As you upgrade each node, you should first perform a drainstop for the host so that any pending client requests are finished before the upgrade.

SKILL SUMMARY

IN THIS LESSON YOU LEARNED:

- High availability is a system design protocol and associated implementation that ensures a certain degree of operational continuity during a given measurement period.
- A cluster is a group of linked computers that work together as one computer. Based on the technology used, clusters can provide fault tolerance (often referred to as availability), load balancing, or both.
- The two most popular forms of clusters are failover clusters and load-balancing clusters.
- A load-balancing cluster for the front end provides the web interface to the back-end servers.
- A failover cluster for back-end servers such as a database (such as SQL Server) or mail server (such as Exchange Server).
- Network Load Balancing (NLB) transparently distributes traffic across multiple servers by using virtual IP addresses and a shared name. By using NLB, you gain fault tolerance and enhanced performance.
- A cluster has two or more servers, known as nodes.
- Each node runs a separate copy of the desired service application such as a web server, an FTP server or a SSH/Remote Desktop Server.
- NLB is able to detect the failure of cluster nodes by sending packets known as *heartbeats*.
- When a node is added or removed from a cluster, a process known as *convergence* occurs, in which the cluster determines its current configuration by building a membership of nodes and mapping clients requests based on the available nodes.

- To configure the NLB cluster, you must configure three types of the parameters: host parameters, cluster parameters, and port rules.
- Port rules specify how NLB directs traffic based on the port and protocol.
- Affinity determines how the servers balance the load. You use affinity settings when you use multiple hosts filter mode.
- For a system with two network cards, you should use unicast. If a server has only a single network card, you should use multicast mode.
- The drainstop action blocks all new connections without terminating existing sessions.
- To upgrade an NLB cluster to Windows Server 2012 R2, you can upgrade all the hosts at one time or upgrade each host, one at a time.

Knowledge Assessment

Multiple Choice

Select the correct answer for each of the following questions.

1. What is used to transparently distribute traffic equally across multiple servers by using virtual IP addresses and a shared name?
   a. Network Load Balancing (NLB)
   b. Failover cluster
   c. DFS distribution
   d. Site replication

2. Which of the following would use NLB to provide fault tolerance?
   a. SQL databases
   b. Exchange database
   c. Websites
   d. Shared folder

3. What is the maximum number of nodes that is supported in a Windows Server 2012 R2 NLB cluster?
   a. 2
   b. 8
   c. 16
   d. 32

4. What is used to detect the failure of cluster nodes?
   a. autoconfig
   b. whoami
   c. Announcements
   d. Heartbeats

5. When you add or remove a node from an NLB cluster, what must happen?
   a. Adaptation
   b. Reset
   c. Convergence
   d. Redefine

6. Which three types of parameters configure the NLB cluster?
   a. Convergence rules
   b. Balance parameters
   c. Cluster parameters
   d. Host parameters
   e. Port rules

7. What specifies how NLB directs traffic based on the port and protocol?
   a. Convergence rules
   b. Balance parameters
   c. Cluster parameters
   d. Host parameters
   e. Port rules

8. What determines how servers are balanced with NLB?
   a. affinity
   b. drainstop
   c. state sequencing
   d. convergence

9. Which mode allows an NLB cluster to use two MAC addresses for the NLB network adapter?
   a. Unicast mode
   b. Multicast mode
   c. Internet Group Management Protocol multicast mode
   d. Converging mode

10. Which action blocks all new connections without terminating existing sessions?
    a. blocking
    b. suspended
    c. drainstop
    d. multimode

Best Answer

Choose the letter that corresponds to the best answer. More than one answer choice may achieve the goal. Select the BEST answer.

1. Typically you would have port rules to be identical on all nodes on the cluster. What are the exceptions where the port rules don't have to be identical?
   a. Handling priority
   b. TCP, UDP, or both
   c. Load weight
   d. Ports

2. Which mode would you choose to configure affinity?
   a. Multiple hosts
   b. Single host
   c. Disable
   d. Converging host

3. You have a two-node NLB cluster. The cluster is intended to provide high availability and load balancing for the Contoso.com website. You have only the default port rule. Which two steps do you need to configure the NLB cluster to accept only HTTP traffic? (Choose two answers.)
   a. Run the `vlbs disable all` command.
   b. Delete the default port rule.
   c. Create a new Allow rule for TCP port 80.
   d. Change the default port rule to a disabled port range rule.

4. You have a two-node NLB cluster. The cluster is intended to provide high availability and load balancing for the Contoso.com website. You have a single port rule that evenly distributes HTTP traffic between Server01 and Server02. What do you need to evenly distribute HTTP traffic while having all HTTPS traffic to go Server01? (Choose two answers.)
   a. On Server02, change the Handling priority for the TCP 443 to a value of 0.
   b. On Server01, change the Handling priority option for the TCP 443 port rule to the value of 0.
   c. In the properties for the cluster, create a new port rule for TCP 443 that has a filtering mode option set to a single host.
   d. In the properties for the cluster, create a new port for port TCP 443 that has the filtering option set to a multiple host and the Affinity set to Single.

5. You have a server called Server01, which hosts the http://www.contoso.com and https://www.contoso.com websites. You created an NLB cluster using Server01 and Server02. What must you do to ensure that users can connect to the https://www.contoso.com website without any security warnings?
   a. Make sure both servers point to the same Enterprise CA.
   b. Create a new digital certificate on Server02 for www.contoso.com.
   c. Export the SSL certificate from Server01 and import the SSL certificate to Server02.
   d. Create an image of the website on Server01 and import into Server02.

Matching and Identification

1. Match the description with the appropriate term. Not all items will be used and items can be used more than once.
   _______ a) Uses two MAC addresses for a host
   _______ b) Only forwards traffic through the switch ports that are part of the NLB cluster
   _______ c) Gracefully shuts down a node in the NLB cluster
   _______ d) Uses only the host with the highest priority to respond
   _______ e) Replaces the network card's original MAC address with the cluster MAC address
   1. Internet Group Management Protocol multicast mode
   2. drainstop
   3. multicast mode
   4. single host
   5. unicast mode
   6. port rule

2. Which of the following would you configure when configuring port rules?
   _______ a) Filtering mode
   _______ b) Convergence mode
   _______ c) Virtual IP address
   _______ d) TCP or UDP port range
   _______ e) TCP, UDP, or both
   _______ f) drainstop

3. Identify the type of cluster (NLB or Failover) that you would use for a particular type of server.
   _______ a) File server
   _______ b) DHCP server
   _______ c) Exchange back-end/mailbox server
   _______ d) Exchange front-end/CAS server
   _______ e) Web server
   _______ f) SQL server

4. Which of the following are prerequisites for NLB?
   _______ a) The MAC address must be user programmable.
   _______ b) All network adapters must be multicast or unicast.
   _______ c) You must use static addresses.
   _______ d) Servers cannot be geographically dispersed.
   _______ e) The adapter must handle client-to-cluster traffic.
   _______ f) All hosts in the cluster must reside on the same subnet.

Build a List

1. Identify the basic steps, in order, to create an NLB cluster in Windows Server 2012 R2. Not all steps will be used.
   _______ Specify the priority of the host.
   _______ Create port rules.
   _______ Configure convergence parameters.
   _______ Type the name of the current server and click Connect.
   _______ Specify failover options.
   _______ Specify a cluster IP address.
   _______ Specify the Internet name for the cluster.

Business Case Scenarios

Scenario 1-1: Upgrading an NLB Cluster

You are the administrator for several web servers that make up the NLB cluster. They run on servers with Windows Server 2008 R2. Explain the best way to upgrade the NLB cluster to Windows Server 2012 R2 without any downtime.

Scenario 1-2: Creating a Fault-Tolerant Website

You are the administrator for the contoso.com website. Recently, the server hosting the corporate websites had a failure that caused the server to go down for a short period of time while the server was being fixed. In the future, you need to take steps to avoid any hardware failure that would cause the websites to go down. What should you do?

Configuring Failover Clustering

70-412 EXAM OBJECTIVE

Objective 1.2 – Configure failover clustering. This objective may include but is not limited to: Configure quorum; configure cluster networking; restore single node or cluster configuration; configure cluster storage; implement Cluster-Aware Updating; upgrade a cluster; configure and optimize clustered shared volumes; configure clusters without network names; configure storage spaces.

LESSON HEADING	EXAM OBJECTIVE
Understanding Failover Clustering	
Installing and Configuring Failover Clustering	Configure cluster networking Configure cluster storage
Configuring and Optimizing Clustered Shared Volumes	Configure and optimize clustered shared volumes
Configuring Quorum	Configure quorum
Configuring Storage Spaces	Configure storage spaces
Configuring Clusters Without Network Names	Configure clusters without network names
Managing the Cluster	
Implementing Cluster-Aware Updating	Implement Cluster-Aware Updating
Upgrading a Cluster	Upgrade a cluster
Troubleshooting Problems with Failover Clusters	
Backing Up and Restoring Failover Cluster Configuration	Restore single node or cluster configuration

KEY TERMS

Active Directory-detached cluster
active-passive cluster
authoritative restore
cluster resource
Cluster Shared Volume (CSV)
cluster storage
cluster virtual server
Cluster-Aware Updating (CAU)
clustered service
dependent resource
failover cluster
heartbeats
Microsoft Failover Cluster Virtual Adapter
nodes
non-authoritative restore
private network
public network
public-and-private network
quorum
Storage Spaces

Understanding Failover Clustering

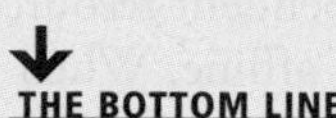

A ***failover cluster*** is a set of servers that work together to increase the availability of services and applications. The clustered servers (called ***nodes***) are connected through a network connection (physical or virtual) and by software. If one of the nodes fails, another node begins to provide services (a process known as *failover*). Failover clusters can be used for a wide range of network services including database applications such as Exchange Server or SQL Server, file servers, or network services such as Dynamic Host Control Protocol (DHCP) services.

The most common failover cluster is the ***active-passive cluster***. In an active-passive cluster, both servers are configured to work as one, but only one at a time. The active node provides the network services whereas the passive node waits for something to happen to the active node where it cannot provide network services. If the active node goes down, the passive node becomes the active node and resumes providing the network services. When the failed node is restored, it becomes the passive node.

Active-passive clusters provide high availability but do not provide scalability. The only exception to the scalability issue is if you implement file servers on Cluster Shared Volumes (CSV), which are discussed later in this chapter. If you need higher performance, you can typically reduce the load or use more powerful hardware for the individual nodes.

Another type of failover cluster is the active-active cluster that is designed to provide fault tolerance and load balancing. Network services are split into two groups. One cluster node runs one set of network services while the other cluster node runs the other set of network services. Both nodes are active. If one of the nodes fails, the remaining node will take over providing all the network services.

Failover clustering is best suited for stateful applications that are derived from a single set of data. For example, a database is stored in a single location and there can be only one database instance running.

To create a failover using Windows Server 2012 R2 you need a minimum of two servers (physical or virtual) that meet the minimum requirements of Windows Server 2012 R2 and that have identical hardware components. In addition, the servers must run the same version and edition, including the same hardware version, 64-bit, and the servers should have the same software updates and service packs. The servers must also be part of the same domain.

When you create the cluster, you assign network resources to the cluster, which can be enabled or disabled when the node is active or inactive. Every cluster has a ***cluster virtual server*** assigned, which includes the network name, and IP address assigned to it.

Clustered services are services or applications that are made highly available by installing them on a failover cluster. Clustered services are active on one node, but can be moved to another node.

A ***cluster resource*** is the most basic and smallest configurable unit that may provide a service to clients, or is an important component that makes up the cluster. It can be a network application server or hardware device, such as a storage device, that is defined and managed by the cluster server. At any time, a resource can run only on a single node in a cluster, and is online on a node when it provides its service to that specific node.

So if you have an active-passive cluster, the active node will have the cluster virtual server with a virtual IP address, and cluster resources (resources that you are providing and making fault tolerant with the cluster). When the active cluster goes offline, the passive cluster becomes the active passive and the resources switch over to the new active node.

A ***dependent resource*** is a resource that depends on or is required by another resource to operate. For example, because a network name must be associated with an IP address, a network name is considered a dependent resource.

To perform graceful failover from one node to another node, the dependent resources are taken offline before the resources upon which they depend are taken offline. When the resources are brought online, the resources that are required for the other services to function are brought online first. A resource can specify one or more resources on which it is dependent. Resource dependencies also determine bindings. For example, clients are bound to the particular IP address on which a network name resource depends.

A failover cluster consists of the following components:

- **Nodes:** Servers that make up the cluster and that run the Cluster service. They host the resources and applications associated to cluster.

TAKE NOTE* In Windows Server 2012 R2, a failover cluster can have 64 physical nodes and can run 4,000 virtual machines on each cluster.

- **Network:** A common network that connects the cluster nodes. Three types of networks can be used in a cluster: public, private, and public-and-private.
- ***Cluster storage*:** A storage system that is shared between cluster nodes and usually connects using fiber channel or iSCSI.
- **Clients:** Computers (or users) that use the Cluster service.
- **Cluster service:** The service that runs on Windows servers that manages and coordinates cluster resources to provide high availability.

Installing and Configuring Failover Clustering

To create a cluster, you first install the Failover Cluster feature. You then validate your hardware configuration, and create a cluster using the Failover Cluster Manager.

TAKE NOTE* If you have previously installed Network Load Balancing (NLB) and have it running, you should remove this feature. In addition, you should also remove any secondary addresses where the same address is used by the same server.

UNDERSTANDING FAILOVER CLUSTERING REQUIREMENTS

To use a failover cluster, you should determine the resources and services that need to be provided by the cluster and that are critical to your organization. Therefore, you need to select the proper hardware to provide a reliable environment.

When creating a cluster, you should think "identical systems are best." Therefore, you should consider the following when selecting systems:

- Each node should have the same or similar hardware on each failover cluster node including network adapters, SAS or Fibre Channel storage connections, motherboard, processor family, and BIOS (including BIOS version). Network adapters and storage connection adapters should have the same firmware and same firmware version.
- All hardware that you select for a failover cluster should meet the Certified for Windows Server 2012 or Windows Server 2012 R2 logo requirements. When hardware is certified, the hardware has been independently tested to ensure that the hardware provides reliability, availability, stability, security, and platform compatibility. In addition, Microsoft provides official support for those items within a cluster.
- If you use iSCSI storage connections, each clustered server should have one or more network adapters or host bus adapters dedicated to the cluster storage. Of course, the adapters should be identical between nodes and it is recommended for 1 Gbps Ethernet or higher.
- Each network adapter in each node should be identical and should be configured identically including the same IP protocol version, speed, duplex, and flow control capabilities.
- When planning the network connections, you should always plan for redundant paths including using network adapter teaming that connect to different switches.
- Each cluster node must run the same version and the same edition of Windows Server 2012.
- Each cluster node must have the same service packs and updates.
- Each node within the cluster should have the same Windows Server 2012 or Windows Server 2012 R2 roles and features.
- It is not recommended that you install the Active Directory Domain Services (AD DS) role on any of the nodes. Remember that multiple domain controllers provide fault tolerance without having a cluster.
- Each node must be in the same Active Directory domain.

CONFIGURING CLUSTER NETWORKING

CERTIFICATION READY
Configure cluster networking.
Objective 1.2

Failover clustering uses only IP-based protocols and is, therefore, suited only to IP-based applications. Failover clustering now supports both IPv4 and IPv6.

When you connect the cluster to the network, you should consider using the following networks:

- ***Private network:*** Used by cluster nodes to communicate with each other.
- ***Public network:*** Used by the clients to access the cluster and its shared resources.
- ***Public-and-private network:*** Used to communicate with external storage systems.

Similar to a Network Load Balancing (NLB) cluster, a failover cluster has full connectivity and communication with the other nodes in the cluster using a private network. In addition, the cluster is aware when a node is added or removed from the cluster. Cluster nodes are kept aware of the status of the other nodes and services through the use of ***heartbeats***. Heartbeats transmit and receive using UDP port 3343 unicast (legacy clusters used UDP broadcast).

Each node of the cluster has a computer name and IP address. In addition, the cluster has a cluster name and cluster IP address. When users connect to the cluster, the users connect using the cluster name and cluster IP address. Therefore, no matter which node is active, users connect to the active node.

Because clusters usually need to access shared storage, the cluster should have a public-and-private network to communicate with the shared storage. If the cluster communicates to shared storage using Fibre Channel, the Fibre Channel will connect using a dedicated network known as a *fabric*. If the cluster connects to shared storage using iSCSI, you can use the public network or use a dedicated public-and-private network to handle iSCSI traffic. Sharing a public network can cause contention and latency issues for the users and the shared resources. However, you can use the public network for a test network.

The Windows Server 2012 R2 Failover Cluster uses a virtual network adapter called ***Microsoft Failover Cluster Virtual Adapter*** to communicate between nodes in the cluster. It is assigned an APIPA address (169.254.0.0/16) and an fe80::/10 prefix. The Microsoft Failover Cluster Virtual Adapter is used as an alternative network if the private network or connection fails.

INSTALLING AND CREATING A FAILOVER CLUSTER

Initially installing a failover cluster is a three-step process:

1. Install the Failover Clustering feature.
2. Validate the cluster configuration.
3. Create the cluster.

You must first install the Failover Clustering feature, which installs the Failover Cluster Manager. You can then use the Failover Cluster Manager to validate the cluster configuration and create the cluster. When you validate the cluster configuration of servers and components that will make up the cluster, you are validating whether everything is compatible with a cluster and that you have the minimum to make a cluster. The four main tests include inventory, network, storage, and system configuration.

INSTALL THE FAILOVER CLUSTERING FEATURE

GET READY. To install the Failover Clustering feature, perform the following steps:

1. On the task bar, click the Server Manager button to open the *Server Manager*.
2. At the top of *Server Manager*, click Manage and click Add Roles and Features. The *Add Roles and Feature Wizard* opens.
3. On the *Before you begin* page, click Next.
4. Select Role-based or feature-based installation and then click Next.
5. On the *Select destination server* page, click Next.
6. On the *Select server roles* page, click Next.
7. On the *Select features* page, click to select the Failover Clustering and click Next.
8. When you are asked to add features required for Failover Clustering, click Add Features.
9. Back on the *Select features* page, click Next.
10. On the *Confirm installation selections* page, click Install.
11. When the installation is complete, click Close.

VALIDATE CLUSTER CONFIGURATION

GET READY. To validate the cluster configuration, perform the following steps:

1. Open Server Manager.
2. Click Tools > Failover Cluster Manager. The *Failover Cluster Manager* opens as shown in Figure 2-1.

Figure 2-1

Opening the *Failover Cluster Manager*

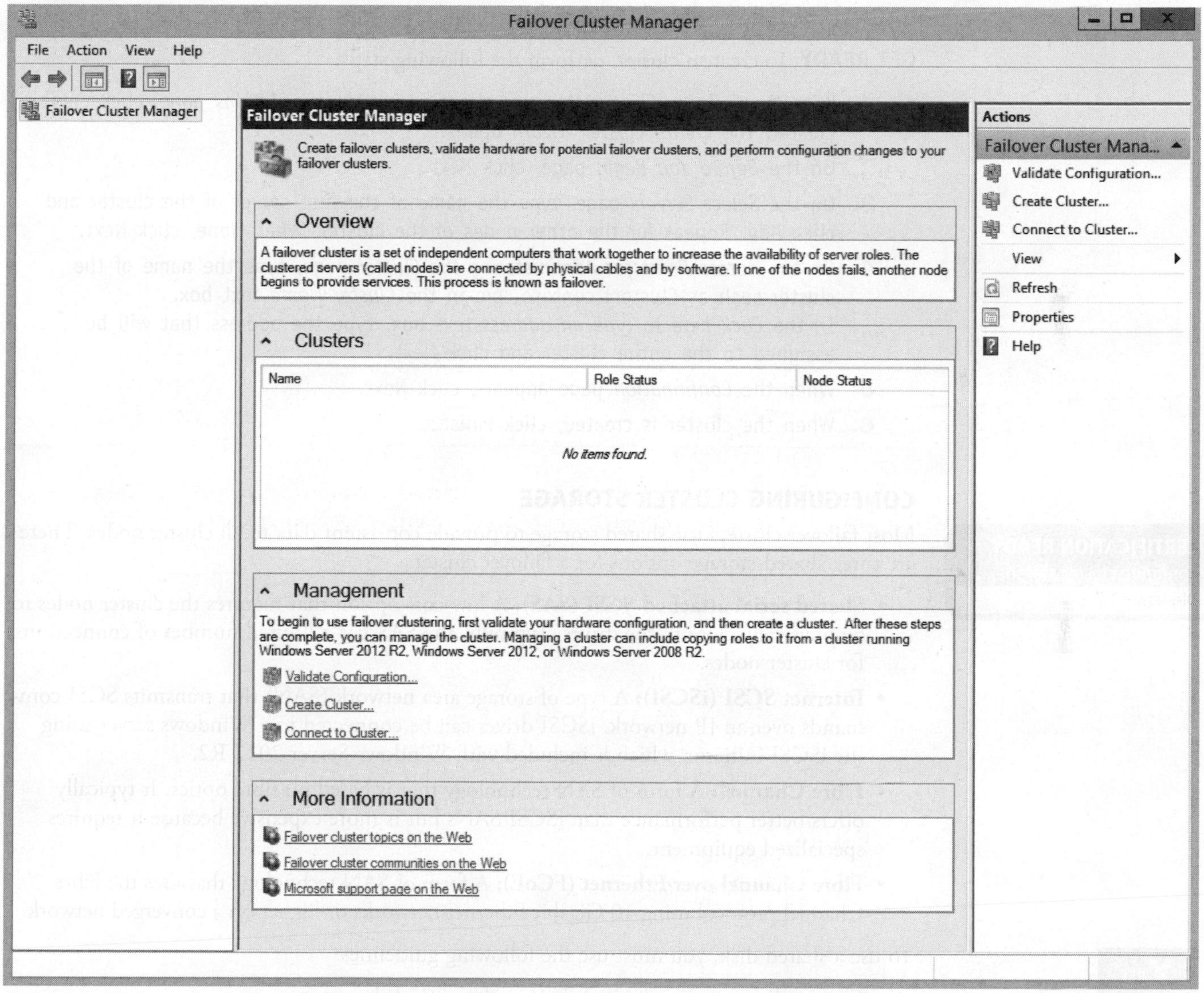

3. In the *Actions* pane, click Validate Configuration. The Validate a Configuration Wizard starts.
4. On the *Before You Begin* page, click Next.
5. In the *Enter* name, type the name of the first server in the cluster such as Server01 and then click Add. Repeat for other servers that will be used within the cluster. After the computers have been added, click Next.
6. With *Run all tests (recommended)* selected, click Next.

7. On the *Confirmation* page, click Next.
8. When the testing is done, the *Summary* page appears. Click View Reports. The *Failover Cluster Validation Report* opens.
9. Close the report.
10. After the cluster has been validated, the *Create Cluster Wizard* opens. For now, click Cancel to close the wizard.

CREATE A CLUSTER

GET READY. To create a cluster, perform the following steps:

1. With the Failover Cluster Manager already open, in the *Actions* pane, click Create Cluster. The *Create Cluster Wizard* opens.
2. On the *Before You Begin* page, click Next.
3. On the *Select Servers* page, type the name of the first server of the cluster and click Add. Repeat for the other nodes of the cluster. When done, click Next.
4. On the *Access Point for Administering the Cluster* page, type the name of the cluster such as Cluster1.contoso.com in the *Cluster Name* text box.
   In the *Click here to type an address* text box, type the address that will be assigned to the entire cluster and click Next.
5. When the *Confirmation* page appears, click Next.
6. When the cluster is created, click Finish.

CONFIGURING CLUSTER STORAGE

CERTIFICATION READY
Configure cluster storage.
Objective 1.2

Most failover clusters use shared storage to provide consistent data to all cluster nodes. There are three shared-storage options for a failover cluster:

- **Shared serial attached SCSI (SAS):** A low-cost option that requires the cluster nodes to be physically close to the drives. Typically, the SAS has a limited number of connections for cluster nodes.
- **Internet SCSI (iSCSI):** A type of storage area network (SAN) that transmits SCSI commands over an IP network. iSCSI drives can be connected to a Windows server using the iSCSI initiator, which is included with Windows Server 2012 R2.
- **Fibre Channel:** A form of SAN technology that is based on fibre optics. It typically offers better performance than iSCSI SANs but is more expensive because it requires specialized equipment.
- **Fibre Channel over Ethernet (FCoE):** A form of SAN technology that uses the Fibre Channel protocol using 10 Gigabit Ethernet networks or higher on a converged network.

To use a shared disk, you must use the following guidelines:

X REF
For more information on iSCSI technology, refer to Lesson 7, "Configuring and Optimizing Storage."

- For the disk type, use basic disks, not dynamic disks.
- For the file system type, format the disk as New Technology File System (NFTS).
- For the partition style of the disk, you can use either master boot record (MBR) or globally unique identifier (GUID) partition table (GPT).
- The storage device must follow the SCSI Primary Commands-3 (SPC-3) standard including supporting Persistent Reservations.
- The miniport driver used for the storage must work with the Storport storage driver.
- A storage device can be assigned to only one cluster. This is usually accomplished with logical unit number (LUN) masking or zoning.

Before you add storage to a cluster, be sure that all nodes can see the storage device and that the storage device has been initialized, partitioned, and formatted and that the same drive letter is assigned to the storage device on all nodes.

ADD A SHARED DRIVE TO THE CLUSTER

GET READY. To add a shared drive to a cluster, perform the following steps:

1. Using Server Manager, open Failover Cluster Manager.
2. In the left pane, expand the cluster, expand Storage, and click Disks. The available shared disks are displayed.
3. Right-click Disks and click Add Disk.
4. When the *Add Disks to a Cluster* dialog box opens, select the disks that you want to include and click OK.

Configuring and Optimizing Clustered Shared Volumes (CSVs)

Traditionally, a single node controls a LUN on the shared storage. However, starting with Windows Server 2008 R2, Windows can use a ***Cluster Shared Volume (CSV)***, which allows multiple nodes to share a single LUN concurrently. Instead of taking control of the entire LUN, a node takes control of an individual file. With CSV, a clustered role can fail over quickly from one node to another node without requiring a change in drive ownership or without dismounting and remounting a volume. After a disk has been added to a CSV, the volumes appear as Cluster Shared Volume File System (CSVFS).

CERTIFICATION READY
Configure and optimize clustered shared volumes.
Objective 1.2

After a disk has been added to a CSV, the volumes appear as Cluster Shared Volume File System (CSVFS). Because volumes appear as CSVFS, applications can quickly see that the volume is a CSV; as a result, the applications know how to handle the volume. To make the volumes available to all cluster nodes, the volumes use a single file namespace, using the same name and path on any node in a cluster.

Using CSV with Windows Server 2012 and Windows Server 2012 R2 offers the following features:

- Multisubnet support for CSVs so that you can achieve faster throughput when integrated with Server Message Block (SMB) Multichannel and
- Allows the network adapters to support Remote Direct Memory Access (RDMA).
- Support for BitLocker volume encryption. Each node performs decryption by using the computer account for the cluster itself.
- Support for SMB 3.0 storage.
- Allows the integration with Storage Spaces, which virtualizes storage on clusters of inexpensive disks.

With Windows Server 2012 R2, the following CSV improvements were made:

- You can use data deduplication.
- Windows Server 2012 R2 can scan and repair CSV volumes with zero offline time.

In Windows Server 2012, a CSV disk can be provisioned with NTFS. With the introduction of Resilient File System (ReFS) in Windows Server 2012 R2, Windows Server 2012 R2 CSV disks can be provisioned with NTFS or Resilient File System (ReFS). CSV applications include:

- Clustered virtual hard disk (VHD) files for clustered Hyper-V virtual machines.
- Scale-Out File file shares to be used with the Scale-Out File Server clustered role. Scale-Out File Server clusters are explained in Lesson 3.

To use CSV:

- The disk or storage space must be a basic disk.
- If you want to use storage space for a CSV, Windows Server 2012 supports simple space or a mirror space, while Windows Server 2012 R2 can also be configured as a parity space. Storage spaces are discussed in the "Configuring Storage Spaces" section later in this lesson.
- On all nodes, the drive letter for the system disk must be the same.
- The NTLM protocol must be enabled on all nodes. This is enabled by default.

A CSV cannot be used as a quorum witness disk and you cannot use disk compression.

To add storage to the CSV, you must make the LUN available as shared storage to the cluster and add the shared disk to the cluster. When you add a disk to CSV, the LUN's drive letter or mount point is removed. It should also be noted that you cannot add shared storage to CSV if it is in use.

ADD A VOLUME TO CSV

GET READY. To add a volume to CSV, perform the following steps:

1. Open Failover Cluster Manager.
2. Expand the Storage node and click the Disks node. Figure 2-2 shows the *Disks* node.

Figure 2-2

The available disks for a cluster

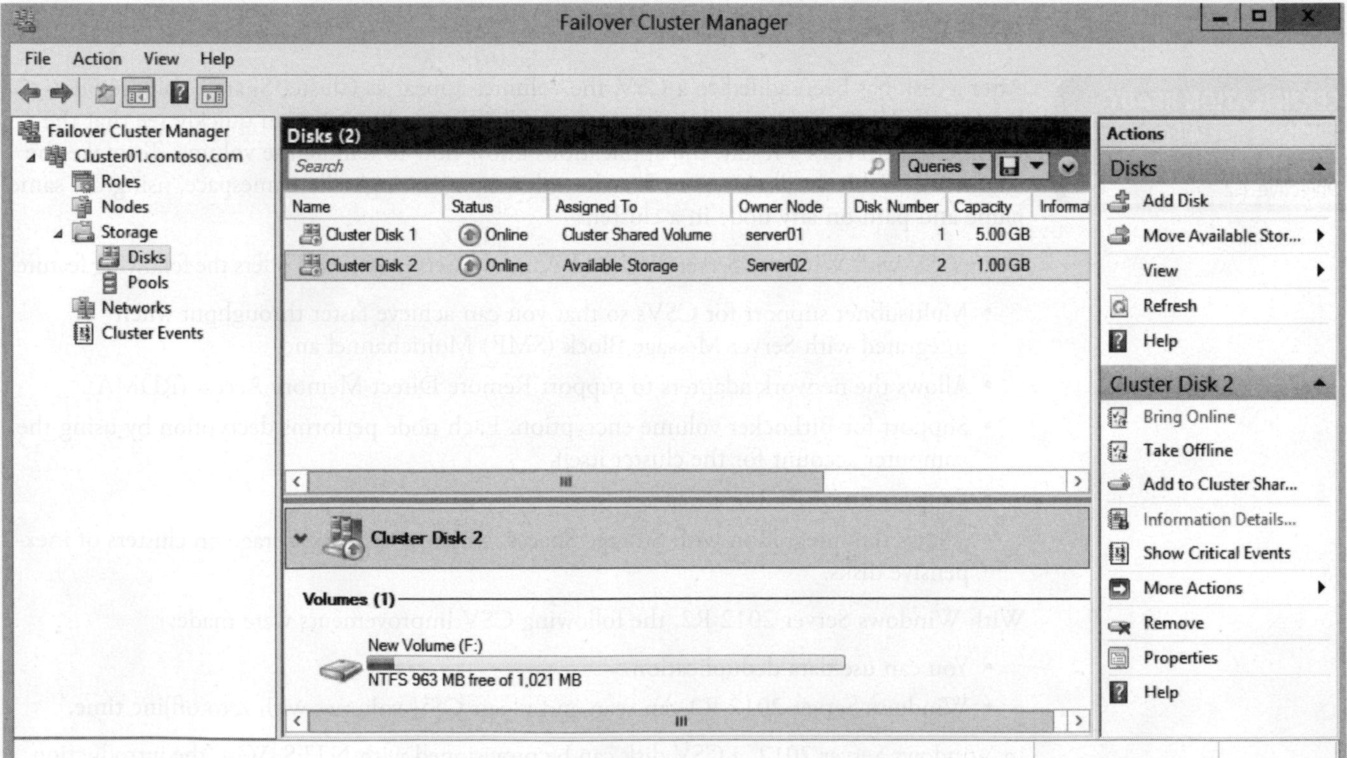

3. Right-click the volume that you want to convert to a Cluster Shared Volume and choose Add to Cluster Shared Volumes. To convert a volume from Cluster Shared Volumes, right-click the CSV and choose Remove from Cluster Shared Volumes.
4. When prompted to confirm this action, click Yes.

Windows Server 2012 R2 has added new CSV functionality, including:

- Optimized CSV placement policies
- Increased CSV resiliency
- CSV diagnosibility
- CSV cache allocation
- CSV interoperability

With Windows Server 2012, one node is the coordinator node or owner for CSV. The coordinator node owns the physical disk resources associated with a LUN, including all I/O operations. With Windows Server 2012 R2, the CSV ownership is automatically distributed and rebalanced across the failover cluster nodes based on the number of CSVs that each node owns. Ownership is automatically rebalanced when a CSV failover occurs, a node rejoins the cluster, a new node is added to the cluster, a cluster node is restarted, or failover is started after being shut down.

In Windows Server 2012, there was only one instance of the Server service per node. With Windows Server 2012 R2, there are multiple Server service instances per failover cluster node so that the default instance can handle incoming traffic from Server Message Block (SMB) clients that access regular file shares and another CSV instance can handle the inter-node CSV traffic.

Problems with the Server service will impact the CSV coordinator node to accept I/O requests from other nodes and to perform the orchestration of metadata updates. In Windows Server 2012 R2, if the Server service becomes unhealthy on a node, CSV ownership will be automatically transitioned to another node.

In Windows Server 2012 R2, you can view the state of a CSV on a per-node basis, including where I/O is direct or redirected or whether the CSV is unavailable. If the CSV is in I/O redirected mode, you can view the reason. To view the state information and the redirection reason, use the Windows PowerShell cmdlet `Get-ClusterSharedVolumeState`.

In Windows Server 2012, the CSV cache (which is a write-through cache) was disabled by default. Also, you could allocate only 20 percent of the total physical RAM to the CSV cache. In Windows Server 2012 R2, however, you can allocate up to 80 percent. Increasing the CSV cache limit is more beneficial for Scale-Out File Server scenarios.

To control the CSV cache, use the following configuration properties:

- `CsvEnableBlockCache`: Allows you to enable CSV Cache on an individual disk. The default setting is 0 for disabled. Setting to a value of 1 enables CSV Block Cache on that disk.
- `SharedVolumeBlockCacheSizeInMB`: Defines how much memory (in megabytes) you wish to reserve for the CSV Cache on each node in the cluster. Configuring a value of 0 disables CSV Block Cache.

To change the CSV cache, use the following Windows PowerShell command:

```
(Get-Cluster).BlockCacheSize = XXX
```

whereby *XXX* is the number in MB.

In Windows Server 2012 R2, CSV functionality has been enhanced to include support for the following features:

- Resilient File System (ReFS)
- Deduplication
- Parity storage spaces
- Tiered storage spaces
- Storage Spaces write-back caching

Configuring Quorum

A ***quorum*** is used with a failover cluster to determine the number of failures that the cluster can sustain. If a quorum (the majority of the votes) is not reached, the cluster will stop running. Each voting element contains a copy of the cluster configuration, and the Cluster service works to keep all copies synchronized at all times.

CERTIFICATION READY
Configure quorum.
Objective 1.2

For example, if a cluster has five nodes, it needs three nodes running to have a majority. Therefore, two nodes can fail and the cluster will still continue to function. If there is an even number of nodes, then the cluster needs to have a witness assigned to the cluster to break the tie. The witness can be either a disk or a file share.

A cluster protects against only hardware failure such as a server with a faulty power supply, motherboard, or processor. A quorum will not protect if a remaining cluster node does not have the resources to run properly such as sufficient disk space, processing power, random access memory (RAM), or network bandwidth.

For a simple failover cluster that has only two nodes, you want to configure a quorum drive. Therefore, you will need to add a shared drive that is seen by all nodes.

When you configure the quorum, there are four possible quorum configurations:

- **Node Majority:** Recommended for clusters with an odd number of nodes. It can sustain failures of half the nodes (rounding up) minus one.
- **Node and Disk Majority:** Recommended for clusters with an even number of nodes. It can sustain failures of half the nodes (rounding up) if the disk witness remains online.
- **Node and File Share Majority:** Used for clusters with special configurations. Instead of using a disk witness, it uses a file share witness.
- **No Majority (Disk Only):** Allows the cluster to function as long as one node is available and the disks are online. However, this configuration is not recommended because the disk might be a single point of failure.

If you use a witness disk, the disk must be at least 512 MB. It must be dedicated for cluster use and not assigned to a clustered role. It cannot be a volume that is a CSV.

In Windows Server 2012, you had to configure a witness and manually adjust the quorum configuration if node membership changed so that you would keep the total number of votes as an odd number. With Windows Server 2012 R2, to reduce the risk that a cluster will go down because of the witness failure, by default, the cluster determines quorum management options, including the quorum witness. Therefore, if you have an odd number of votes, the quorum witness does not have to vote; if you have an even number of votes, the quorum witness has a vote. In addition, if the witness resource is offline or has failed, the cluster sets the witness vote to "0".

In Windows Server 2012, you had to run the Validate Quorum Configuration validation report or use Windows PowerShell to view the vote status. In Windows Server 2012 R2, you can view the assigned quorum vote and the current quorum vote for each cluster node in the Failover Cluster Manager user interface (UI) by clicking the Nodes node (as shown in Figure 2-3). However, the quorum mode terminology–such as node majority (no witness), node majority with witness (disk or file share) or no majority (disk witness only)–are not longer being used.

Figure 2-3

The Nodes node showing the status of the nodes

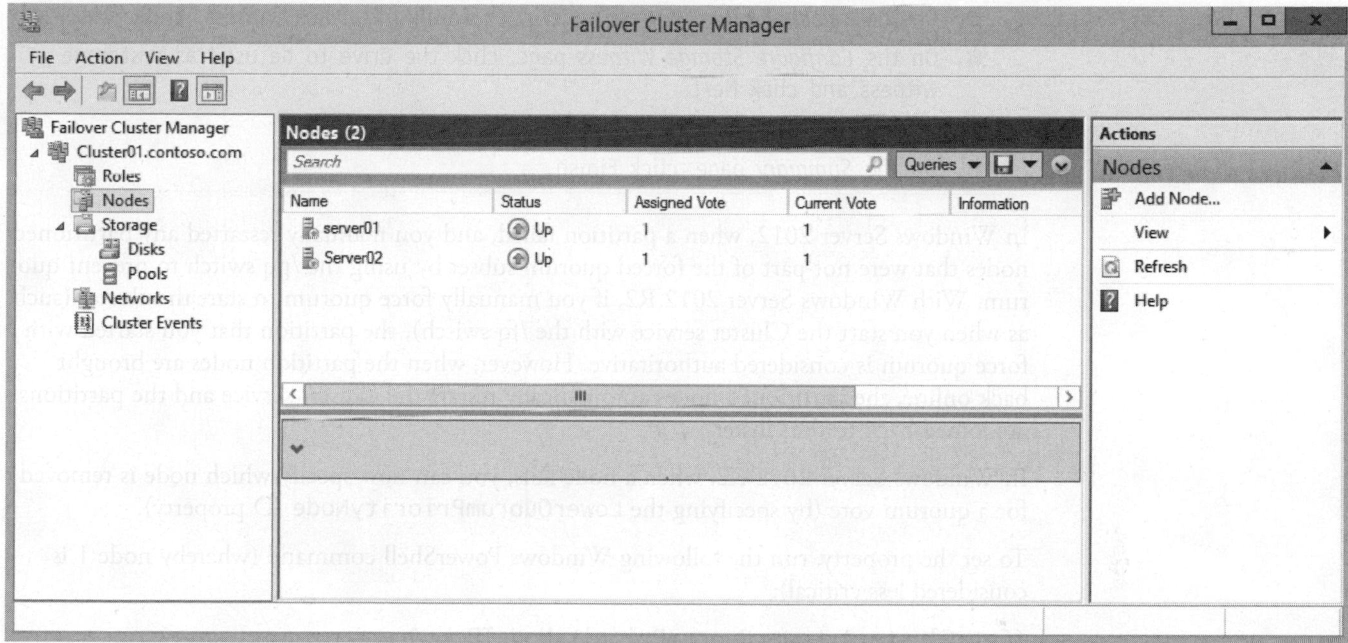

To view the quorum witness vote, use the following Windows PowerShell command:

```
(Get-Cluster).WitnessDynamicWeight
```

A value of "0" indicates that the witness does not have a vote. A value of "1" indicates that the witness has a vote.

CONFIGURE THE CLUSTER QUORUM SETTINGS USING TYPICAL SETTINGS

GET READY. To configure the Cluster Quorum settings using typical settings, perform the following steps:

1. Open Server Manager, and then open Failover Cluster Manager.
2. In the left pane, right-click the cluster, click More Actions, and click Configure Cluster Quorum Settings.
3. When the *Configure Cluster Quorum Wizard* starts, click Next.
4. On the *Select Quorum Configuration Option* page, verify that Use typically settings (recommended) is already selected. Click Next.
5. On the *Confirmation* page, click Next.
6. On the *Summary* page, click Finish.

ADD OR CHANGE THE QUORUM WITNESS

GET READY. To add or change the Cluster Quorum settings, perform the following steps:

1. Open Server Manager, and then open Failover Cluster Manager.
2. In the left pane, right-click the cluster, click More Actions, and then click Configure Cluster Quorum Settings.

3. When the *Configure Cluster Quorum Wizard* starts, click Next.
4. On the *Select Quorum Configuration Option* page, click Add or change the quorum witness and click Next.
5. On the *Select Quorum Witness* page, click Configure a disk witness, and click Next.
6. On the *Configure Storage Witness* page, click the drive to be used as a storage witness and click Next.
7. On the *Confirmation* page, click Next.
8. On the *Summary* page, click Finish.

In Windows Server 2012, when a partition failed, and you manually restarted any partitioned nodes that were not part of the forced quorum subset by using the /pq switch to prevent quorum. With Windows Server 2012 R2, if you manually force quorum to start the cluster (such as when you start the Cluster service with the /fq switch), the partition that you started with force quorum is considered authoritative. However, when the partition nodes are brought back online, the partitioned nodes automatically restart the Cluster service and the partitions are joined back to the cluster.

In Windows Server 2012 R2, when a node fails, you can now specify which node is removed for a quorum vote (by specifying the `LowerQuorumPriorityNode` ID property).

To set the property, run the following Windows PowerShell command (whereby node 1 is considered less critical):

```
(Get-Cluster).LowerQuorumPriorityNodeID = 1
```

Configuring Storage Spaces

As you recall from the 70-410 exam, you can group local disks–USB, Serial ATA (SATA) or Serial Attached SCSI (SAS)–into storage pools and then create virtual disks called ***Storage Spaces*** from the available capacity in the storage pools. Storage Spaces can also provide resiliency (such as using mirroring or parity) and scalability. You can deploy clustered storage spaces by using Storage Spaces and Failover Clustering to provide solutions that are resilient, highly available, and cost efficient.

CERTIFICATION READY
Configure storage spaces.
Objective 1.2

Although you cannot use a storage space to host the Windows system drive, you can use clustered storage spaces to help protect against the following:

- Physical disk failures
- Data access failures
- Data corruptions and volume unavailability
- Server node failures

By using CSVs, you can combine the storage access into a single namespace, which all cluster nodes can access at the same time, and you can easily take a server offline for maintenance.

To deploy clustered storage spaces, you will need a small collection of servers and a set of shared Serial Attached SCSI enclosures, which must be connected to all servers with redundant paths. All physical disks used to create a clustered pool must pass the failover cluster validation tests. Clustered storage spaces must use fixed provisioning. Simple and mirror storage spaces are supported, but Parity Spaces are not supported. Storage spaces formatted with ReFS cannot be added to the CSV.

CONFIGURE A CLUSTERED STORAGE SPACE

GET READY. To configure a Clustered Storage Space, perform the following steps:

1. Using *Server Manager*, click Manage > Add Roles and Features.
2. On the *Before You Begin* page, click Next.
3. On the *Select installation type* page, click Next.
4. On the *Select destination server* page, click the server to which you want to install and then click Next.
5. On the *Select server roles* page, click the File Server role and then click Next.
6. On the *Select features page*, click Next.
7. On the *Confirm installations selections* page, click Install.
8. When the installation is complete, click Close.
9. Using *Server Manager*, click Tools > Failover Cluster Manager.
10. In the left pane, expand the cluster node, expand the Storage node, and then click the Pools node (see Figure 2-4).

Figure 2-4
The Pools node

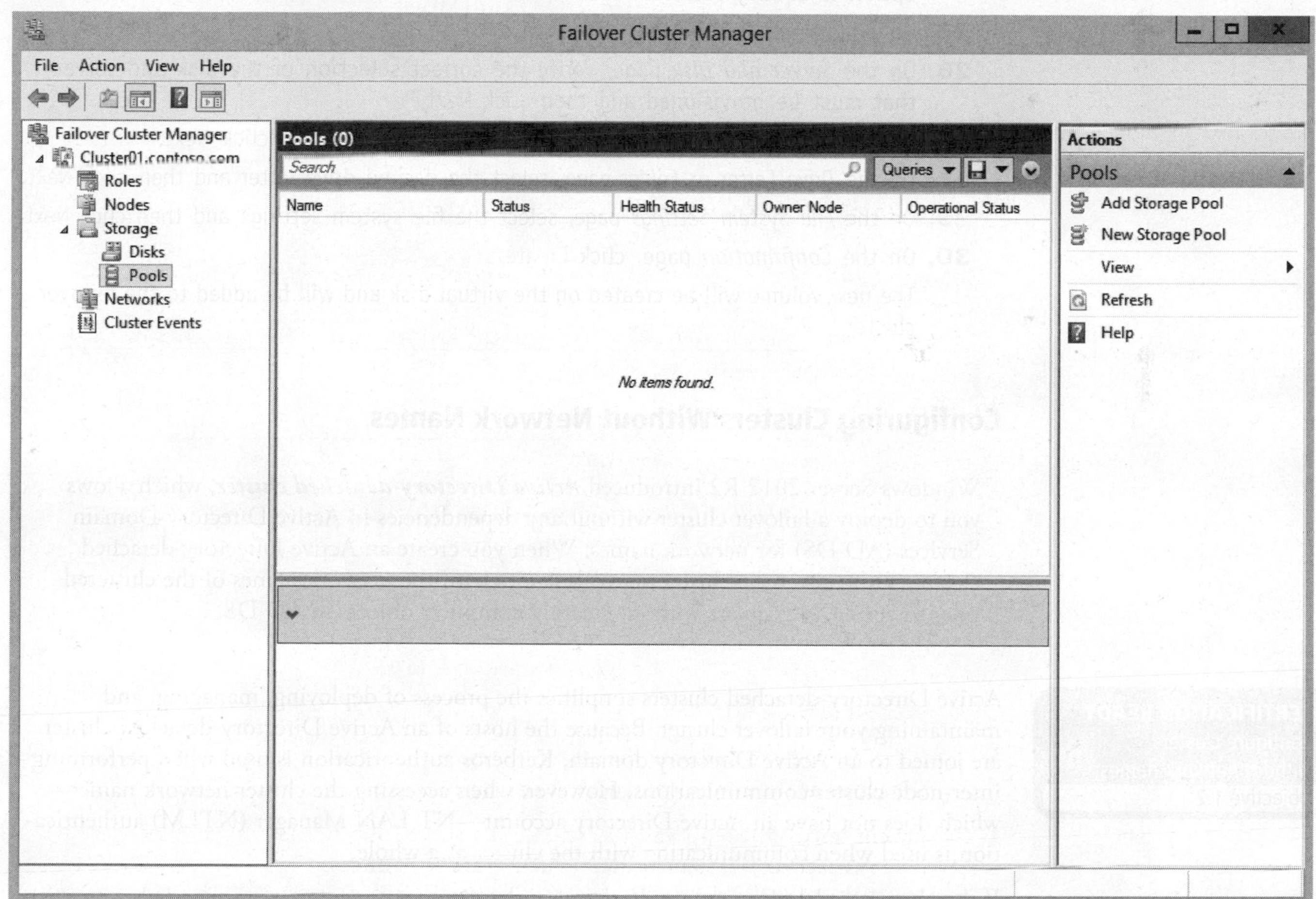

11. Right-click Pools and choose New Storage Pool.
12. On the *Before You Begin* page, click Next.

13. On the *Storage Pool Name* page, in the *Name* text box, type the name of the storage pool. Then select the storage subsystem that is available to the cluster and click Next.
14. Select a minimum of three physical disks and then click Next.
15. On the *Confirmation* page, click Create.
16. Once the storage pool is created, click Close.
17. Right-click the storage pool and choose New Virtual Disk.
18. On the *Before You Begin* page, click Next.
19. On the *Storage Pool* page, select the server and storage pool for the virtual disk and then click Next.
20. On the *Virtual Disk Name* page, in the *Name* text box and the *Description* text box, provide a name and description for the virtual disk and then click Next.
21. On the *Storage Layout* page, specify the desired *Storage Layout* (Simple or Mirror). Remember, parity is not supported in a failover cluster. Click Next.
22. On the *Size* page, specify the size of the virtual disk and then click Next.
23. On the *Confirmation* page, click Create.
24. Once the virtual disk is created, the *Create a volume when this wizard closes* option is already selected. Click Close.
25. On *Before You Begin* page, click Next.
26. On the *Server and Disk* page, verify the correct selection of the disk and server that must be provisioned and then click Next.
27. On the *Size* page, specify the size of the volume and then click Next.
28. On the *Drive Letter or Folder* page, select the desired drive letter and then click Next.
29. On the *File System Settings* page, select the file system settings and then click Next.
30. On the *Confirmation* page, click Create.

    The new volume will be created on the virtual disk and will be added to the failover cluster.

Configuring Clusters Without Network Names

Windows Server 2012 R2 introduced ***Active Directory-detached cluster***, which allows you to deploy a failover cluster without any dependencies in Active Directory Domain Services (AD DS) for network names. When you create an Active Directory-detached cluster, you register the cluster network names with the network names of the clustered roles to your DNS servers without creating computer objects in AD DS.

CERTIFICATION READY
Configure clusters without network names.
Objective 1.2

Active Directory-detached clusters simplifies the process of deploying, managing, and maintaining your failover cluster. Because the hosts of an Active Directory-detached cluster are joined to an Active Directory domain, Kerberos authentication is used when performing inter-node cluster communications, However, when accessing the cluster network name—which does not have an Active Directory account—NT LAN Manager (NTLM) authentication is used when communicating with the cluster as a whole.

If the cluster applications require Kerberos authentication, it is not recommended to use Active Directory-detached clusters. Therefore, you should consider the following:

- Since the Server Message Block (SMB) traffic recommends using Kerberos, you should not use Active Directory-detached clusters.
- If you require live migration, which requires Kerberos authentication, you should not use Active Directory-detached cluster for Hyper-V.

- Since Message Queuing stores properties in AD DS, you cannot use Active Directory-detached clusters.
- If you have an Active Directory-detached cluster with a SQL server, you should use SQL Server authentication.
- BitLocker Drive Encryption is not supported with Active Directory-detached clusters.
- Cluster-Aware Updating (CAU) in self-updating mode is not supported with Active Directory-detached clusters. However, CAU is supported in remote-updating mode.
- If you deploy a highly available file server by using this deployment method, you cannot use Server Manager to manage the file server. Instead, you must use Windows PowerShell or Failover Cluster Manager.
- After you create the cluster, you cannot change the cluster to an Active Directory-detached cluster or an Active Directory-attached cluster.

Before you create the failover cluster, you must ensure that all servers that you want to add as cluster nodes meet the following prerequisites:

- All servers must be running Windows Server 2012 R2.
- All servers must be joined to the same Active Directory domain.
- All servers must have the Failover Clustering feature installed.
- All servers must use supported hardware and the collection of servers must pass all cluster validation tests.

To deploy an Active Directory-detached cluster, you must create the failover cluster with the Windows PowerShell `New-Cluster` cmdlet with the

`-AdministrativeAccessPoint` parameter set to a value of `Dns`.

For example, to create a failover cluster called Cluster1 using the two nodes (Node1 and Node2) and using an administrative access point of type DNS (Active Directory-detached), use the following command:

```
New-Cluster Cluster1 -Node Node1,Node2 -StaticAddress 192.168.1.16
-NoStorage -AdministrativeAccessPoint Dns
```

To verify the type of administrative access point for a failover cluster, use the following Windows PowerShell command:

```
(Get-Cluster).AdministrativeAccessPoint
```

Managing the Cluster

The Failover Cluster Manager is used to manage and monitor the cluster and its nodes. Most common options can be accessed from the cluster page, as shown in Figure 2-5.

Figure 2-5
Managing the failover cluster

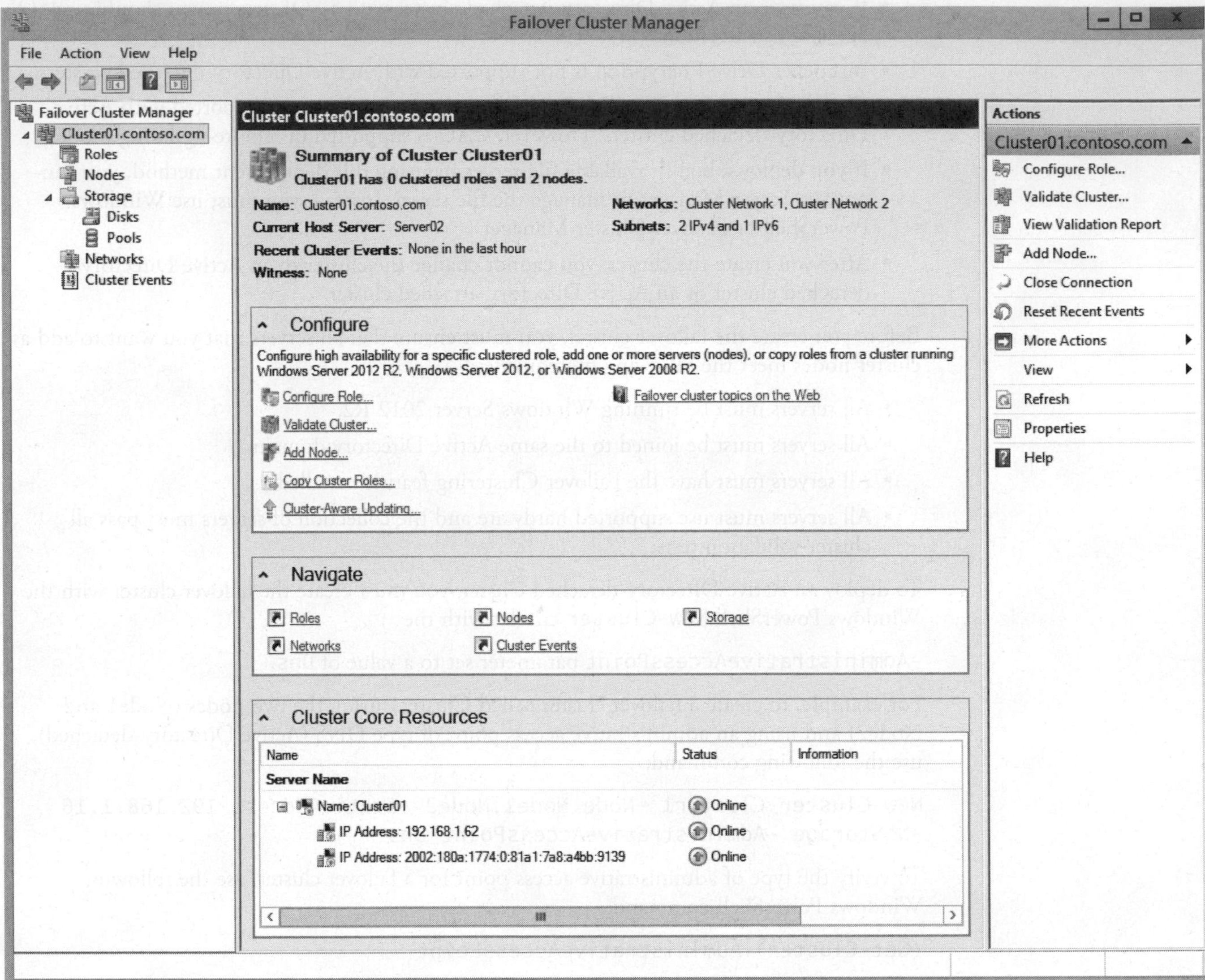

When a failover occurs (intentionally triggered by an administrator or an unplanned event such as a hardware failure), the failover attempt will consist of the following steps:

1. The Cluster service takes all the resources in the instance offline, in an order that is determined by the instance's dependency hierarchy. To perform a graceful shutdown of the resources, dependent resources are taken offline first, and then the supporting resources are taken offline.
2. The Cluster service transfers the instance to the node that is listed next on the instance's list of preferred owners.
3. If the instance is moved successfully, the Cluster service attempts to bring the resources online. The components that provide services for other components are started first, and then the dependent resources are brought online.

Failover is complete when all the resources are online on the new node. Depending on how you have the cluster configured, when the offline node becomes active again, the Cluster service can fail back the instance to the original offline node, or continue with the current node.

Most of the maintenance tasks performed on a cluster are done using the failover cluster, including the following:

- To drain the roles (change roles to other nodes gracefully), you right-click a node, click *Pause*, and click *Drain Roles*.
- To resume a node, you right-click the node, click *Resume*, and choose either *Fail Roles Back* or *Do Not Fail Roles Back*.
- To stop the Cluster service, right-click the node, click *More Actions*, and then click *Stop Cluster Service*.
- To take a shared storage device offline used by a cluster, right-click the disk and click *Take Offline*. When it asks if you are sure, click *Yes*.
- To bring a shared storage device that has been taken offline, right-click the drive and click *Bring Online*.
- To manually change a shared disk or role (roles are discussed more in Lesson 3, "Managing Failover Clustering"), right-click the shared disk or role, click *Move*, select *Best Possible Node*, or *Select Node*. When you choose Select Node, you will then be prompted for the node to change the disk or resource to.
- To add a new node to the cluster, right-click *Node* and click *Add Node* to run the Add Node Wizard.
- To permanently remove a node from the cluster, right-click the server that you want to remove, click *More Actions* and click *Evict*.
- To delete a cluster, right-click the cluster, click *More Actions*, and click *Destroy Cluster*.

USING WINDOWS POWERSHELL

You can configure and manage failover clusters using Windows PowerShell. Some of the cmdlets include the following:

- `Add-ClusterCheckpoint`: Adds a cryptographic or registry checkpoint for a resource.
- `Add-ClusterDisk`: Makes a new disk available for use in a failover cluster.
- `Add-ClusterFileServerRole`: Creates a clustered file server resource group that includes one or more disks, on which shared folders can be created for users.
- `Add-ClusterGenericApplicationRole`: Configures high availability for an application that was not originally designed to run in a failover cluster.
- `Add-ClusterGenericScriptRole`: Configures an application controlled by a script that runs in Windows Script Host, within a failover cluster.
- `Add-ClusterGenericServiceRole`: Configures high availability for a service that was not originally designed to run in a failover cluster.
- `Add-ClusterGroup`: Adds an empty resource group to the failover cluster configuration, in preparation for adding clustered resources to the group.
- `Add-ClusteriSCSITargetServerRole`: Creates a highly available iSCSI Target server.
- `Add-ClusterNode`: Adds a node, or server, to a failover cluster.
- `Add-ClusterPrintServerRole`: Creates a clustered print server, a resource group that includes a printer, and a disk for storing print job information and printer drivers.
- `Add-ClusterResource`: Adds a resource to a clustered role, resource group, in a failover cluster.
- `Add-ClusterResourceDependency`: Adds a resource to the list of resources on which a particular resource depends, using AND as the connector, within a failover cluster.
- `Add-ClusterResourceType`: Adds a resource type to a failover cluster and specifies information such as the dynamic-link library (DLL) to be used with that resource type.
- `Add-ClusterScaleOutFileServerRole`: Creates a clustered file server for scale-out application data.
- `Add-ClusterServerRole`: Creates a highly available basic server.
- `Add-ClusterSharedVolume`: Makes a volume available in CCSVs in a failover cluster.

(continued)

- `Add-ClusterVirtualMachineRole:` Creates a clustered virtual machine, that is, a virtual machine that can be failed over if necessary to a different server in the failover cluster.
- `Add-ClusterVMMonitoredItem:` Configures monitoring for a service or Event Tracing for Windows (ETW) event in a virtual machine.
- `Block-ClusterAccess:` Prevents the specified user or users from accessing a failover cluster.
- `Clear-ClusterDiskReservation:` Clears the persistent reservation on a disk in a failover cluster.
- `Clear-ClusterNode:` Clears the cluster configuration from a node that was evicted from a failover cluster.
- `Get-Cluster:` Gets information about one or more failover clusters in a given domain.
- `Get-ClusterAccess:` Gets information about permissions that control access to a failover cluster.
- `Get-ClusterAvailableDisk:` Gets information about the disks that can support failover clustering and are visible to all nodes, but are not yet part of the set of clustered disks.
- `Get-ClusterCheckpoint:` Retrieves a cryptographic or registry checkpoint for a resource in a failover cluster.
- `Get-ClusterGroup:` Gets information about one or more clustered roles, or resource groups, in a failover cluster.
- `Get-ClusterLog:` Creates a log file for all nodes, or a specific node in a failover cluster.
- `Get-ClusterNetwork:` Gets information about one or more networks in a failover cluster.
- `Get-ClusterNetworkInterface:` Gets information about one or more network adapters in a failover cluster.
- `Get-ClusterNode:` Gets information about one or more nodes, or servers, in a failover cluster.
- `Get-ClusterOwnerNode:` Gets information about which nodes can own a resource in a failover cluster or information about the order of preference among owner nodes for a clustered role.
- `Get-ClusterParameter:` Gets detailed information about an object in a failover cluster, such as a cluster resource.
- `Get-ClusterQuorum:` Gets information about the quorum configuration of a failover cluster.
- `Get-ClusterResource:` Gets information about one or more resources in a failover cluster.
- `Get-ClusterResourceDependency:` Gets information about the dependencies that have been configured between clustered resources in a failover cluster.
- `Get-ClusterResourceDependencyReport:` Generates a report that lists the dependencies between resources in a failover cluster.
- `Get-ClusterResourceType:` Gets information about one or more resource types in a failover cluster.
- `Get-ClusterSharedVolume:` Gets information about CSVs in a failover cluster.
- `Get-ClusterVMMonitoredItem:` Retrieves the list of services and events currently being monitored in the virtual machine.
- `Grant-ClusterAccess:` Grants access to a failover cluster, either full access or read-only access.
- `Move-ClusterGroup:` Moves a clustered role, a resource group, from one node to another in a failover cluster.
- `Move-ClusterResource:` Moves a clustered resource from one clustered role to another within a failover cluster.
- `Move-ClusterSharedVolume:` Moves a CSV to ownership by a different node in a failover cluster.
- `Move-ClusterVirtualMachineRole:` Moves the ownership of a clustered virtual machine to a different node.
- `New-Cluster:` Creates a new failover cluster.
- `Remove-Cluster:` Destroys an existing failover cluster.
- `Remove-ClusterAccess:` Removes a user from the access list on the cluster.
- `Remove-ClusterCheckpoint:` Removes a cryptographic or registry checkpoint for a resource in a failover cluster.
- `Remove-ClusterGroup:` Removes a clustered role, also called a *resource group,* from a failover cluster.
- `Remove-ClusterNode:` Removes a node from a failover cluster.
- `Remove-ClusterResource:` Removes a clustered resource from the failover cluster.
- `Remove-ClusterResourceDependency:` Removes a dependency between two resources in a clustered role within a failover cluster.
- `Remove-ClusterResourceType:` Removes a resource type from a failover cluster.

- `Remove-ClusterSharedVolume`: Removes a volume from the CSVs in a failover cluster and places it in Available Storage in the cluster.
- `Remove-ClusterVMMonitoredItem`: Removes monitoring of a service or custom event that is currently being monitored.
- `Repair-ClusterSharedVolume`: Runs repair tools on a CSV locally on a cluster node.
- `Reset-ClusterVMMonitoredState`: Resets the Application Critical state of a virtual machine, so that the virtual machine is no longer marked as being in a critical state in the cluster.
- `Resume-ClusterNode`: Resumes activity on a failover cluster node after it has suspended it, or paused.
- `Resume-ClusterResource`: Turns off maintenance for a disk resource or CSV within a failover cluster.
- `Set-ClusterLog`: Sets the size and level of detail for the cluster log.
- `Set-ClusterOwnerNode`: Specifies which nodes can own a resource in a failover cluster or specifies the order of preference among owner nodes for a clustered role, or a resource group.
- `Set-ClusterParameter`: Controls specific properties of an object in a failover cluster, such as a resource, a group, or a network.
- `Set-ClusterQuorum`: Configures quorum options for a failover cluster.
- `Set-ClusterResourceDependency`: Specifies the resources that a particular resource depends on within a failover cluster.
- `Start-Cluster`: Starts the Cluster service on all nodes of the cluster on which it is not yet started.
- `Start-ClusterGroup`: Brings one or more clustered services and applications, also known as *resource groups*, online on a failover cluster.
- `Start-ClusterNode`: Starts the Cluster service on a node in a failover cluster.
- `Start-ClusterResource`: Brings a resource online in a failover cluster.
- `Stop-Cluster`: Stops the Cluster service on all nodes in a failover cluster, which will stop all services and applications configured in the cluster.
- `Stop-ClusterGroup`: Takes one or more clustered services and applications, also known as *resource groups*, offline on a failover cluster.
- `Stop-ClusterNode`: Stops the Cluster service on a node in a failover cluster.
- `Stop-ClusterResource`: Takes a resource offline in a failover cluster.
- `Suspend-ClusterNode`: Suspends activity on a failover cluster node, that is, pause the node.
- `Suspend-ClusterResource`: Turns on maintenance for a disk resource or CSV so that you can run a disk maintenance tool without triggering failover.
- `Test-Cluster`: Runs validation tests for failover cluster hardware and settings.
- `Test-ClusterResourceFailure`: Simulates a failure of a cluster resource.
- `Update-ClusterIPResource`: Renews or releases the DHCP lease for an IP address resource in a failover cluster.
- `Update-ClusterNetworkNameResource`: Registers existing Network Name resources with a DNS server in a way that does not interrupt cluster availability.

Implementing Cluster-Aware Updating

Applying Windows updates to nodes in a cluster always needs more attention and planning because having one update on one node and not on the other node can cause problems or corruption of data. If you don't want downtime, you must move resources manually from the node that you are updating, perform the updates on the first node, and then change the resources to another node and perform the updates on the next node. Starting with Windows Server 2012, ***Cluster-Aware Updating (CAU)*** lets administrators update cluster nodes automatically, with little or no downtime, particularly if you use Hyper-V with live migration.

CERTIFICATION READY
Implement Cluster-Aware Updating.
Objective 1.2

You can use CAU in one of the following two modes:

- Remote-updating mode
- Self-updating mode

With remote-updating mode, you install the failover clustering administrative tools on a CAU orchestrator (a remote computer running Windows 8.1 or Windows Server 2012 R2 that is not a member of the cluster). The CAU is included in the Remote Server Administration Tool (RSAT). The administrator triggers the update process on the orchestrator computer. Remote-updating mode is useful for monitoring real-time progress during the Updating Run, and for clusters that run on Server Core installations of Windows Server 2012 R2.

With self-updating mode, the CAU (installed on a node on the cluster) updates the cluster at scheduled times by using a default or custom Updating Run profile. During the Updating Run, the CAU orchestrator process starts on the node that currently owns the CAU clustered role, and the process sequentially performs updates on each cluster node. You can use a self-updating mode, which allows the CAU to update the failover cluster by using a fully automated, end-to-end updating process, or you can trigger the updates manually. When using self-updating mode, you can check the progress of updates by connecting to the cluster and running the `Get-CauRun` Windows PowerShell cmdlet.

UPDATE THE SERVER USING CLUSTER-AWARE UPDATING

GET READY. To update the server using Cluster-Aware Updating, perform the following steps:

1. Open Server Manager, and then open Cluster-Aware Updating. The *Cluster–Aware Updating* dialog box opens.
2. Click the Connect to a failover cluster option and select your cluster. Click Connect. The cluster nodes appear as shown in Figure 2-6.

Figure 2-6
Connecting to a cluster

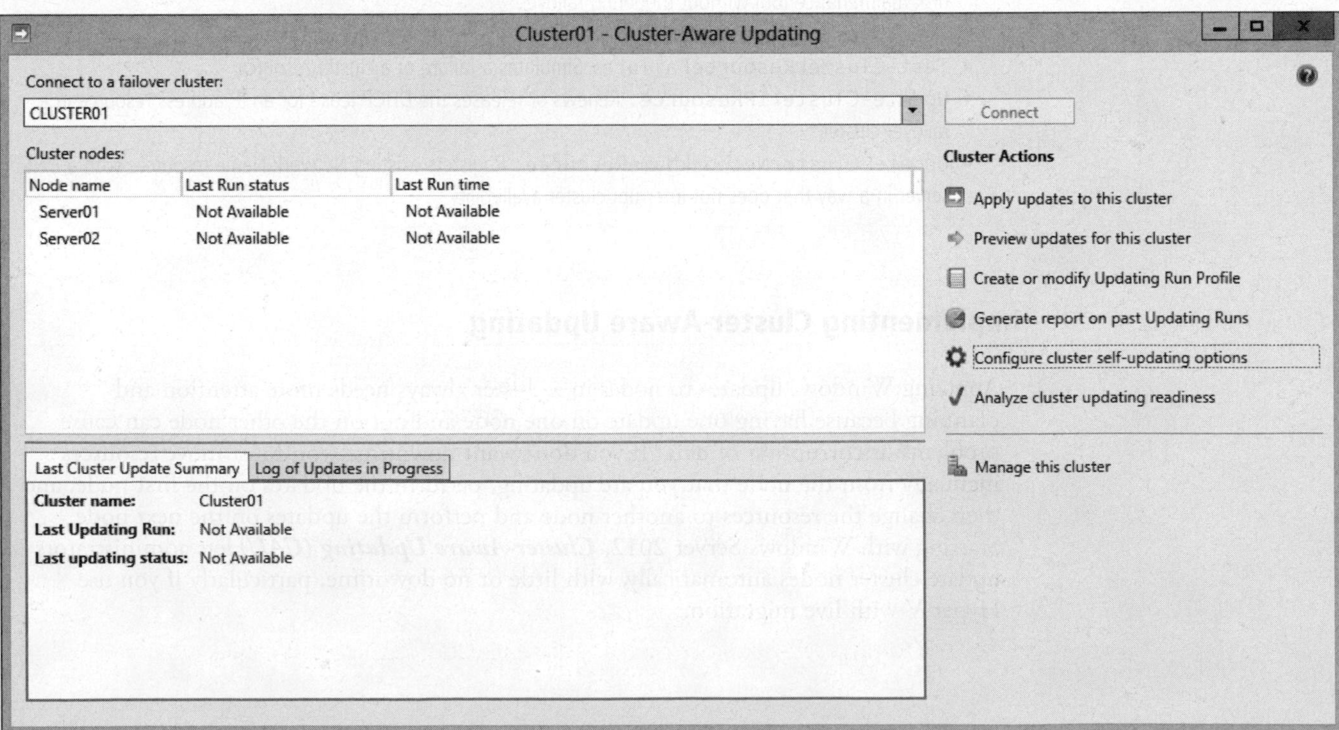

3. To install the cluster-aware role on the cluster, click Configure cluster self-updating options.
4. When the *Configure Self-Updating Options Wizard* starts, click Next.
5. Click the Add the CAU clustered role, with self-updating mode enabled, to this cluster and click Next.
6. On the *Specify self-updating schedule* page, specify how often it should do self-updating and when it should occur. Click Next.
7. On the *Advanced Options* page (see Figure 2-7), you can modify the options that define how self-updating runs. Click Next.

Figure 2-7

Modifying advanced options

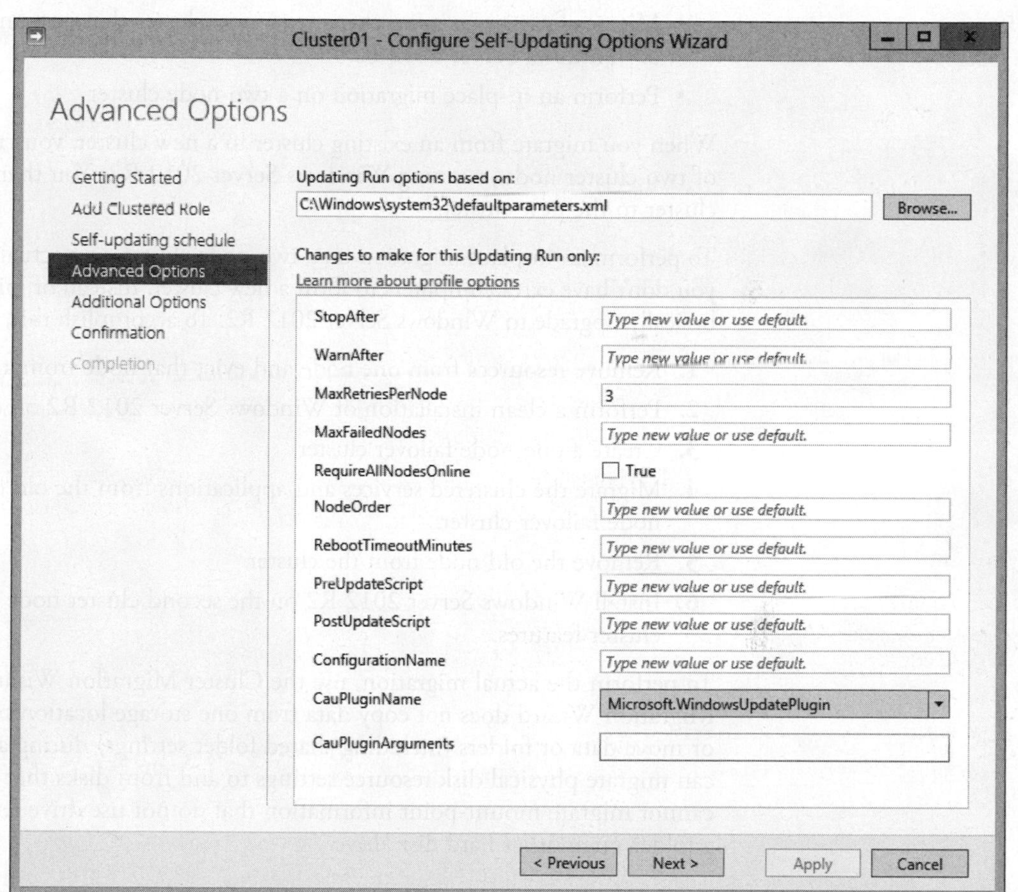

8. If you want recommended updates, click Give me recommended updates the same way that I receive important updates option and click Next.
9. On the *Confirmation* page, click Apply.
10. On the *Completion* page, click Close.
11. To manually apply updates, click Apply updates to this cluster.
12. When the *Cluster-Aware Updating Wizard* starts, click Next.
13. On the *Confirmation* page, click Update.
14. When the scheduling of the immediate updating is successful, click Close.

Upgrading a Cluster

If you have a cluster running on Windows Server 2008 or Windows Server 2008 R2, and you want to upgrade Windows to Windows Server 2012 or Windows Server 2012 R2, upgrading a cluster is more difficult if you want little or no downtime. Therefore, in these situations, you need to plan your upgrade.

CERTIFICATION READY
Upgrade a cluster.
Objective 1.2

To replace cluster nodes or upgrade to a newer version of Windows, you need to migrate cluster roles or services from one cluster to another. You can migrate clusters running Windows Server 2008, Windows Server 2008 R2, Windows Server 2012, and Windows Server 2012 R2. You can migrate these roles and configuration in one of the two ways:

- Migrate from an existing cluster to a new cluster that is running Windows Server 2012 or Windows Server 2012 R2
- Perform an in-place migration on a two-node cluster

When you migrate from an existing cluster to a new cluster, you create a new cluster consisting of two cluster nodes running Windows Server 2012 R2. You then migrate from the existing cluster to the new cluster.

To perform an in-place migration on a two-node cluster, you actually perform a migration when you don't have extra computers to form a new cluster. Instead of migrating to a new cluster, you basically upgrade to Windows Server 2012 R2. To accomplish this, perform the following:

1. Remove resources from one node and evict that node from a cluster.
2. Perform a clean installation of Windows Server 2012 R2 on the evicted server.
3. Create a one-node failover cluster.
4. Migrate the clustered services and applications from the old cluster node to the new one-node failover cluster.
5. Remove the old node from the cluster.
6. Install Windows Server 2012 R2 on the second cluster node and configure the failover cluster features.

To perform the actual migration, use the Cluster Migration Wizard. Because the Cluster Migration Wizard does not copy data from one storage location to another, you must copy or move data or folders (including shared folder settings) during a migration. Although you can migrate physical disk resource settings to and from disks that use mount points, you cannot migrate mount-point information that do not use drive letters, and are mounted in a folder on another hard disk drive.

RUN THE MIGRATE A CLUSTER WIZARD

GET READY. To run the Migrate a Cluster Wizard, perform the following steps:

1. On a node of the new cluster, use Server Manager to open the *Failover Cluster Wizard*.
2. Right-click the cluster, click More Actions, and click Migrate Roles.
3. When the *Migrate a Cluster Wizard* starts, click Next.
4. On the *Specify Old Cluster* page, type the name of the cluster or a name of one of the cluster nodes in the *Cluster or cluster node to migrate from* text box and click Next.
5. On the *Select Services and Applications* page, select the resources that you want to migrate and click Next.
6. On the *Customize Virtual Machine Networks*, select the virtual network switch and click Next.

7. On the *Confirmation* page, click Next.
8. When the wizard is complete, click Finish.

At this point, the target cluster is ready to take over. So during a scheduled maintenance window, you need to shut down all servers on the old cluster, configure the storage, and start the servers on the Windows Server 2012 R2 cluster.

Troubleshooting Problems with Failover Clusters

Although clusters provide availability to network resources, the cluster brings complexity to the network resources. Therefore, anytime you make something more complex, the troubleshooting also becomes more complex. However, when troubleshooting any problem, don't forget the basics: identify the perceived problem by collecting and documenting the symptoms of the problem and identifying the scope of the problem. Determine whether the problem is with the entire cluster or a specific node within the cluster. As you collect additional information, make a list of possible problems, and then prioritize them by probability and the impact of the repair. When you are ready, complete and test the repair until the problem is fixed. Lastly, document the fix and discuss what you can do in the future to prevent the same type of failure in the future.

When troubleshooting problems with failover clusters, you can use many tools. You should always start with opening the Failover Cluster Manager to see which resources are online and which resources are offline. You can even run the Validate a Configuration Wizard and look at the results. If some of the resources are offline, try to make the resources online. If you cannot access shared disks, make sure that the disks are available on the network and that all network and fabric cables are connected. If you use storage from a SAN, check the masking or security settings that specify which servers can access the storage.

Using Failover Cluster Manager, you can also click the *Cluster Events*, to show the events associated with clusters. In addition, you can use the Event Viewer and Performance and Reliability Monitor snap-in to review cluster and cluster-related events and performance metrics.

When a specific disk or role fails, you can right-click the failed disk or role, click *More Actions*, and click *Show Dependency Report* to identify dependent resources that allow the disk or role to function.

Backing Up and Restoring Failover Cluster Configuration

Because configuring a cluster is time-consuming and sometimes complex, it is important that you back up the cluster configuration. You can back up the cluster configuration and restore using Windows Server Backup or a non-Microsoft Backup tool.

CERTIFICATION READY
Restore single node or cluster configuration.
Objective 1.2

Before you put a cluster into production, you should test failover to make sure it is functioning properly. In addition, be sure that each node runs with the necessary resources. Lastly, you should test the backup and recovery process so that if a disaster occurs, you will know the steps to bring the cluster back in a timely manner.

Assuming that you have installed the Windows Server Backup feature, before you can perform a backup, the cluster needs to be running and you must have quorum. The Cluster service keeps track of the cluster configuration. When a change is made, it replicates the configuration to all cluster nodes. If the cluster has a witness disk, the Cluster service also replicates the configuration to the witness disk. Therefore, be sure to back up the System State, Cluster folders, and the witness disk.

You still have to back up the individual applications running the server and the associated data such as SQL databases, Exchange databases, or shared files. To back up application data, you can install backup software on the cluster node that owns the disk resource, or you can run the backup against the clustered resource over the network. If you use CSV volumes, you can run backup from any node that is attached to the CSV volume.

To restore the cluster, you can perform one of the two types of restores:

- ***Non-authoritative restore:*** A type of restore that restores the information that was performed when originally backed up but is overwritten by current information stored on other cluster nodes.
- ***Authoritative restore:*** A type of restore that restores the information that was performed when originally backed up but is marked as the current and authoritative configuration, which will then overwrite the configuration on the other nodes.

If you have a single cluster node that has failed, you can perform the non-authoritative restore. After fixing or replacing the failed node, perform a non-authoritative restore including the system state. When you restart the node, the restored node will join the cluster and automatically receive the latest cluster configuration from the other nodes or the witness disk.

Alternatively, you can remove a node and add a new node to the cluster. The new node will automatically receive the cluster information.

If an administrator accidently removed clustered resources or modified other cluster settings and you need to restore the cluster back to a specific point in time before the changes were made, you will perform an authoritative restore. To perform an authoritative restore, you will need to stop the cluster restores on all nodes. You then perform a system state recovery on a single node. After the restore, restart the cluster service so that the cluster service will mark the current configuration as the most recent configuration. As you bring the remaining cluster nodes online and start the cluster service, the other nodes will receive the restored configuration.

SKILL SUMMARY

IN THIS LESSON YOU LEARNED:

- A failover cluster is a set of independent computers that work together to increase the availability of services and applications.
- The clustered servers (called nodes) are connected through a network connection (physical or virtual) and by software.
- Failover clustering is best suited for stateful applications that are derived from a single set of data.
- A cluster resource is the most basic and smallest configurable unit that can provide a service to clients, or is important component that makes up the cluster. It can be a network application server or hardware device, such as a storage device, that is defined and managed by the cluster server.
- Cluster storage is a storage system that is shared between cluster nodes and usually connects using Fibre Channel or iSCSI.

- Initially installing a failover cluster is a three-step process: install the Failover Clustering feature, validate the cluster configuration, and create the cluster.
- Before you add storage to a cluster, be sure that all nodes can see the storage device and that the storage device has been initialized, partitioned, and formatted, and that the same drive letter is assigned to the storage device on all nodes.
- Traditionally, a single node controls a LUN on the shared storage. However, starting with Windows Server 2008 R2, Windows can use a Cluster Shared Volume (CSV), which allows multiple nodes to share a single LUN concurrently.
- A quorum is used with a failover cluster to determine the number of failures that the cluster can sustain. If a quorum (the majority of the votes) is not reached, the cluster will stop running.
- With Windows Server 2012 R2, you can deploy clustered storage spaces by using Storage Spaces and Failover Clustering to provide a resilient, highly available, and cost efficient solution.
- Windows Server 2012 R2 introduced Active Directory-detached cluster, which allows you to deploy a failover cluster without any dependencies in Active Directory Domain Services (AD DS) for network names.
- The Failover Cluster Manager manages and monitors the cluster and its nodes.
- Cluster-Aware Updating (CAU) lets administrators update cluster nodes automatically, with little or no downtime, particularly if you use Hyper-V with live migration.
- You can back up the cluster configuration and restore using Windows Server Backup or a non-Microsoft Backup tool.

Knowledge Assessment

Multiple Choice

Select the correct answer for each of the following questions.

1. Which type of clustering is used for back-end databases?
   a. Network Load Balancing (NLB) cluster
   b. failover cluster
   c. aggregated cluster
   d. power cluster

2. What is the maximum number of nodes you can have in a single cluster?
   a. 2
   b. 8
   c. 32
   d. 64

3. Which of the following can networks can you use in a Windows failover cluster? (Choose all that apply.)
   a. public-and-private
   b. private
   c. public
   d. central

4. What port do heartbeats use?
   a. 80
   b. 2232
   c. 3343
   d. 3389
5. Which of the following are SAN technologies that are used for centralized storage when configuring failover clusters? (Choose all that apply.)
   a. SAS
   b. Fibre Channel
   c. Serial ATA
   d. iSCSI
6. Which type of storage allows multiple nodes to access the storage at the same time?
   a. Cluster Shared Volume (CSV)
   b. FAT Volume
   c. LAN Volume
   d. WAN Volume
7. What is used to provide quorum when you have only two nodes in a cluster? (Choose all that apply.)
   a. heartbeat
   b. witness disk
   c. CSV disk
   d. shared folder
8. What allows you to automatically patch a cluster node with little or no downtime?
   a. Cluster-Aware Updating
   b. Cluster Auto Update
   c. Cluster Free Update
   d. Orchestrated Updates
9. What type of quorum would you use if you have three nodes in a failover cluster?
   a. Node Majority
   b. Node and Disk Majority
   c. Node and File Share Majority
   d. No Majority
10. What Windows PowerShell cmdlet would you use to check the progress of updates when using CAU?
    a. `InspectCAU`
    b. `Show-CAU`
    c. `Run-CAU`
    d. `Get-CAURUN`
11. Which of the following are improvements for CSV introduced with Windows Server 2012? (Choose all that apply)
    a. Support for SMB 3.0
    b. Support for dynamic disks
    c. Allows scan and repair of the CSV volumes with no downtime
    d. Supports NTFS and ReFS

12. Which of the following allows you to deploying a failover cluster without creating an Active Directory computer account for the cluster network name?
    a. `-Administrative AccessPoint`
    b. a Kerberos-free cluster
    c. a virtual failover cluster
    d. An Active Directory-detached cluster

Best Answer

Choose the letter that corresponds to the best answer. More than one answer choice may achieve the goal. Select the BEST answer.

1. You have an Active Directory domain called *contoso.com*. You have two servers called *Server1* and *Server 2*, both of which are running Windows Server 2012 R2. Server1 and 2 make up the failover cluster called *Cluster1*. You add a third node. What do you need to configure so that the cluster will stop if two of the nodes fail?
   a. Failover settings
   b. Host priority
   c. Cluster Quorum settings
   d. Quick migration
2. You are going to create a failover cluster that connects to an iSCSI SAN. What is the minimum number of network adapters recommended for each node?
   a. 1
   b. 2
   c. 3
   d. 4
3. You are an administrator for the Contoso Corporation. You have a two-node failover cluster with a witness disk. One of the servers failed and the entire server has been replaced. How should you add the replacement server to the cluster?
   a. Perform an authoritative restore
   b. Perform a non-authoritative restore
   c. Create an image from the remaining server and restore to the new server
   d. Install Windows and the cluster, and copy the cluster folder from the witness disk to the new server
4. For a failover cluster, what type of network would you use to communicate with an iSCSI device?
   a. private
   b. public
   c. public-and-private
   d. internal
5. You are an administrator for the Contoso Corporation. You have a two-node failover cluster with a witness disk. You need to take one of the servers down for maintenance. What should you do?
   a. Stop the Cluster service
   b. Unplug the network connections of the server before shutting down
   c. Drain the roles for the server that you want to shut down
   d. Add a new node and then remove the node that you need to take down for maintenance

Matching and Identification

1. Match the appropriate term with its description.
   _______ a) failover cluster
   _______ b) node
   _______ c) quorum
   _______ d) Cluster Shared Volume (CSV)
   _______ e) Cluster-Aware Updating (CAU)
   _______ f) heartbeat
   1. Used by nodes to keep aware of the status of other nodes
   2. Computers that make up a cluster
   3. A set of independent computers to provide high availability for a service
   4. Updates cluster nodes automatically
   5. A volume that allows multiple nodes to share a single LUN
   6. Determines the number of failures that a cluster can sustain at the same time

2. Identify the appropriate quorum configuration. Options may be repeated.
   _______ a) Recommended for odd number of nodes
   _______ b) Specifies that at least half the nodes and a witness is up
   _______ c) Uses a shared folder instead of a witness disk
   _______ d) Specifies that more nodes must be up than down
   _______ e) Requires only at least one node to be active
   _______ f) Recommended for cluster with even numbers
   1. Node Majority
   2. Node and Disk Majority
   3. Node and File Share Majority
   4. No Majority

3. Where would you find the following options? (Options may be repeated.)
   _______ a) Drain a role
   _______ b) Add a new node
   _______ c) Configure the quorum settings
   _______ d) Bring a shared storage online
   _______ e) Migrate a cluster
   _______ f) Stop a cluster
   _______ g) Delete a cluster
   1. Right-click the cluster and select More Actions
   2. Right-click a node and click Pause
   3. Right-click the shared volume
   4. Right-click the node

Build a List

1. Identify the three basic steps necessary to install and create a failover cluster by placing the number of the step in the appropriate space. Not all steps will be used.
   _______ Create the cluster
   _______ Validate the cluster configuration
   _______ Define the heartbeats parameters
   _______ Install the Failover Clustering feature
   _______ Install the Microsoft Failover Cluster Virtual Adapter

2. Identify the basic steps necessary to upgrade a cluster to Windows Server 2012 R2 by placing the number of the step in the appropriate space.
   _______ Create a one-node failover cluster
   _______ Evict the node from a cluster
   _______ Remove the last node from the cluster and install Windows Server 2012 R2
   _______ Perform a clean installation of Windows Server 2012 R2
   _______ Add second node to new cluster
   _______ Remove resources from one node
   _______ Migrate the clustered services and applications from the old cluster node to that failover cluster

Business Case Scenarios

Scenario 2-1: Configuring a Redundant Server

You work for the Contoso Corporation. You have a server that acts as a file server for clients. You must make sure that the server is up at all times. What would you recommend?

Scenario 2-2: Upgrading a Cluster to Windows Server 2012 R2

You work for the Contoso Corporation. You have a cluster used as a file server that is running Windows Server 2008 R2. You do not have any other free servers. How would you upgrade the cluster to Windows Server 2012 R2?

Managing Failover Clustering Roles

70-412 EXAM OBJECTIVE

Objective 1.3 – Manage failover clustering roles. This objective may include but is not limited to: Configure role-specific settings including continuously available shares; configure virtual machine (VM) monitoring; configure failover and preference settings; configure guest clustering.

LESSON HEADING	EXAM OBJECTIVE
Managing Failover Clustering Roles	
Configuring Roles	
Configuring Role-Specific Settings	Configure role-specific settings including continuously available shares Configure guest clustering
Configuring Failover and Preference Settings	Configure failover and preference settings
Configuring VM Monitoring	Configure virtual machine (VM) monitoring

KEY TERMS

cluster-aware clustered role
General Use File Server
generic application
generic clustered role
generic script
generic service
guest cluster
highly available virtual machines
preferred node
Scale-Out File Server
Server Message Block (SMB) 3.0
transaction
virtual machine (VM)
VM monitoring

■ Managing Failover Clustering Roles

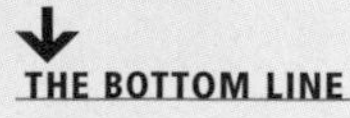

THE BOTTOM LINE

Failover clusters provide high availability and scalability to many server applications such as Microsoft Exchange, Microsoft SQL, and Hyper-V. You can use the High Availability Wizard to configure a *clustered role* (formerly called a *clustered service* or *application*), which is a service or application that you make highly available.

Similar to storage, if a server has a problem, a clustered role can fail over to another server. Clustered roles are divided into the following two types:

- Cluster-aware
- Generic

A ***cluster-aware clustered role*** is designed to work with Windows Server 2012 and Windows Server 2012 R2 fail-over clusters. Examples include the File Server clustered role and the Virtual Machine clustered role.

A ***generic clustered role*** provides high availability for a service, application, or script that is not originally designed to run in a cluster. As a result, the cluster cannot detect the state of the generic application, script, or service as it can with a cluster-aware role.

- ***Generic application:*** The cluster software starts the generic application, and then periodically queries the operating system to see whether the application still runs.
- ***Generic script:*** You create a script that runs in Windows Script Host, which monitors and controls an application. The state of the application is determined by the script.
- ***Generic service:*** The cluster software starts the service. Similar to generic applications, the cluster services periodically queries the Service Controller to determine whether the service is still running.

Depending on the cluster role or application that you try to run, one or more server roles or applications on each node might be required. In addition, some applications, such as mail and database applications might require additional configuration to work properly in a clustered environment. Microsoft provides thorough documentation to configure Microsoft Exchange or Microsoft SQL to run on a failover cluster on the technet.microsoft.com website.

Configuring Roles

To add a clustered role, you right-click the *Roles* node and click *Configure Role*, which starts the High Availability Wizard.

In the High Availability Wizard, you can choose from the following services and applications (see Figure 3-1):

- **DFS Namespace Server:** Provides a virtual view of shared folders in an organization, which allows users to access shared folders that are distributed among multiple folders.
- **DHCP Server:** Automatically provides TCP/IP hosts with valid IP addresses.
- **Distributed Transaction Coordinator (DTC):** Supports distributed applications that perform transactions. A ***transaction*** is a set of related tasks, such as updates to databases that either succeed or fail as a unit.
- **File Server:** Provides a central location on your network where you can store and share files with users.
- **Generic Application:** Allows you to run an application that is not specifically designed to run on a cluster.
- **Generic Script:** Allows you to run scripts that are used to start and monitor applications.
- **Generic Service:** Allows you to run services that are not specifically designed to run on a cluster.
- **iSCSI Target Server:** Allows you to provide iSCSI storage devices to iSCSI clients known as *iSCSI initiators*.
- **Internet Storage Name Service (iSNS) Server:** Provides a directory of iSCSI targets.
- **Message Queuing:** Enables distributed applications that are running at different times to communicate across heterogeneous networks and with computers that might be offline.

- **Other Server:** Provides a client access point and storage only. Add an application after completing the wizard.
- ***Virtual Machine (VM):*** Runs on a physical computer as a virtualized computer system. Multiple virtual machines can run on one computer.
- **WINS Server:** Enables users to access resources by a NetBIOS name instead of requiring them to use IP addresses that are difficult to recognize and remember.

Figure 3-1

Selecting a role to install on a cluster

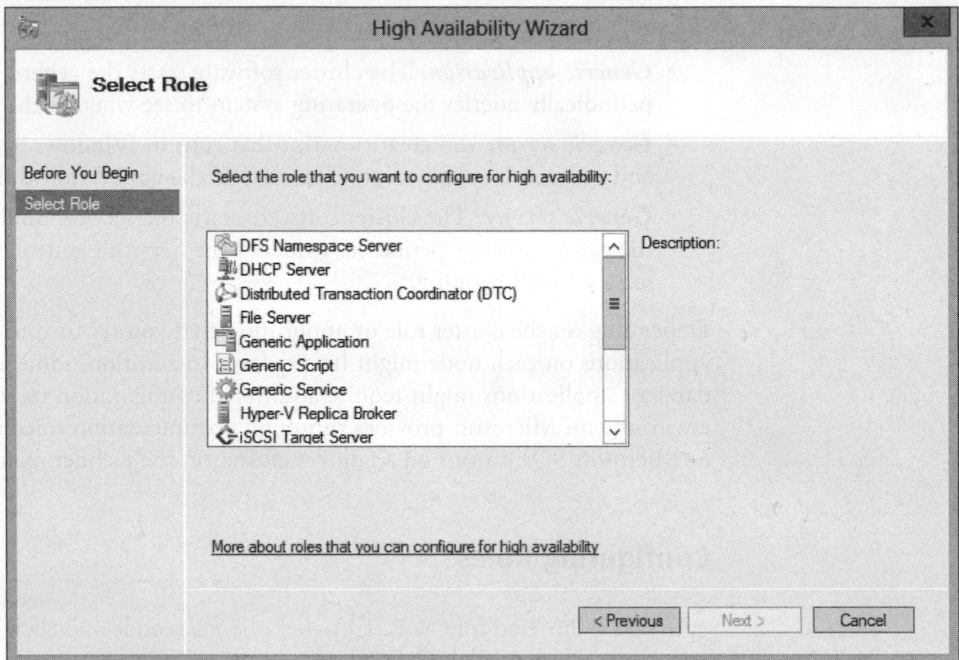

Configuring Role-Specific Settings

Clusters can be used for a wide range of applications to provide high availability. However, popular uses of clustering include file services and VMs.

CERTIFICATION READY
Configure role-specific settings including continuously available shares.
Objective 1.3

When you deploy high-available file services and VMs, you use a shared disk to store data files or VM files. Therefore, you need to choose a shared disk that is highly available and has high performance.

UNDERSTANDING SMB 3.0

Server Message Block (SMB) 3.0 (previously named *SMB 2.2*) is the newest version of the SMB protocol, which was introduced with Windows 8 and Windows Server 2012. It brings significant changes to add functionality and improve performance, particularly in virtualized data centers.

SMB 3.0 has the following additional features:

- **SMB Transparent Failover:** Provides Continuously Available properties that allow SMB 3 clients to not lose an SMB session when failover occurs. Both the SMB client and SMB server must support SMB 3.0 to take advantage of the SMB Transparent Failover functionality.
- **SMB Scale Out:** Allows users to scale shared bandwidth by adding cluster nodes. Both the SMB client and SMB server must support SMB 3.0 to take advantage of the SMB Scale Out feature. SMB 1.0 clients do not contain the required client functionality to access

SMB scale-out file shares and will receive an "Access Denied" error message when they try to connect to a scale-out file share. SMB 2.x clients will be able to connect to SMB scale-out file shares but will not benefit from the SMB Transparent Failover functionality.

- **SMB Multichannel:** Uses multiple network interfaces to provide both high performance through bandwidth aggregation and network fault tolerance through the use of multiple network paths to data on an SMB share. SMB 1.0 and SMB 2.x clients will use a single SMB connection.
- **SMB Direct (SMB over Remote Direct Memory Access [RDMA]):** Enables direct memory-to-memory data transfers between servers, with minimal CPU utilization and low latency, using standard RDMA-capable network adapters (iWARP, InfiniBand, and RoCE). It also minimizes the processor utilization when performing large file I/O operations. SMB Direct Functionality requires that the SMB client and SMB server support SMB 3.0.
- **SMB Encryption:** Performs encryption by selecting a check box. Both the SMB client and SMB server must support SMB 3.0 to take advantage of the SMB Encryption functionality.
- **VSS for SMB file shares:** Extends the Windows Volume Shadow Copy Service infrastructure to enable application-consistent shadow copies of server application data stored on SMB file shares, for backup and restore purposes. Both the SMB client and SMB server must support SMB 3.0 to take advantage of the Volume Shadow Copy Service (VSS) for SMB file shares functionality.
- **SMB Directory Leasing:** Reduces the latency when accessing files over slow WAN links by caching directory and file meta-data for longer periods, which reduces the associated round-trips to fetch the meta-data from the server. Both the SMB client and SMB server must support SMB 3.0 to take advantage of the SMB Directory Leasing functionality.
- **SMB PowerShell:** SMB PowerShell management cmdlets were introduced in Windows Server 2012 and in Windows 8.

DEPLOYING THE GENERAL USE FILE SERVER ROLE

File servers in a cluster can be configured for general use—***General Use File Server***—which is almost the same as it was in Windows Server 2008 R2. It provides a central location for users to share files or for server applications that open and close files frequently. It also supports SMB, Network File System (NFS), Data Deduplication, File Server Resource Manager, DFS Replication, and other File Services role services. The only significant difference between Windows Server 2008 R2 and Windows Server 2012/Windows Server 2012 R2 is that Windows Server 2012/Windows Server 2012 R2 supports SMB 3.0.

Before you install and configure the File Server role, be sure that you install the appropriate file server roles for Windows Server 2012 and Windows 2012 R2 such as File Server or Server for NFS. Then when you deploy the General Use File Server role, you will first add the File Server role, and then create the file shares.

DEPLOY THE GENERAL USE FILE SERVER ROLE

GET READY. To deploy the General Use File Server role, perform the following steps:

1. Open Server Manager and click Tools > Failover Cluster Manager. The *Failover Cluster Manager* opens.
2. Right-click Roles and click Configure Roles. Alternatively, you can click the cluster and under *Actions,* click Configure Role.
3. When the *High Availability Wizard* opens, click Next.
4. On the *Select Role* page, click File Server and then click Next.
5. On the *File Server Type* page (see Figure 3-2), click File Server for general use, and then click Next.

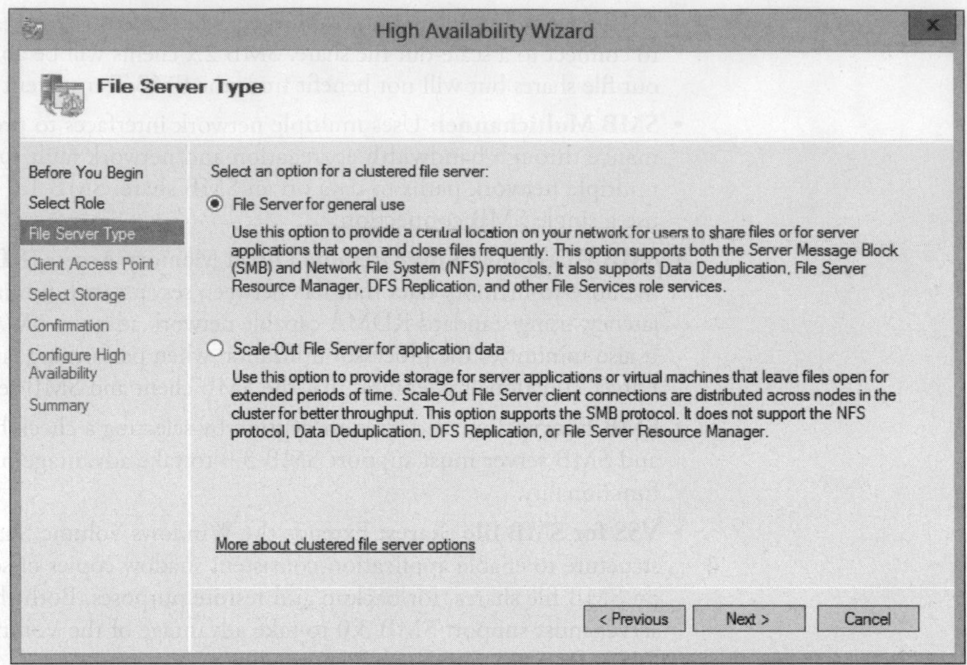

Figure 3-2
Selecting the file server type

6. On the *Client Access Point* page, type a NetBIOS name that the clients will access for the clustered role in the Name text box. Next, type an IP address in the *Address* column.
7. On the *Select Storage* page, enter a storage location for the data and click Next. The disk cannot be assigned as a Cluster Shared Volume (CSV).
8. On the *Confirmation* page, click Next.
9. On the *Summary* page, click Finish.
10. To create a file share, right-click the File Server Role, and click Add File Share.
11. When the *New Share Wizard* opens, select the appropriate file share profile. Click SMB Share – Quick and click Next.
12. On the *Share Location* page, be sure that the File Server cluster role is selected. Then with the Type a custom path selected, type a path (such as E:\Data) in the text box. Click Next.
13. On the *Share Name* page, type a name in the *Share name* box and click Next.
14. On the *Other Settings* page (see Figure 3-3), select or deselect the desired options and click Next.
15. On the *Permissions* page, configure the NTFS and Share permissions as necessary by clicking Customize permissions. When done, click Next.
16. On the *Confirmation* page, click Create.
17. When the installation is complete, click Close.

Figure 3-3

Select other settings

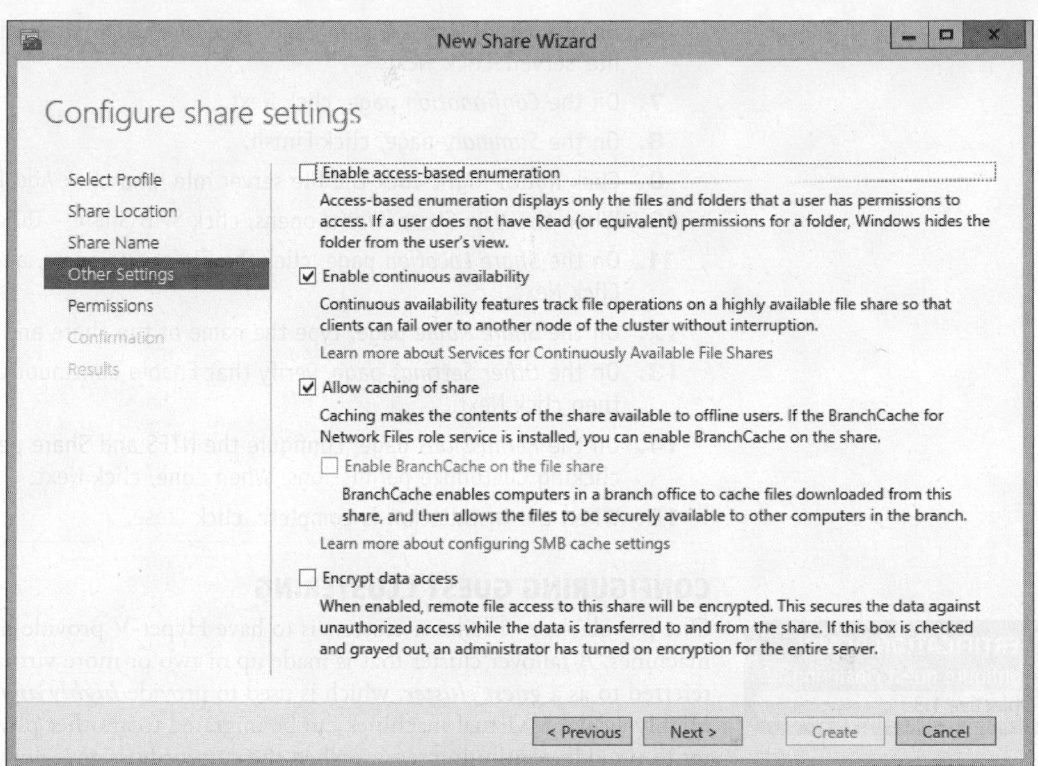

TAKE NOTE*

The Enable continuous availability and Encrypt data access options are selected by default. The Enable continuous availability takes advantage of SMB v3 functionality (Transparent Failover), whereas the Encrypt data access enables to encrypt the SMB connections.

DEPLOYING SCALE-OUT FILE SERVER

The type of file server that you can use with a cluster is the Scale-Out File Server (introduced in Windows Server 2012), which is intended for application data, such as Hyper-V VM files, file shares that require reliability, manageability, and high performance. Different from a General Use File Server cluster, the ***Scale-Out File Server*** cluster is an active-active failover cluster where all file shares are online on all nodes simultaneously. Although the Scale-Out File Server supports SMB, it does not support NFS, Data Deduplication, DFS Replication, or File Server Resource Manager.

To support multiple nodes to access the same volume at the same time, the Scale-Out File Server uses a CSV. It also uses a CSV cache, which reads cache that significantly improves performance in certain scenarios, such as Virtual Desktop Infrastructure.

DEPLOY A SCALE-OUT FILE SERVER

GET READY. To deploy a Scale-Out File Server, perform the following steps:

1. Open Server Manager and click the Tools > Failover Cluster Manager. The *Failover Cluster Manager* opens.
2. Right-click Roles and click Configure Roles. Alternatively, you can click the cluster and under *Actions*, click Configure Role.
3. When the *High Availability Wizard* opens, click Next.
4. On the *Select Role* page, click File Server and click Next.
5. On the *File Server Type* page, click Scale-Out File Server for application data, and click Next.

6. On the *Client Access Point* page, type the name that clients will use to access the file server. Click Next.
7. On the *Confirmation* page, click Next.
8. On the *Summary* page, click Finish.
9. Click Roles. Right-click the file server role, and click Add File Share.
10. When the *New Share Wizard* opens, click SMB Share – Quick, and then click Next.
11. On the *Share Location* page, click the file server name, and click Select by volume. Click Next.
12. On the *Share Name* page, type the name of the share and click Next.
13. On the *Other Settings* page, verify that Enable continuous availability is selected, and then click Next.
14. On the *Permissions* page, configure the NTFS and Share permissions as necessary by clicking Customize permissions. When done, click Next.
15. When the installation is complete, click Close.

CONFIGURING GUEST CLUSTERING

CERTIFICATION READY
Configure guest clustering.
Objective 1.3

One popular use of failover clusters is to have Hyper-V provide highly available virtual machines. A failover cluster that is made up of two or more virtual machines is typically referred to as a ***guest cluster***, which is used to provide ***highly available virtual machines***. Highly available virtual machines can be migrated to another physical host in a failover cluster to provide continuing service when the current host goes down or needs maintenance. Different from the other types of clusters, the Hyper-V nodes must be composed of physical hosts. You cannot run Hyper-V on a VM. In addition, to avoid losing network connectivity, you must create the same virtual networks on all physical hosts that participate in the cluster.

To make a VM highly available, all the VM storage location must be on shared storage that all nodes can access. In addition, the storage needs to be configured as a CSV.

In addition to the network and storage requirements, to deploy Hyper-V on a failover cluster, you must meet the following hardware requirements:

- Physical hosts should have similar hardware.
- Physical hosts require an x64-based processor with hardware-assisted virtualization, and hardware-enforced Data Execution Prevention (DEP).
- The processors should be the same architecture and version.
- To provide network redundancy, you can connect cluster nodes to multiple networks and/or use teamed network adapters, redundant switches, and redundant routers.
- To provide inter-host communications, you need one network adapter for each host to form the private network.
- If you use a Serial Attached SCSI (SAS) or Fibre Channel, the mass-storage device controllers in all physical hosts should be identical and should use the same firmware version.
- If you use iSCSI, each physical host should have one or more network adapters that are dedicated to the cluster storage.
- The network adapters that you use to connect to the iSCSI storage target should be identical, and you should use a gigabit Ethernet or faster network adapter.
- When creating shared storage, use basic disks, not dynamic disks.
- Format the disks with the NTFS file system.
- Use either master boot record (MBR) or GUID partition table (GPT).
- If you use a storage area network (SAN), the miniport driver that the storage uses must work with the Microsoft Storport storage driver.

- If you use a SAN, consider using multipath I/O software.
- To protect against host failure, it is recommended that you place virtual machines that are part of the same guest cluster on different physical hosts.

TAKE NOTE*

Microsoft supports a Windows Server 2012 R2 failover cluster solution only if all the hardware features are marked as "Certified for Windows Server 2012 R2."

To deploy Hyper-V on a failover cluster, you must meet the following software requirements:

- All physical hosts must run the Windows Server 2012 R2 Standard Edition or Windows Server 2012 R2 Datacenter Edition. In addition, you must have the same edition.
- All physical hosts must be either Full installation or Server Core installations.
- All physical hosts should have the same Windows updates and service packs.
- Network settings such as speed, duplex mode, flow control, and media type settings are the same.
- Make sure that the private network uses a unique subnet.
- Use DNS Dynamic update protocol.
- All servers must be in the same Active Directory Domain Services (AD DS) domain.
- When you first create a cluster or add servers to a cluster, you must be logged on to the domain with an administrator's account on all the cluster's servers. If the account is not a domain administrator, the account must have the Create Computer Objects permission in the domain.

DEPLOY A GUEST CLUSTER

To deploy a guest cluster, perform the following steps:

1. Connect both host computers to the network and storage.
2. Install and configure the required versions of Windows Server 2012 R2.
3. Configure the network settings and join the computers to the AD DS domain.
4. Configure the connection to the shared storage and partition and format the disks with Disk Manager.
5. Install the Hyper-V role.
6. Create the necessary virtual switches.
7. Install the failover clustering features on the host servers.
8. Validate the cluster configuration using the Validate This Cluster Wizard.
9. Create the cluster.
10. Enable Clustered Shared storage for the cluster.
11. Create a VM on one of the cluster nodes. Be sure that the virtual hard disk and VM configuration files are stored on the shared CSV volume.
12. Using the High Availability Wizard, select the *Virtual Machine role* and select the VMs that you want to make highly available.
13. Install the guest operating system on the VM.
14. Test VM failover.

DEPLOYING HYPER-V OVER SMB 3

Another way to make a VM highly available is to store the VM files on a highly available SMB 3.0 file share, instead of using host or guest clustering. To accomplish this, you need the following:

- One or more computers that are running Windows Server 2012 and Windows Server 2012 R2 PR with the Hyper-V role installed.

- One or more computers that are running Windows Server 2012 and Windows Server 2012 R2 with the File and Storage Services role installed.
- The servers must be part of the same Active Directory domain.

After you have the servers in place, you create a scale-out file server cluster and deploy the new SMB file share for applications. When the file shares are ready, you can deploy new servers or migrate existing VMs to the SMB file share. Hyper-V migration is discussed in Lesson 4, "Managing VM Movement."

Configuring Failover and Preference Settings

Usually, in a cluster, one node is the same as another. However, you do have some control over which server is the preferred node, and whether a server fails back when the server is brought back online.

CERTIFICATION READY
Configure failover and preference settings.
Objective 1.3

You have multiple nodes in a cluster. To specify that one node is the ***preferred node***, you can right-click a role and click *Properties*. When the Properties dialog box opens, select the *General* tab (see Figure 3-4). You can then click the server that you prefer and click the *Up* button to make it first in the list.

The default value for the maximum number of failures is $n - 1$, where n is the number of nodes. Although you can change this value, it is recommended that you keep the value relatively low or the application or service will keep bouncing between nodes.

If a cluster has multiple roles, you can categories the priority for each role. Roles with higher priorities are started before roles with lower priorities. If you don't want a role to start, you select *No Auto Start*.

Figure 3-4

Specifying the preferred owner

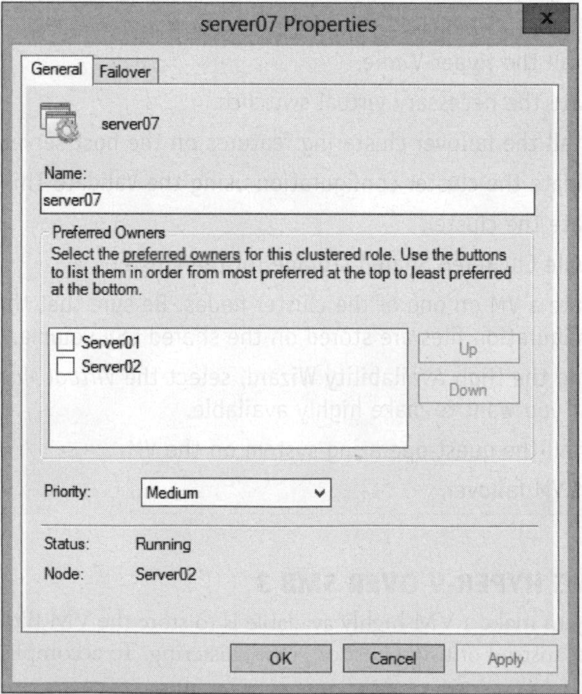

When you click the *Failover* tab (see Figure 3-5), you can specify the number of times the Cluster service will attempt to restart or failover. In the Failback option, you can specify not to failback to the preferred owner after the preferred owner is brought back online and when the failback will occur.

Figure 3-5

Specifying Failover and Failback options

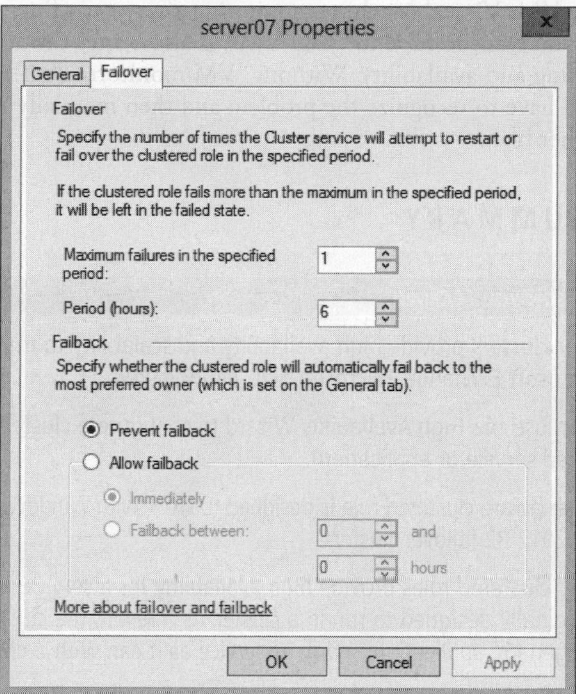

Configuring VM Monitoring

With Windows Server 2012 R2, you can use ***VM monitoring***, which is used to monitor specific services within the VM and reacts if there is a problem with a service.

CERTIFICATION READY
Configure VM monitoring.
Objective 1.3

Lesson 2, "Configuring Failover Clustering," discusses how you can use the Failover Cluster Manager, Event Viewer, and Performance and Reliability Monitors to verify that a cluster runs and how well the cluster is doing. However, you cannot monitor the health of applications running inside the guest operating systems of a Hyper-V VM.

Before you can set up VM monitoring on the Failover Cluster Manager, you must have the following:

- The Hyper-V Host operating system must be Windows Server 2012 R2 or Microsoft Hyper-V Server 2012 R2.
- The guest operating system of the VM must be Windows Server 2012.
- The VM guest operating system needs to be on the same domain as the Hyper-V host.
- The administrator of the Hyper-V Cluster needs to have local administrator rights on the VM guest.
- The VM guest firewall needs to allow VM monitoring.

To enable VM monitoring, right-click the *VM* in the Failover Cluster Manager, choose *More Actions*, and click *Choose Configure Monitoring*. When the Select Services dialog box opens, select the services that you want to monitor and click *OK*. You can also enable VM monitoring with the following Windows PowerShell command:

```
Add-ClusterVMMonitoredItem -VirtualMachine
"VM_Name" -Service Name_of_Service
```

When the service is determined to be unhealthy, the Event ID 1250 will be shown in the System Logs. VM monitoring will then restart the VM gracefully on the host that it's currently running on. If the VM fails again, VM monitoring will move the VM to another node and start the VM. Virtual Machine monitoring gives you a finer granularity of the kind of monitoring you want to have for your VMs. It also brings the added benefit of additional health-checking and availability. Without "VM monitoring", if a particular service has a problem, you will have to recognize the problem and then manually restart the service or move the VM to another host.

SKILL SUMMARY

IN THIS LESSON YOU LEARNED:

- Failover clusters provide high availability and scalability to many server applications such as Microsoft Exchange, Microsoft SQL, and Hyper-V.
- You can use the High Availability Wizard to configure a clustered role (formerly called a clustered service or application).
- A cluster-aware clustered role is designed to work with Windows Server 2012 and Windows Server 2012 R2 failover clusters.
- Generic clustered roles provide high availability for a service, application, or script that is not originally designed to run in a cluster. As a result, the cluster cannot detect the state of the generic application, script, or service as it can with a cluster-aware role.
- Server Message Block (SMB) 3.0 (previously named *SMB 2.2*) is the newest version of the SMB protocol, which was introduced with Windows 8 and Windows Server 2012. It brings significant changes to add functionality and improve performance, particularly in virtualized data centers.
- File servers in a cluster can be configured for general use (General Use File Server), which is almost the same as it was in Windows Server 2008 R2. It provides a central location for users to share files or for server applications that open and close files frequently.
- Different from a General Use File Server cluster, the Scale-Out File Server cluster is an active-active failover cluster where all file shares are online on all nodes simultaneously.
- To support multiple nodes to access the same volume at the same time, the Scale-Out File Server uses a Cluster Shared Volume (CSV).
- A failover cluster that is made up of two or more virtual machines is typically referred to as a guest cluster, which is used to provide highly available virtual machines.
- To make a VM highly available using guest clustering, all the VM storage location must be on share storage that all nodes can access. In addition, the storage needs to be configured as a CSV.
- Another way to make a VM highly available is to store the VM files on a highly available SMB 3.0 file share, instead of using host or guest clustering.
- Usually, in a cluster, one node is the same as another. However, you do have some control over which server is the preferred node, and whether a server fails back when the server is brought back online.
- With Windows Server 2012 R2, you can use Virtual Machine monitoring to monitor specific services within the VM and react if there is a problem with a service.

Knowledge Assessment

Multiple Choice

Select the correct answer for each of the following questions.

1. Which do you configure to make a service or application highly available?
   a. role
   b. resource
   c. device
   d. storage

2. Which type of role is designed to work with Windows Server 2012 R2 failover cluster?
   a. generic clustered role
   b. available role
   c. cluster-aware clustered role
   d. clustered update role

3. Which of the following is a benefit of Server Message Block (SMB) 3.0? (Choose all that apply.)
   a. SMB Encryption
   b. SMB Multichannel
   c. SMB General Use File Services
   d. SMB Directory Leasing

4. Which SMB feature allows multiple nodes to access a clustered disk at the same time?
   a. SMB Transparent Failover
   b. SMB Scale Out
   c. SMB Direct
   d. VSS for SMB file shares

5. Which type of file server resembles the file server used in Windows Server 2008 R2?
   a. General Use File Server
   b. Scale-Out File Server
   c. Highly Available CSV
   d. Direct Access File Server

6. Which type of volume should you use for highly available virtual machine?
   a. SAS
   b. GPT
   c. DEP
   d. CSV

7. What do you configure if you want one node to be an active node while it is available?
   a. Failback partner
   b. Prioritized member
   c. Preferred owner
   d. Primary Active node

8. What Windows PowerShell cmdlet is used to enable VM monitoring?
   a. `Set-ClusterVMMonitoredItem`
   b. `Get-ClusterVMMonitoredItem`
   c. `Configure-ClusterVMMonitoredItem`
   d. `Add-ClusterVMMonitoredItem`

9. Which type of application or services would you configure on a cluster for an application or service that was not made for a cluster?
   a. generic clustered role
   b. available role
   c. cluster-aware clustered role
   d. clustered update role

10. Which of the following is supported by a Scale-Out Server? (Choose all that apply.)
   a. NFS
   b. Data Deduplication
   c. SMB
   d. DFS Replication

Best Answer

Choose the letter that corresponds to the best answer. More than one answer choice may achieve the goal. Select the BEST answer.

1. You are an administrator for contoso.com. You have two servers called *Server1* and *Server2* that run Windows Server 2012 R2 and have the Failover Clustering feature installed. You decide to add two more nodes to the cluster. You have a folder that you want all the servers to provide service for. What should you configure?
   a. File server for general use
   b. Scale-Out File Server
   c. Preferred Server
   d. handling priority

2. You are an administrator for contoso.com. You have two servers called *Server1* and *Server2* that run Windows Server 2012 R2 and have the Failover Clustering feature installed. You have configured the application named *APP1* on the cluster. You need to make sure that Server02 handles all requests for APP1. What should you configure?
   a. preferred owner
   b. possible owner
   c. host priority
   d. handling priority

3. You are an administrator for contoso.com. You have two servers called *Server1* and *Server2* that run Windows Server 2012 R2 and have the Failover Clustering feature installed. You want to make a highly available file server that supports DFS. What should you configure?
   a. File server for general use
   b. Scale-Out File Server
   c. Preferred Server
   d. handling priority

4. You are an administrator for contoso.com. You have two servers called *Server1* and *Server2* that run Windows Server 2012 R2 and have the Failover Clustering feature installed. You install a cluster that provides high availability for DHCP and a shared folder. You want to make sure that if two heartbeats are missed, the DHCP service is switched to another node on the cluster. What should you configure?
   a. preferred owner
   b. failover settings
   c. host priority
   d. handling priority

5. You are an administrator for contoso.com. You have two servers called *Server1* and *Server2* that run Windows Server 2012 R2 and have the Failover Clustering feature installed. You configure the server to run a highly available virtual machine that is the DHCP server. What do you configure to monitor the DHCP service?
   a. Enable event forwarding
   b. Enable VM monitoring
   c. Enable service monitoring
   d. Enable event subscriptions

Matching and Identification

1. Identify which of the following can be made highly available using the High Availability Wizard?
   _______ a) DFS Namespace Server
   _______ b) iSCSI client
   _______ c) Print services
   _______ d) DHCP Server
   _______ e) Message Queuing
   _______ f) Name resolver
   _______ g) WINS Server
   _______ h) Virtual machine
2. Match the appropriate SMB 3.0 feature with its description.
   _______ a) SMB Direct
   _______ b) SMB Encryption
   _______ c) SMB Directory Leasing
   _______ d) SMB Multichannel
   _______ e) SMB Transparent Failover
   1. Use multiple network interfaces to provide high performance
   2. Direct memory-to-memory data transfers between servers with minimum assistance from the processor is enabled
   3. Encrypts SMB traffic
   4. SMB session continues during failover
   5. Latency is reduced when accessing files over slow WAN links by caching directory and file meta-data for longer periods

Build a List

1. Identify the basic steps in order to create a general use file server by placing the number of the step in the appropriate space.
   _______ Select File Server
   _______ Install the Failover Cluster feature
   _______ Create the cluster
   _______ Select File Server for general use
   _______ Start the High AvailabilityWizard
   _______ Select the storage to be used
   _______ Specify a name and IP address for the clients to access
   _______ Define a share by selecting a file share profile

2. Identify the basic steps in order to create a Scale-Out file server by placing the number of the step in the appropriate space.
   _______ Select File server for general use
   _______ Install the Failover Cluster feature
   _______ Create the cluster
   _______ Enable continuous availability
   _______ Define a share by selecting a file share profile
   _______ Start the High AvailabilityWizard
   _______ Select File Server

3. Identify the basic steps, in order, when deploying a highly available virtual machine by placing the number of the step in the appropriate space.
   _______ Create the cluster
   _______ Install Windows Server 2012 R2
   _______ Validate the cluster
   _______ Connect both computers to network and storage
   _______ Test the virtual machine failover
   _______ Install Hyper-V
   _______ Install the Failover Clustering feature
   _______ Prepare disk to be used as a shared volume
   _______ Create a virtual machine
   _______ Use the High AvailabilityWizard to make the VM highly available
   _______ Create the necessary virtual switches
   _______ Enable the Clustered Shared storage

■ Business Case Scenarios

Scenario 3-1: Deploying a Clustered File Server

You are an administrator for the Contoso Corporation. You have client software that receives its configuration from a shared folder. Therefore, you need to make sure that this shared folder is highly available. Because it is used by hundreds of users, many at the same time, you want to make sure that performance is high. What would you do?

Scenario 3-2: Deploying a High Availability Virtual Machine

You are an administrator for the Contoso Corporation. You have an enterprise database application that has to be highly available. The application currently runs on a VM. What do you need to make the VM highly available?

Managing Virtual Machine Movement

LESSON 4

70-412 EXAM OBJECTIVE

Objective 1.4 – Manage Virtual Machine (VM) movement. This objective may include but is not limited to: Perform live migration; perform quick migration; perform storage migration; import, export, and copy VMs; configure virtual machine network health protection; configure drain on shutdown

Lesson Heading	Exam Objective
Understanding Virtual Machine Movement	
Understanding Live Migration	
Performing LM	Perform live migration
Performing Quick Migration	Perform quick migration
Performing Storage Migration	Perform storage migration
Configuring Virtual Machine Network Health Protection	Configure virtual machine network health protection
Configuring Drain on Shutdown	Configure drain on shutdown
Importing, Exporting, and Copying Virtual Machines	Import, export, and copy VMs
Migrating from Other Platforms – Understanding P2V and V2V	
Converting a Virtual Machine to Virtual Machine (V2V) Using SCVMM	

KEY TERMS

Credential Security Support Provider (CredSSP)
live migration (LM)
Microsoft System Center 2012 SP1 Virtual Machine Manager (SCVMM)
Open Virtualization Format (OVF)
quick migration
Physical Machine to Virtual Machine (P2V)
protected network
storage migration
VHDX
virtual hard disks (VHD)
Virtual Machine to Virtual Machine migration (V2V)

Understanding Virtual Machine Movement

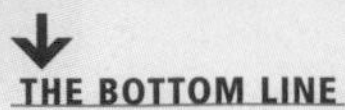

Because of the ease with which virtual machines (VMs) can be created and the speed with which the services they provide grow, VM management can quickly become a problem. When this happens, you need a way to move the VM and its storage quickly and with as little inconvenience to your users as possible.

As a server administrator, VMs are one of the best tools to use for providing functionality on demand. With relative speed and ease, you can deliver additional applications as soon as they are needed rather than waiting for the purchase of new hardware.

However, there comes a time when that new application grows from being hardly used to being a mission-critical application that everyone in your organization relies on daily or even hourly. When that happens, inevitably, the server with which you started is no longer powerful enough to handle the load.

In these growth scenarios—when a more powerful server or more storage space is required—because the application started as a VM, it can be moved to that more powerful server or larger disk with relative ease and no server downtime. The challenge, however, is to move the existing VM from one physical computer to another *and* not impact your users.

In prior versions, moving VMs required either a cluster or powering the VM down and moving the files manually. Starting with Windows Server 2012, Live VM movement is no longer limited to a cluster. You can now move an entire VM and its storage to another physical machine with ease while it is online and being used. Three processes are used to move an entire VM or its parts while it runs:

- ***Live Migration (LM):*** The process of moving an entire VM or parts of a VM to another physical server without a cluster.
- ***Quick Migration:*** The process of moving an entire VM or parts of a VM to another physical server using a cluster.
- ***Storage Migration:*** The process of moving the storage of a VM from one physical server to another without a cluster.

Understanding Live Migration

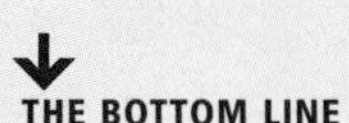

LM is the process of moving a VM or its storage from one physical server to another without turning off the VM and without any perceived or actual downtime. In prior versions, the process of performing LM required the VM to be hosted within a clustered environment. In Windows Server 2012 and Windows Server 2012 R2, although that is still possible, it is no longer a requirement.

LM allows you to move the entire VM or its storage from one physical host to another without interrupting your users. This process is sometimes referred to as a *shared nothing* migration because the storage is mirrored over the network to the destination server while the VM continues to run and provide network services

CERTIFICATION READY
Perform live migration.
Objective 1.4

Performing LM

LM requires four steps performed in order to properly move a running VM.

To perform an LM, your systems must perform the following steps:

1. Configure LM prerequisites.
2. Configure LM security (constrained delegation, if needed).
3. Configure the source and destination computers for LM.
4. Move a running VM or VM storage.

CONFIGURING LM PREREQUISITES

To support LM, you need two or more Windows Server 2012 and Windows Server 2012 R2 servers with the Hyper-V Role enabled, and they must meet the following requirements:

- They must use processors from the same manufacturer (for example, all Intel or all AMD).
- All hosts must support hardware virtualization.
- They must belong to the same Active Directory domain or two domains that trust one another; LM does not work with servers that are in a workgroup.
- The VMs must be configured to use ***virtual hard disks (VHD)***, which is the older VM file format, or ***VHDX***, the new VM file format, or virtual Fibre Channel disks.
- It is recommended they use a private network dedicated to LM traffic.
- Membership in one of the following groups on both the source and destination machines or in Active Directory for both domains (if using trusted domains) is required:
  a. Administrators
  b. Domain Admins
  c. Hyper-V Administrators

In addition, you need to ensure the following is configured and available:

- Windows 8.1 computer
- Hyper-V Remote Management tools installed and configured to remotely manage both Hyper-V servers

Finally, you need to consider how you will perform the actual migration and from where you can or need to sign in to perform it. Will you perform the LM via a Keyboard, Video, and Monitor switch (KVM), through an attached monitor session, a Remote Desktop, Remote Management tools, or a Windows PowerShell session?

The answer to this consideration determines whether you will utilize ***Credential Security Support Provider (CredSSP)*** protocol, which enables you to securely delegate a user's credentials from a client to a target server, or Kerberos to authenticate LM traffic.

If you are not using remote management tools to perform a LM, you must sign on to the source server and use CredSSP to authenticate the LM.

If you are using remote management tools, you need to configure constrained delegation and select Kerberos as the authentication protocol.

CONFIGURE CONSTRAINED DELEGATION

GET READY. To configure constrained delegation, perform the following steps:

1. Open the Active Directory Users and Computers snap-in.
2. In the navigation pane, expand the *domain name* and select the Computers folder.
3. In the *Computers* folder, identify the two (or more) servers you will use in this process: *Server01* and *Server02*.
4. Right-click the account of Server01, (the server you are moving from), and then select Properties.

5. In the *Properties dialog box,* click the Delegation tab.
6. On the *Delegation tab,* select Trust this computer for delegation to the specified services only, and then select Use Kerberos only.
7. Click Add.
8. In the *Add Services* dialog box, click Users or Computers. The *Select Users or Computers* dialog box opens.
9. Type the name Server02 (the server you are moving to).
10. Click Check Names to verify that you typed the name correctly, and then click OK. The *Add Services* dialog box opens.
11. The *List of Available Services* dialog box opens. Select both of the following, and then click OK.
    - To move VM storage, select CIFS. This is required for moving the VM storage either with or without the VM.
    - To move VMs, select Microsoft Virtual System Migration Service.
12. Verify your selections on the *Delegation* tab of the *Properties* dialog box, and then click OK (see Figure 4-1).

Figure 4-1

Verifying selections on the Delegation tab

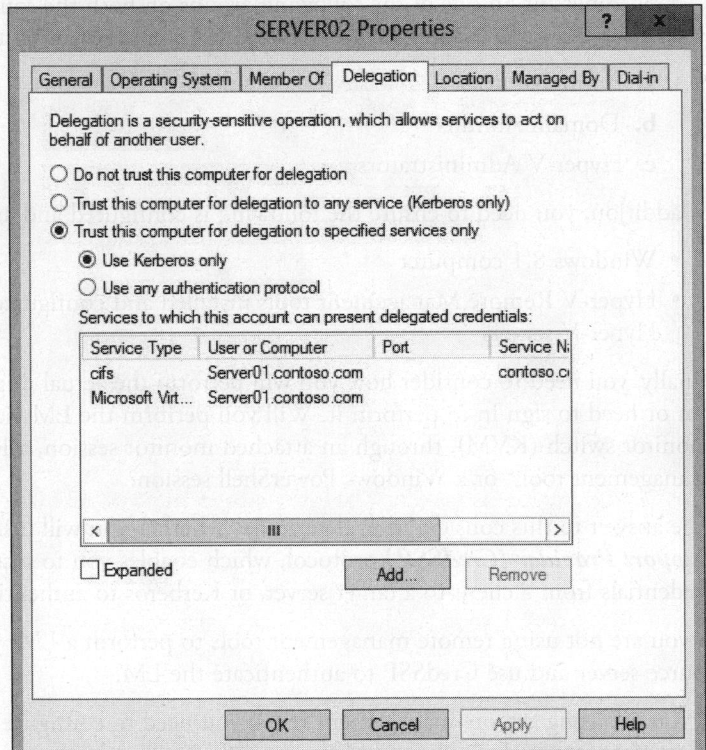

13. For the next part of the process, repeat steps 3 through 12, substituting the appropriate server names where needed.

CONFIGURE THE SOURCE AND DESTINATION COMPUTERS FOR LM

GET READY. To prepare both the source and destination computers for an LM, perform the following steps:

1. Click Server Manager, click Tools, and then select the Hyper-V Manager.
2. In the navigation pane, select the first server you want to configure for LMs.

3. In the *Action* pane, select Hyper-V Settings.
4. In *Hyper-V Settings* dialog box, click Live Migrations.
5. In the *Live Migrations* pane, select Enable incoming and outgoing live migrations (see Figure 4-2).

Figure 4-2

Enabling Live Migrations pane

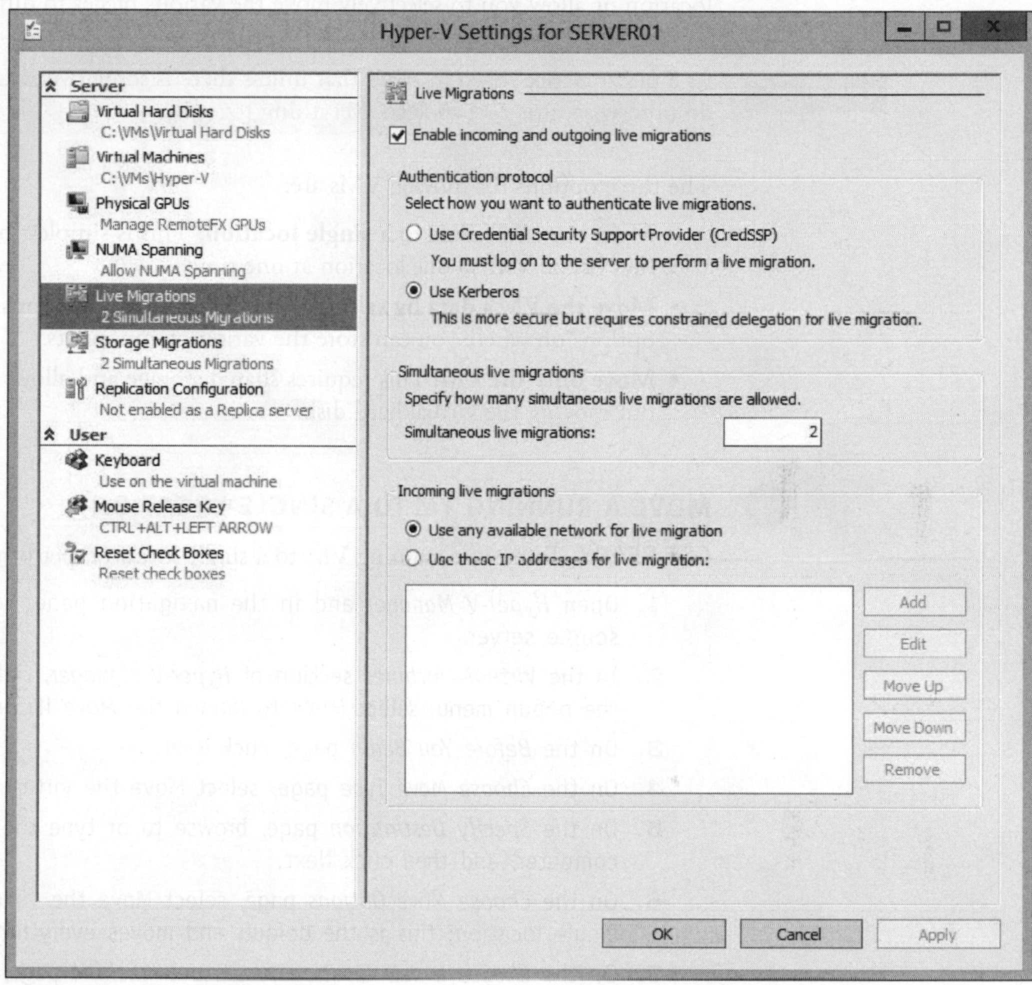

6. In the *Authentication protocol*, select Use Kerberos if you are using the Hyper-V Remote Management Tools and have configured constrained delegation; otherwise, leave Use Credential Security Support Provider (CredSSP) selected.
7. In *Simultaneous live migrations*, specify a different number if you don't want to use the default of 2.
8. In *Incoming live migrations*, if you have configured dedicated network connections to accept LM traffic, select Add to type the IP address information. If you have not configured a dedicated network for LM, select Use any available network for live migration, and then click OK.
9. Select the second server in Hyper-V Manager and repeat steps 3 through 8.

USING WINDOWS POWERSHELL

You can configure and manage LM using the following cmdlets:

- PS C:\> Enable-VMMigration
- PS C:\> Set-VMMigrationNetwork [IP Address]
- PS C:\> Set-VMHost –VirtualMachineMigrationAuthenticationType Kerberos

MOVING VMS USING LM

The machines are now ready for the LM.

In the sixth step of the following exercise, you are presented with three options for moving virtual machines. These options allow you the flexibility to either move the entire VM to one location or allow you to selectively move the various pieces to different locations.

TAKE NOTE* As a best practice, keep in mind that unless there is some overwhelming technical need to do otherwise, it is best to keep everything together.

The three options for moving VMs are:

- **Move the VM's data to a single location:** This is simplest because it moves all of the files of the VM to one location at one time.
- **Move the VM's data by selecting where to move the items:** This provides the most options on where you can store the various components.
- **Move only the VM:** This requires shared storage and allows you to move the VM without moving the virtual hard disk.

MOVE A RUNNING VM TO A SINGLE LOCATION

GET READY. To move a running VM to a single location, perform the following steps:

1. Open *Hyper-V Manager* and in the navigation pane, select the name of the source server.
2. In the *Virtual Machines* section of *Hyper-V Manager*, right-click the VM and, from the popup menu, select Move to launch the *Move Wizard*.
3. On the *Before You Begin* page, click Next.
4. On the *Choose Move Type* page, select Move the virtual machine.
5. On the *Specify Destination* page, browse to or type the name of the destination computer, and then click Next.
6. On the *Choose Move Options* page, select Move the virtual machine's data to a single location; this is the default and moves everything. Click Next.
7. On the *Choose a new location for virtual machine* page, in the *Destination location Folder* box, specify the path of the folder on the destination computer or browse to it and select the folder where you wish to place the VM, and then click Next.
8. On *the Completing Move Wizard*, verify that your selections are correct, and then click Finish.

MOVE A RUNNING VM'S DATA BY SELECTING WHERE TO MOVE THE ITEMS

GET READY. To move a running VM's data by selecting where to move the items, perform the following steps:

1. Open *Hyper-V Manager* and in the navigation pane, select the name of the source server.
2. In the *Virtual Machines* section of *Hyper-V Manager*, right-click the virtual machine and, from the popup menu, select Move to launch the *Move Wizard*.
3. On the *Before You Begin* page, click Next.
4. On the *Choose Move Type* page, select Move the virtual machine.

5. On the *Specify Destination* page, browse to or type the name of the destination computer, and then click Next.
6. On the *Choose Move Options* page, select Move the virtual machine's data by selecting where to move the items, and then click Next.
7. On the *Choose Advanced Options for the Move* page, select Move the virtual machine's data automatically. This maintains the file and folder structure of the source on the destination.
8. On the *Completing Move Wizard*, verify that your selections are correct, and then click Finish.

On the Choose Advanced Options for the Move page, there are three:

- **Move the VM's data automatically:** Maintains the file and folder structure of the source on the destination
- **Move the VM's hard disks to different locations:** Allows you to move the VM's hard disks and other files to a suitable location on the destination
- **Move the VM's items to different locations:** Allows you to specify the location of each moving item.

MOVE A RUNNING VIRTUAL MACHINE

GET READY. To move a running VM's data, you select where to move the items. To do this, perform the following steps:

1. Open *Hyper-V Manager* and in the navigation pane, select the name of the source server.
2. In the *Virtual Machines* section of *Hyper-V Manager*, right-click the VM and, from the popup menu, select Move to launch the *Move Wizard*.
3. On the *Before You Begin* page, click Next.
4. On the *Choose Move Type* page, select Move the virtual machine.
5. On the *Specify Destination* page, browse to or type the name of the destination computer, and then click Next.
6. On the *Choose Move Options* page, select Move only the virtual machine, and then click Next.
7. On the *Completing Move Wizard*, verify that your selections are correct, and then click Finish.

■ Performing Quick Migration

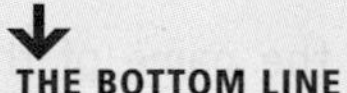

Windows Server 2012 and Windows Server 2012 R2 includes a way to move a running VM that is hosted in a cluster called a Quick Migration.

CERTIFICATION READY
Perform Quick Migration.
Objective 1.4

Quick Migration is another process of moving a running VM from one physical host to another. However, Quick Migration occurs within the confines of a cluster.

Quick Migration allows you to:

- Consolidate physical servers.
- Maintain availability of a production VM during host maintenance.
- Quickly restore services after service outages.

The process by which Quick Migration works is as follows:

- Quick Migration saves the state of the running guest VM to disk or shared storage.
- It moves the storage connection from the source physical server to the destination server.
- It restores the state of the running guest VM to the destination server.

The speed of the Quick Migration is dependent upon how much memory needs to be written to disk and the speed of the network connection between the source and destination servers.

■ Performing Storage Migration

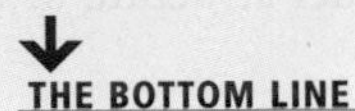

THE BOTTOM LINE

As VMs grow, they can outgrow their initial storage. ***Storage Migration*** is yet another way to move live VM data without disrupting users.

CERTIFICATION READY
Perform Storage Migration.
Objective 1.4

Storage is the heart of the VM. As long as you have the VHD/VHDX file, you can rebuild the configuration and the VM. It is a powerful file.

Whether facing a server or storage hardware maintenance, upgrades, or other performance issues, during the course of normal operations, there may be times when the VM storage needs to be moved.

Just as there are three options for moving VMs, there are also three options for moving storage. These options give you the flexibility to either move the entire VM to one location or to selectively move the various pieces to different locations.

TAKE NOTE* As a best practice, keep in mind that unless there is some overwhelming technical need to do otherwise, it is best to keep everything together.

The three options for moving storage are:

- **Move the VM's data to a single location:** This is simplest because it moves all of the files of the VM to one location at one time.
- **Move the VM's data by selecting where to move the items:** This provides the most options on where you can store the various components.
- **Move only the VM:** This requires shared storage and allows you to move the VM without moving the virtual hard disk.

MOVE THE VM'S DATA TO A SINGLE LOCATION

GET READY. To move a running VM's data to a single location, perform the following steps:

1. Open *Hyper-V Manager* and in the navigation pane, select the name of the source server.
2. In the *Virtual Machines* section of *Hyper-V Manager*, right-click the VM and, from the popup menu, select Move to launch the *Move Wizard*.
3. On the *Before You Begin* page, click Next.
4. On the *Choose Move Type* page, select Move the virtual machine's storage, and then click Next.
5. On the *Choose Options for Moving Storage* page, select *Move the virtual machine's data to a single location*. This is the default and moves everything. Click Next.

6. On the *Choose a new location for virtual machine* page, in the *Destination location Folder* box, specify the path of the folder on the destination computer or browse to it and select the folder where you wish to place the VM storage. Click Next.
7. On *the Completing Move Wizard*, verify that your selections are correct, and then click Finish.

MOVE A RUNNING VM'S DATA TO DIFFERENT LOCATIONS

GET READY. To move a running VM's data to different locations, perform the following steps:

1. Open *Hyper-V Manager* and in the navigation pane, select the name of the source server.
2. In the *Virtual Machines* section of *Hyper-V Manager*, right-click the VM and, from the popup menu, select Move to launch the *Move Wizard*.
3. On the *Before You Begin* page, click Next.
4. On the *Choose Move Type* page, select Move the virtual machine's storage, and then click Next.
5. On the *Choose Options for Moving Storage* page, select Move the virtual machine's data to different locations, and then click Next.
6. On the Select Items to Move page, select any or all of the items you want to move, and then click Next.
7. On the *Chose a new location for attached virtual hard disk* page, in the *Destination location Folder:* box, specify the path of the folder on the destination computer or browse to it and select the folder where you wish to place the VM storage. Click Next.
8. On the Chose a new location for current configuration page, in the *New location Folder:* box, specify the path of the folder on the destination computer or browse to it and select the folder where you wish to place the current configuration, and then click Next.
9. On the *Chose a new location for snapshot* page, in the *New location Folder:* box, specify the path of the folder on the destination computer or browse to it and select the folder where you wish to place the current configuration, and then click Next.
10. On the *Chose a new location for smart paging* page, in the *New location Folder:* box, specify the path of the folder on the destination computer or browse to it and select the folder where you wish to place the Smart Paging files, and then click Next.
11. On *the Completing Move Wizard*, verify that your selections are correct, and then click Finish.

MOVE ONLY THE VM'S HARD DISKS

GET READY. To move a running VM's virtual hard disks, perform the following steps:

1. Open *Hyper-V Manager* and in the navigation pane, select the name of the source server.
2. In the *Virtual Machines* section of *Hyper-V Manager*, right-click the VM and, from the popup menu, select Move to launch the *Move Wizard*.
3. On the *Before You Begin* page, click Next.
4. On the *Choose Move Type* page, select Move the virtual machine's storage, and then click Next.

5. On the *Choose Options for Moving Storage* page, select Move only the virtual machine's virtual hard disks, and then click Next.
6. On the *Select Items to Move* page, select the disk(s) you want to move, and then click Next.
7. On the *Choose a new location for attached virtual hard disk* page, in the *Destination location Folder:* box, specify the path of the folder on the destination computer or browse to it and select the folder where you wish to place the VM storage, and then click Next.
8. On the *Completing Move Wizard*, verify that your selections are correct, and then click Finish.

■ Configuring Virtual Machine Network Health Protection

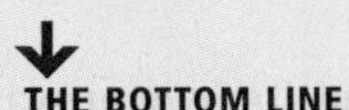

Starting with Windows Server 2012 R2, the network health detection and recovery option called ***Protected network*** is available at the virtual machine level for a Hyper-V host cluster. When a virtual machine becomes disconnected from the network, a live migration will occur to a host where the external virtual network is available. Of course, for this to occur, you must have multiple network paths between cluster nodes.

CERTIFICATION READY
Configure virtual machine network health protection.
Objective 1.4

In Windows Server 2012, if a virtual machine was disconnected from the network, the virtual machine continued to run on the host computer (but the virtual machine might not be available to users). In Windows Server 2012 R2, if the virtual machine has the Protected network option enabled, the availability of the machine is increased. If live migration occurs, there is no downtime because live migration maintains the session state of the virtual machine. If there are no available networks, the cluster removes the node from the cluster, transfers ownership of the virtual machine files, and then restarts the virtual machines on another node. Protected network option is enabled by default.

ENABLE THE PROTECTED NETWORK OPTION

GET READY. To enable the protected network option, perform the following steps:

1. Using *Server Manager,* open the Tools menu and click Hyper-V Manager.
2. In *Hyper-V Manager,* right-click a virtual machine and choose Settings.
3. In the *Settings* dialog box, in the left pane, expand the Network Adapter node and then click Advanced Features, as shown in Figure 4-3.

Figure 4-3

Enabling the protected network option

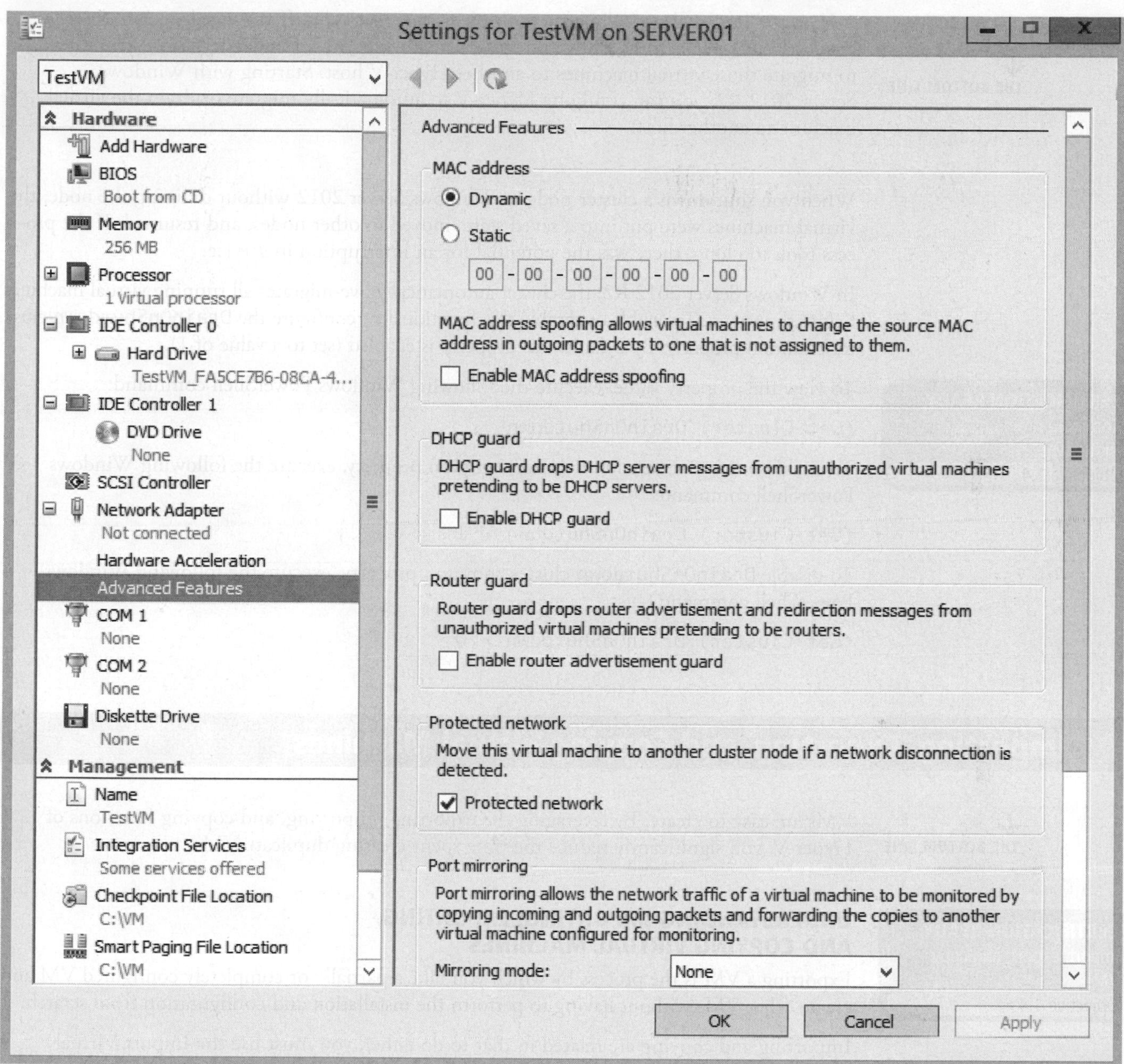

4. To enable the *Protected network* option, make sure the Protected network check box is selected. To disable the Protected network, deselect the Protected network option.
5. Click OK to close the Settings dialog box.

■ Configuring Drain on Shutdown

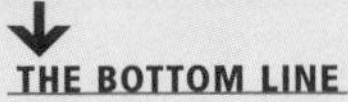

A Hyper-V host will typically have multiple virtual machines. If you need to shut down or reboot a Hyper-V host, and want those virtual machines to continue to run, you need to migrate those virtual machines to another Hyper-V host. Starting with Windows Server 2012 R2, you can configure Hyper-V to automatically migrate or drain the virtual machine to another host.

When you shut down a cluster node in Windows Server 2012 without draining the node, the virtual machines were put into a saved state, moved to other nodes, and resumed. If the process took too long, there was the potential for an interruption in service.

In Windows Server 2012 R2, the cluster automatically live-migrates all running virtual machines before shutdown. To enable or disable this functionality, configure the `DrainOnShutdown` cluster common property. By default, this property is enabled (set to a value of 1).

CERTIFICATION READY
Configure drain on shutdown.
Objective 1.4

To view the property value, execute the following Windows PowerShell command:

```
(Get-Cluster).DrainOnShutdown
```

To enable `DrainOnShutdown` cluster common property, execute the following Windows PowerShell command:

```
(Get-Cluster).DrainOnShutdown = 1
```

To disable `DrainOnShutdown` cluster common property, execute the following Windows PowerShell command:

```
(Get-Cluster).DrainOnShutdown = 0
```

■ Importing, Exporting, and Copying Virtual Machines

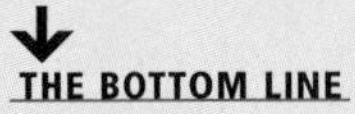

VMs are easy to create. By leveraging the exporting, importing, and copying functions of Hyper-V, you significantly reduce the time spent creating duplicate VMs.

CERTIFICATION READY
Import, export, and copy VMs.
Objective 1.4

UNDERSTANDING IMPORTING, EXPORTING, AND COPYING VIRTUAL MACHINES

Exporting a VM is the process by which you take a partially or completely configured VM and create other VMs without having to perform the installation and configuration from scratch.

Importing and copying are related in that to do either, you must use the Import Virtual Machine Wizard.

- Importing is the process by which you take an existing set of VM files and recreate the exact same VM.
- Copying is the process of using an exported VM like a template to create as many additional VMs as you need.

In Windows Server 2012 and Windows Server 2012 R2, there are three options available when you select the Import Virtual Machine Wizard:

- **Register the virtual machine in place (use the existing unique ID):** Used when you have manually placed the VM files where you want them, there is no other VM on the machine that has the same unique ID, and you just want Hyper-V to register the VM.

- **Restore the virtual machine (use the existing unique ID):** Used when you have VM files on other media (external drive, file server, and so on), there is no other VM on the machine that has the same unique ID, and you want Hyper-V to organize the files and register the VM.
- **Copy the virtual machine (create a new unique ID):** Used when you have an exported VM that you are using as a template and want to import many times.

TAKE NOTE* If you want to use an exported VM as a template to create multiple VMs, you should run Sysprep on the VM prior to performing the export.

EXPORT A VM

GET READY. To export a VM, perform the following steps:

1. Open *Hyper-V Manager* and in the navigation pane, select the name of the source server.
2. In the *Virtual Machines* section of *Hyper-V Manager*, right-click the GM and, from the popup menu, select Export to launch the *Move Wizard*.
3. In the *Export Virtual Machine* dialog box, in the *Location* box, specify the path of the folder or browse to it and select the folder where you wish to place the exported VM, and then select Export.
4. In the *Virtual Machines* section of *Hyper-V Manager*, scroll to the right to view the status of the export.

TAKE NOTE* If your intention is to use your exported VM multiple times, it is important to name the VM something generic to avoid confusion later.

COPY A VM

GET READY. To copy a VM, perform the following steps:

1. Open *Hyper-V Manager* and in the navigation pane, select the name of the source server.
2. In the *Actions s* section of *Hyper-V Manager*, click Import Virtual Machine. The *Import Virtual Machine Wizard* opens.
3. On the *Before You Begin* page, click Next.
4. On the *Locate Folder* page, specify the path of the folder or browse to it and select the folder of the exported VM, and then click Next.
5. On the *Select Virtual Machine* page, select the name of the VM to import, and then click Next.
6. On the *Choose Import Type* page, select from the following choices:
   - **Register the virtual machine in-place (use the existing ID):** This takes the existing VM and corresponding files and folder structure as it is and registers the VM with the host.
   - **Restore the virtual machine (use the existing ID):** This is similar to registering; however, it enables you to specify different paths for the files and folders.

   Click Next.

TAKE NOTE* This should be the same name as the VM you are replacing.

7. If you selected the *Register* option, you are presented with the *Completing Import Wizard* box. Verify that your selections are correct, and then click Finish.
8. If you selected the *Restore* option, you are presented with the *Choose Folders for Virtual Machine Files* box. Select the Store the virtual machine in a different location checkbox.
9. In the *Virtual machine configuration folder* box, specify the path of the folder or browse to it and select the folder where you wish to place the current configuration.
10. In the *Snapshot store* box, specify the path of the folder or browse to it and select the folder where you wish to place the current configuration.
11. In the *Smart Paging Folder* box, specify the path of the folder or browse to it and select the folder where you wish to place the Smart Paging files.
12. Click Next.
13. On the *Chose Folders to Store Virtual Hard Disks* page, in the *Location:* box, specify the path of the folder or browse to it and select the folder where you wish to place the VM hard disk, and then click Next.
14. On *the Completing Move Wizard,* verify that your selections are correct, and then click Finish.

IMPORT A VIRTUAL MACHINE

GET READY. To import a VM, perform the following steps:

1. Open *Hyper-V Manager* and in the navigation pane, select the name of the source server.
2. In the *Actions s* section of *Hyper-V Manager*, click Import Virtual Machine. The *Import Virtual Machine Wizard* opens.
3. On the *Before You Begin* page, click Next.
4. On the *Locate Folder* page, specify the path of the folder or browse to it and select the folder of the exported VM, and then click Next.
5. On the *Select Virtual Machine* page, select the name of the VM to import, and then click Next.
6. On the *Choose Import Type* page, select Copy the virtual machine (create a new unique ID), and then click Next.

TAKE NOTE*

When importing a VM multiple times, remember that the actual name of the VM will be the same as the exported VM in Hyper-V Manager. The VM name can be changed in Hyper-V Manager, but the file names should remain the same.

Prior to importing, copy the entire exported VM folder to the location where you want to store the new VM. This will avoid duplicate file naming conflicts.

7. In the *Choose Folders for Virtual Machine Files* box (see Figure 4-4), if you want to move the files from their current location, select the Store the virtual machine in a different location checkbox. Then, choose one of the following:
   - In the *Virtual machine configuration folder* box, specify the path of the folder or browse to it and select the folder where you wish to place the current configuration.
   - In the *Snapshot store* box, specify the path of the folder or browse to it and select the folder where you wish to place the current configuration.

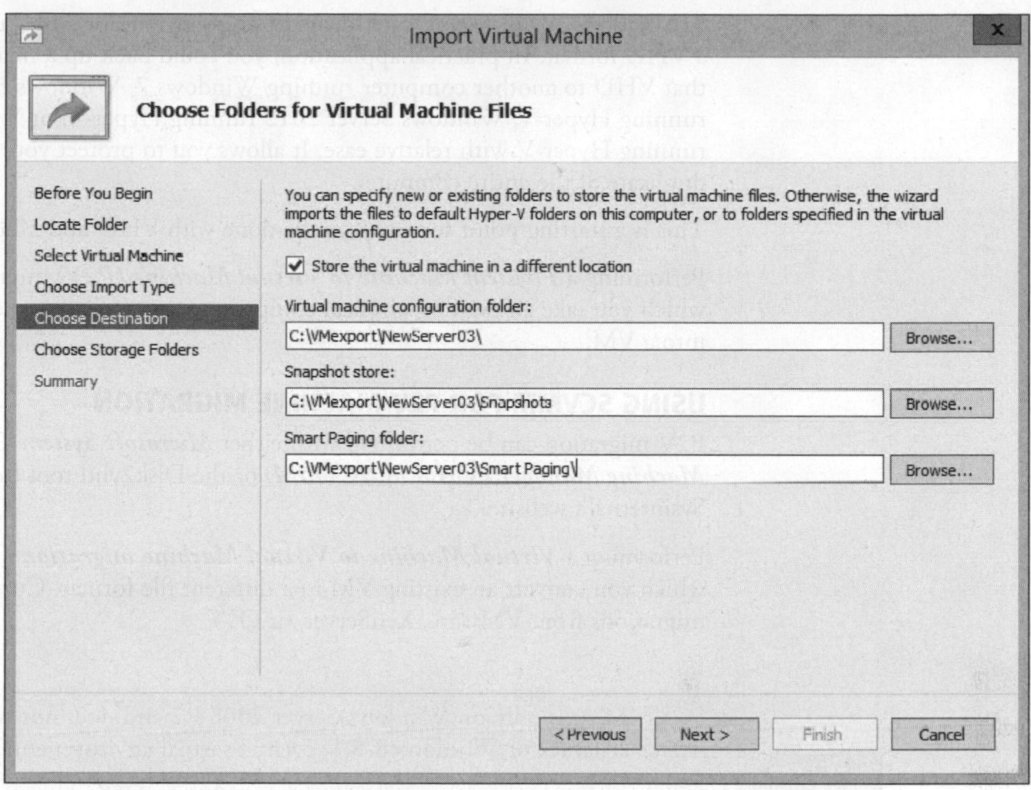

Figure 4-4
The Choose Folders for Virtual Machine Files page

- In the *Smart Paging Folder* box, specify the path of the folder or browse to it and select the folder where you wish to place the Smart Paging files.
- Then, click Next.

8. On the Choose Folders to Store Virtual Hard Disks page, if you want to move the files from their current location, in the Location box, specify the path of the folder or browse to it and select the folder where you wish to place the VM hard disk, and then click Next.
9. On *the Completing Move Wizard*, verify that your selections are correct, and then click Finish.

Migrating from Other Platforms – Understanding P2V and V2V

THE BOTTOM LINE

P2V and V2V are additional methods to quickly create VMs using physical or virtual machines previously created.

Hardware replacements because of failures or upgrades are commonplace. Most users accept that. In many cases, however, users do not look forward to getting a new computer because of the risk of losing data.

The challenge then becomes how to ensure you grab all of the data prior to that failure or upgrade occurring.

In Windows 7, full backups performed using the Windows Backup utility have stored files in a VHD format. In practical application, you could back up a machine to a VHD and deploy that VHD to another computer running Windows 7, Windows 8/8.1, Windows Server 2008 running Hyper-V, Windows Server 2012 running Hyper-V, or Windows Server 2012 R2 running Hyper-V with relative ease. It allows you to protect your data by having an exact duplicate of the entire computer.

This is a starting point for what can be done with VHD and VHDX files.

Performing a ***Physical Machine to Virtual Machine (P2V)*** migration is the method by which you take an existing physical computer, either a client or server, and transform it into a VM.

USING SCVMM FOR P2V MACHINE MIGRATION

P2V migration can be performed with either ***Microsoft System Center 2012 R2 Virtual Machine Manager (VMM or SCVMM)*** or the Disk2vhd tool from the Microsoft Sysinternal's website.

Performing a ***Virtual Machine to Virtual Machine migration (V2V)*** is the method by which you convert an existing VM in a different file format. Currently, SCVMM supports migrations from VMware, XenServer, or OVF.

TAKE NOTE*

SCVMM runs only on Windows Server 2008 R2 and does not work well with Windows Server 2012 R2 or Windows 8/8.1, even in virtual environments.

SCVMM R2 runs only on Windows Server 2012 or Windows Server 2012 R2 and works well with Windows Server 2012/Windows Server 2012 R2 or Windows 8/8.1.

Open Virtualization Format (OVF) is an open standard for packaging and distributing virtual machines and needs the OVF Import/Export tool, which is available from the Microsoft Download Center. The OVF Import/Export tool must be installed into an existing VMM management server that has the VMM console installed.

P2V SOURCE MACHINE REQUIREMENTS

To perform a P2V migration using SCVMM, SCVMM SP1, or SVCMM R2, the source machine must meet the following requirements:

- 512 minimum RAM
- No volume larger than 2040 GBs
- An Advanced Configuration and Power Interface (ACPI) BIOS
- Accessible by the VM host and VMM
- Cannot be located in a perimeter network
- Cannot have encrypted volumes
- VMM does not support P2V conversion for computers with Itanium-based systems, NT Server 4.0, or Windows Server 2003 SP1.
- Any of the following Windows operating systems:

  32-bit: Windows XP Pro SP3; Windows Server 2003 Web, Standard, Enterprise, or Datacenter Edition; Windows Vista SP1; Windows Server 2008 Web, Standard, Enterprise, or Datacenter; and Windows 7

  64-bit: Windows XP Pro SP3; Windows Server 2003 Web, Standard, Enterprise, or Datacenter Edition; Windows Small Business Server 2003; Windows Vista SP1; Windows Server 2008 Standard, Enterprise, or Datacenter; Windows 7; Windows Server

2008 R2 Web, Standard, Enterprise, or Datacenter; Windows 8/8.1; Windows Server 2012 Standard, or Datacenter; and Windows Server 2012 R2 Standard or Datacenter.

P2V DESTINATION MACHINE REQUIREMENTS

To perform a P2V conversion using SCVMM, the destination machine, the computer to which you are moving the VM, also known as the host, must meet or exceed the following system requirements, which are:

- Enough RAM for both the host OS and ALL guest VMs that will reside on the host; i.e. if you plan on hosting four VMs on one machine, if the RAM requirements for each of the four VMs is 4GBs and the host OS requires 4 GBs, you will need at least 20 GBs of RAM on the destination machine
- Cannot be located in a perimeter network
- If using SC12VMM, one of the following operating systems:
  a. Windows Server 2008 R2 SP1 or later; full or Server Core installation (Standard, Enterprise, or Datacenter)
  b. Hyper-V Windows Server 2008 R2
  c. Windows Server 2008 SP2 or later; full or Server Core installation (Enterprise or Datacenter)
- If using SC12VMM SP1, one of the following operating systems:
  a. Windows Server 2008 R2 SP1 or later; full or Server Core installation (Standard, Enterprise, or Datacenter)
  b. Hyper-V Windows Server 2008 R2
  c. Windows Server 2012; full or Server Core installation (Standard or Datacenter)
  d. Hyper-V Windows Server 2012
- If using SC12VMM R2, one of the following operating systems:
  a. Windows Server 2008 R2 SP1 or later; full or Server Core installation (Standard, Enterprise, or Datacenter)
  b. Hyper-V Windows Server 2008 R2
  c. Windows Server 2012 or Windows Server 2012 R2; full or Server Core installation (Standard or Datacenter)
  d. Hyper-V Windows Server 2012

P2V SUGGESTED PREREQUISITES

It is suggested that the following be performed prior to starting a P2V conversion using SCVMM:

- Run Disk Defragmenter on the source computer.
- Disable standby power mode on all machines.
- Run the System Center Virtual Machine Manager Configuration Analyzer (VMMCA) on the SCVMM management server, the destination hosts, and the source computers.

TAKE NOTE*

As of this writing, the VMMCA tool has not been updated to run on Windows Server 2012 R2 and Microsoft System Center 2012 SP1. It requires a full installation of Windows Server 2008 R2 and Microsoft System Center 2012 without SP1.

- Enable a gigabit or greater network connection between the source computer and the VM host.
- Use dynamic virtual hard disks (VHDs) to conserve disk space on the destination host.
- For an online P2V conversion, ensure that all applications running on the source computer have VSS-aware writers or are stopped.
- For an offline P2V, ensure that any and all NIC and storage drivers are available on the VMM server.

CONVERTING PHYSICAL COMPUTERS TO VMS

With SCVMM, P2V conversions can be done either online or offline. You can perform an online P2V conversion if you cannot take the physical machine offline. This is the default action. Should you choose to do this, ensure that all critical applications running on the source computer have Volume Shadow Copy Service (VSS)-aware writers or that the applications have been stopped.

In an online P2V conversion, SCVMM creates a copy of the source NTFS volumes and data of VSS-aware applications. SCVMM uses the VSS to:

- Verify that data is reliably backed up while the source computer continues to service user requests.
- Create a VHD based on the read-only snapshot created.

An offline P2V conversion is the only way to ensure a consistent conversion. Also, it is the only way to migrate FAT volumes and domain controllers.

SCVMM restarts the source computer into Windows PE. Then it clones the volume(s) as a VHD and restarts the source computer.

Additional information on online versus offline conversion can be obtained from Microsoft's TechNet website.

P2V ANOTHER WAY—DISK2VHD

The Disk2vhd tool from the Microsoft Sysinternals website is another tool that will allow a physical machine to be converted to the older VHD format. Should you wish to convert the VHD to the VHDX format; a simple Windows PowerShell script will do the job.

■ Converting a Virtual Machine to Virtual Machine (V2V) Using SCVMM

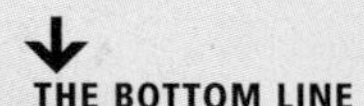

In Hyper-V, there are no native functions that permit the conversion of a VM from another vendor to a native Hyper-V VM.

There are three formats which SCVMM can convert

- Citrix XenServer
- VMware ESX
- The Open Virtualization Format (OVF)

CONVERT CITRIX XENSERVER VIRTUAL MACHINES TO HYPER-V

To convert a Citrix XenServer VM to Hyper-V, you need to use the P2V conversion process in SCVMM on a XenServer VM that runs a Windows-based guest operating system.

Although it is not required, you should remove the Citrix Tools for Virtual Machines before you start the conversion.

CONVERT VMWARE ESX/ESXI VIRTUAL MACHINES TO HYPER-V

To convert a VMware ESX/ESXi VMs to Hyper-V, you need to use the V2V conversion process in SCVMM.

The prerequisites for V2V using SCVMM are as follows:

- VMware ESX/ESXi version 3.5 update 5 or higher (4.0, 4.1 or 5.1).
- The VMware Tools must be removed.
- VMware virtual hard disks cannot be connected to an IDE bus.

CONVERT VIRTUAL MACHINES TO HYPER-V USING THE OVF IMPORT/EXPORT TOOL

The OVF Import/Export Tool is a series of cmdlets that allows SCVMM to both import and export VMs in the OVF format. OVF is a file packaging standard created and maintained by Distributed Management Task Force, Inc., to help move and deploy virtual machines and appliances on different platforms.

The OVF package is a combination of an XML file with an OVF extension and the virtual disk(s). There are a few things to know about the OVF tool, including the following:

- In addition to OVF packages, it can import VMs from Citrix XenServer or VMware vCenter platforms.
- It can export to the OVF file format.
- Currently, it supports the import or export of a single VM.
- It does not convert virtual hard disk formats.
- If the virtual hard disk is not in VHD/VHDX format, you need a third-party tool to convert it.
- If you convert the file type of the virtual hard disk, it should be as a fixed or thick disk.
- In the OVF XML file, all instances of the virtual hard disk file name should be updated to reflect the converted file name.

TAKE NOTE* As of this writing, the OVF Import/Export tool has not been updated to run on Windows Server 2012 R2 and Microsoft System Center 2012 SP1. It requires a full installation of Windows Server 2008 R2 and Microsoft System Center 2012 WITHOUT SP1.

SKILL SUMMARY

IN THIS LESSON YOU LEARNED:

- Live Migration (LM) is the process of moving an entire VM or parts of a VM to another physical server with or without a cluster.
- If using Hyper-V Remote Management tools to perform migrations, you need to configure constrained delegation and use Kerberos authentication.
- If you are not using Hyper-V Remote Management tools to perform migrations, CredSSP is used to authenticate during migrations.
- Both Source and Destination computers must have incoming and outgoing LMs enabled in Hyper-V settings.
- When moving VMs via LM, there are three options for moving the virtual machine's data: to a single location, selecting where to move the items, and move only the virtual machine.
- Quick Migration is the process of moving an entire VM or parts of a VM to another physical server using a cluster.
- Starting with Windows Server 2012 R2, the Network health detection and recovery is available at the virtual machine level for a Hyper-V host cluster that will perform a live migration when a virtual machine becomes disconnected from the network.
- Starting with Windows Server 2012 R2, you can configure the Hyper-V to automatically migrate or drain the virtual machine to another host.
- Storage Migration is the process of moving the storage of a VM from one physical server to another without a cluster.
- Exporting a VM is the process by which you take a partially or completely configured VM and create other VMs without having to perform the installation and configuration from scratch.
- Importing a VM is the process by which you take an existing set of VM files and recreate the exact same VM.
- Copying is the process of using an exported VM like a template to create as many additional VMs as you need.
- P2V migration is the process of migrating a physical machine to a virtual machine.
- P2V migration can be performed with either Microsoft System Center 2012 – Virtual Machine Manager or the Disk2vhd tool from Microsoft Sysinternals.
- V2V is the method by which SCVMM converts an existing virtual machine from VMware, XenServer, or OVF into a Hyper-V virtual machine.

Knowledge Assessment

Multiple Choice

Select the correct answer for each of the following questions.

1. Which of the following options are available when you select the Import Virtual Machine Wizard? (Choose two answers.)
   a. Copy the virtual machine
   b. Move the virtual machine's data by selecting where to move the items
   c. Register the virtual machine in place
   d. Move the virtual machine's data automatically

2. Windows Server 2012 R2 Hyper-V files are stored in what file types? (Choose two answers.)
   a. .NSF
   b. .HTM
   c. .VHD
   d. .VHDX

3. Which of the following advanced options are available when you select where to move items during an LM? (Select two answers)
   a. Copy the virtual machine
   b. Move the virtual machine's data by selecting where to move the items
   c. Register the virtual machine in place
   d. Move the virtual machine's data automatically

4. When using remote management tools to perform LM, what needs to be configured?
   a. CredSSP
   b. Kerberos
   c. OVF
   d. Constrained Delegation

5. Which process takes an existing partially or completely configured VM and creates other VMs without having to perform the installation and configuration from scratch?
   a. Importing
   b. Exporting
   c. Copying
   d. Extracting
   e. Migrating

6. Which process takes an existing set of VM files and recreates the exact same VM?
   a. Importing
   b. Exporting
   c. Copying
   d. Extracting

7. What is the name of the process for moving an entire VM or parts of a VM to another physical server without a cluster?
   a. Quick Migration
   b. Storage Migration
   c. Constrained Delegation
   d. Live Migration

8. What is the name of the process for moving an entire VM or parts of a VM to another physical server using a cluster?
   a. Quick Migration
   b. Storage Migration
   c. Constrained Delegation
   d. Live Migration

9. In which file should all instances of the virtual hard disk file name be updated to reflect the converted file name?
   a. .VHD
   b. .NSF
   c. OVF XML
   d. .VHDX

10. Which of the following tools do you need to perform V2V conversions?
    a. SCVMM
    b. VMMCA
    c. Disk2VHD
    d. Any VSS-aware application

Best Answer

Choose the letter that corresponds to the best answer. More than one answer choice may achieve the goal. Select the BEST answer.

1. You need to migrate a physical computer to a Windows Server 2012 R2 running Hyper-V server. You also need to capture all local user accounts in your migration. Which of the following tools should you use?
   a. XenServer
   b. Active Directory Users and Computers
   c. Disk2VHD
   d. OVF Import/Export Tool

2. The server hosting your mission-critical email server is failing. The email server has been created in a VM that is not in a cluster; however, its storage is maintained on an SAN. You need move the VM to a new host and maintain server availability. How should you proceed?
   a. Power down and export and import the VM registering the VM in place with the existing unique ID
   b. Power down and export and import the VM restoring the VM in place with the existing unique ID
   c. Power down and export and import the VM copying the VM in place to create a new unique ID
   d. Use Live Migration to move only the VM and keep the storage in place

3. You need to perform a LM but are unable to. You are a member of the Hyper-V Administrators group on the source Hyper-V server and a member of the Domain Admins group on the destination sever. You are using the Hyper-V Remote Management Tools on your Windows 7 Workstation. What do you need to do to perform the LM?
   a. Have an Enterprise Admin add your account to the Hyper-V Administrators group on the destination server
   b. Upgrade your workstation to Windows 8
   c. Upgrade your Hyper-V Remote Management Tools to the latest version
   d. Reconfigure Constrained Delegation and reboot both the source and destination severs

4. You need to create a VM template to create 20 identical VMs. How do you do this?
   a. Run Sysprep on the VM, power it down, and export and import the VM registering the VM in place with the existing unique ID
   b. Power down and export and import the VM restoring the VM in place with the existing unique ID
   c. Run Sysprep on the VM, power it down, and export and import the VM copying the VM in place to create a new unique ID
   d. Use Live Migration to move only the VM as many times as you want

5. You need to migrate a VM created in the VirtualBox hypervisor. You do not need to capture local user accounts in your migration. Which of the following tools do you use?
   a. XenServer
   b. Active Directory Users and Computers
   c. Disk2VHD
   d. OVF Import/Export Tool

Matching and Identification

1. The three options for moving virtual machine storage are:
   _______ **a)** Move the virtual machine's data automatically
   _______ **b)** Move the virtual machine's data to a single location
   _______ **c)** Move the virtual machine's hard disks to different locations
   _______ **d)** Move the virtual machine's data by selecting where to move the items
   _______ **e)** Move the virtual machine's items to different locations
   _______ **f)** Move only the virtual machine

2. Which of the following are prerequisites for LM?
   _______ **a)** Using processors from the same manufacturer (i.e. all Intel or all AMD)
   _______ **b)** All hosts must support hardware virtualization
   _______ **c)** Belong to the same Active Directory domain or trusted domains
   _______ **d)** Belong to the same workgroup
   _______ **e)** The VMs must be configured to use either virtual hard disks (VHD or VHDX) or virtual Fibre Channel disks
   _______ **f)** Membership in Administrators, Domain Admins, or Hyper-V Administrators group
   _______ **g)** Windows 7 Computer

3. To perform a P2V migration, SCVMM uses which of the following operating systems as a source machine?
   _______ **a)** Windows XP SP3 – 64-bit
   _______ **b)** Windows 7
   _______ **c)** Windows Vista – 32-bit
   _______ **d)** Windows Server 2003
   _______ **e)** Windows Server 2000
   _______ **f)** Windows Server 2012 – 32-bit

4. The OVF Import/Export tool can import VMs from which of the following?
   _______ **a)** Citrix XenServer
   _______ **b)** Microsoft Excel
   _______ **c)** VMware vCenter
   _______ **d)** Raw XML files
   _______ **e)** OVF file packages
   _______ **f)** VMM files

5. Which of the following Windows PowerShell cmdlets can be used to configure and manage LM?
   _______ a) `Enable-VMMigration`
   _______ b) `Add-VMMigrationNetwork`
   _______ c) `Enable-VMReplication`
   _______ d) `Export-VM`
   _______ e) `Set-VMMigrationNetwork`
   _______ f) `Set-VMHost)`

Build a List

1. Identify the basic steps to export a VM in Windows Server 2012 R2. Not all steps will be used.
   _______ Launch the Move Wizard
   _______ Select Store as the OVF file
   _______ Specify the path of the storage location
   _______ Choose Export Type
   _______ Select Export
   _______ Register the VM in place
   _______ Select Export

■ Business Case Scenarios

Scenario 4-1: Exporting and Importing a VM

Management has decided to migrate all servers to Windows Server 2012 R2 and all users to Windows 8. As the senior administrator for Contoso, management has tasked you with preparing a lab quickly so that the new features of both operating systems can be tested along with the current set of standard corporate applications and division-specific applications for three divisions. In a virtual environment, you need to create a simple Active Directory domain with DNS and DHCP, LOB application servers and workstations to test each configuration. How many servers and workstations do you need and what do you do?

Scenario 4-2: Using Live Migration

Server01 is in need of maintenance. You use LM to move a VM from Server01 to Server02. When the maintenance is complete, you try to move the VM back to Sever01 from the Hyper-V Manager on Server01 and encounter the following error: `Virtual machine migration operation failed at migration Source. Failed to establish a connection with host Server01: No credentials are available in the security package (0x8009030E.`

Why does this occur?

Scenario 4-3: Using V2V Migration

Your manager has decided to migrate all existing Windows-based XenServer VMs to Hyper-V and has tasked you with planning and performing the migration. There are no domain controllers, DNS, or DHCP servers in the migration but there are LOB application servers. How should you perform the migration?Lesson

Configuring Advanced File Services

LESSON 5

70-412 EXAM OBJECTIVE

Objective 2.1 – Configure advanced file services. This objective may include but is not limited to: Configure Network File System (NFS) data store; configure BranchCache; configure File Classification Infrastructure (FCI) using File Server Resource Manager (FSRM); configure file access auditing.

LESSON HEADING	EXAM OBJECTIVE
Configuring NFS Data Store	
Obtaining User and Group Information	
Creating an NFS Share	
Installing and Configuring the NFS Data Store	Configure Network File System (NFS) data store
Configuring BranchCache	Configure BranchCache
Configuring File Classification Infrastructure	Configure File Classification Infrastructure (FCI) using File Server Resource Manager (FSRM)
Configuring File Access Auditing	Configure file access auditing

KEY TERMS

auditing
authentication
authorization
BranchCache
distributed cache mode
file classification
File Server Resource Manager (FSRM)
group identifier (GID)
hosted cache mode
Identity Management for UNIX
Network File System (NFS)
NFS Data Store
Server for NFS role
user identifier (UID)

Configuring NFS Data Store

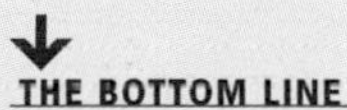

Network File System (NFS) is a distributed file system protocol that is used to access files over a network, similar to accessing a file using a shared folder in Windows (which uses Server Message Block (SMB). It is used with UNIX and Linux file server clients and VMware. Therefore, to support these clients, Windows Server 2012 and Windows Server 2012 R2 supports NFS.

NFS was originally developed by Sun Microsystems in the 1980s. NFS was later released to the public, and by 1995, the Internet Engineering Task Force (IETF) standardized it as RFC 1813, "NFS Version 3 Protocol Specification." Virtually all UNIX and Linux distributions available today include both NFS client and server support.

By installing the Network File System role service, you can provide NFS Server and NFS Client capabilities. Different from using a Universal Naming Convention (UNC), which uses a \\servername\sharename, or mounting a UNC to a drive letter, NFS takes part of a remote file system and mounts it or connects to a local file system. The client can then access the server's files as if they were a local resource.

Obtaining User and Group Information

Natively UNIX and Linux machines have their own user accounts, which are not part of Windows or Active Directory. As Active Directory is common among corporations, there are several technologies that can be used to link or add the Unix/Linux machines to Active Directory. To prevent NFS clients running on UNIX or Linux systems from having to perform a separate logon when accessing NFS shares, the Windows Server 2012 R2 NFS Server implementation can look up the user information sent by the client and the associated UNIX/Linux account with a particular Windows account.

Similar to Windows, with UNIX and Linux, you log in and authenticate with an account name and password. The user is identified with a ***user identifier (UID)*** value and a ***group identifier (GID)***. Whenever a file is accessed using NFS, the UID and GID are sent to the NFS server to see whether the user has the proper permissions to access.

For the Windows Server 2012 and Windows Server 2012 R2 NFS server to grant the UNIX user access to the requested file, it must associate the UID and GID with a Windows or Active Directory account and use that account to authenticate the client. NFS uses Active Directory lookup and User Name Mappings to obtain user and group information when accessing NFS shared files.

Identity Management for UNIX enables you to integrate Windows users into an existing UNIX or Linux environment, including managing user accounts and passwords on Windows and UNIX systems using Network Information Service (NIS), and enables you to automatically synchronize passwords between Windows and UNIX operating systems. To use this method, you must install the Identity Management for UNIX using the Deployment Image Servicing and management command-line tool, Dism.exe.

INSTALL THE IDENTITY MANAGEMENT FOR UNIX USING DISM.EXE

GET READY. To install the Identity Management for UNIX using Dism.exe, on a Windows Server 2012 R2 domain controller, perform the following steps:

1. Click Windows PowerShell on the taskbar to open the *Windows PowerShell* window.
2. To install the administration tools for Identity Management for UNIX, execute the following command:
   ```
   Dism.exe /online /enable-feature /featurename:adminui /all
   ```
   When you are asked to restart the computer, type N.
3. To install the Server for NIS, execute the following command:
   ```
   Dism.exe /online /enable-feature /featurename:nis /all
   ```
   When you are asked to restart the computer, type N.
4. To install Password Synchronization, execute the following command:
   ```
   Dism.exe /online /enable-feature /featurename:psync /all
   ```
5. When you are asked to restart the computer, type Y.

When you use Active Directory lookup, NFS searches the Active Directory database for the UID and GID values in the NFS file access request and uses the accounts associated with those values to authenticate the client.

When you install the ***Server for NFS role***, it extends the Active Directory schema by adding UNIX attributes. These attributes can be set with Active Directory Users and Computers (see Figure 5-1).

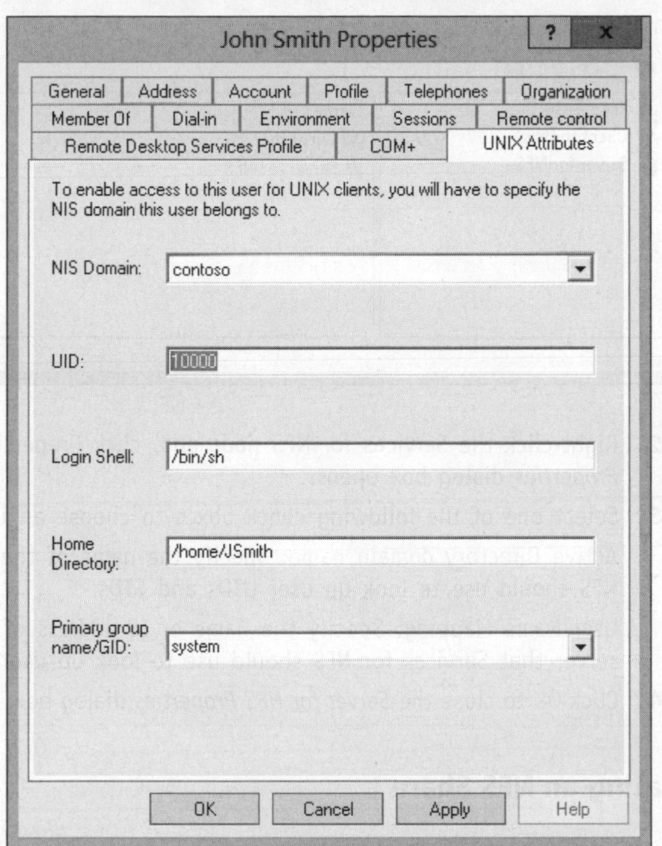

Figure 5-1
Setting UNIX attributes

INSTALL THE SERVER AND CLIENT FOR NFS

GET READY. To install the Server for NFS and Client for NFS, perform the following steps:

1. On the task bar, click the Server Manager button to open the *Server Manager*.
2. At the top of *Server Manager*, click Manage and click Add Roles and Features. The *Add Roles and Feature Wizard* opens.
3. On the *Before you begin* page, click Next.
4. Select Role-based or feature-based installation and then click Next.
5. On the *Select destination server* page, click Next.
6. On the *Select server roles* page, expand File and Storage Services, expand File and iSCSI Services, and click to select Server for NFS. Click Next.
7. When you are asked to add features required for Server for NFS, click Add Features.
8. On the *Select features* page, click to select Client for NFS and click Next.
9. Back on the *Select features* page, click Next.
10. On the *Confirm installation selections* page, click Install.
11. When the installation is complete, click Close.

CONFIGURE ACCOUNT LOOKUPS

GET READY. To configure Account Lookup for NFS, perform the following steps:

1. Using Server Manager, open the Tools menu and click Services for Network File System (NFS). The *Services for Network File System* console opens (see Figure 5-2).

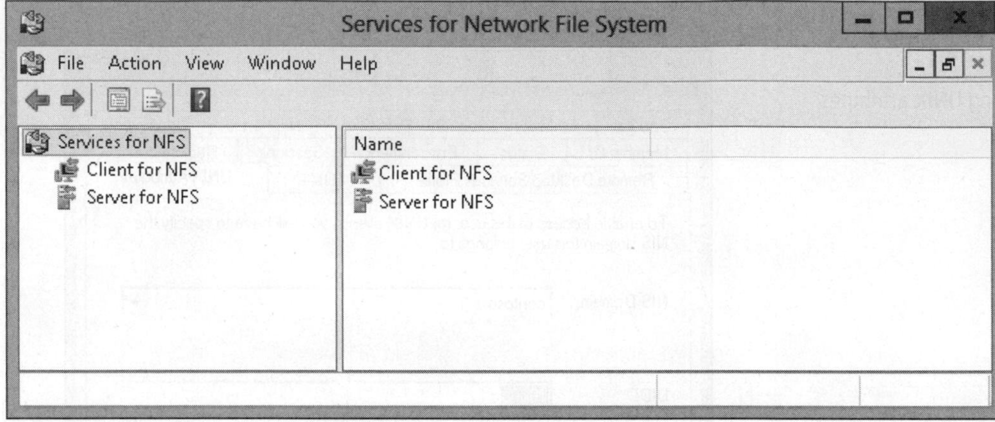

Figure 5-2
Opening the Services for Network File System console

2. Right-click the Services for NFS node and, click Properties. The *Services for NFS Properties* dialog box opens.
3. Select one of the following check boxes to choose an identity mapping source:

   Active Directory domain name: Specify the name of the domain that Services for NFS should use to look up user UIDs and GIDs.

   User Name Mapping: Specify the name or IP address of the User Name Mapping server that Services for NFS should use to look up user UIDs and GIDs.
4. Click OK to close the *Server for NFS Properties* dialog box.

Creating an NFS Share

When you install the Services for NFS role service, an NFS Sharing tab is added to the properties of every volume and folder on the computer's drives.

To make a volume or folder available to NFS clients, you need to open the properties for the volume or folder and configure the appropriate values.

CREATE AN NFS SHARE

GET READY. To create an NFS share, perform the following steps:

1. Browse to a volume or folder on a local NTFS drive, right-click it, and click Properties. The *Properties* dialog box opens.
2. Click the NFS Sharing tab.
3. Click Manage NFS Sharing (see Figure 5-3). The *NFS Advanced Sharing* dialog box appears.

Figure 5-3
Sharing an NFS folder

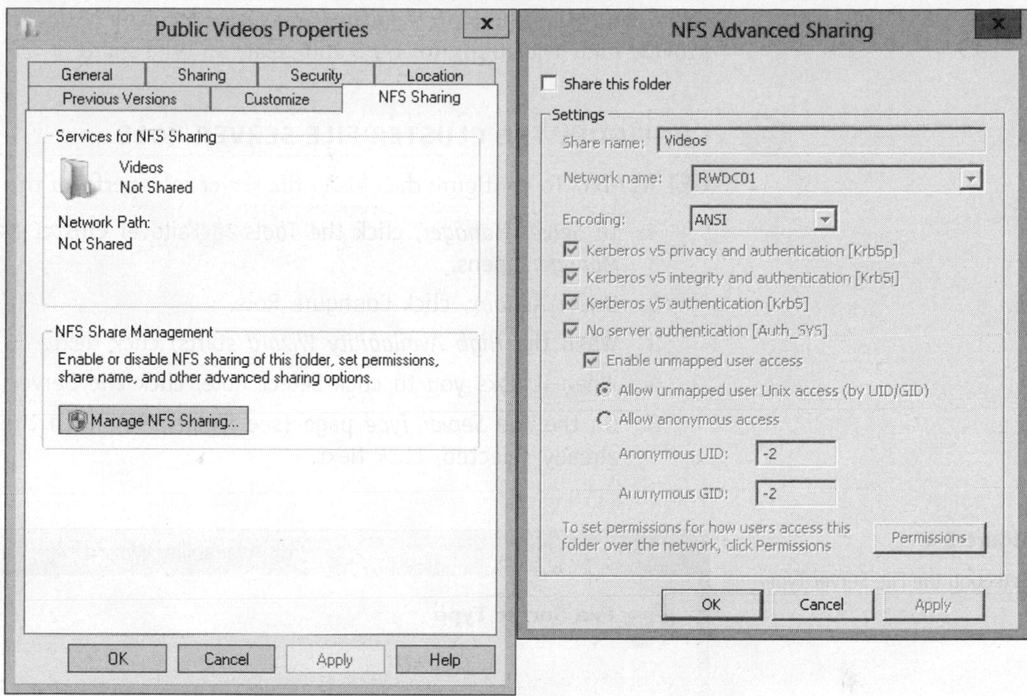

4. Select the Share this folder check box.
5. In the *Share Name* text box, type the name that you want NFS clients to use when accessing the folder and select one of the encoding schemes from the Encoding drop-down list.
6. If you want NFS clients to be able to access the share without authenticating, click to select the Allow anonymous access, and modify the *Anonymous UID* and *Anonymous GID* values, if necessary.
7. Click Permissions. The *NFS Share Permissions* dialog box appears.
8. By default, all NFS clients have read-only access to the share. If you want clients to have Read-Write, change the type of access. You can also grant root access by clicking the Allow root access option.
9. You can click Add to select users or groups and create new permission assignments.
10. Click OK to close the *NFS Share Permissions* dialog box.
11. Click OK to close the *NFS Advanced Sharing* dialog boxes.
12. Click OK to close the *Properties* dialog box.

Installing and Configuring the NFS Data Store

Starting with Windows Server 2012, Server for NFS can be used with failover clustering so that you can deploy NFS while providing fault tolerance. The shared folder within a cluster is known as a ***NFS Data Store***.

CERTIFICATION READY
Configure NFS data store.
Objective 2.1

To create an NFS shared folder on a cluster, you need to install the following on each cluster node:

- The File Services role
- The Server for NFS role service
- The Failover Clustering feature

After you install these prerequisites and create a cluster, you can configure the cluster to provide high availability for NFS and create an NFS share.

CONFIGURE THE CLUSTER FILE SERVER ROLE

GET READY. To configure the cluster file server role, perform the following steps:

1. In *Server Manager*, click the Tools > Failover Cluster Manager. The *Failover Cluster Manager* opens.
2. Under *Actions*, click Configure Role.
3. When the *High Availability Wizard* starts, click Next.
4. When it asks you to click Select Role, click File Server and click Next.
5. On the *File Server Type* page (see Figure 5-4), with the File Server for general use already selected, click Next.

Figure 5-4

Selecting the File Server Type

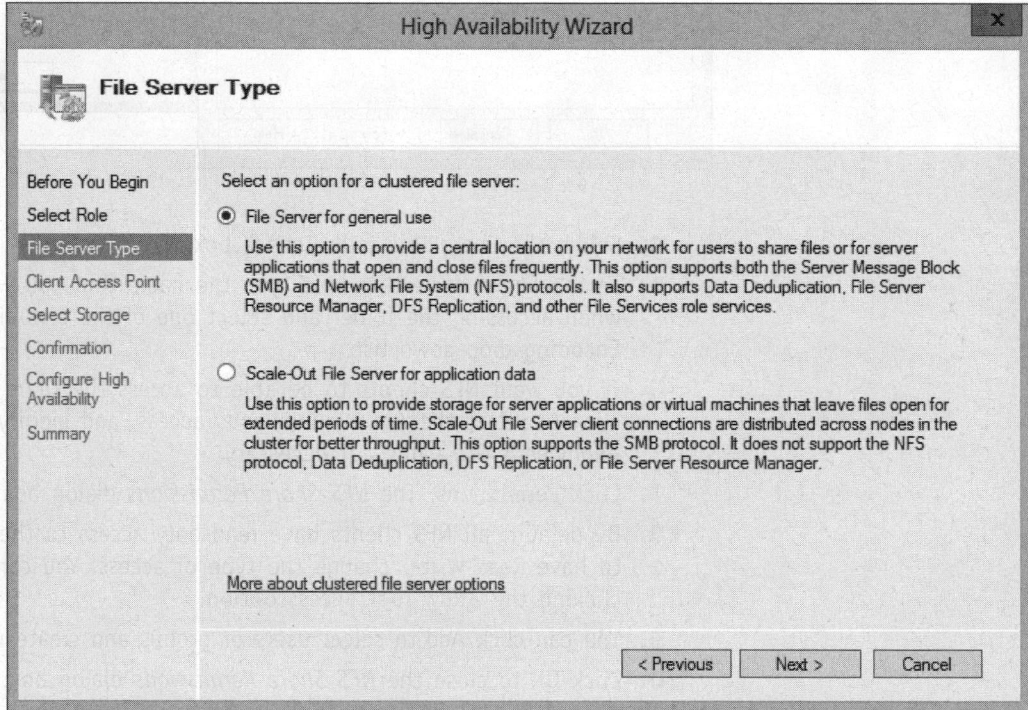

6. For the *Client Access Point* page, type a name for the cluster in the *Name* text box.
7. In the Click here to type an address box, type an address for the cluster.
8. On the *Select Storage* page, click the available storage and click Next.
9. On the *Confirmation* page, click Next.
10. On the *Summary* page, click Finish.

To create an NFS share to be used with the cluster, you need to choose an *NFS Share–Quick or NFS Share–Advanced.* The NFS Share–Quick is the quickest way to create an NFS file share. The Advanced profile allows you to set the folders' owners for access-denied assistance, configure default classification of data in the folder for management and access polices, and enable quotas. If you want to use the NFS Share–Advanced, you need both the Server for NFS and File Server Resource Manager role servers installed.

CREATE A REDUNDANT NFS SHARE

GET READY. To create a redundant NFS share, perform the following steps:

1. In *Failover Cluster Manager*, click Roles in the left pane.
2. Right-click the cluster under *Roles* and click Add File Share.
3. When the *New Share Wizard* opens, it will ask to select a profile as shown in Figure 5-5. Click NFS Share – Quick and click Next.

Figure 5-5

Selecting a profile for a file server failover cluster

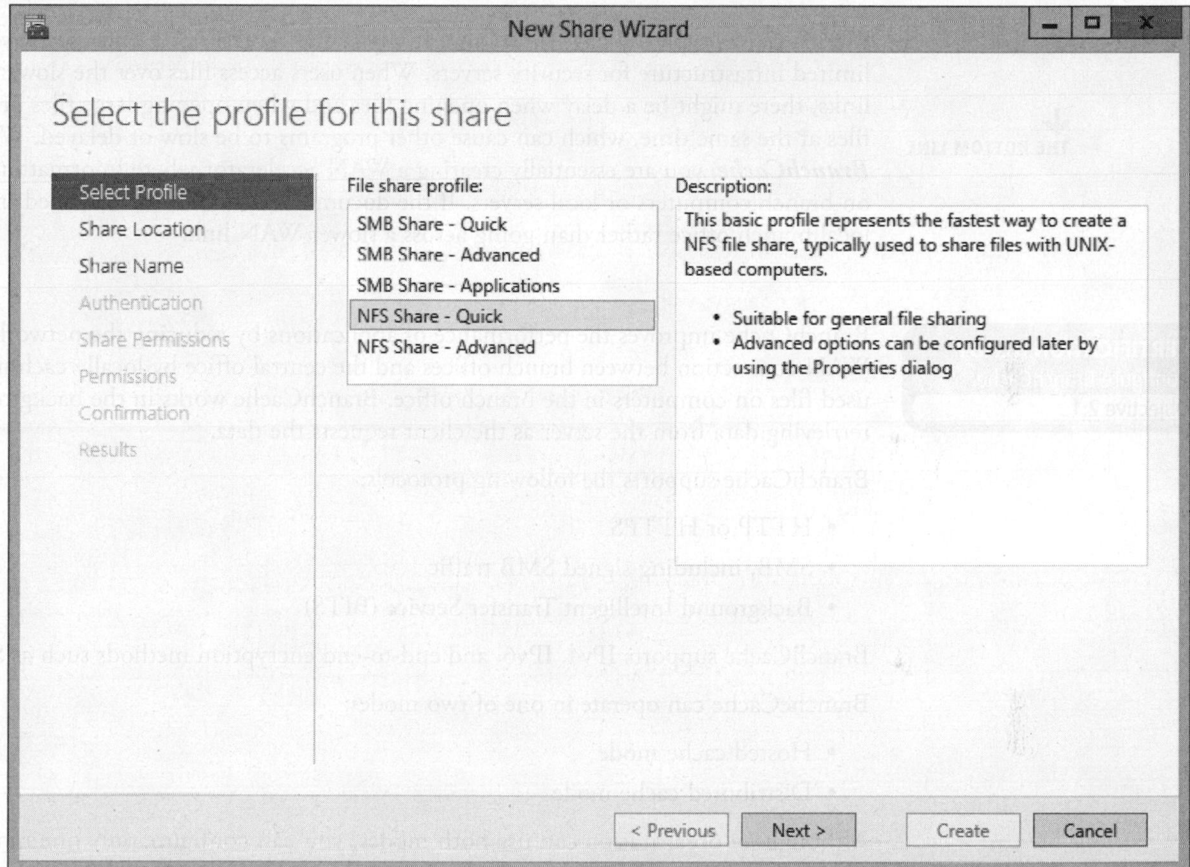

4. On the *Share Location* page, select the volume and click Next.
5. On the *Specify share name* page, type a share name in the *Share name* text box. In the *Local path to share* text box, specify the local path to share. If the folder does not exist, it will create the folder.
6. On the *Authentication* page, click the desired authentication method and click Next.
7. To specify the share permissions, click the Add button.
8. When the *Add Permissions* dialog box opens, *Host* will already be selected. In the text box, type the name of the host that can access the NFS share. Then specify the language encoding and specify the Share permissions. If desired, you can click Allow root access. Click Add.
9. Repeat step 8 as necessary to add additional hosts or groups.
10. On the *Share Permissions* page, click Next.

11. On the *Permissions* page, you can customize the permissions by clicking the Customize permissions. When done, click the Next button.
12. On the *Confirmation* page, click Create.
13. When the share has been created, click Close.

Configuring BranchCache

THE BOTTOM LINE

Branch offices typically have slow connectivity to the central office and typically have limited infrastructure for security servers. When users access files over the slower WAN links, there might be a delay when opening files and when opening large files or many files at the same time, which can cause other programs to be slow or delayed. When using ***BranchCache***, you are essentially creating a WAN accelerator where information is cached on branch computers or local servers. If the document is cached, it is accessed from the local branch office rather than going across a slower WAN link.

CERTIFICATION READY
Configure BranchCache.
Objective 2.1

BranchCache improves the performance of applications by reducing the network use on the WAN connection between branch offices and the central office by locally caching frequently used files on computers in the branch office. BranchCache works in the background by retrieving data from the server as the client requests the data.

BranchCache supports the following protocols:

- HTTP or HTTPS
- SMB, including signed SMB traffic
- Background Intelligent Transfer Service (BITS)

BranchCache supports IPv4, IPv6, and end-to-end encryption methods such as SSL and IPsec.

BrancheCache can operate in one of two modes:

- Hosted cache mode
- Distributed cache mode

Although an organization can use both modes, you can configure only one mode per branch office.

The ***hosted cache mode*** uses one or more dedicated servers to host the cache. If the content is not available in the hosted cache, the content will be retrieved over the WAN link and added to the hosted cache so that clients requesting the same content in the future will benefit. By default, BranchCache allocates five percent of the disk space on the active partition for hosting cache data. However, this size can be changed by using Group Policy or the `netsh branchcache set cachesize` command.

Instead of having a centralized cache, ***distributed cache mode*** has the cache distributed among the local Windows 7 or 8/8.1 clients at the local site. Content on an individual client is shared with the other clients at the site. Distributed cache mode is designed for branch offices with fewer than 50 users that do not have a dedicated server in the branch office. BranchCache works across a single subnet only.

Windows 8/8.1, Windows Server 2012, and Windows Server 2012 R2 Clients can be configured through Group Policy as distributed cache mode clients by default. However, the clients will search for a hosted cache server, and if one is found, it will automatically configure itself into hosted cache mode clients so that it can use the local server.

To use BranchCache, you perform the following:

- For each web server that you want to cache, you must install the BranchCache feature.
- For each file server, you must install the BranchCache for Network Files role service on the file server that is hosting the data. In addition, you have to configure a hash publication for BranchCache and create BranchCache-enabled file shares.
- For the clients to use BranchCache, you must configure the clients using Group Policy or the netsh command.
- If you use the hosted cache mode, you just add the BranchCache feature to the computer running Windows Server 2012 R2 that will be holding the hosted cache.

INSTALL AND CONFIGURE THE BRANCHCACHE FEATURE

GET READY. To install and configure the BranchCache feature, perform the following steps:

1. Open Server Manager, and then click Manage > Add Roles and Features.
2. When the *Add Roles and Features Wizard* opens, click Next.
3. On the *Select Installation Type* page, make sure that *Role-based or feature-based installation* is selected, and then click Next.
4. On the *Select destination server* page, make sure that the correct server is selected, and then click Next.
5. In *Select server roles*, click Next.
6. In *Select features*, click BranchCache, and then click Next.
7. When installation is complete, click Close.

Alternatively, to install BranchCache, you can open Windows PowerShell and execute the following commands:

```
Install-WindowsFeature BranchCache
Restart-Computer
```

INSTALL BRANCHCACHE FOR NETWORK FILES

GET READY. To install BranchCache for Network Files, perform the following steps:

1. With Server Manager, open the Manage menu, and click Add Roles and Features.
2. When the *Add Roles and Features Wizard* opens, click Next.
3. On the *Select Installation Type* page, make sure that *Role-based or feature-based installation* is selected, and then click Next.
4. On the *Select destination server* page, make sure that the correct server is selected, and then click Next.
5. In *Select Server Roles*, under *Roles*, expand File and Storage Services, and expand File and iSCSI Services. Click to select the check boxes for File Server and BranchCache for Network Files. Click Next.
6. In *Select features*, click Next.
7. In *Confirm Installation Selections*, review your selections, and then click Install.
8. When installation is complete, click Close.

Because all the file servers that participate in the BranchCache infrastructure must have the same hash publication policy, it is best to place all of the servers in the same Active Directory OU and then assign the appropriate Group Policy object (GPO).

CONFIGURE THE BRANCHCACHE HASH PUBLICATION GROUP POLICY OBJECT

GET READY. To configure the BranchCache hash publication Group Policy object, perform the following steps:

1. In *Server Manager*, click Tools > Group Policy Management. The *Group Policy Management* console opens.
2. Right-click the GPO that is assigned to the OU that the file servers are in and click Edit. The *Group Policy Management Editor* opens.
3. In the *Group Policy Management Editor* console, expand the following path: Computer Configuration, Policies, Administrative Templates. Click Network, Lanman Server.
4. Double-click Hash Publication for BranchCache. *The Hash Publication for BranchCache* dialog box opens.
5. In the *Hash Publication for BranchCache* dialog box, click Enabled (see Figure 5-6).

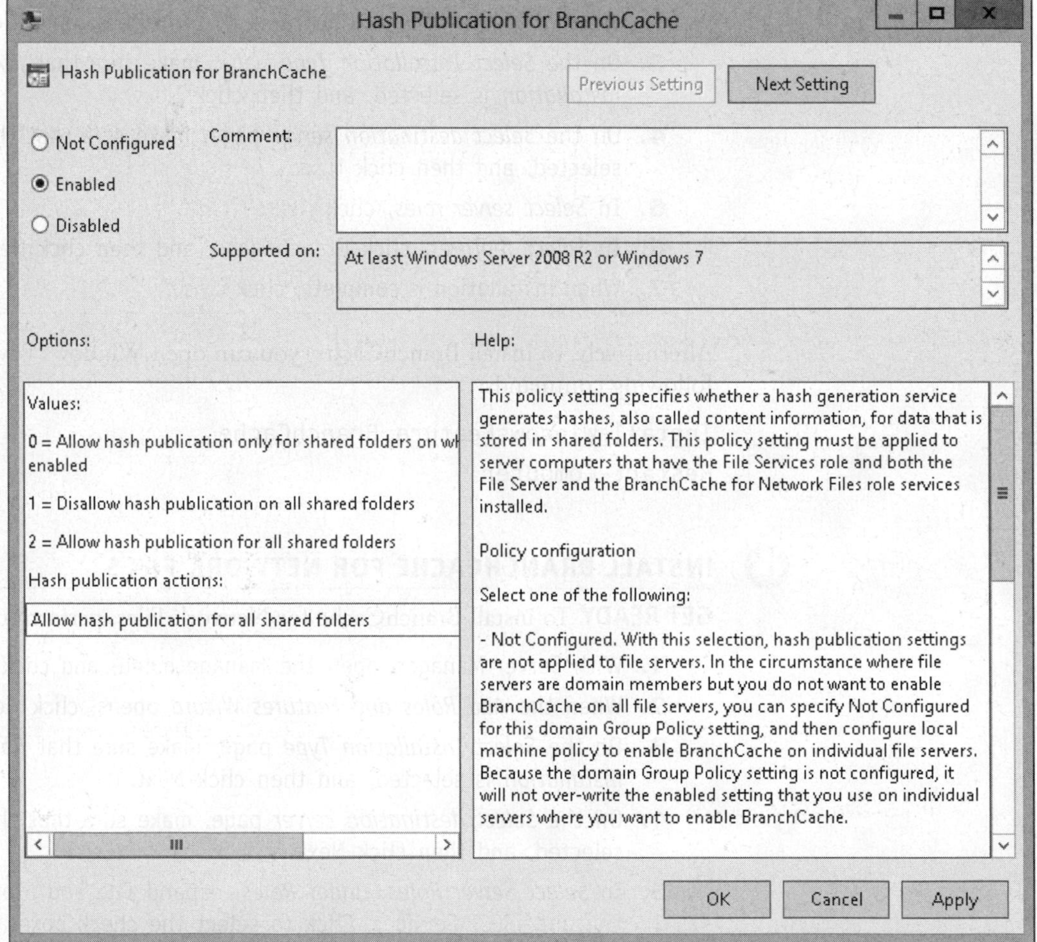

Figure 5-6

Configuring Hash Publication for BranchCache using group policies

6. In *Options*, click Allow hash publication for all shared folders, and then click one of the following:
   a. To enable hash publication for all shared folders for all file servers that you added to the OU, click Allow hash publication for all shared folders.
   b. To enable hash publication only for shared folders for which BranchCache is enabled, click Allow hash publication only for shared folders on which BranchCache is enabled.

c. To disallow hash publication for all shared folders on the computer even if BranchCache is enabled on the file shares, click Disallow hash publication on all shared folders.

7. Click OK to close the *Hash Publication for BranchCache* dialog box.
8. Close *Group Policy Management Editor*.

ENABLE BRANCHCACHE ON A FILE SHARE

GET READY. To enable BranchCache on a File Share, perform the following steps:

1. In *Server Manager*, click Tools > Computer Management. The *Computer Management* console opens.
2. Under *System Tools*, expand Shared Folders and click Shares.
3. In the details pane, right-click a share, and then click Properties. The share's *Properties* dialog box opens.
4. In the *Properties* dialog box, on the *General* tab, click Offline Settings. The *Offline Settings* dialog box opens (see Figure 5-7).

Figure 5-7
Configuring offline settings

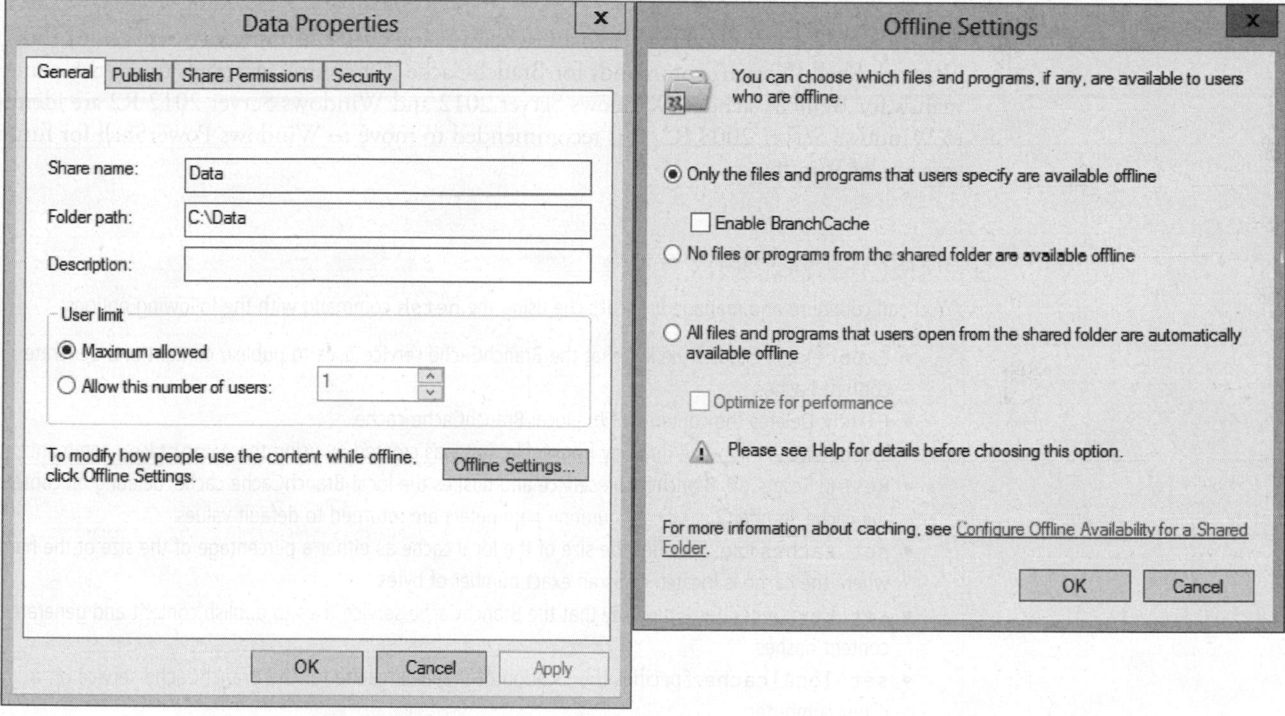

5. Ensure that Only the files and programs that users specify are available offline is selected, and then click Enable BranchCache.
6. Click OK twice.
7. Close Computer Management.

BranchCache is disabled by default on client computers. To enable and configure BranchCache, you need to perform the following steps:

1. Enable BranchCache.
2. Enable the *Distributed Cache* mode or *Hosted Cache* mode.
3. Configure the client firewall to allow BranchCache protocols.

Before the clients can use the BrancheCache, you need to enable BranchCache on the clients. To configure BranchCache settings by using group policy, you open a group policy and navigate to *Computer Configuration > Policies > Administrative Templates > Network*, and then click *BranchCache*. Then Turn on BranchCache and set either the *Distributed Cache* mode or the *Hosted Cache* mode.

To configure BranchCache settings by using the `netsh` command, perform one of the following:

- Use the following `netsh` syntax for the distributed mode:

  ```
  netsh branchcache set service mode=distributed
  ```

- Use the following `netsh` syntax for the hosted mode.

  ```
  netsh branchcache set service mode=hostedclient
  location=<Name of Hosted Cache server>
  ```

You can configure and manage BranchCache by using either Windows PowerShell or the Network Shell (Netsch) commands for BranchCache. Of course, although the `netsh` commands for BranchCache in Windows Server 2012 and Windows Server 2012 R2 are identical to Windows Server 2008 R2, it is recommended to move to Windows PowerShell for future versions of Windows.

USING THE NETSH COMMAND

You can configure and manage BranchCache using the `netsh` command with the following options:

- `Exportkey`: Exports the key that the BranchCache service uses to publish content and generate content hashes.
- `Flush`: Deletes the contents of the local BranchCache cache.
- `Importkey`: Imports a new key from a file that was created by using the `exportkey` command.
- `Reset`: Resets the BranchCache service and flushes the local BranchCache cache, deleting all content in the cache. In addition, all configuration parameters are returned to default values.
- `set cachesize`: Specifies the size of the local cache as either a percentage of the size of the hard disk where the cache is located or as an exact number of bytes.
- `set key`: Generates a new key that the BranchCache service uses to publish content and generate content hashes.
- `set localcache`: Specifies the location of the local cache for the BranchCache service on a client computer.
- `set publicationcache`: Sets the location of the local publication cache for the BranchCache service on a content server.
- `set publicationcachesize`: Sets the size of the publication cache on the local computer.
- `set service`: Configures the BranchCache service.
- `show hostedcache`: Displays the folder location of the hosted cache on the local computer.
- `show localcache`: Displays the status of the local cache.
- `show publicationcache`: Displays the status of the publication cache.
- `show status`: Displays the status of the BranchCache service.
- `smb`: Changes to the smb subcontext of the BranchCache context.
- `set latency`: Specifies the minimum allowed network link latency, in milliseconds, between the branch office and the content source office.
- `show latency`: Displays the configured minimum link latency value in milliseconds.

USING WINDOWS POWERSHELL

You can configure and manage BranchCache using the following cmdlets:

- `Add-BCDataCacheExtension`: Increases the amount of cache storage space that is available on a hosted cache server by adding a new cache file.
- `Clear-BCCache`: Deletes all data in all data and hash files.
- `Disable-BC`: Disables the BranchCache service.
- `Enable-BCDistributed`: Enables BranchCache and configures a computer to operate in distributed cache mode.
- `Enable-BCHostedClient`: Configures BranchCache to operate in hosted cache client mode.
- `Enable-BCHostedServer`: Configures BranchCache to operate in hosted cache server mode.
- `Enable-BCLocal`: Enables the BranchCache service in local caching mode.
- `Export-BCCachePackage`: Exports a cache package.
- `Export-BCSecretKey`: Exports a secret key to a file.
- `Get-BCClientConfiguration`: Retrieves the current BranchCache client computer settings.
- `Get-BCContentServerConfiguration`: Retrieves the current BranchCache content server settings.
- `Get-BCDataCache`: Retrieves the BranchCache data cache.
- `Get-BCDataCacheExtension`: Retrieves the BranchCache data cache extensions from a hosted cache server.
- `Get-BCHashCache`: Retrieves the BranchCache hash cache.
- `Get-BCHostedCacheServerConfiguration`: Retrieves the current BranchCache hosted cache server settings.
- `Get-BCNetworkConfiguration`: Retrieves the current BranchCache network settings.
- `Get-BCStatus`: Retrieves a set of objects that provide BranchCache status and configuration information.
- `Import-BCCachePackage`: Imports a cache package.
- `Import-BCSecretKey`: Imports the cryptographic key that BranchCache uses for the generation of segment secrets.
- `Publish-BCFileContent`: Generates hashes, also called *content information,* for files in shared folders on a file server that have BranchCache enabled and the BranchCache for Network Files role service installed.
- `Publish-BCWebContent`: Creates hashes for web content when deploying content servers that are running Windows Server 2012 R2 with the Web Services (IIS) server role installed.
- `Remove-BCDataCacheExtension`: Deletes a data cache file.
- `Reset-BC`: Resets BranchCache to the default configuration.
- `Set-BCAuthentication`: Specifies the BranchCache computer authentication mode.
- `Set-BCCache`: Modifies the cache file configuration including the cache size.
- `Set-BCDataCacheEntryMaxAge`: Modifies the maximum amount of time that data can remain in the cache.
- `Set-BCMinSMBLatency`: Sets the minimum latency that must exist between client and server before transparent caching functions are utilized.

Configuring File Classification Infrastructure

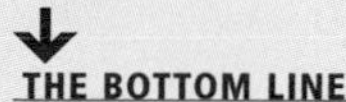

THE BOTTOM LINE

File Server Resource Manager (FSRM) is a suite of tools that enables you to control and manage the quantity and type of data stored on a file server. It enables you to define how much data a person can store, define what type of files that a user can store on a file server, and generate reports about the file server being used. In this section, you classify files based on defined properties and apply policies based on the classification. You can restrict access to files, encrypt files, and have files expire.

CERTIFICATION READY
Configure File Classification Infrastructure (FCI) using File Server Resource Manager (FSRM).
Objective 2.1

File classification allows you to configure automatic procedures for defining a desired property on a file, based on the conditions specified in classification rules. For example, if the content contains "sales figure," you can automatically set the *Confidentiality* property to *High*. By using file classification, you can automate file and folder maintenance tasks, such as deleting old data or protecting sensitive information.

To use file classification, you perform the following steps:

1. Define classification properties and values, which you can assign to files by running classification rules.
2. Create, update, and run classification rules, which are based assigning a single predefined property and value to files within a specified directory based on installed classification plug-ins.
3. When running a classification rule, reevaluate files that are already classified. You can choose to overwrite existing classification values, or add the value to properties that support multiple values. You can also use classification rules to declassify files that are not in the classification criterion anymore.

To configure file classifications, you use the File Server Resource Manager console to create classification rules that scan files for a standard text string, or a string that matches a pattern. When a match is found, the file is classified as specified in the classification rule.

When planning for file classifications, you should do following:

1. Identify which classification or classifications that you want to apply on documents.
2. Determine the method you to want to use to identify documents for classification.
3. Determine the schedule for automatic classifications.
4. Establish a review of classification success.

After you define the classifications, you can then use Dynamic Access Control to enable control on who can access the classified files. Dynamic Access Control is discussed in Lesson 6, "Implementing Dynamic Access Control."

Similar to the previous Windows server roles, the FSRM is installed with Server Manager as a server role.

INSTALL FILE SERVER RESOURCE MANAGER

GET READY. To install FSRM, perform the following steps:

1. Open Server Manager.
2. At the top of *Server Manager*, click Manage > Add Roles and Features to open the *Add Roles and Feature Wizard*.
3. On the *Before you begin* page, click Next.
4. Select Role-based or feature-based installation and then click Next.
5. Click Select a server from the server pool, click the name of the server to install FSRM to, and then click Next.
6. Scroll down and expand File and Storage Services and expand File and iSCSI Services. Select File Server Resource Manager.
7. When you are asked to add features, click Add Features.
8. On the *Select server roles* page, click Next.
9. On the *Select features* page, click Next.
10. On the *Confirm installation selections*, click Install.
11. When the installation is complete, click Close.

CREATE A CLASSIFICATION PROPERTY AND RULE

GET READY. To create a classification property and rule using FSRM, perform the following steps:

1. In *Server Manager*, click Tools > File Server Resource Manager. The *File Server Resource Manager* opens.
2. In *File Server Resource Manager*, under *Classification Management*, click, then right-click Classification Properties and click Create Local Property. The *Create Local Classification Property* dialog box opens (see Figure 5-8).

Figure 5-8

Creating a classification property

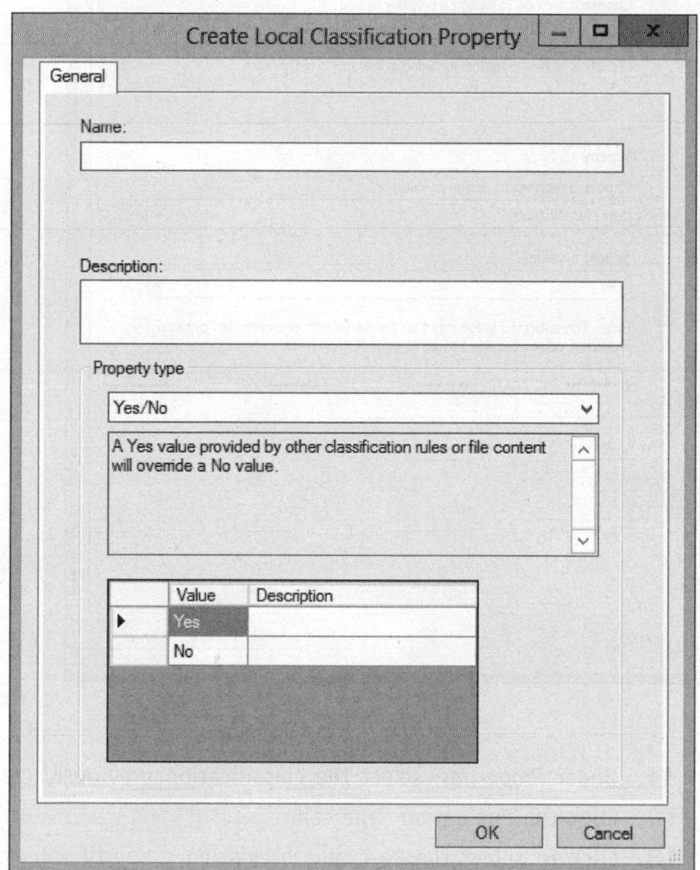

3. In the *General* tab, type the name and an optional description for the local classification.
4. You can choose different property types such as Yes/No, Date-time, number, Multiple Choice List, Ordered List, Single Choice, String, or Multi-String. For the *Property* type, select Yes/No, and click OK.
5. Click, then right-click Classification Rules, and click Create Classification Rule. The *Create Classification Rule* dialog box opens.
6. In the *General* tab, type a rule name and description. Make sure the rule is enabled.
7. Click the Scope tab.
8. Click the Add button. When the *Browse For Folder* dialog box opens, navigate to the folder such as C:\Data.

9. Click the Classification tab.
10. In the *Classification method* section, you can use Content Classifier to search for specified content in the file. To select that the classification is based on its location, for the *Choose a method to assign a property to files*, select Folder Classifier (see Figure 5-9).

Figure 5-9

Defining the classification in a classification rule

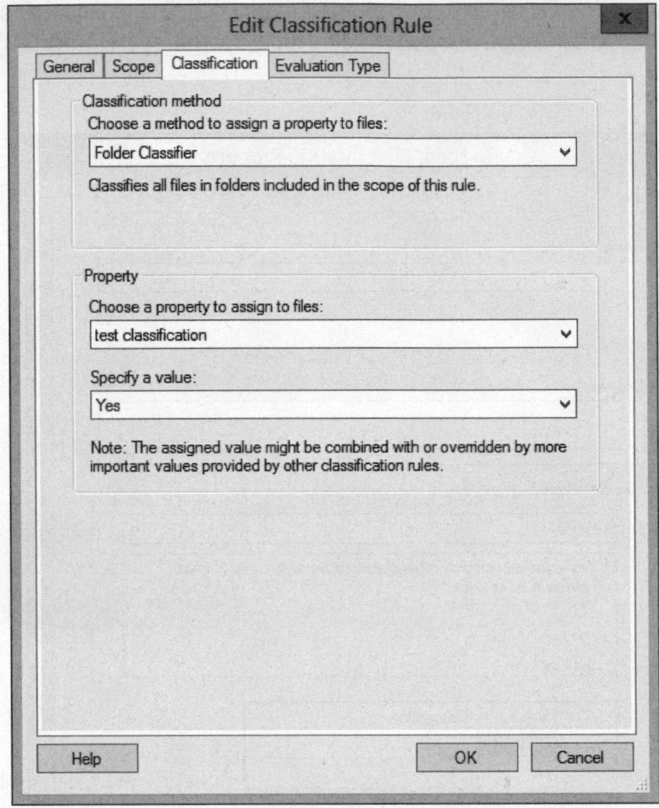

11. Under *Properties*, select the classification previously created and the Yes value.
12. Click the Evaluation Type tab.
13. Click to select the Re-evaluate existing property values. Aggregate the value should already be selected.
14. Click OK to close the *Create Classification Rule* dialog box.
15. In *File Server Resource Manager*, under *actions*, click Run Classification with All Rules Now.
16. When the *Run Classification* dialog box opens, click Wait for classification to complete. When the classification is complete, the *Automatic Classification Report* opens.
17. Close the Automatic Classification Report.
18. Close File Server Resource Manager.

Configuring File Access Auditing

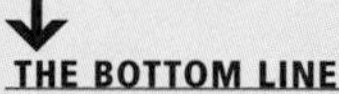

Security can be divided into three areas: authentication, authorization, and auditing. ***Authentication*** is used to prove the identity of a user. ***Authorization*** gives access to the user who was authenticated. To complete the security picture, you need to enable ***auditing*** so that you can have a record of the users who have logged in, what the users accessed or tried to access, and what action the users performed such as rebooting, shutting down a computer, or accessing a file. When you want to audit files, you must first enable object access auditing. Then you must specify which files you want to audit.

CERTIFICATION READY
Configure file access auditing.
Objective 2.1

Most audit settings require you to enable only specific audit settings. However, object auditing is more complex. After you enable object access (using standard audit policy settings or using the detailed audit policy (specifically audit file system), you have to enable auditing on the specific object (including a folder or file) that you want to enable.

ENABLE OBJECT AUDITING

GET READY. To audit account logon successes and failures, perform the following steps:

1. Open Server Manager.
2. Click Tools > Group Policy Management to open the *Group Policy Management* console.
3. Expand the Domain Controllers to show the *Default Domain Controllers Policy*. Then right-click the Default Domain Control Default Policy and click Edit. *Group Policy Management Editor* appears.
4. Expand Computer Configuration, Policies, Windows Settings, Security Settings, Local Policies, and select Audit Policy.
5. Double-click Audit object access. The *Audit account logon events Properties* dialog box opens.
6. Select Define these policy settings and select both Success and Failure.
7. Click OK to close the *Audit account logon events Properties* dialog box.

CONFIGURE FILE SYSTEM AUDITING

GET READY. To audit files and folders, perform the following steps:

1. Right-click the file or folder that you want to audit, click Properties, and then click the Security tab.
2. Click the Advanced button. The *Advanced Security Settings for Updates* dialog box opens.
3. In the *Advanced Security Settings for Updates* dialog box, click the Auditing tab.
4. To add an auditing entry, click Add. The *Auditing Entry for Data* dialog box opens.
5. To specify a user or group, click Select a principal. When the *Select User, Computer, Service Account, or Group* dialog box opens, type a name for a *username* or *group*, and then click OK. See Figure 5-10.

Figure 5-10

Creating auditing entries for file auditing

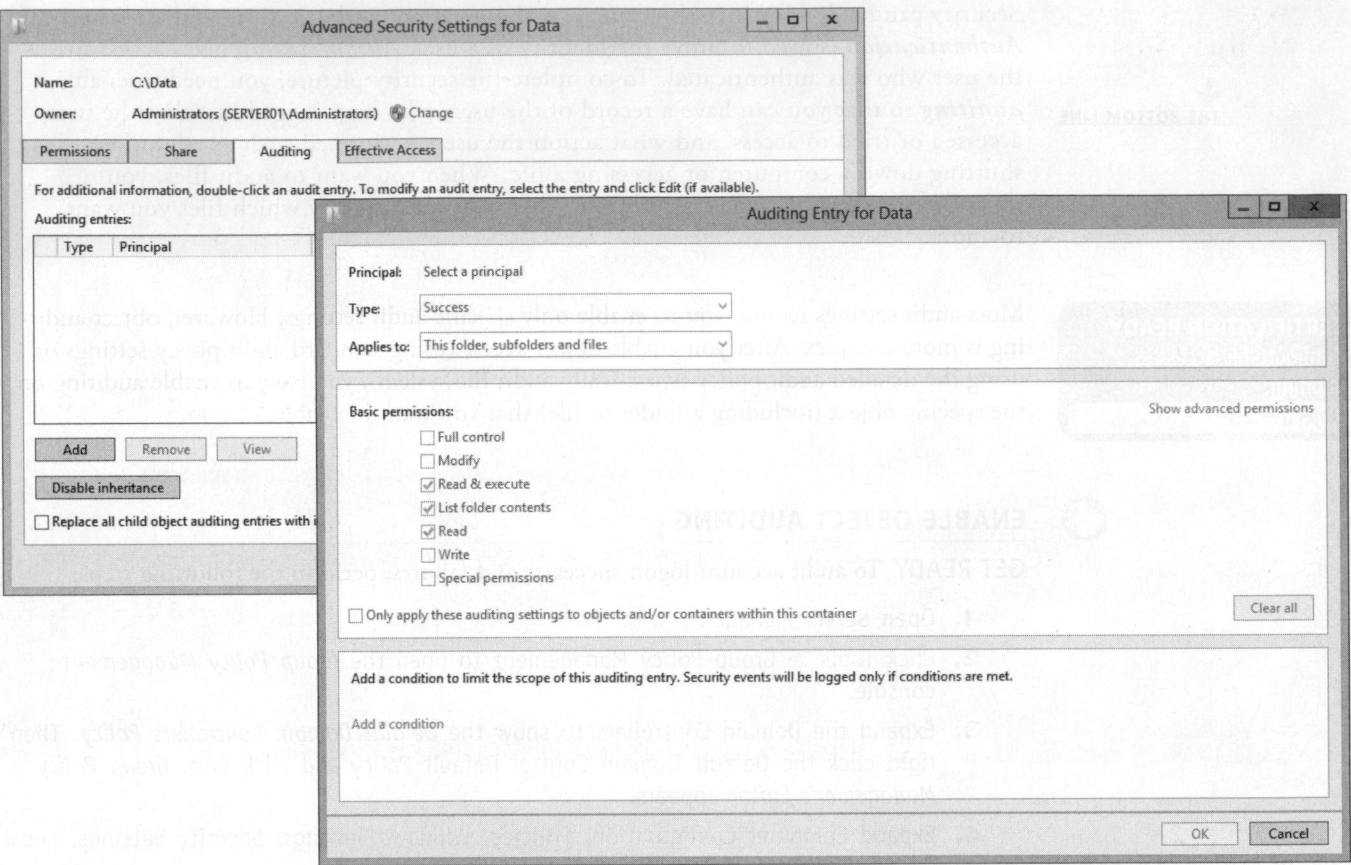

6. For *Type*, select Success, Fail, or All.
7. Specify the permissions that you want to audit by selecting or deselecting the appropriate permission.
8. Click OK to close the *Auditing Entry for Updates* dialog box.
9. Click OK to close the *Advanced Security Settings for Updates* dialog box.
10. Click OK to close the *Properties* dialog box.

Starting with Windows 7 and Windows Server 2008 R2, you can enable Global Object Access Auditing, which enables you to configure object access auditing for every file and folder in a computer's file system. This allows you to centrally manage and configure Windows to monitor files without actually going to each computer and configuring the auditing of each computer or each folder.

You can also take this one step further by using Dynamic Access Control to create targeted audit policies based on resource properties and expressions so that you don't have to audit every file, which can be a burden to the systems performing the auditing and generate a huge number of log entries. As mentioned previously, Dynamic Access Control is discussed in the next lesson.

To use global object access to audit files, you must enable the following two settings:

- Computer Configuration\Windows Settings\Security Settings\Advanced Audit Policy\Audit Policies\Object Access\Audit File System
- Computer Configuration\Windows Settings\Security Settings\Advanced Audit Policy\Audit Policy\Global Object Access Auditing\File System (see Figure 5-11).

Figure 5-11

Configuring the SACL for Global Object Access Audit

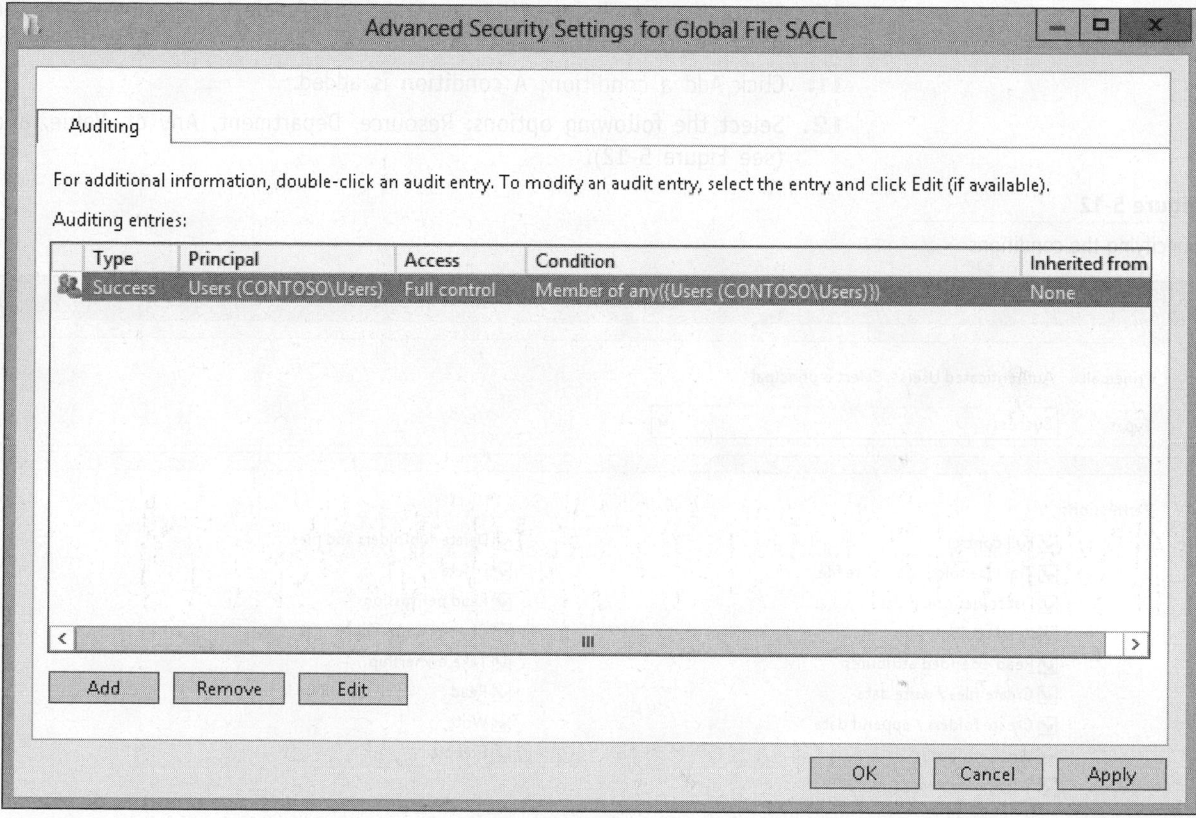

As you configure the Global Object Access Auditing, you have to configure the System Access Control List (SACL), where you define the principal that you want to monitor, the type of event (success, failure, or all), the permission that you want to monitor, and a condition.

DEFINE GLOBAL OBJECT ACCESS AUDITING

GET READY. To define Global Object Access Auditing, perform the following steps:

1. Open Server Manager.
2. Click Tools > Group Policy Management to open the *Group Policy Management* console.
3. Expand the Group Policy Objects folder, right-click a group policy and click Edit. *Group Policy Management Editor* opens.
4. Expand Computer Configuration\Policies\Windows Settings\Security Settings\Advanced Audit policy Configuration\Audit Policies and click Global Object Access Auditing to display the *Global Object Access Auditing* settings.
5. In the right pane, under *Resource Manager*, double-click File system to display the *File system Properties* dialog box.

6. Select Define this policy setting and click Configure. The *Advanced Security Settings for Global File SACL* dialog box opens.
7. In the *Advanced Security Settings for Global File SACL* dialog box, click Add. The *Auditing Entry for Global File SACL* dialog box opens.
8. Click Select a principal. The *Select User, Computer, Service Account, or Group* dialog box opens. Type a name of a user or group in the *Enter the object name to select* box and click OK.
9. For the *Type*, select Success, Fail, or All.
10. Select the permissions that you want and deselect the permissions that you don't want.
11. Click Add a condition. A condition is added.
12. Select the following options: Resource, Department, Any of, Value, and Finance (see Figure 5-12).

Figure 5-12

Specifying the conditions

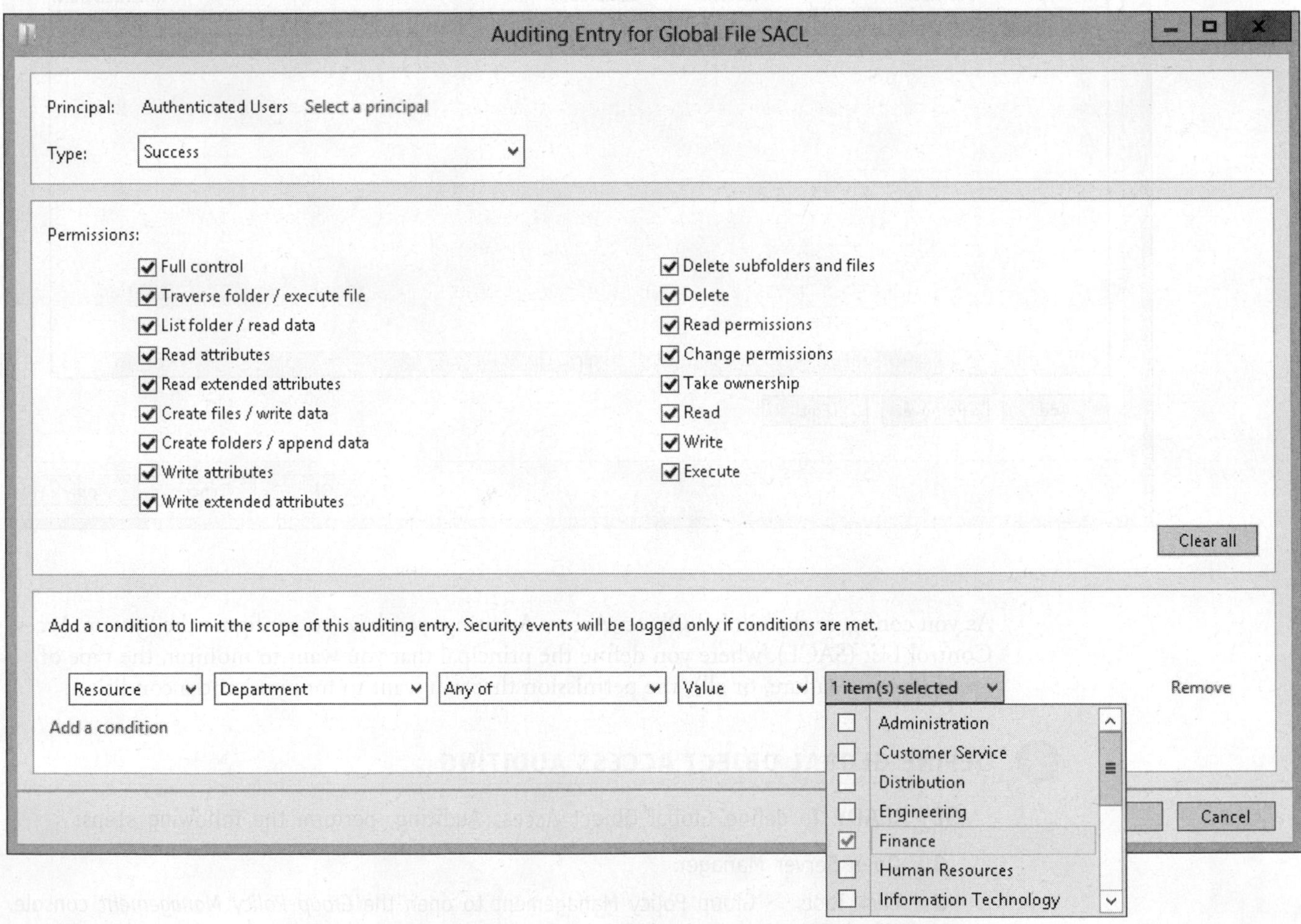

13. Click OK to close the *Auditing Entry for Global File SACL* dialog box.
14. Click OK to close the Advanced Security Settings for Global File SACL dialog box.
15. Click OK to close the *File system Properties* dialog box.
16. Close the *Group Policy Management Editor* and *Group Policy Management*.

SKILL SUMMARY

IN THIS LESSON YOU LEARNED:

- Network File System (NFS) is a distributed file system protocol that is used to access files over a network, similar to accessing a file using a shared folder in Windows (which uses Server Message Block (SMB)).
- Install the Network File System role service to provide NFS Server and NFS Client capabilities.
- Similar to Windows, with UNIX and Linux, you log in and authenticate with an account name and password. The user is identified with a user identifier (UID) value and a group identifier (GID).
- Identity Management for UNIX allows you to integrate Windows users into an existing UNIX/Linux environment including managing user accounts and passwords on Windows and UNIX systems using Network Information Service (NIS) and automatically synchronize passwords between Windows and UNIX operating systems.
- When you install the Services for NFS role service, an NFS Sharing tab is added to the properties of every volume and folder on the computer's drives.
- Server for NFS can be used with failover clustering so that you can deploy NFS while providing fault tolerance. The shared folder within a cluster is known as an *NFS Data Store*.
- BranchCache improves the performance of applications by reducing the network use on the WAN connection between branch offices and the central office by locally caching frequently used files on computers in the branch office.
- BrancheCache can operate in one of two modes: hosted cache mode and distributed cache mode.
- The hosted cache mode uses a dedicated server to host the cache. If the content is not available in the hosted cache, the content will be retrieved over the WAN link and added to the hosted cache so that clients requesting the same content in the future will benefit.
- Instead of having a centralized cache, distributed cache mode has the cache distributed among the local Windows 7 or 8/8.1 clients at the local site.
- File Server Resource Manager (FSRM) is a suite of tools that enables you to control and manage the quantity and type of data stored on a file server.
- File classification allows you to configure automatic procedures for defining a desired property on a file, based on the conditions specified in classification rules.
- Auditing allows you to create a record of the users who have logged in, what the users accessed or tried to access, and what action the users performed such as rebooting, shutting down a computer, or accessing a file.
- To audit files, you must first enable object access auditing. Then you must specify which files you want to audit.
- Starting with Windows 7 and Windows Server 2008 R2, you can enable Global Object Access Auditing, which allows you to configure object access auditing for every file and folder in a computer's file system.

Knowledge Assessment

Multiple Choice

Select the correct answer for each of the following questions.

1. What method of file sharing is used with UNIX and Linux machines?
   a. SMB
   b. CIFS
   c. NTFS
   d. NFS

2. When using NFS, how do you connect to the shared folder?
   a. You mount the volume to a local folder
   b. You mount the volume to a remote folder
   c. You access the shared folder using a UNC
   d. You access the shared folder using a URL

3. What allows you to integrate Windows users into an existing UNIX or Linux environment?
   a. NFS snap-in
   b. UNIX translator
   c. Identity Management for UNIX
   d. UNIX plug-in

4. What command do you use to install Identity Management for UNIX?
   a. `install.exe`
   b. `feature.exe`
   c. `dism.exe`
   d. `msiexec.exe`

5. When you define access to NFS, which two items must you include? (Choose two answers.)
   a. domain name
   b. GID
   c. admin access
   d. UID

6. What are the three requirements for the NFS Data Store? (Choose three answers.)
   a. File Services role
   b. Server for NFS role service
   c. Failover Clustering feature
   d. Identity Manage for UNIX

7. Which Windows Server 2012 R2 server acts as a WAN accelerator?
   a. NFS accelerator
   b. BranchCache
   c. File Server Resource Manager
   d. GPO Cache

8. Which mode in BranchCache allows you to store the cache among multiple computers running Windows 8.1?
   a. hosted cache mode
   b. distributed cache mode
   c. WSCache
   d. WideRanceCache

9. Which primary tool is used when classifying files?
   a. File Administrator
   b. Server Manager
   c. Computer Management
   d. File Server Resource Manager

10. What are the two items that you have to create when using file classification?
    a. classification property
    b. classification attribute
    c. classification syntax
    d. classification rule

Best Answer

Choose the letter that corresponds to the best answer. More than one answer choice may achieve the goal. Select the BEST answer.

1. What are the two actions that need to be done when you need to audit whether a file is being read by a certain user? (Choose two answers.)
   a. You need to specify which folders and files to audit
   b. You need to add a checksum to the file to be audited
   c. You need to enable object auditing
   d. You need to add an audit digital certificate to the system where the files reside
2. What do you use to extend the Active Directory schema to store UNIX attributes?
   a. NFS Management console
   b. Server for NFS role
   c. Computer Management console
   d. Identity Management for UNIX
3. At the corporate office, you have a file server called Server01. At a remote site, you installed BranchCache on Server02, which is acting as a BranchCache hosted cache server. To move things along, you decide to preload the data from the file shares on Server1 to the cache on Server02. What would generate the hashes for the file share on Server01?
   a. Use the `Enable-BCCache` PowerShell cmdlet
   b. Use the `Publish-BCCache PowerShell` cmdlet
   c. Use the `Export-BCCachepackage` PowerShell cmdlet
   d. Use the `Set-BCCache PowerShell` cmdlet
4. To fully use Identity Management for UNIX, what are the three components that you have to install? (Choose three answers.)
   a. nis
   b. adminui
   c. Unix-add
   d. psync
5. Which two commands allow you to specify the cache size for BranchCache hosted cache server?
   a. `netsh set cachsize` command
   b. `netsh set publicationcachezie` command
   c. `Set-BCCacheSize` PowerShell cmdlet
   d. `Set-BCCache` PowerShell cmdlet

Build a List

1. Identify the basic steps in order to create an NFS data store by placing the number of the step in the appropriate space. Not all steps will be used.
   _______ Install the Failover Clustering feature
   _______ Create an NFS Share using Failover Cluster Manager
   _______ Install the File Services role
   _______ Use Windows Explorer to create the NFS share
   _______ Install the Identity Management of UNIX
   _______ Install the Server for NFS role service
   _______ Configure the role using Cluster Manager
   _______ Share the folder using Windows Explorer

2. Identify the steps that must be completed before you can use BranchCache at a remote site with a server configured as a hosted cache server by placing the number of the step in the appropriate space.
   _______ Configure BranchCache Hash Publication for each File Server
   _______ Install and configure BranchCache feature on a server at the remote site
   _______ Install BranchCache feature on each web server
   _______ Install BranchCache feature on each file server
   _______ Install BranchCache for Network File Server on each file server
   _______ Install BranchCache for Network File Server on each web server
   _______ Use GPOs to configure each file server
   _______ Use GPOs to configure each shared folder
   _______ Use GPOs to configure each client to use BranchCache

3. Identify the basic steps in order to classify a set of files by placing the number of the step in the appropriate space. Not all steps will be used.
   _______ Create a Classification Property
   _______ Create a Classification Rule
   _______ Configure the attributes of each file or folder using Windows Explorer
   _______ Run a classification report to verify results
   _______ Run the classification rules
   _______ Configure a GPO for the folder to classify the folder or file
   _______ Install FSRM

4. Identify the basic steps in order to audit all files on all file servers that are located in the File Server OU. Not all steps will be used.
   _______ Configure the system attribute of the file or folders to be audited
   _______ Define the type of auditing
   _______ Enable Global Object Access\File System
   _______ Use Computer Management to pre-scan the files to audit
   _______ Specify the principal
   _______ Define the condition of the audit event
   _______ Enable Audit File System

Choose an Option

1. You have a central office and several remote sites. To help with system performance, you decide to implement BranchCache. Each remote site has between 15 and 25 users/computers with no dedicated server. What options within the GPO would you need to configure BranchCache for a remote site? Circle the necessary options in Figure 5-13.

Figure 5-13

Viewing GPO Settings

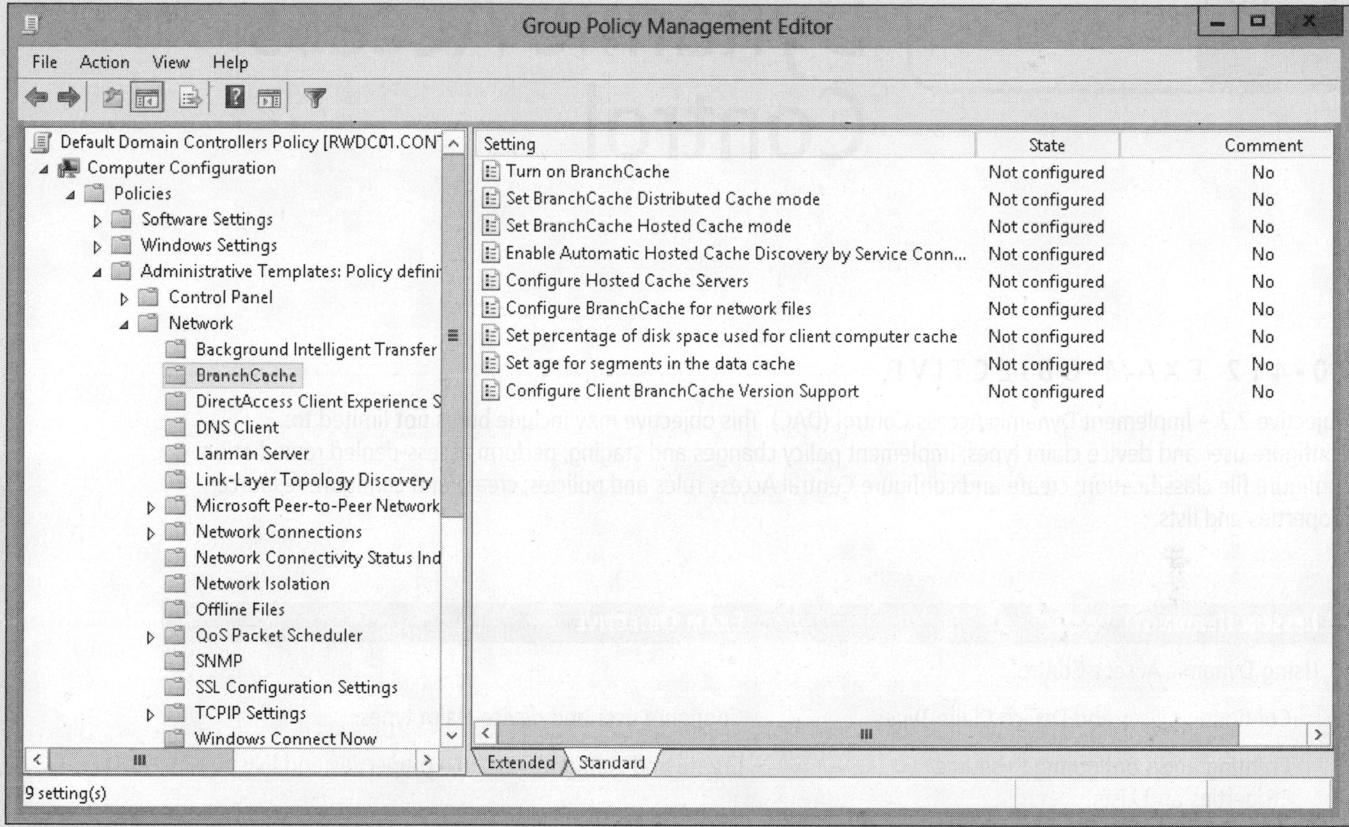

Business Case Scenarios

Scenario 5-1: Configuring BranchCache for a Remote Site

You have a site (Site1) that has about 20 users. For the last few months, users at Site1 have been complaining about the performance when accessing multiple large files at the corporate office, particularly if the files are relatively large. They have no dedicated server to configure DFS replication. Therefore, what else can you do to improve the performance when accessing these files?

Scenario 5-2: Classifying Human Resource Documents

You have a bunch of files on Server01 that belong to the Human Resources department. You need to classify these documents as confidential so that you can define some auditing and make sure that the documents are secure. What should you do?

Implementing Dynamic Access Control

70-412 EXAM OBJECTIVE

Objective 2.2 – Implement Dynamic Access Control (DAC). This objective may include but is not limited to: Configure user and device claim types; implement policy changes and staging; perform access-denied remediation; configure file classification; create and configure Central Access rules and policies; create and configure resource properties and lists.

Lesson Heading	Exam Objective
Using Dynamic Access Control	
Configuring User and Device Claim Types	Configure user and device claim types
Creating and Configuring Resource Properties and Lists	Create and configure resource properties and lists
Configuring File Classification	Configure file classification
Creating and Configuring Central Access Rules and Policies	Create and configure Central Access rules and policies
Implementing Policy Changes and Staging	Implement policy changes and staging
Creating Expression-Based Audit Policies	
Performing Access-Denied Remediation	Perform access-denied remediation

KEY TERMS

Access-Denied Assistant
Central Access Policy
Central Access Rules
claim
claim type
claims-based access control
classification rules
Dynamic Access Control (DAC)
Global Object Access Auditing
Security Token Service (STS)
token
trusted identity provider

Using Dynamic Access Control

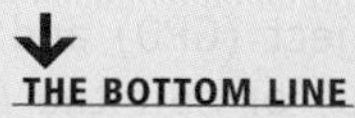

THE BOTTOM LINE

Dynamic Access Control (DAC), originally called *claims-based access control*, was introduced with Windows Sever 2012, is used for access management. It provides an automatic mechanism to secure and control access to resources.

Claims-based access control uses a trusted identity provider to provide authentication. The ***trusted identity provider*** issues a token to the user, which the user then presents to the application or service as proof of identity. Identity is based on a set of information. Each piece of information is referred to as a ***claim*** (such as who the user or computer claims to be), and stored as a token, which is a digital key. The ***token*** is digital identification for the user or computer that is accessing a network resource. The token has a digital signature of the identity provider to verify the authenticity of the information stored within the token. As users or computers need access to a resource, the user or computer presents the token to get access to the resource.

In Windows Server 2012 R2 the identity provider is the ***Security Token Service (STS)*** and the claims are the Active Directory attributes assigned to a user or device (such as a computer). The claims, the user's security identifier (SID), and group membership are stored inside the Kerberos ticket. The ticket is then used to access protected resources. Of course, claims authorization relies on the Kerberos Key Distribution Center (KDC).

In Windows Server 2012 R2 DAC allows you to perform the following:

- Identify data by using automatic and manual classification or tagging files in an organization.
- Control access to files by applying automatic policies that are controlled by Central Access Policies.
- Audit access by using a Central Audit Policy to ensure compliance and to be used in forensic analysis.
- Use Active Directory Rights Management Service (RMS) to encrypt sensitive documents. Active Directory Management Services is discussed in Lesson 21, "Installing and Configuring Active Directory Rights Management Services."
- Offer Access-Denied Assistance, which provides a method for users to request access from the owner of data when he or she is denied access.

To use claims-based authorization, you need the following:

- Windows Server 2012 R2 must be installed on the file server that hosts the resources that DAC protects.
- At least one Windows Server 2012 R2 domain controller must be accessible by the requesting client.
- If you use claims across a forest, you must have a Windows Server 2012 R2 domain controller in each domain.
- If you use device claims, clients must run Windows 8.1.

When you enable DAC, you have the option to support claims, compound authentication, and Kerberos armoring. Compound authentication is an extension to Flexible Authentication Secure Tunneling (FAST), which allows Kerberos to create service tickets to devices. The Kerberos armoring fully encrypts Kerberos messages and signs Kerberos errors. Although Kerberos armoring enhances security, it also increases processing time.

ENABLE DAC FOR ACTIVE DIRECTORY DOMAIN SERVICES

GET READY. To enable DAC for Active Directory Domain Services (AD DS), perform the following steps:

1. To enable AD DS for DAC, create a new Group Policy Object (GPO) and link the GPO to the *Domain Controllers* organization unit (OU) or edit the *Default Domain Controllers Policy* GPO. Open Server Manager, and then open Group Policy Management.
2. When the *Group Policy Management* console opens, double-click the GPO assigned to the Domain Controllers OU that you want to use to enable DAC.
3. When the *Group Policy Management Editor* opens, navigate to Computer Configuration\Policies\Administrative Templates\System\KDC and double-click KDC support for claims, compound authentication and Kerberos armoring.
4. Click Enabled.
5. Under *Options*, you can choose one of the following:
   - Not supported: Does not provide support for claims, compound authentication, or armoring.
   - Supported: Supports claims, compound authentication, and Kerberos armoring for DAC.
   - Always provide claims: Provides support for claims.
   - Fail unarmored authentication requests: Rejects unarmored Kerberos requests.
6. Click Close to close the *KDC support for claims, compound authentication and Kerberos armoring* dialog box.
7. Close the Group Policy Management Editor.

Configuring User and Device Claim Types

CERTIFICATION READY
Configure user and device claim types.
Objective 2.2

After you enable support for DAC in AD DS, you must create and configure claims and resource property objects. To create and configure claims, you primarily use the Active Directory Administrative Center.

The most common types of claims are attribute-based claims, which are usually configured with Active Directory Administrative Center, specifically using the Dynamic Access Control node (see Figure 6-1). All claims are stored in the configuration partition in AD DS, which is a forest-wide partition. As a result, all domains in the forest share the claim dictionary.

Figure 6-1

Managing DAC using Active Directory Administrative Center

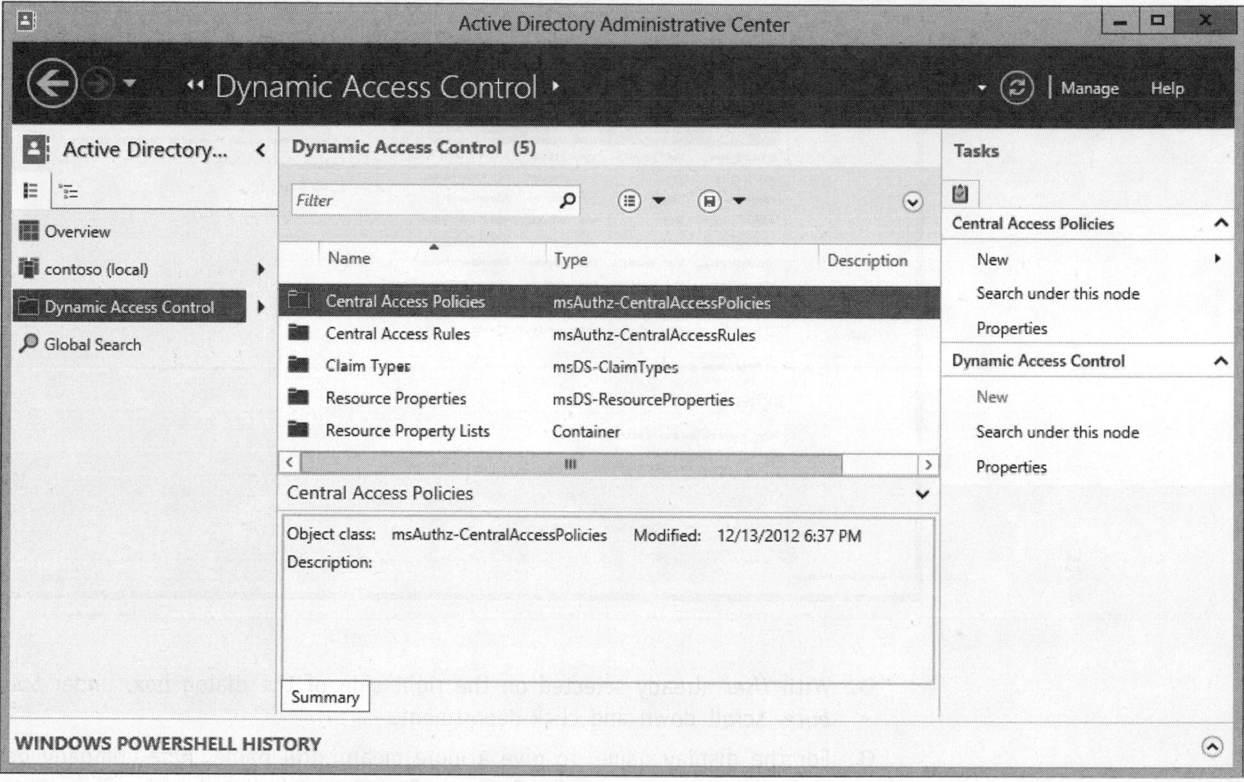

To create a ***claim type***, you specify a specific attribute from Active Directory. Of course, for DAC to be effective, Active Directory must contain accurate information. By default, the claim name is the name of the selected attribute name. However, you can modify this to give a more meaningful name. Lastly, you have the option to provide suggested values for the claim.

CREATE CLAIM TYPES

GET READY. To create a claim type, perform the following steps:

1. Open Server Manager.
2. Click Tools > Active Directory Administrative Center. The *Active Directory Administrative Center opens.*
3. Navigate to the Dynamic Access Control node and click the Claim Types container.
4. In the *Tasks* pane, under *Claim Types*, click New, and then click Claim Type. The *Create Claim Type* dialog box opens (see Figure 6-2).

Figure 6-2

Creating a claim type

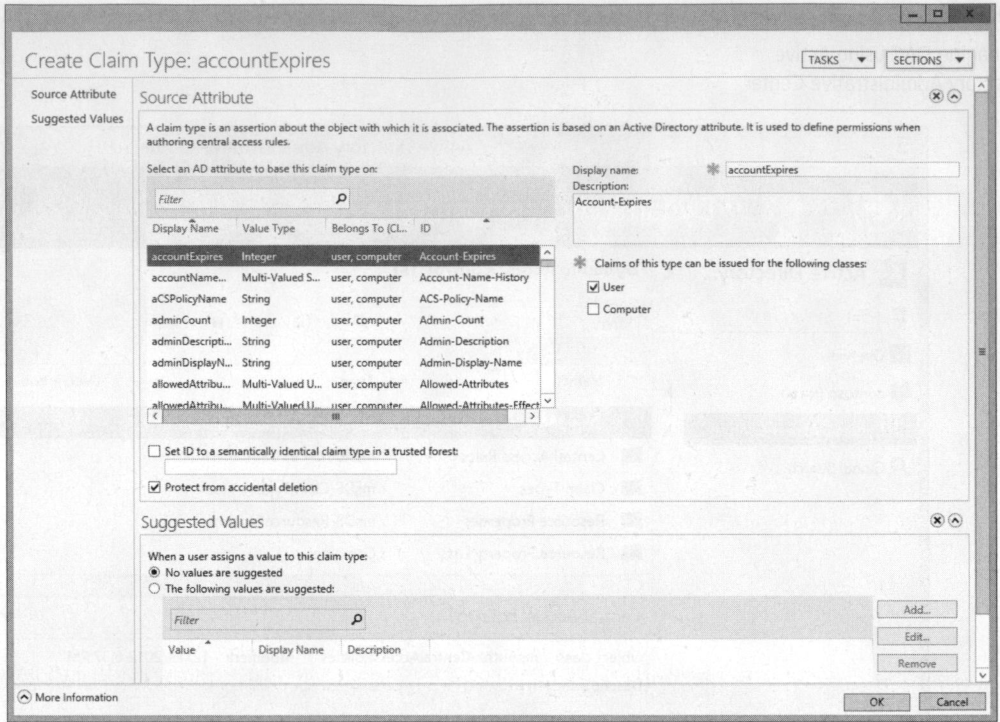

5. With *User* already selected on the right side of the dialog box, under *Source Attribute,* scroll down and click department.
6. For the display name, to give a more meaningful name, type Company Department and click OK. An entry for *Company Department* is listed under *Claim types.*
7. In the *Tasks* pane, under *Claim Types,* click New, and then click Claim Type.
8. Click to deselect User and click to select Computer.
9. Under *Source Attribute*, scroll down and for *Source Attribute,* click description.
10. Click OK to close the *Create Claim Type* dialog box. The *description* claim type appears.
11. When the installation is complete, click Close.

After you create the claim types, you must configure the resource property objects such as a folder or a file using the Active Directory Administrative Center. You can create your own resource property, or you can use preconfigured properties, such as Project, Department, or Folder Usage. If you choose to use a preconfigured property, they are disabled by default. Therefore, you have to enable the preconfigure property.

Each resource property must be added to at least one resource property list and each resource property list must then be downloaded to the file servers. The Global Resource Property List is downloaded by all servers.

ENABLE RESOURCE PROPERTIES

GET READY. To enable a resource property, perform the following steps:

1. With Active Directory Administrative Center, navigate to and click the Dynamic Access Control node. Next, double-click Resource Properties.
2. To enable the Department resource property, under *Resource Property*, right-click Department, and click Enable.

3. To enable the *Confidentiality* resource property, under *Resource Property*, right-click Confidentiality, and click Enable.
4. To view the *Confidentiality* settings, double-click Confidentiality. The *Confidentiality* dialog box opens (see Figure 6-3).

Figure 6-3

Viewing the Confidentiality resource property

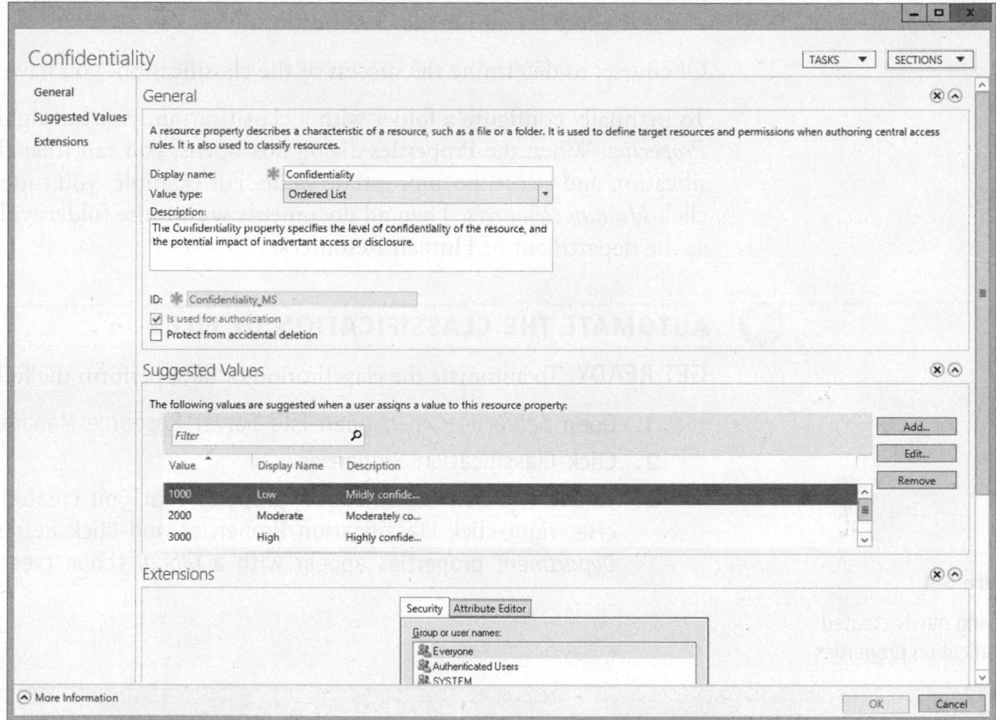

5. Click Cancel to close the *Confidentiality* dialog box.
6. Close *Active Directory Administrative Center*.

Creating and Configuring Resource Properties and Lists

CERTIFICATION READY
Create and configure resource properties and lists.
Objective 2.2

When you configure the properties that are downloaded by files servers and used to classify files or directories, you will use DAC rules to compare user attribute values with resource properties, which are assigned to Resource Properties Lists. You can enable existing properties or create new ones.

Configuring File Classification

When planning DAC implementation, you should include file classification. Although file classification is not mandatory for DAC, it can enhance the automation of access control because it can be used to identify documents that you need to protect, and classify them appropriately.

CERTIFICATION READY
Configure file classification.
Objective 2.2

Classification management and file management tasks enable administrators to manage groups of files based on various file and folder attributes. After folders and files are classified, you can automate file and folder maintenance tasks, such as cleaning up stale data or protecting sensitive information. Although classification management can be done manually, you can automate this process with the File Server Resource Manager console.

Classification rules can be created and then scheduled to be applied on a regular basis so that files are automatically scanned and classified based on the content of the file. When you want to perform file classification, you need to determine the following:

- Classifications that you want to apply to documents
- Method that you will use to identify documents for classification
- Schedule for automatic classifications

Of course, to determine the success of the classification, you have to establish periodic reviews.

To manually configure a folder with a classification, you can right-click the folder and click *Properties*. When the Properties dialog box opens, you can then choose the name of the classification and select the appropriate value. For example, you can select *Department*, and then click *Human Resources*. Then all documents within the folder will automatically be classified as the department of Human Resources.

AUTOMATE THE CLASSIFICATION OF FILES

GET READY. To automate the classification of files, perform the following steps:

1. Open Server Manager, open File Server Resource Manager.
2. Click Classification Properties.
3. To see the new classification property that you created in the previous exercise, right-click Classification Properties and click Refresh. The *Confidentiality* and *Department* properties appear with a *Global* scope (see Figure 6-4).

Figure 6-4

Viewing newly created classification properties

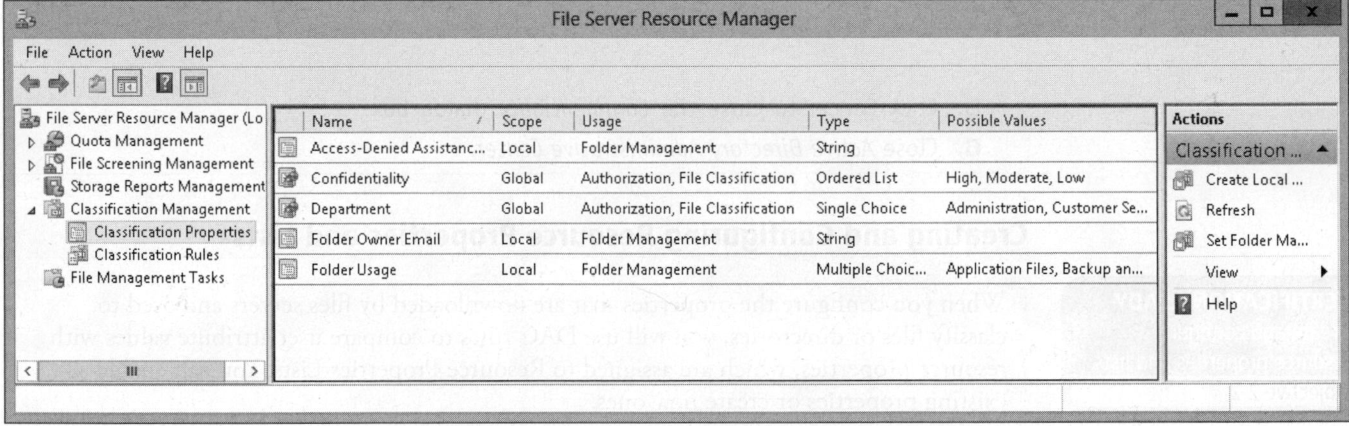

4. Click Classification Rules. Next, right-click Classification Rules and click Create Classification Rule. The *Create Classification Rule* dialog box opens.
5. In the *General* tab, in the *Rule name* text box, type Confidentiality.
6. Click the Scope tab.
7. At the bottom of the dialog box, click Add. Browse to the C:\Data folder and click OK. *C:\Data* is listed under *The following folders are included in this scope* section.
8. Click the Classification tab.
9. The *Classification method* should already be *Content Classifier*, the *Confidentiality* and *High* are set under *Property*. To configure the Classification parameter, under *Parameters*, click Configure. The *Classification Parameters* dialog box opens.

10. Change the Regular expression to String. Under *Expression*, type HR. This means that if any of the documents have the string *HR*, they will be automatically tagged as *High* confidentiality.
11. Click OK to close the *Classification Parameters* dialog box.
12. Click Evaluation Type tab.
13. Click to select Re-evaluate existing property values. Then select Overwrite the existing value.
14. Click OK to close the *Create Classification Rule* dialog box.
15. With *File Server Resource Manager* open, click Run Classification with All Rules Now. When you are asked how you want to run the classification rules, click Wait for classification to complete and click OK.
16. When the *Automatic Classification Report* opens, review the results and close the report.
17. If you have a document that has the *HR* string, right-click the document and click Properties.
18. When the *Properties* dialog box opens, click the Classification tab, and notice that *Confidentiality* has been set to *High* (see Figure 6-5).

Figure 6-5

Viewing a document file classifications

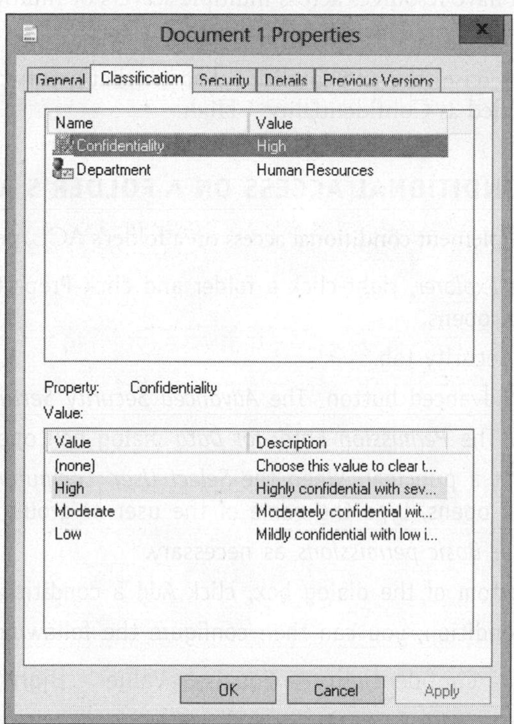

19. Click OK to close the *Properties* dialog box.
20. Close the *File Server Resource Manager*.

Creating and Configuring Central Access Rules and Policies

Similar to file classification, a Central Access Policy is not mandatory for DAC. However, it is recommended to implement at least one Central Access Policy.

CERTIFICATION READY
Create and configure Central Access rules and policies.
Objective 2.2

Files stored in shared folders are data files that need to be accessed by multiple users. However, when you apply shared and NTFS permissions, the permissions apply to all files in a specific folder. Unless you constantly monitor the folder and modify the permissions for the folder or the individual files in the folder, the shared and NTFS permissions might not always be a good fit to keep the files secure.

A ***Central Access Policy*** contains ***Central Access Rules*** that grant permissions to objects for a defined group of resources. By default the rules apply to all resources, but you can limit the resources to which the rule will apply. Once the rule is defined, you can choose to apply it live or you can choose to use a "staging" mode.

Before you implement a Central Access Policy, you should do the following:

1. Identify the resources that you want to protect.
2. Define the authorization policies.
3. Translate the authorization policies into expressions.
4. Break down the expressions that you have created, and determine what claim types, resource properties, and device claims that you must create to deploy the policies.

If you have one file server, or one folder, you don't necessarily need to implement a Central Access Policy. Instead, you can implement conditional access on the folder's Access Control List (ACL). If you have resources across multiple servers or multiple folders, you would most likely benefit from a Central Access Policy.

During the next exercise, you add conditional access that grants permissions to files in a folder that is classified as Confidentiality – High.

IMPLEMENT CONDITIONAL ACCESS ON A FOLDER'S ACL

GET READY. To implement conditional access on a folder's ACL, perform the following steps:

1. Using *File Explorer*, right-click a folder and click Properties. The *Properties* dialog box opens.
2. Click the Security tab.
3. Click the Advanced button. The *Advanced Security Settings* dialog box opens.
4. Click Add. The *Permission Entry for Data* dialog box opens.
5. Click Select a principal. When the *Select User, Computer, Service Account, or Group* dialog box opens, type the name of the user or group and click OK.
6. Specify the *Basic permissions* as necessary.
7. At the bottom of the dialog box, click Add a condition.
8. For the condition, you can then configure the following:

   Resource > Confidentiality > Equals > Value > High (see Figure 6-6). Click OK.
9. Back on the *Advanced Security Settings* dialog box, click OK to close the *Advanced Security Settings for Data* dialog box.
10. Click OK to close the *Properties* dialog box.

Figure 6-6

Configuring a condition for an ACL

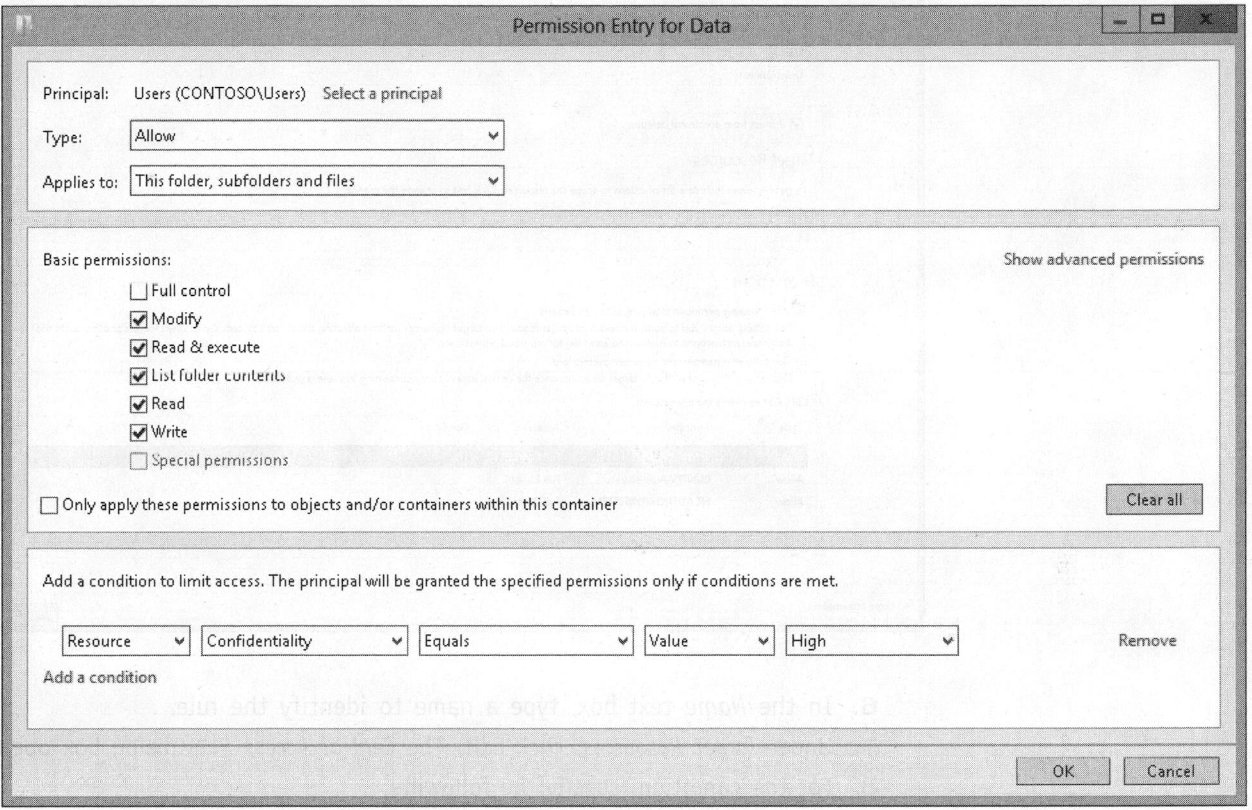

During the next exercise, you create a Central Access Rule that grants permissions to files in a folder that is classified as Confidentiality – High.

CREATE A CENTRAL ACCESS POLICY

GET READY. To create and apply a Central Access Policy, perform the following steps:

1. In the *Active Directory Administrative Center*, navigate to and click the Dynamic Access Control node. Next, double-click Central Access Policies.
2. Under *Tasks*, click New, and click Central Access Policy. The *Central Access Policy* dialog box opens.
3. In the *name* text box, type a name of the Central Access Policy.
4. Under the *Member Central Access Rules* section, click Add.
5. Because you do not have a Central Access Rule defined, click Add a new central access rule. The *Create Central Access Rule* dialog box is shown in Figure 6-7.

Figure 6-7

Using the Create Central Access Rule dialog box

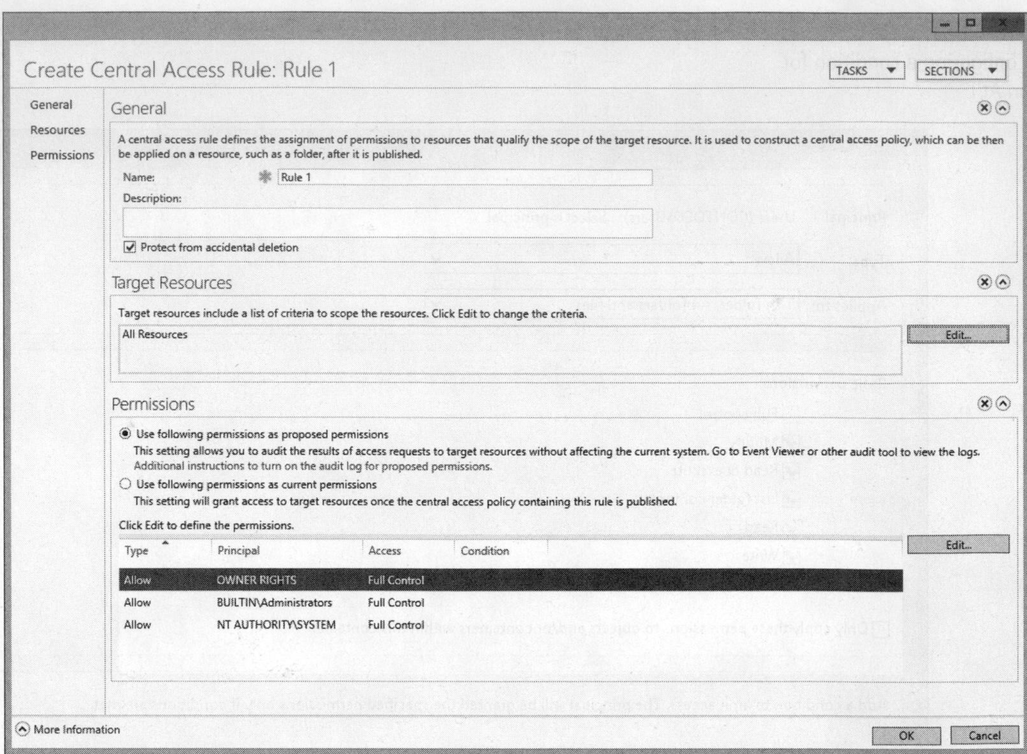

6. In the *Name* text box, type a name to identify the rule.
7. Under *Target Resources*, click Edit. The *Central Access Rule* dialog box opens.
8. For the condition, specify the following:

   Resource > Confidentiality > Equals > Value > High

   Click OK to close the *Central Access Rule* dialog box.
9. Click OK to close the *Create Central Access Rule* dialog box.
10. Back on the *Central Access Rule* dialog box, the rule should be listed in the right pane. Click OK to close the *Add Central Access* dialog box.
11. Click OK to close the *Create Central Access Policy* dialog box.
12. Click Cancel to close the *Confidentiality* dialog box.
13. Close the *Active Directory Administrative Center.*

    You can also take this a step further and specify that access is granted only if the user is part of the Human Resources department:

    Resource > Department > Equals > Value > Human Resources

Implementing Policy Changes and Staging

As you probably already have figured out, DAC can be a powerful tool that helps secure your environment and automates the configuration to make your resources secure. However, if you do not properly plan out DAC, when you first implement DAC or when you make changes, you can either grant more access than desired, or you can restrict access to the files too much, resulting in an increase of help desk calls.

CERTIFICATION READY
Implement policy changes and staging.
Objective 2.2

To help you test implementing DAC or making changes, Windows Server 2012 R2 allows you to perform staging, which allows you to verify the proposed policy updates before enforcing them. To use staging, you deploy the proposed polices along with the enforced policies, but you do not actually grant or deny permissions. You then open the Event Viewer on the file server search for Audit Event 4818 in the security logs. The Audit Event 4818 shows the result of the access check that is using the staged policy is different than the access check that is using the enforced policy. However, before the staging appears, you need to first enable *Audit Central Access Policy Staging* using *Group Policies*.

CONFIGURE STAGING OF CENTRAL ACCESS POLICY

GET READY. To configure staging of Central Access Policy, perform the following steps:

1. Open Server Manager, and then open Group Policy Management.
2. Using the *Group Policy Management* console, right-click a group policy that you are using to configure DAC and click Edit. The *Group Policy Management Editor* opens.
3. Navigate to Computer Configuration\Policies\Windows Settings\Security Settings\Advanced Audit Policy Configuration\Audit Policies and double-click Object Access.
4. Double-click Audit Central Access Policy Staging, select all three check boxes, and then click OK.
5. Double-click Audit File System.
6. When the *Audit Central Access Policy Staging Properties* dialog box opens, click to select Configure the following audit events, Success, and Failure.
7. Click OK to close the *Audit Central Access Policy Staging Properties* dialog box.
8. Close the *Group Policy Management Editor* and the *Group Policy Management* console.

Another way to test DAC changes is to use effective permissions. Of course, you should test for users who should have access and users that do not have access.

VIEW THE EFFECTIVE PERMISSIONS OF A USER ON A FILE RESOURCE

GET READY. To view the effective permissions of a user on a file, perform the following steps:

1. Using *File Explorer*, navigate to a test folder with documents that you are protecting with DAC.
2. Right-click a test document and click Properties. The *Properties* dialog box opens.
3. Click the Advanced button. The *Advanced Security Settings* dialog box opens.
4. Click the Effective Access tab.
5. Click Select a user. If you need to test computer access, you would instead click Select a device. When the *Select User, Computer, Service Account, or Group* dialog box opens, type a name of a test user in the *Enter the object name to select* text box and click OK.
6. Click Include a user claim. Select the resource, and type a value as shown in the Figure 6-8.

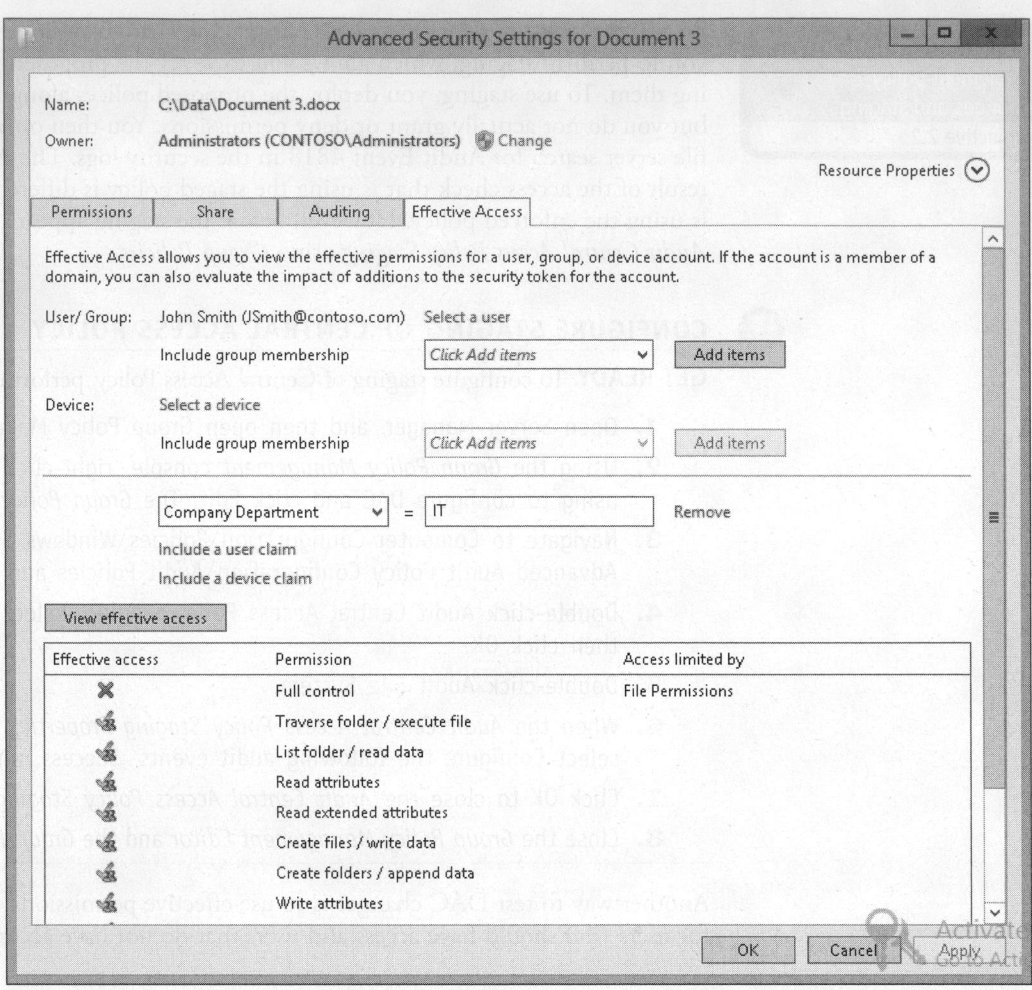

Figure 6-8
Viewing effective permissions

7. On the *Confirm installation selections* page, click Install.
8. When the installation is complete, click Close.

Creating Expression-Based Audit Policies

Windows Server 2012 R2 features advanced audit policies to implement more detailed and more precise auditing on the file system including configure global-based audit policies and expression-based auditing. Expression-based audit policies allow you to specify what to audit based on defined properties or attribute for documents (such as a department or country).

Global Object Access Auditing lets you define computer-wide system access control lists for either the file system or registry. Therefore, instead of manually altering and maintaining System Access Control Lists (SACLs) on large sets of shared files or registry entry. In addition, the auditing is implicitly specified, which does not actually modify the files.

For example, with DAC, you can define certain attributes that define what department a file belongs to, such as the Finance department, which is assigned to a large set of files. You would then specify auditing based on the attribute.

DEFINE GLOBAL OBJECT ACCESS AUDITING

GET READY. To define Global Object Access Auditing, perform the following steps:

1. With Server Manager, click Tools > Group Policy Management to open the *Group Policy Management* console.
2. Right-click a GPO and click Edit. The *Group Policy Management Editor* opens.
3. Expand Computer Configuration\Policies\Windows Settings\Security Settings\Advanced Audit Policy Configuration\Audit Policies and click Global Object Access Auditing to display the *Global Object Access Auditing* settings.
4. In the right-hand pane, under *Resource Manager*, double-click File system to display the *File system Properties* dialog box.
5. Select Define this policy settings and click Configure. The *Advanced Security Settings for Global File SACL* dialog box opens.
6. In the *Advanced Security Settings for Global File SACL* dialog box, click Add. The *Auditing Entry for Global File SACL* dialog box opens.
7. Click Select a principal. The *Select User, Computer, Service Account, or Group* dialog box opens. Type a name of a user or group in the *Enter the object name to select* box and click OK.
8. For the *Type*, select Success, Fail, or All.
9. Select the permissions that you want and deselect the permissions that you don't want.
10. Click Add a condition. A condition is added.
11. Select the following options: Resource, Department, Any of, Value, and Finance.
12. Click OK to close the *Auditing Entry for Global File SACL* dialog box.
13. Click OK to close the *Advanced Security Settings for Global File SACL* dialog box.
14. Click OK to close the *File system Properties* dialog box.
15. Close the *Group Policy Management Editor* and *Group Policy Management*.

Performing Access-Denied Remediation

When a user is denied access to a shared folder or file, Windows Server 2012 R2 provides the ***Access-Denied Assistant***, which helps users determine why they cannot access the folder or file, and directs users to resolve the issue without calling the help desk. At this time, Access-Denied Assistance works only with Windows 8.1 and Windows Server 2012 R2.

CERTIFICATION READY
Perform access-denied remediation.
Objective 2.2

When Access-Denied Assistant is combined with DAC, Access-Denied Assistant can inform an administrator so that the administrator can make adjustments to the policy or user attribute. For example, it might help to identify that the department was HR instead of Human Resources.

When planning for Access-Denied Assistance, you need to include the following:

- The message that users will see when they are denied when accessing a resource
- The e-mail text that users use to request access
- The recipients for the Access Request e-mail messages

Access-Denied Assistance is configured with group policies. If you navigate to *Computer Configuration\Policies\Administrative Templates\System\Access-Denied Assistance*, you can enable Access-Denied Assistance, and specify the customized messages for users. You can also configure Access-Denied using *File Server Resource Manager*, but this feature will be disabled if you enable with Group Policies.

ENABLE ACCESS-DENIED ASSISTANCE

GET READY. To enable Access-Denied Assistance, perform the following steps:

1. Open Server Manager, and then open Group Policy Management.
2. In the *Group Policy Management* console, right-click a group policy that you are using to configure DAC and click Edit. The *Group Policy Management Editor* opens.
3. Navigate to Computer Configuration\Policies\Administrative Templates\System\Access-Denied Assistance, and double-click Enable access-denied assistance on client for all file types.
4. When the *Enable access-denied assistance on client for all file types* dialog box opens, click Enabled.
5. Click OK to close *the Enable access-denied assistance on client for all file types* dialog box.
6. Double-click Customize message for Access Denied errors. The *Customize message for Access Denied errors* dialog box opens.
7. Click Enabled.
8. Under *Options*, type a message to the users in the *Display the following message to users who are denied access* text box.
9. If desired, click to select the Enable users to request assistance. Then type the text that will be in the e-mail in the *Add the following text to the end of the email* text box.
10. If desired, specify the e-mail recipients. Options include Folder owner, File server administrator, or additional recipients.
11. Click OK to close *the Customize message for Access Denied errors* dialog box.
12. Close the *Group Policy Management Editor*.
13. Close the *Group Policy Management* console.

USING WINDOWS POWERSHELL

You can configure and manage DAC using the following cmdlets:

- `Add-ADCentralAccessPolicyMember`: Adds Central Access Rules to a Central Access Policy in Active Directory.
- `Add-ADResourcePropertyListMember`: Adds one or more resource properties to a resource property list in Active Directory.
- `Get-ADCentralAccessPolicy`: Retrieves Central Access Policies from Active Directory.
- `Get-ADCentralAccessRule`: Retrieves Central Access Rules from Active Directory.
- `Get-ADClaimType`: Returns a claim type from Active Directory.
- `Get-ADResourceProperty`: Gets one or more resource properties.
- `Get-ADResourcePropertyList`: Retrieves resource property lists from Active Directory.
- `Get-ADResourcePropertyValueType`: Retrieves a resource property value type from Active Directory.
- `New-ADCentralAccessPolicy`: Creates a new Central Access Policy in Active Directory containing a set of Central Access Rules.
- `New-ADCentralAccessRule`: Creates a new Central Access Rule in Active Directory.
- `New-ADClaimType`: Creates a new claim type in Active Directory.
- `New-ADResourceProperty`: Creates a new resource property in Active Directory.
- `New-ADResourcePropertyList`: Creates a new resource property list in Active Directory.
- `Remove-ADCentralAccessPolicy`: Removes a Central Access Policy from Active Directory.
- `Remove-ADCentralAccessPolicyMember`: Removes Central Access Rules from a Central Access Policy in Active Directory.

- `Remove-ADCentralAccessRule`: Removes a Central Access Rule from Active Directory.
- `Remove-ADClaimType`: Removes a claim type from Active Directory.
- `Remove-ADResourceProperty`: Removes a resource property from Active Directory.
- `Remove-ADResourcePropertyList`: Removes one or more resource property lists from Active Directory.
- `Remove-ADResourcePropertyListMember`: Removes one or more resource properties from a resource property list in Active Directory.
- `Set-ADCentralAccessPolicy`: Modifies a Central Access Policy in Active Directory.
- `Set-ADCentralAccessRule`: Modifies a Central Access Rule in Active Directory.
- `Set-ADClaimType`: Modifies a claim type in Active Directory.
- `Set-ADResourceProperty`: Modifies a resource property in Active Directory.
- `Set-ADResourcePropertyList`: Modifies the resource property in Active Directory.

SKILL SUMMARY

IN THIS LESSON YOU LEARNED:

- Dynamic Access Control (DAC), originally called *claim-based access control*, was introduced with Windows Sever 2012, which is used for access management. It provides an automatic mechanism to secure and control access to resources.
- Claims-based access control uses a trusted identity provider to provide authentication.
- The trusted identity provider issues a token to the user, which the user then presents to the application or service as proof of identity.
- After you enable support for DAC in Active Directory Domain Services (AD DS), you must next create and configure claims and resource property objects. To create and configure claims, you primarily use the Active Directory Administrative Center.
- When planning a DAC implementation, you should include file classification. Although file classification is not mandatory for DAC, it can enhance the automation of access control because it can be used to identify documents that you need to protect and classify them appropriately.
- Classification rules can be created and then scheduled to run on a regular basis so that files are automatically scanned and classified based on the content of the file.
- A Central Access Policy contains Central Access Rules that grant permissions to those objects for a defined group of resources.
- If you do not properly plan out DAC, when you first implement DAC or when you make changes, you can either grant more access than desired, or you can restrict access to the file too much, resulting in an increase of help desk calls.
- Global Object Access Auditing lets you define computer-wide system access control lists for either the file system or registry. Therefore, instead of manually altering and maintaining SACLs on large sets of shared files or registry entry. In addition, the auditing is implicitly specified, which does not actually modify the files.
- When a user is denied access to a shared file or folder, Windows Server 2012 R2 provides Access-Denied Assistant, which helps users determine why they cannot access a file or folder, and directs users to resolve the issue without calling the help desk.

Knowledge Assessment

Multiple Choice

Select the correct answer for each of the following questions.

1. Which of the following uses a trusted identity provider to provide authentication?
   a. centralized access control
   b. physical-based access control
   c. password access control
   d. claims-based access control
2. Which digital identification is used by a user or computer?
   a. passport
   b. token
   c. SID
   d. GUID
3. Which identity provider is in Windows Server 2012 R2?
   a. Security Token Service
   b. Kerberos Key Generator
   c. Trust Replicator
   d. Rights Management Service (RMS)
4. What is used to automatically label files based on content?
   a. token rules
   b. claim rules
   c. resource properties
   d. classification rules
5. What do you specify when you create a claim type?
   a. claim resource
   b. claim name
   c. claim token
   d. claim property
6. What is used to grant permissions to those objects on multiple file servers within your domain?
   a. Classification Policy
   b. Central Access Policy
   c. Token Policy
   d. Distributed Access Policy
7. How do you enable staging of Dynamic Access Control (DAC)?
   a. Use the netsh command
   b. Use Active Directory Administrative Center
   c. Use GPOs
   d. Use the Dynamic Access Control console
8. Which log do you view when you enable staging when using DAC?
   a. Application
   b. Security
   c. System
   d. Forwarded

9. How can you test DAC changes before you implement the changes?
   a. Use the DAC emulator
   b. Use the Dynamic Access Control console
   c. Use the Computer Management console
   d. Use staging
10. What is included with devices when using DAC?
    a. users
    b. files
    c. computers
    d. phones

Best Answer

Choose the letter that corresponds to the best answer. More than one answer choice may achieve the goal. Select the BEST answer.

1. What is the best way to enable Access-Denied Assistant for all of your file servers?
   a. Dynamic Access Control console
   b. File Server Resource Manager
   c. Active Directory Administrative Center
   d. Group Policy Objects
2. Which of the following can you perform when using DAC? (Choose all that apply.)
   a. Audit access by using an audit policy
   b. Encrypt all files on a server
   c. Classify and tag data
   d. Provide Access-Denied Assistance when a user is denied access to a shared file
   e. Allow connections from mobile phones to files protected by DAC
3. Which of the following are required when using DAC? (Choose two answers.)
   a. Classification rules
   b. Resource properties
   c. Claim types
   d. Staging
4. What would you use to perform targeted auditing?
   a. Staging
   b. Advanced logging
   c. Dynamic logging
   d. Global Object Access Auditing
5. How can you manually classify files in a folder?
   a. Folder properties
   b. File Server Resource Manager
   c. Dynamic Access Control console
   d. Active Directory Administrative Center

Build a List

1. You want to create an expression that indicates all users that are assigned to the Contoso Corporation. What components would make up the expression when creating a Central Access Policy? Place a number of the step in the appropriate space. Not all answers will be used.
   ________ Values
   ________ Device
   ________ User
   ________ Department
   ________ Resource
   ________ Company
   ________ Equals
   ________ Contoso

2. What are the steps to automatically control access to the file shares on Server01 based on the Division attribute and the Division resource property? Place a number of the step in the appropriate space. Not all answers will be used.
   ________ On the shared folders, set the classification value
   ________ From the Active Directory Administrative Center, create a claim type
   ________ From the Active Directory Administrative Center, configure the delegation settings of Server01
   ________ From the Active Directory Administrative Center, create a reference resource property
   ________ From the Active Directory Administrative Center, create a resource property list

3. In Active Directory, you have all your file servers in an OU called *File Servers*, with a GPO1 linked to it. You want to modify the NTFS permissions for many folders on the file servers using Central Access Policies. What steps would you need to perform to identify the users who will be denied access to resources after you implement the new policies?
   ________ On GPO1, modify the Audit Central Access Policy Staging settings and configure the Central Access Policy settings
   ________ Pre-scan the documents
   ________ Modify the Security settings of the shared folder on the file servers
   ________ Create a Central Access Rule
   ________ Stage the files
   ________ Create a Central Access Policy
   ________ Search for failure events in the security logs on the file server
   ________ Create a claim type

4. Identify the four basic steps in order when you want to implement a Central Access Policy by placing the number of the step in the appropriate space. Place the number of the step in the appropriate space. Not all steps will be used.
   ________ Translate the authorization policies into expressions
   ________ Identify the resource that you want to protect
   ________ Create claim types and resource properties
   ________ Define the authorization policy

5. What are the three basic steps used when automatically classifying files? Place the number of the step in the appropriate space. Not all steps will be used.
   ________ Define the location of the documents
   ________ Define the schedule for automatic classification
   ________ Pre-scan the documents
   ________ Determine what you will use to identify the documents for classification
   ________ Identify the classifications that you want to apply to documents

Business Case Scenarios

Scenario 6-1: Controlling Access to Files

You are an administrator for the Contoso Corporation. Many of the HR documents have Social Security numbers, which are considered confidential. What can you do to make sure that only people from HR can access those files and they are labeled as Highly confidential?

Scenario 6-2: Implementing and Testing a Central Access Policy

You are an administrator for the Contoso Corporation. You have just replaced a senior administrator. During your first week, you discover that certain users have access to the HR documents that should not. The HR documents preside on three file servers at the corporate office. Therefore, you want to make sure that only HR personnel have access to the HR documents, and no one else. However, when you make the changes, you need to ensure that the users who need to access them still have access. What would you recommend?

Configuring and Optimizing Storage

70-412 EXAM OBJECTIVE

Objective 2.3 – Configure and optimize storage. This objective may include but is not limited to: Configure iSCSI target and initiator; configure Internet Storage Name server (iSNS); implement thin provisioning and trim; manage server free space using Features on Demand; configure tiered storage.

LESSON HEADING	EXAM OBJECTIVE
Understanding Shared Storage	
Using iSCSI	
Configuring iSCSI Target	Configure iSCSI target and initiator
Configuring iSCSI Initiator	Configure iSCSI target and initiator
Configuring iSCSI for High Availability	
Configuring Internet Storage Name Server	Configure Internet Storage Name server (iSNS)
Configuring Tiered Storage	Configure tiered storage
Implementing Thin Provisioning and Trim	Implement thin provisioning and trim
Managing Server Free Space Using Features on Demand	Manage server free space using Features on Demand

KEY TERMS

discovery domains (DD)
dynamically expanding disks
Features on Demand
Fibre Channel
Internet Small Computer System Interface (iSCSI)
Internet Storage Name server (iSNS)
iSCSI initiators
iSCSI Qualified Name (IQN)
iSCSI targets
Logical Unit Number (LUN)
Multipath (I/O)
Multiple Connection Session (MCS)
network attached storage (NAS)
shared storage
storage area networks (SANs)
storage tiers
thin provisioning
trim

Understanding Shared Storage

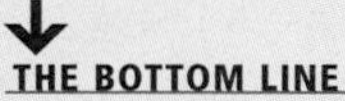

THE BOTTOM LINE

Many of the servers used in an organization require large amounts of disk space to provide the services and resources. For example, file servers need to store data files, mail servers, and database servers need to store large databases. Therefore, these servers typically need many hard drives connected directly to the machine, or servers connected to shared storage. ***Shared storage*** devices have many hard drives to provide huge amounts of disk space.

There are two network storage solutions used in networking:

- ***Network attached storage (NAS):*** A NAS is a file-level data storage device that is connected to the server over a computer network to provide shared drives or folders usually using Server Message Block (SMB) or Network File System (NFS).
- ***Storage area networks (SANs):*** A SAN is a storage architecture that allows systems to attach to the storage in the SAN, and present the drives to the server just as it is locally attached.

Accessing the shared files on a NAS is like accessing a shared folder on a server. To provide fault tolerance and better performance, most NAS devices use redundant array of independent disks (RAID). NAS devices can be managed with a web interface, and some enterprise NAS devices include a command-line interface accessible using Secure Shell (SSH).

If a server fails, the data is still stored in the SAN. You can then bring up another server, present the same storage to the server, and you have all your data intact. Typically when you use clustering in a production environment and for a virtual environment such as Hyper-V, it is common and recommended to use a SAN. Of course, the robust SANs usually have a higher level of RAID such as RAID 10, spare drives, redundant power supplies, redundant network connections, and built-in monitoring tools.

Most SANs use the SCSI protocol for communication between servers and disk drive devices. By using SCSI protocol, you can attach disks to a server using copper Ethernet cables or fiber optic cables. The two standards used in SANs include:

- Fibre Channel
- iSCSI

Both of these technologies use a fabric, which is a network topology where devices are connected to each other through one or more high-efficient data paths. Besides allowing multiple servers to access the SAN, both of these technologies also allow the SAN to be in a different rack in the server room, in a separate room, or even a separate building. Of course, when deciding on what is an acceptable performance, it always comes down to bandwidth and latency.

Fibre Channel is a gigabit-speed or higher network technology primarily used for a storage network. With Fibre Channel fabric, the network includes one or more Fibre Channel switches that enable the servers and storage devices to connect to each other through a virtual point-to-point connection. The switches route the packets in the fabric. Servers use a host bus adapter (HBA) to connect to the storage device.

Internet Small Computer System Interface (iSCSI) is a protocol that enables clients to send SCSI commands over a TCP/IP network using TCP port 3260. Different from Fibre Channel, you use standard Ethernet cabling and switches to connect servers to the SAN. Because you connect to the SAN over the network, you should use a minimum of two network adapters on the server, one for the SAN communications and one for standard network communications. Currently, the fastest network connection is Fibre Channel of Ethernet (FCoE), which is capable of 10 gigabits per second or more.

A ***Logical Unit Number (LUN)*** is a logical reference to a portion of a storage subsystem. The LUN can be a disk, part of a disk, an entire disk array, or part of the disk array. So when configuring servers to attach to a SAN, you usually configure the SAN to assign a LUN to a specific server. In other words, the LUN allows the administrator to break the SAN storage into manageable pieces. If the LUN is not mapped to a specific server, the server cannot see or access the LUN.

Using iSCSI

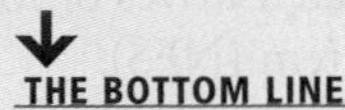

iSCSI is an Internet Protocol-based storage network standard that allows servers and other devices to connect to a data storage device or devices. As the name indicates, it carries SCSI commands over IP networks. Different from standard local SCSI drives, iSCSI allows data transfers over intranets and can be used over long distances. iSCSI allows clients, which are called ***iSCSI initiators***, to send SCSI commands to iSCSI storage devices, which are known as ***iSCSI targets***.

Storage devices provided by iSCSI are often used as storage devices that contain sensitive or critical data. Therefore, you need to protect the iSCSI infrastructure. The best approach for security is to use a Defense-in-Depth security strategy consisting of the following:

- Policies, procedures, and awareness that include security best practices, enforcing a strong user password policy and strong administrator password policy for accessing iSCSI storage devices and computers that have iSCSI management software installed.
- Physical security that protects servers and iSCSI storage devices that can be accessed by authorized personnel only.
- Perimeter security that includes firewalls to protect attacks from outside the organization and prevent attacks on the iSCSI devices.
- Network protection including authentication such as target access lists, Challenge-Handshake Authentication Protocol (CHAP), virtual LANs (VLANs), and physical isolation. You might also consider using Internet Protocol security (IPsec).
- Keeping your servers updated with the latest security updates.
- Protecting the data stored on the iSCSI storage devices including encryption (using BitLocker and Encrypted File System (EFS)) and Access Control Lists (ACLs).
- Performing backups on a regular basis and storing the backups in a safe place.

Of these, iSCSI targets and initiators have the following security features built in:

- Limit which iSCSI initiators can connect to an iSCSI target.
- Use CHAP to provide authentication between an iSCSI initiator and an iSCSI target.
- For encryption of traffic between an iSCSi initiator and an iSCSI target, you can use IPsec.

iSCSI Qualified Name (IQN) are unique identifiers that are used to address initiators and targets on an iSCSI network. The IQN uses the following format:

- Literal iqn
- Date (yyyy-mm) that the naming authority took ownership of the domain
- Reversed domain name of the authority
- Optional ":" prefixing a storage target name specified by the naming authority.

An example of an IQN is:

```
iqn.1991-05.com.contoso:storage01-target1-target
```

When you configure an iSCSI target, you define which iSCSI initiators can connect to an iSCSI LUN by the client's IQN. You can also specify which servers can connect to the iSCSI target based on MAC addresses, IP address, and DNS name. The iSCSI initiators use IQNs to connect to the iSCSI targets. If name resolution is possible, you can also use IP addresses to identify initiators and targets.

Configuring iSCSI Target

Starting with Windows Server 2012 R2, you can install the iSCSI Target Server role, so that other Windows servers can provide iSCSI storage to other clients (including other Windows servers). After you install the iSCSI Target Server role, you use Server Manager to create the volumes that will be presented to clients and specify which servers can access the iSCSI LUNs.

CERTIFICATION READY
Configure iSCSI target and initiator.
Objective 2.3

The iSCSI Target Server included in Windows Server 2012 R2 provides the following functionality:

- By using boot-capable network adapters or a software loader, you can use iSCSI targets to deploy diskless servers.
- By using virtual disks, you can save up to 90 percent of the storage space for the operating system images by using differencing disks.
- Supports server application storage that requires block storage.
- Supports iSCSI initiators for Windows and non-Windows operating systems.
- Supports lab environments.

When you install iSCSI Target Server, you should install the following two components:

- **iSCSI Target Server:** Provides tools to create and manage iSCSI targets and virtual disks. Enabling iSCSI Target Server can provide application block storage, consolidate remote storage, provide for diskless boots, and run in a failover cluster environment.
- **iSCSI Target Storage Provider:** Enables applications on a server that is connected to an iSCSI target to perform volume shadow copies of data on iSCSI virtual disks. It also enables you to manage iSCSI virtual disks by using older applications that require a Virtual Disk Service (VDS) hardware provider, such as using the DiskRAID command-line tool.

INSTALL iSCSI TARGET SERVER

GET READY. To install the iSCSI Target Server, perform the following steps:

1. Open Server Manager.
2. At the top of *Server Manager*, click Manage > Add Roles and Features. The *Add Roles and Feature Wizard* opens.
3. On the *Before you begin* page, click Next.
4. Select Role-based or feature-based installation and then click Next.
5. On the *Select destination server* page, select the server that you are installing to and click Next.

6. On the *Select server roles* page, expand File and Storage Services, expand File and iSCSI Services, and click iSCSI Target Server and iSCSI Target Storage Provider (VDS and VSS hardware providers). Click Next.
7. On the *Select features* page, click Next.
8. On the *Confirm installation selections* page, click Install.
9. When the installation is complete, click Close.

Virtual disks or targets are created on an iSCSI disk storage subsystem that is not directly assigned to a server. Targets are created to manage the connections between an iSCSI device and the servers that need to access it. Instead of having its own console, managing iSCSI virtual disks and iSCSI targets are done with Server Manager.

CREATE AN iSCSI VIRTUAL DISK

GET READY. To create an iSCSI virtual disk, perform the following steps:

1. Open Server Manager, click File and Storage Services, and then click iSCSI.
2. Click To create an iSCSI virtual disk, start the New iSCSI Virtual Disk Wizard (see Figure 7-1). Alternatively, you can open the Tasks menu in the *iSCSI Virtual Disks* section and click New iSCSI Virtual Disk.

Figure 7-1
Managing iSCSI virtual disks

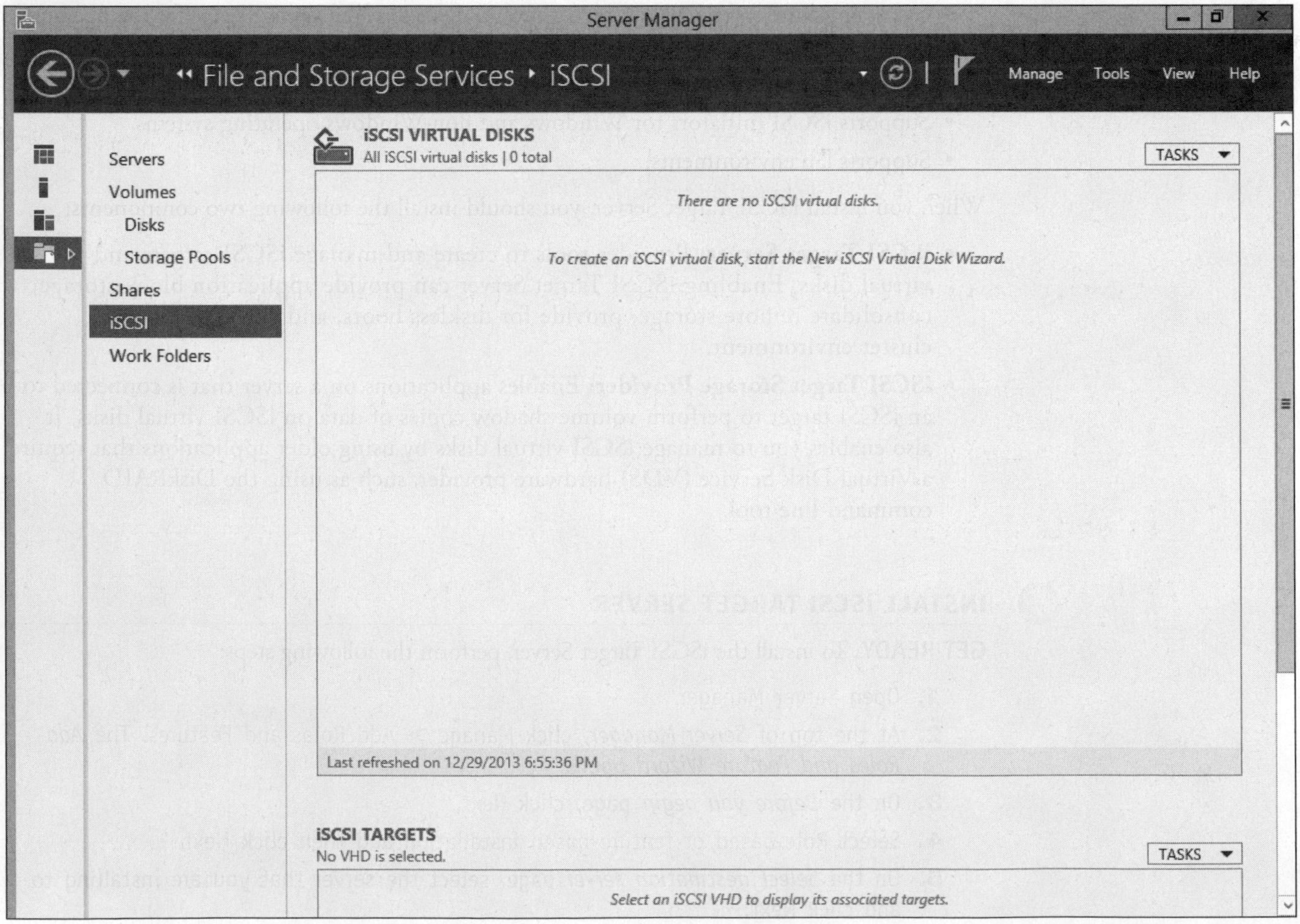

3. On the *Select virtual disk location* page, click a drive to store the iSCSI virtual disk, and then click Next.
4. On the *iSCSI Virtual Disk Name* page, in the *Name* text box, type the name of the iSCSI virtual disk. Click Next.
5. In the *iSCSI Virtual Disk Size* page, specify the size in GB of the iSCSI virtual disk. Click Next.
6. On the *iSCSI Target* page, if targets have been defined previously, you can click a target and click Next. To create a new target, click New iSCSI target and click Next.
7. If you chose the *New iSCSI target*, on the *Target Name and Access* page, type the name of the target. Click Next.
8. On the *Access Servers* page, click Add.
9. When the *Add initiator ID* page opens (see Figure 7-2), for the type, select IQN, DNS Name, IP Address, or MAC address. Then in the *Value* text box, type the corresponding value for the initiator that matches the type. Click OK.

Figure 7-2

Specifying the iSCSI initiators that can connect to the target

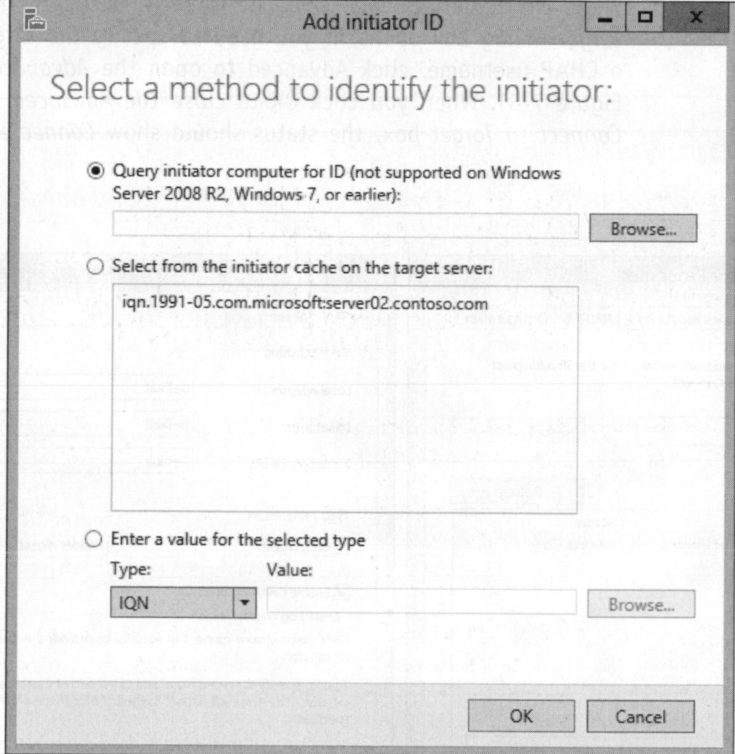

10. On the *Access Servers* page, add any additional iSCSI initiators. Then click Next.
11. On the *Enable Authentication* page, if you want to use authentication, click to select the Enable CHAP. Then type a username and password. When done, click Next.
12. On the *Confirmation* page, click Create.
13. When the iSCSI virtual disk is created, click Close.

You can assign a current iSCSI virtual disk to an initiator by right-clicking the virtual disk and clicking *Assign iSCSI Virtual Disk*. You can modify the iSCSI targets by right-clicking an iSCSI target and clicking *Properties*.

CERTIFICATION READY
Configure iSCSI target and initiator.
Objective 2.3

Configuring iSCSI Initiator

To connect to an iSCSI target, you use an iSCSI initiator. As mentioned previously, the iSCSI Initiator is already included with Windows.

After the targets are configured and registered, you open the iSCSI initiator, as discussed in the following procedure.

CONFIGURE THE iSCSI INITIATOR

GET READY. To configure the iSCSI initiator, perform the following steps:

1. Click Tools > iSCSI Initiator. The *iSCSI Initiator Properties* dialog box opens. If it is the first time launching, Microsoft iSCSI will not be running. Therefore, when it asks to start automatically each time the computer restarts, click Yes.
2. On the *Targets* tab, the iSCSI target should be listed in the *Discovered targets* section. If you just created one and it does not show up, click Refresh.
3. When the target appears, click the target and click Connect. When the *Connect to Target* dialog box opens, if you need to specify the target portal IP address or a CHAP username, click Advanced to open the *Advanced Settings* dialog box (see Figure 7-3). When you click OK to close the *Advanced Settings* dialog box and *Connect to Target* box, the status should show *Connected*.

Figure 7-3
Connecting to a target

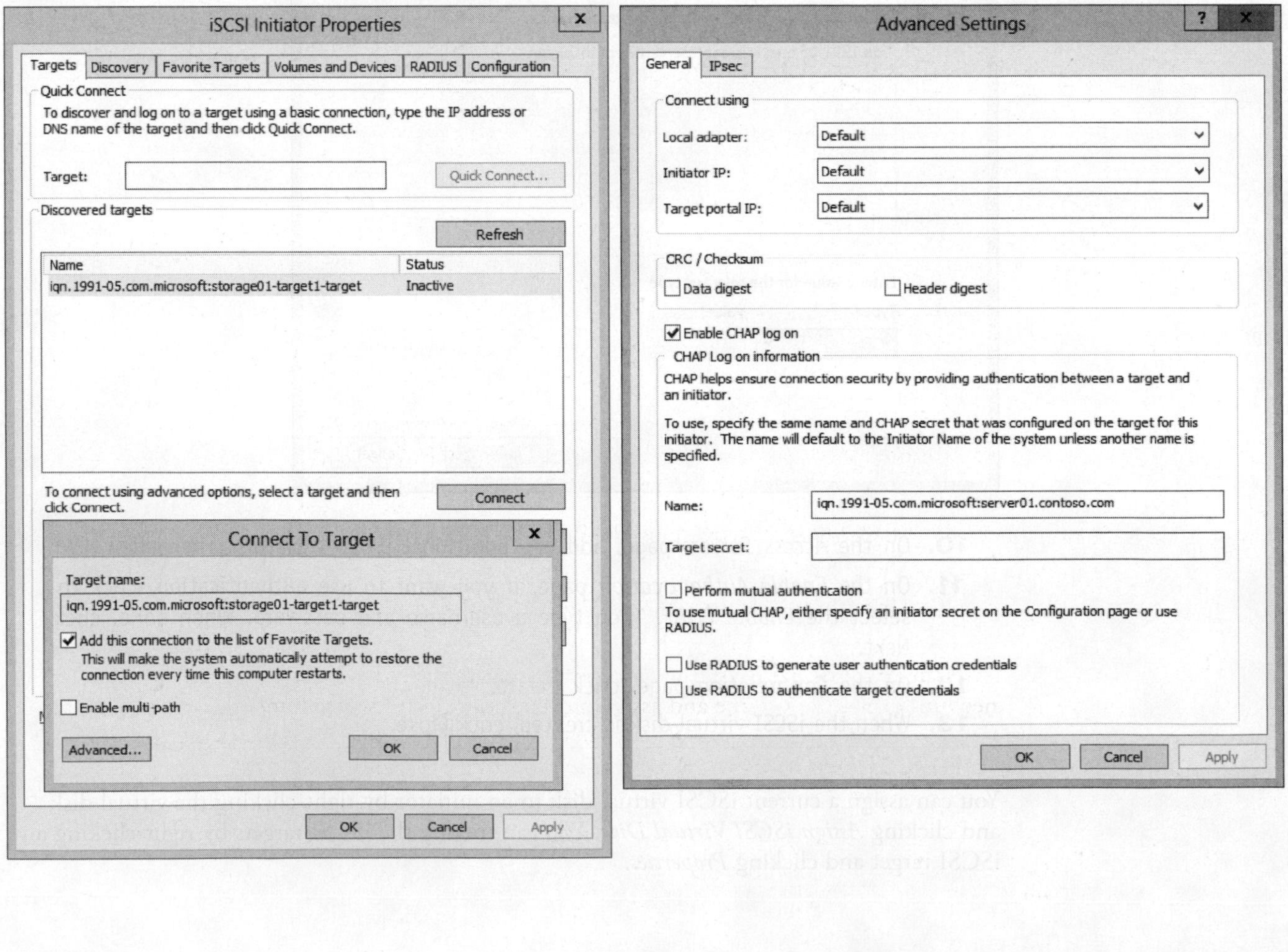

TAKE NOTE* If the target does not show up, verify that the initiator ID is specified correctly in the iSCSI target access server list.

4. Click the Volumes and Devices tab.
5. Click Auto Configure. The available iSCSI targets should appear in the Volume List as shown in Figure 7-4.

Figure 7-4

Showing the Volume List

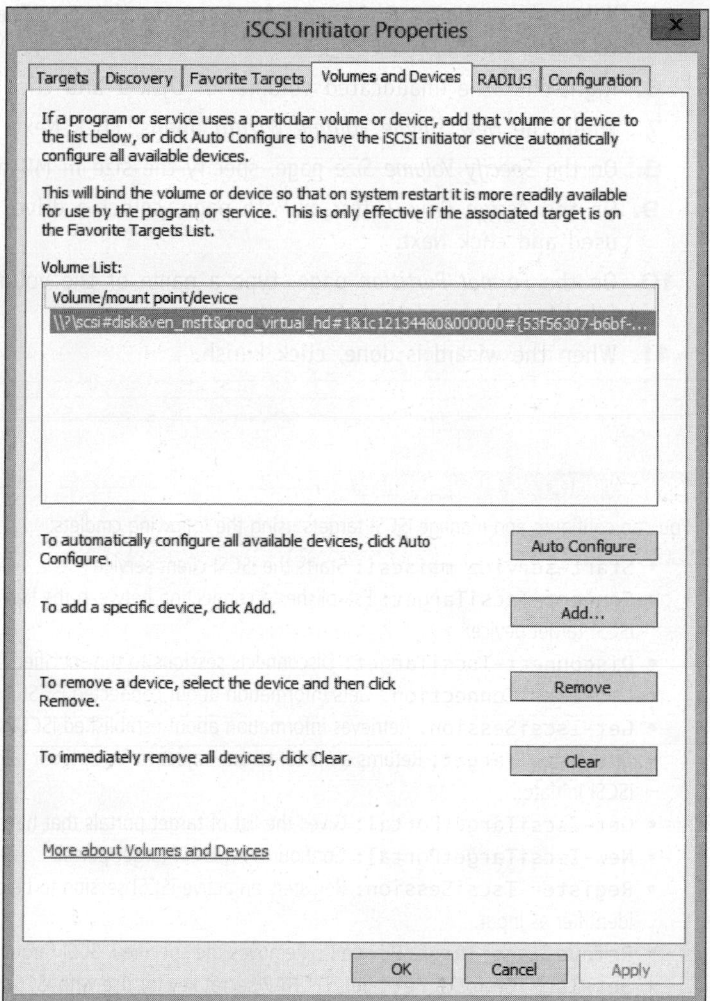

6. If you need to configure CHAP or IPsec to connect to the iSCSI target, click the Configuration tab.
7. Click OK to close the *iSCSI Initiator Properties* dialog box.

After an iSCSI device is attached to a server running Windows Server 2012 R2, you might need to format the volume and assign a drive letter to the new volume. To accomplish this, you use *Computer Management*. After opening Computer Management, if the disk does not show up, right-click *Disk Management* and try to perform a Rescan disk.

PREPARE AN iSCSI VOLUME

GET READY. To prepare an iSCSI volume, perform the following steps:

1. In Server Manager, click Tools > Computer Management. The *Computer Management* console opens.
2. Under *Storage*, click Disk Management. The *Disk Management* snap-in is displayed.
3. To bring Disk 1 online, right-click Disk 1, and click Online. The status of Disk 1 changes to not initialized.
4. To initialize a disk, right-click Disk 1, and click Initialize Disk.
5. When *the Initialize Disk* dialog box opens, click OK. The status of Disk 1 changes to Basic, Online.
6. Right-click the unallocated volume for Disk 1 and click New Simple Volume.
7. When the *New Simple Volume Wizard* opens, click Next.
8. On the *Specify Volume Size* page, specify the size in MB of the volume and click Next.
9. On the *Assign Drive Letter or Path* page, select a drive letter that is not being used and click Next.
10. On the *Format Partition* page, type a name of the volume label on the *Volume label* text box and click Next.
11. When the wizard is done, click Finish.

USING WINDOWS POWERSHELL

You can configure and manage iSCSI targets using the following cmdlets:

- `Start-service msiscsi`: Starts the iSCSI client service.
- `Connect-IscsiTarget`: Establishes a connection between the local iSCSI initiator, and the specified iSCSI target device.
- `Disconnect-IscsiTarget`: Disconnects sessions to the specified iSCSI target object.
- `Get-IscsiConnection`: Gets information about connected iSCSI initiator connections.
- `Get-IscsiSession`: Retrieves information about established iSCSI sessions.
- `Get-IscsiTarget`: Returns an iSCSI target object for each iSCSI target that is registered with the iSCSI initiator.
- `Get-IscsiTargetPortal`: Gives the list of target portals that have been set for discovery.
- `New-IscsiTargetPortal`: Configures an iSCSI target portal.
- `Register-IscsiSession`: Registers an active iSCSI session to be persistent using the session identifier as input.
- `Remove-IscsiTargetPortal`: Removes the specified iSCSI target portal.
- `Set-IscsiChapSecret`: Sets a CHAP secret key for use with iSCSI initiator connections.
- `Unregister-IscsiSession`: Removes an active iSCSI session from being persistent using the session identifier as input.
- `Update-IscsiTarget`: Refreshes the information about connected iSCSI target objects.

Configuring iSCSI for High Availability

A single connection to an iSCSI storage device makes the storage available, it does not make the storage highly available. If the network connection fails, or a switch fails, the server connecting to the iSCSI storage will lose access to its storage. Because many of the servers require high availability, you need to use high availability technologies such as Multiple Connection Session (MCS) and Multipath I/O (MPIO).

Multiple Connection Session (MCS) enables multiple TCP/IP connections from the initiator to the target for the same iSCSI session. If a failure occurs, all outstanding commands are reassigned to another connection automatically. Typically, MCS has better failover recovery and better performance than MPIO.

ENABLE A MULTIPLE CONNECTION SESSION

GET READY. To enable multiple connection sessions, perform the following steps:

1. In Server Manager, click Tools > iSCSI Initiator. The *iSCSI Initiator Properties* dialog box opens.
2. On the *Targets* tab, click Properties. The *Properties* dialog box opens.
3. On the *Sessions* tab, under the *Configure Multiple Connected Session (MCS)* section, click MCS. The *Multiple Connected Session (MCS)* dialog box opens.
4. To add a second connection, click the Add button and click Connect.
5. When the *Advanced* dialog box opens, specify an IP address for a second local network card in the *Initiator IP* box and the second remote target portal on the *iSCSI target* box.
6. Click OK to close the *Multiple Connected Session (MCS)* dialog box and click OK to close the *Properties* dialog box.
7. Click OK to close *iSCSI Initiator Properties* dialog box.

As mentioned in Lesson 1, "Understanding Fault Tolerance," often organizations need to have redundancy to provide high availability. Because a SAN can provide central storage that will be used by multiple servers, the entire SAN infrastructure needs to be highly available including disks and connections. ***Multipath (I/O)*** is a multipath solution that supports iSCSI, Fibre Channel, and serial attached storage (SAS) SAN connectivity by establishing multiple sessions or connections to the storage array. Multipathing solutions use redundancy path components including adapters, cables, and switches, to create logical paths between the server and the storage device. To use MPIO, you can install the Multipath I/O as a feature.

Configuring Internet Storage Name Server

The ***Internet Storage Name server (iSNS)*** protocol is used to automatically discover, manage, and configure iSCSI devices on a TCP/IP network. iSNS is used to emulate Fibre Channel fabric services to provide a consolidated configuration point for an entire storage network.

CERTIFICATION READY
Configure Internet Storage Name server (iSNS).
Objective 2.3

iSNS is installed as a feature. The iSNS provides a registration function to allow entities in a storage network to register a query in the iSNS database. Both targets and initiators can register in the iSNS database. After information is entered in the database, targets and initiators can query information about other initiators and targets. For information to be entered into the database, you specify iSNS server on the iSCSI Initiator's Discovery tab.

INSTALL ISNS

GET READY. To install iSNS, perform the following steps:

1. Open Server Manager.
2. At the top of *Server Manager*, click Manage > Add Roles and Features. The *Add Roles and Feature Wizard* opens.

3. On the *Before you begin* page, click Next.
4. Select Role-based or feature-based installation and then click Next.
5. On the *Select destination server* page, select the server that you are installing to and click Next.
6. On the *Select server roles* page, click Next.
7. On the *Select features* page, click to select iSNS Server service and click Next.
8. On the *Confirm installation selections* page, click Install.
9. When the installation is complete, click Close.

The iSNS Server can be started from Administrative Tools or the Server Manager Tools menu. Registered iSCSI initiators and targets are listed in the iSNS Server Properties (see Figure 7-5). For more information about the initiator or target, click the iSCSI initiator or target and click *Details*.

The ***discovery domain (DD)*** service allows the partitioning of storage nodes into management groupings (called discovery domains) for administrative and logon control purposes. The iSNS Server Properties start with the Default DD (see Figure 7-6). You can create a new discovery domain by using the *Creating* button and typing the name of the discovery domain. Then use the *Add* button to add members.

Figure 7-5

Viewing registered iSCSI initiators and targets

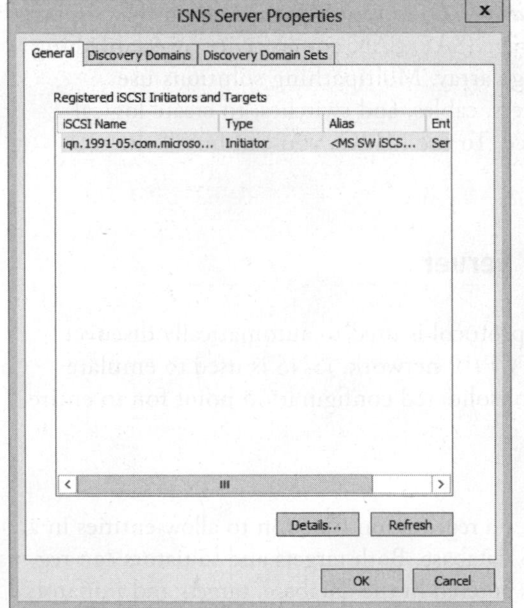

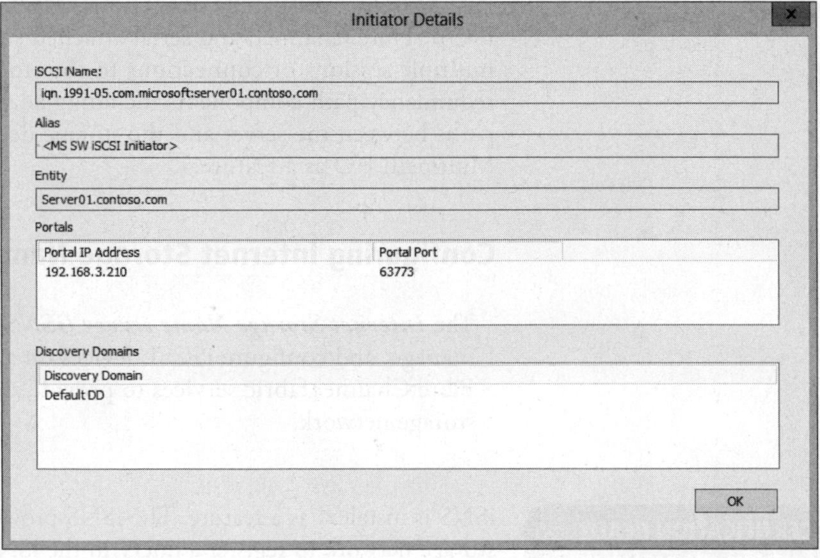

Figure 7-6
Managing discovery domains

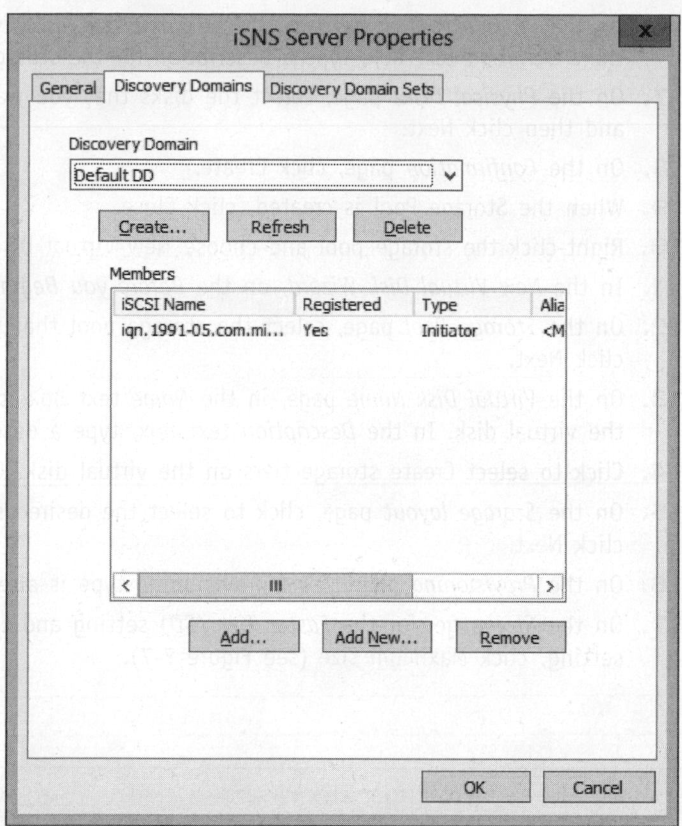

Configuring Tiered Storage

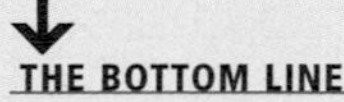

THE BOTTOM LINE

A new feature of Windows Server 2012 R2 is ***storage tiers***, which allow you to use solid-state drives (SSDs) and hard drive storage within the same pool. To get acceptable performance while managing costs, you will store more frequently accessed data on SSD media.

CERTIFICATION READY
Configure tiered storage.
Objective 2.3

Typically, faster disk drives cost more than slower disk drives. So while you always desire faster disk drives, it might not be cost-effective to use all SSD disks. However, if you use the faster disks for programs that are accessed more often than others, you can realize better performance while still managing costs effectively. Windows Server 2012 R2 offers tiered storage, in which you can combine the two types of disks into one virtual disk and volume. You should keep in mind that you cannot remove storage tiers from a virtual disk after it is created. In addition, storage tiers require fixed provisioning.

CONFIGURE TIERED STORAGE

GET READY. To configure tiered storage, perform the following steps:

1. Open Server Manager.
2. Click File and Storage Services. In the *Volumes* section, click Disks to view the current disks that are available.
3. In the *Volumes* section, click Storage Pools.
4. In the main pane, under *Storage Spaces*, right-click Primordial pool and choose New Storage Pool.
5. On the *Before you Begin* page, click Next.

6. On the *Storage Pool Name* page, in the *Name* text box, type a descriptive name. In the *Description* text box, type a description for the storage pool and then click Next.
7. On the *Physical Disks* page, select the disks that you want to include in the pool and then click Next.
8. On the *Confirmation* page, click Create.
9. When the Storage Pool is created, click Close.
10. Right-click the storage pool and choose New Virtual Disk.
11. In the *New Virtual Disk Wizard*, on the *Before you Begin* page, click Next.
12. On the *Storage Pool* page, select the storage pool that you just created and then click Next.
13. On the *Virtual Disk Name* page, in the *Name* text box, type a descriptive name for the virtual disk. In the *Description* text box, type a description.
14. Click to select Create storage tiers on the virtual disk. Click Next.
15. On the *Storage layout* page, click to select the desired storage layout and then click Next.
16. On the *Provisioning* page, *Fixed* provisioning type is already selected. Click Next.
17. On the *Size* page, for the *Faster Tier (SD)* setting and the *Standard Tier (HDD)* setting, click Maximum size (see Figure 7-7).

Figure 7-7

The available disks for a cluster

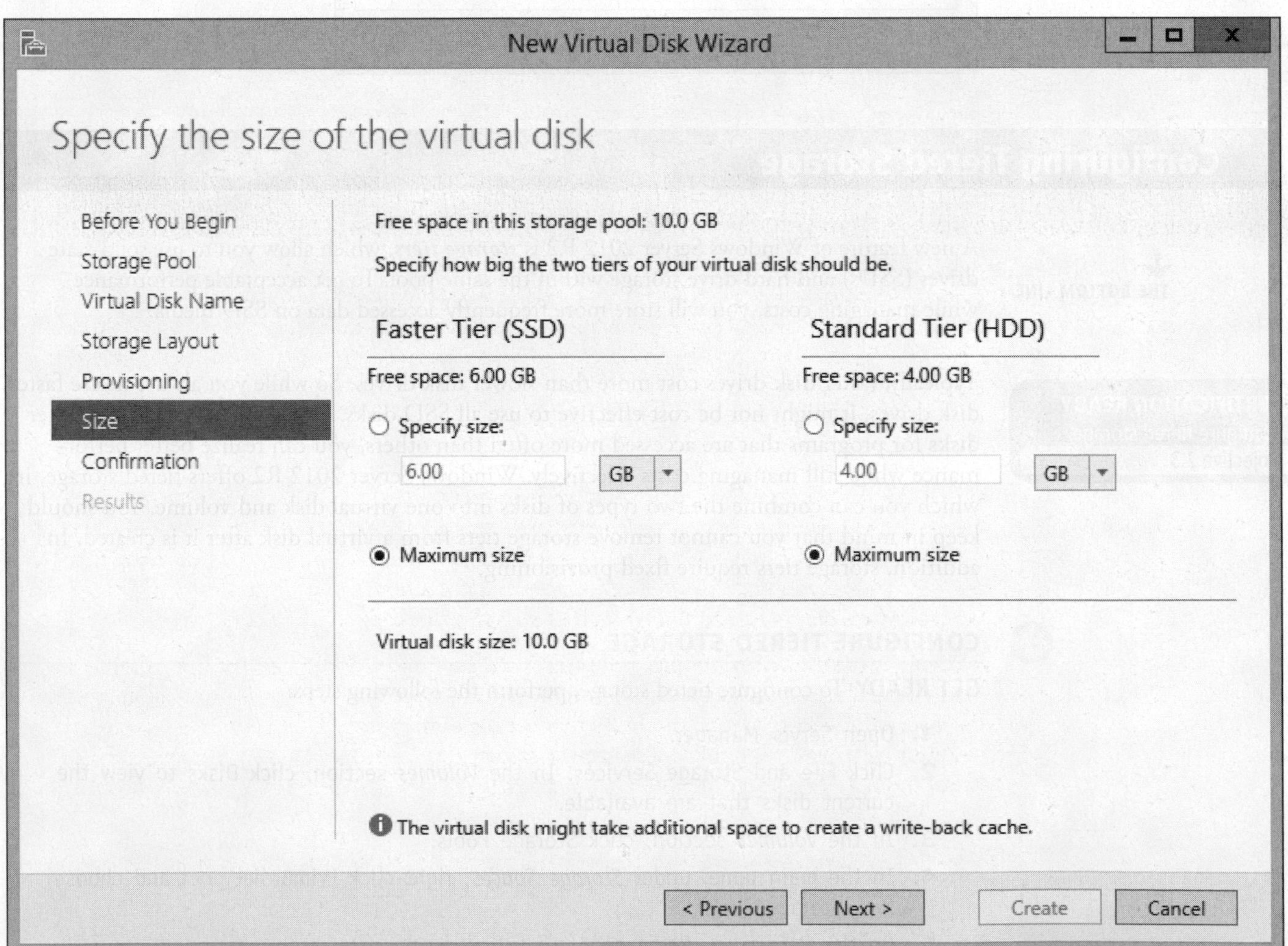

18. Click Next.
19. On the *Confirmation* page, click Create.
20. When the virtual disk is created, click Close.
21. In the *New Volume Wizard*, on the *Before You Begin* page, click Next.
22. On the *Server and Disk* page, select the server and virtual disk and then click Next.
23. On the *Size* disk, specify the size of the volume and then click Next.
24. On the *Drive Letter or Folder* page, specify the desired drive letter and then click Next.
25. On the *Select file system settings* page, for the *File system* setting, select NTFS or ReFS. In the *Volume label* text box, type a volume name. Click Next.
26. On the *Confirmation* page, click Create.
27. When the volume is created, click Close.

Sometimes, disks are identified as "Unspecified," which means they are not identified as SDD or HDD disks. To view the current disks for the storage pool named StoragePool, you would execute the following Windows PowerShell command:

```
get-storagepool StoragePool |get-Physicaldisk |FT FriendlyName, Size,
MediaType
```

To change all unspecified disks to SDD disks, use the following Windows Powershell command:

```
Get-StoragePool StoragePool | Get-PhysicalDisk | ? MediaType -eq
"Unspecified" |Set-PhysicalDisk -MediaType SSD
```

To change `PhysicalDisk5` to `HDD`, execute the following Windows PowerShell command:

```
Set-PhysicalDisk -FriendlyName PhysicalDisk5

-MediaType HDD
```

Implementing Thin Provisioning and Trim

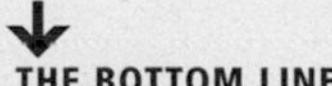

The advantage of running virtual machines is to share resources and to make use of wasted or idle resources on a computer. For example, although a physical server might have two processors, much of what the processors do is nothing as it waits for something to do. The same can be said for storage. Therefore, Hyper-V introduces ***thin provisioning*** using ***dynamically expanding disks*** in Windows Server 2012 R2.

CERTIFICATION READY
Implement thin provisioning and trim.
Objective 2.3

With dynamically expanding disks, rather than creating a file equivalent in size of the disk, it creates a small file that grows as data is written to it, up to the limitations set forth in the configured size of the disk. Therefore, if you designate a 100 GB disk but you have only 5 GB of data, the disk will take only 5 GB. When you combine the amount of disk space that is not used with several servers on the LUN, the amount of wasted space is often significant.

When you use thin provisioning, you must make sure that you do not have a disk that suddenly expands a lot causing a disk to run out of disk space on the Hyper-V host. If you run out of space on Hyper-V, virtual machines that use the same storage device and LUN could fail. In addition, you need to monitor disk growth so that if you need to move a VM or virtual disk from the LUN or expand the LUN, you can do so before running of disk space becomes a problem. When you create a disk in Hyper-V, you have a choice of the following:

- **Fixed size:** The virtual hard disk that is created initially uses the size of the virtual hard disk and does not change when data is deleted or added.
- **Dynamically expanding:** The virtual hard disk file that is created is initially small and grows as data is added.

- **Differencing:** Allows you to build on top of a parent disk. Changes to the virtual disk are written to a child disk. As a result, the parent disk does not change.

After a virtual disk is created, you can change the parameters of the disk by opening the properties of the virtual machine, clicking on the virtual disk, and clicking *Edit* to open the Edit Virtual Hard Disk Wizard dialog box. You can then perform the following actions (see Figure 7-8):

TAKE NOTE*

To perform some of these actions, the VM needs to be powered off. If not, the option may be greyed out.

- **Compact:** Compacts the file size of a virtual hard disk by removing blank space that is left behind when data is deleted from the virtual hard disk. The storage capacity of the virtual hard disk is unchanged.
- **Convert:** Converts a virtual disk by copying the contents to a new virtual hard disk. It can be used to convert from an expanding virtual hard disk to a fixed virtual hard disk or vice versa.
- **Expand:** Expands the capacity of the virtual hard disk.
- **Shrink:** Reduces or ***trims*** the storage capacity of the virtual hard disk.

Figure 7-8

Editing a virtual disk

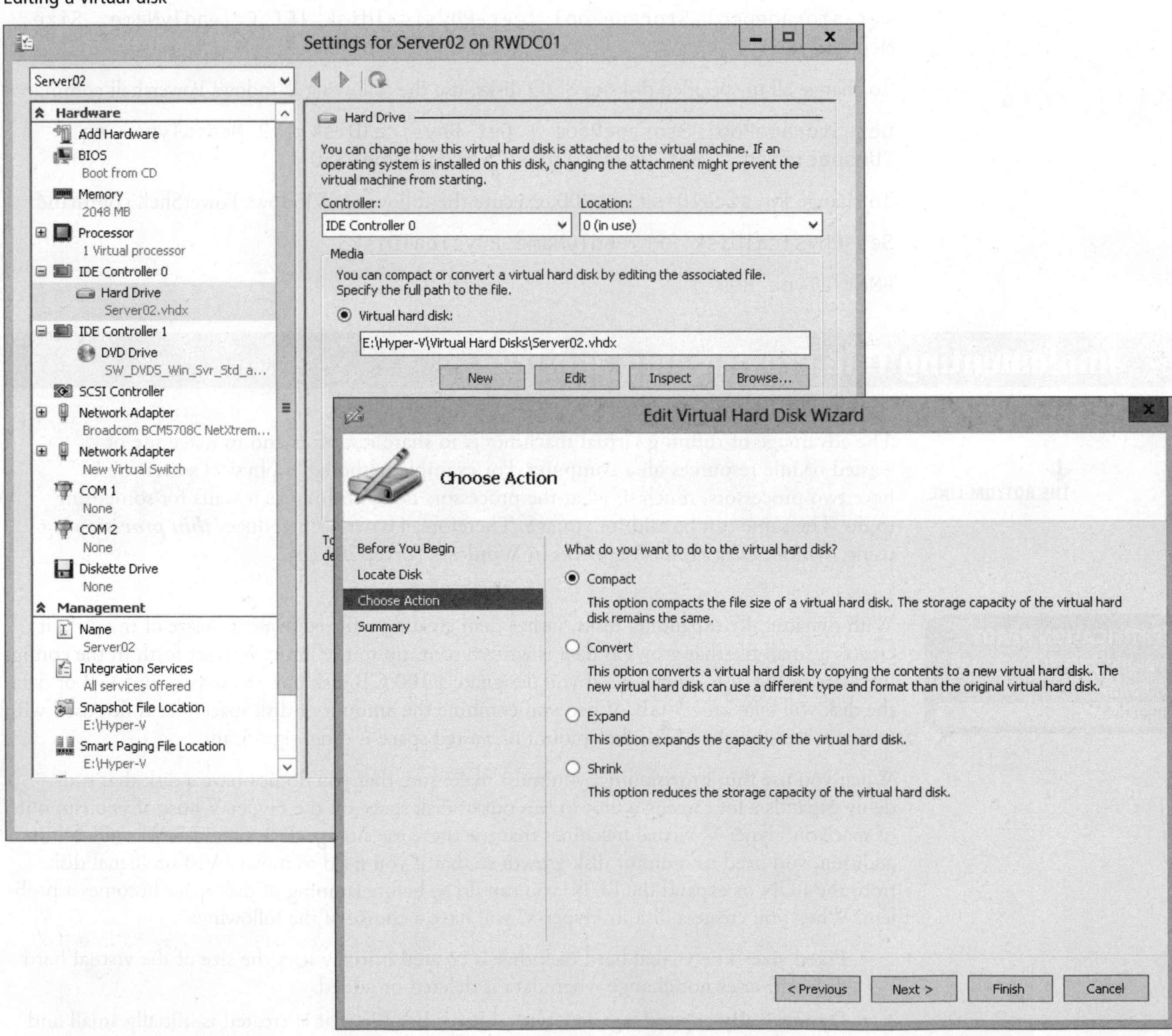

Managing Server Free Space Using Features on Demand

THE BOTTOM LINE

Features on Demand allows administrators to completely remove the installation binaries for roles and features that are not needed for the server. Of course, by using ***Features on Demand***, you save disk space and enhance the security by removing binaries for features that will not be needed.

CERTIFICATION READY
Manage server free space using Features on Demand.
Objective 2.3

To view the available features for Windows, you can execute Windows PowerShell command:

```
Get-WindowsFeature
```

or the following command at a command prompt:

```
dism /online /get-features /format:table
```

Then to remove the binaries of a feature, you use the *Uninstall-WindowsFeature PowerShell* cmdlet with the `-Remove` parameter. For example, if you do not need BitLocker, you can perform the following command:

```
uninstall-WindowsFeature Bitlocker -Remove
```

After the binaries are removed, the previous `dism` command shows `Disabled with Payload Removed`.

SKILL SUMMARY

IN THIS LESSON YOU LEARNED:

- A SAN is a storage architecture that allows systems to attach to the storage in the SAN, and presents the drives to the server just as it is locally attached.
- Internet Small Computer System Interface (iSCSI) is a protocol that enables clients to send SCSI commands over a TCP/IP network using TCP port 3260.
- A Logical Unit Number (LUN) is a logical reference to a portion of a storage subsystem. The LUN can be a disk, part of a disk, an entire disk array, or part of the disk array.
- iSCSI allows clients, which are called *iSCSI initiators*, to send SCSI commands to SCSI storage devices, which are known as *iSCSI targets*.
- iSCSI Qualified Name (IQN) are unique identifiers that are used to address initiators and targets on an iSCSI network.
- Virtual disks or targets are created on an iSCSI disk storage subsystem that is not directly assigned to a server.
- Because many of the servers require high availability, you need to use high availability technologies such as Multiple Connection Session (MCS), and Multipath I/O (MPIO) can be used with iSCSI.
- The Internet Storage Name server (iSNS) protocol is used to automatically discover, manage, and configure iSCSI devices on a TCP/IP network.
- A new feature of Windows Server 2012 R2 is to use **Storage Tiers**, which allow for use of SSD and hard drive storage within the same pool and which stores more frequently accessed data on the SSD media.

- With dynamically expanding disks, rather than creating a file equivalent in size of the disk, you create a small file that grows as data is written to it, up to the limitations set forth in the configured size of the disk.
- With Features on Demand, you save disk space and enhance the security by removing binaries for features that are not needed.

Knowledge Assessment

Multiple Choice

Select the correct answer for each of the following questions.

1. What protocol allows a server to connect to a SAN by sending SCSI commands over a TCP/IP network?
   a. Fibre Channel
   b. iSCSI
   c. SATA
   d. MPIO
2. Which port does iSCSI use?
   a. 1080
   b. 8080
   c. 3260
   d. 4800
3. Which client connects to an iSCSI SAN?
   a. iSCSI target
   b. iSCSI source
   c. iSCSI receiver
   d. iSCSI initiator
4. What can be installed so that Windows Server 2012 R2 can be used to present iSCSI volumes to Windows servers?
   a. iSCSI target
   b. iSCSI source
   c. iSCSI receiver
   d. iSCSI initiator
5. What is a unique identifier that is used to identify iSCSI initiators and targets?
   a. iSNS
   b. IQN
   c. MPIO
   d. MPC
6. Which protocol is used for authentication for iSCSI?
   a. PAP
   b. CHAP
   c. MS-CHAPv2
   d. SPAP
7. How do you install iSCSI Target on Windows Server 2012 R2?
   a. You install the MMC snap-in
   b. You install an add-in program
   c. You install as a Windows feature
   d. You install as a Windows Server role

8. What can you use to encrypt iSCSI traffic?
   a. CHAP
   b. IPsec
   c. BitLocker
   d. EFS
9. Which two technologies can help make iSCSI highly available? (Choose two answers.)
   a. MCS
   b. EFS
   c. LUNX
   d. MPIO
10. What is used to automatically discover, manage, and configure iSCSI devices?
   a. LUN
   b. IQN
   c. MPIP
   d. iSNS

Best Answer

Choose the letter that corresponds to the best answer. More than one answer choice may achieve the goal. Select the BEST answer.

1. You have around 30 servers, all running Windows Server 2012 R2 and each using iSCSI storage. Your small team of administrators is complaining that it is becoming difficult to locate the available iSCSI resources on the network. What can you use to help administrators quickly locate iSCSI resources?
   a. DNS
   b. iSNS
   c. iSCSI Target Storage Provider
   d. Windows Standard-Based Storage Management feature
2. You have a new virtual machine running Windows Server 2012 R2. It has a C drive and a D drive. The D drive is a 200 GB fixed disk. However, you notice that after a couple of months, much of the drive is not being used. What should you do so that you don't use as much space?
   a. Convert the disk to the dynamically expanding disk
   b. Create a differencing disk so that you can remove the unused space
   c. Compact the disk
   d. Run a defrag
3. You have a physical server running Windows Server 2012 R2. It has a 40 GB fixed disk. You are running out of space on the C drive and you don't want to replace the hard drive. Therefore, what can you do to free up disk space on the C drive?
   a. Convert the drive to a dynamically expanding disk
   b. Compact the disk
   c. Defrag the hard drive
   d. Remove binaries for features that are not being used
4. Which Windows PowerShell cmdlet would you use to view the iSCSI initiator connections?
   a. `Get-IscsiConnection`
   b. `Get-IscsiSession`
   c. `Get-IscsiTarget`
   d. `Connect-IscsiTarget`

5. You are configuring an iSCSI Target Server role and multiple volumes that will be assigned to multiple servers using iSCSI initiators. Because these servers contain confidential information, you want to make sure that they are not accessed by other servers using an iSCSI initiator. What should you do?
   a. Specify the initiator ID that can connect when creating the iSCSI virtual disk
   b. Specify the initiator ID that can connect when creating the iSCSI target
   c. Enable IPSec
   d. Configure the iSCSI ACL list when you configure the iSCSI initiator

Matching and Identification

1. Match the following action with the appropriate command:
   _______ a) `uninstall-WindowsFeature`
   _______ b) `dism /online /get-features`
   _______ c) `Unregister-IscsiSession`
   _______ d) `New-IscsiTargetPortal`
   _______ e) `Get-IscsiSession`
   _______ f) `Connect-IscsiTarget`
   1. Uninstalls the binaries
   2. Views the available features on Windows
   3. Establishes a connection between an iSCSI initiator and an iSCSI target device
   4. Gets information about connected iSCSI initiator connections
   5. Configures an iSCSI target portal
   6. Removes an active iSCSI session from being persistent

2. Identify the type of address used in the Add initiator ID page.
   _______ E069956EE51A
   _______ storage.contoso.com
   _______ iqn.1992-01.com.contoso
   _______ 192.168.32.42

Build a List

1. Identify the steps in order when creating an iSCSI virtual disk by placing the number of the step in the appropriate space. Not all steps will be used.
   _______ Specify the access servers
   _______ Specify the IP address of the iSCSI volumes
   _______ Specify the size of the virtual disk
   _______ Specify the location of the iSCSI virtual disk
   _______ Specify the IPsec password
   _______ Specify the name of the iSCSI virtual disk
   _______ Specify the type of volume

2. Identify the basic steps in order to configure a server to use the iSCSI initiator to connect to an iSCSI volume by placing the number of the step in the appropriate space. Not all steps will be used.
   _______ Use Computer Management to partition the disk
   _______ Use Computer Management to initialize the disk
   _______ Use Computer Management to format the disk
   _______ On the Connection tab, click the target and click Connect
   _______ On the Targets tab, click the target and click Connect
   _______ Click the Volumes and Devices tab and click Auto Configure
   _______ Click the Attachment tab and click Auto Configure
   _______ Click the Connection tab and click Auto Configure

3. Identify the order of the IQN components that make up an IQN string.
   _______ microsoft
   _______ 1992-03
   _______ iqn
   _______ :storage01-targetnew-target
   _______ com

Business Case Scenarios

Scenario 7-1: Using iSCSI Devices

You are an administrator for the Contoso Corporation. You have a large server that is running Windows Server 2012 R2 and that has about 8 TB of disk space that you can allocate to be used by other servers. What can you do so that two other servers running Windows Server 2012 R2 can use the disk space just as if the disk space was local?

Scenario 7-2: Reducing Disk Space

You are an administrator for the Contoso Corporation. You have several virtual machines running on Hyper-V that get their disk space from a local SAN. The SAN is running out of disk space. What can you do to reduce the space used on the SAN?

Configuring and Managing Backups

70-412 EXAM OBJECTIVE

Objective 3.1 – Configure and manage backups. This objective may include but is not limited to: Configure Windows Server backups; configure Microsoft Azure backups; configure role-specific backups; manage VSS settings using VSSAdmin.

LESSON HEADING	EXAM OBJECTIVE
Configuring and Managing Backups	
Installing the Windows Server Backup Feature	Configure Windows Server backups
Configuring Windows Server Backups	
Configuring Microsoft Azure Backups	Configure Microsoft Azure backups
Configuring Role-Specific Backups	Configure role-specific backups
Managing VSS Settings Using VSSAdmin	Manage VSS settings using VSSAdmin
Creating System Restore snapshots	

KEY TERMS

bare metal recovery
Hyper-V checkpoints
Microsoft Azure Online Backup
Shadow Copies for Shared Volumes (SCSV)
source volume
storage volume
system state
Volume Shadow Copy Administrative Command-line Tool (VSSAdmin)
Volume Shadow Copy Service (VSS)
VSS provider
VSS requester
VSS writer
wbadmin
Windows Server Backup

■ Configuring and Managing Backups

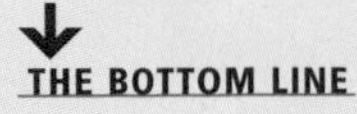

When an organization loses data, the results can range from a loss of productivity to an entire meltdown of the company itself. Having a solid backup strategy along with the systems, processes, and tools to execute the strategy is the key to your ability to recover.

There is an old saying that nothing lasts forever, which means one should live it up, take chances, and never have any regrets. That might be sound advice in some situations, but it's not the approach you want to take when it comes to protecting your data.

If you've been administering servers for any length of time, you most likely have experienced or heard of someone who lost data due to one of the following:

- Hardware failure
- Software failure
- Human Error
- Computer virus
- Theft
- Natural disaster (flooding, earthquakes, severe weather, and so on)
- Fire

When an organization loses data, the impact can range from a loss of productivity (employees having to recreate their data or wait for it to be restored) to a complete financial collapse of the company itself. In between these two extremes are costly downtimes that result from restoring or rebuilding your data, delayed responses to customer inquiries, and the overall negative perceptions your customers will have of your organization as a whole.

Unfortunately, most people and companies take backups seriously only after they've experienced the impact of losing their data. It's inevitable; it will happen sooner or later, and you must be prepared by implementing a backup strategy and executing it when the time comes.

Determining what needs to be backed up, the frequency and types of backups, as well as where they are stored (onsite/offsite/cloud) should all be part of your backup strategy. In addition to protecting your data, you must also consider the roles performed by the servers on the network. The role(s) assigned to a server (Active Directory Domain Services, DHCP Server, DNS Server, File and Storage Services, Application Server, Web Server, and so on) can dramatically change its configuration, what you back up, and the frequency the backup is performed.

You also need to consider the impact the backups will have on users as well as the ability to keep critical applications running. Users need to get their work done, so critical applications cannot be taken down in order for a backup to be performed. Fortunately, Windows Server utilizes the Volume Shadow Copy Service (VSS) and shadow copies to create point-in-time snapshots allowing you to keep any downtime to a minimum.

To protect data on your servers, you might have some form of fault tolerance such as RAID or clustering in place. Although these solutions can protect you from single or multiple drive failures, they are not a substitute for performing backups. With these issues in mind, let's take a look at how to protect your data and servers using the tools provided by Windows Server 2012 and Windows Server 2012 R2.

Installing the Windows Server Backup Feature

Windows Server Backup, ***wbadmin***, and Windows PowerShell cmdlets provide the tools you need to back up and restore your critical data and servers.

To prepare for a server backup, you need to first install the Windows Server Backup feature. Once installed, you have access to the following tools:

- Windows Server Backup Microsoft Management Console (MMC) snap-in
- wbadmin command-line tool (wbadmin.exe)
- Windows PowerShell cmdlets for Windows Server Backup

CERTIFICATION READY
Configure Windows Server backups.
Objective 3.1

The Windows Server Backup MMC snap-in is not installed on Windows Server 2012 R2 systems running the Server Core installation option only. To run backups on these systems, you need to use either the command-line tool wbadmin or the Windows PowerShell cmdlets, or manage them remotely from another computer using the Windows Server Backup MMC. You can also use the Windows 8 Remote Server Administration Tools (RSAT) for Windows 8.1.

INSTALL THE WINDOWS SERVER BACKUP FEATURE

GET READY. To install the Windows Server Backup feature on Server01, perform the following steps:

1. Log in to Server01 and open Server Manager.
2. Click Manage > Roles and Features.
3. Click Next when the *Add Roles and Features Wizard* appears.
4. Click Next on the *Select installation type* screen.
5. Click Next on the *Select destination server* screen.
6. Click Next on the *Select server roles* screen.
7. Select Windows Server Backup and click Next (see Figure 8-1).

Figure 8-1
Installing the Windows Server Backup feature

Add Roles and Features Wizard
Select features
DESTINATION SERVER
Server01.contoso.com
Before You Begin
Installation Type
Server Selection
Server Roles
Features
Confirmation
Results
Select one or more features to install on the selected server.
Features
User Interfaces and Infrastructure (2 of 3 installed)
Windows Biometric Framework
Windows Feedback Forwarder
Windows Identity Foundation 3.5
Windows Internal Database
Windows PowerShell (2 of 5 installed)
Windows Process Activation Service
Windows Search Service
Windows Server Backup
Windows Server Migration Tools
Windows Standards-Based Storage Management
Windows TIFF IFilter
WinRM IIS Extension
WINS Server
Description
Windows Server Backup allows you to back up and recover your operating system, applications and data. You can schedule backups, and protect the entire server or specific volumes.
< Previous Next > Install Cancel

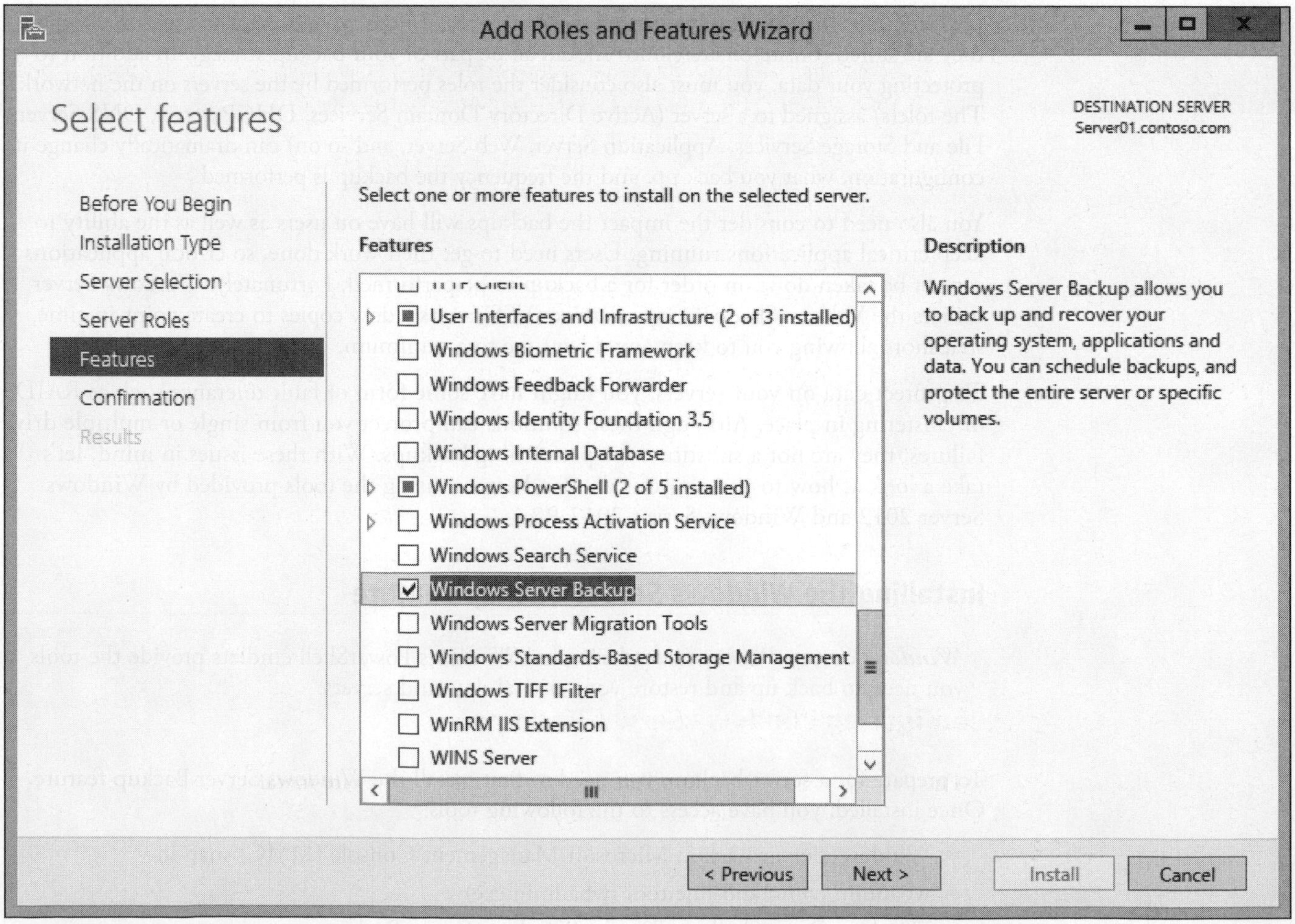

8. Select Restart the destination server automatically if required and click Yes to allow automatic restarts.
9. Click Install and then click Close.

After the installation completes, you can launch the Windows Server Backup Microsoft Management Console (MMC) snap-in by selecting *Server Manager > Tools > Windows Server Backup*.

To view the list of commands supported by the wbadmin command-line tool, open a command prompt while logged on with administrative rights and use the following command:

```
wbadmin /?
```

To view the Windows PowerShell cmdlets available for Windows Server Backup module, use the following command from within Windows PowerShell:

```
PS C:\Get-Command -Module WindowsServerBackup -CommandType Cmdlet
```

INSTALL WINDOWS SERVER BACKUP FEATURES ON A SERVER CORE USING WINDOWS POWERSHELL (OPTIONAL)

GET READY. To install the Windows Server Backup features on a Server Core installation, perform the following steps:

1. Log in to the Server Core installation.
2. Enter the following command from within the command window that appears, and then press Enter to start a Windows PowerShell session:

   powershell
3. Enter the following command to make the Server Manager features available from within the Windows PowerShell session:

   PS C:\Import-Module Servermanager
4. Enter the following command to add the Windows Server Backup feature:

   PS C:\Install-WindowsFeature Windows-Server-Backup
5. Enter the following command to confirm the Windows Server Backup feature is installed:

   PS C:\Get-WindowsFeature | where {$_.Name -eq "Windows-Server-Backup"}
6. Type Exit to end the Windows PowerShell session and return to the command window.
7. Type wbadmin /? and confirm wbadmin tools are installed.

Configuring Windows Server Backups

The Windows Server Backup feature provides full server, bare metal recovery, system state, system reserve, and local/remote volume backup capabilities.

Once the Windows Server Backup feature is installed, it's time to refer to your backup strategy to answer several key questions. Before we review those questions, there are two important things to consider that will shape your overall strategy:

- The maximum amount of time you will have to bring a system back online before it has a significant impact on your organization. This is called the Recovery Time Objective (RTO).
- The amount of data you can afford to lose before it has a significant impact on your organization. This is called the *Recovery Point Objective (RPO)*.

As you review the following questions, keep the RTO and RPO in mind:

- How often will you perform the backup (hourly, daily, or weekly)?
- When should you perform the backup (which days and times)?
- Where will you store your backups (external hard drive, remote share, or DVD)?
- What will you back up (full server, system state, files, folders, or volumes)?
- What will you use the backup for (full server, system state recovery, or bare metal)?

Here are a few things to keep in mind when working with Windows Server Backup on Windows Server 2012 R2:

- Backing up directly to a tape drive is not supported, although you can still back up to this media if you have System Center 2012 R2 - Data Protection Manager (DPM). This works by using a disk-to-disk-to-tape (D2D2T) approach in which data is initially copied to backup storage on a disk, and then copied again to the tape storage system. Third-party backup programs can also be used if you need to back up to tape.
- If your backup strategy incorporates multiple disks, you must have all the disks online when performing the initial setup of the backup. These disks should be dedicated to the backup job, which means they will be formatted and configured as a single New Technology File System (NTFS) volume. NTFS is a proprietary file system developed by Microsoft.
- The system state, which includes the core files and registry settings used by the operating system (boot files, system-protected files, shared system volume (SYSVOL), the COM+ class registration database, and Active Directory files) cannot be backed up to a DVD drive. Active Directory service files and SYSVOL are included as part of the system state on domain controllers.
- Applications can be backed up to attached disks or remote shared folders but not to a DVD drive, optical, or removable media. These disks must be attached and online and should support either USB 2.0 or IEEE 1394 as well as provide at least 1.5 times the storage capacity of the items you are backing up. The additional space allows you to store a couple of backup versions.
- When backing up to folders on a local or remote volume, only one copy of the backup can be stored in the folder. Subsequent backups overwrite the contents from the previous one.
- When using remote shares, you specify the Universal Naming Convention (UNC) path (\\servername\share) to provide the location for storing the backup. If you decide to change this after backups are executed, you will no longer be able to recover your backup data without performing a full restore and creating a new UNC path or resetting the share back to its original configuration.
- Backing up to a folder on a volume where users access data frequently results in a degradation of performance while the backup is in process.

REVIEWING BACKUP CONFIGURATION OPTIONS

When configuring your backup, you select either a full server (recommended) or a custom configuration.

The following provides an overview of the configuration options:

- **Full server (recommended):** This option backs up all hard disk volumes (except for the volume where the backup is stored) as well as any critical data required for recovery. This includes your server data, applications, and system state. Full server backups can be used to recover the Active Directory Domain Services (AD DS), bare metal recovery restores, as well as specific files/folders.
- **Custom:** This option allows you to specify the items you want to include in the backup. The options include:
  - ***Bare metal recovery:*** This option allows you to recover your server from a hard drive failure to a machine running the same/different hardware. It does not support cross-architecture (x86 to x64) and requires Windows Server installation media to start the recovery process. Selecting this option automatically includes system state, system reserved, and the critical volumes that are necessary for the operating system to run. Examples of critical volumes include those that hold the boot files (Bootmgr and the Boot Configuration Data [BCD] store), the operating system and registry, the SYSVOL, Active Directory database, and Active Directory database log files. When selecting this option as a substitute for a full backup, keep in mind that it will not automatically back up non-critical volumes that contains data you need.
  - ***System state:*** This option backs up all the files needed to recover Active Directory. The system state includes the registry, boot files, the COM+ class registration database, the Active Directory database (ntds.dit) and its associated log files, the Active Directory Certificate Services database, the SYSVOL folder, and system files under the protection of Windows Resource protection. Additional data can be included if the server performs additional roles.
  - **System Reserved:** This option contains the Windows Recovery Environment (WinRE) files and can be used to boot the server in situations where the operating system becomes corrupted or fails to boot.
  - **Local disk (x:):** This option represents local disks and volumes on the server.

After selecting the backup configuration, your next decision involves determining whether you want to run the backup manually or schedule it to start automatically.

EXPLORING YOUR SCHEDULING OPTIONS

You can run a manual backup (one-time backup) by using the Backup Once Wizard, which can be accessed via the Actions pane in the Windows Server Backup console. These types of backups can also be initiated using wbadmin and Windows PowerShell.

Never use manual backups as a replacement for your regularly scheduled backup. Instead, use them as a complement to your ongoing backups in the following situations when you want to:

- Back up a volume that isn't included in your regularly scheduled backups.
- Make a backup outside of your current backup schedule window.
- Store a backup in a location that is different from the one currently being used by your automatic backups.
- Make a change to the server (for example, install new programs and service packs).

Outside of the previous scenarios, schedule your backups to run automatically. Depending upon the needs of your organization, you have the option to schedule a backup to occur once a day or multiple times during the day at the times you specify.

Once you have a schedule in place, you're ready to select the target location to store your backups.

SELECTING WHERE TO STORE YOUR BACKUPS

Windows Server Backup provides three options to select from when deciding where to store your backups. These options include:

- Backing up to hard disk(s) (recommended)
- Backing up to a volume
- Backing up to a shared network folder

The first two options involve storing your backups on the server locally. When backing up to a hard disk, you should dedicate the disks to the Windows Backup program, which means they will be formatted and used exclusively for storing backups and not for holding other data. In other words, you will no longer see them appear in File Explorer, and they will be managed by Windows Server Backup exclusively.

When backing up to hard disks, use multiple external hard disks and then rotate the disks offsite to further aid in disaster recovery. When setting up the backup, Windows Server Backup labels each disk with the server name, the current date and time, and the disk name you assign. To avoid any confusion while rotating disks between sites and when performing a restore, attach a physical label for identification purposes that matches the information provided during their setup.

Because a single NTFS volume is created to span across all the disks, you don't have control over exactly which disks the backup will use in the set. If for some reason you want to backup to a specific disk, you can detach or disable the other disks. The same goes for taking a disk offsite. When the disk is removed, the backup program will use the remaining disks for the next scheduled backup.

If you don't have the disk capacity to back up to a hard disk, you can target your backups to a local volume. Storing your backups on a local volume impacts the volume's performance; therefore, you should not place any additional server data on the volume. Windows Server Backup supports only backing up to a single volume per disk.

The last option, back up to a shared network folder, allows you to store your backups on a remote folder share that will hold only one backup at a time. This means that each time the backup is run, it overwrites the previous backup in the folder. An alternative approach, often used by administrators to avoid overwriting of the remote folder backup, is to create a Windows PowerShell script. The script is used to automate the process of moving the backup on a daily basis to a longer term storage location. To maintain multiple versions of your backups, consider using dedicated disks. Prior to backing up to a remote share, make sure the appropriate permissions are set on the share and its contents to maintain security and integrity of your backups.

After selecting a storage location for your backups, you are ready to perform the actual backup. Before you do, let's take a quick look at what the folder and file structure of a backup looks like and options for optimizing the backup process.

REVIEWING THE FOLDER AND FILE STRUCTURE CREATED DURING A BACKUP

When your backup starts, Windows Server Backup creates a folder structure in the target location you specified. The parent folder, named *WindowsImageBackup*, includes a subfolder with the name of the server you performed the backup on. If you expand this folder, you can see the following folder/file structure:

- Backup <Date> <ID number>
- Catalog
- Logs
- SPPMetadataCache
- MediaID

These files and folders contain information and details about your backup. For example, the Backup <Date><ID number> folder contains several XML files that provide backup history details along with virtual hard disk (VHD) files that are basically duplicates of your volumes.

The Catalog folder contains information about the volumes backed up and where your backups are stored. The MediaID file contains the identifier tagged to the backup storage location, whereas the Logs folder contains a text file that documents errors that occur during the backup process. The SPPMetadataCache folder contains files used by Metadata Cache Management to store information about metadata caches. You need to keep all of these folders/files together in order to perform a restore.

OPTIMIZING YOUR BACKUPS (FULL VERSUS INCREMENTAL)

After you complete the first full backup, you can then automatically run incremental backups, which saves only the data that has changed from the last backup. By default, Windows Server Backup creates incremental backups that function much like full backups allowing you to restore from a single backup. In the past, you had to restore a full backup followed by the necessary incremental backup(s) to complete the restore process.

Windows Server Backup also provides performance enhancements by using block-level technology and Volume Shadow Copy Service (VSS). Block-level backup technology increases performance by bypassing the files and file system. In other words, Windows Server Backup reads the blocks in the order they appear on the disk instead of reading them in the order they appear in files, which are usually fragmented across the disk. ***Volume Shadow Copy Service (VSS)*** takes a snapshot of the volume's current data, which is used by Windows Server Backup to back up the data. The snapshot, or shadow copy, is then deleted when the backup has completed.

If you are backing up full volumes, you have the option to optimize the backup process by selecting *Configure Performance Settings...* under the Actions panel in the Windows Server Backup console.

The following provides a brief overview of each option:

- **Normal backup performance (default):** Indicates you are performing full backups and that you want the volume's contents transferred in their entirety.
- **Faster backup performance:** Indicates you are performing incremental backups; therefore, Windows keeps a shadow copy on the source volume, which it will use to track changes. The next time you perform a backup, only the changes made since the last backup will be transferred. This is accomplished by reading from the "diff" area of the shadow copy. The "diff" area is storage space on a volume that is used to maintain a set of information that represents the differences between the current content and the content from a previous point in time. These differences are called *snapshots* and you look at them closer later in this lesson. To protect against data loss, Windows Server Backup still performs a full backup when you reach 14 incremental backups and more than 14 days have passed since the last full backup.
- **Custom:** Allows you to configure each volume separately.

TAKE NOTE* A remote share (\\server02\volbackup) needs to be created on Server02 before starting this exercise, and Server01 needs to have a simple volume named *CorpData* mapped to drive (E:) with a few sample folders and files to include in the backup.

PERFORM A MANUAL BACKUP OF A LOCAL VOLUME TO A REMOTE SHARE

GET READY. To complete a backup on a volume on Server01 to a remote share on Server02, perform the following steps:

1. Log in to the Server01 and open Server Manager.
2. Click Tools > Windows Server Backup.
3. Select Backup Once from the *Actions* panel.
4. Select Different Options when prompted to select a Backup option and click Next.
5. Select Custom for the backup configuration and click Next.

6. Select Add Items, select the CorpData (E:) volume, and then click OK.
7. Select Next to continue.
8. On the *Specify Destination type* screen, select Remote shared folder, and then click Next.
9. Enter the location \\server02\volbackup and click the More information link to read and understand the security implications of backing up to a shared folder. Click OK and then click Next to continue.
10. Review the backup items to confirm your settings and then click Backup.
11. Click Close after the backup status changes to completed for the Corpdata volume.

PERFORM A SCHEDULED FULL BACKUP TO A REMOTE SHARE

GET READY. To complete a full backup on Server01 to a remote share on Server02, perform the following steps:

TAKE NOTE* A remote share (\\server02\fullbackup) needs to be created on Server02 before starting this exercise.

1. Log in to the Server01 and open Server Manager.
2. Click Tools > Windows Server Backup.
3. From the *Actions* panel, select Backup Schedule and click Next when the *Getting Started Wizard* appears.
4. Select Full server (recommended) and click Next.
5. Select Once a day, select a time of day that is closest to your current time, and click Next.
6. Select Backup to a shared network folder and click Next.
7. Click OK after reading the message that each backup will erase the previous backup when using a remote shared folder as a storage destination.
8. Enter the location for the backup \\server02\fullbackup, and then click Next.
9. Enter the user name and password to use for scheduling the backup, and then click Next.
10. Review the settings and click Finish.
11. Click Close.
12. Confirm the backup was successful by viewing the status in Windows Server Backup after the scheduled time has passed.

PERFORM A BARE METAL RECOVERY BACKUP OF A SERVER

GET READY. To complete a bare metal recovery backup on Server01 to a remote share on Server02, perform the following steps:

TAKE NOTE* A remote share (\\server02\BMbackup) needs to be created on Server02 before starting this exercise.

1. Log in to the Server01 and open Server Manager.
2. Click Tools > Windows Server Backup.
3. From the *Actions* panel, select Backup Once.
4. Select Different Options when prompted to select a Backup option and click Next.
5. Select Custom for the backup configuration and click Next.
6. Select Add Items and select the Bare metal recovery. Notice that a bare metal recovery includes the system state, system reserved, and c: but not data drives. To restore volumes that include data to a new system, you need to include them as part of the backup. Click OK.
7. Click Next.

8. Select Remote shared folder for the storage location, and then click Next.
9. Enter the location for the backup \\server02\BMbackup, and then click Next.
10. Confirm the settings and click Backup.
11. Click Close after the backup has completed successfully.

Configuring Microsoft Azure Backup

Storing your backups in the cloud allows you to retrieve them from any location where you have Internet access as well as provides you with an offsite storage location to protect against disasters.

CERTIFICATION READY
Configure Microsoft Azure backups
Objective 3.1

Microsoft Azure Online Backup is a feature available with Windows Server 2012 R2 that allows you to back up your files and folders to the Microsoft Azure Online Backup service. Microsoft Azure is a cloud-based storage service managed by Microsoft. The backups are compressed, which means the backup is smaller and reduces bandwidth requirements. The backups are also encrypted to protect the data while it's stored. Storing your data in the cloud allows you to recover it from any location that has Internet access and provides offsite protection against disasters (for example, floods, earthquakes, fire, and theft).

A Windows Azure Backup Online Agent, installed on each server and integrated with the Windows Server Backup console, connects to the Microsoft Azure Recovery Services service and transfers file and folder data. Prior to transferring the data, the agent compresses and encrypts it using a passphrase you create during setup. The agent, which is an add-on for Windows Server 2012 or Windows Server 2012 R2, can also be integrated with System Center 2012 (SP1) or System Center 2012 R2 DPM.

When using Microsoft Azure Recovery Services, you need to keep the following in mind:

- It's only used with Windows Server 2012 or Windows Server 2012 R2.
- If BitLocker is enabled to protect your data files, it must be turned off in order for the software agent to back up your data files.
- You can back up only files and folders (data); system state and system drives are not supported.

There are eight steps to get a server up and running with Microsoft Azure Recovery Services.

1. Install and enable the Windows Server Backup feature on each server you want to back up.
2. Generate a digital certificate for the server. The certificate must have at least 2048 bit key, the enhanced key usage is Client Authentication, and the expiration date is not more than 3 years from current date.
3. Export the certificate to a file.
4. Register and set up an account for the Microsoft Azure Recovery Services.
5. Log in to Microsoft Azure with the account.

6. Access Recovery Services, create a New Vault (as shown in Figure 8-2), click Backup Vault, and then click Quick Create. You then specify the name and region of the vault, and then click Create Vault.

Figure 8-2
Creating a new vault

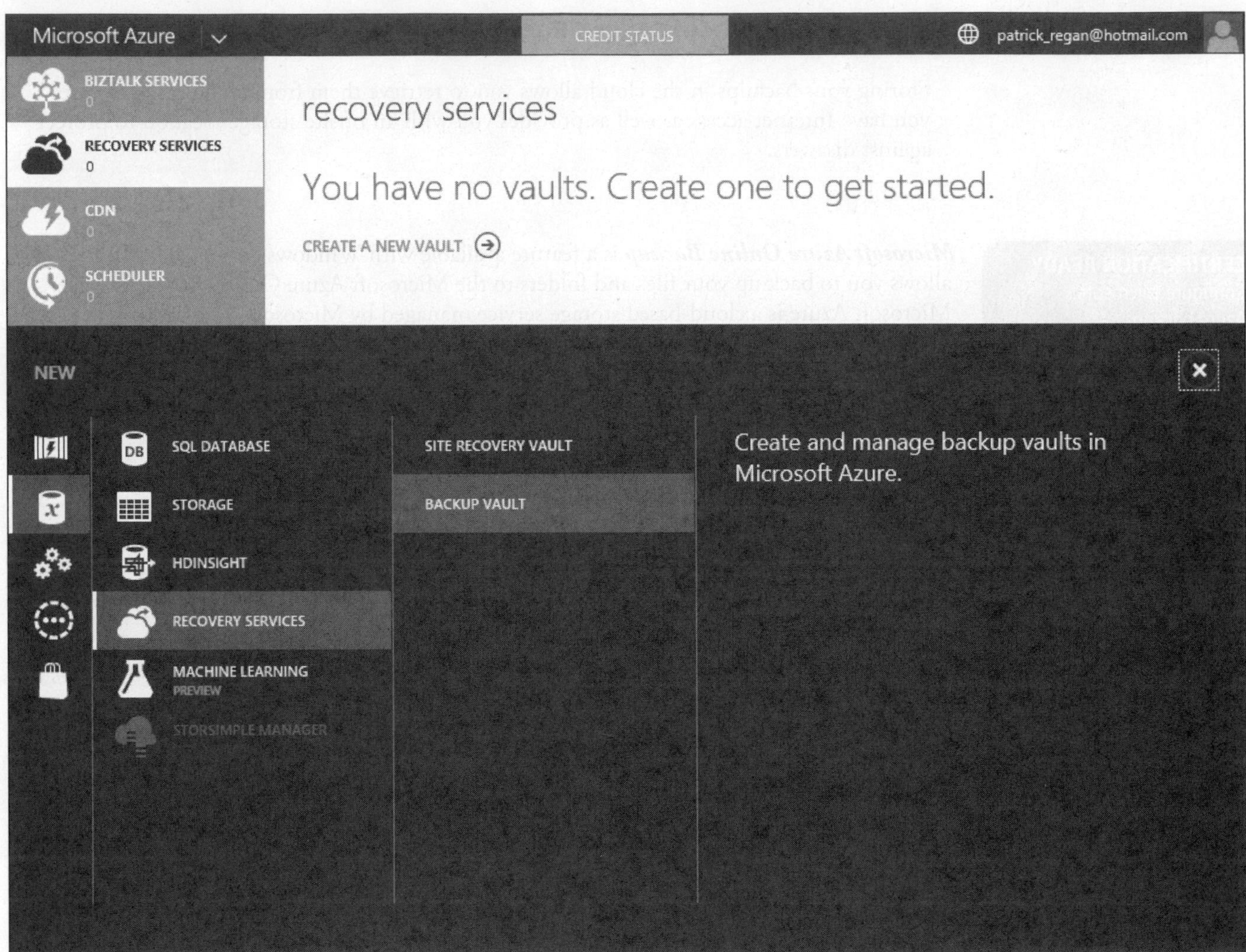

7. After the vault is created, open the vault by clicking the vault.
8. Click Manage certificate (see Figure 8-3) to upload the server certificate that you exported in Step 3.
9. Download and install the Windows Azure Online Backup Agent, and then verify the installation.
10. Using the Start button, start Windows Azure Backup.
11. When the Windows Azure Backup opens, click Register Server to register the current server for backup. You will choose the same certificate that you uploaded previously, select the Backup Vault, and then specify a passphase (which will be used with the backups).
12. Set up a backup schedule.

Figure 8-3

Uploading the server certificate

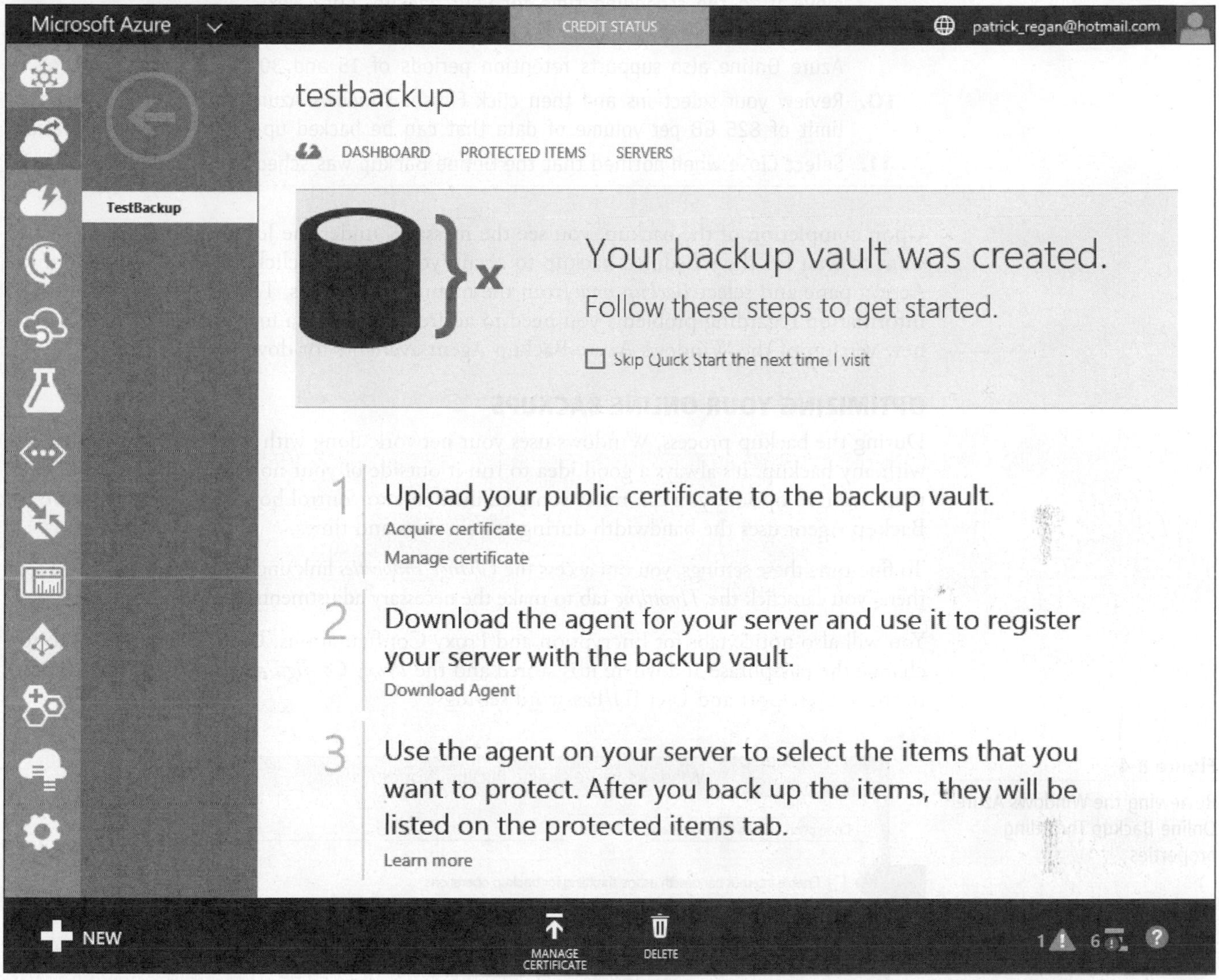

SCHEDULE A MICROSOFT AZURE ONLINE BACKUP

GET READY. To back up a data folder on Server01 using the Microsoft Azure Online Backup service, perform the following steps:

> **TAKE NOTE***
> Before starting this activity, create a folder named *OnlineBackups* on the C: drive and add a text file to the folder.

1. Open the Windows Azure Backup console if it is not already open.
2. Select Schedule Backup under the *Actions* panel.
3. Click Next when the wizard launches.
4. On the *Select Items to Backup* screen, select Add Items.
5. Expand the C: drive, select OnlineBackups, and then click OK.
6. Click Next to continue.

7. Select the current day for your backup.
8. Select an available time that is closest to your current time and click Add to move it to the scheduled time for your backup. Click Next.
9. Confirm the retention period is set to its default (7 days) and click Next. Windows Azure Online also supports retention periods of 15 and 30 days.
10. Review your selections and then click Finish. Windows Azure Online Backup has a limit of 825 GB per volume of data that can be backed up in one backup operation.
11. Select Close when notified that the Online Backup was scheduled successfully.

Upon completion of the backup, you see the message, under the Jobs tab. If you don't want to wait for the scheduled backup to occur, you can right-click *Online Backup* from the Action pane and select *Backup now* from the menu that appears. The Alerts tab provides information regarding problems you need to address as well as a message when there is a new version of the Windows Azure Backup Agent available for download.

OPTIMIZING YOUR ONLINE BACKUPS

During the backup process, Windows uses your network along with Internet bandwidth. As with any backup, it's always a good idea to run it outside of your normal work hours but if that is not an option, you can make some adjustments to control how the Windows Azure Backup Agent uses the bandwidth during certain days and times.

To fine-tune these settings, you can access the *Change Properties* link under the Actions panel. From there, you can click the *Throttling* tab to make the necessary adjustments as shown in Figure 8-4. You will also notice tabs for Encryption and Proxy Configurations. Use the *Encryption* tab to change the passphrase and where it is stored and the *Proxy Configuration* tab to make changes to the address/port and User ID/Password settings.

Figure 8-4

Reviewing the Windows Azure Online Backup Throttling properties

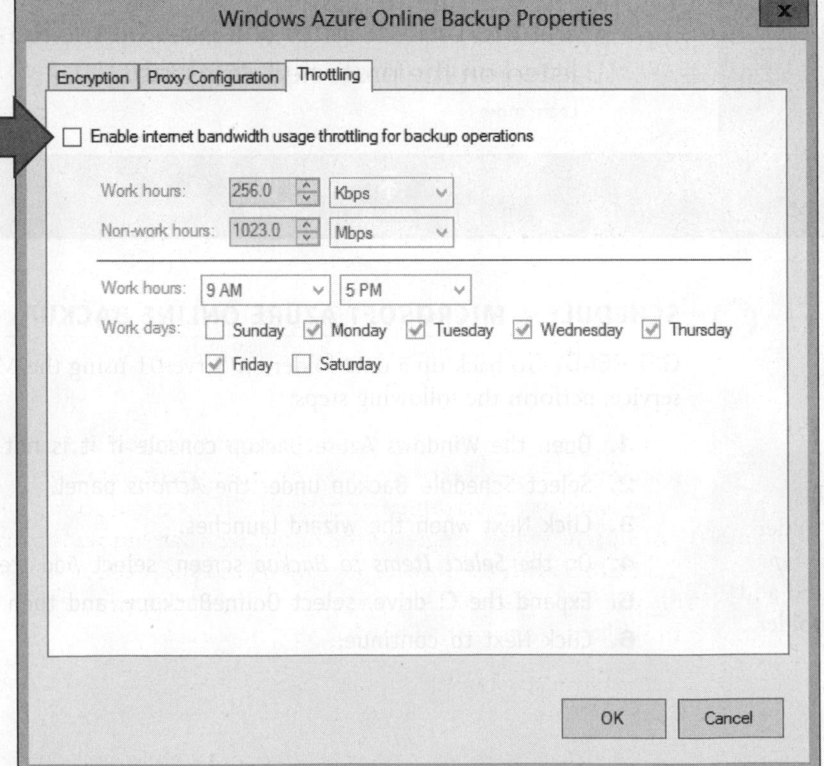

MONITORING THE HEALTH STATUS OF YOUR WINDOWS AZURE ONLINE BACKUP SERVICE

You learned the process for downloading and installing the Microsoft Azure Online Backup Agent. This involved logging into the Microsoft Azure dashboard located on the Microsoft Online Backup website and accessing the download link under the setup menu.

In addition to downloading the agent, you can also learn more about Microsoft Azure by taking advantage of the links under the Support section, which provides resources such as How To videos, Customer Support options, and access to the Microsoft Azure online communities.

On the service health tab, you can review the current health status for each sub-region. The status is color coded as green (normal service availability), orange (performance degradation), and red (service interruption). You can use your mouse to hover over an icon to view additional details.

Configuring Role-Specific Backups

The roles assigned to a server can dramatically impact its configuration as well as the frequency and type of backup needed to restore it in the future.

As part of your overall backup strategy, take into consideration the roles installed on each of your servers. As you learned, the role performed by the server can have an impact on how you approach the backup and eventually the restore of the server. Let's take a closer look at some of these roles and what can be done to back them up.

BACKING UP DHCP AND DNS

CERTIFICATION READY
Configure role-specific backups.
Objective 3.1

The Dynamic Host Configuration Protocol (DHCP) database contains information about IP address leases, reservations, scopes, scope options, and DHCP registry key settings. It's backed up automatically at 60-minute intervals to the %systemroot%\System32\Dhcp\Backup directory. It is also backed up as part of a system state or full backup, and by using the DHCP Manager console.

You can back up DHCP via the DHCP Manager console by performing the following steps:

1. Open the *DHCP Manager* console.
2. Select the DHCP Server that contains the scopes you want to back up.
3. Select *Action* > *Backup*.
4. Browse to the folder where you want to store the backup and click *OK*. By default this will be the %systemroot%\Windows\System32\Dhcp\Backup.
5. Click *OK*.

Active Directory-integrated DNS zone configuration information is stored in the registry; therefore, it's also backed up as part of the system state and during full backups. In situations where you have a corrupted or failing DNS, you can recover it only by restoring the entire system state, which might or might not be what you want to do. An alternative is to use DNSCMD with the /zoneexport switch to export the Active Directory-integrated zones to a file you can back up. This file can be restored as a primary zone file and then converted into an Active Directory-integrated zone if necessary.

The following command creates a copy of the DNS zone contoso.com in the %systemroot%\system32\dns\backup\contoso.com.dns.bak file.

```
DNSCMD /zoneexport contoso.com \backup\contoso.com.dns.bak
```

The XCOPY command can be used to back up primary and secondary zone files to a backup folder you specify.

```
Example: XCOPY %systemroot%\system32\dns c:\backups\dns /y
```

The command backs up all zone text files into the c:\backups folder.

You can then restore them by using XCOPY to copy the backup to the %systemroot%\system32\Dns folder.

BACKING UP WINS

The Windows Internet Name Service (WINS) maintains a distributed database used to register and query dynamic mappings of NetBIOS names for computers and groups. It maps NetBIOS names to IP addresses. Although the database is backed as part of system state and full backups, you can also back up the WINS database from the WINS console.

Because most of the entries in the database are dynamically entered by the servers and workstations, the only reason to back it up would be if you had created static entries in the WINS database. You can back up the WINS database by performing the following steps:

1. Open the *WINS* console.
2. Right-click the *WINS Server*.
3. Select *Back Up Database*.
4. Browse to the folder where you want to store the backup and click *OK*. By default this will be %systemroot%\Windows\System32\WINS.
5. Click *OK*.

BACKING UP CERTIFICATE SERVICES

Certificate Services stores a database in the C:\Windows\system32\Certlog location by default. When certificates are issued to users and computers, the associated information is maintained in the Certificate Services database.

If this database becomes corrupted or is accidentally deleted, certificates issued by the server will be considered invalid. Although Certificate Services is backed as part of a system state and a full backup, you can also back it up via the Certificate Services console by performing the following steps:

1. Open the *Certificate Service* console.
2. Right-click the server and select *All Tasks* >*Backup CA* …
3. Select *Next* to start the Certification Authority Wizard.
4. Select *Private Key and CA Certificate* and the *Certificate database and certificate database log* options.
5. Enter *C: \Windows\System32\CABackup* and click *Next*.
6. Click *OK* to create the directory.
7. Enter and confirm a password to gain access to the private key and the CA certificate file and click *Next*.
8. Click *Finish* to back up the Certificate Authority.

BACKING UP ACTIVE DIRECTORY DOMAIN SERVICES

Active Directory is backed up as part of system state and full backups. The components included in the system state are as follows:

- **System startup (boot) files:** These files are required to boot Windows.
- **System registry:** This contains registry files that include information about the system hardware, low-level operating system components, and installed programs and their settings.

- **COM+ Class registration database:** The Component Object Model (COM) is a standard for writing component software in a distributed systems environment. COM uses the registry database for storing component registration information. The database supports a VSS writer allowing VSS requesters to back up the database on a shadow-copied volume.
- **System volume (SYSVOL):** This folder, on a domain controller, contains the net logon shared folders used to host user logon scripts and policy settings for pre-Windows 2000 network clients. The user logon scripts for Active Directory-enabled clients, system policies, group policy settings, and the File Replication service (FRS) directories used to stage directories and files that must be available and synchronized between domain controllers.
- **Active Directory:** This includes the Active Directory database (ntds.dit), the checkpoint file (edb.chk), transaction logs (edb*.log), and the reserved transaction logs (Res1.log and Res2.log).

In most Active Directory environments, changes to user passwords, computer accounts, and other domain objects occur on a daily basis. When performing restores, you return the domain controller back to a former state, which can affect authentication and replication; therefore, the more frequently you back up domain controllers, the fewer problems you will encounter after a restore. In general, back up your domain controller at least once per day. In situations where you are upgrading a domain controller or installing a new service pack or hotfix, perform a backup immediately.

Another common mistake regarding Active Directory is the deletion of Active Directory objects by accident. For example, if you delete an organizational unit (OU) by mistake that just happens to contain multiple user accounts, the deletion will be replicated to all other domain controllers. When this happens, you need to perform an authoritative restore to return the OU to its original state. This involves restoring the system state and using the Ntdsutil tool. Fortunately, with Windows Server 2012 R2, there is a more efficient way to handle the restoring of deleted Active Directory objects without having to restore the system state. It's called the *Active Directory Recycle Bin*.

ENABLING THE ACTIVE DIRECTORY RECYCLE BIN

To use Active Directory Recycle Bin, your forest functional level should be set to at least Windows Server 2008 R2 or greater and all domain controllers must be running Windows Server 2008 R2, Windows Server 2012, or Windows Server 2012 R2. This can be confirmed by selecting *Server Manager > Tools > Active Directory Administrative Center*. In the following exercise, you confirm the functional level and enable the Active Directory Recycle Bin.

ENABLE THE ACTIVE DIRECTORY RECYCLE BIN

GET READY. To enable the Active Directory Recycle Bin on RWDC01, perform the following steps:

1. Log in to the RWDC01 with administrative privileges.
2. Select Server Manager > Tools > Active Directory Administrative Center.
3. Right-click the domain name contoso (local) and select Properties.
4. Confirm the forest functional level is set to at least Windows Server 2008R2 or later and click Cancel.
5. Right-click the domain name contoso (local) and select Enable Recycle Bin.
6. Click OK when prompted; you cannot disable the feature.
7. Select OK to refresh the Active Directory Administrative Center.
8. Open Windows PowerShell.
9. Type the following to confirm that the Active Directory Recycle Bin is enabled:

```
Get-ADOptionalFeature -filter *
```

10. Confirm that a partition is listed for the EnabledScopes parameter:

```
EnabledScopes
 ;{CN=Partitions,CN=Configuration,DC=contoso,DC=com
 , CN=NTDS
Settings,CN=RWDC01,CN=Servers,CN=Default-First-
Site-Name,CN=Sites,
CN=Configuration,DC=contoso,DC=com
```

If EnabledScopes shows < >, then Active Directory Recycle Bin is not enabled.

PROTECTING ACTIVE DIRECTORY OBJECTS FROM DELETION

To further protect against the accidental deletion of objects in Active Directory (Computers, OUs, and Users), Windows Server 2012 R2 provides the "protect from accidental deletion" option. This setting can be found by opening the Active Directory Administration Center, right-clicking the object, and selecting *Properties*.

To streamline the process of protecting OUs, you can use the following Windows PowerShell cmdlet to determine which OUs are not protected from deletion:

```
Get-ADOrganizationalUnit -filter * -Properties
ProtectedfromAccidentalDeletion | where {$_.
ProtectedFromAccidentalDeletion -eq $false} |ft
name,DistinguishedName -AutoSize
```

TAKE NOTE*

In this exercise, you back up to a remote share (\\Server02\ADbackup) in which network backups will save only the latest version of the backup. This is used only for training purposes. In a production environment, you back up to attached disks that are rotated offsite to provide additional security and protection. It's also recommend that you perform a scheduled full backup to occur on a daily basis for your domain controllers.

PERFORM A BACKUP OF THE SYSTEM STATE OF AN ACTIVE DIRECTORY DOMAIN CONTROLLER USING WBADMIN

GET READY. To complete a backup of the system state on RWDC01, perform the following steps:

1. Log in to the RWDC01 with administrative privileges.
2. Start Windows PowerShell, enter the following commands to install Windows Server Backup, press Enter after each command. If Windows Server Backup is already installed, you can skip this step.

   ```
   PS C:\Add-WindowsFeature Windows-Server-BackupPS C:\Exit
   ```

3. Open a command prompt and type the following to perform a system state backup of the domain controller using wbadmin:

   ```
   wbadmin start backup systemstatebackup -backuptarget:
   \\server02\ADbackup -quiet
   ```

4. Type Exit to close the command window after the backup operation successfully completes.
5. Browse to the share on \\server02\ADbackup to view the files/folders created as part of the system state backup of the domain controller.

Managing VSS Settings Using VSSAdmin

Volume Shadow Copy Administrative Command-line Tool (VSSAdmin) can be used to create and delete volume shadow copies/associations, list shadow copy providers and writers, and resize a volume shadow storage association.

The VSSAdmin is used to manage the VSS. Before you take a closer look at this tool and the information it provides, it's important that you have a good understanding of VSS and its components.

The VSS coordinates several components, which allow you to back up your server without impacting running applications or users. It accomplishes this through the use of shadow copies. A shadow copy (also called a *snapshot*) of a volume is a duplicate of the data on the volume at a specific point in time.

The VSS components communicate with each other via the VSS Framework to both create and restore your shadow copies. The following provides a brief overview of the tasks performed by each component:

- ***VSS requester:*** Requests that a shadow copy be taken. The Windows Server Backup program and the System Center Data Protection Manager are examples of VSS requesters.
- ***VSS writer:*** Makes sure the data is ready for the shadow copy to be created. The writer is usually provided by the application software itself and each Windows Server has one or more writers. Examples of VSS writers include Hyper-V, SQL Server, Exchange Server, Active Directory System Service, Performance Counter Writer, ASR Writers, System Writer, Registry Writer, WINS Jet Writer, DHCP Jet Writer, WMI Writer, Certificate Authority Writer, NTDS Writer, and so on.
- ***VSS provider:*** Creates and maintains the shadow copies. Examples of VSS providers (fileshare and system types) include the Microsoft File Share Shadow Copy provider and the Microsoft Software Shadow Copy provider. Hardware vendors also include VSS providers with their storage arrays.
- ***Source volume:*** Contains the data you want to copy.
- ***Storage volume:*** Holds the shadow copy storage files for the VSS provider.

The following provides a basic overview of how VSS components interact with each other during a typical backup:

1. When you launch Windows Server Backup (VSS requester), it queries the VSS and asks it to list the VSS writers.
2. Each VSS writer then describes the components and data stores that need to be backed up and provides the information to VSS. VSS provides the information to the VSS requester (for example, Windows Server Backup), which then selects the components to back up.
3. VSS then notifies all VSS writers to prepare their data in order to make a shadow copy. Preparing the data involves completing any open transactions, flushing their caches, and/or rolling any transaction logs. Once the VSS writer has completed its pre-backup tasks, it informs VSS.
4. VSS tells the VSS writers to quiesce (pause) their data and temporarily queue any I/O write requests from applications. This is necessary to ensure a consistent backup and allows VSS to create a shadow copy of the volume. The VSS freezes the file system to ensure its metadata is written in a consistent order.
5. The VSS provider tells VSS to create the shadow copy.
6. After the copy is complete, VSS unfreezes the file system and releases the VSS writers, which allows them to process their queue of I/O write requests.

7. VSS then queries the VSS writers to make sure they held I/O write requests during the time period the snapshot was taken. If they did not, the shadow copy is deleted and Windows Server Backup (VSS requester) is notified. If the VSS writers handled their queues appropriately, VSS provides Windows Server Backup (VSS requester) with information on where it can locate the shadow copy.

When an application attempts to write to the protected sector, VSS makes a copy of the sector before it allows the application to write to it. The copied sector is the one stored in the backup.

CERTIFICATION READY
Manage VSS settings using VSSAdmin.
Objective 3.1

Now that you have a better idea of the components that make up VSS and how they interact with each other, you can use the VSSAdmin to view the list of writers and providers on your server, see a list of volume shadow copies on your server, and view how much storage space (currently, in the future, and maximum) is used by shadow copies.

MANAGE VSS SETTINGS USING VSSADMIN

GET READY. To manage VSS settings using VSSAdmin, perform the following steps:

1. Log in to Server01 with administrative privileges.
2. Open a command prompt.
3. Type the following to see a list of commands supported with vssadmin:

   ```
   c:\vssadmin /?
   ```
4. Type the following to see a list of VSS writers on Server01 and their current state.

   ```
   c:\vssadmin list writers
   ```

   If this were a server and you noticed one or more of the VSS writers with a state set to Failed, you can most likely fix them with a quick server reboot. In situations where you cannot reboot the server, you can search the registry or the Internet for the Writer ID to identify the service associated with it. You can then restart that specific service and rerun the list writers command to confirm the fix.
5. Type the following to see a list of VSS providers on Server01:

   ```
   c:\vssadmin list providers
   ```
6. Type the following to see a list of existing volume shadow copies:

   ```
   c:\vssadmin list shadows
   ```
7. To list the volumes that are eligible for shadow copies, enter the following:

   ```
   c:\vssadmin list volumes
   ```
8. To view used, allocated, and maximum shadow copy storage space, type the following:

   ```
   c:\vssadmin list shadowstorage
   ```

After running the command, you see the amount of shadow copy storage space being used, the amount allocated for the future, and the maximum space that can be used. If you notice the amount of storage space that is being used is almost as large as the maximum, you might need to move the VSS storage area to another location. This can be accomplished by accessing the computer's volume that is currently used for the volume shadow copy storage area, right-clicking it, and selecting *Configure Shadow Copies*. Select *Settings* and then choose another volume to store the shadow copies on.

Creating System Restore Snapshots

Shadow Copies for Shared Volumes (SCSV) and Hyper-V checkpoints provide you with the ability to return to a specific point in time.

Although Windows client operating systems support the ability to create system restore points, Windows Server 2012 and Windows Server 2012 R2 don't. What they do provide is the ability to use Shadow Copies for Shared Volumes (SCSV) as well as Hyper-V checkpoints as mechanisms for returning to a specific point in time. You can also utilize the Hyper-V VSS writer and VSS to back up virtual machines (VMs) using Window Server Backup.

ENABLING SHADOW COPIES FOR SHARED VOLUMES

Shadow Copies for Shared Volumes (SCSV) uses the capabilities of the VSS to capture and store copies of folders and files (located on shared network resources) at a specific point in time.

When SCSV is implemented on a volume, both end users and administrators can recover accidentally deleted or overwritten files as well as compare different versions of the same file. Because end users can restore their own files, implementing SCSV can dramatically reduce not only the time but the associated costs of having to recover their folder and files via their IT support desk.

You enable SCSV on a per-volume basis by selecting *Server Manager > Tools > Computer Management*. The volumes must be formatted using NTFS and should not contain any mounted drives or mount points. If the volume has either, their contents will not be included in the shadow copies. The first shadow copy of the volume is a complete copy of the data; subsequent shadow copies include only the changes made since the last shadow copy was created. The source volume is the volume that contains the data you want to copy. The storage volume is where your shadow copies will be located and if possible should be placed on a separate disk from the one that holds the source volume.

You need at least 300 MB of free space to create a shadow copy on the selected volume. By default, a shadow copy is created at 7:00 AM (Monday-Friday) and at 12:00 PM (Monday-Friday). You can modify the schedule by selecting the *Settings* button. You can also click the *Create Now* button to take a manual snapshot between scheduled times (see Figure 8-5).

ENABLE SHADOW COPIES FOR SHARED VOLUMES

GET READY. To enable Shadow Copies for Shared Volumes on Server01, perform the following steps:

TAKE NOTE*

The folder created in this exercise is used in Lesson 9, "Recovering Servers," as part of the restore process.

1. Log in to Server01 with administrative privileges.
2. Create a shared folder called CorpDocs on a simple volume (E:) on Server01 and share the folder so that administrators have full access.
3. Create a file in the *CorpDocs* folder named Agenda.txt, enter sample text, and then save and close.
4. Open Server Manager, and select Tools > Computer Management.
5. Expand the Storage item and select Disk Management.
6. Right-click the volume you created the shared folder on and select Properties.
7. Select the Shadow Copies tab.
8. Confirm the volume you selected in Step 4 is highlighted and then click Enabled.
9. Click Yes to confirm you want to enable shadow copies on the volume. A snapshot is taken immediately and the date/time stamp is noted (see Figure 8-5).
10. Click Create Now to create a second snapshot of the selected volume and then click OK to close.

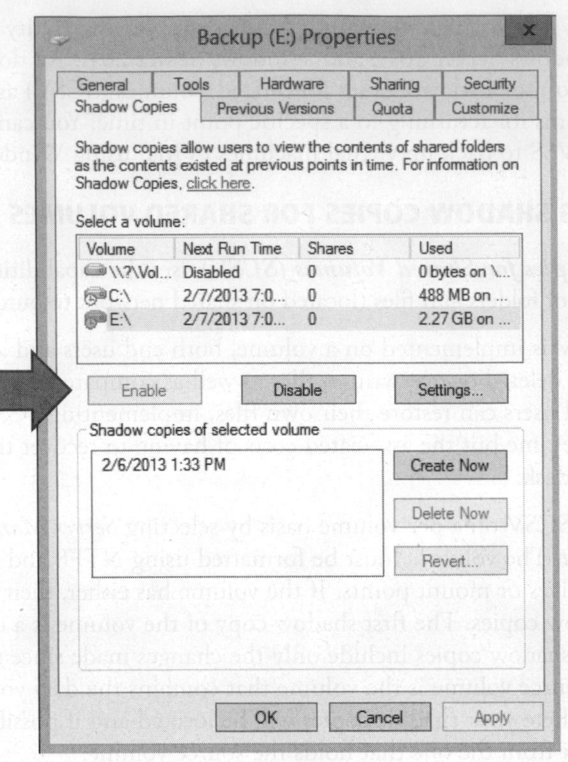

Figure 8-5

Enabling Shadow Copy for a Shared Volume/Taking snapshot

BACKING UP HYPER-V VIRTUAL MACHINES

VMs, created using Hyper-V, are stored as files on your hard disk. These files contain the VHDs, saved state files, checkpoint files, and configuration files. Because these are stored on a volume on your server, Windows Server Backup can be used to protect them in combination with the VSS.

VSS writers are responsible for preparing their data in order to make the shadow copy and are instructed by VSS to quiesce its associated application to ensure a consistent backup is made. By using the Microsoft Hyper-V VSS writer, Windows Server Backup can create the checkpoints while the VM is running.

Windows Server Backup supports only a volume-based backup for VMs; therefore, you need to select all volumes that contain your VM files. For example, if you store your VM configuration files on one volume and your VHD files on another, both volumes need to be backed up.

VMs containing dynamic disks need to be backed up offline. Machines running operating systems that do not support VSS and those that do not have Integration Services installed will be put in a saved state while the VSS snapshot is created.

TAKING HYPER-V CHECKPOINTS

Hyper-V checkpoints (formerly called snapshots in Windows Server 2012 and earlier) offer another way to capture the state, data, and hardware configurations for a VM at a specific point in time. These checkpoints, which can be taken when the VM is running or stopped, are created in the Hyper-V Manager. The checkpoint includes the configuration and network settings for the VM as well as the current state of the VHD(s) attached to the machine and any saved state information. Hyper-V uses the VSS to make a copy of the guest machine's hard disk.

By default, a Hyper-V checkpoint's data is stored in an automatic VHD (.avhd) file and then it's attached to the VM. When you take a snapshot of a VM, you are basically converting its VHD into a differencing disk.

Although not designed as a recovery option in production environments, you can use Hyper-V checkpoints to troubleshoot potential problems with applications or the impact a service pack/upgrade will have on a server.

If you enabled VSS on a volume where the Hyper-V checkpoints are stored, they can be backed up by default, as part of a shadow copy created at 7:00 AM (Monday–Friday) and at 12:00 PM (Monday–Friday).

If you have the backup (volume snapshot) Integration Services installed on the guest operating system, a VSS requester is installed that allows the VSS writers in the guest OS to participate in the VM's backup.

The following outlines the steps used to take a snapshot of a VM using the Hyper-V Manager on the host:

1. Log on to the server with administrative privileges.
2. Open *Server Manager* and select *Tools* > *Hyper-V Manager*.
3. Select the VM host that manages the VMs.
4. Highlight the VM.
5. Right-click and select *checkpoint* from the menu.

Each checkpoint taken of a VM is documented in a tree structure. The first (root) node represents the first checkpoint taken, and the Now node is the current version of the VM that is running. Each checkpoint is labeled using the VM's name (as created in Hyper-V Manager) along with a time stamp based on the date/time the checkpoint was created.

EXPLORING ENTERPRISE BACKUP SOLUTIONS FOR WINDOWS SERVER 2012 R2

If you are looking for an enterprise backup solution, then System Center 2012 R2-Data Protection Manager should be considered. It provides the ability to not only back up to disk but to tape as well. It can be used to protect and recover Exchange (2007, 2010, 2013), SQL (2008, 2008R2, 2012), SharePoint (2013, 2010), Windows SharePoint Server 3.0, Microsoft Office SharePoint Server 2007, Windows desktops/laptops (Windows 7, Windows 8/8.1, Windows Vista), virtual servers (Hyper-V Windows Server 2008/2008R2, Windows Server 2012/Windows Server 2012 R2), and file servers (Windows Server 2008/2008R2, Windows Server 2012/Windows Server 2012 R2) within and across Active Directory domains.

DPM also provides you with the ability to manage system state and bare metal recovery from a central location. The following vendors also provide enterprise backup solutions for Windows Server 2012 R2:

- Acronis Backup and Restore
- Symantec Backup Exec 2012 and NetBackup
- IBM Tivoli Storage Manager
- Carbonite
- CA Technologies ARCserve
- Commvault Simpana

SKILL SUMMARY

In this lesson you learned:

- Hardware/software failures, human error, computer viruses, theft, natural disasters, and fire can result in loss of data; therefore, you need to have a backup strategy in place and be prepared to execute it.
- When the Windows Server Backup feature is installed, it includes the Windows Server Backup console, wbadmin, and Windows PowerShell cmdlets that can be used to back up your server.
- Windows Server Backup on Windows Server 2012 R2 does not support backing up to tape, but you can still use System Center 2012 R2 Data Protection (DPM) Manager to perform a disk-to-disk-to-tape (D2D2T) and third-party software if necessary.
- Windows Server Backup offers both full server (recommended) and custom backup configuration options. Custom options include bare metal recovery, system state, system reserved, and local disk.
- Bare metal recovery backups can be used to recover your server from a hard drive failure to a machine running the save/different hardware, but it does not support cross-architecture (x86 to x64) restores.
- Manual backups should not be a replacement for regularly scheduled backups.
- Windows Server provides three options to select from when deciding where to store your backups: hard disk, volumes, and shared network folders. When backing up to hard disk, the best practice is to dedicate them to the Windows Server Backup job set and use a rotation schedule to take disks offsite for additional protection.
- Backups to shared network folders are overwritten with each subsequent backup.
- Backups are stored in a folder named *WindowsImageBackup* under the name of the server being backed up (for example, \\<server>\<sharedfolderpath>\WindowsImageBackup\<serverbackedup>).
- Backup performance is enhanced through the use of block-level technology and Volume Shadow Copy Service (VSS). Block-level technology bypasses the files and file system, and reads the blocks in the order they appear on the disk. VSS takes snapshots of the volume's current data allowing users and applications to continue to use the volume without interruption.
- Backups of full server volumes can be optimized by selecting the faster backup performance setting (incremental backups) available in the Configure Performance Settings.
- File classification allows you to configure automatic procedures for defining a desired property on a file, based on the conditions specified in classification rules.
- Windows Online Backups allows you to back up your files and folders to the Microsoft Azure Online Backup service. It does not support the backup of system drivers/system state. This involves setting up a Microsoft Azure Online account, installing a software agent, registering the server, and then scheduling the backup to occur. You can also monitor the health of the online service with the Windows Azure dashboard.
- As part of your overall backup strategy, you need to take into consideration the roles installed on each of your servers. Depending upon the role performed, the impact on how you approach the backup, and eventually restore the system is impacted.
- The Volume Shadow Copy Administrative Command-line tool (VSSAdmin) can be used to manage VSS. VSS consists of VSS requesters, writers, and providers that work with each other using the VSS Framework.

- Shadow Copies for Shared Volumes (SCSV) uses the capability of VSS to capture and store copies of folders located on shared network resources, at a specific point in time. This can be used by end users to restore their own files, which can reduce the time and costs associated with recovering files.
- Hyper-V checkpoints can be used to capture the state, data, and hardware configurations for a virtual machine (VM) at a specific point in time.

Knowledge Assessment

Multiple Choice

Select the correct answer for each of the following questions.

1. Which tools do you have access to after installing the Windows Server Backup feature? (Select all that apply.)
   a. Windows Server Backup MMC snap-in
   b. wbadmin.exe
   c. Windows PowerShell cmdlets for Windows Server Backup
   d. RSAT
2. Which of the following are true statements regarding Windows Server Backup in Windows Server 2012 R2? (Select all that apply.)
   a. You can back up to tape drives and attached hard drives.
   b. Applications can be backed up to a DVD drive.
   c. Applications can be backed up to a remote shared folder.
   d. Backing up to folders on a local or remote volume supports only one copy of the backup. Subsequent backups overwrite the contents of the previous backup.
3. Which of the following types of backups will back up all of the files needed to recover Active Directory? (Select all that apply.)
   a. system state
   b. full backup
   c. bare metal recovery
   d. system reserved
4. What is the name of the folder where your backups are stored?
   a. WindowsBackup
   b. WindowsImageBackup
   c. WindowsBkup
   d. WindowsImageBkup
5. Which of the following are true regarding Windows Online Backups? (Select all that apply.)
   a. It's only available with Windows Server 2012 R2
   b. It supports bandwidth throttling
   c. It uses an agent that supports backing up BitLocker-enabled drives
   d. It supports backup of files and folders
6. Which of the following server roles should be backed up only in situations where you have static entries in the database?
   a. DHCP
   b. DNS
   c. RAS
   d. WINS

7. Which Windows PowerShell command installs the Windows Server Backup feature?
   a. PS C:\Add-WindowsFeature Windows-Server-Backup
   b. PS C:\Add-WindowsFeature WindowsServerBackup
   c. PS C:\Install-WindowsFeature Windows-Server-Backup
   d. PS C:\Install-WindowsFeature WindowsServerBackup

8. Which wbamin command backs up the system state on a domain controller to a remote volume located on Server02 named SysState?
   a. wbadmin start backup –backuptarget: \\server02\SysState
   b. wbadmin start backup –systemstate \\server02\SysState
   c. wbadmin start backup –systemstate –backuptarget: \\server02\SysState
   d. wbadmin start backup –systemstate –target: \\server02\SysState

9. This Volume Shadow Copy Service (VSS) component is responsible for making sure the data is ready for the shadow copy to be created.
   a. VSS requester
   b. VSS provider
   c. VSS writer
   d. VSS ShadowWriter

10. Which of the following are characteristics of Shared Copies for Shadow Volumes (SCSV)?
   a. It's enabled on a per-volume basis.
   b. By default, shadow copies are taken at 7:00 AM and 12:00 AM (Monday-Friday).
   c. The volumes must be formatted using NTFS.
   d. Mount points are supported.

Best Answer

Choose the letter that corresponds to the best answer. More than one answer choice may achieve the goal. Select the BEST answer.

1. A bare metal recovery backup includes which of the following?
   a. system state
   b. system reserved
   c. critical volumes
   d. volumes containing user data files

2. When should you perform a manual backup in place of a regularly scheduled backup?
   a. The volume isn't included in your regular backups
   b. The backup needs to be done outside the normally scheduled window
   c. The backup needs to be stored in a location that is different from the one used for automatic backup
   d. You need to make a change to the server (for example, install a new service pack)

3. You would like to back up the system state. Which of the following tools/programs can you use?
   a. Windows Server Backup
   b. wbadmin
   c. ntbackup
   d. Microsoft Azure Online Backup

4. This type of backup technology bypasses the files and file system to increase performance during backups.
   a. segment-level technology
   b. block-level technology
   c. sector-level technology
   d. file-level technology

5. You select the faster backup performance option via the Windows Server Backup console > Actions panel > Configure Performance Settings. What is the impact of making this configuration change on future backups?
   a. This indicates you are performing incremental backups after the initial full backup
   b. After you reach 14 incremental backups and more than 14 days have passed, Windows Server Backup will still perform a full backup
   c. After you reach 21 incremental backups and more than 10 days have passed, Windows Server Backup will still perform a full backup
   d. After you reach 14 incremental backups and more than 30 days have passed, Windows Server Backup will still perform a full backup

Build a List

1. Identify the six basic steps in order to install and confirm the installation of the Windows Server Backup feature on a Server Core installation by placing the number of the step in the appropriate space. Not all steps will be used.
   _______ Log in to the Server Core installation
   _______ Log in to the server and open Server Manager
   _______ Click Next on the Select installation type screen
   _______ Enter Windows PowerShell from the command windows to start a Windows PowerShell session
   _______ Enter `PS C:\Import-Module Servermanager`
   _______ Select Manage > Roles and Features
   _______ Enter `PS C:\Get-WindowsFeature | where {$_.Name -eq "Windows-Server-Backup"}`
   _______ Enter `PS C:\Install-WindowsFeature Windows-Server-Backup`
   _______ Type Exit to end the Windows PowerShell session and return to the command window

2. Identify the seven steps that must be completed to enable SCSV by placing the number of the step in the appropriate space.
   _______ Select Tools > Computer Management
   _______ Select the Shadow Copies tab
   _______ Log in to the server with administrative privileges and open Server Manager
   _______ Right-click the volume you want to enable shadow copies on and select Properties
   _______ Click Enabled
   _______ Expand the Storage item and select Disk Management
   _______ Click Yes to confirm you want to enable shadow copies on the volume

3. Identify the four basic steps in order to back up the system state using the wbadmin and Windows PowerShell commands on a domain controller without the Windows Server backup feature installed, by placing the number of the step in the appropriate space. Not all steps will be used.
   _______ Log in to the domain controller with administrative privileges
   _______ Run a wbadmin /verify to confirm the backup was successful
   _______ Open a command prompt and run the following command to back up the system state:

   ```
   C:\wbadmin start backup -systemstate -back++++uptarget:
   \\server02\ADBackup -quiet
   ```

   _______ Start Windows PowerShell and enter the following command:

   ```
   PS C:\Add-WindowsFeature Windows-Server-Backup
   ```

   _______ Type Exit to close the command window after the backup operation completes successfully

4. Identify the five basic steps in order to back up the DHCP database.
   _______ Stop the DHCP service
   _______ Log in to the DHCP Server with administrative privileges
   _______ Open the DHCP Manager console
   _______ Select OK to start the backup
   _______ Select the DHCP Scope
   _______ Browse to the folder where you want to store the backup
   _______ Select Action > Backup

Choose an Option

1. You would like to improve the performance of your backups while still ensuring that a full backup is performed when you reach 14 incremental backups and more than 14 days have passed since the last full backup. Select the option in Figure 8-6 that will accomplish your goal. (Note: Normal backup performance is checked as the default setting.)

Figure 8-6

Improving backup performance

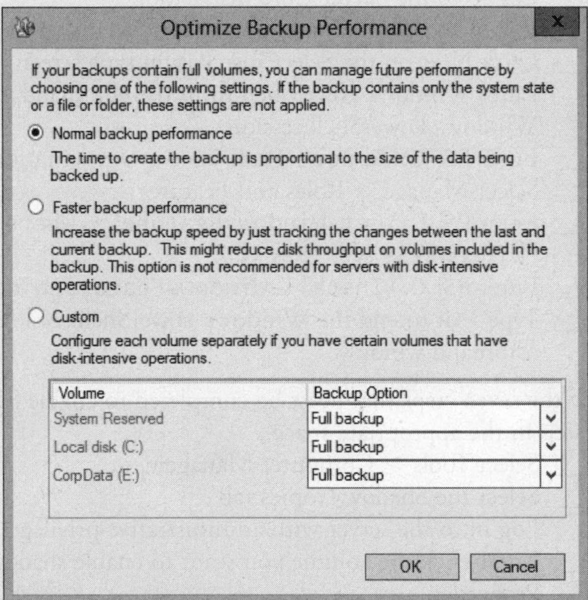

Business Case Scenarios

Scenario 8-1: Recovering the System State of DNS

You are currently running system state backups on a server that has Active Directory-integrated DNS zones. Will this be sufficient to allow you to restore the DNS zones should they become corrupted? What are the restore implications to consider when using this backup approach?

Scenario 8-2: Running Out of Space

After running the `vssadmin list shadowstorage` command, you noticed that the amount of storage space used for shadow copies is almost as large as the maximum configured size. What should you do?

Recovering Servers

LESSON 9

70-412 EXAM OBJECTIVE

Objective 3.2 – Recover servers. This objective may include but is not limited to: Restore from backups, perform a Bare Metal Restore (BMR); recover servers using Windows Recovery Environment (WinRE) and safe mode; configure the Boot Configuration Data (BCD) store.

LESSON HEADING	EXAM OBJECTIVE
Preparing For Windows Server 2012 R2 Restores	
Restoring Files and Folders	Restore from backups
Restoring Volumes	Restore from backups
Restoring the System State	Restore from backups
Performing a Bare Metal Recovery Restore	Perform a Bare Metal Restore (BMR)
Recovering Servers Using WinRE and Safe Mode	Recover servers using Windows Recovery Environment (WinRE) and safe mode
Applying System Restore Checkpoints	
Configuring the Boot Configuration Data Store	Configure the Boot Configuration Data (BCD) store

KEY TERMS

Active Directory Recycle Bin
authoritative restore
Boot Configuration Data Editor (bcdedit.exe)
Boot Configuration Data (BCD) store
boot loader/application
Boot Recovery Tool (bootrec.exe)
Directory Service Restore Mode (DSRM)
MSConfig
non-authoritative restore
ntdsutil.exe
reverting
safe mode
System File Checker
Windows Boot Manager
Windows Recovery Environment (WinRE)

■ Preparing For Windows Server 2012 R2 Restores

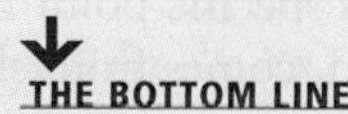
THE BOTTOM LINE

Having a written server recovery plan that outlines roles and responsibilities as well as the steps necessary to recover your servers is critical to reducing the overall downtime and loss of productivity in your organization.

Do you have a written plan that describes how you will recover a server in your organization? If so, when is the last time you reviewed it to make sure it was current and applicable to your existing environment?

If you're like most, you either don't have a plan or the one you do have is probably out of date. You might be thinking, "No problem! I'll figure it out when the time comes." If so, that would be a mistake! When users need access to data that has become corrupted or lost or in situations where a server is no longer functional, you will discover quickly how stressful and hostile those around you can become.

Here are just a few questions to consider when developing a recovery plan for your servers:

1. Who will be on the recovery team from IT and what will each of their recovery responsibilities be?
2. Do you know how many servers you have and where they are located (main office, branch office, and so on)?
3. Do you have a current network topology map that shows all critical servers, roles/features, IP addressing information, and network connections?
4. Do you have the specs on each server (memory, drive space, and volume info)? In other words, the information you need to know to rebuild the server from scratch?
5. Which server(s) will you need to recover first?
6. What is the step-by-step procedure for how the data recovery process will occur on each?
7. How will you know/test that things are back to normal after the restore?
8. When is the last time you performed a test restore to make sure your backups were working correctly?

When the time comes to restore a server, you need to decide whether you want to restore the entire system, restore a single volume, or spend some time trying to troubleshoot the problem and hopefully get the server back into production. The option you choose depends upon the situation you find yourself in at the time.

In this lesson, you look at how to address and perform some of the most common restores you will experience when running Windows Server 2012 R2. The backups that you restore from were created in Lesson 8, "Configuring and Managing Backups."

Restoring Files and Folders

Windows Server provides two options when it comes to restoring files and folders. You can take advantage of the Previous Version option if shadow copies are available or use Windows Server Backup to restore your data.

If a user accidentally deletes or overwrites a file or folder on a network share, you have two options for restoring the data:

- Access the share and restore the previous version.
- Use Windows Server Backup to restore the data.

The simplest approach for restoring files is to access the share and restore the previous version of the file. Of course, this assumes you enabled Shadow Copies for Shared Volumes (SCSV) on the volume prior to the point in time the data was deleted. As you recall from Lesson 8, SCSV uses the capabilities of the Volume Shadow Copy Service (VSS) to capture and store copies of folders and files (located on a shared network resource) at a specific point in time. The previous version of the file, which is read-only until it is restored, comes from shadow copies that are saved automatically on the server.

When working with previous versions of files, you have two options: copy a previous version of the file to a new location or restore a previous version of the file.

If you select *Copy*, you will be prompted to select a new location. The file's permissions will default to those of the directory where you place the file. The following lists the basic steps to copy a previous version of the file:

1. Connect to the shared folder.
2. Right-click the folder and select *Restore previous versions.*
3. Select the version of the file you want to copy from the Previous Versions tab and click *Copy.*
4. Select the place where you want to copy the file to.
5. Select *Copy.*
6. Select *OK* to close.

CERTIFICATION READY
Restore from backups.
Objective 3.2

If you choose restore, you will delete the current version and restore the file to the state it was in at the date and time you selected. This means any changes that were made after that time will be lost, but the file retains its permission settings. The following lists the basic steps to restore a previous version of the file:

1. Connect to the shared folder.
2. Right-click the folder and select *Restore previous versions.*
3. Select the version of the file you want to restore from the Previous Versions tab and click *Restore.*
4. Read the prompt and click *Restore.*

You can store a maximum of 64 copies per volume. Once you reach the limit, the oldest shadow copy will be permanently deleted.

If you did not enable shadow copies on the volume, you can use the Windows Server Backup program to restore the data. Windows Server Backup provides similar options when it comes to restoring your data. You can overwrite the existing data or restore a copy with a different name. You can also determine whether you want to restore permissions to the file or folder that you are recovering.

The following lists the basic steps to restore a previous version of a file previously backed up from the local computer, to its original location overwriting existing versions with the recovered version:

1. Open *Server Manager* and select *Tools* > *Windows Server Backup.*
2. Select *Local Backup.*
3. Click *Recover* under the Actions pane.
4. Select the location of the backup (local server).
5. Select the backup you want to restore by date/time.
6. Select *Files and Folders* on the Select Recovery Type page.
7. Select the files to be restored.
8. Specify that the files will be restored to their original location.
9. Select *Overwrite the existing versions with the recovered versions.*
10. Verify your selections and click *Recover.*

RESTORE A FILE USING SCSV

GET READY. To restore a file using the Copy option, perform the following steps:

1. Log in to Server02 with administrative privileges.
2. Select the Windows logo key + R and enter the following command in the *Run* dialog box, to view the shared folders on Server01:

   \\server01
3. Right-click the CorpDocs shared folder and select Restore previous versions.
4. Select the CorpDocs folder with the latest date modified and click Copy (see Figure 9-1).

TAKE NOTE*

This exercise uses a folder created on Server01 in Lesson 8.

Figure 9-1

Selecting the latest date modified for the CorpDocs folder

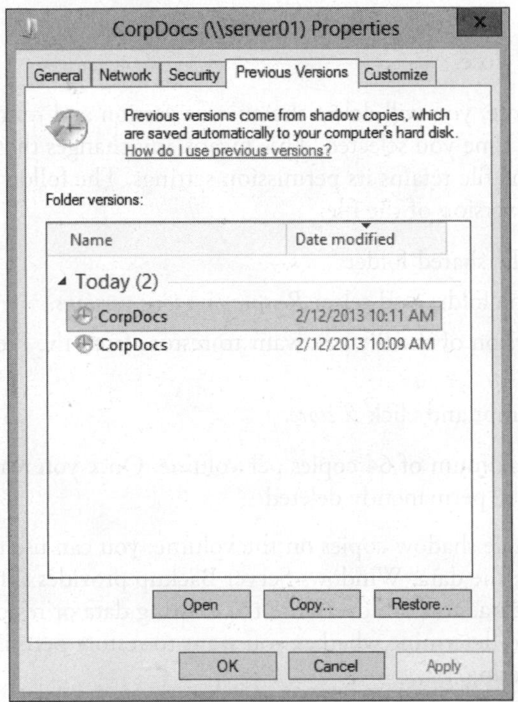

5. Select Desktop as the place where you want to copy the Agenda.txt file to, and then click Copy.
6. Click OK.

Restoring Volumes

The approach used to restore a volume depends on the type of volume you need to recover. Data volumes can be restored using Windows Server Backup, whereas system volumes require you to use the WinRE and Windows installation media.

If the volume you lose contains data only and you still have access to the operating system, you can perform the restore using Windows Server Backup.

CERTIFICATION READY
Restore from backups.
Objective 3.2

To restore a system volume, you must restore using the ***Windows Recovery Environment (WinRE)*** and the Windows installation media. WinRE provides a set of utilities that can assist you in troubleshooting and recovering a system that will not boot due to problems with the operating system files, services, and device drivers.

Here are a few things to keep in mind when restoring a system volume:

- The server's hardware must not have changed and your data volumes must still be operational.
- The server's current system volume will be erased and replaced with the restored system volume.
- If there are any data volumes on the same disk that contain the system volumes, they will be erased as part of the restore process.

RESTORE A DATA VOLUME

GET READY. To restore a data volume on Server01, perform the following steps:

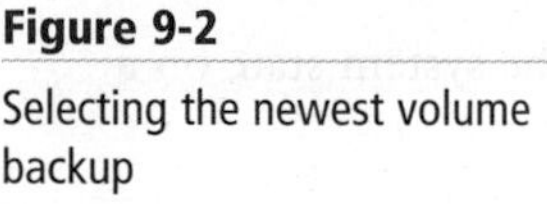

TAKE NOTE*

This exercise uses the \\server02\Volbackup created in Lesson 8.

1. Log in to Server01 and open Server Manager.
2. Select Tools > Computer Management.
3. Expand Storage and select Disk Management.
4. Right-click the CorpData volume (E:\) and select Delete Volume.
5. Select Yes after reading the warning message.
6. Create a new volume that is the same size or larger than the previous Corpdata volume, assign it the letter (E:\), and name it CorpData.
7. Expand Windows Server Backup under the *Storage* node and select Local Backup.
8. Select Recover under the *Actions* pane.
9. Select a backup stored on another location and click Next.
10. Select Remote shared folder for the location type and click Next.
11. Enter \\server02\volbackup and click Next.
12. Select the newest available backup (see Figure 9-2) and click Next.

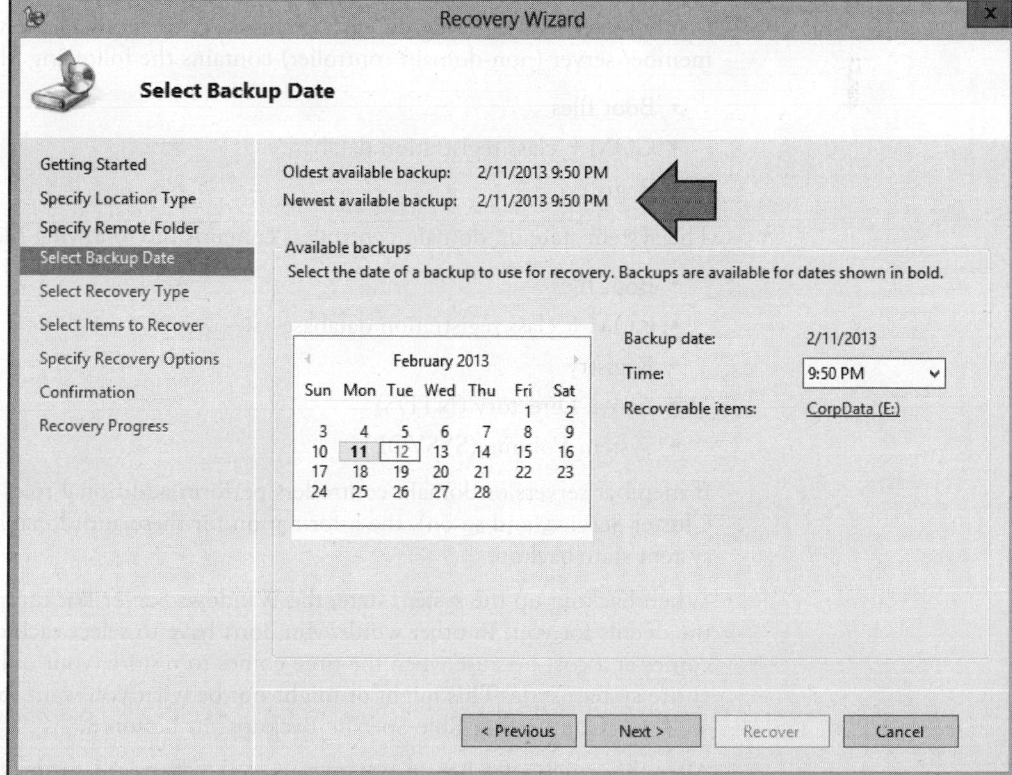

Figure 9-2

Selecting the newest volume backup

13. Select Volumes for the recovery type and click Next.
14. Select CorpData (E:) and click Next.
15. Select Corpdata (E:) as the *Source Volume* and select the drop-down arrow under *Destination Volume* to select the new volume you created in Step 6. Click Next to continue.
16. Select Yes to confirm you want to continue the recovery operation.
17. Click Recover.
18. Click Close once the volume has been recovered.
19. Select Disk Management and confirm the recovered volume shows as healthy.
20. Right-click the recovered volume and select Explore. You should see the sample folder/files you created in Lesson 8.

Restoring the System State

The system state includes the operating system configuration files. What is included in the system state differs depending upon the role(s) performed by the server. This also impacts the process used to restore the system state when the time comes.

The system state is included in the following backup configuration options:

- Full backups (recommended)
- Bare metal recovery backups
- System state backups

CERTIFICATION READY
Restore from backups.
Objective 3.2

In addition to regularly scheduled backups, you should also perform a manual backup prior to installing a new service pack, driver, or program on the server. In either case, you are preparing for the operating system crash that will inevitably happen.

Before we discuss restoring the system state, let's do a quick review. The system state on a member server (non-domain controller) contains the following files:

- Boot files
- COM+ class registration database
- Registry

The system state on domain controllers contains the following files:

- Boot files
- COM+ class registration database
- Registry
- Active Directory (NTDS)
- System Volume (SYSVOL)

If member servers or domain controllers perform additional roles (Certificate Services, IIS, Cluster Service, and so on), the information for these additional roles is also included in the system state backup.

When backing up the system state, the Windows Server Backup program will take care of the details for you. In other words, you don't have to select each component. Of course, this comes at a cost because when the time comes to restore, your only option is to restore the entire system state. This might or might not be what you want to do as discussed in the section, "Configuring Role-Specific Backups" in Lesson 8.

After this quick refresher on system state, let's take a look at the steps needed to restore the system state on a member server.

RESTORING THE SYSTEM STATE ON A MEMBER SERVER

Recovering the system state of a member server can be performed via the Windows Server Backup program. The following steps are typically performed after you replace the faulty hardware and install the Windows operating system:

1. Log in to the member server and open *Server Manager.*
2. Select *Tools > Windows Server Backup.*
3. Select *Local Backup* and then select *Recover* from the Actions pane.
4. Select the location where the backup is stored.
5. Select the specific backup you want to restore by date/time.
6. Select system state as the recovery type option.
7. Select the location to restore to.
8. Review your selections and select *Recover.*
9. Reboot the server and confirm functionality.
10. Perform a full backup.

RESTORING THE SYSTEM STATE ON A DOMAIN CONTROLLER

Recovering the system state of a domain controller requires that you boot into ***Directory Service Restore Mode (DSRM).*** DSRM is a special boot mode that is used to repair and recover Active Directory. To log in to DSRM, you need to have the password created when you first promoted the server to a domain controller. This password, which is unique to each domain controller, is required to take its copy of Active Directory offline.

There are two ways you can configure your server to boot into DSRM:

- Use msconfig to configure the server to reboot into DSRM.
- Enter the following from a command prompt:

  ```
  bcdedit /set safeboot dsrepair
  ```

  If you use the bcdedit command, you can return the server to normal boot by entering the following:

  ```
  bcdedit /deletevalue safeboot
  ```

Regardless of the method you use to prepare the server to boot into DSRM, you need to log in with the local administrator account and use the DSRM password. For example, if you are logging in to restore the system state on a domain controlled named *RWDC01,* don't log in as CONTOSO\Administrator but as RWDC01\Administrator.

Once logged in, you can open the Windows Server Backup or wbadmin.exe to start the recovery process. The process is similar to recovering a system state on a member server. You need to tell the Windows Server Backup where the backup is stored (this server or another location), indicate the location type (local drive, remote shared folder), select from the available backups based on date/time, and select system state as the recovery type.

Once you make the previous decisions, things get a little more involved when it comes to restoring the system state on a domain controller. You need to decide whether you want to recover the system state of Active Directory to the original location or to an alternate location and determine whether you need to perform an authoritative restore.

NON-AUTHORITATIVE RESTORES

If you don't select the "perform an authoritative restore of Active Directory files" option, you're performing a ***non-authoritative restore.*** This means you are returning the domain controller to the state it was in when you performed the backup. The restored domain controller will then use normal replication with other replication partners (domain controllers) to gather information that was changed after the backup was taken. These changes overwrite the state you restored and bring the domain controller up to date with the current copy of the Active Directory database.

AUTHORITATIVE RESTORES

Performing an ***authoritative restore*** provides you with the ability to increment the version number of the object in Active Directory you want to restore. This object will then appear to be newer than the existing version of the same object being held by the other replication partners (domain controllers). Because the object appears as newer, it will be replicated to the other domain controllers and overwrite their data.

You perform an authoritative restore when someone accidentally deletes one or more objects and the change is replicated to other domain controllers. For example, let's say you ask one of your administrators to delete a specific user's account. When performing the task, the administrator selects the organizational unit (OU) containing the account instead and deletes it. By the time you discover what happened, the change has been replicated to all the other domain controllers. Assuming you did not have Active Directory Recycle Bin enabled prior to this event, you have a new item on your To Do list—performing an authoritative restore.

To perform an authoritative restore, you need to boot into DSRM and use the Ntdsutil.exe tool. ***Ntdsutil.exe*** is a command-line tool used to access and manage an Active Directory database. The authoritative restore consists of two steps.

1. Perform the non-authoritative restore from your backup.
2. Perform the authoritative restore of the deleted object(s).

Once the non-authoritative restore of the system state is complete and the server reboots into DSRM mode, you open a command window and enter the following to restore an OU named *Sales* and all objects beneath it in the Contoso.com domain. (Press *Enter* after each command.)

```
C:>Ntdsutil
Ntdsutil: Activate Instance NTDS
Ntdsutil: Authoritative Restore
Restore subtree "cn=OU,dc=contoso,dc=com"
```

Once the object is restored, you can reboot the server and confirm the change has been made and replicated to your other domain controllers.

When performing this type of restore, you should realize that the restore can produce some unexpected results. If you restore a user account, the password will default to what it was at the time of the backup. If the user password was changed since the last backup and other services and accounts are configured to use it, they will fail to authenticate because the older object along with its previous attributes will be seen as authoritative. The restore can also impact things such as changes to home directories, profile paths, and group membership that were made after the backup. The general rule of thumb is to restore the smallest unit necessary in the Active Directory tree when performing an authoritative restore. This helps you to avoid these types of issues.

RESTORE THE SYSTEM STATE OF A DOMAIN CONTROLLER

GET READY. To restore the system state of a domain controller (RWDC01), perform the following steps:

> **TAKE NOTE***
> This exercise uses the \\server02\ADbackup created in Lesson 8.

1. Log in to RWDC01 with administrative privileges.
2. Select Windows logo key + R and enter msconfig in the *Run* dialog box and press Enter.
3. Select the Boot tab and check Safe boot under *Boot* options and *Active Directory Repair.*
4. Click OK and select Restart when prompted.

5. Log in as RWDC01\Administrator using the DSRM password for your domain controller.
6. Select Tools > Windows Server Backup from within *Server Manager*.
7. Select Local Backup and then Recover from the *Actions* pane.
8. Select a backup stored on another location and click Next.
9. Select Remote shared folder and click Next.
10. Enter \\server02\ADbackup and click Next.
11. Select the newest available backup and click Next.
12. Select System state and click Next.
13. Select Original location and click Next.
14. Click OK after reading the message regarding the need to re-synchronize after recovery.
15. Click OK to continue after reading the message about recovering the system state over network connections.
16. Click Recover.
17. Click Yes when prompted that system state cannot be paused or cancelled once it has started.
18. Restart the server once the system state restore has completed.
19. Log in as RWDC01\Administrator using the DSRM password for your domain controller.
20. Select Enter to continue after logging back in.
21. Select Windows logo key + R and enter msconfig in the *Run* dialog box.
22. Select the Boot tab, uncheck Safe boot, and click OK.
23. Select Restart.
24. Log in to the domain controller with administrative credentials (for example, contoso\administrator).
25. Open Server Manager and review all roles/services via the dashboard to confirm that the domain controller has been restored successfully. Remember, in a production environment, you should always follow this procedure with a full backup of the server once it's operational.

In the previous exercise, you used the Windows Server Backup program to restore the system state created originally using wbadmin.exe. Wbadmin.exe can also be used to restore the backup by using the following command after booting into DSRM:

```
Wbadmin start systemstaterecovery -version:
02/13/2013-18:39 -backuptarget:\\server02\ADBackup
-machine:RWDC01 -quiet
```

To obtain the version number for the backup, you need to enter the following command. This returns a list of the backups performed on RWDC01 along with their version identifiers and share labels:

```
wbadmin get versions
```

To perform an authoritative restore using wbadmin, you need to add the `-authsysvol` parameter to the command. Adding the `-quiet` parameter runs the command without prompting for user input.

RESTORING ACTIVE DIRECTORY OBJECTS USING THE ACTIVE DIRECTORY RECYCLE BIN

You can avoid performing lengthy authoritative restores using ntdsutil if you have the ***Active Directory Recycle Bin*** enabled before the Active Directory object was deleted. Active Directory Recycle Bin restores objects and their attributes in their entirety. This is possible due to a new Active Directory state that replaces tombstone states that were in previous versions of Active Directory.

When an Active Directory object is deleted, Active Directory creates a tombstone of the object. It then keeps the tombstone object(s) in the database for 180 days before the object is physically removed. Tombstones are replicated to all domain controllers in the Active Directory environment during this time period. Once Active Directory creates a tombstone of the object, the object is marked as deleted, renamed, and moved to the CN=Deleted Objects container and most of its attributes are removed.

With Active Directory Recycle Bin, a new deleted state is used in place of a tombstone. Active Directory Recycle Bin then moves the object to a recycled state when it expires (after 180 days). At this point, some of the attributes of the object are removed and the object is maintained for an additional 180 days before it is deleted.

As you recall from Lesson 8, you can determine whether the Active Directory Recycle Bin is enabled by using the following Windows PowerShell commands on the domain controller:

```
Get-ADOptionalFeature -filter *
```

Look for the EnabledScopes parameter:

```
EnabledScopes;
{CN=Partitions,CN=Configuration,DC=contoso,DC=com,
CN=NTDS Settings,CN=RWDC01,CN=Servers,CN=Default-
First-Site-Name,CN=Sites,
CN=Configuration,DC=contoso,DC=com
```

If EnabledScopes shows < > then Active Directory Recycle Bin is not enabled.

RESTORE A DELETED OU BY USING ACTIVE DIRECTORY RECYCLE BIN

GET READY. To restore a deleted OU on (RWDC01) by using the Active Directory Recycle Bin, perform the following steps:

1. Log in to RWDC01 with administrative privileges.
2. Open Server Manager and select Tools > Active Directory Administration Center.
3. Right-click the contoso (local) domain and select New > Organizational Unit.
4. Enter a name for the OU using the first initial from your first and last name followed by OUtest (for example, BWOUtest).
5. Uncheck the Protect from accidental deletion option. This allows you to test the restore function using Active Directory Recycle Bin.
6. Click OK and then confirm the OU appears.
7. Right-click the OU you created in the previous step and select New > User.
8. Create a new user. Enter a first name, last name, and the user's UPN logon name for the new user.
9. Create and confirm a password for the user account and click OK.
10. Right-click the OU you created and select Delete.
11. Click Yes when prompted to confirm the deletion of the OU.
12. Click Yes when prompted that the OU contains other objects.
13. Select the arrow next to the contoso (local) domain and then double-click Deleted objects.
14. Hold the Shift key down and select the OU you deleted as well as the user account and select Restore.

TAKE NOTE*

You must have the Active Directory Recycle Bin enabled from Lesson 8 before starting this exercise.

Performing a Bare Metal Recovery Restore

> **TAKE NOTE***
> Selecting *Restore* restores the objects to their original parent container. Selecting *Restore To* allows you to select another container for the restore target.

A bare metal recovery restore allows you to restore the server without having to load the operating system beforehand. It does require that you have your Windows installation media from which to boot.

When your server suffers a catastrophic failure, Windows Server 2012 R2 provides you with the option to perform a Bare Metal Restore.

Remember that bare metal recovery backup does not include your data volumes unless you specifically included them in your selection when you set up the backup job.

> **CERTIFICATION READY**
> Perform a Bare Metal Restore (BMR).
> Objective 3.2

Although most of the steps in the restore process are straight-forward, there is one point in the recovery process that you need to make a critical decision: whether or not you want to format and repartition your disks or only restore your system drives.

If you select to format and repartition disks, the restore process will delete and reformat the existing partitions on the target drive to be the same as the one included in the backup. You have the option to exclude disks if there are disks that you want to omit from the formatting and partitioning process. If you are restoring from a backup on a locally attached disk, it will automatically be excluded. If all disks are not visible when using the exclude disks option, you might need to use the *Install drivers* button to add the drivers for the storage device you are recovering to. To recover only the operating system, you can select the option to only restore system drives option.

The Advanced option allows you to indicate whether you want to automatically restart the server and determine whether you want to check the disks for errors after the recovery process is complete.

For example, if the disk that contains the operating system has failed and you are restoring to a new disk, *Format and repartition disks* will be the appropriate option. If the server is corrupt, refuses to start, and the disk that contains the system partitions is functional, then you should select to restore only system drives.

> **TAKE NOTE***
> You need to set up a VM without an operating system installed and use the *\\server02\BMbackup* you created during Lesson 8 to complete this exercise. The existing VM (Server01) should be shut down before the new VM is started.

PERFORM A BARE METAL RESTORE OF A SERVER

GET READY. To complete a bare metal recovery of Server01 onto another server VM, perform the following steps:

1. Open Hyper-V Manager and create a new virtual machine (VM).
2. Insert a DVD with the Windows Server installation files or configure the appropriate ISO image file to use in the settings for the VM machine.
3. Start the new VM.
4. Select Next after confirming the language, time/currency format, and keyboard or input methods.
5. Select Repair your computer.
6. Select the Troubleshoot tile.
7. Select the System Image Recovery tile.
8. Close the *Re-image your computer* dialog box and click Next.
9. Select the Advanced button and click Search for a system image on the network.
10. Select Yes when asked if you want to connect to the network.
11. Enter the path to the system image: \\server02\BMBackup and click OK.

12. Enter a user name and password to connect to the share on Server02 (for example, Administrator) and its associated password, and click OK.
13. Select the image and click Next.
14. Select the date and time of the system image to restore and click Next.
15. Select Format and repartition disks.
16. Click Next to continue.
17. Review the information provided and click Finish.
18. Select Yes when prompted that all disks to be restored will be formatted and replaced with the layout and data in the system image.
19. Log in with administrative credentials once the server reboots.
20. Confirm the server is operational.

Recovering Servers Using WinRE and Safe Mode

If you experience problems that prevent Windows Server 2012 R2 from booting, you can use the Windows Recovery Environment (WinRE) to troubleshoot and repair the system.

CERTIFICATION READY
Recover servers using Windows Recovery Environment (WinRE) and safe mode.
Objective 3.2

There are several ways to access the Windows Recovery Environment (WinRE) in Windows Server 2012 R2:

- The server enters WinRE in situations after two consecutive failed attempts to start Windows, after two consecutive shutdowns that were unexpected, or due to secure boot errors. Secure boot is a security feature built into Windows Server that captures a signature of the operating system. Windows checks against the signature the last time it booted up. If the signatures don't match, the system enters WinRE.
- Select *Settings* from the Charms bar, choose *Power*, and click *Restart* while holding down the *Shift* key.
- Boot the server from Windows installation media and select *Repair Computer*.
- Enter the command `shutdown /r /o` from a command prompt.

Upon entering the WinRE environment, you have the following options as shown in Figure 9-3:

Figure 9-3
Exploring the Windows Recovery Environment (WinRE)

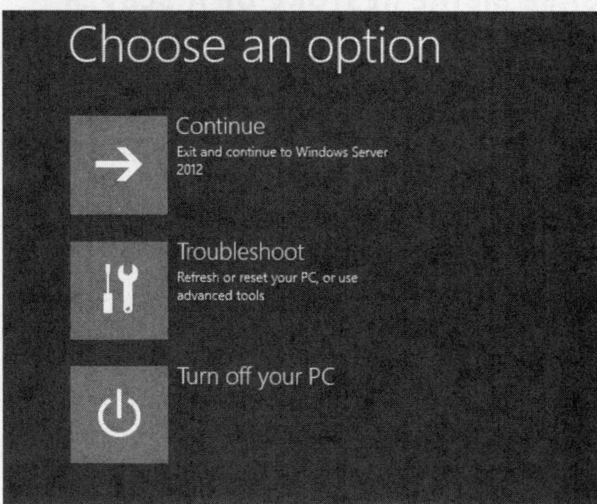

- **Continue:** Exits the WinRE environment and continues to the Windows Server 2012 R2 operating system.
- **Turn off PC:** Shuts down the server.
- **Troubleshoot:** Provides access to the following tools as shown in Figure 9-4.

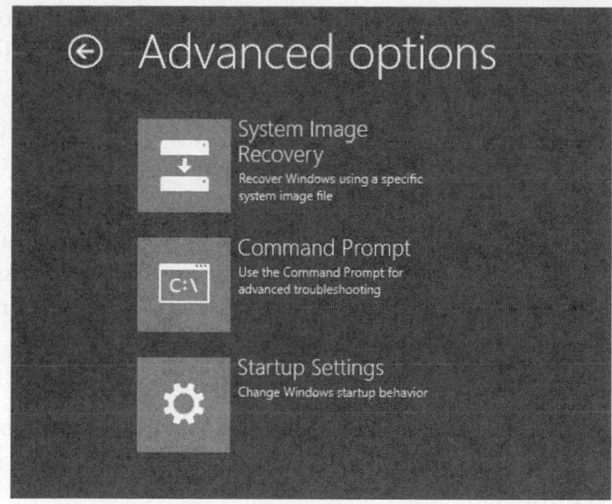

Figure 9-4

Troubleshooting using the Windows Recovery Environment (WinRE) tools

- **System Image Recovery:** Restores the entire system to a previous state by using an image created by Windows Backup. This option should be used only after you try other options and assumes you have a current backup of your server to restore from.
- **Command Prompt:** Provides command-line access with administrator privileges to the Windows Server file system. You can use it for tools such as Diskpart, System File Checker, bootrec, bcdedit, and format.
- **Startup Settings:** Provides access to the Advanced Boot options menu.

From the Advanced Boot Options menu (see Figure 9-5), you can select from the following:

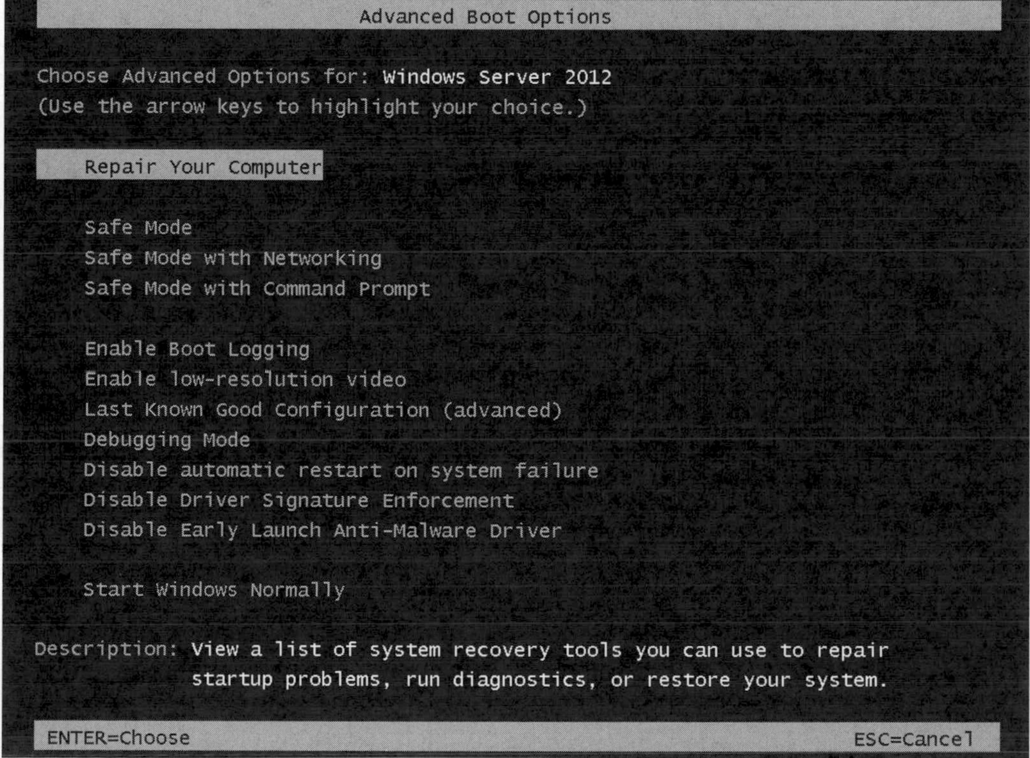

Figure 9-5

Understanding the Advanced Boot Options menu

- **Repair Your Computer:** Provides a list of system recovery tools that you can use to repair your system, run diagnostics, or restore your system (for example, System Image Recovery, Command Prompt, and Startup Settings).
- **Start Safe Mode:** Starts Windows using only the core drivers and services. This option should be used when you cannot boot after the installation of a new driver and/or device.
- **Start Safe mode with Networking:** Similar to safe mode but with networking support. Use this option to create a network connection to gain access to files on servers, connect and compare settings on other computers, and use the Internet to download updates.
- **Start Safe mode with Command Prompt:** Similar to safe mode but opens a command prompt.
- **Enable Boot Logging:** Creates ntbt.log.txt that lists all of the drivers that are loaded during setup. This includes the last driver loaded before the system failed. It's stored in the %systemroot%.
- **Enable low resolution video:** Starts Windows in low resolution display mode; allows you to set or reset the display resolution.
- **Last Known Good Configuration (advanced):** Starts Windows using the settings from the last time that Windows booted successfully.
- **Debugging Mode:** Enables the Windows kernel debugger.
- **Disable automatic restart on system failure:** The settings here prevent Windows from automatically rebooting after a crash.
- **Disable Driver Signature Enforcement:** Allows drivers containing improper signatures to be loaded.
- **Disable Early Launch Anti-Malware Driver:** Allows drivers to initialize without being measured by the anti-malware driver.

EXPLORING COMMAND-LINE TOOLS

If you select the Command Prompt option, you have access to several different tools that can assist you in recovering a server that will not boot into the operating system:

- **Bootrec:** Troubleshoots and repairs the master boot record, boot sector, and Boot Configuration Data (BCD) store.
- **Bcdedit:** Displays how Windows is configured to boot and can also be used to troubleshoot issues with the Windows Boot Manager.
- **Format:** Formats partitions.
- ***System File Checker:*** Checks the integrity of your hard drive. If a file is missing or corrupt, it can be restored with this tool. SFC validates the digital signatures of all the Windows system files and restores any that it finds that are incorrect.
  - **Sfc /scannow:** Scans all of your protected system files and repair problems it finds by replacing incorrect versions with the correct Microsoft versions.
  - **Sfc /verifyonly:** Scans for integrity of all protected system files but does not perform a repair operation.
- **Diskpart:** Loads the Windows Disk management program. Using this program, you can shrink, expand, create, and delete existing partitions as well as gather information about your hard drives.

BOOTING INTO SAFE MODE

In Windows Server 2012 R2, you can boot into safe mode by using one of the options discussed previously. Starting in ***safe mode*** allows you to troubleshoot situations where you cannot access the system due to faulty hardware, software, device drivers, and virus infections.

Safe mode loads a minimal set of drivers and services; therefore, if you can boot into safe mode but can't boot normally, the system most likely has a conflict with hardware settings, services, drivers, or some type of registry corruption.

Once you can access your system via safe mode, you should check the event viewer (System and Application logs) for errors. You can also run the Windows System Information tool (msinfo32.exe) to gather details about the computer, operating system, and software including drivers. You can also search for problem devices.

You can review the ntbtlog located in the %systemroot% folder. You can open this file using a text editor (Notepad) to review the devices and services that loaded and did not load. The file shows the path of each item and identifies them as BOOTLOG_LOADED or BOOTLOG_NOT_LOADED.

Another option is to run MSConfig and use the process of elimination to identify the source of the problem that is keeping Windows from booting correctly. ***MSConfig*** (also called *System Configuration)* is a tool used to troubleshoot the system startup process (see Figure 9-6). It can be used to disable or enable, software, device drivers, and services that run at startup. MSconfig can also be used to change boot parameters if necessary.

Figure 9-6

Using MSConfig to troubleshoot

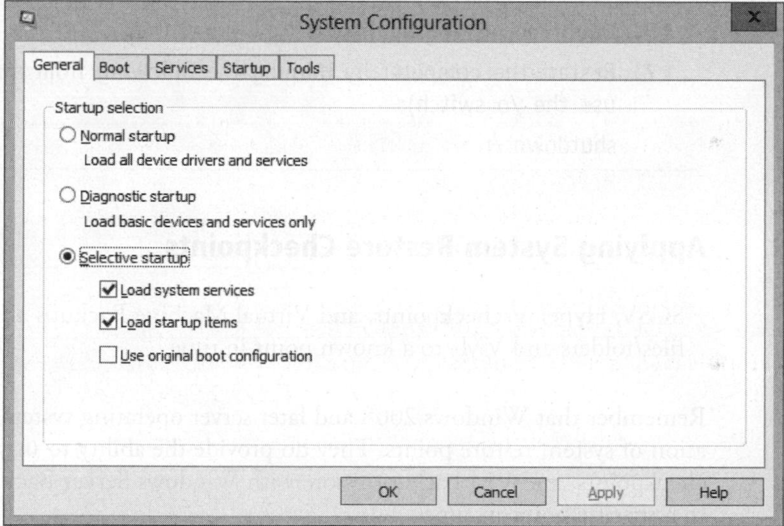

The general process for troubleshooting using MSConfig is as follows:

1. Start Windows in Diagnostic startup mode in the General tab. If the problem occurs during a diagnostic startup, files and drivers are suspect. If the problem does not occur, proceed to Step 2.
2. Start Windows in Select startup mode in the General tab.
3. Select the services tab and disable each service one at a time and restart the server. If the problem does not go away, you can eliminate the services as the source.
4. Select the *Startup* tab and turn off all startup items except the first one. Reboot the server. This process can be used to isolate a startup item.

BOOT INTO SAFE MODE

GET READY. To boot into safe mode on Server01, perform the following steps:

1. Log in to Server01 and enter the following at a command prompt: shutdown /r /o
2. Select Close when prompted the system will shutdown in less than a minute.

TAKE NOTE*

The /r switch tells the server to restart; the /o option tells the server to end the current Windows session and open the Advanced Boot options menu.

3. Select the Troubleshoot tile.
4. Select the Startup Settings tile.
5. Select Restart.
6. Select Safe Mode and press Enter.
7. Enter the password for the Administrator account and press Enter.
8. Confirm your system is now in safe mode. The word "safe mode" should appear on each corner of your desktop.
9. Select the Windows logo key + R to open the *Run* dialog box.
10. Enter MSConfig and select OK.
11. Review each tab of the *System Configuration* tool for options you can configure and then close the dialog box.
12. Select the Windows logo key + R to open the *Run* dialog box.
13. Enter compmgmt.msc to open the *Computer Management* console.
14. Expand Event Viewer > Windows logs and review the *System and Application* logs. Close the *Computer Management* console.
15. Use File Explorer to navigate to %systemroot% and locate the ntbtlog.txt file.
16. Open the ntbtlog.txt file to view its contents.
17. Restart the computer by running the following from a command prompt (do not use the /o switch):

    shutdown /r

Applying System Restore Checkpoints

SCSV, Hyper-V checkpoints, and Virtual Machine Backups all offer options for returning files/folders and VMs to a known point in time.

Remember that Windows 2008 and later server operating systems do not support the creation of system restore points. They do provide the ability to use the SCSV feature, Hyper-V checkpoints, and VM backup/restore with Windows Server Backup as options for returning to a specific point in time.

In the section, "Restoring the Previous Version of a File using Shadow Copies and Windows Server Backup," you learn the steps necessary to copy and restore a previous version of a file that was stored on a volume protected by SCSV.

You now turn your attention to the steps needed to return a VM to the previous checkpoints (called ***reverting***) or to a selected checkpoint and use Windows Server Backup to restore a VM.

RETURNING A VM TO A PREVIOUS STATE

To return a VM to the last checkpoint that was taken, you can use the Revert option. The steps are as follows:

1. Log on to the server with administrative privileges.
2. Open *Server Manager* and select *Tools > Hyper-V Manager.*
3. Select the VM host that manages the VMs.
4. Highlight the VM.
5. Select *Revert* from the Actions pane.
6. Click *Revert* when asked if you are sure you want to revert this virtual machine to its previous checkpoint.

Selecting the Revert option returns the VM to the state and the configuration it was at the time the last checkpoint was taken. This process does not change the hierarchy of the tree and continues to show all checkpoint taken of the VM. To return to a specific checkpoint, you need to perform the following steps:

1. Log on to the server with administrative privileges.
2. Open *Server Manager* and select *Tools* > *Hyper-V Manager*.
3. Select the VM host that manages the VMs.
4. Highlight the VM.
5. Select the checkpoint you want to return to.
6. Select *Apply* from the Actions pane.
7. Select *Apply*.

RESTORING VMS USING WINDOWS SERVER BACKUP

The process for restoring VMs using Windows Server Backup involves the following steps:

1. Open *Server Manager* and select *Tools* > *Windows Server Backup*.
2. Select *Recover* from the Actions pane.
3. Choose the server you want to recover the backup from.
4. Select the date/time of the backup you want to restore.
5. Select *Applications* recovery type.
6. Select *Hyper-V*.
7. Select the restore location.
8. Click *Recover*.

Configuring the Boot Configuration Data Store

The Boot Configuration Data (BCD) store, a replacement for the boot.ini file in previous releases, stores boot configuration information.

CERTIFICATION READY
Configure the Boot Configuration Data (BCD) store.
Objective 3.2

The ***Boot Configuration Data (BCD) store*** contains information that controls how your server boots. It replaces the boot.ini text file that was used in Windows Server 2003 to manage the boot configuration information. The BCD store is located in the \Boot\Bcd directory on BIOS-based operating systems and on the Extensible Firmware Interface (EFI) system partition on EFI-based systems.

Windows Boot Manager displays a list of boot loader entries when your server boots. When you select one of these entries, the Windows Boot Manager loads the system specific boot loader for that operating system and passes those parameters for that boot entry to the system-specific boot loader. The boot loader then loads the operating system based on the parameters it finds.

Because the BCD store is a binary file, you can't modify it by using a standard text editor such as Notepad. Instead, you need to use the ***Boot Configuration Data Editor (bcdedit.exe)*** tool from a command prompt. Here are a few things you can do with bcdedit.exe:

- Add, modify, and delete entries in the BCD store.
- Import/Export entries to/from a BCD store.
- List the current settings of the BCD store.
- Apply a global change to all entries in the BCD store.
- Change the default time-out value.
- Query entries of a specific type in the BCD store.

To see the list of entries in BCD store, you can enter the following command:

```
Bcdedit /enum
```

In Figure 9-7, you can see the boot environment is split into two components:

- Windows Boot Manager
- Boot loaders/applications

Figure 9-7

Viewing the BCD store with only one operating system loaded

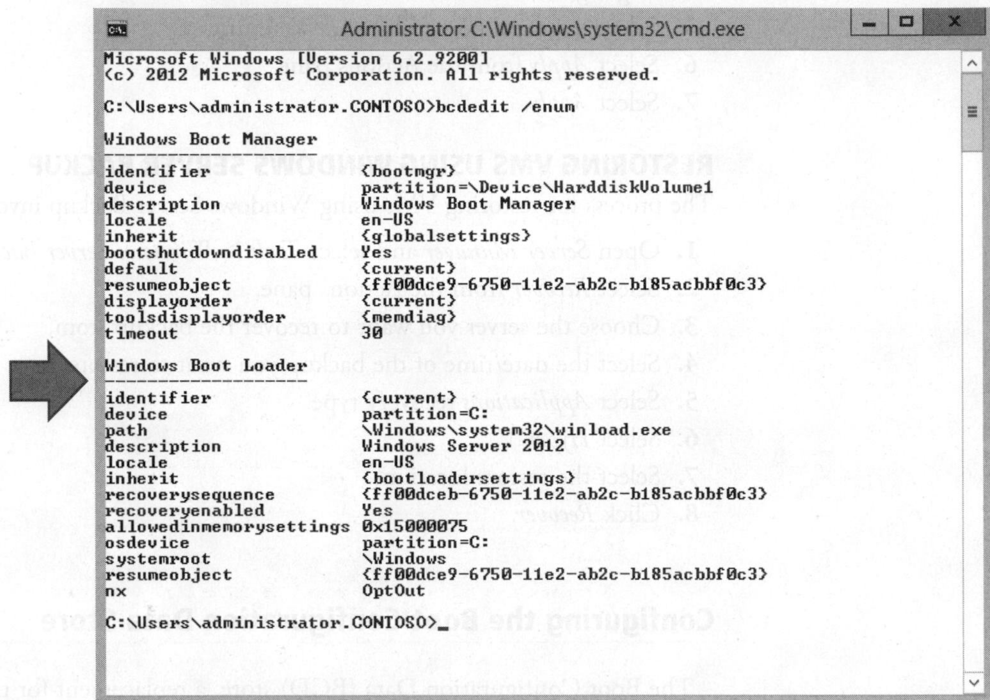

The ***Windows Boot Manager*** makes it possible for you to choose which boot loader/application to load. A ***boot loader/application*** is a small program that moves the operating system into memory. In Figure 9-7, you see a computer that is running Windows Server 2012 R2 only; therefore, only one boot loader is listed. In situations where you are running multiple operating systems on the same system, you see more than one, as shown in Figure 9-8.

This is a client computer running both Windows 7 and Windows 8/8.1 in a multi-boot configuration. As you can see from the Figure 9-8, Windows Boot Manager displays two boot loaders.

Figure 9-8

Viewing the BCD store with more than one operating system

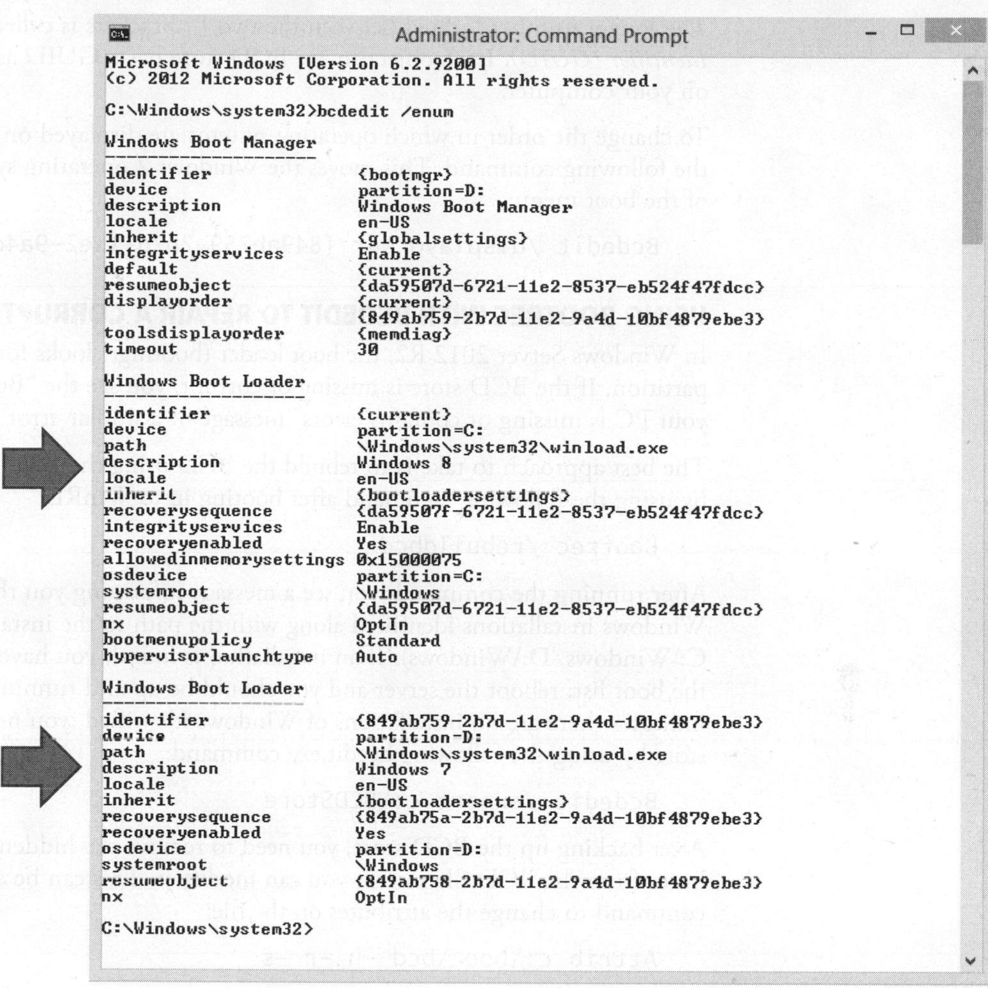

USING BCDEDIT TO MODIFY SETTINGS IN THE BCD STORE

`Bcdedit /timeout <value>` can be used to configure the length of time the computer waits until the default operating system loads. For example, in Figure 9-8, the multi-boot system is configured to boot to Windows 8.1 after 30 seconds pass. To change this setting to only wait for 10 seconds, you enter the following command:

```
bcdedit /timeout 10
```

To create a backup of this BCD store to a folder named *BcdStore* on drive D:\, you enter the following command:

```
bcdedit /export D:\BcdStore
```

You can use `bcdedit /import D:\BcdStore\bcdbackup` to import and restore the backup created using the /export switch.

In the previous multi-boot example, Windows 8.1 is configured as the default operating system to launch if you don't make a selection after the time-out value is reached (for example, 30 seconds). To make Windows 7 the default operating system to boot after the time-out value is reached, you enter the following command:

```
Bcdedit /default {849ab759-2b7d-11e2-9a4d-10bf4879ebe3}
```

The longer number located between the two { } brackets is called a *Globally Unique Identifier (GUID)*. Each object in the BCD store has a GUID as well as every drive/partition on your computer.

To change the order in which operating systems are displayed on the boot menu, you can use the following command. This moves the Windows 7 operating system boot loader to the top of the boot menu:

```
Bcdedit /displayorder {849ab759-2b7d-11e2-9a4d-10bf4879ebe3}
```

USING BOOTREC WITH BCDEDIT TO REPAIR A CORRUPTED/MISSING BCD STORE

In Windows Server 2012 R2, the boot loader (bootmgr) looks for the BCD store on the active partition. If the BCD store is missing or corrupt, you see the "Boot Configuration Data for your PC is missing or contains errors" message or a similar error during the boot process.

The best approach to take is to rebuild the BCD using the ***Boot Recovery Tool (bootrec.exe)*** by using the following command after booting in to WinRE:

```
Bootrec /rebuildbcd
```

After running the command, you see a message informing you that there is one or more Windows installations identified along with the path to the installation(s) (for example, C:\Windows, D:\Windows). If an installation is found, you have the option to add it to the boot list; reboot the server and you should be up and running again. If the message indicates there are no installations of Windows identified, you need to export the BCD store by using the following bcdedit.exe command:

```
Bcdedit /export c:\BCDStore
```

After backing up the BCD store, you need to remove the hidden, read-only, and system attributes from the BCD file so that you can modify it. This can be done by using the attribute command to change the attributes on the file:

```
Attrib c:\boot\bcd -h -r -s
```

TAKE NOTE*

This exercise simulates a corruption of the BCD store allowing you to take the steps necessary to rebuild it. You need access to Windows Server installation media before starting this exercise.

After modifying the BCD file's attributes, rename the existing BCD store by using the Ren command:

```
Ren c:\boot\bcd bcd.old
```

Next, rebuild the BCD store by entering the following command:

```
Bootrec /rebuildbcd
```

Once the rebuild of the BCD store is completed successfully, you should see that a Windows installation was identified and be prompted to add the installation to the boot list. After doing so, reboot the server and you should be up and running. Refer to Table 9-1 for examples of common BCDedit command switches.

REBUILD A BCD STORE

GET READY. To rebuild a BCD store on Server01, perform the following steps:

TAKE NOTE*

The /r switch tells the server to restart; the /o option tells the server to end the current Windows session and open the Advanced Boot options menu.

1. Log in to Server01 and enter the following at a command prompt:

   shutdown /r /o
2. Select the Troubleshoot tile.
3. Select the Command Prompt tile.
4. Choose an account to continue.
5. Enter the password for the account you chose in the previous step and click Continue.

Table 9-1

Common BCDedit command switches

Command	Description
Commands that operate on the store	
/createstore	Creates a new empty boot configuration store.
/export	Exports the contents of the system store to a file. This file can be used later to restore the state of the system store.
/import	Restores the state of the system store using a backup file created with the /export command.
Commands that operate on entries in the store	
/copy	Makes copies of the entries of the store.
/create	Creates new entries in the store.
/delete	Deletes entries from the store.
/mirror	Creates a mirror of entries in the store.
Commands that control the boot manager	
/bootsequence	Sets the one-time boot sequence for the boot manager.
/default	Sets the default entry that the boot manager will use.
/displayorder	Sets the order in which the boot manager displays the multiboot menu.
/timeout	Sets the boot manager time-out value.

6. Type bcdedit /enum to view the boot loaders on Server01.
7. Export your current BCD database by typing the following and press Enter:

   bcdedit /export c:\BCDbkup
8. Remove the hidden, read-only, and system attributes from the BCD store file by typing the following and pressing Enter:

   attrib c:\boot\bcd -h -r -s
9. Rename the existing BCD store by typing the following and pressing Enter:

   Ren c:\boot\bcd bcd.old
10. Reboot the server and you will see the error message shown in Figure 9-9:

TAKE NOTE By rebooting the server at this point, you are able to simulate a missing BCD store because you renamed the current store to bcd.old. If you don't want to simulate this error, skip to Step 16 and rebuild the store.

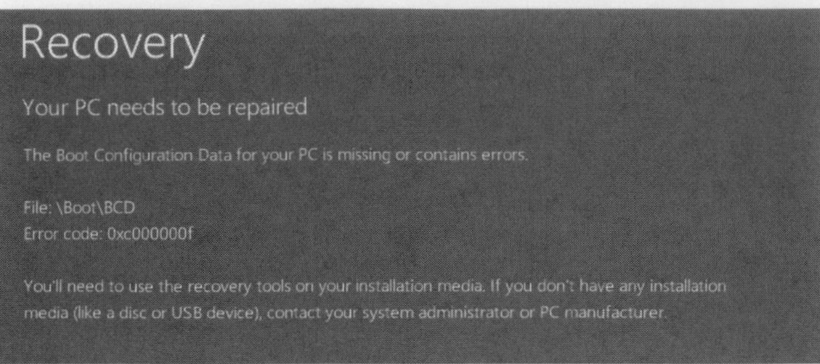

Figure 9-9
Receiving the error message that the BCD for your PC is missing or contains errors

11. Boot back into the server using installation media or by pointing your VM to the ISO image of the installation media.
12. Select Next to install the language, time, and keyboard input methods.
13. Select Repair your computer.
14. Select the Troubleshoot tile.
15. Select the Command Prompt tile.
16. Rebuild the BCD store by typing the following command:
    Bootrec /rebuildbcd
17. Select Yes when prompted to add the installation found to the boot list and press Enter.
18. Type Exit after the rebuild operation reports it was successful.
19. Select Continue from the options provided to boot into Windows Server.
20. Log in and confirm the server is operational.

SKILL SUMMARY

IN THIS LESSON YOU LEARNED:

- You should have a written plan when it comes to recovering your servers.
- Windows Server 2012 R2 provides two options when it comes to restoring files and folders: previous versions and Windows Server Backup.
- There are two options for recovering previous versions of files. You can copy the files to a new location where they will inherit the permissions of the target directory or restore the files, which means it deletes the current version while retaining the file's permission settings.
- The approach used to restore a volume depends upon the type of volume to recover. Data volumes can be restored using Windows Server backup, whereas system volumes require you to use the WinRE and Windows installation media.
- WinRE provides a set of utilities that can assist you in troubleshooting and recovering a system that will not boot due to problems with the operating system files, services, and device drivers.
- The system state includes the operating system configuration files. Additional items might be included depending upon the role of the server (for example, domain controller's system state includes NTDS and SYSVOL). The system state is included in full backups, bare metal recovery backups, and system state backups.
- Recovering the system state on a domain controller requires you to boot into Directory Service Restore Mode (DSRM).

- Non-authoritative restores means you are returning the domain controller to the state it was in when the backup was performed; the restored domain controller will then use normal replication with replication partners to obtain updated information.
- Authoritative restores are used when you want to restore an Active Directory object(s) that was accidentally deleted and the change has already replicated to other domain controllers. The goal of this type of restore is to overwrite the copies located on the other domain controllers.
- Ntds.util is used to perform an authoritative restore, whereas Active Directory Recycle Bin can be used to avoid the labor-intensive process used to perform an authoritative restore if it is enabled prior to the Active Directory object being deleted.
- Performing authoritative restores can impact passwords, home directory and profile paths, and group membership changes that occurred after the backup was made. To avoid these types of issues, always restore the smallest unit necessary to return your Active Directory to an operational state.
- A bare metal recovery restore allows you to restore a server without having to load the operating system beforehand. By default, a Bare Metal Restore includes only the system state, system reserved, and the critical volumes (those that hold the boot files, operating system and registry, SYSVOL, Active Directory database, and Active Directory database log files) unless you add the data volumes as part of the setup.
- There are several ways to access the Windows Recovery environment to troubleshoot problems keeping your system from booting: shut down /r /o, booting from the Windows installation media and selecting Repair Computer, selecting the Charms bar, choosing Power, and clicking Restart while holding down the SHIFT key.
- Booting into safe mode allows you to troubleshoot situations where you cannot access the system due to faulty hardware, software, device drivers, and virus infections. Once booted into safe mode, you can check system/application logs, run msinfo32.exe to gather details, review the ntbtlog file, and use MSConfig to troubleshoot and repair your server.
- You can use the Revert option within Hyper-V Manager to return to the previous checkpoint.
- Boot Configuration Data (BCD) store contains information that controls how your server boots. You can use Bcdedit and Bootrec to make modifications to the store as well as repair a corrupted/missing BCD store.

■ Knowledge Assessment

Multiple Choice

Select the correct answer for each of the following questions.

1. When restoring files protected by SCSV, which of the following statements are true? (Select all that apply.)
   a. Copying a file causes it to lose its original permission settings
   b. Copying a file allows it to retain its original permission settings
   c. Restoring a file causes it to lose its original permission settings
   d. Restoring a file allows it to retain its original permission settings

2. What is the maximum number of shadow copies allowed per volume?
   a. 24
   b. 128
   c. 64
   d. unlimited
3. Which of the following statements is incorrect regarding restoring a system volume?
   a. The server's hardware must not have changed and your data volumes must still be operational
   b. The server's current system volume will be erased
   c. If there are any data volumes on the same disk that contains the system volumes, they are erased as part of the restore process
   d. If there are any data volumes on the same disk that contains the system volumes, they will not be erased as part of the restore process
4. You would like to recover the system state for a member server from a backup. Which backup types include them by default? (Select all that apply.)
   a. full backups
   b. system state backups
   c. bare metal backups
   d. simple volume backups
5. Which command can be used to boot into a special mode that allows you to repair and recover Active Directory?
   a. bcdedit /set safeboot dsrepair
   b. bcdedit /set safeboot dsrm
   c. bcdedit /set safeboot ad repair
   d. bcdedit /set safeboot repairDS
6. Someone accidentally deleted an organizational unit (OU) in Active Directory. What type of restore do you need to perform if you do not have Active Directory Recycle Bin enabled?
   a. non-authoritative restore
   b. ntdsutil.exe restore
   c. authoritative restore
   d. ntdsutil.exe auth restore
7. What is the maximum number of days you can fully recover an Active Directory-deleted object and all of its attributes if you have Active Directory Recycle Bin enabled?
   a. 60 days
   b. 180 days
   c. 30 days
   d. 360 days
8. Which of the following are inaccurate statements regarding performing a bare metal recovery restore? (Select all that apply.)
   a. You can restore cross architecture
   b. You can recover to a server that has the different hardware
   c. You will include the system state, system reserved, and critical volumes by default
   d. If you are restoring from a backup that is on the server's locally attached disk, that disk will be excluded automatically from being formatted if you select Format and repartition disks

9. Which of the following command-line tools can be used to display the boot loader/applications configured on a server?
   a. bcdedit.exe
   b. bootrec
   c. sfc /verify
   d. diskpart

10. Which of the following would you select, within Hyper-V Manager, to return a virtual machine (VM) to the last checkpoint that was taken after selecting the VM in the console?
   a. Action Menu > Apply
   b. Action Menu > Return
   c. Action Menu > Revert
   d. Action Menu > Undo

Best Answer

Choose the letter that corresponds to the best answer. More than one answer choice may achieve the goal. Select the BEST answer.

1. Which tool provides you with the best information on which devices and services were loaded and not loaded during startup?
   a. Device Manager
   b. ntbtlog
   c. Computer Management console
   d. Netstart

2. What tools should be used to rebuild a corrupted BCD store?
   a. Full backup restore using Windows Server Backup
   b. bcdedit / bootrec
   c. Bare metal recovery restore
   d. bcedit

3. Which of the following allows you to set the length of time the computer waits to load the default operating system to 10 seconds?
   a. bcdedit
   b. bcdedit /timeout
   c. bcdedit /timeout 10
   d. bcconfig /timeout 10

4. Which of the following files are included as part of the system state on a member server after a default installation?
   a. Boot files, COM+ class registration database, Registry, NTDS
   b. Boot files, COM+ class registration database, Registry, SYSVOL
   c. Boot files, COM+ class registration database, SYSVOL, NTDS
   d. Boot files, COM+ class registration database, Registry

5. You have just rebooted a server named *DC01*, which is part of the Contoso.com domain into DSRM. Which of the following will you use to log in and restore the system state?
   a. Contoso\Administrator
   b. DC01\Admin
   c. DC01\Administrator
   d. Contoso.com\Admin

Build a List

1. Identify the ten basic steps in order to restore the system state on a member server using Windows Server Backup.
   _____ Select the location to restore to
   _____ Select Local Backup and then select Recover on Actions pane
   _____ Review your selections and select Recover
   _____ Log in to the member server and open Server Manager
   _____ Select system state as the recovery type option
   _____ Select the specific backup you want to restore by date/time
   _____ Select Tools > Windows Server Backup
   _____ Select the location where the backup is stored
   _____ Reboot the server and confirm functionality
   _____ Perform a full backup

2. Identify the four steps that must be completed to restore a previous version of a file.
   _____ Read the prompt and click Restore
   _____ Right-click the folder and select Restore previous versions
   _____ Connect to the shared folder
   _____ Select the version of the file you want to restore from the Previous Versions tab and click Restore

3. Identify the commands in the order they will be used to rebuild the BCD store.
   _____ shutdown /r /o
   _____ attrib c:\boot\bcd –h –r –s
   _____ bcdedit /export c:\BCDbkup
   _____ Ren c:\boot\bcd bcd.old
   _____ Bootrec /rebuildbcd

4. Identify the seven basic steps in order to return to a specific checkpoint in Hyper-V Manager.
   _____ Select Apply
   _____ Select Apply form the Actions pane
   _____ Select the checkpoint you want to return to
   _____ Highlight the VM
   _____ Select the VM host that manages the VMs
   _____ Open Server Manager and select Tools > Hyper-V Manager
   _____ Log on to the server with administrative privileges

Choose an Option

1. A junior administrator has accidentally deleted the Sales OU and the change has replicated to all of the domain controller's replication partners. You do not have Active Directory Recycle Bin enabled and have decided to restore the system state. Which option would you select to make sure the Sales OU is restored correctly so that it is recreated on all of the replication partners? Refer to Figure 9-10, which shows the dialog box in its default state.

Figure 9-10

Restoring system state

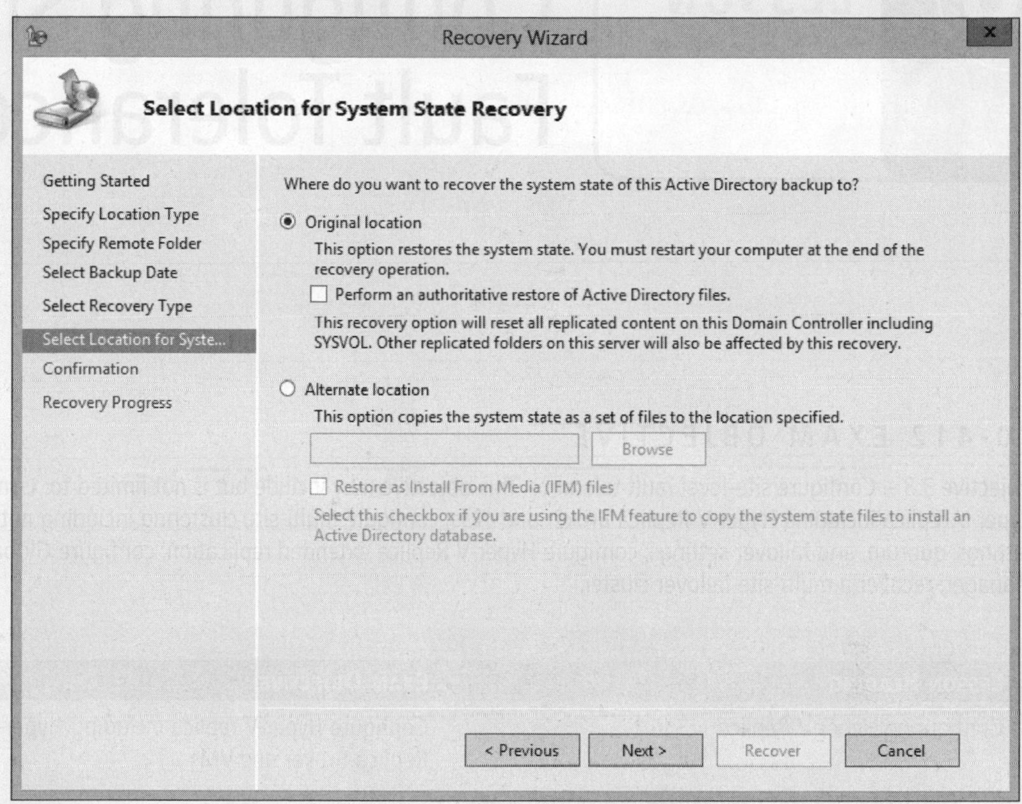

■ Business Case Scenarios

Scenario 9-1: Recovering from a Corrupt Virtual Server

You are currently running a virtual server on a server named *VMHOST*. After installing a service pack and a new Line of Business application on the virtual server, you discover the system is no longer stable. How can you resolve the issue?

Scenario 9-2: Recovering from a Missing BCD

It's 5:00 PM on a Friday evening and you receive a call that one of your servers has an error message displayed on the screen. The error message is as follows:

```
The Boot Configuration Data for your PC is missing or contains errors

File: \Boot\BCD
Error code: 0xc000000f
```

How would you resolve this issue?

Configuring Site-Level Fault Tolerance

70-412 EXAM OBJECTIVE

Objective 3.3 – Configure site-level fault tolerance. This objective may include but is not limited to: Configure Hyper-V replica including Hyper-V Replica Broker and VMs; configure multi-site clustering including network settings, quorum, and failover settings; configure Hyper-V Replica extended replication; configure Global Update Manager; recover a multi-site failover cluster.

LESSON HEADING	EXAM OBJECTIVE
Configuring Hyper-V Replica	Configure Hyper-V replica including Hyper-V Replica Broker and VMs
Configuring Hyper-V Replica Between Two Servers	
Configuring Hyper-V Replica Extended Replication	Configure Hyper-V Replica extended replication
Configuring Multi-Site Clustering	Configure multi-site clustering including network settings, quorum, and failover settings
Configuring Multi-Site Storage and Network Settings	
Configuring Quorum and Failover Settings	
Configuring Multi-Site Failure Cluster	
Configuring Global Update Manager	Configure Global Update Manager
Recovering a Multi-Site Failover Cluster	Recover a multi-site failover cluster

KEY TERMS

asynchronous replication
Global Update Manager
Hyper-V replica
Hyper-V Replica Broker server role
Hyper-V Replica extended replication
multi-site failover cluster
synchronous replication

Configuring Hyper-V Replica

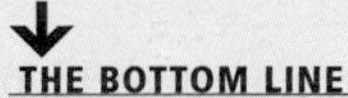

THE BOTTOM LINE

The reason that you perform backups is to be ready when you need to perform data recovery. Using clustering, you can provide fault tolerance for servers. However, when disasters occur that cause the cluster to fail or the virtual machine (VM) or data that you have on the central storage device becomes corrupted, it takes time to perform any repairs and restore from backup. To help overcome this problem, Hyper-V replica was created.

CERTIFICATION READY
Configure Hyper-V replica including Hyper-V Replica Broker and VMs.
Objective 3.3

Hyper-V replica (offline copy) allows you to replicate a Hyper-V VM from one Hyper-V host at a primary site to another Hyper-V host at the Replica site. The Hyper-V replica is used as a spare server, which is stored on another central storage device at another site. To keep the replica updated, Hyper-V replica tracks the write operations on the primary VM and then replicates the changes to the replica over a wide area network (WAN) link. If the primary site goes down, you can then bring up the replica server in minutes. In addition, Hyper-V replica enables you to restore virtualized workloads to a point in time depending on the Recovery History selections for the VM.

Hyper-V replica consists of the following components:

- **Replication engine:** The component that manages the replication configuration details and manages initial replication, delta replication, failover, and test-failover operations.
- **Change tracking:** The component tracks changes on the primary copy of the VM. It tracks the changes regardless of where the VM .vhdx files reside.
- **Network module:** The network module provides a secure and efficient way to transfer VM replicas between primary hosts and replica hosts by using compression and encryption (using HTTPS and certification-based authentication).
- ***Hyper-V Replica Broker server role:*** A new server role (introduced in Windows Server 2012) that redirects all VM specific events to the appropriate node in the replica cluster. It is configured as part of the failover cluster.

Configuring Hyper-V Replica Between Two Servers

Hyper-V replica is part of the Hyper-V server role. It can be used on servers that are not part of a cluster. To replicate servers that are part of a cluster, use the Hyper-V Replica Broker server role.

To deploy Hyper-V replica, perform the following steps:

1. Enable replication between two Hyper-V hosts.
2. Configure replication of one or more VMs.
3. Test the replication deployment.

To enable Hyper-V replica, you configure the Hyper-V server settings, including selecting the authentication and port options and configuring authorization options. In addition, you must configure the location for replica files.

To use encryption for the replication, you need to use certificate-based authentication (HTTPS). You then need to use an existing X.509v3 certificate or create a self-signed certificate. In either case, the certificate needs to meet the following criteria:

- The certificate must not be expired or revoked.
- The certificate must include both client and server authentication extensions for enhanced key usage (EKU) and an associated private key.
- The certificate must terminate at a valid root certificate in the Trusted Root Certification Authorities store on the Replica server.

- If the VM is hosted by a standalone server, the subject common name (CN) contains the fully qualified domain name (FQDN) of the host. If the VM is hosted by a failover cluster, the subject common name (CN) should contain the FQDN of the Hyper-V Replica Broker.

ENABLE HYPER-V REPLICATION

GET READY. To enable Hyper-V replication, perform the following steps on both Hyper-V hosts:

1. Using Server Manager, open Hyper-V Manager. The *Hyper-V Manager* console opens.
2. Right-click the Hyper-V host, and click Hyper-V Settings.
3. When the *Hyper-V Settings* dialog box opens, click Replication Configuration.
4. In the *Replication Configuration* section (see Figure 10-1), click to enable the Enable this computer as a Replica server option.

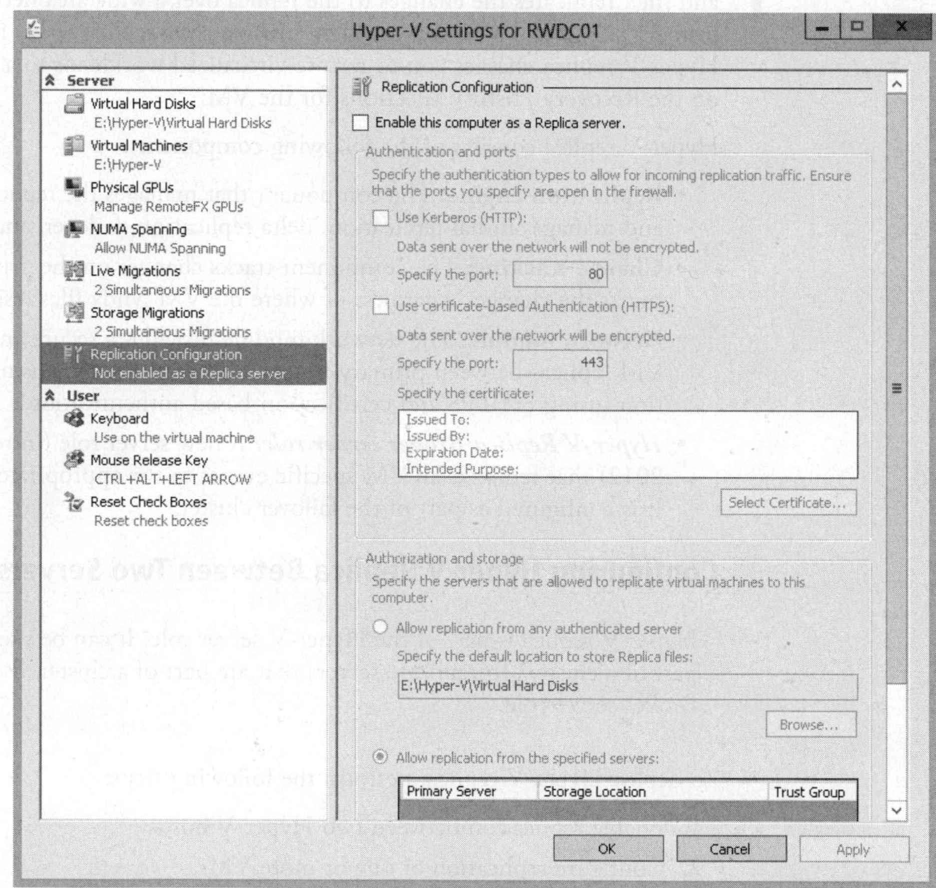

Figure 10-1
Configuring host replication

5. To enable Kerberos authentication, click to select Use Kerberos (HTTP).
6. To use certificate-based authentication, click to select Use certificate based authentication (HTTPS).
7. In the *Authorization and storage* section, click to select Allow replication from any authenticated server, and then click Browse.
8. Click Computer, double-click Local Disk (E), click New folder, in the *Name* text box, type VMReplica, and then press Enter.
9. Select the E:\VMReplica\ folder, and then click Select Folder.
10. Click OK to close the *Hyper-V Settings* dialog box.
11. When Inbound traffic needs to be allowed in the Firewall, click OK.

12. Open the Control Panel, click System and Security, and then click Windows Firewall.
13. Click Advanced settings.
14. In the *Windows Firewall with Advanced Security* console, click Inbound Rules.
15. In the center pane, in the Inbound Rules list, right-click Hyper-V Replica HTTP Listener (TCP-In), and then click Enable Rule.
16. Close the Windows Firewall with Advanced Security console, and then close Windows Firewall.

If the VM is running in a failover cluster, the replication options in Hyper-V will be greyed out and will not be available. Instead, you have to open the *Failover Cluster Manager*, right-click the host server and click *Hyper-V Settings*. When the Hyper-V Settings dialog box opens, click *Replication Configuration* to open the same options that you see when you open the Hyper-V Settings.

INSTALL AND CONFIGURE THE HYPER-V REPLICA BROKER

GET READY. To configure Hyper-V Replica Broker, perform the following steps:

1. Using Server Manager, open Failover Cluster Manager.
2. Right-click Roles and click Configure Role.
3. When the *High Availability Wizard* opens, click Next.
4. On the *Select Role* dialog box, click Hyper-V Replica Broker and click Next.
5. On the *Client Access Point* page, specify the name and IP address of the client access point and click Next.
6. In the *Confirmation* page, click Next.
7. On the *Summary* page, click Finish.
8. With Failover Cluster Manager, click Roles, right-click Hyper-V Replica Broker, and click Replication Settings.
9. In the *Replication Configuration* section (refer to Figure 10-1), click to enable Enable this computer as a Replica server.
10. To enable Kerberos authentication, click to select Use Kerberos (HTTP).
11. To use certificate-based authentication, click to select Use certificate based authentication (HTTPS).
12. In the Authorization and storage section, click to select Allow replication from any authenticated server, and then click Browse.
13. Click Computer, double-click Local Disk (E), click New folder, in the *Name* text box, type VMReplica, and then press Enter.
14. Select the E:\VMReplica\ folder, and then click Select Folder.
15. Click OK to close the *Hyper-V Replica Broker Configuration* dialog box.

After you enable replication on the host, you need to configure the VMs to replicate. During this configuration, you must specify the replica server name, options for the connection, and the virtual hard disks drives that you want to replicate. Lastly, you can configure the recovery history and the initial replication method.

CONFIGURE REPLICATION FOR A VM

GET READY. To configure replication for a VM, perform the following steps:

1. Using Server Manager, open Hyper-V Manager.
2. Right-click the VM that you want to replicate and click Enable Replication.
3. When the *Enable Replication Wizard* begins, click Next.

4. On the *Specify Replica Server* page, type the name of the Replica server that you want to copy to in the *Replica server* text box. Click Next.
5. On the *Specify Connection Parameters* dialog box, click Next.
6. On the *Choose Replication VHDs* page, the virtual hard disks are already selected. Click Next.
7. On the *Configure Recovery History* page, the *Only the latest recovery point* is already selected. Click Next.
8. On the *Choose Initial Replication Methods* page, *Send initial copy over the network* and *Start replication immediately* are already selected. Click Next.
9. On the *Summary* page, click Finish.
10. If you get an *Enable Replication* dialog box saying that Replication enabled successfully but the network adapters for the Replica VM is not connected to any network, click Settings.
11. When the *Settings* dialog box opens, select the virtual switch that you want to use and click OK. After a period of time, the server will be replicated to the second Hyper-V host.

After you start the replication, you can check on the status of the replication by right-clicking the VM, clicking *Replication*, and clicking *View Replication Health*. Figure 10-2 shows the replication health of a VM.

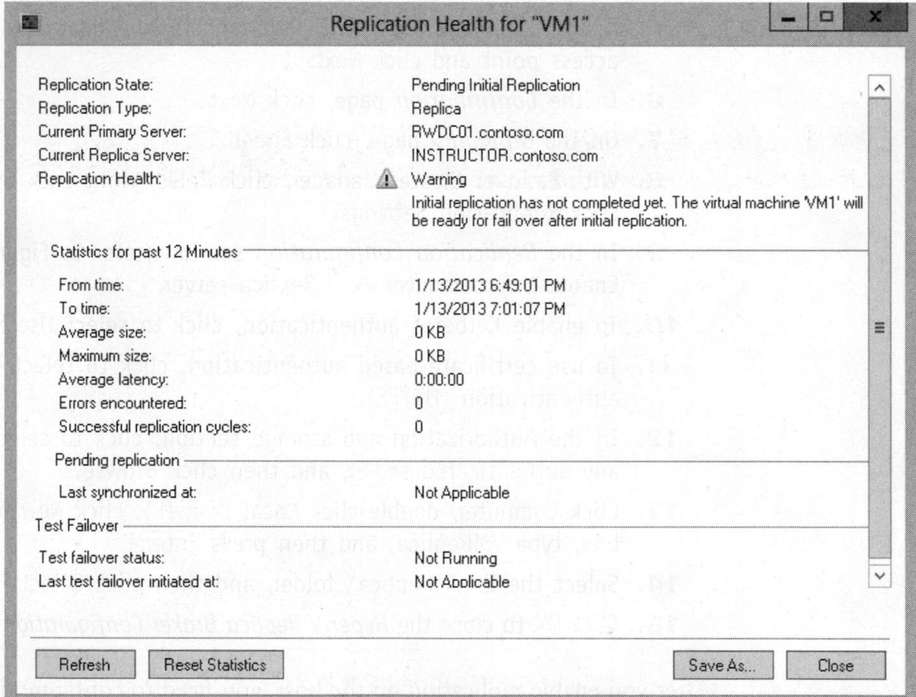

Figure 10-2
Viewing replication health

Configuring Hyper-V Replica Extended Replication

CERTIFICATION READY
Configure Hyper-V Replica extended replication.
Objective 3.3

Starting with Windows Server 2012 R2, you can use ***Hyper-V Replica extended replication***, which is used create a second replica from another replica. By having an extra replica, you can replicate to one local server and remote site or you can replicate to two remote sites.

Just as the name implies, when you extend the replica, the second replica is created from first replica. Since you are essentially running a second wizard to configure the replica, you can define different replication intervals between the first and second replica.

CONFIGURE HYPER-V REPLICA EXTENDED REPLICATION

GET READY. To configure Hyper-V Replica Extended Replication, perform the following steps:

1. Using *Server Manager*, open Hyper-V Manager.
2. Right-click a virtual machine that is replicated and choose Replication > Extend Replication.
3. In the *Extend Replication* Wizard, on the *Before You Begin* page, click Next.
4. On the *Specify Replica Server* page, in the *Replica server* text box, type the name of a Hyper-V host. Click Next.
5. On the *Specify Connection Parameters* page, *Use Kerberos authentication (HTTP)* and *Compress the data that is transmitted over the network* options are already selected. Click Next.
6. On the *Configure Replication Frequency* page, select the desired frequency (5 minutes or 15 minutes). The default is 5 minutes. Click Next.
7. On the *Configure Additional Recovery Points* page, *Maintain only the latest recovery point* is already selected. Click Next.
8. On the *Choose Initial Replication Method* page, the *Send initial copy over the network* and *Start replication immediately* options are selected. Click Next.
9. On the *Completing the Extend Replication Wizard* page, click Finish.

Configuring Multi-Site Clustering

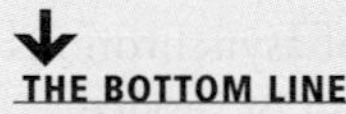

Many companies have only one office, which is used to define a single site. If the site goes down, such as from a fire or flooding, the company would be at a stand-still until a minimum number of servers were brought up and the data was restored from backups that were stored offsite. For larger companies, this type of solution is unacceptable. Therefore, assuming that the company has the money and resources, a backup site needs to be established so that it can be brought online and allow the company to function while the primary site is fixed and brought back online.

At the beginning of this lesson, using Hyper-V replicas was used to make a backup copy of servers. The replicas can be used to replicate to a second site. However, the Hyper-V replica is a cold server that must be brought online when the primary site is unavailable.

Another solution is to create a ***multi-site failover cluster***. A multi-site failover cluster has the following advantages, as compared to a replica VM:

CERTIFICATION READY
Configure multi-site clustering including network settings, quorum, and failover settings.
Objective 3.3

- When a failure occurs, a multi-site cluster automatically fails over the clustered service or application to another.
- Because a site fails over automatically, a multi-site cluster has less administrative overhead than a cold standby server, which needs to be turned on and configured.

A multi-site failover cluster is similar to a standard failover cluster, however, you must take into account that the two sites are usually connected with a significantly slower WAN link as compared to links found in Local Area Networks (LANs).

Configuring Multi-Site Storage and Network Settings

Because of the slower WAN link, there is no shared storage that cluster nodes on the two sites can use. Therefore, you need to use two separate storage systems, one at each site, and have some method to replicate the data between the two sites.

Because Microsoft Windows does not include a built-in mechanism for data replication, you need to use one of the following three methods:

- Block level hardware-based replication
- Software-based file replication
- Application-based replication

Some SANs have the capability to replicate data between SAN units. If not, you need to purchase another hardware system or software-based replication system to perform the replication. You should also check whether the shared application or service that you are running on the cluster has built-in replication. For example, both Microsoft Exchange and Microsoft SQL server have replication built in to the software. Exchange Server has continuous replication, and SQL Server has several types of replication including log shipping. In some situations, if the data that you replicate are small files that are typically closed, you can use Distributed File System (DFS) replication.

When you configure multi-site replication, the replication is either synchronous or asynchronous. With ***synchronous replication***, data is written to the remote site and then waits for a receive message stating that the data has been written to the remote site properly. If the message is not received, the data will be sent again. Although the synchronous replication keeps both sites the same, any slowness or delays over a WAN link slows the cluster application or service because the application or service waits for the data to be written to the remote site. Therefore, to use synchronous replication, you need high bandwidth between the two sites and low latency.

With ***asynchronous replication***, the data is written to the primary storage device and then is written separately to the remote storage device, typically on its own schedule. However, most of these systems are written only after a short delay. The advantage of asynchronous replication is that it keeps the performance high for the clustered application or service.

Lastly, your network needs basic network services functioning when a site goes down, which includes Active Directory Domain Services (AD DS) and Domain Name System (DNS). Therefore, you need multiple domain controllers through your organization including at least one at the secondary site. In addition, you should have multiple DNS servers including at least one at the secondary site. Of course, for clients to use DNS at the secondary site, make sure that the secondary DNS server for the clients point to the DNS server at the secondary site.

Configuring Quorum and Failover Settings

Any time you deal with WAN links, you have to take into account that those links will have slower bandwidth and higher latency. Since failover is triggered by missing heartbeats, you may need to tweak the quorum and failover settings so that the failover will work more efficiently if it is a multi-site cluster.

By default, the heartbeat occurs once every second (1,000 milliseconds). If a node misses five heartbeats in a role, another node will initiate failover.

For a cluster to operate properly over multiple sites, you should have have at least one low-latency and reliable network connection between sites to carry the cluster heartbeats.

If not, you will need to use the Failover settings (right-click the role, click *Properties*, and click the *Failover* tab) to specify the maximum failures in a specified period, so that a cluster does not failover prematurely or unnecessarily.

As discussed in Lessons 3, “Managing Failover Clustering,” and 4, “Managing VM Movement,” you need enough nodes and votes to reach quorum, even if a site is down. Because the sites are geographically dispersed, you cannot use quorum configuration that requires a witness disk. If there is an odd number of nodes, then use the Node Majority quorum. If there is an even number of nodes, which is typical in a geographically dispersed cluster, you can use the Node Majority with File Share Majority quorum.

If you use Node Majority with File Share Majority quorum, you need to place the file share witness at a third site. In a multi-site cluster, a single server can host the file share witness. However, you must create a separate file share for each cluster.

With Windows Server 2012 and Windows Server 2012 R2, you can adjust cluster quorum settings including specifying which nodes can vote and which nodes cannot vote when determining quorum (see Figure 10-3). This might help you implement solutions across multiple sites and tweak settings after a major failure has occurred.

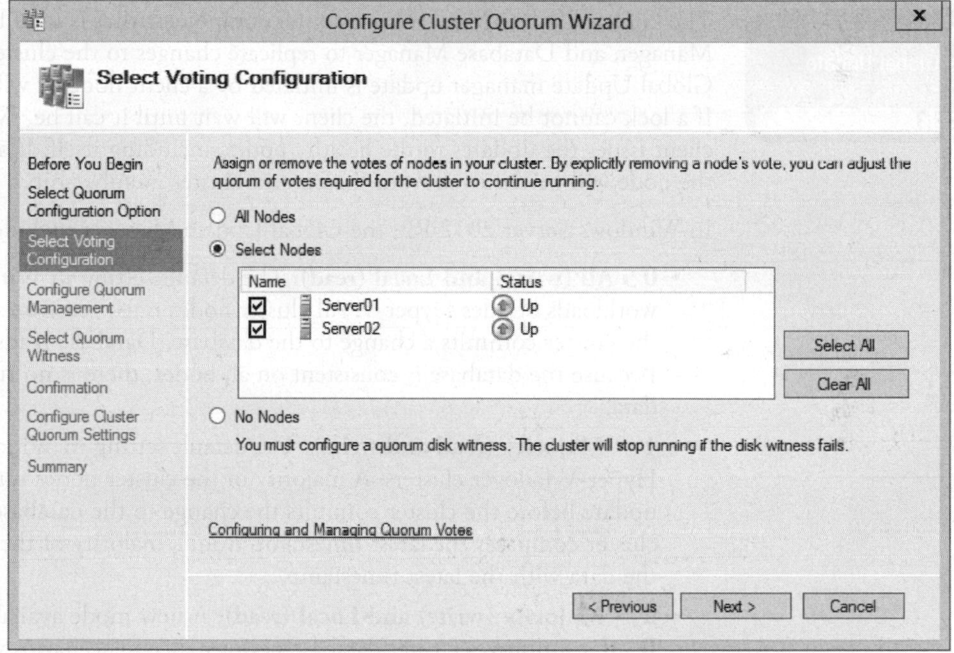

Figure 10-3

Selecting which nodes can vote

Configuring Multi-Site Failure Cluster

When you set up the multi-site failure cluster, you use much of the knowledge that you learned in Lessons 3 and 4, which discuss failover clusters.

The high level steps that you should perform when configuring a multi-site failover cluster are the following:

1. Ensure that you have enough cluster nodes at each site and that each node has similar hardware configuration and the same version of operating system and service packs.
2. Ensure that sites have stable connections, with sufficient bandwidth and low network latency. Latency validates when you run the Validate Configuration Wizard in Failover Cluster Manager.

3. Ensure that you have a reliable storage replication mechanism between sites.
4. Make sure you have the basic network services available on each site including AD DS, DNS, and DHCP.
5. Run the Validate a Configuration Wizard on all nodes and fix any problems that it might indicate.
6. Create a cluster.
7. Configure the cluster quorum mode.
8. Configure failover/failback settings.
9. Create the clustered role.
10. Test failover and failback.

Configuring Global Update Manager

Global Update Manager is used to coordinate state changes within the cluster, such as when a cluster node is taken offline. Starting with Windows Server 2012 R2, you can configure how the cluster manages global updates.

CERTIFICATION READY
Configure Global Update Manager.
Objective 3.3

The Global Update Manager is a cluster component that is used by Failover Manager, Node Manager, and Database Manager to replicate changes to the cluster database nodes. When a Global Update manager update is initiated by a client node, it will first request a global lock. If a lock cannot be initiated, the client will wait until it can be. When the lock is granted, the client issues the updates to the healthy nodes, including itself. If an update fails on a node, the node will be removed from the current cluster membership.

In Windows Server 2012 R2, the Global Update Manager includes the following modes:

- **0 5 All (write) and Local (read):** The default setting in Windows Server 2012 R2 for all workloads besides Hyper-V. All cluster nodes must receive and process the update before the cluster commits a change to the database. Database reads occur on the local node. Because the database is consistent on all nodes, there is no risk of out of date or "stale" data.
- **1 = Majority (read and write):** The default setting in Windows Server 2012 R2 for Hyper-V failover clusters. A majority of the cluster nodes must receive and process the update before the cluster commits the change to the database. For a database read, the cluster compares the latest timestamp from a majority of the running nodes, and uses the data with the latest timestamp.
- **2 = Majority (write) and Local (read):** A new mode available in Windows Server 2012 R2 that improves cluster database performance in scenarios where there is significant network latency between the cluster nodes (for example, with a stretch multi-site cluster). A majority of the cluster nodes must receive and process the update before the cluster commits the change to the database. Database reads occur on the local node. Because the cluster does not compare the latest timestamp on a majority of nodes, the data may be out of date or "stale."

You should not use either of the majority modes (1 or 2) for scenarios that require strong consistency guarantees from the cluster database, such as for Microsoft SQL Server failover cluster that uses AlwaysOn availability groups or for Microsoft Exchange Server.

In Windows Server 2012, you cannot configure the Global Update Manager mode. However, in Windows Server 2012 R2, you can configure the Global Update Manager mode with the DatabaseReadWriteMode property. To view the Global Update Manager mode, start Windows PowerShell as an administrator, and then execute the following command:

```
(Get-Cluster).DatabaseReadWriteMode
```

To change the Global Update Manager Mode to Majority (write) and Local (read), execute the following command:

```
(Get-Cluster).DatabaseReadWriteMode=2
```

Recovering a Multi-Site Failover Cluster

The best method to restore a cluster is to restore from backup. However, because the cluster configuration is replicated between cluster nodes, you can fix and restore a single node and the configuration information will be replicated to the newly restored node. If you have to restore a cluster configuration from backup, you will have to perform an authoritative restore.

CERTIFICATION READY
Recover a multi-site failover cluster.
Objective 3.3

To ensure that you can recover a failed cluster is to make sure that you have a backup of the failover cluster including backing up the cluster configuration, and the data on clustered disks. To back up the cluster configuration, the cluster must be running and must have quorum.

When you restore to a failover cluster from backup, you can restore the cluster configuration, the data on clustered disks, or both. The Cluster service keeps track of which cluster configuration is the most recent, and it replicates that configuration to all cluster nodes, including a disk witness.

When you restore a single cluster node from backup, you can perform one of the following:

- **Non-authoritative restore:** Restore the failed node to normal function, which while restore the node to normal function and join the node to the cluster. Cluster configuration will be automatically replicated to the restored node.
- **Authoritative restore:** By restoring the failed node, but marking the configuration as the most recent. The Cluster service will then overwrite the configuration across all nodes.

When you restore data on clustered disk, data can be written only to disks that are online and owned by that cluster node when the backup is being restored.

SKILL SUMMARY

IN THIS LESSON YOU LEARNED:

- Hyper-V replica (offline copy) allows you to replicate a Hyper-V VM from one Hyper-V host at a primary site to another Hyper-V host at the Replica site. The Hyper-V replica is used as a spare server, which is stored on another central storage device on another site.
- To keep the replica updated, Hyper-V replica tracks the write operations on the primary VM and then replicates the changes to the Replica over a WAN link.
- Hyper-V Replica Broker server role is a new server role (introduced in Windows Server 2012) that redirects all VM specific events to the appropriate node in the replica cluster.
- Hyper-V Replica Broker is configured as part of the failover cluster.
- Hyper-V replica is part of the Hyper-V server role.
- To deploy Hyper-V replica, you enable replication between two Hyper-V hosts and then configure replication of one or more VMs.

- Because failover is triggered by missing heartbeats, you might need to tweak the quorum and failover settings so that the failover will work more efficiently if it is a multi-site cluster, particularly if you are using slow or high latency WAN links. Because of the slower WAN link, there is no shared storage that cluster nodes on the two sites can use. Therefore, you need to use two separate storage systems, one at each site, and have some method to replicate the data between the two sites.
- If there is an odd number of nodes, then use the Node Majority quorum. If there is an even number of nodes, which is typical in a geographically dispersed cluster, you can use the Node Majority with File Share Majority quorum.
- If you use Node Majority with File Share Majority quorum, you need to place the file share witness at a third site.
- Global Update Manager is used to coordinate state changes within the cluster, such as when a cluster node is taken offline. Starting with Windows Server 2012, you can configure how the cluster manages global updates.

■ Knowledge Assessment

Multiple Choice

Select the correct answer for each of the following questions.

1. What allows you to place an offline copy of a VM that is regularly updated?
  a. Data Deduplication
  b. DFS replication
  c. Cluster replication
  d. Hyper-V replica

2. Which component of the Hyper-V replica performs the replication of VMs?
  a. Replication Engine
  b. Change Tracker
  c. Network Module
  d. Change Manager

3. How is data replicated when replicating to a Hyper-V replica?
  a. HPPT
  b. Telnet
  c. FTP
  d. TFTP

4. What program is normally used to enable Hyper-V replication?
  a. Hyper-V Manager
  b. Hyper-V Replica
  c. Failover Cluster Manager
  d. Hyper-V Replica Broker

5. When a VM is replicated as a Hyper-V replica, what is the replicated VM considered?
  a. cold server
  b. warm server
  c. hot server
  d. dynamic server

6. What type of quorum is recommended for multi-site clusters consisting of two nodes on the primary site and two nodes on the backup site?
   a. Node Majority with File Share Majority
   b. Node Majority with Disk Witness
   c. No Majority
   d. Node Majority
7. You have a total of five cluster nodes that are used by a multi-site cluster. Which type of quorum should you use?
   a. Node Majority with File Share Majority
   b. Node Majority with Disk Witness
   c. No Majority
   d. Node Majority
8. What provides encryption for Hyper-V replication over the network?
   a. HTTPS
   b. SSH
   c. SFTP
   d. TFTP
9. What is the advantage of using synchronous replication?
   a. It keeps the source and target storage devices the same
   b. It is faster
   c. It accommodates high latency
   d. It accommodates low bandwidth
10. If you have a secondary site to be used as a backup site, what basic network services will you need? (Choose all that apply.)
    a. SMTP
    b. SQL Server
    c. AD DS
    d. DNS
11. What is used to enable Hyper-V replica if you have a failover cluster installed on a server where you have Hyper-V installed?
    a. Hyper-V Manager
    b. Hyper-V Replica
    c. Failover Cluster Manager
    d. Hyper-V Replica Broker
12. You have two servers, Server1 and Server2, running Windows Server 2012 R2. Both servers have the Hyper-V server role installed. Server1 is in the primary site and Server2 is in the secondary site, which are connected over a slow WAN link. Server1 is running a VM. If Server1 fails, how can you start a copy of the VM on Server2, while keeping the cost low?
    a. Install MPIO on Server1 and modify the storage locations of the VM
    b. Install MPIO on Server1 and modify the storage locations of the VM
    c. On Server1, modify the Replication Configuration settings and enable the replication of VM
    d. On Server2, modify the Replication Configuration settings, and enable the replication of the VM

13. You have two servers, Server1 and Server2. Both are running Windows Server 2012 R2 and the Hyper-V server role. You need to replicate VMs between Server1 and Server2. You need to use encryption with SSL. Of course, you need a digital certificate for SSL. What two intended purposes of the certificate would you need?
    a. client authentication
    b. server authentication
    c. IP security
    d. KDC authentication

14. You have three physical hosts called Server1, Server2, and Server3, all of which are running Windows Server 2012 R2. Server1 and Server2 make up the failover cluster Cluster1. Cluster1 has the Hyper-V Replica Broker role installed and is hosting several VMs. What tools do you need use to configure the VMs to replicate to Server3?
    a. Hyper-V Manager console connected to Server3
    b. Hyper-V Manager console connected to Cluster1
    c. Failover Cluster Manager console connected to Cluster1
    d. Failover Cluster Manager console connected to Server3

15. What is desirable when you purchase a WAN link to connect two sites? (Choose two answers.)
    a. low latency
    b. low bandwidth
    c. high latency
    d. high bandwidth

Matching and Identification

1. Identify which of the following are components of Hyper-V replica.
   _______ a) Hyper-V Replica console
   _______ b) Network module
   _______ c) Change tracking
   _______ d) Address module
   _______ e) Replication Engine
   _______ f) Replication Authentication Module
   _______ g) Repl plug-in

2. Identify which of the following are requirements for the digital certificates needed for HTTPS transfers Hyper-V replica?
   _______ a) Cert must be expired or revoked
   _______ b) If the certificate is used by a failover cluster, the cert must contain the CN of the Hyper-V Replica Broker
   _______ c) Cert must have a valid root certificate
   _______ d) Cert must have the password extension
   _______ e) Cert must have the user authentication extension
   _______ f) Cert must have the server authentication extension
   _______ g) Cert must have the client authentication extension
   _______ h) Cert must be an X.509v3 certificate
   _______ i) Cert must be an X.400 certificate

Build a List

1. Identify the three basic steps in order to deploy Hyper-V replica by placing the number of the step in the appropriate space. Not all steps will be used
   _______ Enable replication between two Hyper-V hosts
   _______ Configure replication of one or more VMs
   _______ Schedule when the system will be replicated each day
   _______ Test the replication deployment
   _______ Enable the Replication Service using the Services console

2. Identify the basic steps in order when configuring multi-site failure cluster by placing the number of the step in the appropriate space.
   _______ Install and configure storage replication mechanism
   _______ Create a cluster
   _______ Test network connectivity between sites
   _______ Configure cluster quorum mode
   _______ Install computers at both sites
   _______ Run the Validate a Configuration Wizard
   _______ Configure failover/failback settings
   _______ Install basic network services at backup site
   _______ Create the clustered role
   _______ Test failover

3. Identify the basic steps in order to enable Hyper-V replication between Server1 and Server2. Not all steps will be used.
   _______ Drag the VM to the Allow side
   _______ Click Replication Configuration
   _______ Open the firewall for replication
   _______ Enable the Replica Service
   _______ Enable the Enable this computer as a replica server
   _______ Install IPSec
   _______ Using Hyper-V Manager, right-click the host and click Hyper-V Settings
   _______ Specify the location to store the replicas

Business Case Scenarios

Scenario 10-1: Replicating a VM to a Secondary Site

You are an administrator at the Contoso Corporation. You have multiple sites within your corporation. At the main office, you have most of the servers for your company. The secondary site is a data recovery site if there is a major problem at the primary site. The primary servers are VMs on Server01 that need to run all the time. What do you need to have a backup copy at the secondary site?

Scenario 10-2: Setting Up a Multi-Site Cluster

You are an administrator at the Contoso Corporation. You have multiple sites within your corporation. At the main office, you have most of the servers for your company. The secondary site is a data recovery site if there is a major problem at the primary site. At the primary site, you have a failover cluster that has two nodes. You want to expand the cluster to the secondary site. What will you need to do and what are some of things that you will need to overcome?

Implementing an Advanced Dynamic Host Configuration Protocol (DHCP) Solution

70-412 EXAM OBJECTIVE

Objective 4.1 – Implement an advanced Dynamic Host Configuration Protocol (DHCP) solution. This objective may include but is not limited to: Create and configure superscopes and multicast scopes; implement DHCPv6; configure high availability for DHCP including DHCP failover and split scopes; configure DHCP Name Protection; configure DNS registration.

Lesson Heading	Exam Objective
Implementing Advanced DHCP Solutions	
Understanding DHCP Basics	
Creating and Configuring DHCP Policies	
Configuring DNS Registration	Configure DNS registration
Creating and Configuring Superscopes	Create and configure superscopes and multicast scopes
Creating and Configuring Multicast Scopes	Create and configure superscopes and multicast scopes
Implementing DHCPv6 Scopes	Implement DHCPv6
Configuring High Availability for DHCP	Configure high availability for DHCP including DHCP failover and split scopes
Configuring DHCP Name Protection	Configure DHCP Name Protection

KEY TERMS

Bootstrap Protocol (BOOTP)
broadcast
DHCP client reservations
DHCP console
DHCP database
DHCP failover
DHCP Name Protection
DHCP options
DHCP policies
DHCP scopes
DHCP server service
Dynamic Host Configuration Protocol (DHCP)
IPv6 address
multicast
multicast scopes
split scopes
superscope
unicast

Implementing Advanced DHCP Solutions

THE BOTTOM LINE

The ***Dynamic Host Configuration Protocol (DHCP)*** is a network protocol that automatically configures the IP configuration of a device including assigning an IP address, subnet mask, default gateway, and primary and secondary Domain Name System (DNS) servers. Most clients and some servers that connect to a network receive their address from a DHCP server including home routers/modems and office networks. In addition, the DHCP technology and protocol has becomes a necessary component of Windows Deployment Services (WDS) to deploy Windows to a client, and Network Access Protection (NAP), which is needed to limit the connectivity of clients that do not have the current Windows updates and proper antivirus software.

DHCP has been included with Windows for years and is included with Windows Server 2012 and Windows Server 2012 R2 as a server role. Starting with Windows Server 2012, DHCP supports failover capability. It helps administrators distribute the appropriate IP addresses and network configuration information automatically to network devices or hosts, which eliminates a lot of time to automatically configure each host that connects to the network and eliminates human error during configuration. The devices or hosts include computers, mobile devices, printers, network appliances, and switches.

Understanding DHCP Basics

DHCP is based heavily on the ***Bootstrap Protocol (BOOTP)***, which was one of the early network protocols used to obtain an IP address from a configuration server. Although the DHCP server functions as a BOOTP server, DHCP is a more advanced protocol and includes additional functionality including the ability to reclaim allocated addresses that are no longer used. DHCP is an open, industry-standard protocol defined by the Internet Engineering Task Force (IETF) in Request for Comments (RFCs) 2131 and 2132.

You can install the DHCP server role on a stand-alone server, a domain member server, or a domain controller. The components that make up the DHCP technology and protocol consist of the following:

- ***DHCP server service:*** A service that works in the background on a server. It distributes IP addresses and other network configuration information.
- ***DHCP scopes:*** A range of IP addresses that can be allocated to clients. A scope consists of a name and description, range of addresses, and a subnet mask. To ease the allocation of addresses, administrators can define IP addresses that are excluded from distribution. The administrators can also specify the duration of the IP address leases. By the end of the lease, the address needs to be renewed or it is released back into the pool so that it can be reallocated to another host. After a scope is created, the scope has to be activated before it can allocate addresses.
- ***DHCP options:*** Options that are assigned when the addresses are assigned or renewed including the default gateway and the primary and secondary DNS servers. Other options include DNS domain suffix, Windows Internet Name Service (WINS) server, and TFTP addresses. Based on how you configure the DHCP options, you can assign the options globally (all scopes), specific to a particular scope, to specific clients based on a Class ID values), or to clients that have specific IP address reservations configured.
- ***DHCP database:*** A database that contains the configuration for the DHCP server, the IP addresses that it has distributed, their current lease time, and the IP addresses that

the server still have to distributed. The database uses the Microsoft Jet Database Engine, which is stored in the %systemroot%\System32\Dhcp folder.

- ***DHCP console:*** The Microsoft Management Console (MMC) that allows you to manage the DHCP server, and the scopes. Figure 11-1 shows the DHCP console.

Figure 11-1

Looking at the DHCP console

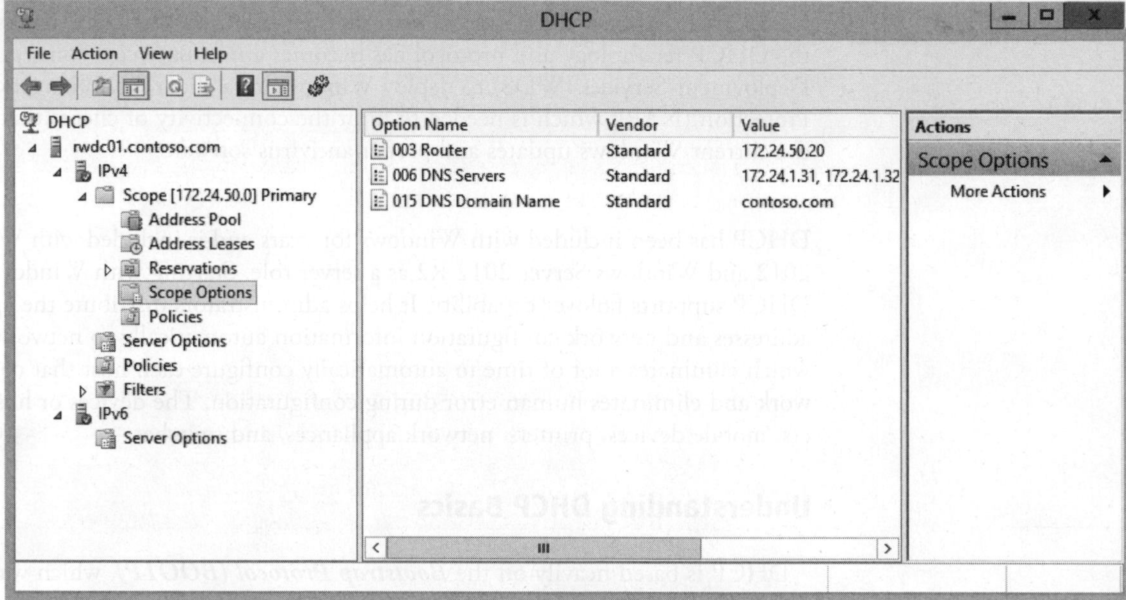

CLIENTS ACQUIRING AND RENEWING IP ADDRESSES

Assuming that a host is configured to use DHCP during startup, the host performs an IP broadcast in its subnet to request IP configuration from any DHCP server that receives the request. Because broadcasts are generally restricted to the local subnet, a DHCP server must be on the subnet, or a relay agent or IP helper grabs the broadcast and forwards it directly to a DHCP server on a remote subnet using unicast packets.

DHCP allocates IP addresses using a lease. The default lease time for a wired client is eight days. When the DHCP lease has reached 50 percent of the lease time, the client attempts to renew the lease. If the DHCP server is down or unreachable, the client will try again from time to time. When the DHCP server comes back up or becomes reachable again, the DHCP client will succeed in contacting it and renew its lease.

DHCP OPTIONS

DHCP options are not required for use by DHCP. However, they can be essential to an organization to automatically configure these options so that they do not have to be manually configured. On today's network, some of these options are taken for granted; they are nonetheless essential for a client to operate properly on a network. For example, if a client does not have the address of a DNS server assigned, the client will not be able to perform name resolution, and will not be able to locate resources on the network or access websites on the Internet.

The most popular DHCP options include:

- **Option 3 Router:** Specifies a list of IP addresses for the default gateway or router on the client's subnet. Multi-homed computers can have only one list per computer, not one per network adapter. The router option is usually configured at the scope level.
- **Option 6 DNS servers:** Specifies a list of IP addresses for DNS name servers available to the client.

- **Option 15 Domain name:** Specifies the DNS domain name that the client should use for DNS computer name resolution.
- **Option 44 WINS/NBNS servers:** Specifies a list of IP addresses for NetBIOS name servers (NBNS).
- **Option 46 WINS/NBT node type:** Allows configurable NetBIOS over TCP/IP (NetBT) clients to be configured as described in RFC 1001/1002, where 1 = b-node, 2 = p-node, 4 = m-node, and 8 = h-node. On multi-homed computers, the node type is assigned to the entire computer, not to individual network adapters.

By default, the DHCP server dynamically updates the DNS address host (A) resource records and pointer (PTR) resource records only if requested by the DHCP clients. By default, the client requests that the DHCP server register the DNS PTR resource record, while the client registers its own DNS A resource record. The DHCP server discards the A and PTR resource records when the client's lease is deleted. To change how DHCP registers and deletes DNS A and PTR resource records, you configure it by right-clicking the IPv4 node or scope, clicking *Properties*, and clicking the *DNS* tab.

RESERVATIONS

DHCP client reservations allow administrators to reserve an IP address for permanent use by a DHCP client. By using reservations, you can ensure that the host will always have the same IP address. As with any other lease, when a client receives a reserved address, the client also receives all assigned options such as addresses of the default gateway and DNS servers. If these options are changed, they will automatically be updated on the client when the lease is renewed.

DHCP SERVER AUTHORIZATION

A rogue DHCP server is a DHCP server on a network that is not under the administrative control of the organization IT department. It can be used to interrupt network access, bypass network security, and capture private information using a man-in-the-middle attack. To help protect a network from rogue DHCP servers (such as a rogue DHCP server handing out bogus IP configuration causing network interruption, or redirect users to servers or websites that may be used to retrieve private information or bypass security), if DHCP server is part of an Active Directory domain, you must authorize the DHCP server before it can hand out IP addresses. You must be an Enterprise Admin to authorize the DHCP server. If the server is a stand-alone server, Windows will verify whether it is a DHCP server on the network, and it will not start the DHCP service if there is one.

Creating and Configuring DHCP Policies

Starting with Windows Server 2012, by using ***DHCP policies***, you can give granular control over scopes to allow you to assign different IP addresses or different options based on the device type, or its role. Policies are applicable for a specific scope with a defined processing order. The options can be configured at the scope or inherited from server-wide policies.

A DHCP policy can support the following scenarios:

- If you have different types of clients (for example, desktop computers, printers, and IP phones) on the same subnets, you can assign different IP address ranges within the subnet.
- If you have a mix of wired and mobile computers, you can assign shorter lease durations for mobile computers and longer lease durations to wired computers.
- You can control who gets access to your network based on MAC address for a subnet.

A DHCP policy consists of conditions and settings. A condition allows you to identify and group clients based on whether a specified criteria is equal or not equal to a specified values. The criteria include:

- MAC address
- Vendor Class
- User Class
- Client identifier
- Relay Agent Information such as remote id, circuit id, and subscriber id

Every DHCP client request is evaluated against the conditions in a policy. If a client request matches the conditions in the policy, the specified settings (IP address and options) assigned to the policy will be applied to the DHCP client. For example, you can identify the type of device, so that wired clients are in one group, and mobile computers are in another group. You can also use a trailing wild card with MAC address, Vendor Class, User Class, and Client identifier conditions to perform a partial match. A client that does not match conditions is leased an IP address from the remaining IP addresses of the scope that are not assigned to a policy and are giving options assigned to the scope.

You can configure more than one policy within a scope or server wide. As a client makes a DHCP request, each policy is evaluated and the settings are combined. If there is a conflict for a specific option, the policy higher up in processing order overrides the previous option.

Every policy has an assigned processing order. While processing client requests, the DHCP server evaluates the client requests against the conditions in the different policies based on the processing order of the policy—with processing order 1 policy processed first. Scope level policies are processed first by the DHCP server followed by server-wide policies.

Depending on your needs, you might need to first build a vendor class. In the first exercise, you create a vendor class for the Nortel IP phone and the HP Jet Direct, which is the primary network interface used for HP network printers. Then in the following exercise, you create a DHCP policy based on the vendor class.

CREATE VENDOR CLASSES

GET READY. To create a vendor class, perform the following steps:

1. Open Server Manager, open the Tools menu, and click DHCP. The *DHCP* console opens.
2. In the *DHCP* console, right-click IPv4 or IPv6, and click Define Vendor Class.
3. When the *DHCP Vendor Classes* dialog box opens, click Add. The *New Class* dialog box opens (see Figure 11-2).

Figure 11-2

Adding a new DHCP vendor class

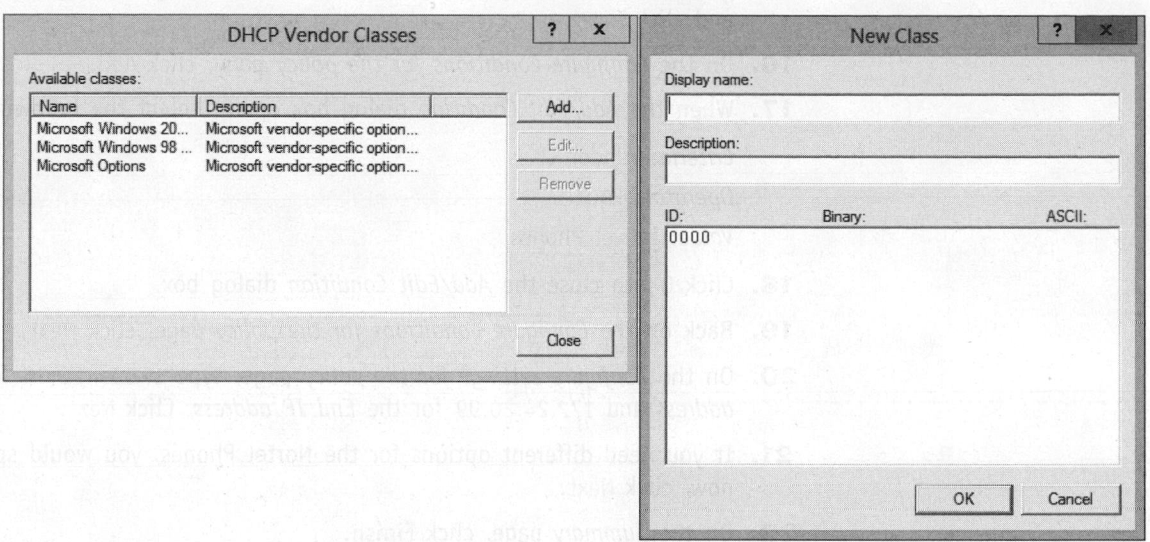

4. In the *Display name* text box, type Nortel Phones. In the *Description* text box, type Desk phone.
5. Click under the *ASCII* field name and type Nortel-i 2004-A. Click OK.
6. Click Add again.
7. In the *Display name*, type HP Printer.
8. Click under the *ASCII* field and type Hewlett-Packard JetDirect. Click OK.
9. Click Close to close the *DHCP Vendor Classes* dialog box.

CREATE A DCHP POLICY FOR A SCOPE

GET READY. To create a DHCP policy for a scope, perform the following steps:

1. Open Server Manager, open the Tools menu, and click DHCP. The DHCP console opens.
2. In the *DHCP* console, right-click IPv4 and click New Scope.
3. When the *New Scope Wizard* starts, click Next.
4. When the *Scope Name* page opens, type NormalScope in the *Name* text box and click Next.
5. On the IP address range, type 172.24.25.50 for the *Start IP address* and type 172.24.25.200 for the *End IP address*. For the *subnet mask*, type 255.255.255.0. Click Next.
6. On the *Add Exclusion and Delay* page, click Next.
7. On the *Lease Duration* page, click Next.
8. On the *Configure DHCP Options* page, click Next.
9. On the *Router (Default Gateway)* page, type 172.24.25.20 for the *IP address* and click Add. Click Next.
10. On the *Domain Name and DNS Servers* page, click Next.
11. On the *WINS Servers* page, click Next.
12. On the *Activate Scope* page, click Next.
13. When the wizard is complete, click Finish.

14. Right-click the Policies node under the *NormalScope* scope.
15. When the *DHCP Policy Configuration Wizard* starts, type Policy1 for the *policy name*, and click Next.
16. On the *Configure Conditions for the policy* page, click Add.
17. When the *Add/Edit Condition* dialog box opens, select the following and click Add:

    Criteria: Vendor Class

    Operator: Equals

    Value: Nortel Phones
18. Click OK to close the *Add/Edit Condition* dialog box.
19. Back on the *Configure Conditions for the policy* page, click Next.
20. On the *Configure settings for the policy* page, type 172.24.20.50 for the *Start IP address* and 172.24.20.99 for the *End IP address*. Click Next.
21. If you need different options for the Nortel Phones, you would specify them. For now, click Next.
22. On the *Summary* page, click Finish.
23. Right-click Policy1, and click Properties.
24. On the *Properties* dialog box opens, click to select the Set lease duration for the policy option.
25. Change the lease time to 7 days. Click OK.

Configuring DNS Registration

With Windows Server 2012 R2, by using the proper FQDN-based condition and a DNS suffix, you can use DHCP policies to fully control DNS registration for computers and devices on the network, including workgroup computers, guest devices, or clients with a specific attribute.

CERTIFICATION READY
Configure DNS registration.
Objective 4.1

With Windows Server 2012 R2, you can use DHCP policies to allow users to configure conditions based on the fully qualified domain name (FQDN) of the client. In addition, DHCP policies can be configured to register DHCP clients using a specific DNS suffix, overriding the DNS suffix that is already configured on the client.

CONFIGURE A POLICY BASED ON THE FQDN

GET READY. To configure a policy based on the FQDN, perform the following steps:

1. Using *Server Manager*, open the DHCP console.
2. In the *DHCP* console, expand the server, expand IPv4, expand a scope, and then click the Policies node. Right-click the Policies node and choose New Policy.
3. In the *DHCP Policy Configuration Wizard,* on the *Policy based IP address and Option Assignment* page, in the *Policy Name* text box, type a name of the policy. In the *Description* text box, type a description for the policy. Click Next.
4. On the *Configure Conditions for the policy* page, click Add.
5. In the *Add/Edit Condition* dialog box, for *Criteria,* select Fully Qualified Domain Name. The *Operator* is already set to *Equals*.

6. In the *Value* text box, type a domain name, such as adatum.com (as shown in Figure 11-3) and click Add. If desired, you can select the Prefix wildcard (*) option or the Append wildcard (*) option. Click OK.

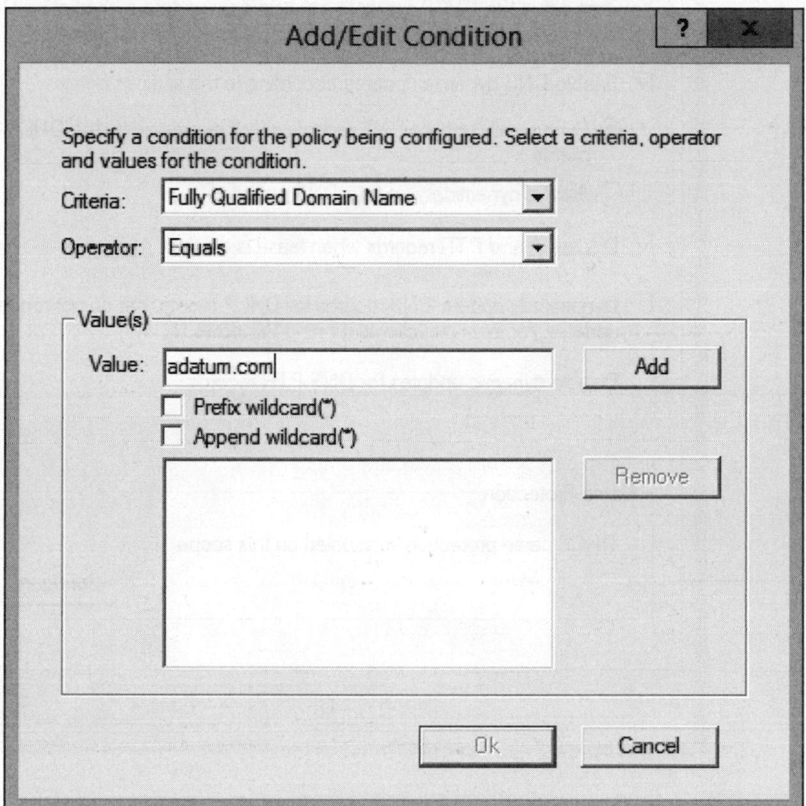

Figure 11-3
Specifying a condition based on the FQDN

7. On the *Configure Conditions for the policy* page, click Next.
8. On the *Summary* page, click Finish.

In addition, with Windows Server 2012 R2, you can configure the DHCP server to register only the A record for clients with the DNS server. By only registering the A record, you avoid failed attempts to register PTR records when the associated reverse lookup zone does not exist. PTR record registration can be disabled for all clients of a DHCP server, or by specific subnet or attribute.

DISABLE DYNAMIC UPDATES FOR DNS PTR RECORDS

GET READY. To disable dynamic updates for DNS PTR records, perform the following steps:

1. Using *Server Manager*, open the DHCP console.
2. In the DHCP console, expand the server, expand IPv4, expand a scope, and then click the scope. Right-click the scope and choose Properties.
3. Click the DNS tab.
4. On the *DNS* tab (as shown on Figure 11-4), click to select the Disable dynamic updates for DNS PTR records option.

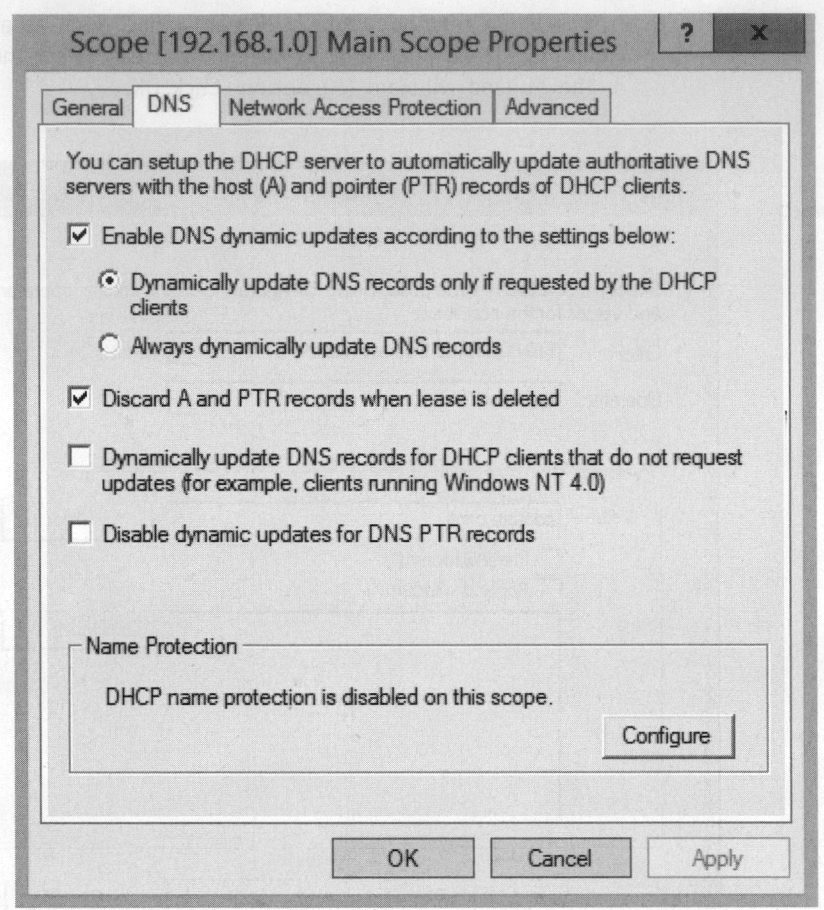

Figure 11-4

The Scope properties showing the DNS tab

5. Click OK to close the *Scope Properties* dialog box.

Creating and Configuring Superscopes

A ***superscope*** is the grouping of multiple scopes into a single administrative entity. By using superscopes, you can support larger subnets.

CERTIFICATION READY
Create and configure superscopes and multicast scopes.
Objective 4.1

A superscope can be used if a scope runs out of addresses and you cannot add more addresses from the subnet. Instead, you can add a new subnet to the DHCP server. You then perform multinetting, where you lease addresses to clients in the same physical network, but the clients will be in a separate network logically by subnet. Once you add a new subnet, you must configure routers to recognize the new subnet so that you ensure local communications in the physical network.

You can also use superscopes to move clients gradually into a new IP number scheme. Having both numbering schemes coexist at the same time allows you to move clients into the new subnet. When you renew all client leases in the new subnet, you can retire the old subnet.

You can create only a superscope if you have two or more IP scopes already created in DHCP. You can use the New Superscope Wizard to select the scopes that you want to combine together to create a superscope.

CREATE A SUPERSCOPE OUT OF TWO SCOPES

GET READY. To create a superscope out of two scopes, perform the following steps:

1. Open Server Manager, open the Tools menu, and click DHCP. The *DHCP* console opens.
2. In the *DHCP* console, click a DHCP server, such as RWDC01.contoso.com. Right-click IPv4, and then click New Scope.
3. When the *New Wizard* opens, click Next.
4. In the *Name* text box, type Scope1, and click Next.
5. In the IP address range, set the *Start IP address* to 172.24.20.50 and *End IP address* to 172.24.20.240. For the Subnet mask, type 255.255.255.0. Click Next.
6. On the *Add Exclusion and Delay* page, click Next.
7. On the *Lease Duration* page, change the duration to 3 days, and click Next.
8. On the Configure DHCP Options page, click Next.
9. On the *Router (Default Gateway)* page, type the address of 172.24.20.20, and click Add. Click Next.
10. On the *Domain name and DNS Servers* page, the *Parent domain* should already be set to contoso.com, and the DNS server should already be defined. Click Next.
11. On the *WINS Servers* page, click Next.
12. On the *Activate Scope* page, click Next.
13. When the wizard is complete, click Finish.
14. Right-click IPv4, and then click New Scope.
15. When the *New Wizard* opens, click Next.
16. In the *Name* text box, type Scope2, and click Next.
17. In the IP address range, set the *Start IP address* to 172.24.21.50 and *End IP address* to 172.24.21.240. For the *Subnet mask*, type 255.255.255.0. Click Next.
18. On the *Add Exclusion and Delay* page, click Next.
19. On the *Lease Duration* page, change the duration to 3 days, and click Next.
20. On the Configure DHCP Options, click Next.
21. On the *Router (Default Gateway)* page, type the address of 172.24.21.20, and click Add. Click Next.
22. On the Domain name and DNS Servers page, the *Parent domain* should already be set to contoso.com, and the DNS server should already be defined. Click Next.
23. On the *WINS Servers* page, click Next.
24. On the *Activate Scope* page, click Next.
25. When the wizard is complete, click Finish.
26. Right-click IPv4, and click New Superscope.
27. When the *New SuperScope Wizard* begins, type Super1 in the *Name* text box, and click Next.
28. On the *Select Scopes* page, press the Control key and hold it down. Then click Scope1 and Scope2. Release the Control key. Click Next.
29. Click Finish. The superscope shows in the DHCP console (see Figure 11-5).

Figure 11-5

Viewing a superscope in the DHCP console

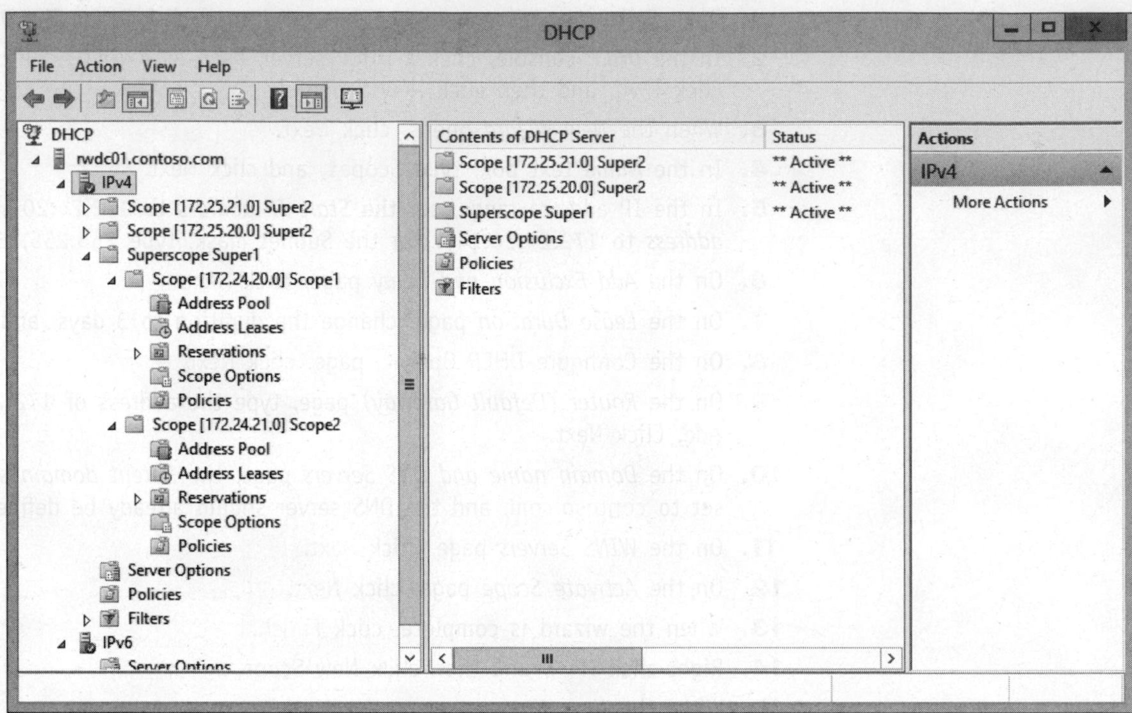

CREATE A SUPERSCOPE FROM SCRATCH

GET READY. To create a superscope from scratch, perform the following steps:

1. Open Server Manager, open the Tools menu, and click DHCP. The *DHCP* console opens.
2. In the *DHCP* console, click the DHCP server, such as RWDC01.contoso.com. Right-click IPv4, and then click New Superscope.
3. When the *New SuperScope Wizard* begins, type Super2 in the *Name* text box, and click Next.
4. In the IP address range, set the *Start IP address* to 172.25.20.50 and *End IP address* to 172.25.21.254. For the subnet mask, type 255.255.255.0. Click Next.
5. When it says that address range is too large for a single scope, click Yes, to create a superscope. Click Next.
6. On the *Lease Duration* page, change the duration to 3 days, and click Next.
7. On the Configure DHCP Options page, click Next.
8. On the *Router (Default Gateway)* page, type the address of 172.25.20.20, and click Add. Click Next.
9. On the *Domain name and DNS Servers* page, the *Parent domain* should already be set to contoso.com, and the DNS server should already be defined. Click Next.
10. On the *WINS Servers* page, click Next.
11. On the *Active Scope* page, click Next.
12. Click Finish. The superscope shows in the *DHCP* console.

Creating and Configuring Multicast Scopes

When a host sends packets to a single host (single point to single point), the communication is ***unicast***. ***Broadcast*** is sent from one host to all other hosts (one point to all other points). ***Multicast*** is when packets are sent from one host to multiple hosts (one point to a set of other points). Multicasting delivers the same packet simultaneously to a group of clients, which results in less bandwidth usage. For example, if you have to send a live video to 100 computers, instead of sending 100 sets of packets (unicast), you would send one set of packets. When multicast packets reach a router, the packets are forwarded only to the networks that have receivers for the packets. Besides live video or audio transmissions, it can also be used in some instances when deploying multiple computers at the same time—you only need to send one set of packets to multiple computers.

CERTIFICATION READY
Create and configure superscopes and multicast scopes.
Objective 4.1

Classful networks include Class A, Class B, and Class C networks. The first octet is the following:

- **Class A:** 0-127 with a default subnet mask of 255.0.0.0
- **Class B:** 128-191 with a default subnet mask of 255.255.0.0
- **Class C:** 192-223 with a default subnet mask of 255.255.255.0

Class D addresses are defined from 224.0.0.0 to 239.255.255.255 and used for multicast addresses.

In DHCP, ***multicast scopes*** (commonly known as a *Multicast Address Dynamic Client Allocation Protocol (MADCAP) scopes*) allow applications to reserve a multicast IP address for data and content delivery. Applications that use multicasting request addresses from the scopes need to support the MADCAP application programming interface (API).

Creating and managing a multicast scope is similar to creating and managing a normal scope; however, multicast scopes cannot use reservations and you cannot set additional options such as DNS and routing. In addition, because multicast is shared by groups of computers, the default duration of a multicast scope is 30 days.

CREATE A MULTICAST SCOPE

GET READY. To create a multicast scope, perform the following steps:

1. Open Server Manager, open the Tools menu, and click DHCP. The *DHCP* console opens.
2. In the *DHCP* console, click the DHCP server, such as RWDC01.contoso.com. Right-click IPv4, and then click New Multicast Scope.
3. When the *New Multicast Scope Wizard* opens, click Next.
4. In the *Name* text box, type Multicast Scope1, and click Next.
5. In the IP address range, set the *Start IP address* to 224.0.0.0 and *End IP address* to 224.255.255.255. Click Next.
6. On the *Add Exclusion and Delay* page, click Next.
7. On the *Lease Duration* page, click Next.
8. On the *Activate Scope* page, click Next.
9. When the installation is complete, click Finish.

Implementing DHCPv6 Scopes

IPv6 address utilizes a 128-bit address space to provide addressing for every device on the Internet with a globally unique address. Because the IPv6 addresses uses 128 bits, the addresses are usually divided into groups of 16 bits, written as 4 hex digits. Hex digits include 0, 1, 2, 3, 4, 5, 6, 7, 8, 9, A, B, C, D, E, and F. Colons separate the groups. An example of an address is the following:

FE80:0000:0000:0000:02C3:B2DF:FEA5:E4F1

Similar to the IPv4 addresses, IPv6 addresses are divided into network bits and host addresses. In addition, IPv6 supports automatic configuration. However, with a Windows DHCP server, you can perform stateful address autoconfiguration.

CERTIFICATION READY
Implement DHCPv6.
Objective 4.1

The first 64 bits of an IPv6 address define the network address, and the second 64 bits define the host address. Therefore, in the previous example address, FE80:0000:0000:0000 defines the network bits and 02C3:B2DF:FEA5:E4F1 defines the host bits. The network bits are also further divided where 48 bits are used for the network prefix and the next 16 bits are used for subnetting. The remaining host bits are 64-bits.

With IPv6, unicast addressing can be divided into the following:

- **Global unicast addresses:** Public addresses that are globally routable and reachable on the IPv6 portion of the Internet.
- **Link-local addresses:** Private non-routable addresses confined to a single subnet. These addresses are used to communicate with neighboring hosts on the same link and are equivalent to the Automatic Private IP addresses (169.254.x.x) used by IPv4 when a DHCP server cannot be contacted. Although they can be used to set up permanent small LANs, link-local addresses can also be used to create temporary networks or ad-hoc networks. Although routers process packets sent to a link-local address, they do not forward the packets to other links.
- **Unique local addresses:** Intended private addressing, so that you can join two subnets together without creating any addressing problems.

An IPv6 host address can be configured with stateful or stateless mode. Because the two address configuration modes are independent of each other and will not trample over each other, a host can use both stateless and stateful address configuration.

Stateless mechanism is used to configure both link-local addresses and additional non-link-local addresses based on Router Solicitation and Router Advertisement messages with neighboring routers. With stateless autoconfiguration, the MAC address is used to generate the host bits. When using stateless configuration, the address is not assigned by a DHCP server. However, a DHCP server can still assign other IPv6 configuration settings.

Stateful configuration has the IPv6 addresses and additional IPv6 configuration, assigned by a DHCPv6 server.

When you create an IPv6 scopes, you define the following properties:

- **Prefix:** Defines the network portion of the IP address.
- **Preference:** Values assigned to a DHCP scope to indicate which the preferred DHCP server to use when an organization has multiple DHCP servers. The scope with the lowest preference value is used first.
- **Exclusions:** Defines single addresses or blocks of addresses that will not be offered for lease.
- **Valid and preferred lifetimes:** Defines how long leased addresses are valid. The preferred lifetime is the preferred amount of time the lease should be valid. The valid lifetime is the maximum amount of time the lease is valid.
- **DHCP options:** IPv6 options such as DNS servers and default gateway.

CREATE A DHCP IPV6 SCOPE

GET READY. To create a DHCP IPv6 scope, perform the following steps:

1. Open Server Manager, open the Tools menu, and click DHCP. The *DHCP* console opens.
2. Right-click IPv6, and click New Scope.
3. When the New Scope Wizard starts, click Next.
4. Type a name such as IPv6Scope1 in the *Name* text box.
5. In the *Scope Prefix* page (see Figure 11-6), specify the *Prefix* such as FEC0::. In addition, specify the *Preference* value, such as 0.

Figure 11-6

Specifying the network prefix

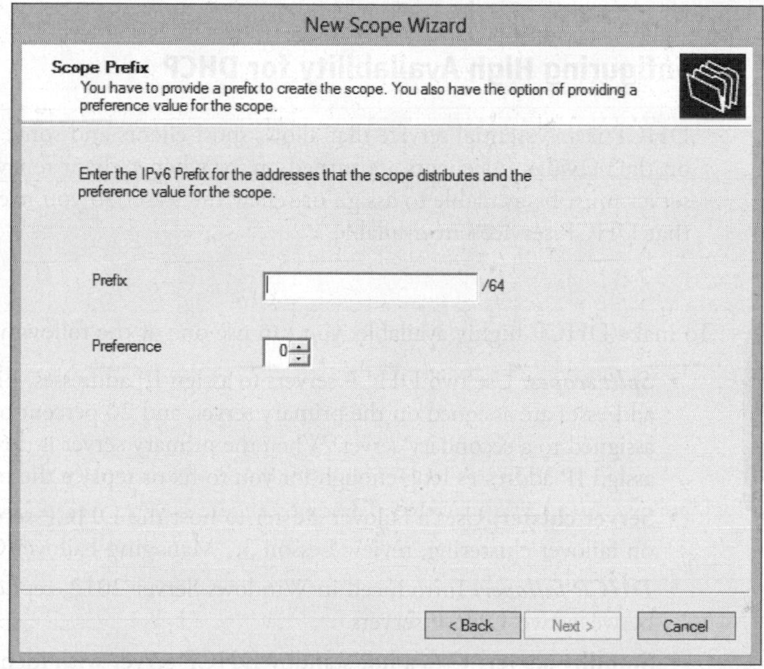

6. On the *Add Exclusions* page, click Next.
7. On the *Scope Lease* page, specify the preferred life time, and valid life time for the host. Change the *Preferred Life Time* to 1 day, and the *Valid Life Time* to 10 days. Click Next.
8. When the wizard is complete, *Yes* is already selected to activate the scope. Click Finish.

DHCP IPv6 options can be assigned at the server level, or the scope level. To configure the server level, right-click *IPv6,* and click *Set Predefined Options*. To configure the options at the scope level, expand the scope, right-click *Scope Options*, and click *Configure Options*. The options available include:

- **00021 SIP Server Domain Name List:** Specifies a list of the domain names of the Session Initiation Protocol (SIP) outbound proxy servers for the client to use.
- **00022 SIP Servers IPv6 Address List:** Specifies a list of IPv6 addresses indicating SIP outbound proxy servers available to the client. If an organization has more than one server, the server with the highest preference is used.
- **00023 DNS Recursive Name Server IPv6 Address:** The DNS server used for DNS queries. If an organization has more than one DHNS server, the server with the highest preference is used.
- **00024 Domain Search List:** Specifies the domain search list the client is to use when resolving hostnames with DNS.

- **00027 NIS IPv6 Address List:** Specifies a list of IPv6 addresses indicating Network Information Services (NIS) servers available to the client.
- **00028 NIS + IPv6 Address List:** Specifies a list of IPv6 addresses indicating Network Information Services v2 (NIS +) servers available to the client.
- **00029 NIS Domain List:** Used by the server to convey the client's list of NIS Domain Name information to the client.
- **00030 NIS + Domain Name List:** Used by the server to convey the client's list of NIS + Domain Name information to the client.
- **00031 SNTP Servers IPv6 Address List:** Provides a list of one or more IPv6 addresses of SNTP servers so clients can perform time synchronization with the SNTP server.

Configuring High Availability for DHCP

DHCP is an essential service that allows most clients and some servers to communicate on the network. As clients are turned on, or when a client renews a lease, the DHCP server must be available to assign or renew the lease. So you need to take steps to ensure that DHCP services are available.

CERTIFICATION READY
Configure high availability for DHCP including DHCP failover and split scopes.
Objective 4.1

To make DHCP highly available, you can use one of the following methods:

- ***Split scopes:*** Use two DHCP servers to assign IP addresses. Eighty percent of the available addresses are assigned on the primary server, and 20 percent of the available addresses are assigned to a secondary server. When the primary server is down, the secondary server can assign IP addresses long enough for you to fix or replace the primary server.
- **Server cluster:** Uses a failover cluster to host the DHCP server. For more information on failover clustering, review Lesson 3, "Managing Failover Clustering."
- ***DHCP failover:*** Introduced in Windows Server 2012, replicates lease information between two DHCP servers.
- **Standby server:** Uses a hot standby DHCP server with identical scopes and options as the production DHCP server.

If you restore a DHCP database server from backup, you need to make sure that DHCP clients do not receive IP addresses that are currently in use on the network. This can be accomplished by opening the *Properties* of a scope, clicking the *Advanced* tab, and setting the *Conflict Detection* value to 2.

CONFIGURING SPLIT SCOPES

For years, if you wanted high availability, you would use a split-scope configuration, also known as the *80/20 configuration*. Split-scope configuration, uses two DHCP servers, with the same scopes and options. However, the scopes have complementary exclusion ranges, so that there is no overlap in the addresses that they lease to clients. You do not want the two servers to hand out the same address to different clients.

It is known as the *80/20 configuration* because the primary server is assigned 80 percent of the available addresses, whereas the secondary server is assigned 20 percent of the available addresses. The secondary server is configured to respond after a delay, giving the primary server the first opportunity to hand out addresses. Because the local server responds first, it leases the address to the clients. If the primary server is not available, the secondary server will respond and lease an address.

To simplify the configuring of split-scopes, Windows Server 2012 and Windows Server 2012 R2 includes a Split-Configuration Wizard. To access this wizard, you need to have the two DHCP servers that are authorized. Then after you create a scope, on one of the servers, you can access the DHCP Split-Scope Wizard.

USE THE DHCP SPLIT-SCOPE WIZARD

GET READY. To use the DHCP Split-Scope Wizard, perform the following steps:

1. Open Server Manager, open the Tools menu, and click DHCP. The *DHCP* console opens.
2. Right-click a scope that you created on the DHCP server, click Advanced, and click Split-Scope.
3. When the *DHCP Split-Scope Configuration Wizard* starts, click Next.
4. On the *Additional DHCP Server* page, type the name of the secondary DCHP server, and click Next.
5. On the *Percentage of Split* page (see Figure 11-7), the slider bar is already set at 80. Click Next.

Figure 11-7

Specifying the 80-20 split

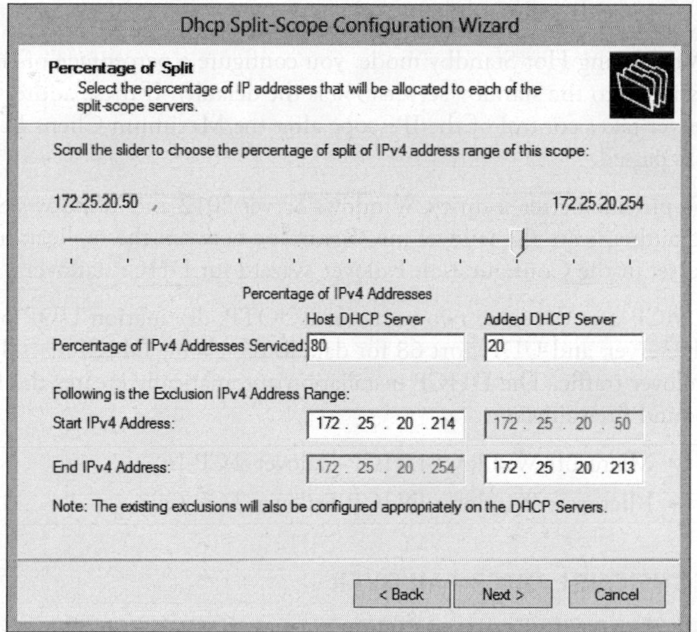

6. On the *Delay in DHCP Offer* page, the host DHCP server and the added DHCP server have a delay of 0 milliseconds. Change the delay of the added DHCP server to 500. Click Next.
7. When the wizard is complete, click Finish.
8. On the *Summary of Split-Scope* page, click Close.

CONFIGURING DHCP FAILOVER

In the past, DHCP failover was not possible because each DHCP server had its own database. So when a lease was granted to a client, the other DHCP server would not be aware of the other lease. So if you assign the same pool of addresses, you would have the same address assigned to two different hosts, causing an IP address conflict. You can use cluster, which requires some manual configuration and monitoring.

Starting with Windows Server 2012, DHCP can replicate lease information between two DHCP servers for IPv4 scopes and subnets. If one DHCP server fails or becomes overloaded, the other server services the clients for the entire subnet.

DHCP failover establishes a failover relationship between the two DHCP servers. Each relationship has a unique name, which is exchanged during configuration. A single DHCP server can have multiple failover relationships with other DHCP servers as long as each relationship has a unique name.

DHCP failover is time sensitive. The time between partners must be no greater than one minute. If the time is greater, the failover process will halt with a critical error.
DHCP failover supports two modes:

- **Load Sharing:** Both servers simultaneously supply IP configuration to clients. By default, the load is distributed evenly, 50:50. However, you can adjust the ratio if you prefer one server over another. Load Sharing is the default mode.
- **Hot Standby:** One server is the primary server that actively assigns IP configuration for the scope or subnet, and the other is the secondary server that assumes the DHCP role if the primary server becomes unavailable. Hot Standby mode is best suited when the disaster recovery site is located at a different location. Because the failover is defined for a scope, you can have one server act as the primary for one scope or subnet, and be the secondary for another.

When using Hot Standby mode, you configure a percentage of the scope addresses to be assigned to the standby server (5% is the default). If these addresses are used, the secondary server takes control of the IP scope after the Maximum Client Lead Time (MCLT) interval has passed.

To provide better security, Windows Server 2012 and Windows Server 2012 R2 can be used to authenticate the failover message traffic between the replication partners using a shared secret in the Configuration Failover Wizard for DHCP failover.

DHCP uses the same two ports for BOOTP: destination UDP port 67 for sending data to the server, and UDP port 68 for data to the client. DHCP uses TCP port 647 to listen for failover traffic. The DHCP installation automatically creates the following inbound and outbound firewall rules:

- Microsoft-Windows-DHCP-Failover-TCP-In
- Microsoft-Windows-DHCP-Failover-TCP-Out

CONFIGURE DHCP FAILOVER

GET READY. To configure DHCP failover, perform the following steps:

1. Open Server Manager, open the Tools menu, and click DHCP. The *DHCP* console opens.
2. Expand IPv4.
3. To configure a single scope, right-click the scope, and click Configure Failover. To configure failover for all scopes, right-click IPv4, and click Configure Failover.
4. When the *Configure Failover Wizard* starts, all scopes will be selected. To select only one scope, deselect the Select all option and click the scope that you want to configure. Click Next.
5. On the *Specify the partner server to use for failover* page, type the name of the partner DHCP server and click Next.
6. On the *Create a new failover relationship* page (see Figure 11-8), specify the maximum client lead time, the mode, the load balance percentage, and the state switch over interval.

Figure 11-8

Creating a new failover relationship

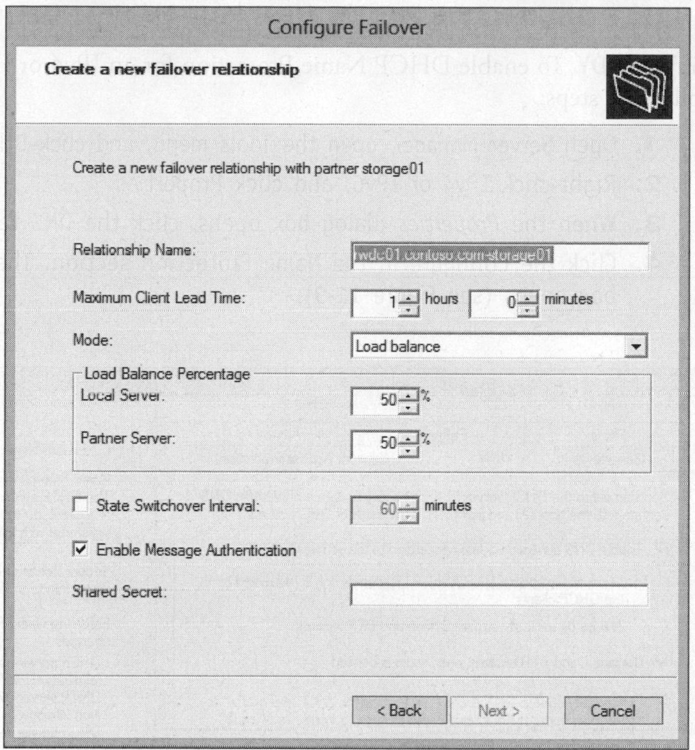

7. By default, *Enable Message Authentication* is enabled. Type a shared secret such as Password01. Click Next.
8. To complete the wizard, click Finish.
9. When the configuration is done, click Close.

Configuring DHCP Name Protection

If an organization uses only Windows systems that are part of an Active Directory domain, each computer will have its own unique computer name, which DHCP registers in DNS on behalf of the client. Name squatting is when a non-Windows based computer registers a name in DNS that is already registered to a Windows-based computer. To prevent non-Microsoft systems from overwriting systems that use static addresses, Windows Server 2012 introduced ***DHCP Name Protection*** to prevent these conflicts.

CERTIFICATION READY
Configure DHCP Name Protection.
Objective 4.1

When one client registers a name with DNS, but the name is already used by another client, the original machine can become inaccessible. DHCP Name Protection addresses uses a resource record known as a *Dynamic Host Configuration Identifier (DHCID)* to track which machines originally requested which names. When DHCP assigns or renews an address, the DHCP server refers to the DHCID in DNS to verify that the machine that is requesting the name is the original machine that used the name. If it is not the same machine, then the DNS resource record is not updated.

Name Protection can be used for both IPv4 and IPv6 and can be configured at the server level or at the scope level. However, configuring DHCP Name Protection at the server level applies only to newly created scopes.

ENABLE DHCP NAME PROTECTION FOR AN IPV4 OR IPV6 NODE

GET READY. To enable DHCP Name Protection for an IPv4 or IPv6 node, perform the following steps:

1. Open Server Manager, open the Tools menu, and click DHCP. The *DHCP* console opens.
2. Right-click IPv4 or IPv6, and click Properties.
3. When the *Properties* dialog box opens, click the DNS tab.
4. Click the Configure in the Name Protection section. The *Name Protection* dialog box opens (see Figure 11-9).

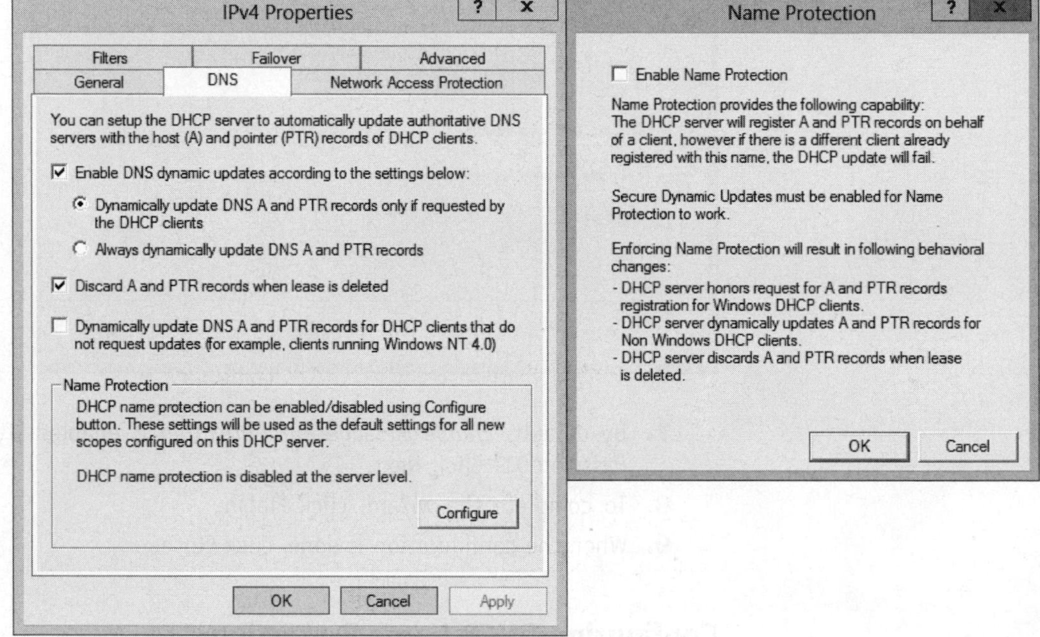

Figure 11-9

Enabling DHCP Name Protection

5. Click to select the Enable Name Protection option.
6. Click OK to close the *Name Protection* dialog box and click OK to close the *Properties* dialog box.

ENABLE DHCP NAME PROTECTION FOR A SCOPE

GET READY. To enable DHCP Name Protection for scope, perform the following steps:

1. Open Server Manager, open the Tools menu, and click DHCP. The *DHCP* console opens.
2. Right-click the scope and click Properties.
3. When the *Properties* dialog box opens, click the DNS tab.
4. Click Configure in the *Name Protection* section. The *Name Protection* dialog box opens.
5. Click to select the Enable Name Protection option.
6. Click OK to close the *Name Protection* dialog box and click OK to close the *Properties* dialog box.

SKILL SUMMARY

In this lesson you learned:

- The Dynamic Host Configuration Protocol (DHCP) is a network protocol that automatically configures the IP configuration of a device including assigning an IP address, subnet mask, default gateway, and primary and secondary DNS servers.
- A superscope is the grouping of multiple scopes into a single administrative entity. By using superscopes, you can support larger subnets.
- Multicast is when packets are sent from one host to multiple hosts (one point to a set of other points). Multicasting delivers the same packet simultaneously to a group of clients, which results in less bandwidth usage.
- In DHCP, multicast scopes (commonly known as a *Multicast Address Dynamic Client Allocation Protocol (MADCAP) scopes*) allow applications to reserve a multicast IP address for data and content delivery.
- IPv6 address utilizes 128-bit address space to provide addressing for every device on the Internet with a globally unique address.
- Stateless mechanism is used to configure both link-local addresses and additional non-link-local addresses based on Router Solicitation and Router Advertisement messages with neighboring routers.
- Stateful configuration has the IPv6 addresses and additional IPv6 configuration, assigned by a DHCPv6 server.
- DHCP is an essential service that allows most clients and some servers to communicate on the network. As clients are turned on, or when a client renews a lease, the DHCP server must be available to assign or renew the lease.
- Split-scope configuration uses two DHCP servers, with the same scopes and options. However, the scopes have complementary exclusion ranges, so that there is no overlap in the addresses that they lease to clients. You do not want the two servers to hand out the same address to different clients.
- It is known as the *80/20 configuration* because the primary server is assigned 80 percent of the available addresses, whereas the secondary server is assigned 20 percent of the available addresses.
- Starting with Windows Server 2012, DHCP can replicate lease information between two DHCP servers for IPv4 scopes and subnets. If one DHCP server fails or becomes overloaded, the other server services the clients for the entire subnet.
- To prevent non-Microsoft systems fromoverwritting systems that use static addresses, Windows Server 2012 introduced DHCP Name Protection to prevent these conflicts.

■ Knowledge Assessment

Multiple Choice

Circle the letter that corresponds to the best answer.

1. You have a scope called *Scope1* (192.168.3.0/24) that is running out of addresses. What can you do to expand the number of addresses?
   a. Create a 192.168.4.0 scope and create a superscope
   b. Create an IPv6 scope
   c. Reassign the scope to 172.24.3.0/16
   d. Create a multicast scope
2. Which type of communication sends a single set of packets to multiple hosts at the same time?
   a. unicast
   b. broadcast
   c. multicast
   d. anycast
3. What type of IPv6 address mechanism is used to generate link-local addresses using the MAC address?
   a. stateless
   b. stateful
   c. prefix-based
   d. multicast
4. What is the default DHCP failover mode?
   a. Stateless
   b. Stateful
   c. Load Sharing
   d. Hot Standby
5. What is used to prevent non-Windows to overwrite DNS information for systems that use static addresses?
   a. Dynamic Protection
   b. Stateful Protection
   c. Stateless Protection
   d. DHCP Name Protection
6. What ports are required for DHCP failover?
   a. 20–21
   b. 67–68
   c. 101–102
   d. 140–141
7. When you add a DHCP reservation for a printer, what two components should you include in the reservation? (Choose two answers.)
   a. the MAC address
   b. the Default gateway
   c. the printer server name
   d. the IP address
8. You have two DHCP servers, Server1 and Server2, running Windows Server 2012 R2. You create a scope called *Scope1*. Server1 is your primary DHCP server. What is the easiest way to assign 80 percent of the addresses to Server1 and 2 percent to Server2?
   a. On Scope1, run the Split-Scope Wizard
   b. Create a multicast scope
   c. Create a DHCP policy
   d. Create a superscope

9. You have just installed a new DHCP server. You try to start the DHCP service, but it will not start. What should you do?
a. Restart the server
b. Configure a scope
c. Activate the scope
d. Authorize the server in Active Directory

10. You replaced your DHCP server due to hardware failure. You restore the server from a backup. You need to ensure that DHCP clients do not receive IP addresses that are currently in use on the network. What should you do?
a. Set the Conflict Detection value to 2
b. Add the DHCP server option 60
c. Add the DHCP server option 44
d. Enable the Retry option

11. You have a server running Windows Server 2012 R2. You want to assign the same IP address from the DHCP server to the server every time. What do you need to do?
a. Create a DHCP policy
b. Create an exclusion policy
c. Create a single scope with the specified address
d. Create a reservation

12. You have a 192.168.1.0/24 subnet. Using DHCP, you want IP phones to be assigned addresses between 192.168.1.51–100 and desktop computers assigned addresses between 192.168.1.101–155. How should you proceed while keeping the administrative effort to a minimum?
a. Create a multicast scope
b. Create a superscope
c. Use DHCP policies
d. Create multiple standard scopes

13. You have the following DHCP scope: 192.168.1.0/24. You need to migrate the clients to 172.24.1.0/16. What type of scope should you create to perform the migration?
a. a multicast scope
b. a superscope
c. a split-scope
d. an IPv6 scope

14. You are an administrator for the Contoso Corporation. Your primary office is in Sacramento and your data recovery site is in Las Vegas. You want to install a DHCP server at both locations to provide high availability. Which configuration should you use?
a. NLB cluster
b. Failover over cluster
c. Load Sharing mode failover partner
d. Hot Standby mode failover partner

15. You have a server running Windows Server 2012 R2 with five networks. You create two teams, each with two NICs. You want to use reservations to always assign the same IP addresses to the interfaces. How many reservations do you need on the DHCP server?
a. 2
b. 3
c. 4
d. 5

Matching and Identification

1. Identify the class (A, B, C, or D) of the following addresses.

_______ a) 10.6.43.34
_______ b) 129.54.5.20
_______ c) 225.225.255.225
_______ d) 201.32.23.1
_______ e) 238.54.1.1

Build a List

1. Identify the steps in order to allocate a different range of IP addresses to network HP printers within a scope and a different lease period by placing the number of the step in the appropriate space. Not all steps will be used.

_______ Create a scope
_______ Set the lease duration for the policy
_______ Create a policy
_______ Create a Client Identifier
_______ Create a User Class
_______ Create a Vendor Class
_______ Configure a condition

2. You have a scope that covers the 172.50.1.0/24 subnet. Identify the steps in order to expand the scope to 172.50.2.0 by placing the number of the step in the appropriate space. Not all steps will be used.

_______ Right-click the IPv4 and create a new superscope
_______ Duplicate the current scope
_______ Create a new scope
_______ Create two new scopes
_______ Select two scopes that you want to combine and finish creating the superscope
_______ Right-click the original scope and expand address range

3. Identify the steps in order when configuring a split-scope by placing the number of the step in the appropriate space. Not all steps will be used.

_______ Create the scope on the primary server
_______ Increase the delay for the primary server
_______ Increase the delay for the secondary server
_______ Specify the percentage of split
_______ Create the scope on the secondary server
_______ Run the DHCP Split-Scope Configuration Wizard

Choose an Option

Circle the tab on Figure 11-10 that you would click to enable Name Protection.

Figure 11-10

Enabling Name Protection

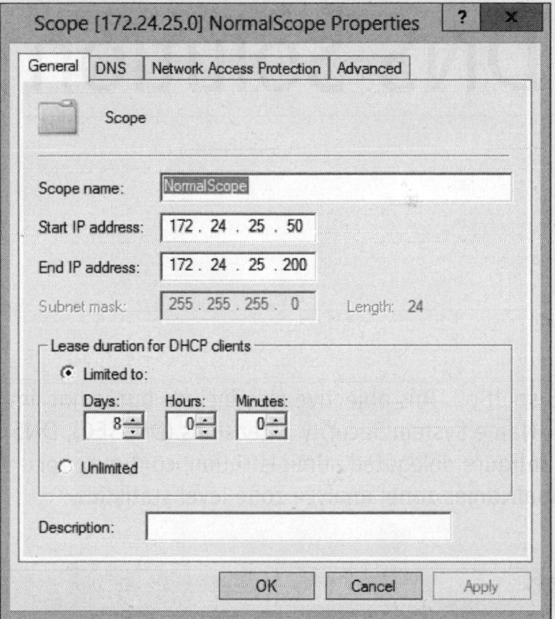

■ Business Case Scenarios

Scenario 11-1: Configuring DHCP High Availability

You are the administrator for the Contoso Corporation. Recently, the DHCP server failed. To fix the problem, you had to fix the server and restore from backup. In the future, you want to make the server fault tolerant in case it fails in the future. In addition, you want to ensure that you add additional sites, and you want to allow the servers to handle a bigger load. What would you recommend?

Scenario 11-2: Performing Granular IP Address Leasing on a DHCP Scope

You are the administrator for the Contoso Corporation. You have 15 sites. You want to create one DHCP scope that includes one set of addresses for computers, one set of addresses for printers, and one set of addresses for IP phones. What would you do?

Implementing an Advanced DNS Solution

70-412 EXAM OBJECTIVE

Objective 4.2 – Implement an advanced DNS solution. This objective may include but is not limited to: Configure security for DNS including Domain Name System Security Extensions (DNSSEC), DNS Socket Pool, and cache locking; configure DNS logging; configure delegated administration; configure recursion; configure netmask ordering; configure a GlobalNames zone; analyze zone level statistics.

Lesson Heading	Exam Objective
Configuring Security for DNS	Configure security for DNS
Configuring DNSSEC	Configure DNSSEC
Configuring DNS Socket Pool	Configure DNS Socket Pool
Configuring DNS cache locking	Configure cache locking
Configuring DNS Logging	Configure DNS logging
Configuring Delegated Administration	Configure delegated administration
Configuring Recursion	Configure recursion
Configuring Netmask Ordering	Configure netmask ordering
Configuring a GlobalNames Zone	Configure a GlobalNames zone
Analyzing Zone Level Statistics	Analyze zone level statistics

KEY TERMS

automated key rollover
debug logging
DNS Security (DNSSEC)
DNSSEC Resource records
Key Signing Key (KSK)
Name Resolution Policy Table (NRPT)
netmask ordering
recursion
signing the zone
socket pool
trust anchor
Zone Signing Key (ZSK)
Zone Signing Parameters

Configuring Security for DNS

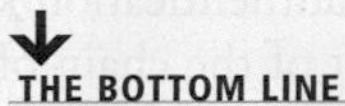

THE BOTTOM LINE

Windows Server 2012 and Windows Server 2012 R2 include a number of new features for domain naming services (DNS) security. Securing the DNS server and DNS records prevents false records from being added and prevents clients from receiving incorrect DNS query responses, which can lead them to visit phishing sites or worse. To prevent DNS being used to attack systems, DNS Security (DNSSEC), cache locking, and other security measures are implemented.

CERTIFICATION READY
Configure Security for DNS including DNSSEC, DNS Socket Pool, and cache locking.
Objective 4.2

Having already deployed DNS servers and configured them successfully in the 70-410 and 70-411 courses, the need arises to secure the DNS servers and caches from spoofing, man-in-the-middle, and cache-poisoning attacks. In the modern world, it is a sad fact that securing all areas of functionality is a necessity. DNS is a common area for attack by interception and tampering. A client that uses DNS to connect is always vulnerable to redirection to an attacker's servers unless the zone has been secured using DNSSEC.

The process for securing a zone using DNSSEC is called ***signing the zone***. Once signed, any queries on the signed zone will return digital signatures along with the normal DNS resource records. The digital signatures are verified using the public key of the server or zone from the ***trust anchor***. DNSSEC uses trust anchors represented by public keys that define the top of a chain of trust. The trust anchor verifies that a digital signature and associated data is valid.

Once this public key has been obtained, the resolver or client is able to validate the responses it receives. The trust anchor is the most important link in this chain. The server, resolver, or zone must be configured with this trust anchor. Once this is achieved, the client will be able to confirm that the DNS information it receives came from a valid server, was unchanged, and does or does not actually exist.

Configuring DNSSEC

DNS Security (DNSSEC) is a suite of protocols defined by the Internet Engineering Task Force (IETF) for use on IP networks. DNSSEC provides DNS clients, or resolvers, with proof of identity of DNS records and verified denial of existence. DNSSEC does *not* provide availability or confidentiality information.

CERTIFICATION READY
Configure Security for DNS including DNSSEC.
Objective 4.2

DNSSEC can be enabled on an Active-Directory Integrated zone (ADI) or on a primary zone. As with all security measures and particularly advanced implementations, planning is important. Which zones do you want to secure? Who has access to the zone? Who has access to the server and the administration of the server security? The answers to these and lots of other questions always depend on the security requirements of your organization. By the time you are ready to implement DNSSEC on your DNS server, the security documentation should have already been created and approved.

DNSSEC is installed as part of the DNS Server role. To enable DNSSEC, Windows Server 2012 and Windows Server 2012 R2 provides a DNSSEC Zone Signing Wizard. This wizard is run from the DNS console and configures the ***Zone Signing Parameters***—all the settings required for ensuring the zone is signed correctly and securely. Follow the instructions to configure DNSSEC for the ADatum.com ADI zone.

Once a zone is signed, there are a number of new ***DNSSEC Resource records*** available. These records are in addition to the standard A, NS, and SRV records in an unsigned zone. These DNSSEC Resource records include DNSKEY, RRSIG, and NSEC. DNSKEY records are used to sign the records. The RRSIG record is returned to the client in response to a successful query along with the A record. The NSEC record is returned to positively deny that the requested A record exists in the zone.

DNSSEC uses a series of keys to secure the server and the zones. These include the ***Key Signing Key (KSK)*** and the ***Zone Signing Key (ZSK)***. The KSK is an authentication key that signs all the DNSKEY records at the root of the zone, and it is part of the chain of trust. The ZSK is used to sign zone data.

Automated key rollover is the process by which a DNSSEC key management strategy for key management is made easier with automated key regeneration.

CONFIGURE DNSSEC ON AN ACTIVE DIRECTORY INTEGRATED ZONE

GET READY. Log on to the computer where you installed the DNS Server role and the ADatum.com ADI zone, with administrative privileges. To configure DNSSEC on an Active Directory integrated zone, perform the following steps:

TAKE NOTE*

Examine all the options in the Zone Signing Wizard. Test items often require you to know where to set a particular choice.

1. Open Server Manager and click Tools > DNS. This loads the *DNS Manager* console.
2. Expand *DNS Server* by clicking the arrow to the left of the server name.
3. Expand the *Forward Lookup Zones* by clicking the arrow to the left of Forward Lookup Zones.
4. Right-click the ADatum.com zone. Click DNSSEC > Sign The Zone. The DNSSEC Zone Signing Wizard opens. It is possible to choose the default options throughout.
5. Click Next. The wizard displays the signing options.
6. There are three options to define the parameters used to sign the zone. Select Customize zone signing parameters, and then click Next.

TAKE NOTE* The greater the key length (in bits), the more secure the DNSSEC keys will be. A long key requires more server resources to encrypt and decrypt. This overhead can be noticeable if the key length is set too long.

7. This screen allows the selection of the DNS server that will manage the keys for the zone. The default is the current server. Click Next.
8. In the *New Key Signing Key (KSK)* dialog box, click Add, and then make the Key Signing Key property selections. Settings include the algorithm, key length, replication, and auto rollover. Click OK when the selections have been made. Click Next, and then click Next again.
9. In the *New Zone Signing Key (ZSK)* dialog box, click Add, and then make the Zone Signing Key property selections. Settings include the algorithm, key length, key storage provider, validity period of the keys, and auto rollover. Click OK when the selections have been made, and then click Next.
10. An NSEC record provides authenticated denial of existence. If a DNS client requests a record that does not exist, the server provides an authoritative denial and the NSEC or NSEC3 record verifies this as genuine. The options are for NSEC or NSEC3. NSEC3 is the default. Click Next.
11. If the DNS server is also a domain controller, when trust anchor distribution is enabled, every other DNS server that is also a domain controller in the forest will receive the trust anchors for the zone. This speeds up the key retrieval. Automated key rollover should be set if trust anchors are required on nondomain-joined computers. Click Next.

TAKE NOTE*

To set automatic key rollover for DNS servers that are not part of a domain, select the check box on this screen. The frequency and initial delay is also set here.

12. The final options screen, Signing and Polling Parameters allows for the configuration of the delegation key record algorithm (DS record) and the polling intervals for the delegated zones. Accept the defaults by clicking Next > Next. The wizard signs the zone. Click Finish. The new DNSSEC records can now be seen in the DNS Manager.

Note that the padlock at the root of the Adatum.com zone (see Figure 12-1) shows the zone is signed. Also note the additional records visible in the zone DNSKEY (Public Key for the zone), RRSIG, NSEC3. Indeed, each original entry now has four records: the A, RRSIG for the A, NSEC3, and the RRSIG for the NSEC3 record.

Figure 12-1

Displaying the signed zone

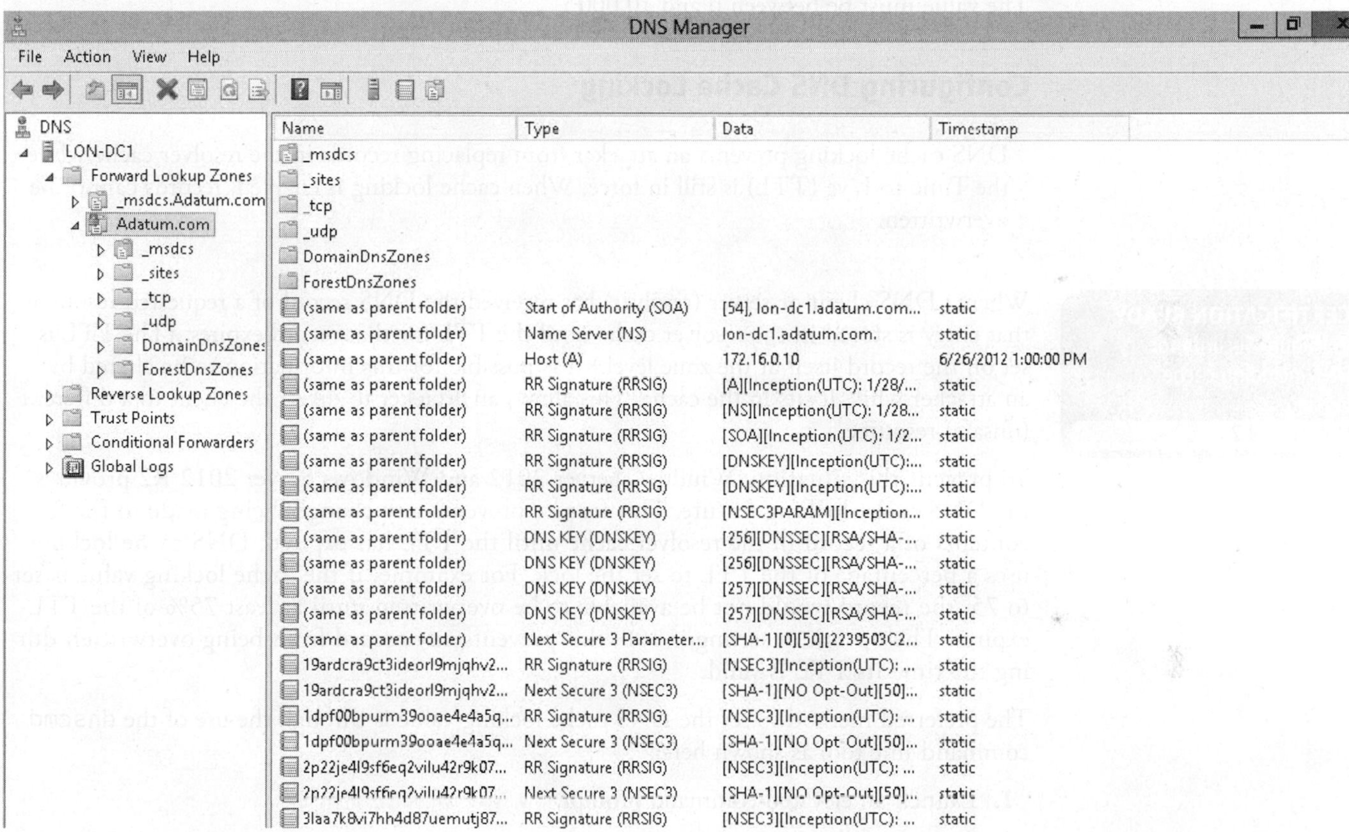

Once the zone is signed, two more options are available on the zone DNSSEC context menu: Properties and Unsign the Zone. The Properties dialog contains the settings you made in the wizard. Unsign the Zone removes all the records and disables DNSSEC for this zone.

The ***Name Resolution Policy Table (NRPT)*** contains a list of rules for DNS client access and response to the DNS server. NRPT is normally set through Group Policy when a zone is signed using DNSSEC.

Configuring DNS Socket Pool

CERTIFICATION READY
Configure Security for DNS including DNS Socket Pool.
Objective 4.2

The DNS ***socket pool*** is a tool used to allow source port randomization for DNS queries, which reduces the chances of an attacker guessing which IP address and port (socket) the DNS traffic uses.

The DNS socket pool protects against DNS spoofing attacks. To be able to tamper with DNS traffic, an attacker needs to know the correct socket and the randomly generated transaction ID.

TAKE NOTE*
Once signed, a zone cannot be removed from the Active Directory unless it is unsigned first.

DNS socket pooling is enabled by default in Windows Server 2012 and Windows Server 2012 R2. The default size of the DNS socket pool is 2500, and the available settings range from 0 to 10,000. The larger the number of ports available to the pool, the more secure the communication.

Windows Server 2012 and Windows Server 2012 R2 also allows for an exclusion list to be created. The preferred method to set the socket pool size is through the use of the `dnscmd` command-line tool as shown here:

1. Launch an elevated command prompt.
2. Type the following command:

```
dnscmd /Config /SocketPoolSize <value>
```

The value must be between 0 and 10,000.

Configuring DNS Cache Locking

DNS cache locking prevents an attacker from replacing records in the resolver cache while the Time to Live (TTL) is still in force. When cache locking is enabled, records cannot be overwritten.

CERTIFICATION READY
Configure Security for DNS including cache locking.
Objective 4.2

When a DNS client or server (resolver) has received the DNS record of a requested resource, that entry is stored in the resolver cache until the TTL for that record expires. (The TTL is set on the record itself at the zone level.) It is possible for this information to be altered by an attacker while it sits in the cache. This allows an attacker to divert the client to a different (unsafe) resource.

To prevent this situation, Windows Server 2012 and Windows Server 2012 R2 provides the DNS cache locking feature. This feature prevents any changes being made to the contents of a record in the resolver cache until the TTL has expired. DNS cache locking uses a percentage of the TTL to set the lock. For example, if the cache locking value is set to 75, the record would not be available to be overwritten until at least 75% of the TTL expires. The optimum setting is 100; this prevents any record from being overwritten during the time its TTL is valid.

The preferred method to set the DNS cache locking value is through the use of the `dnscmd` command-line tool as shown here:

1. Launch an elevated command prompt.
2. Type the following command:

```
dnscmd /Config /CacheLockingPercent <percent>
```

3. Restart the DNS Service to apply the new settings. From the command prompt enter `net stop DNS`, wait for the service to stop, and then enter `net start DNS`

USING WINDOWS POWERSHELL
To change the cache locking value using Windows PowerShell, run the following cmdlet from a Windows PowerShell window `Set-DnsServerCache -LockingPercent 100`

■ Configuring DNS Logging

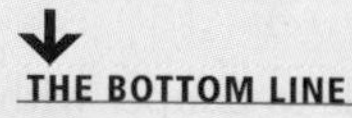
THE BOTTOM LINE

DNS logging is a troubleshooting tool to allow for detailed, file-based analysis of all DNS packets and messages. The full title is DNS ***debug logging***. There is a processing and storage overhead in the use of debug logging.

CERTIFICATION READY
Configure DNS logging.
Objective 4.2

Event Viewer is an essential tool in the successful management and troubleshooting of a DNS server. Windows Server 2012 and Windows Server 2012 R2 provides a specific DNS server application log. This log records events such as starting and stopping the DNS Service, changes to DNS configurations, warnings, and other events. In addition, the DNSSEC zone signing and zone loading events are recorded. There are, however, many occasions when more detailed logging of events, packets, and protocols is required. To facilitate this, Windows Server provides file-based debug logging.

TAKE NOTE*

Dns.log contains the debug logging activity. By default, this is located in the %SYSTEMROOT%\System32\Dns folder.

Debug logging is enabled at the server level and accessed through the DNS Server Properties dialog box.

CONFIGURE DNS DEBUG LOGGING

GET READY. Log on with administrative privileges to the computer where you installed the DNS Server role. Ensure that the ADatum.com ADI zone is present, and then perform the following steps:

1. Open Server Manager and click Tools > DNS. This loads the *DNS Manager* console.
2. Expand the DNS server by clicking the arrow to the left of the server name.
3. Right-click on the LON-DC1 server. Click Properties, click the Debug Logging tab (see Figure 12-2), and then check the Log Packets for debugging check box.

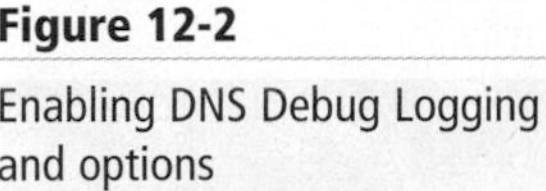

Figure 12-2
Enabling DNS Debug Logging and options

The following DNS debug logging options are available:

- **Direction of packets:** Send packets sent by the DNS server are logged in the DNS server log file. Receive packets received by the DNS server are logged in the log file.
- **Content of packets:** Queries specify that packets containing standard queries (per RFC 1034) are logged in the DNS server log file. Updates specify that packets containing dynamic updates (per RFC 2136) are logged in the DNS server log file.

- **Notifications:** Specifies that packets containing notifications (per RFC 1996) are logged in the DNS server log file.
- **Transport protocol:** UDP specifies that packets sent and received over UDP are logged in the DNS server log file. TCP specifies that packets sent and received over TCP are logged in the DNS server log file.
- **Type of packet:** Request specifies that request packets are logged in the DNS server log file (a request packet is characterized by a QR bit set to 0 in the DNS message header). Response specifies that response packets are logged in the DNS server log file (a response packet is characterized by a QR bit set to 1 in the DNS message header).
- **Enable filtering based on IP address:** Provides additional filtering of packets logged in the DNS server log file. This option allows logging of packets sent from specific IP addresses to a DNS server, or from a DNS server to specific IP addresses.
- **File name:** Lets you specify the name and location of the DNS server log file.
- **Log file maximum size limit:** Lets you set the maximum file size for the DNS server log file. When the specified maximum size of the DNS server log file is reached, the DNS server overwrites the oldest packet information with new information. If left unspecified, the DNS server log file's size can take up a large amount of hard disk space.

Debug logging can be highly resource-intensive and can impact the performance of the DNS server itself. It is recommended that debug logging be used as a temporary measure to gain detailed information regarding DNS server performance, only when it is required. For this reason, the debug logging is disabled by default. The debug logging settings allow for granular control of the types of events or DNS messages that are logged, which reduces the impact to a degree.

Configuring Delegated Administration

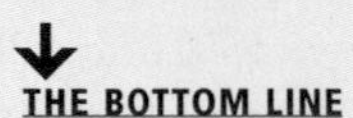

DNS is a key service within your network. Administration of the service should be restricted to those who really need it. The principle of least privilege should always apply to DNS administration.

CERTIFICATION READY
Configure delegated administration.
Objective 4.2

Domain Admins have full permissions by default to manage all aspects of the DNS server, but only in the domain where the Domain Admins security group is located. A member of the Enterprise Admins group has similar permissions but throughout the entire forest.

To delegate administration privileges to a specific user or security group, you add that user or group to the DNS Admins security group. Members of this group can view and modify all DNS data, settings, and the configuration of DNS servers within their home domain.

The DNS Admins group is a Domain Local security group. By default, this group is empty.

TAKE NOTE*

It is best practice to add individual users to the Global or Universal group and then to add the Global or Universal groups to the Domain Local Groups (such as the DNS Admins Group).

Configuring Recursion

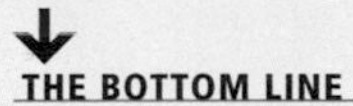

THE BOTTOM LINE

Recursion in DNS is the process by which a client makes a query to a DNS server for an IP address associated with a Fully Qualified Domain Name (FQDN). The server then establishes that IP address through one or many separate queries to other servers and returns the address to the querying client.

CERTIFICATION READY
Configure recursion.
Objective 4.2

In most business networks, the DNS servers are configured to allow recursive queries. That is, the querying client requests the IP address related to an FQDN such as www.adatum.com. The client then makes a recursive query to the configured DNS server.

The local DNS server must either provide an authoritative response (from its own zone) or a positive response (from its cache). If the DNS server has no copy of the namespace requested, it provides an authoritative response (stating the record does not exist).

If the DNS server is configured for recursion, the server makes a recursive query to other DNS servers (usually through root hints on the Internet) and eventually provides the authoritative answer to the querying client.

If recursion is not enabled and no forwarders are configured, the DNS server makes no further queries and responds only from the zones it holds.

The restriction of recursion is a good way of securing a DNS server and maintaining control of DNS query traffic.

To prevent all DNS servers from making recursive queries, forward all external queries to a single server and enable recursion and root hints (or a different forwarder such as an ISP DNS server). This configuration directs all Internet queries through a single internal DNS server, while all local domain or forest DNS queries are resolved locally.

DISABLE RECURSION

WARNING If recursion is disabled and root hints and forwarders are not used on any DNS servers, then *no* external queries will ever be resolved. In short, your network will never be able to connect to named resources on the Internet.

GET READY. Log on with administrative privileges to the computer where you installed the DNS Server role. Ensure that the ADatum.com ADI zone is present, and then perform the following steps:

1. Open Server Manager and click Tools > DNS. This loads the *DNS Manager* console.
2. Expand the DNS server by clicking the arrow to the left of the server name.
3. Right-click the LON-DC1 server. Click Properties, click the Advanced tab (see Figure 12-3) under *Server options*, and then check the Disable recursion (also disables forwarders) check box.

Figure 12-3

Disabling recursion—DNS Advanced dialog options

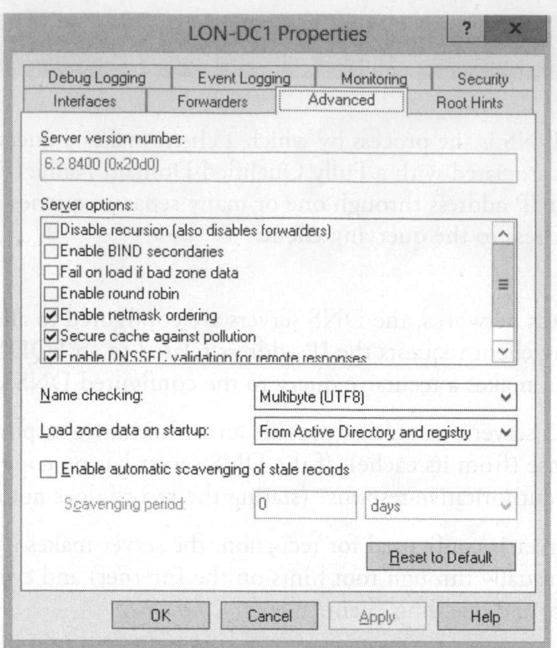

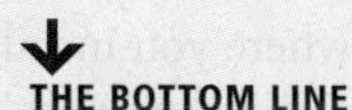 **WARNING** There is a difference between disabling recursion on a server and preventing the server from making recursive queries for a client. If a client can only make iterative queries, then performance will be degraded because every request requires several iterative DNS queries from the client rather than a single recursive one. Recursion and recursive queries are entirely different things!

If the previous option is not set, then the DNS server will try to resolve queries in the following order:

Local Zones, Conditional Forwarders, Forwarders, Root Hints

■ Configuring Netmask Ordering

 **THE BOTTOM LINE**

Netmask ordering prioritizes DNS responses based on the subnet of the requesting client. If several A records exist for a single name, then the one that exists in the subnet of the client is returned.

CERTIFICATION READY
Configure netmask ordering.
Objective 4.2

It is common for a DNS zone to hold more than one A record for a particular hostname. The netmask ordering feature allows the DNS server to return the record that is most local to the client requesting the IP address.

As an example, the FQDN AddressBook.adatum.com has several instances throughout the network and also has several A resource records associated with it. Each subnet has a copy of this address book that rarely changes.

It makes sense that a DNS server will always provide the most local copy for a client to access. Because the subnet identifies the location or site in which a client resides, it is easy to identify where the query originated and thereby to provide the client with the correct A resource record in response. The alternative to this method is to provide a round-robin type of response each time the FQDN is requested, regardless of the location of the client. This method increases network traffic and is not as efficient.

CONFIGURE NETMASK ORDERING

GET READY. Log on with administrative privileges to the computer where you installed the DNS Server role. Ensure that the ADatum.com ADI zone is present. Then, to configure Netmask ordering, perform the following steps:

ANOTHER WAY
You can use the `dnscmd` command-line tool to configure netmask ordering. From an elevated command prompt, enter the following `dnscmd` and press *Enter*: `Dnscmd /Config /LocalNet PriorityNetMask`

1. Open Server Manager and click Tools > DNS. This loads the *DNS Manager* console.
2. Expand the DNS server by clicking the arrow to the left of the server name.
3. Right-click the LON-DC1 server. Click Properties and click the Advanced tab. Under Server options, check the Enable netmask ordering check box.

Netmask ordering is enabled by default in Windows Server 2012 and Windows Server 2012 R2. It is also possible to change the subnet mask used to define the subnets. The default is for a Class C network.

Table 12-1 lists other classfull netmask ordering settings.

Table 12-1
Netmask Ordering (LocalPriorityNet Options)

NETMASK	LOCALPRIORITYNET
255.255.255.0	0x000000ff
255.255.0.0	0x0000ffff
255.0.0.0	0x00ffffff

Configuring A GlobalNames Zone

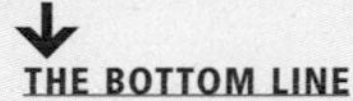

THE BOTTOM LINE

Windows Server 2012 and Windows Server 2012 R2 DNS provides support for single-label names without the need for NETBIOS or WINS. This allows a large multi-DNS environment to support a single name, such as addressbook, rather than an FQDN, such as addressbook.adatum.com.

CERTIFICATION READY
Configure a GlobalNames zone.
Objective 4.2

In an environment where there are several DNS suffixes such as contoso.com, adatum.com, and fabrikam.net, it is necessary to manually create a GlobalNames zone within DNS to allow a single-label name to be resolved.

As an example, the company address book is accessed throughout the enterprise by entering *addressbook* into an Internet Explorer address bar. Without the use of a GlobalNames zone, in this scenario, the name would not be resolved. In an environment with a single DNS suffix such as contoso.com, the suffix would be appended automatically and the name would be resolved.

The only other method for achieving this would be the use of a Windows Internet Naming Service server (WINS). This is a deprecated technology and GlobalNames zone is now the preferred method for achieving single-label name resolution.

Windows Server 2012 and Windows Server 2012 R2 provides built-in support for a GlobalNames zone; however, it must be manually configured and enabled in several steps, as shown in the following section.

CONFIGURE A GLOBALNAMES ZONE

GET READY. Log on with administrative privileges to the computer where you installed the DNS Server role. Ensure that the ADatum.com ADI zone is present. Then, to configure a GlobalNames zone, perform the following steps:

1. From the start screen, type CMD, right-click the CMD icon, and then click Run As administrator from the bottom of the screen.

2. In the command window, type dnscmd <servername> /Config /EnableGlobalnamessupport 1 and wait for the *Command completed successfully* message.
3. Close the command window, and repeat steps 1 and 2 on every DNS server in the forest.
4. Open Server Manager and click Tools > DNS. The *DNS Manager* console opens.
5. Expand the DNS server by clicking the arrow to the left of the server name.
6. Right-click the LON-DC1 server. Click on New Zone to start the New Zone Wizard. Click Next four times. This creates a new primary forward lookup zone replicated to all DNS servers in the domain.
7. Enter the name GlobalNames (this is not case-sensitive), as shown in Figure 12-4, and then click Next.

Figure 12-4

Creating a GlobalNames zone—DNS New Zone Wizard

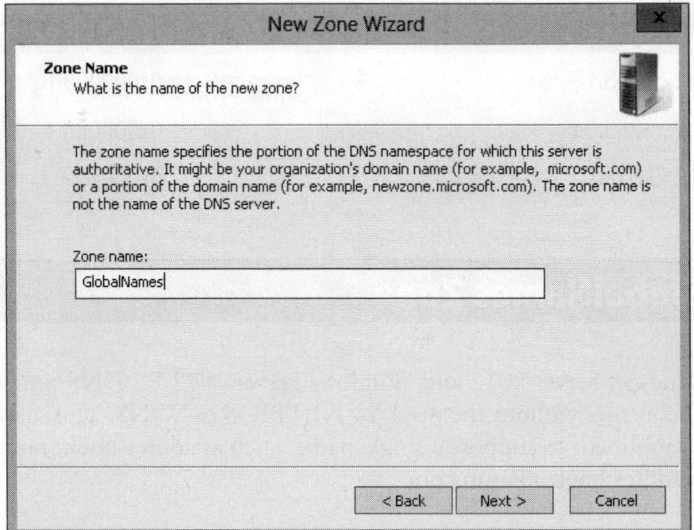

8. Select Do not allow dynamic updates. Because all entries in this zone will be manually created, this is not required and would be a security loophole. Click Next > Finish.
9. The GlobalNames zone is visible (see Figure 12-5).

Figure 12-5

Displaying GlobalNames zone—DNS manager

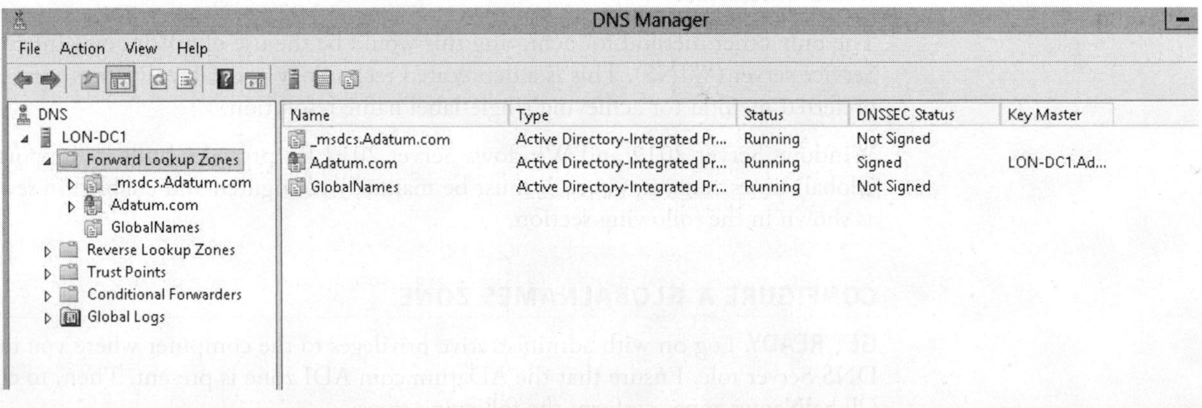

To access the addressbook, create a CNAME record in the GlobalNames zone that points to any records that already exist in the other zones on the Forest DNS servers.

In this instance, a single CNAME record of addressbook in the zone pointing to addressbook.adatum.com would allow any client to resolve this FQDN by entering the label addressbook.

Analyzing Zone Level Statistics

While logging can be used to see what records are being queried and can be used for troubleshooting, logging is not the best tool to determine DNS zone level statistics. Therefore, starting with Windows Server 2012 R2, Microsoft DNS Server provides zone level statistics, which allow you track the usage pattern or monitor DNS server performance.

CERTIFICATION READY
Analyze zone level statistics.
Objective 4.2

Statistics that can be retrieved for DNS servers using the Windows PowerShell Get-DnsServerStatistics cmdlet include the following:

- Server wide query statistics
- Zone query statistics
- Zone transfer statistics
- Zone update statistics
- Packet statistics
- Different record statistics
- DNSSEC statistics

To get the complete zone level statistics for the contoso.com domain, execute the following Windows PowerShell command:

```
Get-DnsServerStatistics -ZoneName contoso.com
```

To the current zone level statistics counter execute the following Windows PowerShell command:

```
Get-DnsServerStatistics -ZoneName contoso.com -Clear
```

SKILL SUMMARY

IN THIS LESSON YOU LEARNED:

- Windows Server 2012 adds new features to domain naming services (DNS) security. You learned how to configure security for your DNS server and DNS zones using DNSSEC, socket pooling, cache locking, and the Name Resolution Policy Table (NRPT).
- DNSSEC can be enabled on an Active-Directory Integrated zone (ADI) or on a primary zone.
- The DNS socket pool is a tool used to allow source port randomization for DNS queries, which reduces the chances of an attacker guessing which IP address and port (socket) the DNS traffic uses.
- The preferred method to set the DNS cache locking value is through the use of the `dnscmd` command-line tool.
- DNS logging is a troubleshooting tool to allow for detailed, file-based analysis of all DNS packets and messages. There are benefits and drawbacks of DNS debug logging and how to configure it.
- Domain Admins have full permissions by default to manage all aspects of the DNS server, but only in the domain where the Domain Admins security group is located. A member of the Enterprise Admins group has similar permissions but throughout the entire forest.

- Recursion in DNS is the process by which a client makes a query to a DNS server for an IP address associated with a Fully Qualified Domain Name (FQDN).
- Netmask ordering prioritizes DNS responses based on the subnet of the requesting client.
- Windows Server 2012 and Windows Server 2012 R2 DNS provides support for single-label names without the need for NETBIOS or WINS.

■ Knowledge Assessment

Multiple Choice

Select the correct answer for each of the following questions.

1. Which of the following actions secures a DNS zone using a public key infrastructure?
 a. Sign the zone
 b. Lock the cache
 c. Increase the socket pool
 d. Create a GlobalNames zone

2. Which of the following allows a DNS server to act as a key master?
 a. KSK
 b. ZSK
 c. Locked Cache
 d. AD CS Certificate Authority

3. Which DNS Resource Record provides a validated denial of existence?
 a. DNSKEY
 b. AAAA
 c. SRV
 d. NSEC3

4. Which dnscmd command-line parameter sets the capability to resolve non-FQDN names?
 a. `/Socketpoolsize`
 b. `/Chachelockingpercent`
 c. `/Enableglobalnamessupport`
 d. `/enumzones`

5. Which of the following actions can you *not* record or perform using DNS debug logging? (Choose all that apply.)
 a. Zone transfers
 b. Start / Stop DNS Service
 c. Log file size
 d. Query request packets

6. Which security group has DNS administration privileges across the forest? (Choose all that apply.)
 a. Enterprise Admins
 b. Domain Admins
 c. Local administrators
 d. DNS Admins

7. Which LocalPriorityNet setting masks a Class A IP address?
 a. 0x000000ff
 b. 0x0000ffff
 c. 0x0000003f
 d. 0x00ffffff

8. Which of the following statements about the GlobalNames zones in Windows Server 2012 R2 DNS Server role are true?
  a. GlobalNames zone is domain-specific
  b. GlobalNames zones require dynamic updates disabled
  c. GlobalNames zones are useful in multi-DNS domain systems
  d. GlobalNames zones are enabled by default

9. Disabling Server recursion has which of the following effects?
  a. Speeds up client queries
  b. Increases the server workload
  c. Restricts a DNS server to its own database
  d. Disables access to the Internet

10. Which built-in Domain Local security group allows full control of the DNS server functions within a single domain?
  a. DNS Users
  b. Power Users
  c. DNS Admins
  d. Enterprise Admins

Best Answer

Choose the letter that corresponds to the best answer. More than one answer choice may achieve the goal. Select the BEST answer.

1. Which security group provides the privileges required for managing DNS within a single domain?
  a. Enterprise Admins
  b. DNS Admins
  c. Power Users
  d. Domain Admins

2. Which key length, in bits, should you choose for a Zone Signing Key (ZSK) that is secure but does not provide too much processing overhead?
  a. 4096
  b. 1024
  c. 2624
  d. 3712

3. Which DNS cache locking setting should you choose?
  a. 30%
  b. 0%
  c. 100%
  d. 50%

4. To provide single name resolution, which of the following should you enable?
  a. WINS
  b. NETBIOS
  c. GlobalNames support
  d. netmask ordering

5. To provide location-specific name resolution for DNS clients, which of the following should you enable?
  a. DNS round-robin
  b. Hardware load-balancing cluster
  c. Netmask ordering
  d. Microsoft Network Load Balancing cluster

Matching and Identification

1. Identify which of the following are DNSSEC resource records.
   _______ a) SRV
   _______ b) AAAA
   _______ c) NSEC
   _______ d) MX
   _______ e) RR
   _______ f) NS
   _______ g) RRSIG
   _______ h) TXT
   _______ i) TSIG
   _______ j) DNSKEY

Build a List

1. Identify the correct order in which a GlobalNames zone and GlobalNames zone record are created. Not all steps will be used.
   _______ Sign the zone
   _______ Enable GlobalNames support
   _______ Enable dynamic updating
   _______ Manually create a host record in the GlobalNames zone
   _______ Create a GlobalNames forward lookup zone
   _______ Create a GlobalNames reverse lookup zone
   _______ Disable dynamic updating on the GlobalNames zone

■ Business Case Scenarios

Scenario 12-1: Administering a DNSSEC Secured Zone

As a member of the DNS Admins domain local security group of the ADatum.com domain, you have created an ADI zone for the contoso.com domain. You implement DNSSEC for this zone and later realize that you need to delegate the zone to a non-active directory controller DNS server. What must you do first?

Scenario 12-2: Managing Delegation

You are the Enterprise administrator for a multi-domain multi-branch forest. The root domain is contoso.com. You need to provide a number of lower level administrators with privileges to create and modify DNS server and zone settings for the following zones: uk.contoso.com, fabrikam.net, and eu.adatum.com. What must you do?

Scenario 12-3: Managing Access to App1

You are responsible for DNS within the enterprise and need to provide access to a company-wide application named *App1*. This is a web-based application that exists in the contoso.com domain with a FQDN of App1.contoso.com. Every user throughout the forest must be able to access the application by typing *App1* into an Internet browser address bar. The forest contains the following DNS zones:

Contoso.com

Fabrikam.net

Adatum.com

The DNS servers have been installed as default and have each had their single zone added. What must you do to allow this application to work in this way?

Deploying and Managing IPAM

LESSON 13

70-412 EXAM OBJECTIVE

Objective 4.3 – Deploy and manage IP Address Management (IPAM). This objective may include but is not limited to: Provision IPAM manually or by using Group Policy; configure server discovery; create and manage IP blocks and ranges; monitor utilization of IP address space; migrate to IPAM; delegate IPAM administration; manage IPAM collections; configure IPAM database storage.

LESSON HEADING	EXAM OBJECTIVE
Configuring IPAM	
Configuring an IPAM Server	Provision IPAM manually or by using Group Policy
Configuring IPAM Database Storage	Configure IPAM database storage
Configuring Server Discovery	Configure server discovery
Creating and Managing IP Blocks and Ranges	Create and manage IP blocks and ranges
Monitoring Utilization of IP Address Space	Monitor utilization of IP address space
Migrating to IPAM	Migrate to IPAM
Delegating IPAM Administration	Delegate IPAM administration
Managing IPAM Collections	Manage IPAM collections

KEY TERMS

address space management (ASM)
IP address block
IP address range
IP addresses
IPAM discovery
IPAM provisioning
multi-server management (MSM)

Configuring IPAM

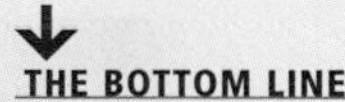

IP Address Management (IPAM) is a new feature in Windows Server 2012 and Windows Server 2012 R2. IPAM provides an administrator with the ability to plan, manage, track, and audit the use of all IP addresses and the DNS services within the network.

CERTIFICATION READY
Configure IPAM manually or by using Group Policy.
Objective 4.3

IPAM is a new feature within Windows Server 2012 and Windows Server 2012 R2, but it is *not* a new network function. Planning, management, tracking, and auditing of IP addresses have been a thorn in every network administrator's side for many years. The only method of managing such facilities prior to Windows Server 2012 and Windows Server 2012 R2 was by the Dynamic Host Configuration Protocol (DHCP) and Domain Naming Service (DNS) management consoles, third-party databases or applications, spreadsheets, or in some cases even scraps of paper with details of every network node recorded. The advent of IPAM in Windows Server 2012 and Windows Server 2012 removes the necessity for all of these alternative methods.

IPAM provides a single point of administration for all DNS and IP management features within an Active Directory Forest. There are a number of key terms that need to be clearly understood prior to implementing IPAM. In addition, there are a number of requirements and functional limitations that need to be taken into consideration.

- ***IP address block:*** IP address blocks are the highest level conceptual entity in an IP address space. They are marked with a starting and ending IP address. For Public IP addresses, the address block is assigned by the Internet Registry (for smaller ranges, this is delegated by your Internet Service provider). An address block is used by network administrators to be the split into address ranges, which is the basis of DHCP scopes. An administrator can use IPAM to add, import, edit, and delete IP address blocks. IPAM automatically tracks the address ranges belonging to an address block. See Figure 13-1 for a hierarchical representation of the address block.
- ***IP address range:*** IP address ranges are the next hierarchical level of an IP address space, beneath the address block. Typically an address range is a subnet marked by a starting and ending address, using a subnet mask. An IP address range normally maps to a DHCP scope. IP address ranges can be added or imported by IPAM.
- ***IP addresses:*** IP addresses are the individual addresses that are contained in an IP address range. IPAM allows complete end-to-end management of both IPv4 and IPv6 IP addresses. IPAM automatically maps IP addresses to the correct range by using the start and end address of a range. IP addresses can be added manually or imported by IPAM from external sources.

Figure 13-1 shows the whole IP address space and how each component fits into the hierarchical model.

Figure 13-1
Displaying the IP address space

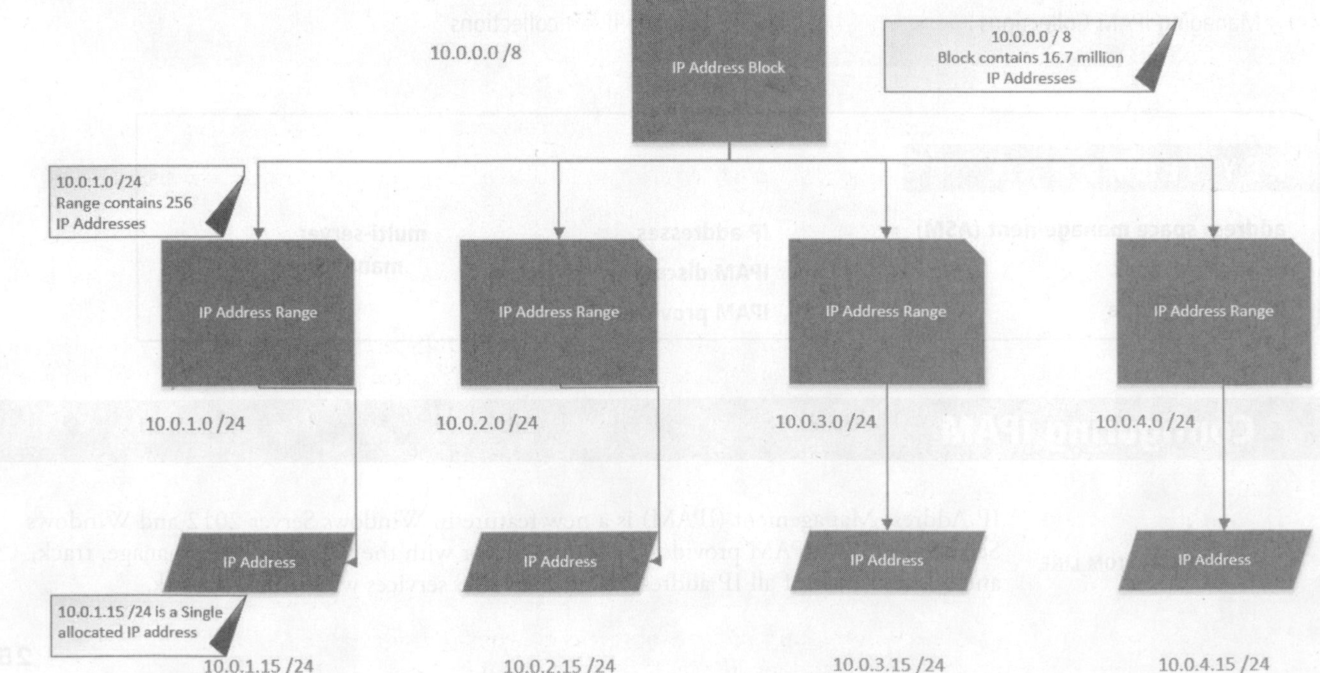

In order to successfully deploy IPAM, the following general requirements should be met:

- An IPAM server *must* be a domain member but *cannot* be a domain controller.
- The IPAM server should be a single purpose server. It is not recommended to install DHCP, DNS, or any other roles on the IPAM server.
- The IPAM server can manage only the IPv6 address space if IPv6 is enabled on that server.
- Always log on to the IPAM server with a domain account, *not* a local account.
- Ensure that the IPAM administrator is a member of the correct local IPAM security group on the IPAM server.
- To use IPAM to track and audit IP addresses, ensure that *log events on all domain controllers and NPS servers* is enabled.

For an IPAM server to be deployed, it must meet the following hardware requirements:

- A dual-core processor of at least 2.0 GHz
- Windows Server 2012 or Windows Server 2012 R2 operating system
- 4 or more Gigabytes of RAM
- 80 Gigabytes of free hard disk space

To be able to manage the DHCP and DNS roles of a Windows Server 2008 using IPAM on Windows Server 2012 or Windows Server 2012 R2, the following requirements should be installed on the Windows Server 2008 or Windows Server 2008 R2 systems:

- Service Pack 2 on Windows Server 2008
- .NET Framework 4.0 full installation
- Windows Management Framework (WMF) 3.0, which provides Windows PowerShell 3.0
- Windows remote management (WinRM) must be enabled

Windows Server IPAM can manage only one Active Directory Forest. IPAM can be deployed in one of three topologies:

- **Centralized:** A single IPAM server for the whole forest.
- **Distributed:** An IPAM server is deployed to every site in the forest.
- **Hybrid:** A central IPAM server and dedicated site-based IPAM servers are deployed at some sites.

Figure 13-2 shows the distributed deployment of IPAM.

There are a number of published specifications for the IPAM feature, which are listed here:

- It is important to understand that an IPAM server never communicates with another IPAM server. For example, they will maintain their own IP address spaces and not share that information within their databases. To effectively manage multiple IPAM servers within a forest, it is necessary to manually configure the discovery scope of each server.
- IPAM manages only Microsoft DHCP and DNS services; no third-party solutions can be managed using Windows Server 2012 or Windows Server 2012 R2 IPAM.
- IPAM supports only domain-joined DNS, DHCP, and NPS servers.
- IPAM supports only the Windows Internal Database (not SQL Server, MYSQL, or any other third-party solution).
- A single IPAM server supports a maximum of 150 DHCP servers and 500 DNS servers.
- A single IPAM server supports up to 6000 DHCP scopes and 150 DNS zones.
- IPAM stores up to 3 years of forensic IP data (IP address leases, MAC address details, and logon and logoff details) for up to 100,000 users.

Figure 13-2
Deploying IPAM

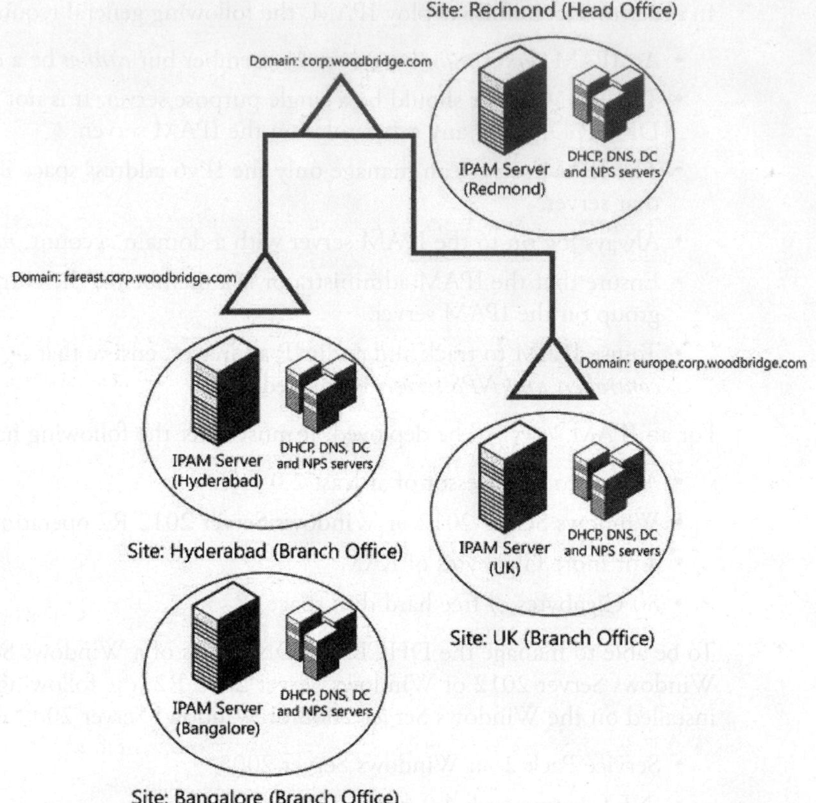

Configuring an IPAM Server

IPAM requires several steps to successfully configure the server, discovery, and address space management. The planning stage is fairly simple, but the servers, services, and administrators must all be configured carefully to ensure the feature adds full value.

There are two main components within IPAM:

- **IPAM server:** Collects data from the managed DNS and DHCP servers within the discovery scope. The IPAM server also manages the Windows Internal Database. Remember that IPAM can use only the Windows Internal Database. The server also provides the Role-Based Access Control (RBAC) for the IPAM installation. All the IPAM security groups and roles are managed from the IPAM server.
- **IPAM client:** Provides the interface with which the IPAM administrator manages and configures the server. The client interfaces with the server and invokes the Windows PowerShell commands to carry out DHCP and DNS tasks as well as any remote management functions. The IPAM client is automatically installed on the IPAM server when the IPAM feature is installed. It is also possible to install the IPAM client on an alternative Windows Server 2012 or Windows Server 2012 R2 server without the IPAM server feature. Finally, it is also possible to manage IPAM using the IPAM client from a Windows 8 client with the Remote Server Administration Tools (RSAT) installed.

INSTALL IPAM ON A MEMBER SERVER

GET READY. Log on to the domain-joined computer where you want to install the IPAM feature, with administrative privileges. To install the IPAM feature, perform the following steps:

1. Open Server Manager, and click Manage > Add Roles and Features. The *Add Role Wizard* begins.

2. Click Next four times, until the *Select Features* dialog box appears.
3. Select the check box next to *IP Address Management (IPAM) Server*. Click Next. This loads the *Add Required Features* dialog box.
4. Click Add Features, click Next, and then click Install. Once the installation begins, click Close.

Once the installation is complete, the IPAM feature appears on the main screen of Server Manager. There are now several stages to configure IPAM (see Figure 13-3).

Figure 13-3

Displaying IPAM server tasks

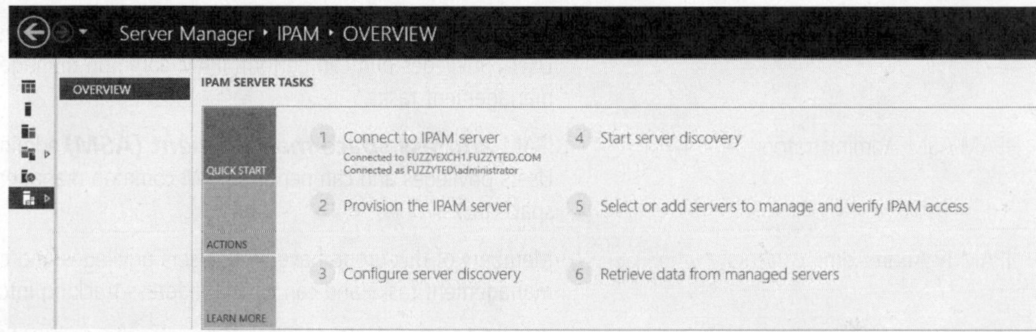

TAKE NOTE*

When installing an IPAM server, the computer must be a domain member, not a domain controller.

Once the IPAM server has been installed, there are a number of steps required to configure it successfully. These are all shown on the main IPAM client screen (refer to Figure 13-3).

The following IPAM tasks are required to configure the IPAM server installation.

Connect to IPAM Server

This step is automatically carried out when the client is running on an IPAM server. If the client is running from a remote server (not an IPAM server), the administrator needs to connect to the chosen IPAM server.

Provision the IPAM Server

IPAM provisioning is the process of allowing the IPAM server to configure and manage the necessary features and functions of the servers, services, and domain objects required for IPAM.

There are two methods of provisioning the IPAM server:

- Automatic Group Policy-based provisioning
- Manual provisioning

The default is Group Policy-based and once this is selected and provisioned, the only method for reversing that decision is to uninstall IPAM and then reinstall. The Group Policy-based provisioning method creates the Group Policy objects (GPOs) that allow the required access settings on all the IPAM managed servers. The GPOs created are:

- IPAM1_DHCP for DHCP servers
- IPAM1_DNS for DNS servers
- IPAM1_DC_NPS for domain controllers and NPS servers

In addition, the IPAM security groups are created, the IPAM database is created and role-based access is configured, and finally the access to the IPAM tasks and folders is configured.

Having performed IPAM provisioning, the following IPAM security groups are now available for managing the IPAM environment both locally and remotely (see Table 13-1).

Table 13-1

IPAM Security Groups

Security Group	Description
IPAM Users	Members of this group can view all information in server discovery, IP address space, and server management. They can view IPAM and DHCP server operational events, but cannot view IP address tracking information.
IPAM MSM Administrators	IPAM ***multi-server management (MSM)*** administrators have IPAM Users privileges and can perform IPAM common management tasks and server management tasks.
IPAM ASM Administrators	IPAM ***address space management (ASM)*** administrators have IPAM Users privileges and can perform IPAM common management tasks and IP address space tasks.
IPAM IP Audit Administrators	Members of this group have IPAM Users privileges and can perform IPAM common management tasks and can view IP address tracking information.
IPAM Administrators	IPAM Administrators have the privileges to view all IPAM data and perform all IPAM tasks.

Starting with Windows Server 2012 R2, IPAM includes role-based access control, which provides the ability to customize roles, access scopes, and access policies so that you can have fine-grained control for which users and groups can access specific administrative operations. The IPAM roles include:

- **DNS record administrator:** Manages DNS resource records.
- **IP address record administrator:** Manages IP addresses but not IP address spaces, ranges, blocks, or subnets.
- **IPAM administrator:** Manages all settings and objects in IPAM.
- **IPAM ASM administrator:** Completely manages IP addresses.
- **IPAM DHCP administrator:** Completely manages DHCP servers.
- **IPAM DHCP reservations administrator:** Manages DHCP reservations.
- **IPAM DHCP scope administrator:** Manages DHCP scopes.
- **IPAM MSM administrator:** Completely manages DHCP and DNS servers.

In addition, all objects in IPAM are included in the global access scope. All additional scopes that are configured are subsets of the global access scope.

WARNING Remember that once chosen, the automatic Group Policy provisioning method cannot be undone without a complete IPAM reinstall.

USE WINDOWS POWERSHELL

The following example shows how the `Invoke-IpamGpoProvisioning` cmdlet can be used to create IPAM provisioning GPOs. In this example, three GPOs are created (IPAM1_DHCP, IPAM1_DNS, and IPAM1_DC_NPS) and linked to the contoso.com domain. These GPOs enable access for the server ipam1.contoso.com using the domain administrator account user1. In this example, the hostname of the IPAM server is used as a GPO prefix, however, this is not required.

```
Invoke-IpamGpoProvisioning -Domain contoso.com -GpoPrefixName IPAM1 -
IpamServerFqdn ipam1.contoso.com -DelegatedGpoUser user1
```

Configuring IPAM Database Storage

With Windows Server 2012 R2, during the IPAM provisioning process, you can use Windows Internal Database (WID) or you can select Microsoft SQL Server so that you can use a dedicated SQL server. By using an external database, you have additional scalability, disaster recovery, and reporting.

CERTIFICATION READY
Configure IPAM database storage.
Objective 4.4

During provisioning, the WID is selected by default and the database is stored in the C:\Windows\System32\IPAM\Database folder. However, if necessary, you can migrate the database from WID to SQL after IPAM has been provided by using the Move-IpamDatabase and Set-IpamDatabase Windows PowerShell cmdlets. Refer to Figure 13-4.

Figure 13-4
Configuring databases for IPAM

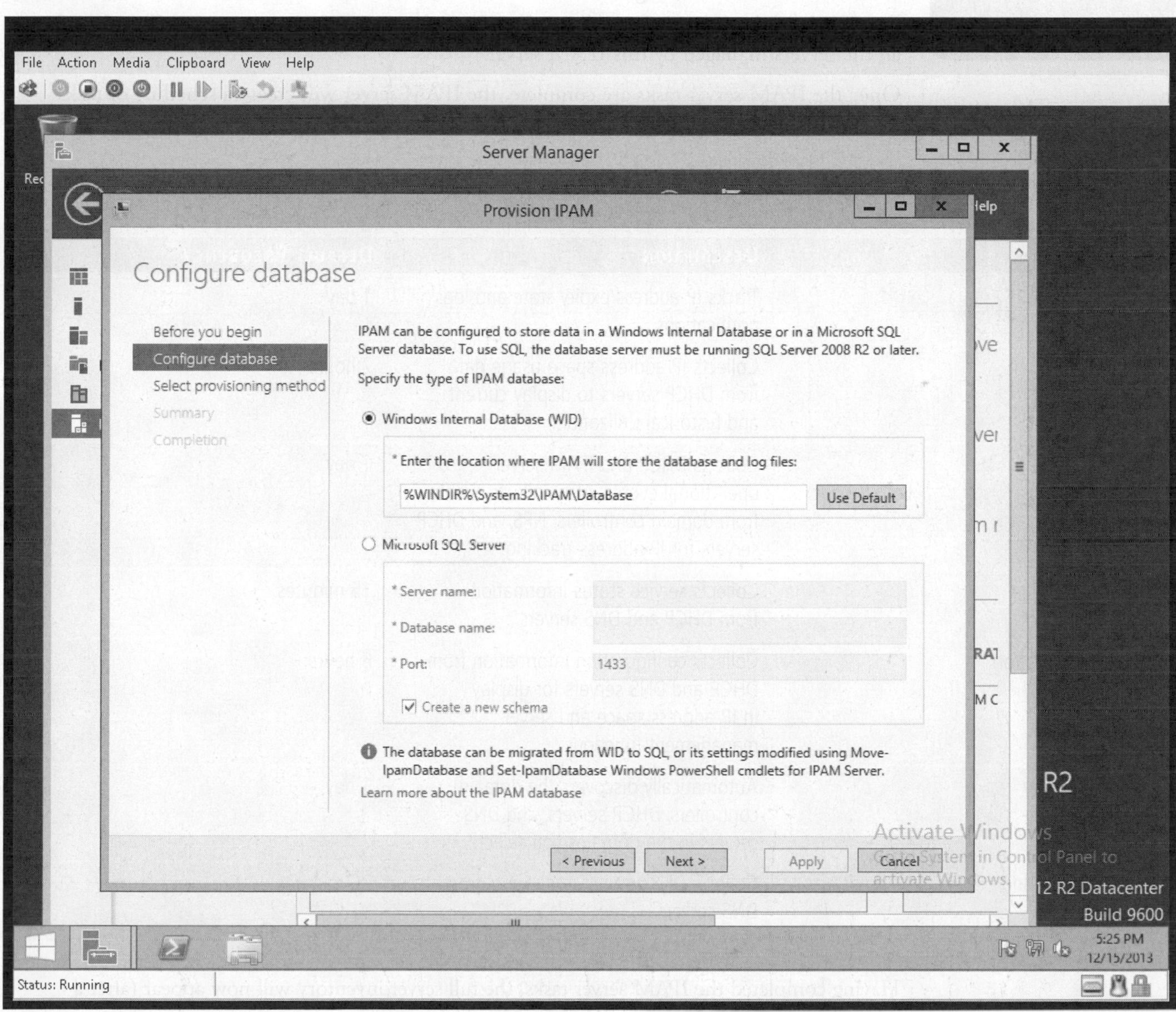

Configuring Server Discovery

Having installed and provisioned the IPAM server, the next step is to configure server discovery.

Configure Server Discovery

Server discovery is the process of defining which domains in the forest that contain servers will be managed by this IPAM server.

Start Server Discovery

IPAM discovery is the process of retrieving a list of all domain controllers, DNS servers, and DHCP servers from the active directory.

Select or add servers to manage and verify IPAM access

Once the IPAM discovery is complete, the IPAM administrator can select which servers, roles, and services will be managed from the list in server inventory.

CERTIFICATION READY
Configure server discovery.
Objective 4.3

Retrieve Data from Managed Servers

This final task launches various data collection tasks on the IPAM server to collect data from all the servers managed by this IPAM server.

Once the IPAM server tasks are complete, the IPAM server will create a schedule of tasks to repeat at various intervals. These tasks are listed in Table 13-2.

Table 13-2
IPAM Server Scheduled Tasks

TASK NAME	DESCRIPTION	DEFAULT FREQUENCY
AddressExpiry	Tracks IP address expiry state and logs notifications.	1 day
AddressUtilization	Collects IP address space usage data from DHCP servers to display current and historical utilization.	2 hours
Audit	Collects DHCP and IPAM server operational events. Also collects events from domain controllers, NPS, and DHCP servers for IP address tracking.	1 day
ServerAvailability	Collects service status information from DHCP and DNS servers.	15 minutes
ServerConfiguration	Collects configuration information from DHCP and DNS servers for display in IP address space and server management functions.	6 hours
Server Discovery	Automatically discovers the domain controllers, DHCP servers, and DNS servers in the domains you select.	1 day
Service Monitoring	Collects DNS zone status events from DNS servers.	30 minutes

Having completed the IPAM server tasks, the full server inventory will now appear (after a refresh) in the Server Manager IPAM console. The server inventory contains a list of managed servers and a panel containing the full relevant details for the selected server.

Creating and Managing IP Blocks and Ranges

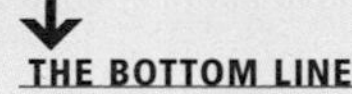

Once the installation and configuration is complete, the IPAM server needs to work with all the IP blocks and ranges.

CERTIFICATION READY
Create and manage IP blocks and ranges.
Objective 4.3

The starting point for the configuration of IP address blocks and IP address ranges is the main IPAM screen, which is reached through Server Manager. Having reviewed the IP address space details previously in Figure 13-1, the first stage is to allocate IP address blocks for the server to track and manage.

CREATE AN IP ADDRESS BLOCK

GET READY. Log on to the IPAM server, with administrative privileges. To create IP address blocks, perform the following steps:

1. Open Server Manager, and click IPAM > IP Address Blocks, Tasks (see Figure 13-5).

Figure 13-5
Creating IP address blocks

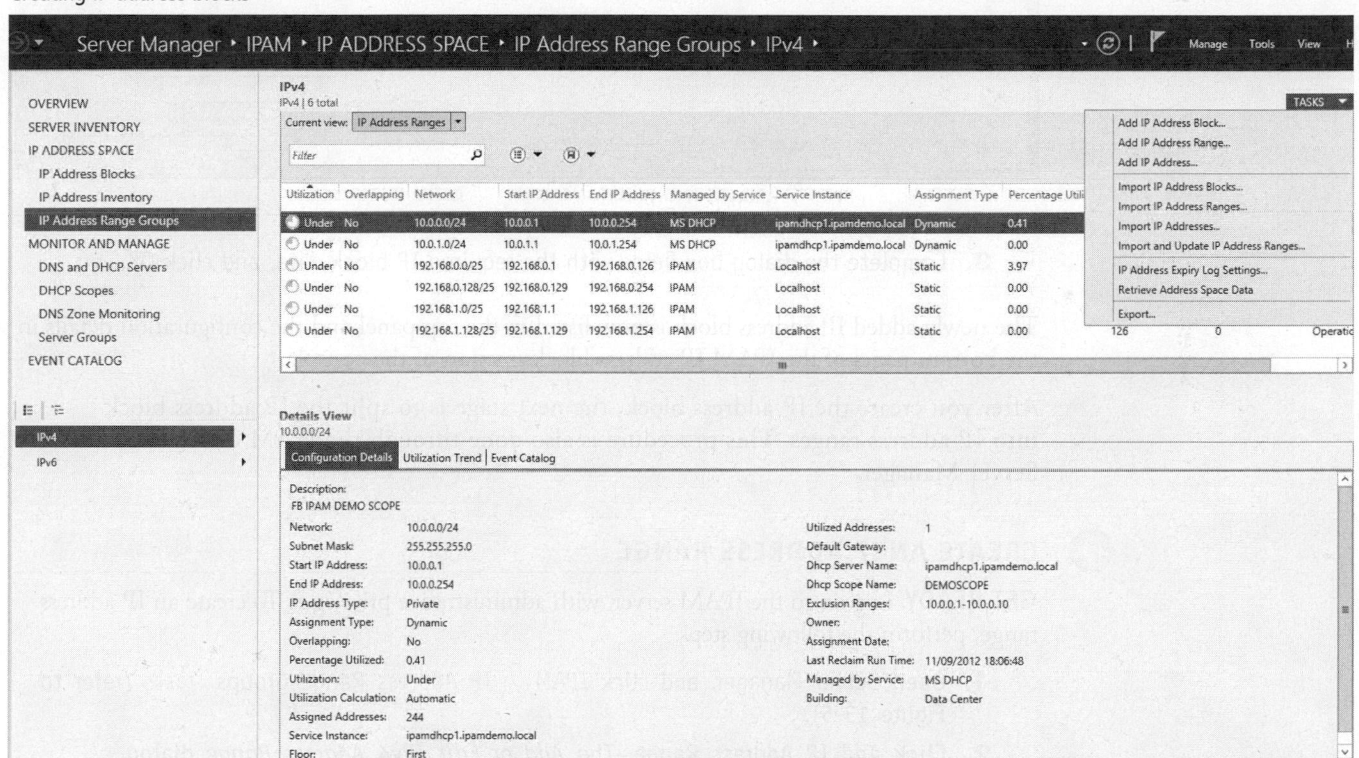

2. Click Add IP Address Block. The *Add or Edit IPv4 Address Block* dialog box opens (see Figure 13-6).

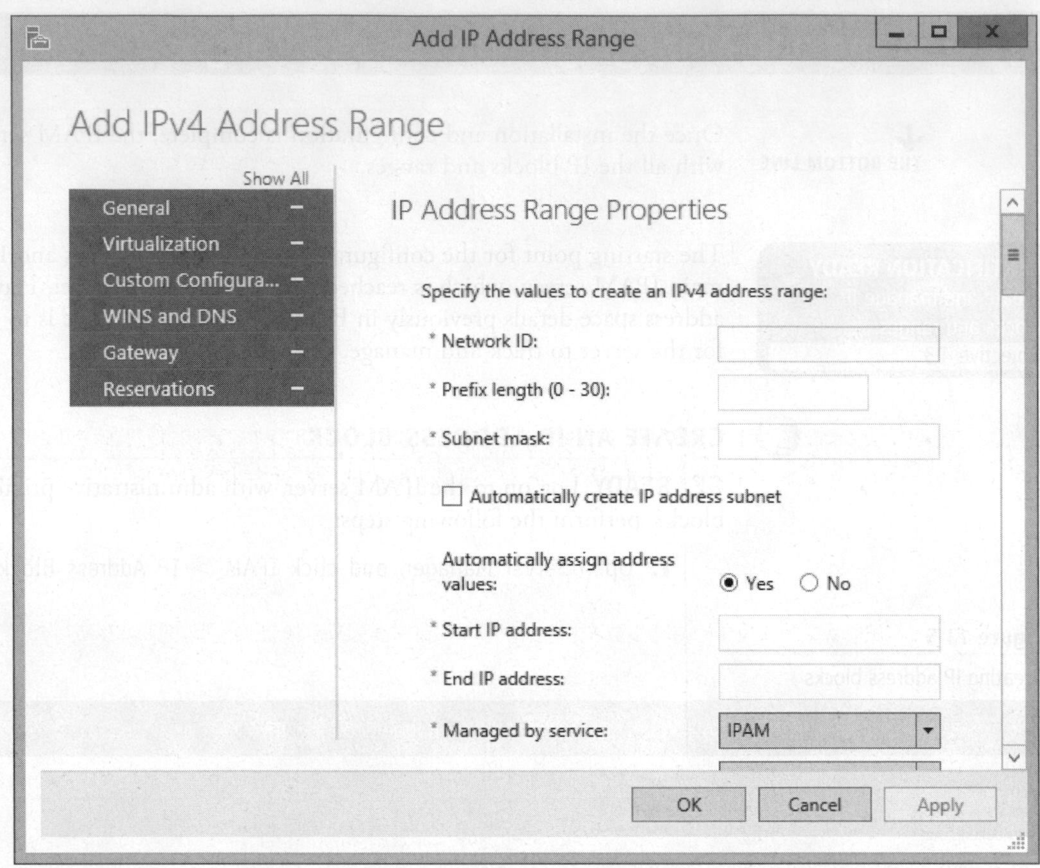

Figure 13-6
Adding an IP address range

3. Complete the dialog box fields with the required IP block data, and click OK.

The newly added IP address block is now listed in the top panel and the configuration details in the bottom panel of the IPAM IP address blocks section of the console.

After you create the IP address block, the next stage is to split the IP address block into IP address ranges. This procedure is also done through the IPAM console in Server Manager.

CREATE AN IP ADDRESS RANGE

GET READY. Log on to the IPAM server, with administrative privileges. To create an IP address range, perform the following steps:

1. Open Server Manager, and click IPAM > IP Address Range Groups, Tasks (refer to Figure 13-5).
2. Click Add IP Address Range. The *Add or Edit IPv4 Address Range* dialog box opens.
3. Complete the dialog box fields with the required Basic IP Range configuration data (see Figure 13-6).
4. In this instance, there are additional custom configuration options to be made. This section allows the IPAM administrator to associate the IP address range with a number of selectable criteria (AD Site, Building, and so on). It is possible to select several user-entered values. Click Add and select the chosen options, entering the required user data, and then click OK.

5. Creating these attributes assists in the tracking and monitoring of IP address range utilization.
6. Click OK to finish the creation of the IP address range.

Having completed the IP configuration, the IPAM server will then maintain accurate records of utilization and allocations. In the situation where the IPAM server manages several IP address ranges, the custom configuration proves most useful to reduce the clutter in the console. Figure 13-7 shows the use of the custom attributes chosen previously to limit the number of IP address ranges as shown.

Figure 13-7

Displaying filtered IP address ranges

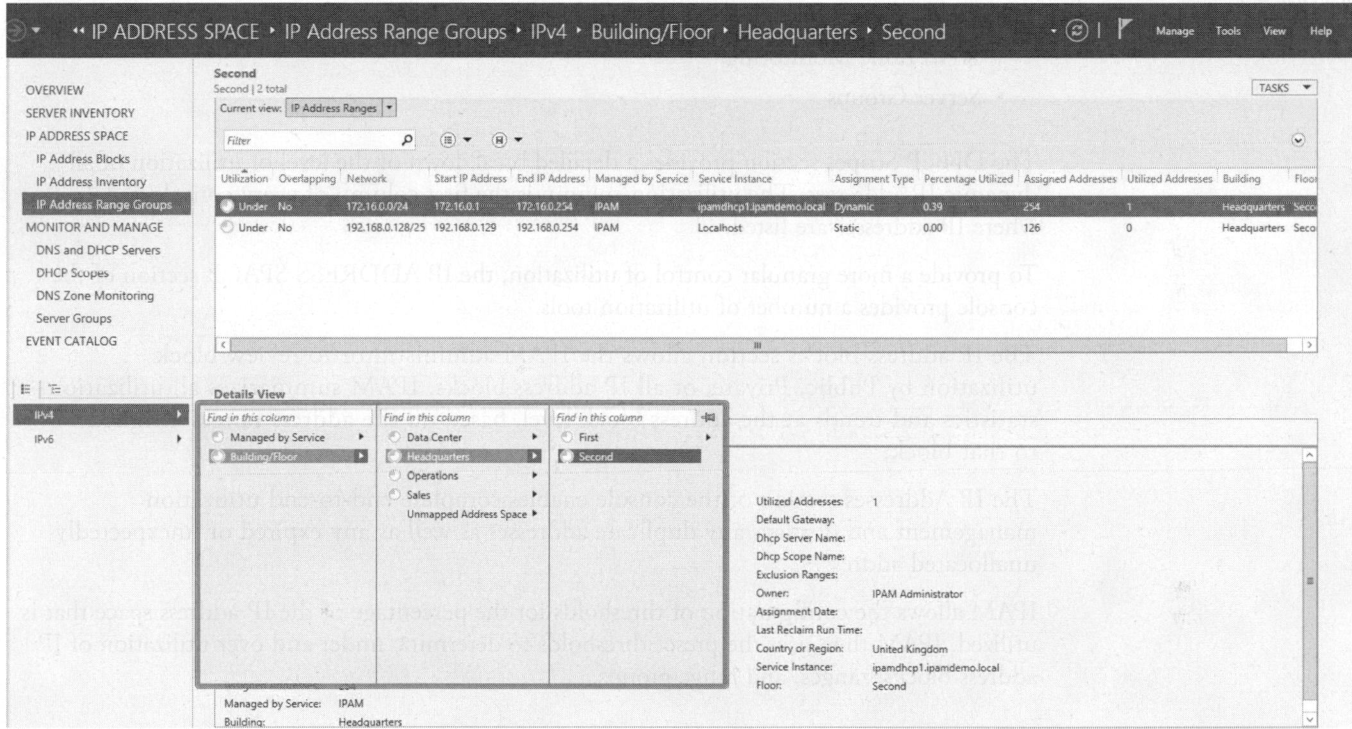

From the IP Address Range Groups console page, an IPAM administrator can carry out a number of actions on each range by right-clicking the IP Address Range Group, to open the context menu. The addition of these options significantly reduces the workload of an IPAM administrator. There is no requirement to remotely log on to a DHCP server and query the data directly.

The IP Address Inventory console allows the IPAM administrator to individually manage and edit any dynamic or static IP addresses monitored by the IPAM server. A number of DHCP and DNS management tasks can also be performed by right-clicking the IP address range to open the context menu. The console also provides detailed information on each address in the bottom panel.

In addition, the MONITOR AND MANAGE section of the console provides detailed DHCP Server and Scope management to ensure that all areas of the IP address space are covered.

Monitoring Utilization of IP Address Space

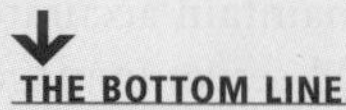

THE BOTTOM LINE

Having installed and configured the IPAM server, an IPAM administrator needs to monitor the utilization of IP addresses within his scope of control. IPAM has many monitoring tools available to make this task easier, preventing ranges from running out of available addresses or blocks running out of ranges.

CERTIFICATION READY
Monitor utilization of IP address space.
Objective 4.3

The IPAM Server console provides a dedicated MONITOR AND MANAGE section. Within this section, there are four categories:

- DNS and DHCP Servers
- DHCP Scopes
- DNS Zone Monitoring
- Server Groups

The DHCP Scopes section provides a detailed breakdown of the level of utilization of all dynamic IP addresses. The utilization column is the first column of every console panel where IP addresses are listed.

To provide a more granular control of utilization, the IP ADDRESS SPACE section of the console provides a number of utilization tools.

The IP address blocks section allows the IPAM administrator to review block utilization by Public, Private, or all IP address blocks. IPAM summarizes all utilization statistics and trends at the address block level, based on the address ranges assigned to that block.

The IP Addresses section of the console enables complete end-to-end utilization management and displays any duplicate addresses as well as any expired or unexpectedly unallocated addresses.

IPAM allows the configuration of thresholds for the percentage of the IP address space that is utilized. IPAM then uses the preset thresholds to determine under and over utilization of IP address blocks, ranges, and range groups.

Migrating to IPAM

Most IP address space management is currently carried out using a mixture of spreadsheets, third-party applications, and printed materials. Having installed the IPAM feature and configured the provisioning and discovery, an IPAM administrator might choose to migrate all the IP address space data into the IPAM database.

CERTIFICATION READY
Migrate to IPAM.
Objective 4.3

Before an IPAM administrator can take advantage of the migration tools available, the feature must be correctly installed, provisioned, and configured for server discovery.

The IPAM client console options for importing IP address data from a Comma Separated Value (CSV) file include the following (refer to Figure 13-5):

- Import IP Address Block
- Import IP Address Ranges
- Import IP Addresses
- Import and Update IP Address Ranges

There is also an export option, which exports all IP address data to a user selected .CSV file. It is important to also consider that when backing up the IPAM server, the Windows Internal Database must be backed up to secure the IPAM data.

MORE INFORMATION

To ensure you format the .CSV file correctly, prepare an export to capture the header information required to import IP address data into the database.

Delegating IPAM Administration

Network administration is a vast topic with many varied and differing roles required to carry it out successfully. Within IP address management, there are several sets of tasks that might require separate staff to carry them out. For this reason, IPAM relies on RBAC to provide the necessary delegate administrative features.

CERTIFICATION READY
Delegate IPAM administration.
Objective 4.3

When the IPAM feature is installed, the provisioning process (if you selected automatic Group Policy-based provisioning) creates the RBAC roles to enable simple delegated administration of the whole IPAM infrastructure.

The roles are controlled by using the previously mentioned IPAM local security groups. These groups allow delegation of tasks to individuals whom you do not want to have full administrative access to your IPAM server and data. Simply place the necessary users or groups in the correct Local group on the IPAM server:

- **IPAM Users:** Users who are members of this group can view server discovery, IP address space, and server management information. Group members can also view IPAM and DHCP server operational events, but they cannot view IP address tracking information.
- **IPAM MSM Administrators:** Members of this group have IPAM Users privileges and can perform common IPAM multi-server management (MSM) tasks and server management tasks.
- **IPAM ASM Administrators:** Members of this group have IPAM Users privileges and can perform common IPAM address space management (ASM) tasks and IP address space tasks.
- **IPAM IP Audit Administrators:** Members of this group have IPAM Users privileges and can perform common IPAM management tasks and can view IP address tracking information.
- **IPAM Administrators:** Members of this group have the privileges to view all IPAM data and perform all IPAM tasks.

Managing IPAM Collections

An IPAM collection refers to the scheduled IPAM server tasks created at the installation of the IPAM feature. The collection of IP address space data, event log data, and DNS data is critical to a successful IPAM implementation.

CERTIFICATION READY
Manage IPAM collections.
Objective 4.3

Table 13-2 shows all the Scheduled IPAM server tasks created at the installation of the IPAM feature. Only a subset of these tasks are actual collection tasks (see Table 13-3).

Table 13-3
IPAM Collection Tasks

TASK NAME	DESCRIPTION	DEFAULT FREQUENCY
AddressUtilization	Collects IP address space usage data from DHCP servers to display current and historical utilization.	2 hours
Audit	Collects DHCP and IPAM server operational events. Also collects events from domain controllers, NPS, and DHCP servers for IP address tracking.	1 day
ServerAvailability	Collects service status information from DHCP and DNS servers.	15 minutes
ServerConfiguration	Collects configuration information from DHCP and DNS servers for display in IP address space and server management functions.	6 hours
Service Monitoring	Collects DNS zone status events from DNS servers.	30 minutes

The collection tasks are first carried out as part of the initial post installation IPAM server tasks.

It is also possible to set off the server tasks at any point in time by selecting the *Retrieve data from the managed server* area of the quick start panel in the IPAM Overview console page or selecting *Retrieve all server data* from the tasks menu of the Server Inventory console page.

Having collected all the server data, it is possible to view the completed (or running tasks) by selecting the *More...* area of the Yellow information bar at the top of the IPAM Server Tasks panel. This option opens the Overview Tasks Details dialog box. This dialog box provides more detailed information than the main Overview console page.

SKILL SUMMARY

IN THIS LESSON YOU LEARNED:

- An installation of an IPAM server and the IPAM feature have specific hardware, software, and infrastructure requirements.
- The correct procedure for installing, configuring, and provisioning the IPAM feature in Windows Server 2012 or Windows Server 2012 R2 uses the automatic Group Policy provisioning option.
- Once an IPAM server is provisioned using the automatic Group Policy option, the only way to undo this is to uninstall and reinstall the IPAM feature.
- Once an IPAM server is installed, there are several post installation IPAM server tasks to successfully implement the IPAM feature.
- In order to delegate administration of IPAM features and IPAM servers, it is necessary to use the correct IPAM server local security group.
- The IPAM client console is the correct place to configure and manage server discovery. The console provides the quick start selections in the overview pane.

- The correct procedure for creating, managing, tracking, and editing IP address blocks, IP address ranges, and IP addresses uses the IPAM client console.
- Using the IPAM client console to monitor the under and over utilization of address ranges and scopes is carried out on the DHCP scopes pane.
- Importing IP data from CSV files into the IPAM database is the way to migrate legacy IP address data.

Knowledge Assessment

Multiple Choice

Select the correct answer for each of the following questions.

1. Which IPAM Security Group allows access to IP address tracking information but not full administration of an IPAM server? (Choose two answers.)
   a. IPAM Users
   b. IPAM ASM Administrators
   c. IPAM Audit Administrators
   d. IPAM Administrators

2. IPAM servers should be installed on which Windows Server 2012 R2?
   a. domain controller
   b. non-domain joined
   c. DNS server
   d. domain-joined sole purpose

3. Which of the following functions does IPAM not carry out?
   a. planning
   b. auditing
   c. tracking
   d. monitoring

4. IPAM can be administered from which operating system?
   a. Windows 7
   b. Windows Server 2008 R2 SP1
   c. Windows 8
   d. Windows Server 2008 SP2

5. Which of the following GPOs is not created when IPAM is provisioned using the automatic Group Policy method?
   a. IPAM1_DHCP
   b. IPAM1_DNS
   c. IPAM1_NPS
   d. IPAM1_DC_NPS

6. How many DNS servers can be managed from a single IPAM server?
   a. 25
   b. 500
   c. 250
   d. 50

7. How much RAM is required to install an IPAM server?
   a. 1 GB
   b. 2 GB
   c. 4 GB
   d. 8 GB

8. Which Windows PowerShell cmdlet commences the automatic Group Policy provisioning on an IPAM server?
   a. `Invoke-IpamGpoProvisioning`
   b. `Start-IpamGpoProvisioning`
   c. `Start-IpamAutoGpoProvisioning`
   d. `Invoke-IpamAutoGpoProvisioning`

9. Which of the following devices will IPAM manage? (Choose all that apply.)
   a. Windows Server 2008 R2 DNS server
   b. Windows Server 2003 DCHP server
   c. Cisco DHCP device
   d. Windows Server 2012 NPS server

10. Which of the following are IPAM collection tasks? (Choose all that apply.)
    a. AddressExpiry
    b. Audit
    c. Service Monitoring
    d. ServerConfiguration

Best Answer

Choose the letter that corresponds to the best answer. More than one answer choice may achieve the goal. Select the BEST answer.

1. Which IPAM local security group should you use to provide IP auditing permissions?
   a. IPAM Audit Administrators
   b. IPAM Administrators
   c. IPAM Users
   d. IPAM ASM Administrators

2. On which Windows Server should you install the IPAM feature?
   a. Windows Server 2008 R2 Domain Controller
   b. Windows Server 2012 R2 DHCP Server
   c. Windows Server 2012 R2 Domain Controller
   d. Windows Server 2012 R2 File Server

3. Which of the following IPAM provisioning methods should you use?
   a. Manual
   b. Group Policy
   c. Automatic Group Policy
   d. Active Directory

4. To alter a DHCP scope using IPAM, which method should you use?
   a. DHCP Scopes console in Server Manager
   b. Directly on the DHCP console on the DHCP server
   c. Directly via Windows PowerShell on the DHCP server
   d. Remotely via Windows PowerShell

Matching and Identification

1. Identify which of the following are IPAM server tasks.
   _______ **a)** AuditTracking
   _______ **b)** IPAM discovery
   _______ **c)** DNSDataCollection
   _______ **d)** ServerConfiguration
   _______ **e)** GPOCollection
   _______ **f)** Audit
   _______ **g)** DHCpDataCollection
   _______ **h)** ForestCollection
   _______ **i)** ServerAvailability
   _______ **j)** EFS recovery
   _______ **k)** AddressExpiry

Build a List

1. Identify the correct order in which IPAM post configuration tasks are carried out. Not all steps will be used.
   _______ Select or add servers to manage
   _______ Start forest discovery
   _______ Provision the IPAM server
   _______ Template
   _______ Configure server discovery
   _______ Start server discovery
   _______ AD Discovery
   _______ Connect to IPAM server
   _______ Retrieve data from managed servers

2. Identify the steps in order in which IP address management is carried out. Not all steps will be used.
   _______ Create IP addresses (static)
   _______ Create DHCP scopes
   _______ Create IP address blocks
   _______ Create DNS zones
   _______ Collect all IP data from servers
   _______ Create IP address ranges

3. Identify the steps in order to create an IP address block. Not all steps will be used.
   _______ Run server manager and select IPAM
   _______ Select tasks and add IP address block
   _______ Select IP address ranges
   _______ Add the IP address block data and click OK
   _______ Select IP address blocks

Business Case Scenarios

Scenario 13-1: Planning IPAM Deployment

You are an administrator of the Contoso Corporation. The Contoso Corporation has a forest root domain called contoso.com. There are subdomains in three trees: Eu.Contoso.com, US.contoso.com, and adatum.com.

The CTO has asked you to recommend an IPAM deployment option but wants each domain administrator to have full control of the infrastructure in his or her own domain.

What do you recommend?

Scenario 13-2: Configuring a Library Computer

You are setting up an IPAM solution for your Active Directory Forest. The forest contains a single domain, adatum.com. All domain controllers are currently running Windows Server 2008 or Windows Server 2008 R2. The forest and domain functional levels are at Windows Server 2008.

Your CTO has asked you to ensure that you can manage all DHCP and DNS servers from the IPAM server. What should you do?

LESSON 14

Configuring a Domain and Forest

70-412 EXAM OBJECTIVE

Objective 5.1 – Configure a forest or a domain. This objective may include but is not limited to: Implement multi-domain and multi-forest Active Directory environments including interoperability with previous versions of Active Directory; upgrade existing domains and forests including environment preparation and functional levels; configure multiple user principal name (UPN) suffixes.

LESSON HEADING	EXAM OBJECTIVE
Implementing Complex Active Directory Environments	Implement multi-domain and multi-forest Active Directory environments including interoperability with previous versions of Active Directory
Implementing Multi-Domain Active Directory Environments	
Implementing Multi-Forest Active Directory Environments	
Upgrading Existing Domains and Forests	Upgrade existing domains and forests including environment preparation and functional levels
Understanding Functional Levels	
Upgrading Windows Server 2008 and Windows Server 2008 R2 to Windows Server 2012 Domain Controllers	
Configuring Multiple UPN Suffixes	Configure multiple user principal name (UPN) suffixes

KEY TERMS

Active Directory	**domain functional levels**	**global catalog servers**
Active Directory schema	**domain trees**	**in-place upgrade**
clean install	**domains**	**organizational units**
directory service	**forest functional levels**	**trust relationships**
domain controllers	**forests**	**user principal names (UPNs)**

Implementing Complex Active Directory Environments

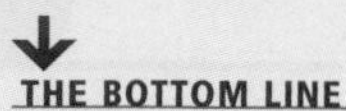

A ***directory service*** stores, organizes, and provides access to information in a directory. Directory services are used for locating, managing, administering, and organizing common items and network resources, such as volumes, folders, files, printers, users, groups, devices, telephone numbers, and other objects. One popular directory service used by many organizations is Microsoft's Active Directory.

CERTIFICATION READY
Implement multi-domain and multi-forest Active Directory environments including interoperability with previous versions of Active Directory.
Objective 5.1

Active Directory is a technology created by Microsoft that provides a variety of network services, including the following:

- Lightweight Directory Access Protocol (LDAP)
- Domain Name System (DNS) based naming and other network information
- Security mechanism for authentication that includes Kerberos-based and single sign-on authentication
- Security mechanism for authorization and auditing
- Central location for network administration and delegation of authority
- Policy-based management for user and computer accounts

You can look at Active Directory from two sides: logical and physical. First, when you think of Active Directory, you most likely focus on the logical components that make up Active Directory. The logical components (which administrators create, organize, and manage) include:

- ***Organizational units:*** Containers in a domain that allow you to organize and group resources for easier administration, including delegating administrative rights.

  You should never create a multiple-domain forest to reflect the organizational structure of your business. The organization structure changes over time. Instead, you should use organizational units to reflect the organizational structure.
- ***Domains:*** An administrative boundary for users and computers, which are stored in a common directory database. A single domain can span multiple physical locations or sites and can contain millions of objects.

  It is easier to manage objects within a single Active Directory Domain Service (AD DS) domain that allows administrators to easily grant rights and permissions within the AD DS domain boundary. It is also easy to implement Group Policy Objects (GPOs) within a domain and to configure auditing.
- ***Domain trees:*** Collection of domains that are grouped together in hierarchical structures and that share a common root domain. A domain tree can have a single domain or many domains. A domain (known as the *parent domain*) can have a child domain. A child domain can have its own child domain. Because the child domain is combined with the parent domain name to form its own unique DNS name, the domains with a tree have a contiguous namespace.

  For example, you can have one domain assigned to an organization's developers and another domain assigned to its salespeople:

  developers.microsoft.com
  sales.microsoft.com

  The developers and sales domains are both child domains of the microsoft.com domain.
- ***Forests:*** A collection of domain trees that share a common AD DS directory schema. A forest can contain one or more domain trees or domains, all of which share a common logical structure, global catalog, directory schema, and directory configuration, as well as automatic two-way transitive trust relationships. A forest can be a single domain tree

or even a single domain. The first domain in the forest is called the *forest root domain*. For multiple domain trees, each domain tree consists of a unique namespace.

A forest differs from a tree because it uses disjointed namespaces between the trees. For example, in a forest, you can have microsoft.com as the root for one tree. Say that Microsoft then purchases another company called *Contoso Corporation (contoso.com)*, and contoso.com then becomes the root of another tree. Both trees can be combined into a forest, yet each tree's identity could be kept separate.

- ***Trust relationships:*** Allow users in one domain to access resources in another domain. Trust relationships form the framework that allows resource sharing and authentication between domains. Domains within a tree and forest are automatically created as two-way transitive trusts. A transitive trust is based on the following concept:

  > If domain A trusts domain B, and domain B trusts domain C, then domain A trusts domain C.

  However, if you have a partnership with another company and you need users from one domain within one organization to access resources in another domain, you can configure an explicit nontransitive trust to be either one way or two way.

The physical components that make up Active Directory include the following:

- ***Domain controllers:*** The servers that contain the Active Directory databases. A domain partition stores only the information about objects located in that domain. All domain controllers in a domain receive changes and replicate those changes to the domain partition stored on other domain controllers in the domain. Eventually, the changes are replicated to all domain controllers within the domain. As a result, all domain controllers are peers in the domain and manage replication as a unit.
- ***Global catalog servers:*** A domain controller that stores a full copy of all Active Directory objects in the directory for its host domain and a partial copy of all objects for all other domains in the forest. Applications and clients can query the global catalog to locate any object in a forest. A global catalog is created automatically on the first domain controller in the forest. Optionally, other domain controllers can be configured to serve as global catalogs.

Active Directory data is stored in an Active Directory database. By default, the Active Directory database is stored in an Active Directory database file (C:\Windows\NTDS\Ntds.dit) and its associated log and temporary files. The Active Directory database uses the Extensible Storage Engine (ESE), which is an indexed and sequential access method (ISAM) database. The ESE (Esent.dll) indexes the data in the database file and provides the mechanism to store and retrieve data. It supports up to a little over 2 billion objects and up to 16 TB in size. The maximum size of a database record is 8110 bytes, based on an 8-kilobyte (KB) page size. The ntds.dit file is approximately 400 MB in size per 1000 users.

An Active Directory database is logically separated into the following directory partitions:

- **Schema partition (one per forest):** Contains definitions of all objects and attributes that can be created in the directory, and the rules for creating and manipulating the objects.
- **Configuration partition (one per forest):** Contains information about the forest-wide Active Directory structure including mapping existing domains and sites, and which domain controllers and services exist within the forest.
- **Domain partition (one per domain):** Contains information about users, groups, computers, and organizational units.
- **Application partition:** Stores information about applications in Active Directory. Each application determines how it stores, categorizes, and uses application-specific information (for example, DNS that is integrated with Active Directory). Depending on how Active Directory-integrated zones are implemented, the information is ForestDNSZones and DomainDNSZones.

Implementing Multi-Domain Active Directory Environments

With the number of objects that can be stored in an Active Directory domain, the use of organizational units to organize and manage those objects, the use of fine-grained Password Policies and Account Lockout Policies, and the ability to span multiple physical sites, many organizations need only one domain. However, sometimes legal or political reasons dictate that multiple domains must be used.

CERTIFICATION READY
Implement multi-domain Active Directory environments.
Objective 5.1

Active Directory is closely tied to DNS, which is used to locate objects and network resources. DNS is often used to represent an Internet presence and maybe used within an organization. When one company purchases or merges with another company, each company might need to keep its own identity and presence.

As large organizations tend to have large Active Directory databases, it might be beneficial to divide a large AD DS database into a more manageable size. In addition, due to replication of information between domain controllers, smaller domains reduce replication traffic, which can be beneficial over slower WAN links. However, this is only a benefit if there are a large number of accounts on the remote domain.

A single domain offers centralized management, where a set of administrators manage everything within the domain; although multiple domains can be centrally managed, multiple domains offer decentralized management, where different administrators manage each domain. If an organization establishes a presence in a foreign country and there are political or legal reasons to have separate security domains, you might consider implementing separate domains.

Some companies define user domains and resource domains. A user domain, as it sounds, is used to manage users. Administrators of the user domain have full administrative control over the user accounts, and create, manage, and remove user accounts. Resource domains are sometimes managed by different management teams, which help secure resources.

Before you decide to use multiple domains and create child domains, you need to do some planning and preparation. Because DNS is so closely tied to Active Directory and Active Directory requires DNS to operate, you might need to define DNS domains for the new Active Directory domain. Because the domain will be within the same tree, you can delegate DNS for the child domain. It should be noted that an existing DNS service might be sufficient and does not necessarily need a separate DNS domain.

DELEGATE DNS FOR A CHILD DOMAIN

GET READY. To delegate DNS for a child domain, perform the following steps:

1. Log in to a domain controller such as RWDC01 as contoso\administrator.
2. Open Server Manager, open the Tools menu, and click DNS. The *DNS Manager* opens.
3. Expand the DNS server, expand Forward Lookup Zones, click Contoso.com, and then click New Delegation.
4. When the *New Delegation Wizard* starts, click Next.
5. To represent North America, type NA in the *Delegated domain* text box, and click Next.
6. On the *Name Servers* page, click Add.
7. In the *New Name Server Record* dialog box, type RWDC01.contoso.com in the Server fully qualified domain name (FQDN). Then click <Click here to add an IP address> (see Figure 14-1), and type 192.168.1.50. Click OK.

Figure 14-1

Delegating a new name server

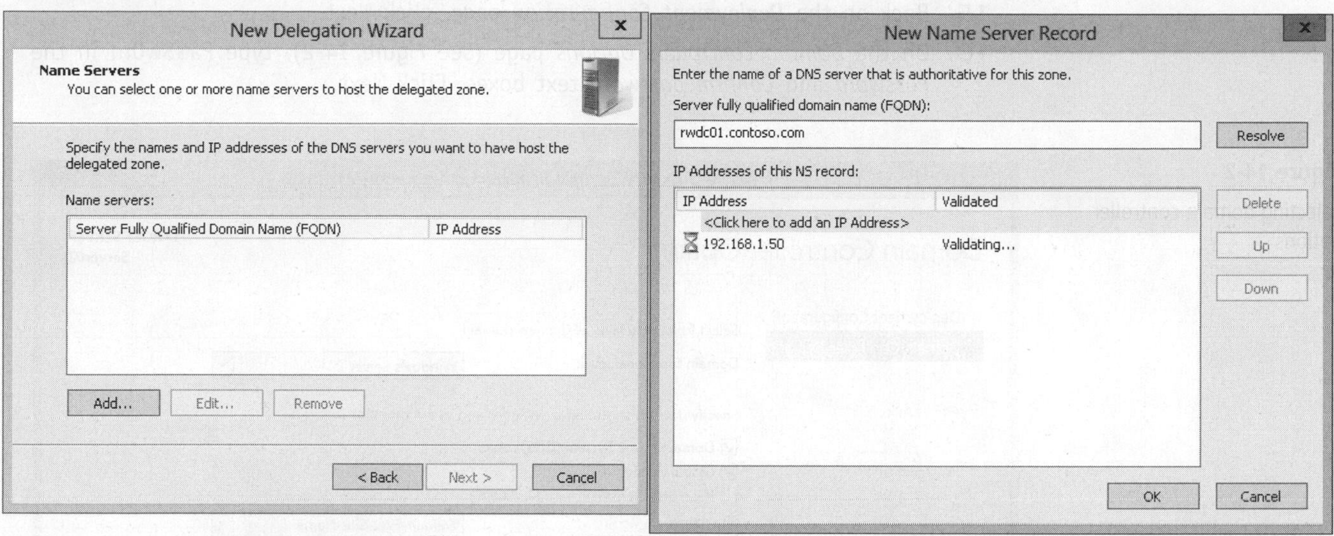

8. When the wizard is complete, click Finish.

Creating a child domain is similar to installing a stand-alone domain controller. The primary difference is that you must link the child domain to the parent domain.

CREATE A CHILD DOMAIN

GET READY. To create a child domain on a stand-alone server that is not part of a domain, perform the following steps:

1. Log in to a domain controller such as RWDC01 as contoso\administrator.
2. Open Server Manager, open the Manage menu, and click Add Roles and Features.
3. When the *Add Roles and Features Wizard* starts, click Next.
4. On the *Select installation type* page, click Next.
5. On the *Select destination server* page, click Next.
6. On the *Select server roles* page, click to select Active Directory Domain Services. When the *Add Roles and Features Wizard* dialog box opens, click Add Features.
7. Back on the *Select server roles* page, click Next.
8. On the *Select features* page, click Next.
9. On the *Active Directory Domain Services* page, click Next.
10. On the *Confirm installation selections* page, click Install.
11. When the installation is complete, click Promote this server to a domain controller link.
12. When the *Active Directory Domain Services Configuration Wizard* starts, click Add a new domain to an existing forest.
13. With the *Select domain type* as *Child Domain*, type contoso.com in the *Parent domain name* text box. In the *New domain name* text box, type NA.

14. Click the Change button. Type the user name of contoso\administrator and the password of Password01. Click OK.
15. Back on the *Deployment Configuration* page, click Next.
16. On the *Domain Controllers Options* page (see Figure 14-2), type Pa$$w0rd in the *Password* and *Confirm password* text boxes. Click Next.

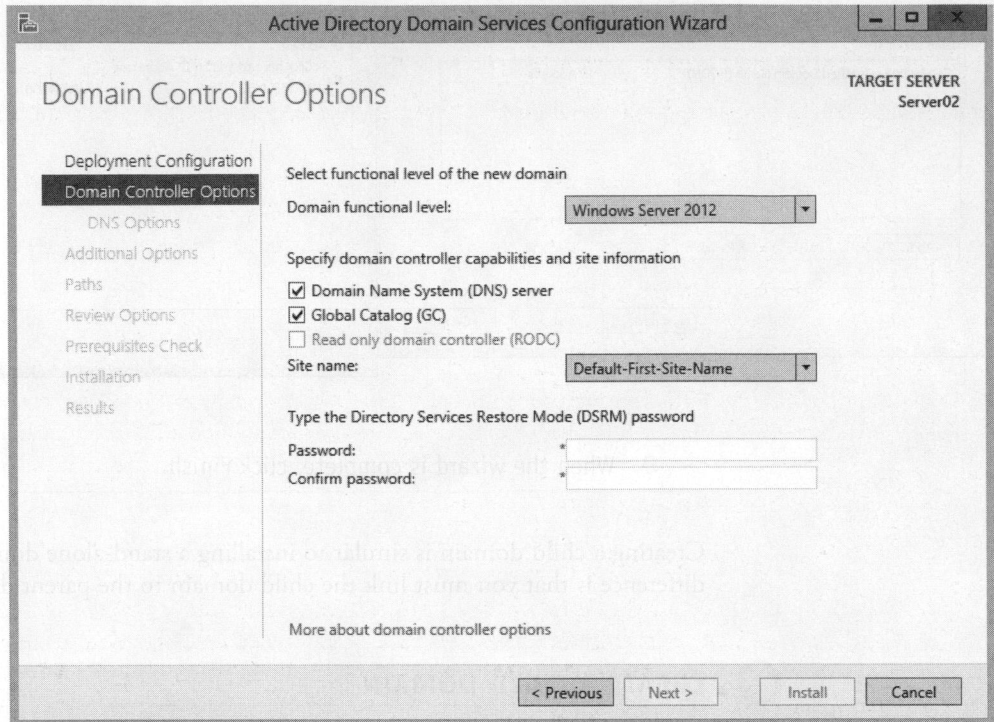

Figure 14-2
Selecting domain controller options

17. On the *DNS Options* page, click Change. Type the user name of contoso\administrator and the password of Pa$$w0rd. Click OK. Click Next.
18. On the *Additional Options* page, click Next.
19. On the *Paths* page, click Next.
20. On the *Review Options* page, click Next.
21. On the *Prerequisites Check* page, confirm that there are no issues, and then click Install.
22. When the installation is complete, click Close.

Implementing Multi-Forest Active Directory Environments

Some organizations need more complex environments that require the organization to have multiple forests. By having a multi-forest organization, each forest has its own configuration, schema, and global catalogs.

CERTIFICATION READY
Implement multi-forest Active Directory environments.
Objective 5.1

Separate Active Directory forests also offer isolated security. By having separate forests, each forest root domain has the Schema Admins and Enterprise Admins AD DS forest. Separate forests are often deployed by government defense contractors and other organizations that require security isolation.

If two or more independent organizations want to share resources, but each organization does not trust the domain administrators of the partner's organization or you need a segmenting of duties, you should use multiple forests with manually implemented trust relationships. Trusts are discussed in Lesson 15, "Configuring Trusts."

The ***Active Directory schema*** defines the objects and attributes of those objects. Because the schema is shared between domains, the domain admins of the various domains must agree on the schema changes. Therefore, if you require different schemas, you can use multiple forests.

Upgrading Existing Domains and Forests

As a general rule, as each version of Windows is introduced, the new version includes new features and functionality that was not available previously. Therefore, to get the most out of Windows servers, you should consider upgrading the domain controllers, domains, and forests to Windows Server 2012 R2.

CERTIFICATION READY
Upgrade existing domains and forests including environment preparation and functional levels.
Objective 5.1

Because Active Directory is a key component to many organizations, you must maintain Active Directory and be careful when upgrading to a newer version. Depending on your needs, the current state of Active Directory, and the hardware that Active Directory is running on, there are several options you can use to upgrade the Active Directory environment. These options include:

- ***In-place upgrade:*** If the domain controller is running Windows Server 2008 or Windows Server 2008 R2, you can upgrade each domain controller one-by-one to Windows Server 2012 R2. Because the Windows Server functional level will be Windows Server 2008 or Windows Server 2008 R2, some schema changes need to be done when using the Server Manager to install AD DS on the first Windows Server 2012 R2 domain controller.
- **Add servers running Windows Server 2012 R2 and promote to domain controllers:** As long as the functional level of the domain and forest is at least Windows Server 2008 mode, you will be able to install Windows Server 2012 R2 servers onto the domain. You can then install the AD DS and promote the server to a domain controller. Similar to an in-place upgrade, the schema is updated when you use the Server Manager to install AD DS on the first Windows Server 2012 domain controller.
- **Create a new AD DS Windows Server 2012 R2 domain and migrate the objects to the new domain or merge the domains together:** By adding new domains, you can perform a gradual upgrade to Windows Server 2012 R2, as you migrate resources to a domain that is running Windows Server 2012. By adding the extra domains, you will have different AD DS domains coexist and share resources until all objects are migrated or merged.

Of these, the "add servers running Windows Server 2012 R2 and promote to domain controllers" is the best option because you start with clean installation of Windows. The "in-place upgrade" option does not start as a clean installation of Windows" and the "create a new domain" option takes the most work to complete and might cause a little confusion when managing resources.

Understanding Functional Levels

To provide backward compatibility with older systems, Windows domains and forests can run at various levels of functionality. However, to get the most out of the domain controllers and utilize all of the available features, you need to upgrade the domain controllers to Windows Server 2012 R2 and raise the domain and forest functional level to Windows Server 2012 R2. However, as you move to the newer domain and forest functional levels, you might prevent older systems from operating in the upgraded environment.

Domain functional levels and ***forest functional levels*** allow administrators to enable domain- or forest-wide Active Directory features within your network environment, while maintaining compatibility with older operating systems. The functional level of the domain or forest depends on the version of the domain controllers in the domain or forest. After all of the domain controllers are upgraded within a domain or forest, the domain or forest functional level can be upgraded so that newer features can be made available.

RAISING DOMAIN FUNCTIONAL LEVELS

As of Windows Server 2012 R2, there are five available domain functional levels: Windows Server 2003, Windows Server 2008, Windows Server 2008 R2, Windows Server 2012 and Windows Server 2012 R2. If you have multiple domains within a tree, you can upgrade the functional level of a domain without affecting the other domains. Windows Server 2012 or Windows Server 2012 R2 domain controllers do not support the Windows 2000 native mode functional level that was available with Windows Server 2008 R2 and earlier.

The Windows Server 2003 domain functional level supports domain controllers running Windows Server 2003, Windows Server 2008, Windows Server 2008 R2, Windows Server 2012 and Windows Server 2012 R2. It does not allow the presence of Windows 2000 domain controllers.

All available domain functional levels now support universal groups, group nesting (one group inside another group), and the conversion between the security and distribution groups. In addition, the Windows Server 2003 domain functional level added the following features:

- **LastLogonTimestamp attribute:** A computer and user attribute that allows the last logon time to be recorded, which is then replicated within the domain.
- **UserPassword attribute:** Allows the UserPassword attribute on the inetOrgPerson object and user objects so that it can be used with other directory services.
- **Constrained delegation:** Allows accounts to be delegated to specific destination services when using Kerberos.

The Windows Server 2008 domain functional level supports domain controllers running Windows Server 2008, Windows Server 2008 R2, Windows Server 2012 R2. It includes all of the features that were available in Windows Server 2003 domain functional mode and includes the following functionality:

- **SYSVOL replication using DFSR instead of NTFRS:** For the SYSVOL, use Distributed File System Replication (DFSR) instead of NT File Replication Service (NTFRS), which allows for more efficient and robust replication between domain controllers.
- **Advanced Encryption Services (AES 128 and 256) support for Kerberos authentication protocol:** AES has become a de facto standard for encryption that is used worldwide. Therefore, the newer versions of Windows support the stronger encryption when authenticating with Kerberos.
- **Improved auditing of user logon information:** Starting with Windows Server 2008, the user's last successful logon, the computer that the user logged into, the number of failed logon attempts for the user, and the time of the last failed logon attempt are recorded. In addition, when making changes in active directory, the old values and new values are recorded in the Event Viewer.
- **Fine-grained password policies:** Before fine-grained password policies, the password policies and account lockout policies could be assigned only for the entire domain. With fine-grained password policies, a password policy or account policy can be configured for a user or global security groups in a domain.
- **Read-only domain controller:** Starting with Windows Server 2008, you can install and place a special type of domain controller in less than secure environments. By using a

read-only domain controller, the domain controller does not perform any outbound replication and you can restrict which accounts do not get replicated to.

The Windows Server 2008 R2 domain functional levels support domain controllers running Windows Server 2008 R2, Windows Server 2012 and Windows Server 2012 R2. It includes all of the features of Windows Server 2008 domain functional mode, and includes the following functionality:

- **Authentication mechanism assurance:** Adds an administrator-designated, universal group membership to a user's access token, which can be used in federated identity management infrastructures and claims-aware applications.
- **Automatic SPN management:** Used for services running on a particular computer under the context of a managed service account to automatically auto-generate passwords so that you don't have to reset passwords manually.

The Windows Server 2012 domain functional levels support only domain controllers running Windows Server 2012 and Windows Server 2012 R2. It includes all of the features of Windows Server 2008 R2 domain functional mode, and includes Key Distribution Center (KDC) support for claims, compound authentication, and Kerberos armoring. By using a KDC administrative template policy setting, you can configure domain controllers to support claims and compound authentication for Dynamic Access Control and Kerberos armoring by using Kerberos authentication.

The Windows Server 2012 R2 domain functional level support only domain controllers running Windows Server 2012 R2. It includes all of the features of Windows Server 2012 domain functional mode, and includes the following features:

- **DC-side protections for Protected Users:** Protects users by not allowing authentication with NTLM, by using DES or RC4 cipher suites in Kerberos pre-authentication. In addition, members cannot be delegated with unconstrained or constrained delegation; they also cannot renew user tickets (TGTs) beyond the initial four-hour lifetime.
- **Authentication Policies:** A forest-based Active Directory policy that is applied to accounts in Windows Server 2012 R2 domains to control which hosts can sign-on from. In addition, you can apply access control conditions for account authentication for services.
- **Authentication Policy Silos:** Used to create containers that define authentication policies for user, managed service and computer accounts.

To raise the domain functional level, you must be a member of the Domain Admins group. In addition, the PDC Emulator must be available.

Before you can raise the domain functional level, you need to ensure that all domain controllers within that domain are running the required version of the Windows operating system. For example, to raise the domain functional level to Windows Server 2012, you must upgrade or retire any domain controllers with Windows Server 2008 R2 or earlier. It should also be noted that generally raising the domain functional level is a one-way process that cannot be reversed, short of performing an authoritative restore of Active Directory. The only exception to date is when you raise the domain functional level to Windows Server 2008 R2. If the forest functional level is Windows Server 2008 or lower, you have the option of rolling the domain functional level back to Windows Server 2008.

RAISE THE DOMAIN FUNCTIONAL LEVEL

GET READY. To raise the domain functional level, perform the following steps:

1. Log in to a domain controller such as RWDC01 as contoso\administrator.
2. Open Server Manager, and open Active Directory Users and Computers.

3. Right-click the Active Directory Domains and Trusts, and click Raise Domain Functional Level.
4. Select the desired domain functional level,and click Raise.
5. When it gives a warning saying that process may not be able to be reversed, click OK.
6. When the functional level has been raised successfully, click OK.
7. Close the Active Directory Users and Computers console.

RAISING FOREST FUNCTIONAL LEVELS

Forest functional levels are similar to domain forest functional levels, except that it affects all domains within the forest. Windows Server 2012 R2 domain controllers support the following forest functional levels: Windows Server 2003, Windows Server 2008, Windows Server 2008 R2, Windows Server 2012 and Windows Server 2012 R2.

When a forest is raised to a functional level, older domain controllers cannot be introduced into the domain. The forest functional level assumes that all domains are raised to the same level before the forest is raised. For example, to raise the forest functional level to Windows Server 2012 R2, you first have to raise the domain functional levels of all domains to Windows Server 2012 R2. Similar to the domain functional level, raising the forest functional level is generally an irreversible procedure.

The Windows Server 2003 forest functional level supports domain controllers running Windows Server 2003, Windows Server 2008, Windows Server 2008 R2, Windows Server 2012 and Windows Server 2012 R2. It does not allow the presence of Windows 2000 domain controllers.

All available forest functional levels now support Universal group caching, and Application Directory partitions. Windows Server 2003 forest functional level adds the following features:

- **Improved replication of group objects by using linked values:** Replicate only the portions of the member list that have actually been added, modified, or deleted.
- **Dynamic auxiliary class objects:** Support dynamically linking auxiliary classes to individual objects, instead of linking only to an entire class of objects.
- **User objects can be converted to inetOrgPerson objects:** The inetOrgPerson object is used by non–Microsoft LDAP directory services, such as Novell.
- **Deactivation and redefinition of attributes and classes in the schema:** Allows to reuse the ldapDisplayName, schemaIdGuid, OID, and mapiID attributes.
- **Domain rename:** The ability to rename a domain.
- **Cross-forest trusts permitted:** Allows linking of two forests using a trust.
- **Improved Knowledge Consistency Checker (KCC):** By using an improved algorithm for the intersite topology generator (ISTG) so that the forest can have a greater number of sites than previously.

The Windows Server 2008 forest functional level is supported by domain controllers running Windows Server 2008, Windows Server 2008 R2, Windows Server 2012 and Windows Server 2012 R2. It does not add any new features. However, it ensures that all new domains and domain controllers are set to Windows Server 2008 or higher.

The Windows Server 2008 R2 forest functional level supports Windows Server 2008 R2, Windows Server 2012 and Windows Server 2012 R2. The Windows Server 2008 R2 forest functional level includes all of the features that are available at the Windows Server 2003 forest functional level. In addition, the Windows Server 2008 R2 forest functional level also includes the Active Directory Recycle Bin (which needs to be activated before its use) that provides the ability to restore deleted objects in their entirety while Active Directory Services is running. All domains that are subsequently added to the forest operate at the Windows Server 2008 R2 domain functional level by default.

The Windows Sever 2012 and the Windows Server 2012 R2 forest functional level does not have any additional features. However, all domain function levels must be Windows Server 2012 or Windows Server 2012 R2.

To raise the forest functional level, you must be a member of the Enterprise Admins group. In addition, the Schema Master role must be available.

Before you can raise the forest functional level, you need to ensure that all domains are running the required version of the Windows operating system. For example, to raise the domain functional level to Windows Server 2012, all domains must be set to Windows Server 2012. Similar to domain functional levels, generally raising the domain functional level is a one-way process that cannot be reversed, short of performing an authoritative restore of Active Directory. The only exception to date is when you raise the forest functional level to Windows Server 2008 R2 and if the Active Directory Recycle Bin is not enabled, you have the option of rolling the forest functional level back to Windows Server 2008.

RAISE THE FOREST FUNCTIONAL LEVEL

GET READY. To raise the forest functional level, perform the following steps:

1. Log in to a domain controller such as RWDC01 as contoso\administrator.
2. Open Server Manager, and open Active Directory Domains and Trusts.
3. Right-click the Active Directory Domains and Trusts, and click Raise Forest Functional Level.
4. Select the desired forest functional level and click Raise.
5. When it gives a warning that when you raise a forest, you may not be able to reverse it, click OK.
6. When the forest has been raised successfully, click OK.
7. Close Active Directory Domains and Trusts.

Upgrading Windows Server 2008 and Windows Server 2008 R2 to Windows Server 2012 Domain Controllers

To upgrade from Windows Server 2008 or Windows Server 2008 R2 Active Directory Domain Services (AD DS), you can upgrade the operating system of the existing domain controllers to Windows Server 2012 or Windows Server 2012 R2 (assuming the hardware can support it), or introduce Windows Server 2012 or Windows Server 2012 R2 servers as domain controllers, and then decommission the older domain controllers.

If you have a server running an old operating system, and you want to move to the new operating system, you can choose to perform an upgrade or perform a clean install. An upgrade usually consists of starting the install program and letting the new files overwrite the old files. Although the upgrade tends to be simple, and quicker, the ***clean install*** allows you to start fresh with no old files or configuration on the machine. Of course, performing a clean install of the operating system, installing any additional software, and configuring Windows and the software require more work. However, when you want the most reliable system, it is always best to perform a clean install.

For a domain that is running in Windows Server 2003, Windows Server 2008, or Windows Server 2008 R2 functional level, you can install Windows Server 2012 and add the computer to the domain. However, before you promote a server running Windows Server 2012 to a domain controller, you must upgrade the schema.

In previous versions of Windows, you would use the adprep.exe tool to upgrade the schema. However, while the Windows Server 2012 includes adprep32.exe has been deprecated. Instead, the Active Directory Domain Services Installation Wizard that is included in Server Manager incorporates the commands necessary to upgrade the AD DS forest schema.

PERFORM AN UPGRADE INSTALLATION

GET READY. To upgrade from Windows Server 2008 or Windows Server 2008 R2 to Windows Server 2012 or Windows Server 2012 R2, perform the following steps:

1. Log in to a domain controller such as RWDC01 as contoso\administrator.
2. Insert the Windows Server 2012 or Windows Server 2012 R2 installation disk into the DVD drive and start the Setup program. This displays the *Windows Setup* window.
3. Click Install Now. The *Windows Setup Wizard* opens, displaying the *Select the operating system you want to install* page.
4. Select the operating system edition and installation option you want to install and click Next. This displays the *License Terms* page.
5. Select the I accept the license terms check box and click Next. This displays the *Which type of installation do you want?* page.
6. Click the Upgrade: Install Windows and keep files, settings, and applications option. This displays the *Compatibility report (saved to your desktop)* page.
7. Note the compatibility information provided by the Setup program and click Next. This displays the *Upgrading Windows* page.
   After several minutes, during which the Setup program upgrades Windows Server 2008 or Windows Server 2008 R2 to Windows Server 2012 or Windows Server 2012 R2 and restarts the computer several times, the system finalizes the installation and the Windows sign-on screen appears.

Before you perform the upgrade, you should always check for hardware and software compatibility. After the installation is completed, you should then open the *Device Manager* and check for missing device drivers, run Windows updates, check for updates for non-Microsoft software, and check the Event Viewer for errors.

■ Configuring Multiple UPN Suffixes

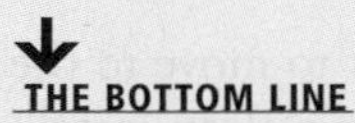

THE BOTTOM LINE

Users can log on by using one of two ways: Domain username (domain_name\username) or the ***user principal names (UPNs)***, which uses an e-mail address format (such as username@domainname.ext). The global catalog resolves the UPN name to a username. Multiple UPN suffixes can be used to allow users to log on using an e-mail account name with different DNS namespace names.

CERTIFICATION READY
Configure multiple user principal name (UPN) suffixes.
Objective 5.1

To add multiple UPN suffixes, you use the Active Directory Domains and Trusts management console to manage the domain properties. After adding the additional UPN suffixes, users can log on with the alternative UPN suffixes. Of course, similar to when two users cannot use the same login name with a multi-domain environment, you must make sure that the UPNs are unique.

CONFIGURE MULTIPLE UPN SUFFIXES

GET READY. To configure multiple UPN suffixes, perform the following steps:

1. Log in to a domain controller such as RWDC01 as contoso\administrator.
2. Open Server Manager, and open Active Directory Domains and Trusts.
3. Right-click Active Directory Domains and Trusts, and then click Properties.
4. On the *UPN Suffixes* tab (see Figure 14-3), type an alternative UPN suffix for the forest, and then click Add. Repeat the process until you add all desired UPN suffixes.

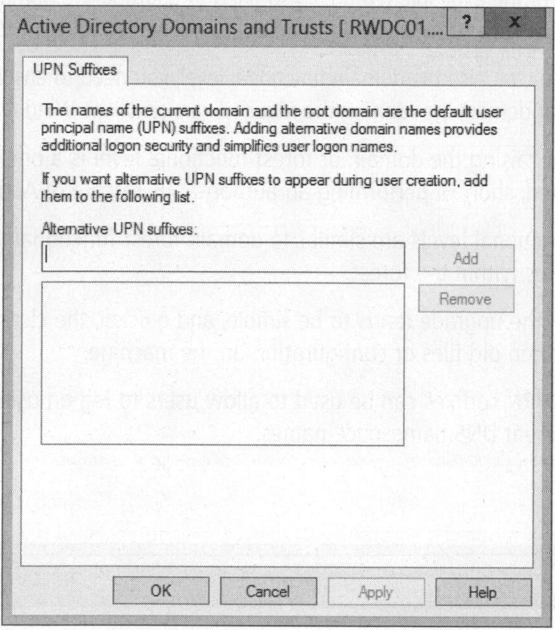

Figure 14-3
Adding an alternative UPN suffix

5. When done, click OK to close the *Properties* dialog box.

SKILL SUMMARY

IN THIS LESSON YOU LEARNED:

- A domain is an administrative boundary for users and computers, which are stored in a common directory database. A single domain can span multiple physical locations or sites and can contain millions of objects.
- A domain tree is a collection of domains that are grouped together in hierarchical structures and that share a common root domain. A domain tree can have a single domain or many domains.
- A forest is a collection of domain trees that share a common Active Directory Domain Services (AD DS) database.
- Creating a child domain is similar to installing a stand-alone domain controller. The primary difference is that you must link the child domain to the parent domain.
- Some organizations need more complex environments that require the organization to have multiple forests. By having a multi-forest organization, each forest has its own configuration, schema, and global catalogs.

- The Active Directory schema defines the objects and attributes of those objects. Because the schema is shared between domains, all domains administrators must agree on the schema changes.
- If the domain controller is running Windows Server 2008 or Windows Server 2008 R2, you can upgrade each domain controller one-by-one to Windows Server 2012 or Windows Server 2012 R2.
- To provide backward compatibility with older systems, Windows domains and forests can run at a various levels of functionality. However, to get the most out of the domain controllers and utilize all of the available features, you need to upgrade the domain controllers to Windows Server 2012 R2 and raise the domain and forest functional level to Windows Server 2012 R2.
- Before you can raise the domain functional level, you need to ensure that all domain controllers within that domain are running the required version of the Windows operating system.
- Generally, raising the domain or forest functional level is a one-way process that cannot be reversed, short of performing an authoritative restore of Active Directory.
- Forest functional levels are similar to domain forest functional levels, except that it affects all domains within the forest.
- Although the upgrade tends to be simple, and quicker, the clean install allows you to start fresh with no old files or configuration on the machine.
- Multiple UPN suffixes can be used to allow users to log on using an e-mail account name with different DNS namespace names.

Knowledge Assessment

Multiple Choice

Select the correct answer for each of the following questions.

1. What should be used to reflect the organizational structure of your organization?
 a. domain
 b. forest
 c. trees
 d. OU

2. Which of the following uses non-contiguous namespace?
 a. domain
 b. forest
 c. trees
 d. OU

3. Which partitions are used by Active Directory? (Choose all that apply.)
 a. configuration partition
 b. domain partition
 c. forest partition
 d. schema partition

4. What utility do you use to update the domain functional level?
 a. Active Directory Users and Computers
 b. Active Directory Domains and Trusts
 c. Active Directory Sites and Services
 d. DNS

5. What is the minimum domain functional level to support fine-grained password policies?
   a. Windows Server 2003
   b. Windows Server 2008
   c. Windows Server 2008 R2
   d. Windows Server 2012

6. What is the minimum domain functional level to support read-only domain controllers?
   a. Windows Server 2003
   b. Windows Server 2008
   c. Windows Server 2008 R2
   d. Windows Server 2012

7. What is the minimum domain functional level to support compound authentication and Kerberos armoring?
   a. Windows Server 2003
   b. Windows Server 2008
   c. Windows Server 2008 R2
   d. Windows Server 2012

8. What forest functional level do you need to support Active Directory Recycle Bin?
   a. Windows Server 2003
   b. Windows Server 2008
   c. Windows Server 2008 R2
   d. Windows Server 2012

9. What domain functional level supports the renaming of domains?
   a. Windows Server 2003
   b. Windows Server 2008
   c. Windows Server 2008 R2
   d. Windows Server 2012

10. What tool is used to raise the forest functional levels?
    a. Active Directory Users and Computers
    b. Active Directory Domains and Trusts
    c. Active Directory Sites and Services
    d. DNS

11. What tool do you use to add additional UPN suffixes?
    a. Active Directory Users and Computers
    b. Active Directory Domains and Trusts
    c. Active Directory Sites and Services
    d. DNS

12. You are ready to upgrade a domain to a domain functional level of Windows Server 2012 R2. Which of the following methods is the most recommended?
    a. Install a new domain controller in a new domain. Migrate the objects into the new domain.
    b. Upgrade the schema, and then upgrade the old domain controllers to Windows Server 2012.
    c. Upgrade the old domain controllers to Windows Server 2012.
    d. Perform a clean install of a new domain controller and retirement of old domain controllers.

13. What domain functional level do you need to support Active Directory Recycle Bin?
    a. Windows Server 2003
    b. Windows Server 2008
    c. Windows Server 2008 R2
    d. Windows Server 2012

14. You have a domain called *Contoso.com*, running the domain functional level Windows 2000. The domain has the following domain controllers: one Windows Server 2000, two Windows Servers 2003 R2, and two Windows Servers 2008 R2. You want to add a domain controller running Windows Server 2012 R2. What should you do first?
    a. Raise the domain functional level to Windows Server 2008 R2
    b. Raise the domain functional level to Windows Server 2012 R2
    c. Decommission the Windows 2000 domain controller
    d. Upgrade the schema

15. You have an Active Directory forest with two domains/trees: contoso.com and litware. com. The contoso.com domain has a domain functional level of Windows Server 2008, whereas the litware.com has a domain functional level of Windows Server 2003. You want to install Windows Server 2012 R2, and promote the server to a domain controller. What should you do?
    a. Run the adprep.xe /domainprep
    b. Raise the domain functional level to Windows Server 2012 R2
    c. Run the Active Directory Domain Services Configuration Wizard
    d. Modify the Computer/Name Domain Changes Properties

Matching and Identification

1. Identify the minimum domain function level (2003, 2008, 2008 R2, 2012 or 2012 R2) for the specified feature.
   _______ a) automatic SPN management
   _______ b) auditing of user logon information
   _______ c) SYSVOL replication using DFSR
   _______ d) KDC support for claims
   _______ e) read-only domain controller

2. Identify the minimum forest function level (2003, 2008, 2008 R2, 2012 or 2012 R2) for the specified feature.
   _______ a) cross-forest trusts
   _______ b) no Windows Server 2003 or Windows Server 2003 domain controllers, but allows Windows Server 2008, Windows Server 2008 R2, and Windows Server 2012 domain controllers
   _______ c) Active Directory Recycle Bin

3. Identify which of the following describes a domain, domain tree, or forest.
   _______ a) Includes one schema partition
   _______ b) Includes a common directory database
   _______ c) Uses disjointed namespace between trees
   _______ d) Has contiguous namespace
   _______ e) Includes one configuration partition

4. Which of the following are features that you find on an environment running the domain functional level Windows Server 2012 and forest functional level Windows Server 2012?
   _______ **a)** authentication mechanism assurance
   _______ **b)** multi-forest global catalogs
   _______ **c)** Advanced Encryption (AES 512 and 1024) support for Kerberos authentication protocol
   _______ **d)** multi-trusted application partition
   _______ **e)** improved KCC
   _______ **f)** Active Directory Recycle Bin
   _______ **g)** resource firewall

Build a List

1. With the Contoso.com domain, you want to create the support.contoso.com child domain. Identify the basic steps in order to accomplish this. Not all steps will be used.
   _____ Choose Add a new domain to the existing forest
   _____ Click Upgrade to DC
   _____ Install Active Directory Domain Services
   _____ Install a domain controller into the contoso.com
   _____ Click Promote this server to a domain controller
   _____ Create a new delegation in DNS for the support.contoso.com
   _____ Create a standalone DNS for the support.com site
   _____ Migrate a contoso.com domain controller to the support.contoso.com

■ Business Case Scenarios

Scenario 14-1: Upgrading the Functional Level

You have a forest that includes five domains and two trees. It contains the following domains:

Contoso.com	3 Windows Server 2003 R2 domain controllers
Support.contoso.com	3 Windows Server 2003 R2 domain controllers and 1 Windows Server 2008 R2 domain controller
Sales.contoso.com	3 Windows Server 2008 domain controllers
Litware.com	2 Windows Server 2003 domain controller and 1 Windows 2000 Server domain controller
Partner.litware.com	2 Windows Server 2003 R2 domain controllers

What are the steps to promote the forest to the Windows Server 2012 R2 functional level?

Scenario 14-2: Working with UPN Suffixes

The Contoso Corporation is a holding company for 20 other companies. Each company has its own independent presence on the Internet and is functionally independent from the other companies. Although you have only one domain, you would like each company to function with its own domain name when logging using the UPN. What do you need to do?

LESSON 15 Configuring Trusts

70-412 EXAM OBJECTIVE

Objective 5.2 – Configure trusts. This objective may include but is not limited to: Configure external, forest, shortcut, and realm trusts; configure trust authentication; configure SID filtering; configure name suffix routing.

Lesson Heading	Exam Objective
Configuring Trusts	Configure external, forest, shortcut, and realm trusts
Understanding Trusts	
Understanding Trust Types	
Understanding Trust Direction	
Understanding Transitivity	
Configuring DNS for Trusts	
Creating External Trusts	Configure external trusts
Creating Forest Trusts	Configure forest trusts
Creating Shortcut Trusts	Configure shortcut trusts
Creating Realm Trusts	Configure realm trusts
Validating Trusts	
Configuring Trust Authentication	Configure trust authentication
Configuring Selective Authentication	
Configuring Domain-Wide Authentication	
Configuring Forest-Wide Authentication	
Configuring SID Filtering	Configure SID filtering
Configuring Name Suffix Routing	Configure name suffix routing

KEY TERMS

automatically generated trusts
domain-wide authentication
external trust
forest-wide authentication
manually created trusts
nontransitive
one-way forest trust
one-way incoming trust direction
one-way outgoing trust direction
resource domain
selective authentication
SID filtering
transitive
trusted domain
trusting domain
trusts
two-way trust
user domain

Configuring Trusts

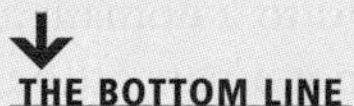

Trusts are relationships between one Windows domain and another Windows domain or non-Microsoft Kerberos v5 realm. Trusts are created to allow users in one domain the ability to authenticate and then access resources on another domain, forest, or realm.

CERTIFICATION READY
Configure external, forest, shortcut, and realm trusts.
Objective 5.2

Understanding Trusts

When you think of trusts, several different scenarios might come to mind. For example, think of a building manager who has several businesses renting the different office spaces in the building. Each business needs separate access to the office spaces. As part of the contract with the businesses, the building manager is required to have garbage removed and to have each office space vacuumed nightly. To meet the requirements of the renting businesses and the cleaners, the building manager needs to have keys made to allow access to the required areas. Each employee to each business needs to own a key to get in the front doors and to his respective offices and nowhere else. The cleaners need to have a master key to get into the front doors, all offices, maintenance closets, and every other room that has a trash receptacle. As you can tell, there are several different types of trust relationships among the building manager, employees, and the cleaning company.

Apply the previous example to domain and forest trusts. Think of the building manager as the Enterprise Administrator, think of each business as its own domain within the forest, and think of each employee as a user account. All have access to the building (forest), but when it comes to specific resources, each is limited by the security permissions required in each domain, essentially an internal forest trust as shown in Figure 15-1.

Now think of the cleaning company; its employees (user accounts) need access to everything in the forest, but they are from an entirely different company. Consider them an external forest. The building manager goes through a bid or interview process to find a trustworthy company to clean the building. Once the building owner finds the right cleaning business, he must "trust" it and provide it and its employees with the required access. This type of trust in a Windows Server environment is a ***one-way forest trust***. The business owner is the trusting root domain, and the cleaning company is the trusted root domain in another forest. The action of the business owner physically passing the keys to the cleaning company indicates the outbound direction of the trust; their receipt and acceptance of the keys is the incoming action.

Figure 15-1

Understanding trusts

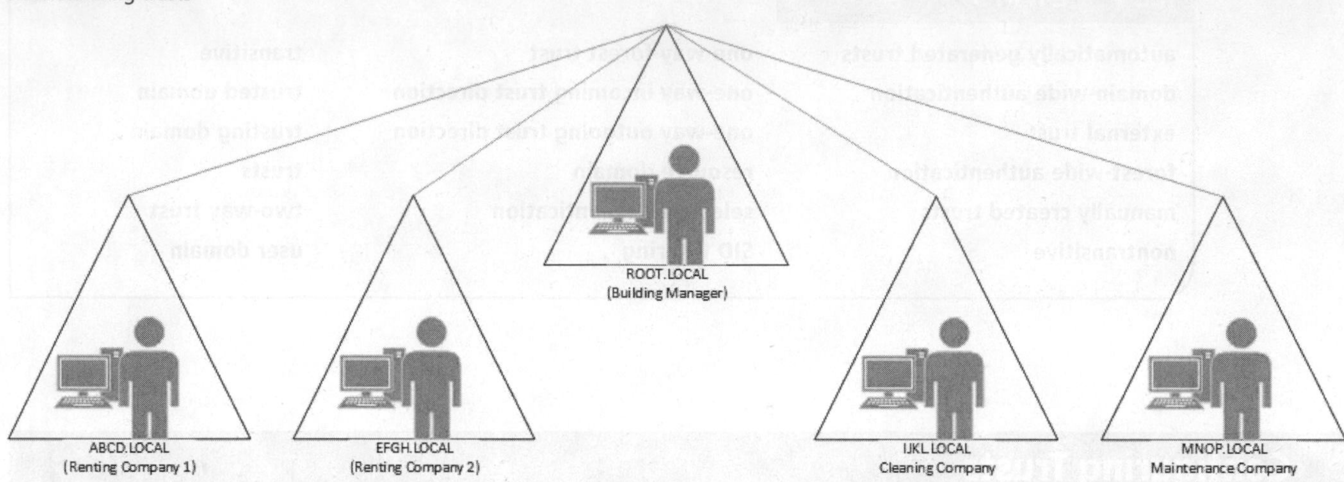

As another example, review how a workstation acts before being added to a domain and how it changes after it has been added to a domain. When a workstation is not a part of the domain, only users that are local to the workstation's Security Account Manager (SAM) database have the ability to log in and access the workstation resources. Users or machines not known to the workstation are unable to authenticate against the workstation.

To add the workstation to the domain, the local user of the workstation must be an administrator or member of the Administrators group on the workstation. To complete the second half of the trust relationship, domain account credentials with the appropriate permissions must be provided to complete the trust. Once authenticated and the request has been made from the workstation to the domain, a trust relationship is created between the workstation and the domain.

When the workstation is added to the domain, domain users have the ability to authenticate and access the workstation's resources.

In this scenario, the workstation is the trusting, ***resource domain***, and the Windows domain is the trusted, ***user domain***. From the workstation's standpoint it is a one-way outgoing trust, and from the Windows domain's standpoint, it is a one-way incoming trust as illustrated in Figure 15-2.

Figure 15-2

Understanding workstation trust relationships during domain join

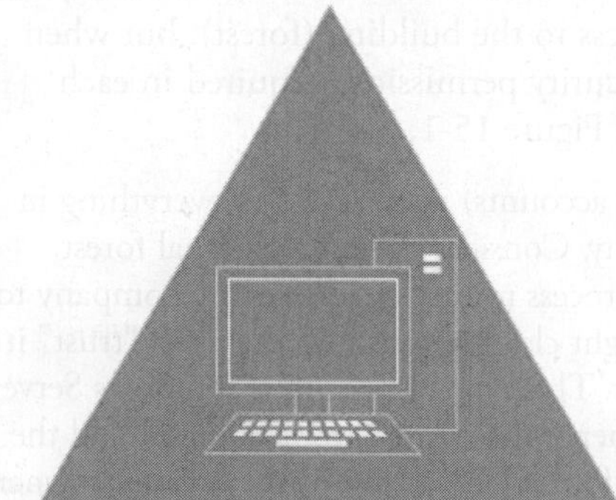

Now, take that concept and apply it to two domains in separate forests. For instance, domains graphics.contoso.local and graphics.adatum.local each have their own Active Directory Domain Services (AD DS) database populated with security principles and resources, such as users, computers, and groups; each security principle and resource has an Access Control List (ACL) associated with it.

Because each domain is in a separate forest, users in the graphics.contoso.local domain cannot access resources in the graphics.adatum.local domain. Each domain allows only security principles within its AD DS forest the ability to log in and/or access resources within that forest. It does not have the ability to grant users from external AD DS domains, the rights to authenticate or access its resources. In order for them to authenticate and access resources with one another or to just one domain, a trust needs to be created.

Similar to the previous workstation scenario, an administrator of the trusting domain, that is a member of the Domain Admins or Enterprise Admins group of the domain or forest, must initiate the outgoing trust request. To complete the request, an administrator of the trusted domain, that is a member of the Domain Admins or Enterprise Admins groups, must initiate an incoming trust request. Once the trust is complete, users in the trusted domain will be able to authenticate and access resources in the trusting domain.

Understanding Trust Types

Two types of trusts can exist in a forest and domain environment. Generated automatically at forest/domain creation or created manually after forest or domain creation, these trusts connect directly to domains and forests inside or outside the existing enterprise.

Trusts can be one of the following:

- ***Automatically generated trusts:*** Trusts that are internal to a forest and are created automatically during domain creation. When a new child domain or tree domain is created within the forest, a two-way trust with the root domain or the parent is created. Automatic trusts are transitive and can traverse trusts, domain to domain, up to the root domain throughout the forest. This allows users in one domain of the forest to authenticate to another domain in the forest. Trusts created within the internal forest during domain creation are all two-way trusts.
- ***Manually created trusts:*** Trusts that can be created to connect two domains within the same forest to one other, or to a forest or domain to a forest or domain in a completely separate enterprise. These trusts can be one-way or two-way trusts and can be transitive or nontransitive in nature. There are four trusts that can be created and configured manually: external trusts, forest trusts, shortcut trusts, and realm trusts.

Understanding Trust Direction

Trust direction indicates the direction in which a trust is given. The ***trusting domain*** is giving trust to the ***trusted domain***. Therefore the trusted domain is "trusted" by the trusting domain. In a one-way trust, direction is from the trusting domain to the trusted domain.

One-way trusts can be one of the following:

- ***One-way incoming trust direction:*** Users in the internal domain or forest can authenticate with a specified external domain or forest. If you create a one-way incoming trust, a user with domain admin or enterprise admin privileges in the other domain needs to create a one-way outgoing trust in the external domain.

- ***One-way outgoing trust direction:*** Users in a specified external domain or forest can authenticate with the internal domain or forest. If you create a one-way outgoing trust in the internal domain, a domain admin or enterprise admin in the other domain will need to create a one-way incoming trust in the external domain. Figure 15-3 illustrates a one-way outgoing and incoming trust direction.

Figure 15-3
Understanding one-way trust direction

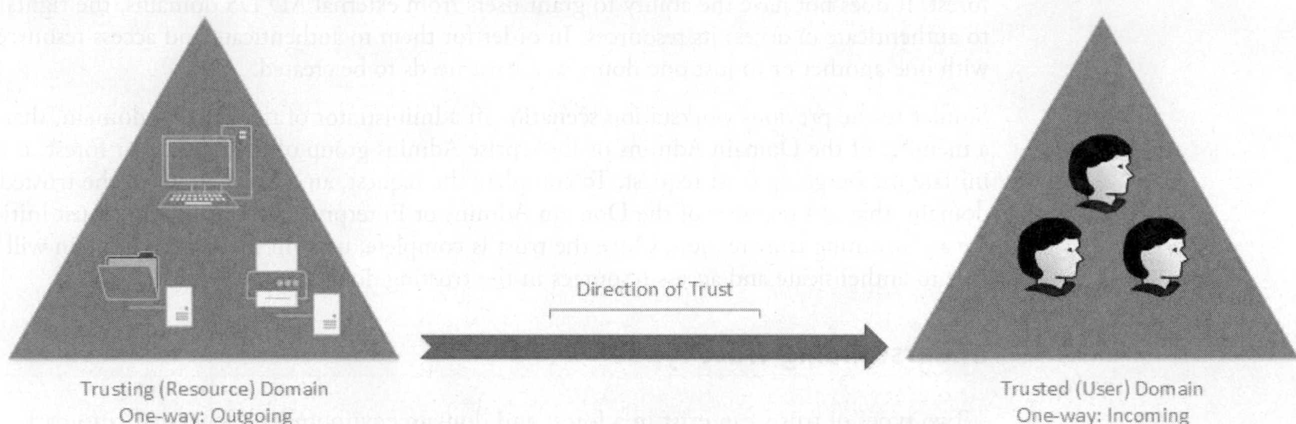

- ***Two-way trust:*** Users in the internal domain or forest can access resources in the specified external domain or forest, and users in the specified, external domain, or forest can access resources in the internal domain or forest. If you create a two-way trust, a user with domain admin or enterprise admin privileges in the other domain needs to create a two-way trust in the external domain. Two-way trusts consist of two one-way trusts. Each domain is trusting the other domain and each domain is trusted by the other domain as illustrated in Figure 15-4.

Figure 15-4
Understanding two-way trust direction

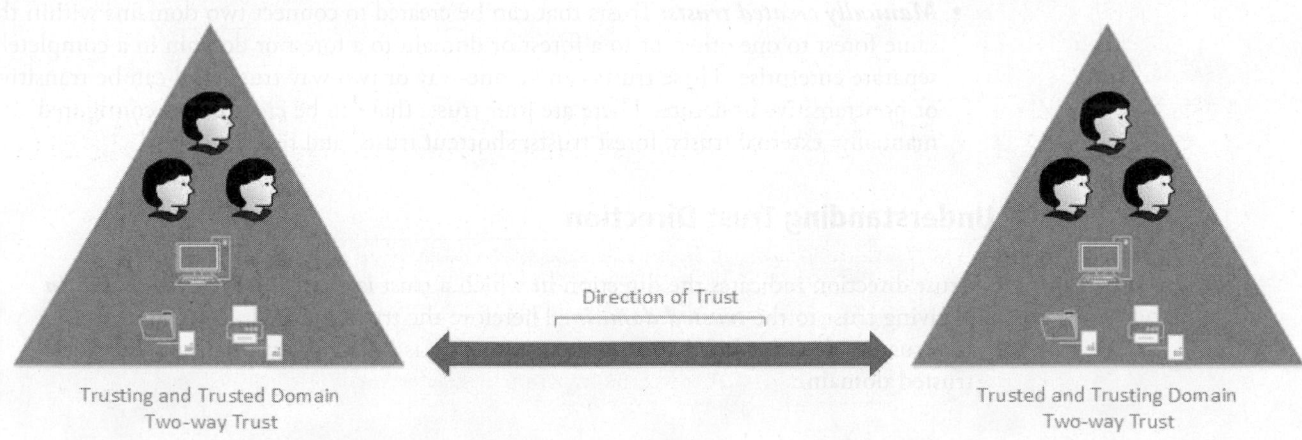

Understanding Transitivity

Transitivity determines how far the trust relationship authentication requests can traverse existing trust authentication paths.

There are two types of transitivity:

- ***Transitive:*** Trust authentication follows the flow of existing trust relationships that are part of the trusted domain; if a transitive trust is created with an external forest, the authentication can traverse the path of the forest's existing trusts.
- ***Nontransitive:*** An explicit trust between two domains, ignoring any existing trusts in the external or internal domain or forest; the domains in the trust only trust each other and will not traverse any existing or future trust paths of either domain.

Configuring DNS for Trusts

For trusts to work properly, they need to be able to resolve the forest or domain names of each side of the trust. Through the use of name resolution, you can configure Domain Name System (DNS) to properly resolve authoritative zones in forests or domains that are part of the trust.

To successfully configure name resolution with the other domains or forests in the trust, consider implementing one of the following DNS solutions:

- **Conditional forwarders in each domain or forest DNS in a Windows Server environment or non-Windows Server environment:** Considered to be the most common configuration in real-world environments, you can configure conditional forwarders in each domain or forest to route name resolution to the DNS servers of the domains or forests included in the trust. By configuring conditional forwarders, DNS changes can be made easily and separately in each domain or forest.
- **Shared Root DNS Server solution:** Create a Shared Root DNS Server solution containing zones that can direct name resolution to the appropriate zones. Once the root servers have been created, add them to the list of root DNS servers in each forest's DNS. After configuring a Shared Root DNS Server solution, DNS changes can be made in a central location without directly affecting local DNS configurations.
- **Secondary DNS zone to connect to DNS server in a Windows Server environment or non-Windows Server environment:** By creating a secondary zone server, you can connect a Windows DNS server to use another Windows DNS server or non-Windows DNS server that serves as the primary way to resolve names in the trusted environments.

Creating External Trusts

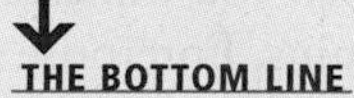

An ***external trust*** is a one-way or two-way nontransitive trust between domains that are not in the same forest, and that are not already included in a forest trust. External trusts connect two domains in separate forests to allow users in the trusted domain the capability to authenticate and/or access resources in the trusting domain. Because external trusts are nontransitive, any existing trusts already in place with the trusting domain cannot be traversed by members of the external trust's trusted domain users.

To accommodate external trusts, the trusting domain generates and stores, in AD DS, Foreign Security Principles for each security principle (Users, Computers, and Groups) of the trusted domain. This allows users of the trusted domain to become members of domain local groups in AD DS and to be added to Access Control Lists (ACL) of resources in the trusting domain. It is highly recommended to *not* modify the automatically generated Foreign Security Principles located in the trusting domain.

CERTIFICATION READY
Configure external trusts.
Objective 5.2

External trusts are also recommended for granting users access to resources in a single domain in an external forest that is not already part of a forest trust as illustrated in Figure 15-5. To create an external trust, you must be a member of the Domain Admins group, Enterprise Admins group, or have been delegated the authority with the appropriate permissions to create the trust. To create a two-way trust, you need the appropriate permissions or work with the other Domain Administrator to create trusts in both domains.

Figure 15-5
Understanding external trusts

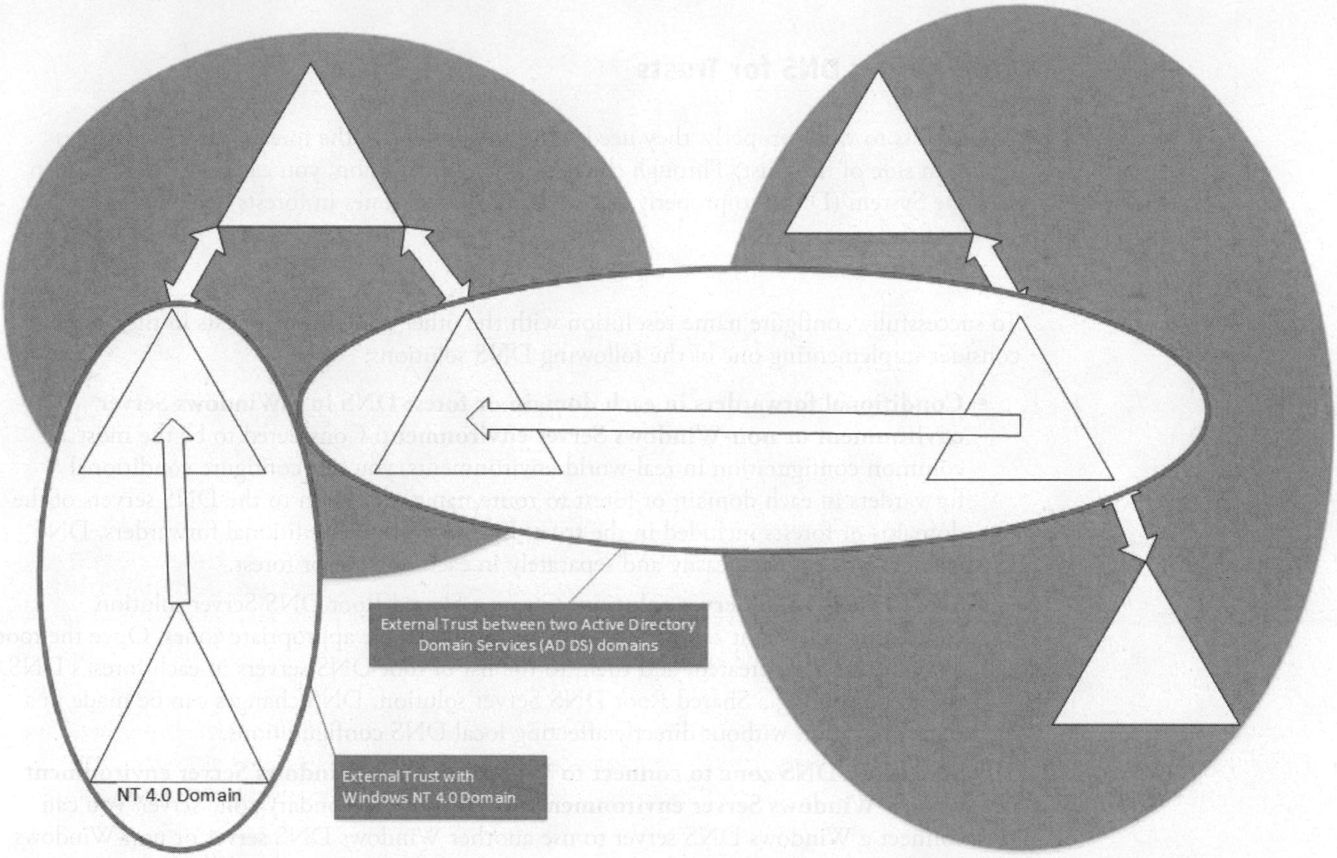

External Trust between two Active Directory Domain Services (AD DS) domains
NT 4.0 Domain
External Trust with Windows NT 4.0 Domain

To create an external trust, use either the Active Directory Domains and Trusts tool or the `netdom` command.

CREATE A ONE-WAY EXTERNAL TRUST USING ACTIVE DIRECTORY DOMAINS AND TRUSTS

GET READY. Log on to the domain controller in your domain in which you will create the trust. You must log in as a user that is a member of the Domain Admins, Enterprise Admins, or delegated equivalent security groups. You must also ensure DNS has been configured to resolve the new trust. To create a one-way, external trust from ADATUM.LOCAL to CONTOSO.LOCAL, perform the following steps:

1. Click Start, right-click the Active Directory Domains and Trusts shortcut and, from the context menu, select Run as Administrator. If it is required, log in with a user account that is a member of the Domain Admins, Enterprise Admins or an equivalent security group. This displays the *Active Directory Domains and Trusts* tool.
2. Right-click the domain that will be the trusting side of the trust and select Properties. This displays the domain name *Properties* window.

3. Click the Trusts tab, and then click the New Trust button. The *New Trust Wizard* opens. Click Next.
4. Type in the Fully Qualified Domain Name (FQDN) of the domain that will be added to the trust, and then click Next.
5. Choose the External trust option if it is not already selected, and then click Next.
6. Select the direction One-way: outgoing option and, then click Next.
7. Select the Both this domain and the selected domain option, and then click the Next button.
8. Enter the username and password of a user with Domain Admin, Enterprise Admin, or equivalent rights in the specified domain, and then click Next.
9. Choose the Domain-wide authentication option, and click Next.
10. The *Trust Selections Complete* prompt appears. Click Next to create the trust.
11. On success, this displays the *Trust Creation Complete* prompt. Click Next.
12. To confirm the trust, select the Yes, confirm the outgoing trust tab, and then click Next.
13. Verify that the trust was successfully created, and then click Finish. Close the *SID Filtering information* box when prompted.
14. You now see the trusted domain listed in the list of outgoing trusts. Click Finish.

CREATE AN EXTERNAL TRUST USING THE NETDOM COMMAND

GET READY. Log on to the domain controller in your domain in which you will create the trust. You must log in as a user that is a member of the Domain Admins, Enterprise Admins, or delegated equivalent security groups. You must also ensure DNS has been configured to resolve the new trust. To create a one-way external trust from ADATUM.LOCAL to CONTOSO.LOCAL, perform the following steps:

1. Click Start, right-click the Windows PowerShell shortcut from the context menu, and select Run as Administrator. If required, log in with a user account that is a member of the Domain Admins, Enterprise Admins, or equivalent security group. This displays the *Active Directory Domains and Trusts* tool.
2. Run the netdom command where *adatum.local* is the Trusting_Domain_Name and *contoso.local* is the Trusted_Domain_Name.

```
netdom trust adatum.local /Domain:contoso.local /add
```

■ Creating Forest Trusts

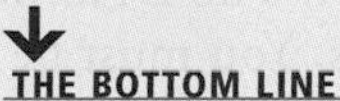

THE BOTTOM LINE

A forest trust is a one-way or two-way transitive trust between two forest root domains.

CERTIFICATION READY
Configure forest trusts.
Objective 5.2

Forest trusts are implemented when users of an internal forest need to authenticate to and/or gain access to all resources of an external forest as illustrated in Figure 15-6. When creating a forest trust, every domain within a forest has a two-way trust with one another from the forest root domain down; therefore, a forest trust is transitive to all domains within the trusting forest.

Figure 15-6
Understanding one-way forest trusts

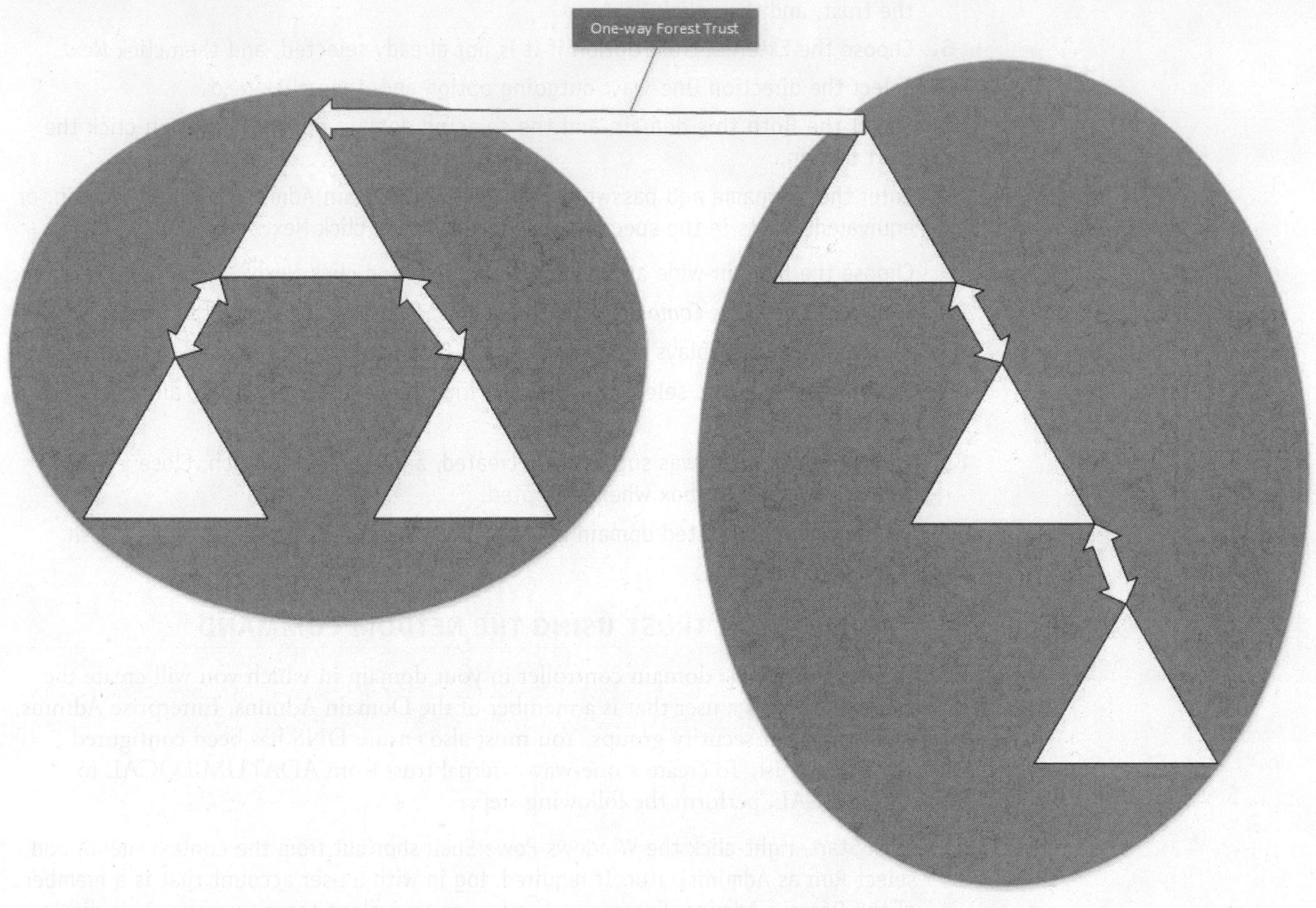

Consider creating forest trusts in the following scenarios:

- Integrating two forests during an acquisition or merger
- Collaborating two businesses closely with one another
- Combining all resources and users of a single company with multiple forests
- Accessing an application provided by a service provider in a forest with another user forest

To create a forest trust, both domains of the trust must be the forest root domain and have a Forest Functional Level of Windows Server 2003 or higher. The DNS infrastructure must be able to accommodate DNS requests between forests. You must be a member of the Domain Admins group, Enterprise Admins group, or have been delegated the authority with the appropriate permissions to create the trust. To create a two-way trust, you need an account in the external domain with the appropriate permissions or work closely with the other Domain Administrator or Enterprise Administrator to complete the two-way trust.

To create a forest trust, use either the Active Directory Domains and Trusts tool or the `netdom` command.

CREATE A ONE-WAY FOREST TRUST USING ACTIVE DIRECTORY DOMAINS AND TRUSTS

GET READY. Log on to the domain controller in your domain in which you will create the trust. You must log in as a user that is a member of the Domain Admins, Enterprise Admins, or delegated equivalent security groups. You must also ensure DNS has been configured to resolve the new trust. To create a one-way forest trust from ADATUM.LOCAL to CONTOSO.LOCAL, perform the following steps:

1. Click Start, right-click the Active Directory Domains and Trusts shortcut and, from the context menu, select Run as Administrator. If required, log in with a user account that is a member of the Domain Admins, Enterprise Admins, or equivalent security group. This displays the *Active Directory Domains and Trusts* tool.
2. Right-click the domain that will be the trusting side of the trust and select Properties. This displays the domain name *Properties* window.
3. Click the Trusts tab, and then click the New Trust button. The *New Trust Wizard* opens. Click Next.
4. Type in the Fully Qualified Domain Name (FQDN) of the domain that will be added to the trust and click Next.
5. Choose the Forest trust option if not already selected, and click Next.
6. Select the direction One-way: outgoing option, and click Next.
7. Select the Both this domain and the selected domain option, and click the Next button.
8. Enter in the username and password of a user with Domain Admin, Enterprise Admin, or equivalent rights in the specified domain, and click Next.
9. Choose the Forest-wide authentication option, and click Next.
10. The *Trust Selections Complete* prompt appears. Click Next to create the trust.
11. On success, this displays the *Trust Creation Complete* prompt. Click Next.
12. To confirm the trust, select Yes, confirm the outgoing trust tab, and click Next.
13. Verify that the trust was successfully created, and click Finish. Close the *SID Filtering information* box if prompted.
14. You now see the trusted forest listed in the list of outgoing trusts. Click Finish.

NOTE*
You cannot create a forest trust using the NETDOM command.

Creating Shortcut Trusts

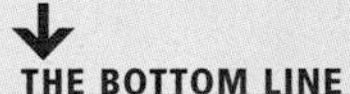
THE BOTTOM LINE

A shortcut trust is a one-way or two-way transitive trust between domains that are in the same forest. Shortcut trusts are primarily used to improve performance when authenticating to and accessing resources in an internal forest.

CERTIFICATION READY
Configure shortcut trusts.
Objective 5.2

Shortcut trusts shorten the authentication trust path between two domains. If you have several domains and/or child domains in a forest, the authentication to the requested domain in the forest will have to travel up the authentication path to the root domain, and then to the domain the user is authenticated to. In some instances, the time for the Kerberos ticket to traverse the authentication path might be unacceptable or cause problems if there are any domain controller outages along the path. This can be resolved by implementing a shortcut trust between two domains in an internal forest. This allows the Kerberos ticket to travel, point-to-point, and allows authentication directly to the destination domain as illustrated in Figure 15-7.

Figure 15-7

Understanding two-way shortcut trusts

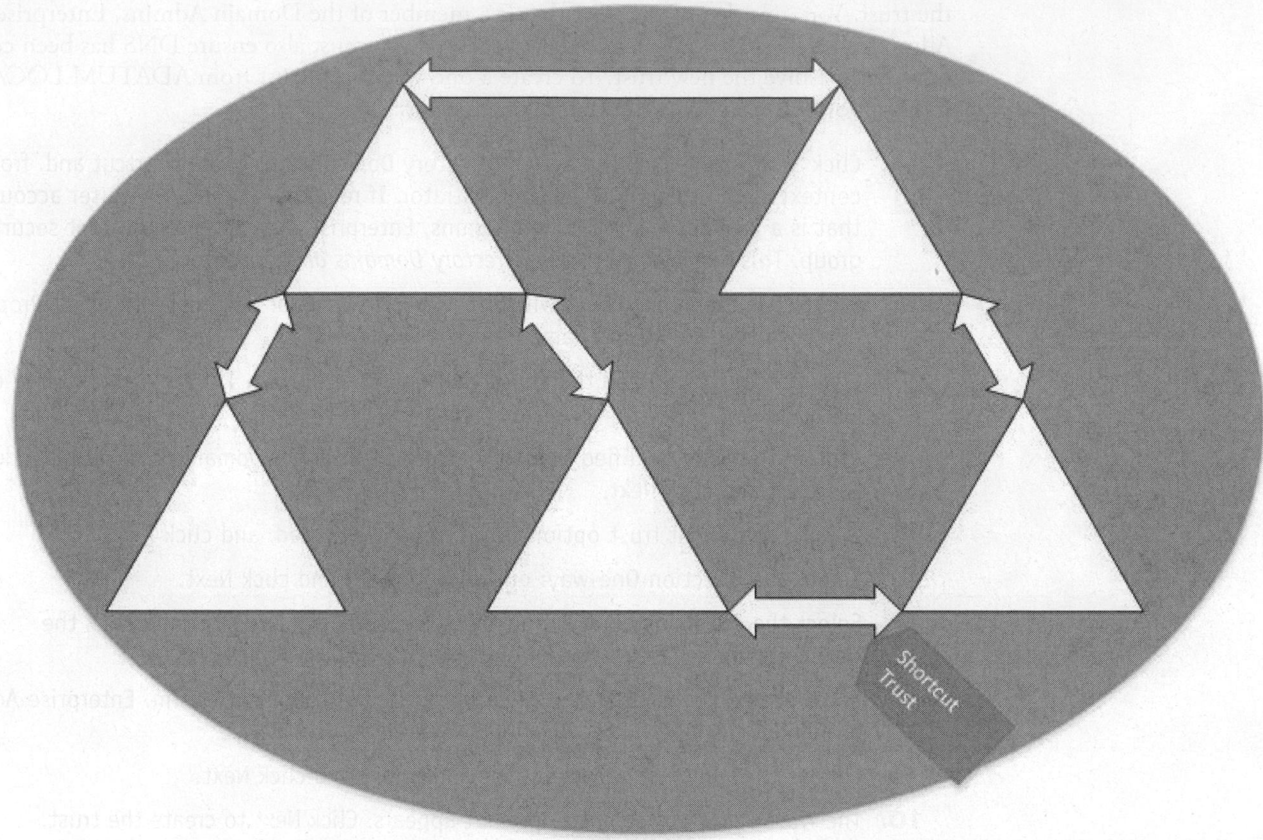

Shortcut trusts can be one-way or two-way trusts, however, keep in mind, if only one, one-way trust is created, the authentication path will be optimized only for authentication to the trusting domain. If users of each domain are authenticating to one another's domain, create a two-way shortcut trust.

Use shortcut trusts in the following scenarios:

- To improve logon times between two domains in a large internal forest
- To shorten the authentication trust path within a forest
- To optimize logon times when multiple users are frequently authenticating to another domain within an internal forest
- To use when users are separated by two domain trees in a forest

You will not be able to create a shortcut trust between two domains in separate forests.

To create a shortcut trust, you must be a member of the Domain Admins group, Enterprise Admins group, or have been delegated the authority with the appropriate permissions to create the trust. To create a two-way trust, you need the appropriate permissions or work with the Domain Administrator or Enterprise Administrator in the other domain to create trusts in both domains.

To create a shortcut trust, use either the Active Directory Domains and Trusts tool, or the `netdom` command.

CREATE A SHORTCUT TRUST USING ACTIVE DIRECTORY DOMAINS AND TRUSTS

GET READY. Log on to the domain controller in your domain in which you will create the trust. You must log in as a user that is a member of the Domain Admins, Enterprise Admins, or delegated equivalent security groups. To create a two-way shortcut trust between TREYRESEARCH.LOCAL and US.ADATUM.LOCAL, perform the following steps:

1. Click Start, right-click the Active Directory Domains and Trusts shortcut and, from the context menu, select Run as Administrator. If required, log in with a user account that is a member of the Domain Admins, Enterprise Admins, or equivalent security group. This displays the *Active Directory Domains and Trusts* tool.
2. Right-click the domain that will be one side of the trust, and then select Properties. This displays the domain name *Properties* window.
3. Click the Trusts tab, and then click the New Trust button. The *New Trust Wizard* opens. Click Next.
4. Type the Fully Qualified Domain Name (FQDN) of the domain that will be added to the trust, and then click Next.
5. Select the direction Two-way option, and click Next.
6. Select the Both this domain and the selected domain option, and then click the Next button.
7. Enter the username and password of a user with Domain Admin, Enterprise Admin, or equivalent rights in the specified domain, and then click Next.
8. The *Trust Selections Complete* prompt appears. Click Next to create the trust.
9. After the trust successfully creates, this displays the *Trust Creation Complete* prompt. Click Next.
10. To confirm the outgoing trust, select Yes, confirm the outgoing trust option, and then click Next.
11. To confirm the incoming trust, select Yes, confirm the incoming trust option, and then click Next.
12. Verify that the trust was successfully created, and then click Finish.
13. You now see the trusted domain listed in the list of outgoing trusts. Click Finish.

CREATE A SHORTCUT TRUST USING THE NETDOM COMMAND

GET READY. Log on to the domain controller in your domain in which you will create the trust. You must log in as a user that is a member of the Domain Admins, Enterprise Admins, or delegated equivalent security groups. To create a two-way shortcut trust between TREYRESEARCH.LOCAL and US.ADATUM.LOCAL, perform the following steps:

1. Click Start, right-click the Windows PowerShell shortcut, and from the context menu, select Run as Administrator. If required, log in with a user account that is a member of the Domain Admins, Enterprise Admins, or equivalent security group. This displays the *Active Directory Domains and Trusts* tool.
2. Run the `netdom` command where *treyresearch.local* is the Trusting_Domain_Name and *us.adatum.local* is the Trusted_Domain_Name.

```
netdom trust treyresearch.local /Domain:us.adatum.local /add /
twoway
```

Creating Realm Trusts

THE BOTTOM LINE

A realm trust is a one-way or two-way, transitive or nontransitive trust between an AD DS domain and a non-Microsoft Kerberos v5 realm.

CERTIFICATION READY
Configure realm trusts.
Objective 5.2

Realm trusts are used to allow users to authenticate and access resources in a non-Windows Kerberos v5 realm, or to allow users in a non-Windows Kerberos v5 realm access to resources in an AD DS domain (see Figure 15-8). Because not all authentication domains and realms are Microsoft, this added benefit allows the non-Microsoft solutions interoperability with one another.

Consider using realm trusts in the following scenarios:

- Users in an AD DS domain need to access resources or log in to clients in a UNIX or MIT realm.
- Users in a UNIX or MIT realm need to access resources in an AD DS domain.

To create a realm trust, you must be a member of the Domain Admins group, Enterprise Admins group, or have been delegated the authority with the appropriate permissions to create the trust. To create a two-way trust, you need the appropriate permissions or work with the Domain Administrator or Enterprise Administrator in the non-Windows Kerberos v5 realm to create trusts in both environments.

Figure 15-8
Understanding two-way realm trusts

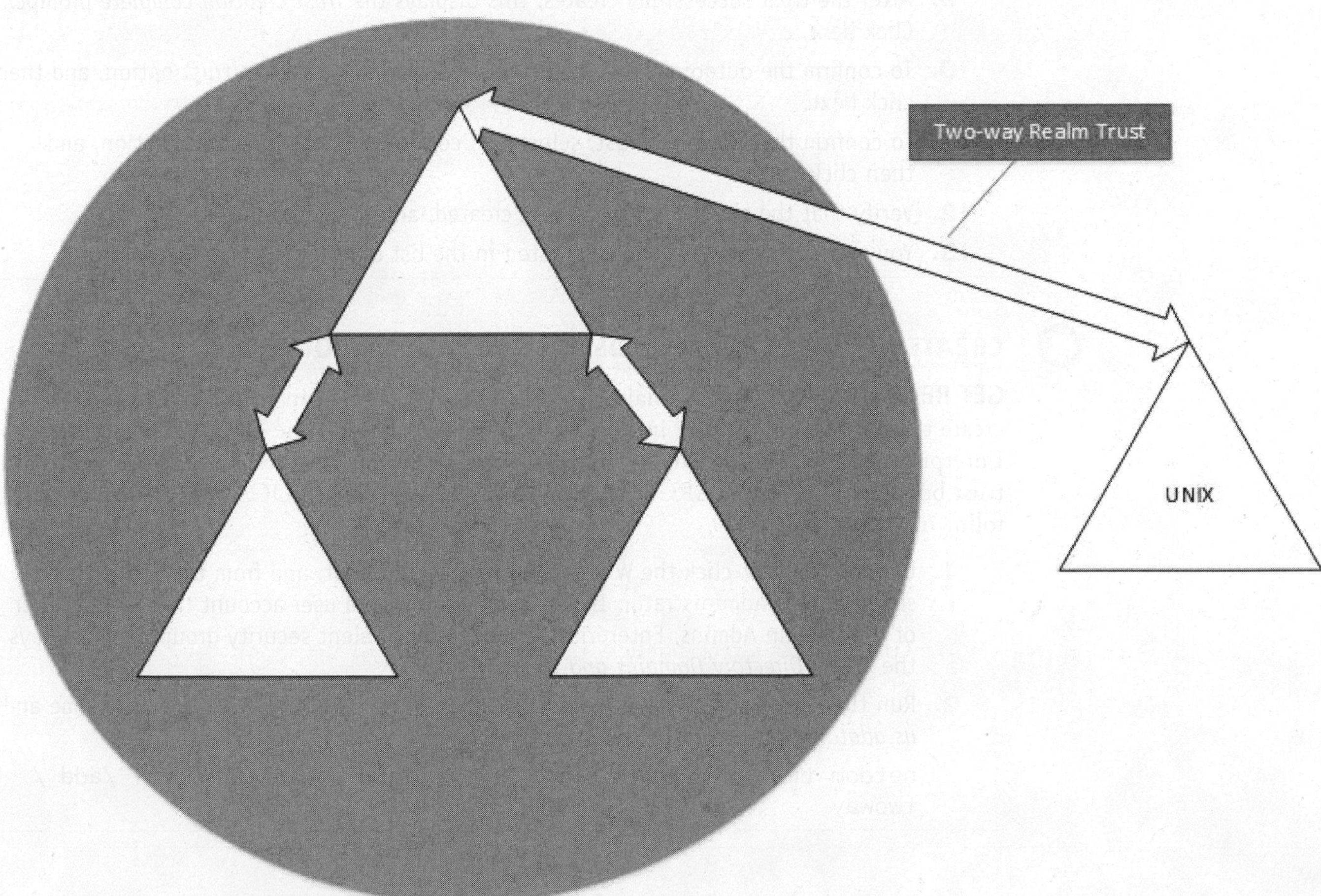

To create a realm trust, use either the Active Directory Domains and Trusts tool, or the `netdom` command.

CREATE A REALM TRUST USING ACTIVE DIRECTORY DOMAINS AND TRUSTS

GET READY. Log on to the domain controller in your domain in which you will create the trust. You must log in as a user that is a member of the Domain Admins, Enterprise Admins, or delegated equivalent security groups. To create a one-way realm trust from ADATUM.LOCAL to CONTOSOREALM.COM, perform the following steps:

1. Click Start, right-click the Active Directory Domains and Trusts shortcut and, from the context menu, select Run as Administrator. If required, log in with a user account that is a member of the Domain Admins, Enterprise Admins, or equivalent security group. This displays the *Active Directory Domains and Trusts* tool.
2. Right-click the domain that will be the trusting side of the trust and select Properties. This displays the domain name *Properties* window.
3. Click the Trusts tab, and then click the New Trust button. The *New Trust Wizard* starts. Click Next.
4. Type in the Fully Qualified Domain Name (FQDN) of the domain that will be added to the trust and click Next.
5. Choose the Realm trust option if not already selected, and click Next.
6. In the *Transitivity of Trust* window, select the transitivity Nontransitive option. Click Next.
7. Select the direction One-way: outgoing option, and click Next.
8. Select a strong *Trust password* to share with the Realm Administrator, and enter and confirm the password. Click Next.
9. The *Trust Selections Complete* prompt appears. Click Next to create the trust.
10. Verify that the trust was successfully created. Remember that you have created only one side of the trust. Contact the Realm Administrator with the secure trust password to finish the trust, and click Finish.

MODIFY TRANSITIVITY OF REALM TRUSTS USING ACTIVE DIRECTORY DOMAINS AND TRUSTS

GET READY. Log on to the domain controller in your domain in which you will create the trust. You must log in as a user that is a member of the Domain Admins, Enterprise Admins, or delegated equivalent security groups. To modify the transitivity of the trust from ADATUM.LOCAL to CONTOSOREALM.COM, perform the following steps:

1. Click Start, right-click the Active Directory Domains and Trusts shortcut and, from the context menu, select Run as Administrator. If required, log in with a user account that is a member of the Domain Admins, Enterprise Admins, or equivalent security group. This displays the *Active Directory Domains and Trusts* tool.
2. Right-click the domain that will be the trusting side of the trust and select Properties. This displays the domain name *Properties* window.
3. Click the Trusts tab, highlight the realm trust you want to modify, and then click the Properties button.
4. At the bottom of the trust's *Properties* window, select the type of transitivity required for the trust. Click OK.
5. Once modified, click OK and close all displayed windows.

CREATE A REALM TRUST USING NETDOM

GET READY. Log on to the domain controller in your domain in which you will create the trust. You must log in as a user that is a member of the Domain Admins, Enterprise Admins, or delegated equivalent security groups. To create a one-way realm trust from ADATUM. LOCAL to CONTOSOREALM.COM, perform the following steps:

1. Click Start, right-click the Windows PowerShell shortcut from the context menu, and select Run as Administrator. If required, log in with a user account that is a member of the Domain Admins, Enterprise Admins, or equivalent security group. This displays the *Active Directory Domains and Trusts* tool.
2. Run the **netdom** command where *adatum.local* is the Trusting_Domain_Name and *contosorealm.com* is the Trusted_Domain_Name.

```
netdom trust adatum.local /Domain:contosorealm.com /add /realm /PasswordT:new_realm_trust_password
```

■ Validating Trusts

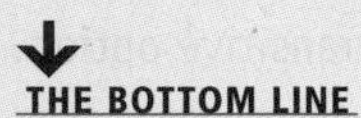

Existing trusts in an environment might need to be validated in the event of failure or problems between trusting and trusted domains. Validating trusts allow you to troubleshoot and reset trust relationships between trusts.

You can validate a trust by using the Active Directory Domains and Trusts tool. Trusts between AD DS domains and forests can be validated; a realm trust cannot be validated.

VALIDATE A TRUST USING ACTIVE DIRECTORY DOMAINS AND TRUSTS

GET READY. Log on to the domain controller in your domain in which you will create the trust. You must log in as a user that is a member of the Domain Admins, Enterprise Admins, or delegated equivalent security groups. To create a one-way external trust from ADATUM. LOCAL to CONTOSO.LOCAL, perform the following steps:

1. Click Start, right-click the Active Directory Domains and Trusts shortcut and, from the context menu, select Run as Administrator. If required, log in with a user account that is a member of the Domain Admins, Enterprise Admins, or equivalent security group. This displays the *Active Directory Domains and Trusts* tool.
2. Right-click the domain that is part of the trust and select Properties. This displays the domain name *Properties* window.
3. Under the General tab, click the Validate button.
4. When a successful validation completes, an information window appears indicating that the trust is in place and active. Click OK. Close all displayed windows when complete.

CREATE A REALM TRUST USING NETDOM

GET READY. Log on to the domain controller in your domain in which you will create the trust. You must log in as a user that is a member of the Domain Admins, Enterprise Admins, or delegated equivalent security groups. To verify the trust between ADATUM.LOCAL to CONTOSO.LOCAL, perform the following steps:

1. Click Start, right-click the Windows Powershell shortcut from the context menu, and select Run as Administrator. If required, log in with a user account that is a member of the Domain Admins, Enterprise Admins, or equivalent security group. This displays the *Active Directory Domains and Trusts* tool.
2. Run the netdom command where *adatum.local* is the Trusting_Domain_Name and *contoso.local* is the Trusted_Domain_Name.

```
netdom trust adatum.local /Domain:contoso.local /verify
```

■ Configuring Trust Authentication

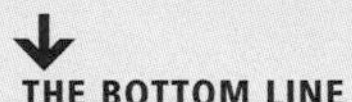
THE BOTTOM LINE

Trust authentication defines how explicit the authentication and access to the trusting domain will be.

CERTIFICATION READY
Configure trust authentication.
Objective 5.2

There are three scopes of trust authentication: selective authentication, domain-wide authentication, and forest-wide authentication. There are instances in which all users are not needed to log in to the trusting domain or forest or only specified users need to authenticate and access resources in the trusting domain. Trust authentication is configured on external and forest trusts.

Configuring Selective Authentication

Selective authentication allows explicit authentication and access to resources in an external trust or forest trust.

In many cases, when you create an external trust or a forest trust, you will not want all users of the trusted domain to authenticate and access all resources in the trusting domain. By enabling selective authentication, you can prevent all users from having access, and then explicitly allow a security group or stand-alone user access to the resources they need access to. The downside of implementing selective authentication is the administrative overhead involved to configure and maintain user access to resources. Each member server or computer account in the trusting domain that holds a required resource needs to be configured to allow authentication to the users in the trusted domain.

Users of the trusted domain are unable to access resources in the trusting domain until they are explicitly configured on the computer object's Discretionary Access Control List (DACL) in the Active Directory Users and Computers tool by checking the *Allowed to Authenticate* check box. By granting them access on the resource DACL, they will access as illustrated in Figure 15-9. It is best practice to configure a security group and add users to the group that need to access the resource.

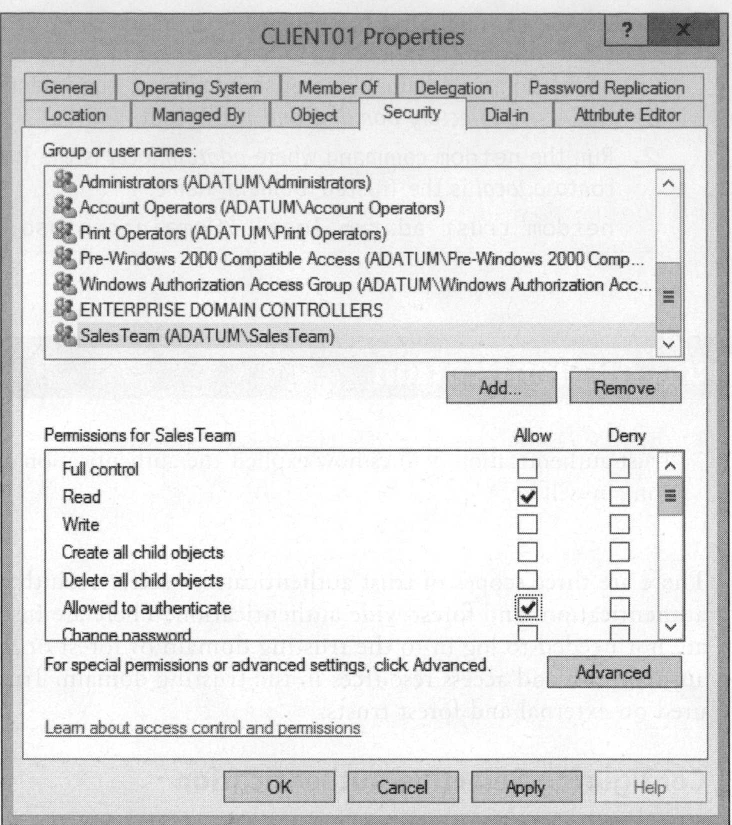

Figure 15-9
Configuring selective authentication

Selective authentication is configurable only on external trusts and forest trusts.

ENABLE SELECTIVE AUTHENTICATION

GET READY. Log on to the domain controller in your domain in which you will create the trust. You must log in as a user that is a member of the Domain Admins, Enterprise Admins or delegated equivalent security groups. To create a one-way external trust from ADATUM.LOCAL to CONTOSO.LOCAL, perform the following steps:

1. Click Start and click the Active Directory Domains and Trusts shortcut. If required, log in with a user account that is a member of the Domain Admins, Enterprise Admins, or equivalent security group. This displays the *Active Directory Domains and Trusts* tool.
2. Right-click the domain that is part of the trust and select Properties. This displays the domain name *Properties* window.
3. Click the Trusts tab, highlight the domain or forest trust you want to modify, and then click the Properties button.
4. Select the Authentication tab and choose Selective Authentication. Click OK. Close all displayed windows when complete.

Configuring Domain-Wide Authentication

In an external trust, ***domain-wide authentication*** allows unrestricted user access by users in the trusted domain to the resources in the trusting domain.

After an external trust is created, all users in the trusted domain will be able to authenticate and access the resources in the trusting domain.

Used in scenarios in which all users must be able to log in to workstations and resources in the trusting domain, domain-wide authentication automatically allows access. Enable or disable domain-wide authentication based on your enterprise requirements:

- Enable domain-wide authentication when all users in the trusted domain need to authenticate against the trusting domain.
- Disable domain-wide authentication when only a select few or a group of users in the trusted domain need to authenticate and access resources in the trusting domain.

Domain-wide authentication is configurable only in an external trust.

Configuring Forest-Wide Authentication

Forest-wide authentication allows unrestricted user authentication and access by users in the trusted forest to the resources in a trusting forest.

After forest trust creation, all users in the trusted forest will be able to authenticate and access the resources in the trusting forest. In a multi-domain forest, all users within each domain in the forest are able to authenticate and access resources in the trusting domain.

Used in scenarios where all users must be able to log in to workstations and resources in the trusting forest, forest-wide authentication automatically allows access to the users. Enable or disable forest-wide authentication based on your enterprise requirements:

- Enable forest-wide authentication when all users in the trusted forest need to authenticate against the trusting forest.
- Disable forest-wide authentication when only a select few or a group of users in the trusted forest need to authenticate and access resources in the trusting forest.

Forest-wide authentication is configurable only in a forest trust.

DISABLE DOMAIN-WIDE OR FOREST-WIDE AUTHENTICATION

GET READY. Log on to the domain controller in your domain in which you will create the trust. You must log in as a user that is a member of the Domain Admins, Enterprise Admins, or delegated equivalent security groups. To create a one-way forest trust from ADATUM.LOCAL to CONTOSO.LOCAL, perform the following steps:

1. Click Start, right-click the Active Directory Domains and Trusts shortcut, and from the context menu, select Run as Administrator. If required, log in with a user account that is a member of the Domain Admins, Enterprise Admins, or equivalent security group. This displays the *Active Directory Domains and Trusts* tool.
2. Right-click the domain or forest that is part of the trust and select Properties. This displays the domain name *Properties* window.
3. Click the Trusts tab, highlight the domain or forest trust you want to modify, and then click the Properties button.
4. Select the Authentication tab and choose Selective Authentication. Click OK. Close all displayed windows when complete.

Configuring SID Filtering

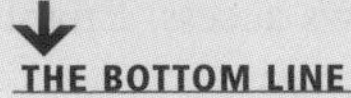

THE BOTTOM LINE

Enabled by default, ***SID filtering*** removes injected SIDs and sIDhistory to allow only the Principle Security Identifier (SID) to be seen by the trusting domain.

CERTIFICATION READY
Configure SID filtering.
Objective 5.2

SID filtering protects trusting domains from malicious users. Malicious users might attempt to inject SIDs of an elevated user or group in the trusting domain to the sIDHistory of a user in the trusted domain.

When SID filtering is disabled, the malicious user can successfully inject the sIDHistory and gain privileged administrative access to resources in the trusting domain. It is best practice to keep SID filtering enabled unless absolutely necessary.

SID filtering can be disabled in the following scenarios:

- User accounts have been involved in a domain migration. If a domain migration has been done, a user will be given a new principle SID in relation to the domain they have been migrated to while maintaining the old SID in the sIDHistory attribute. If the administrator migrated the previous SIDs, the sIDHistory attribute will be populated with the old SID. The previous SID might have been kept to retain access to network resources in the old domain. This can cause problems because if the old SID is filtered off within a trust, the user will lose access to resources still pointing to the old SID.
- There is complete personal trust between all Domain Admins and Enterprise Admins within both trusts.

DISABLE SID FILTERING FOR AN EXTERNAL TRUST

GET READY. Log on to the domain controller in your domain in which you will create the trust. You must log in as a user that is a member of the Domain Admins, Enterprise Admins, or delegated equivalent security groups. To disable SID filtering on ADATUM.LOCAL with its external trust to CONTOSO.LOCAL, perform the following steps:

1. Click Start, right-click the Windows PowerShell shortcut, and from the context menu, select Run as Administrator. If required, log in with a user account that is a member of the Domain Admins, Enterprise Admins, or equivalent security group. This displays the *Active Directory Domains and Trusts* tool.
2. Run the netdom command where *adatum.local* is the Trusting_Domain_Name and *contoso.local* is the Trusted_Domain_Name. Notice external trusts SID filtering uses the "QUARANTINE" switch.

```
netdom trust abldatum.local /Domain:contoso.local /
quarantine:No /userD:[DomainAdminUser] /
passwordD:[password | *]
```

DISABLE SID FILTERING FOR A FOREST TRUST

GET READY. Log on to the domain controller in your domain in which you will create the trust. You must log in as a user that is a member of the Domain Admins, Enterprise Admins, or delegated equivalent security groups. To disable the SID filtering on ADATUM.LOCAL with its forest trust to CONTOSO.LOCAL, perform the following steps:

1. Click Start, right-click the Windows PowerShell shortcut, from the context menu, select Run as Administrator. If required, log in with a user account that is a member of the Domain Admins, Enterprise Admins, or equivalent security group. This displays the *Active Directory Domains and Trusts* tool.
2. Run the **netdom** command where *adatum.local* is the Trusting_Domain_Name and *contoso.local* is the Trusted_Domain_Name. Notice forest trust SID filtering uses the "ENABLESIDHISTORY" switch.

```
netdom trust adatum.local /Domain:contoso.local /
enablesidhistory:No /userD:[DomainAdminUser] /
passwordD:[password | *]
```

Configuring Name Suffix Routing

THE BOTTOM LINE

Name suffix routing manages how authentication requests are passed to each AD DS forest in a forest trust.

CERTIFICATION READY
Configure name suffix routing.
Objective 5.2

When a forest trust is created, all unique suffixes are routed across the trust by default. This allows users in each forest the ability to authenticate to resources in the trusting forest through the means of a unique name suffix.

Unique name suffixes must be unique to the forest and include the following suffixes:

- User principle name (UPN)
- Service principle name (SPN)
- Domain Name System (DNS) name
- Forest or domain tree name that is not a child to the tree

In a forest trust, it is common and recommended that users authenticate by using a forest unique identifier, such as an e-mail address. Because e-mail addresses are truly unique, this solution allows for a smoother authentication process between two forests.

Name suffixes can be modified or excluded from being routed across a forest trust. By excluding an already routed name suffix, future authentication requests by those unique name suffixes will be disallowed.

By default, after a forest trust is created, any new name suffixes added to the trusted forest are disabled. To enable new name suffixes that have been added after the forest trust creation, enable the name suffix by using the Active Directory Domains and Trusts tool.

CONFIGURE NAME SUFFIX ROUTING

GET READY. Log on to the domain controller in your domain in which you will create the trust. You must log in as a user that is a member of the Domain Admins, Enterprise Admins, or delegated equivalent security groups. To modify name suffix routing for names in the CONTOSO.LOCAL trusted domain, perform the following steps:

1. Click Start, right-click the Active Directory Domains and Trusts shortcut and, from the context menu, select Run as Administrator. If required, log in with a user account that is a member of the Domain Admins, Enterprise Admins, or equivalent security group. This displays the *Active Directory Domains and Trusts* tool.
2. Right-click the domain that is part of the trust and select Properties. This displays the domain name *Properties* window.
3. Click the Trusts tab, highlight the forest trust you want to modify, and then click the Properties button.
4. Select the Name Suffix Routing tab and review the name suffixes listed for the trusted forest.
5. Highlight the name suffix you want to modify and choose Disable or Enable to modify the routing of the name suffix (see Figure 15-10).

Figure 15-10

Enabling new name suffixes

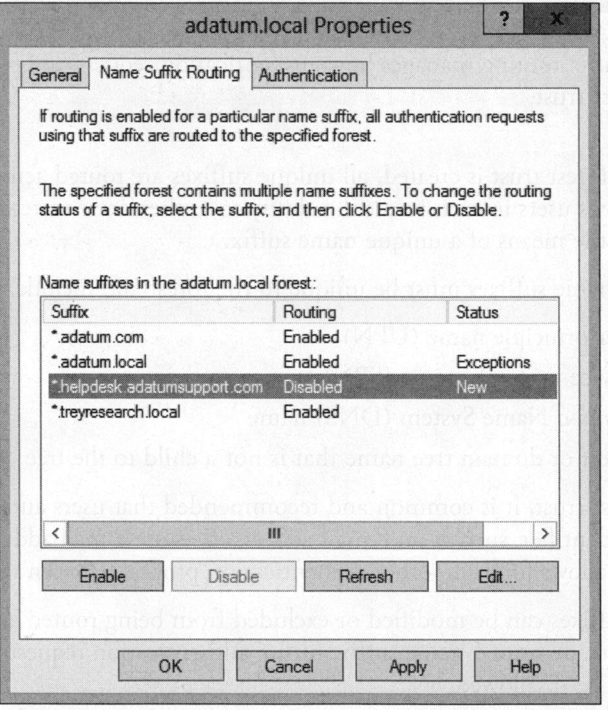

6. If you want to exclude names not included in the list, click the Edit button. In the *Edit name suffix* window, click Add. Type the name suffix in the *Add Excluded Name Suffix* window, and click OK to add the selection. Notice that you can also change the routing status of a name suffix and its children. Click OK to save.
7. Click OK on each displayed window to save changes. Close all displayed windows when completed.

TAKE NOTE*

Any name suffixes added to the trusted domain after forest creation will be disabled by default. In order to use them they must be enabled.

SKILL SUMMARY

IN THIS LESSON YOU LEARNED:

- The trusting domain holds the resources, and the trusted domain is where the users that will authenticate and access the resources are located.
- There are five types of trusts that must be configured: manual, external, forest, shortcut, and realm trusts.
- There are three types of configurable, trust authentication scopes: selective authentication, domain-wide authentication, and forest-wide authentication.
- There are benefits to keeping SID filtering enabled and also certain conditions might require it to be disabled.
- Name suffix routing allows users from one domain or forest to authenticate to another domain or forest in a forest trust. There are also exclusions that can be created to prevent certain name suffixes from being routed. New name suffixes added after forest trust creation are disabled by default.

Knowledge Assessment

Multiple Choice

Select the correct answer for each of the following questions.

1. After using the Active Directory Migration tool to migrate users to your new domain, what concerns should you have when creating a new external trust or forest trust?
   - **a.** You will not be able to create new trusts
   - **b.** Recently migrated accounts will have a new Security Identifier (SID) and an updated sIDHistory
   - **c.** Elevated privileges will not cross the trusts
   - **d.** The RID Master role must be seized
2. Users in a UNIX Realm need to access resources in a Windows Server 2012 R2 domain. What type of trust will you create?
   - **a.** external trust
   - **b.** forest trust
   - **c.** shortcut trust
   - **d.** none of the above
3. You have two domains in a single internal forest. What type of trust should you create so all users can log in to computers in both domains?
   - **a.** external trust
   - **b.** forest trust
   - **c.** shortcut trust
   - **d.** none—automatic trust

4. You have just created a two-way forest trust between Forest A and Forest B and are using forest-wide authentication. Some users complain that they cannot log in to their domain-joined computers in the other forest. What should you do?
   a. Re-create the trust
   b. Have users log in with a generic domain user account
   c. Have users log in with their e-mail address
   d. Have users log in with a username local to the workstation
5. You are the Domain Administrator for support.adatum.local and have been working with the Enterprise Administrator for contoso.local to create a one-way external trust between support.adatum.local and support.contoso.local. Your domain, support.adatum.local will be the trusted domain. The Contoso Enterprise Admins have created a one-way incoming trust with your domain. What will you need to do?
   a. Create a one-way shortcut trust
   b. Create a two-way realm trust
   c. Ask the Contoso Enterprise Admins to remove the recently created trust and create a one-way outgoing trust
   d. Create a one-way outgoing trust with support.contoso.local
6. You are attempting to create a trust between Adatum.local and Contoso.local, both Windows Server 2012 R2 domains. You run the New Trust Wizard and enter in the domain name for Contoso.local. The next screen of the wizard says, "The name you specified is not a valid Windows domain name. Is the specified name a Kerberos v5 realm?" What will you do to resolve the problem?
   a. Configure DNS
   b. Configure DHCP Split-Scope
   c. Manually add contoso.local to the hosts file of the Adatum.local domain controllers
   d. Configure selective authentication
7. You are tasked with creating a forest trust and will work closely with the Enterprise Administrator in the second forest. What tool(s) can you use to create the trust?
   a. `netdom`
   b. Active Directory Domains and Trusts tool
   c. Windows PowerShell
   d. DNS
8. Which of the following statements about external trusts are true?
   a. Domains in an external trust must be at Windows Server 2003 Domain Functional Level
   b. Both domains in the trust must be the forest root domains
   c. External trusts allow Windows NT 4.0 users to authenticate and access resources in an Active Directory Domain Services (AD DS) domain
   d. External trusts connect two domains in different forests with one another
9. When troubleshooting a trust, what tool(s) can you use? (Select all that apply.)
   a. Failover Cluster Manager
   b. `netdom`
   c. Active Directory Sites and Services tool
   d. DNS
10. The company CIO invites you to his office to investigate possible malicious misuse of elevated permissions involving an individual from another domain in your trust. What should be reviewed in your investigation?
    a. selective authentication
    b. SID filtering
    c. WMI filtering
    d. NTLM authentication

Best Answer

Choose the letter that corresponds to the best answer. More than one answer choice may achieve the goal. Select the BEST answer.

1. Which of the following types of trusts connects two domains within a forest for faster authentication?
   a. external trust
   b. shortcut trust
   c. forest trust
   d. realm trust
2. What type of DNS configuration for trusts is the most common and has the least administrative overhead?
   a. stub zones
   b. shared root
   c. conditional forwarders
   d. cache only
3. Selective authentication allows administrators to do what?
   a. Log in with new UPN suffixes
   b. Prevent unwanted users from accessing resources
   c. Allow a user or group access to authenticate to resources
   d. Easily manage authentication across trusts
4. A transitive forest trust allows users in one forest to do what?
   a. Authenticate to all transitive linked domains in the trusting domain
   b. Authenticate to all domain controllers in the trusting domain
   c. Authenticate to the root domain in the trusting domain
   d. Authenticate to all transitive linked domains in the trusted domain
5. After creating a new User Principal Name (UPN) suffix, what must you do to allow users to authenticate in a trusting forest with the new name suffix?
   a. Authenticate on the domain with *UPNSuffix\Username*
   b. Exclude the old UPN suffix in the Name Suffix Routing tab
   c. Remove the old UPN suffix in the Name Suffix Routing tab
   d. Enable the new suffix in the Name Suffix Routing tab

Matching and Identification

1. Match the description with the appropriate term. Not all items will be used and items can be used more than once.
   _______ a) Allowed to Authenticate check box
   _______ b) EnableSIDHistory:NO
   _______ c) Quarantine:NO
   _______ d) Optimize logon times
   _______ e) Traverse Authentication Path
   1. external trust
   2. transitive
   3. forest trust
   4. selective authentication
   5. nontransitive
   6. shortcut trust

2. Match the description with the appropriate term. Not all items will be used and items can be used more than once.

   ________ a) users are located here
   ________ b) resources are located here
   ________ c) resolves trusted domain name
   ________ d) non-Windows Kerberos v5 environment
   ________ e) nontransitive trust

   1. DNS
   2. external trust
   3. trusted domain
   4. UPN suffix
   5. trusting domain
   6. realm trust

3. Identify the scopes of trust authentication.

   ________ forest-wide authentication
   ________ UPN authentication
   ________ external-wide authentication
   ________ shortcut-wide authentication
   ________ selective authentication
   ________ domain-wide authentication

4. Identify the types of trusts

   ________ temporary trusts
   ________ automatically generated trusts
   ________ one-to-many trusts
   ________ one-to-one trusts
   ________ manually created trusts
   ________ requested trusts

Build a List

1. Identify the basic steps to enable a new UPN name suffix for routing. Not all steps will be used.

   ________ Open Windows PowerShell
   ________ Select the UPN suffix
   ________ Run Set-UPNSuffix—Identity "*NewUPNSuffix*" –Enable
   ________ Modify the properties of the forest trust
   ________ Click the Enable button
   ________ Open the Active Directory Domains and Trusts tool
   ________ Open the Name Suffix Routing tab

■ Business Case Scenarios

Scenario 15-1: Planning for Trusts

You are the Enterprise Administrator for a high-end graphics company, contosographics.com. The company recently announced that it will purchase another quality graphics company, adatumgraphics.com. You are tasked to plan for and to integrate both forests with one another. As part of the plan, you need to take into consideration the following needs:

- Users will not be allowed to log into workstations in the other forest.
- The sales teams will need to access all files in the following shares: filesrv.contosographics.local\Sales and dfssrv01.adatumgraphics.local\MoneyMaking.
- The graphics teams needs to access all files in the following shares: contgsrv1.contosographics.local\Working_Pubs, contgsrv2.contosographics.local\Completed_Pubs, dfsgrfx01.adatumgraphics.local\InProgress and dfsgrfx02.adatumgraphics.local\Finals.
- The company managers need to access all shares accessible by the Sales and Graphics teams and nothing else.

What will you recommend as the best solution to meet the needs during the acquisition? What other solutions you can think of that might meet the requirements?

Scenario 15-2: Resolving a Bring Your Own Device Dilemma

Your company consists of ten separate forests spread out across the country and have no existing trusts in place. Your team is investigating implementing a remote desktop infrastructure for all employee workstations. As part of the plan, in some cities the workstations will be replaced with thin clients, and in others, employees will be required to bring their own device. All server infrastructure will be housed at the company headquarters datacenter. All users in all cities need to be able to log in to the virtual machines served from the datacenter with their company e-mail address. What problems do you see with the current setup? What should be included in your plan to meet the company's authentication requirements and future growth needs?

LESSON 16 Configuring Sites

70-412 EXAM OBJECTIVE

Objective 5.3 – Configure sites. This objective may include but is not limited to: Configure sites and subnets; create and configure site links; manage site coverage; manage registration of SRV records; move domain controllers between sites.

Lesson Heading	Exam Objective
Configuring Sites and Subnets	
Configuring Sites	Configure sites
Configuring Subnets	Configure subnets
Creating and Configuring Site Links	Create and configure site links
Managing Site Coverage	Manage site coverage
Managing Registration of SRV Records	Manage registration of SRV records
Moving Domain Controllers between Sites	Move domain controllers between sites

KEY TERMS

bridgehead servers
Hub-and-Spoke Topology
Intersite replication
Intersite Topology Generator (ISTG)
Intrasite replication
IP Transport
Knowledge Consistency Checker (KCC)
replication interval
replication schedule
site link bridges
sites
SMTP Transport
subnets

■ Configuring Sites and Subnets

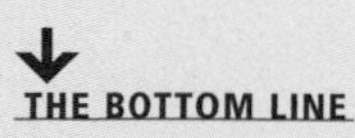
THE BOTTOM LINE

Sites and subnets define the physical design of an Active Directory Domain Services (AD DS) domain. Sites allow clients, authentication, and applications to access domain controllers and services within a physical location before needing to cross a Wide Area Network (WAN) link. Sites also utilize the high speed networks of the local network to quickly replicate data between domain controllers within the site.

One of the best examples of sites and subnets is to compare it to the postal system. Think of each site as having its own zip code, AD DS is the national postal system, and each client IP address and subnet is considered a home or business' physical address. Each post office knows how to route the mail to the next closest zip code for additional processing ensuring reliable and timely deliveries. Each physical address is unique to the zip code that the address resides.

When you send snail mail to a recipient in your city, or any other city, you address the envelope with both a destination and a source address. Once the envelope is ready to be sent, you take it to the closest drop-off point, or the most convenient post office. At this point, you turn over your request for delivery to the post office for them to handle and process the envelope to its final destination.

The post office analyzes the envelope for destination and source addresses, and sorts it to be delivered within the city, to the destination city, or to send it onto the next hub processing center.

If the envelope is intended to be delivered within the city, it is again sorted and put on a truck to be delivered within the city. If it is intended to be sent to another city or state, the envelope is sorted to go to the next closest hub post office for additional processing until it reaches its final zip code, and is finally sorted on the truck for delivery.

Zip codes are a solution to sort mail by physical location and to ensure that mail is routed and delivered to the proper city, as efficiently and inexpensively as possible, to reach its final destination. Without zip codes to define the physical addresses, it would be extremely difficult for mail to be delivered.

Similarly, with AD DS sites, each site represents a physical location. When a client attempts to authenticate or look for resources within the forest, it will send its request to the closest domain controller. The domain controller utilizes the client's IP address and subnet, for the optimal way to allow authentication. Using AD DS, the domain controller examines the client IP address and subnet, and compares it against the defined sites and subnets to determine its location. If a client's network address and subnet belong in the same site as the domain controllers, it will authenticate the client to domain controllers within the site storing the client site information in the client's registry. If the client belongs to another site, it will store the site information in the client's registry and direct it to ask a domain controller in the remote site for authentication.

If there are no sites defined or if they are defined improperly, the authentication or service request might get sent to another physical site. By crossing over the WAN to find resources and to authenticate against domain controllers in a separate site, increased latency and decreased response time to the client are highly likely across slow connections.

Configuring Sites

It is important to configure sites and subnets within your environment to allow for efficient use of domain resources. A misconfigured site or subnet can lead to slow logon times, latent access of file shares across the WAN, and latent access to business resources.

CERTIFICATION READY
Configure sites.
Objective 5.3

Sites are representative of the physical AD DS domain topology and contain domain controllers, clients, and services. At forest creation, the default site created is called *Default-First-Site-Name* and contains all domain controllers added to the domain until new sites and subnets are created.

Sites group together domain controllers at the same physical location to allow efficient replication between one another on high speed internal networks before sending any directory changes to remote locations or branch offices.

Sites and subnets allow clients to authenticate to domain controllers in the same site, locally access resources such as Distributed File System (DFS), and to access to site-aware applications such as Microsoft Exchange by contacting the resources within the site before traversing the WAN to find the next closest domain controller or resource.

All domain controllers within a site replicate with one another in a process called ***Intrasite replication***, which is the replication of compressed data that occurs across site links between domain controllers located in different sites.

Intersite replication, through the use of Bridgehead servers, replicates directory partitions from one site's bridgehead server to another site's bridgehead server. Each bridgehead server then replicates the changes internal to its replica domain controllers through Intrasite replication.

Sites are not limited for use with only AD DS. Sites can also be configured for use in Active Directory Lightweight Directory Services (AD LDS) instances.

In a large environment, with multiple branch offices containing users and domain computers, placing a domain controller at the branch office can prevent problems if a WAN link fails. Because sites and subnets affect all domain controller replication and client connectivity, you must have Domain Administrator rights in the forest root domain or in a multi-domain environment, Enterprise Administrator rights in the forest, to perform any forest-affecting changes within the AD DS.

ADD A SITE

GET READY. Log on to a domain controller as a user who is a member of one of the following groups, forest root domain Domain Admins, Enterprise Admins, or delegated equivalent security group. To create a site, perform the following steps:

1. Click Start, and click the Active Directory Sites and Services shortcut. This displays the *Active Directory Sites and Services* tool.
2. Right-click the Sites container found within the *Active Directory Sites and Services* tool and select New Site... This displays the *New Object – Site* window.
3. Type in the name of the new site.
4. Select the corresponding site link object from the list (see Figure 16-1).

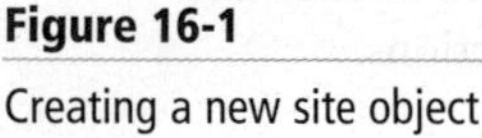

Figure 16-1

Creating a new site object

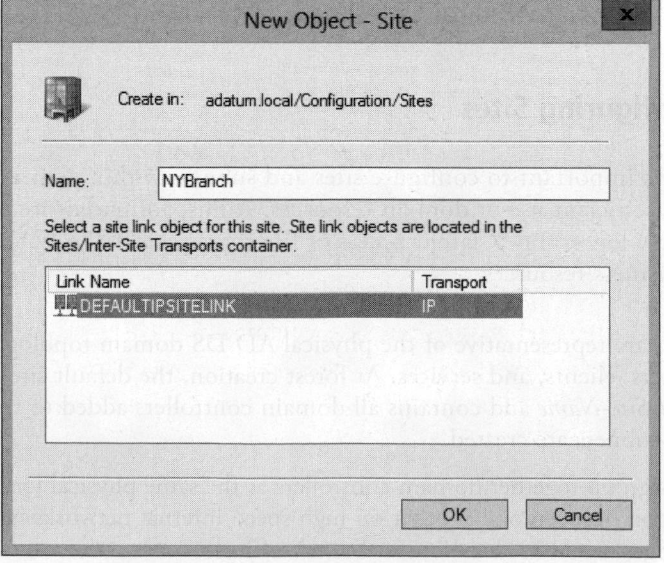

5. Click OK.
6. Confirm that the new site is now listed in the *Active Directory Sites and Services* tree.
7. Close the *Active Directory Sites and Services* tool.

USING WINDOWS POWERSHELL

You can create a site using the following cmdlet:

```
New-ADReplicationSite
```

Configuring Subnets

Subnets are created to group and assign computers within the same network subnet to a site. Subnets can be assigned only to one site and can be IPv4 or IPv6 subnets. At logon, domain controllers assign clients to sites based on their network address and subnet.

CERTIFICATION READY
Configure subnets.
Objective 5.3

When designing an AD DS site topology, make sure all IP ranges used by clients and servers are added to subnets list and assigned to a site for optimized service access and domain controller referencing.

Once assigned to a site, clients and services become "site-aware" to other clients, services, and servers within the same subnet and site. Site-aware clients look for and utilize resources within the same site before looking to other sites for references.

When using private IP address ranges, ensure that they are created and assigned to the correct site. In multi-domain forests, ensure that the Enterprise Administrators, or the Domain Administrators, across the separate domains communicate the use of private IP addresses and subnets, to avoid conflicts. Because subnets can be assigned only to one site, the use of private IP address ranges in multiple domains might become an issue during client logon and service requests are initiated if duplicate private subnets are used in more than one domain.

When clients are unable to assign themselves to a site, the domain controller that authenticates the client at logon logs a NO_CLIENT_SITE entry in `%SystemRoot%\debug\ netlogon.log` and `%SystemRoot%\debug\netlogon.bak`, indicating which IP and hostname cannot find a client site to be a part of. To prevent this from happening, create the subnet of the clients being logged and assign to the correct site.

ADD A SUBNET

GET READY. Log on to a domain controller as a user who is a member of one of the following groups, forest root domain Domain Admins, Enterprise Admins, or delegated equivalent security group. To create a subnet, perform the following steps:

1. Click Start, and click the Active Directory Sites and Services shortcut. This displays the *Active Directory Sites and Services* tool.
2. If needed, expand the Sites container.
3. Right-click the Subnets container and select New Subnet... This displays the *New Object – Subnet* window.
4. Using network prefix notation, type in the address prefix within the *Prefix:*: text box (for example: 192.168.100.0/24).
5. Select the corresponding site object from the list as displayed in Figure 16-2, and click OK.

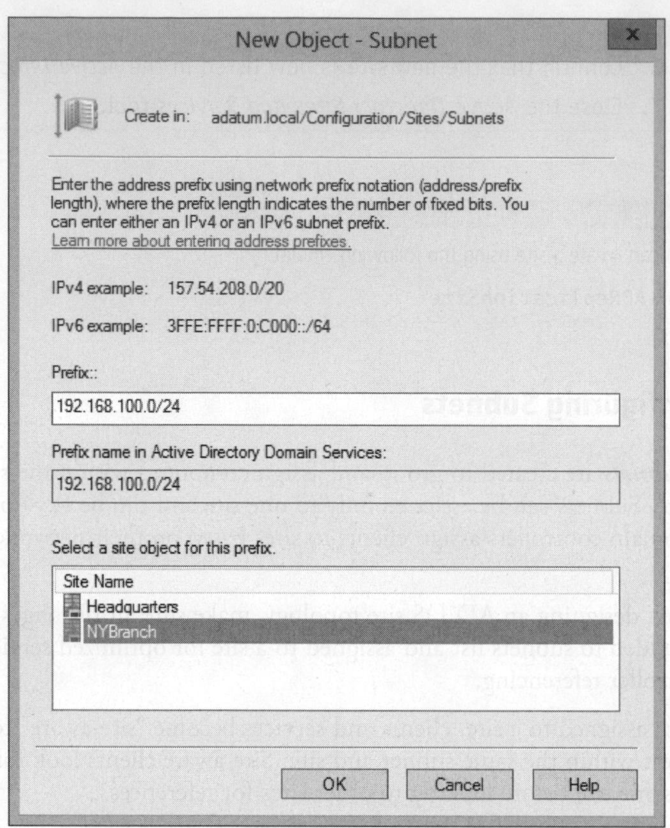

Figure 16-2

Creating a new subnet object

6. Confirm that the new subnet is now listed within the *Subnets* container found in the *Active Directory Sites and Services* tree.
7. Close the *Active Directory Sites and Services* tool.

USING WINDOWS POWERSHELL

You can create a subnet using the following cmdlet:

```
New-ADReplicationSubnet
```

To better understand how sites and subnets work during the authentication process, review the process that a client must do the first time it authenticates on the domain.

1. The client asks the Domain Name Server (DNS) for a list of domain controllers within the domain.
2. The DNS server responds providing the client with a list of Service Record (SRV) records for all domain controllers in the domain.
3. The client contacts all domain controllers for which it has been provided the SRV record.
4. The first domain controller responds, gathering IP and subnet information of the client.
5. The domain controller compares the client's IP address and subnet information to determine what site the client belongs to and responds to the client with its site name.
6. The client stores the site name within its registry for future reference.
7. The client asks the DNS server for a list of domain controllers that are in its site.

8. The DNS server responds with the SRV records of all domain controllers within the client's site.
9. The client attempts to authenticate to all domain controllers within its site, and the first one that responds provides the authentication.
10. The client uses the domain controller for all future authentication requests until it is not reachable or until the client attempts authentication in another site. At that point, it starts the process over again.

This process allows the client to authenticate to the closest domain controller possible. It is important that sites and subnets are configured correctly to allow optimal client authentication and resource access to services on the domain. If sites and subnets are not configured correctly, clients might attempt to connect to domain controllers and resources in a different physical site than where they are located.

Creating and Configuring Site Links

Site links define the logical replication link between sites to perform Intersite replication, allowing for faster and optimized replication between sites based on configured costs and frequencies. Site links manage the logical flow of replication between physical sites.

CERTIFICATION READY
Create and configure site links.
Objective 5.3

Created by default, the DEFAULTIPSITELINK site link object is created at forest creation. When new domains and domain controllers are added to the forest, if new sites links are not manually created, they will all become members of the DEFAULTIPSITELINK site. In large enterprise environments, spanning several physical locations, replication traffic is at the mercy of the WAN links between physical locations. This situation can cause replication issues when there is a mix of reliable and unreliable network paths between sites. Physical infrastructure between sites might differ and have different requirements of when to utilize bandwidth.

To resolve the problem of costly bandwidth and timing restrictions of physical connections, you can implement site links. By creating site links, you can tell AD DS who to replicate with, where to replicate, when to replicate, what path to attempt replication on first, and how often to replicate. This allows the optimization of AD DS replication traffic between sites by using the optimal, least expensive, available route. To modify site links, you must be a member of the Domain Admins group.

Newly created sites should follow a standard naming scheme representing the sites involved within the link or by using another type of descriptor for ease of troubleshooting and recognition throughout the forest. New sites are created using the Active Directory Sites and Subnets tool by expanding *Inter-Site Transports*, right-clicking the *Transport* type, and selecting *New Site Link*….

KNOWLEDGE CONSISTENCY CHECKER (KCC)

The ***Knowledge Consistency Checker (KCC)*** dynamically creates connection objects between domain controllers allowing for addition and removal of domain controllers without having to manually configure replication partners within the Active Directory Sites and Services tool. When domain controllers are added, removed, failed, or modifications are made to the replication schedule, the KCC actively monitors and makes the required changes to keep replication running efficiently between all domain controllers.

Although the KCC can be disabled, it is not an efficient use of administrative resources when numerous changes are to be made within an Enterprise Environment. It is recommended to leave the KCC enabled, and let it dynamically make the changes for you to eliminate unneeded administrative overhead.

INTERSITE TOPOLOGY GENERATOR

Assigned by the KCC, the ***Intersite Topology Generator (ISTG)*** is a domain controller, one in each site, used to monitor and make connections with domain controllers in other sites to domain controllers in its site, managing inbound replication objects for bridgehead servers within its site.

INTERSITE TRANSPORT PROTOCOLS

IP Transports replicate all AD DS partitions synchronously to domain controllers in well-connected sites. Because of its efficiency and reliability, IP Transport is the preferred method of replication between Intersite partners.

SMTP Transports, configured with the Simple Mail Transport Protocol (SMTP) protocol, send replication asynchronously via e-mail messages. SMTP transports require the implementation of Active Directory Certificate Services (AD CS), and replicate only the schema, configuration, and Global Catalog partitions. Using SMTP does not replicate the domain partition. SMTP can be used in situations where RPC over TCP/IP is not configured between two sites.

BRIDGEHEAD SERVERS

Bridgehead servers are automatically configured by AD DS. Bridgehead servers take the changes made during Intrasite replication and then replicate those changes to the bridgehead server in a connected site (see Figure 16-3).

Figure 16-3
Understanding the bridgehead server role

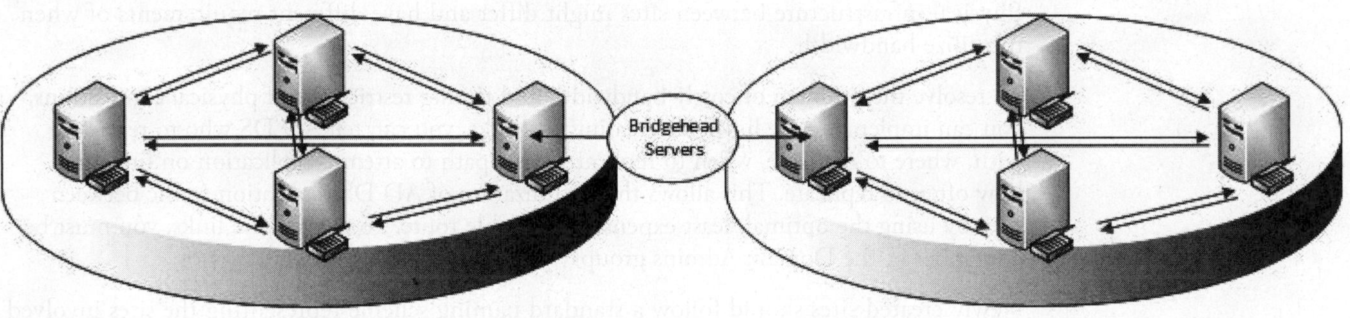

It is best practice to allow AD DS to handle the assignment of the bridgehead server tasks to the domain controller it sees best fit. In certain environments, you might need to manually configure a bridgehead server to dedicate for the additional processing and traffic requirements.

Configuring bridgehead servers manually introduces risks into your environment. If a primary bridgehead server has been configured by an administrator and not dynamically set by AD DS, and that server fails, replication will not take place across to other sites. To prevent this from happening, allow AD DS to dynamically choose a bridgehead server behind the scenes. If you must manually configure a bridgehead server, configure two per site for availability. Ensure that the domain controller that will be a bridgehead server is a DNS and Global Catalog server.

REMOVE A MANUALLY CONFIGURED BRIDGEHEAD SERVER

GET READY. Log on to a domain controller as a user who is a member of one of the following groups: forest root domain Domain Admins, Enterprise Admins, or delegated equivalent security group. To remove a manually configured bridgehead server, perform the following steps:

1. Click Start, and click the Active Directory Sites and Services shortcut. This displays the *Active Directory Sites and Services* tool.
2. If needed, expand the Sites container.
3. If needed, expand the site containing the manually created bridgehead server.
4. Right-click the server holding the manually configured bridgehead server role, and select Properties. This displays the *ServerName Properties* window.
5. Select the transport type from the *This server is a preferred bridgehead server for the following transports:* selection box, and click Remove (see Figure 16-4).

Figure 16-4

Modifying manual bridgehead server configuration

6. Click OK.
7. Verify that all other sites replicating with this site do not contain a manually configured bridgehead server. If one is manually configured, remove it to allow automatic bridgehead server selection.
8. Close the Active Directory Sites and Services tool.

SITE LINK BRIDGES

Site link bridging allows transitive linking between all sites in the forest. By default, Bridge All Site Links is enabled, permitting site link bridging between all sites in the forest.

In scenarios in which a Hub-and-Spoke Topology are preferred and a transitive link between two or more sites, but not all, is required, implement a site link bridge to allow transitivity between the required sites.

A ***Hub-and-Spoke Topology*** is created by an Enterprise Administrator disabling the Bridge All Site Links option, and then creating site link bridges between a central "hub" site and each of its remote "spoke" sites (see Figure 16-5). This forces all replication to between the hub-and-spoke bridge site members. Remote sites in a Hub-and-Spoke Topology are not configured to replicate with each other unless a site link bridge is configured. Configuring a Hub-and-Spoke Topology forces all replication to take place through the hub site before replicating back to branch offices. A disadvantage of the Hub-and-Spoke Topology is the inability to directly replicate directory partitions between branch offices. All replication must cross the WAN to replicate with the hub site and then traverse through a WAN connection again to reach the second branch office. This increases the time it takes for the second branch office to receive directory changes.

Figure 16-5

Understanding Hub-and-Spoke Topology

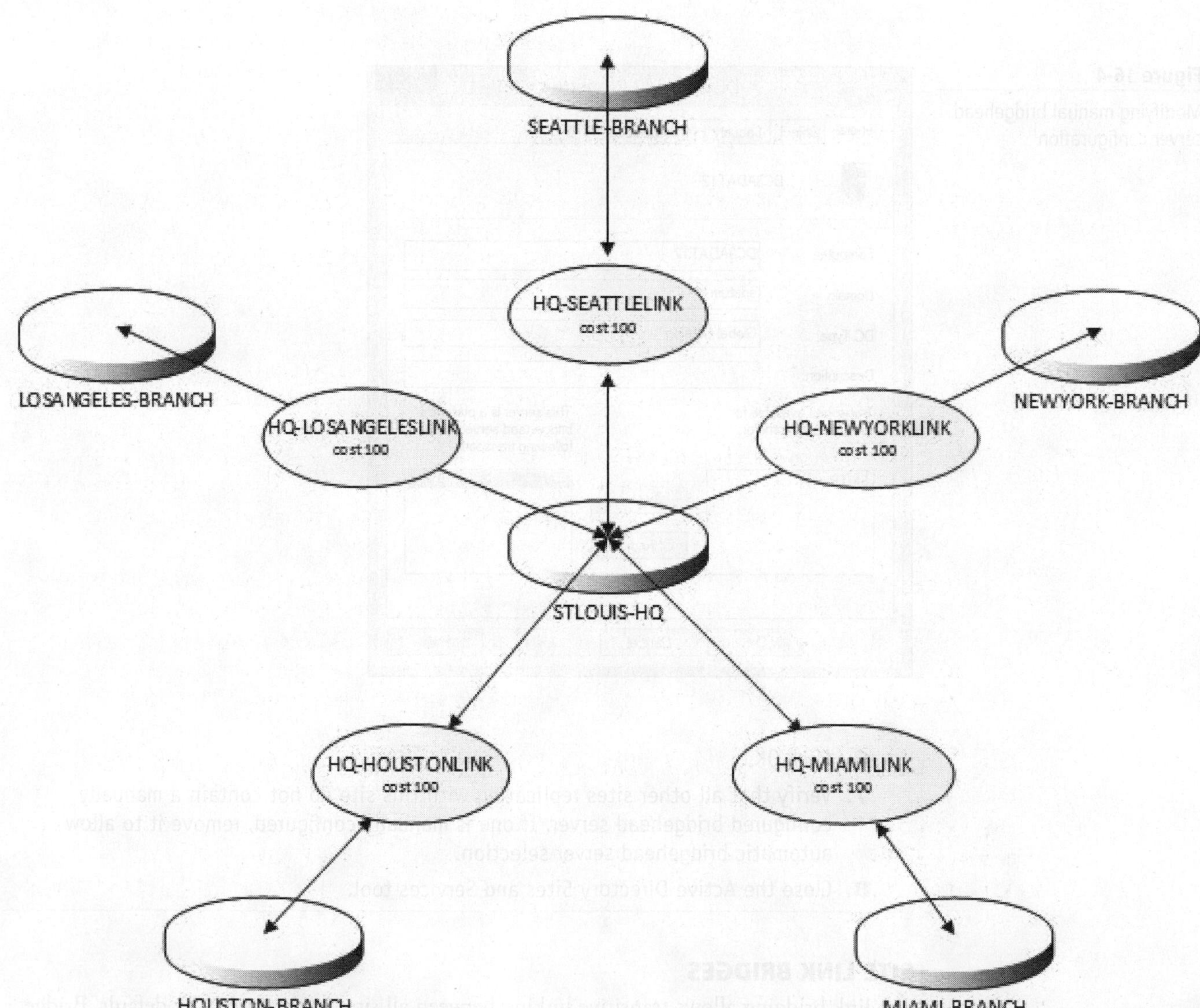

Site link bridges are used when the Bridge All Site Links option is disabled to allow transitive linking between sites not directly connected (see Figure 16-6).

Figure 16-6

Understanding site link bridge integration

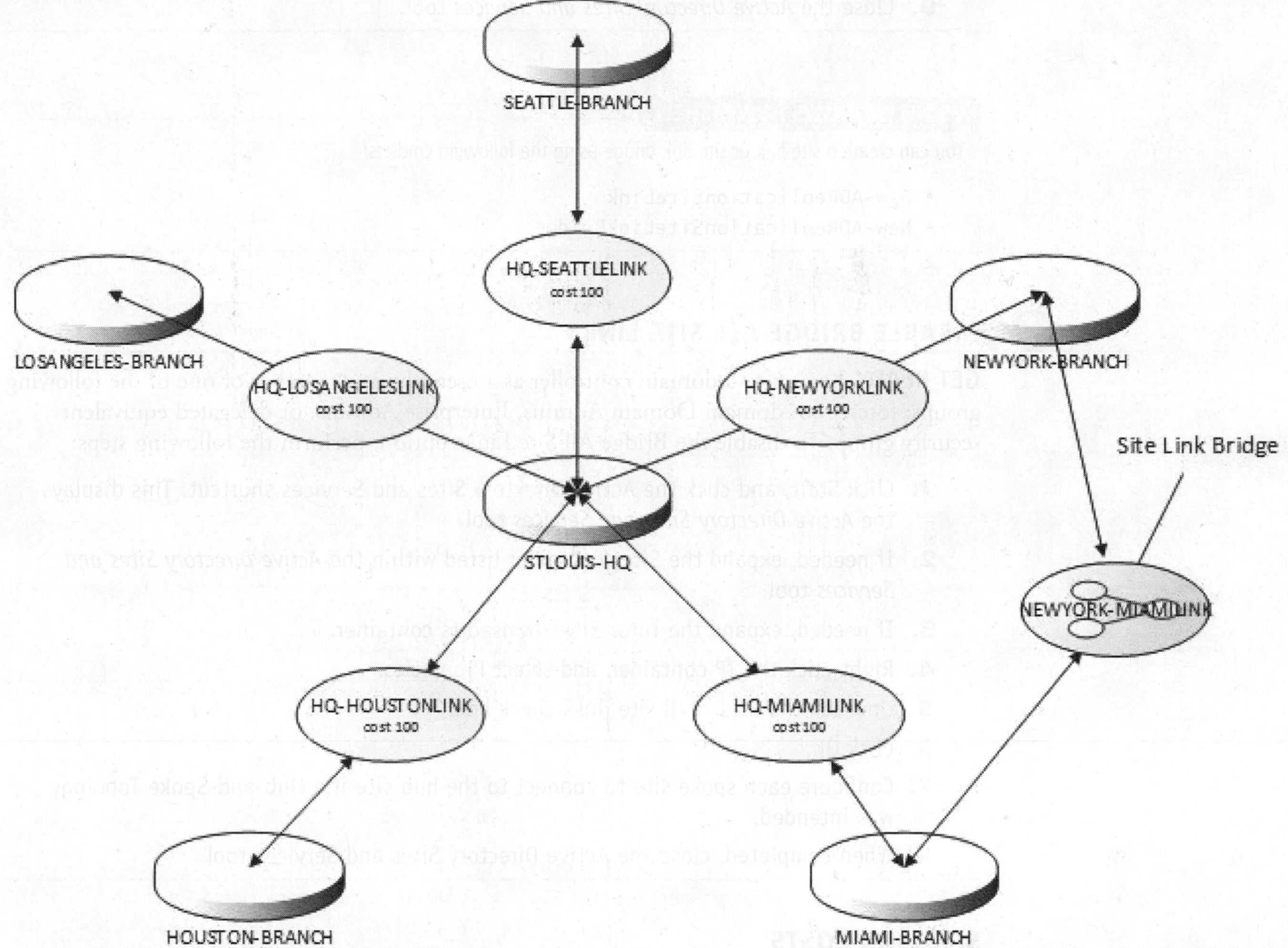

CREATE A SITE LINK AND SITE LINK BRIDGE

GET READY. Log on to a domain controller as a user who is a member of one of the following groups: forest root domain Domain Admins, Enterprise Admins, or delegated equivalent security group. To create a site link or site link bridge, perform the following steps:

1. Click Start, and click the Active Directory Sites and Services shortcut. This displays the *Active Directory Sites and Services* tool.
2. If needed, expand the Sites container.
3. If needed, expand the Inter-Sites Transports container.
4. Right-click the IP container and select New Site Link... This displays the *New Object—Site Link* window. To create a new site link bridge, select New Site Link... This displays the *New Object—Site Link Bridge* window.
5. Provide the name for the new *Site Link* or *Site Link Bridge*, within the text box.
6. Add at least two sites to the link, by selecting the sites from the *Sites not in this link:* selection box, and clicking the Add button.

7. Click OK.
8. Confirm that the new site link is now listed within the *Sites* > *Inter-Site Transports* > *IP* container found in the *Active Directory Sites and Services* tree.
9. Close the *Active Directory Sites and Services* tool.

USING WINDOWS POWERSHELL

You can create a site link or site link bridge using the following cmdlets:

- `New-ADReplicationSiteLink`
- `New-ADReplicationSiteLinkBridge`

DISABLE BRIDGE ALL SITE LINKS

GET READY. Log on to a domain controller as a user who is a member of one of the following groups: forest root domain Domain Admins, Enterprise Admins, or delegated equivalent security group. To disable the Bridge All Site Links option, perform the following steps:

1. Click Start, and click the Active Directory Sites and Services shortcut. This displays the *Active Directory Sites and Services* tool.
2. If needed, expand the Sites container listed within the *Active Directory Sites and Services* tool.
3. If needed, expand the Inter-Sites Transports container.
4. Right-click the IP container, and select Properties.
5. Uncheck the Bridge all site links check box.
6. Click OK.
7. Configure each spoke site to connect to the hub site if a Hub-and-Spoke Topology was intended.
8. When completed, close the Active Directory Sites and Services tool.

SITE LINK COSTS

By default, site link costs are configured with a cost value of 100. Site link costs can be configured to allow AD DS to replicate over one link before replicating over another one. Replication always replicates over the lowest cost link between sites.

As an example, think of a hub spoke configuration between four sites. With the hub site as the primary datacenter for the domain and each branch office as a spoke to the hub, each branch office connects to the primary datacenter on a high-speed WAN. With the Bridge All Site Links option off, all replication is replicated to the hub site, and then down to the other spokes, not branch office to branch office. Now, imagine that you have a slow and costly satellite connection between two of the branch offices. Though it is less efficient and expensive to use the satellite link, you plan to use the satellite link as a backup path in the event that the link between the branch office and the primary datacenter fails.

You can configure a new site link between the branch offices to utilize the satellite link as a backup link if the optimal site link between the sites is down. To do so, you create a new site link between the branch offices and assign a higher cost to those links.

When replicating between sites, the total cost of the replication path to the destination is added and assessed. If the total cost of the replication is cheaper by going over one route than over another, the lowest total cost route will perform the replication.

MODIFY SITE LINK COSTS

GET READY. Log on to a domain controller as a user who is a member of one of the following groups: forest root domain Domain Admins, Enterprise Admins, or delegated equivalent security group. To modify site link costs, perform the following steps:

1. Click Start, and click the Active Directory Sites and Services shortcut. This displays the *Active Directory Sites and Services* tool.
2. If needed, expand the Sites container.
3. If needed, expand the Inter-Sites Transports container.
4. Select the IP container. Notice the site links listing in the window.
5. From the list of site links, right-click the site link you want to modify and select Properties. This displays the *LinkName Properties* window.
6. Modify the Cost: value to reflect the requirements of the enterprise (see Figure 16-7).

Figure 16-7

Modifying site link cost

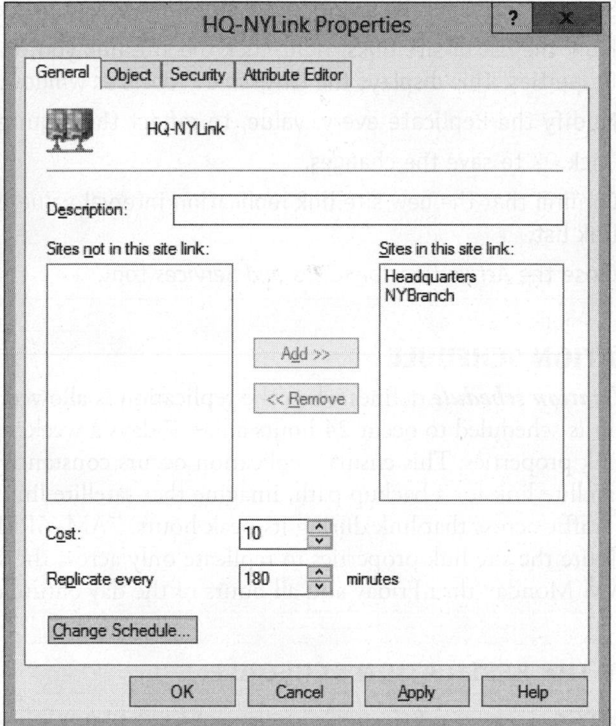

7. Click OK to save the changes.
8. Confirm that the new site link cost is reflected within the site link list.

REPLICATION INTERVAL

The ***replication interval*** defines how often replication across the site link occurs. By default, replication on site links are configured to occur every 180 minutes and can be modified within the site link properties. Replication between sites might need to occur more frequently if there are constant changes to AD DS that need to be seen in branch offices immediately. The replication interval can be configured to allow replication every 15 minutes across site links.

USING WINDOWS POWERSHELL

You can modify site link cost and the replication interval using the following cmdlet:

```
Set-ADReplicationSiteLink LinkName -Cost 100
-ReplicationFrequencyInMinutes 15
```

MODIFY THE REPLICATION INTERVAL

GET READY. Log on to a domain controller as a user who is a member of one of the following groups: forest root domain Domain Admins, Enterprise Admins, or delegated equivalent security group. To modify the replication interval, perform the following steps:

1. Click Start, and click the Active Directory Sites and Services shortcut. This displays the *Active Directory Sites and Services* tool.
2. If needed, expand the Sites container.
3. If needed, expand the Inter-Sites Transports container.
4. Select the IP container. Notice the site links listing in the window.
5. From the list of site links, right-click the site link you want to modify and select Properties. This displays the *LinkName Properties* window.
6. Modify the Replicate every: value, to reflect the requirements of the enterprise.
7. Click OK to save the changes.
8. Confirm that the new site link replication interval value is reflected within the site link list.
9. Close the *Active Directory Sites and Services* tool.

REPLICATION SCHEDULE

The ***replication schedule*** defines when the replication is allowed to occur. By default, replication is scheduled to occur 24 hours a day, 7 days a week, and can be modified within the site link properties. This ensures replication occurs constantly. In the previous example of using a satellite link for a backup path, imagine that satellite link is three times more costly to replicate traffic across that link during its peak hours, 7AM–6PM, Monday thru Friday. You can configure the site link properties to replicate only across the satellite network between 6PM–7AM Monday thru Friday and all hours of the day Saturday and Sunday.

MODIFY THE REPLICATION SCHEDULE

GET READY. Log on to a domain controller as a user who is a member of one of the following groups: forest root domain Domain Admins, Enterprise Admins, or delegated equivalent security group. To modify the replication schedule, perform the following steps:

1. Click Start, and click the Active Directory Sites and Services shortcut. This displays the *Active Directory Sites and Services* tool.
2. If needed, expand the Sites container.
3. If needed, expand the Inter-Sites Transports container.
4. Select the IP container. Notice the site links listing in the window.
5. From the list of site links, right-click the site link you want to modify and select Properties. This displays the *LinkName Properties* window.
6. Click the Change Schedule... button.
7. Using your mouse, click and hold the left mouse button dragging the cursor over the range of time you want to modify, releasing the mouse button after selected.

8. Choose Replication Not Available or Replication Available to remove or add the time range to the replication schedule (see Figure 16-8).

Figure 16-8

Modifying replication schedule

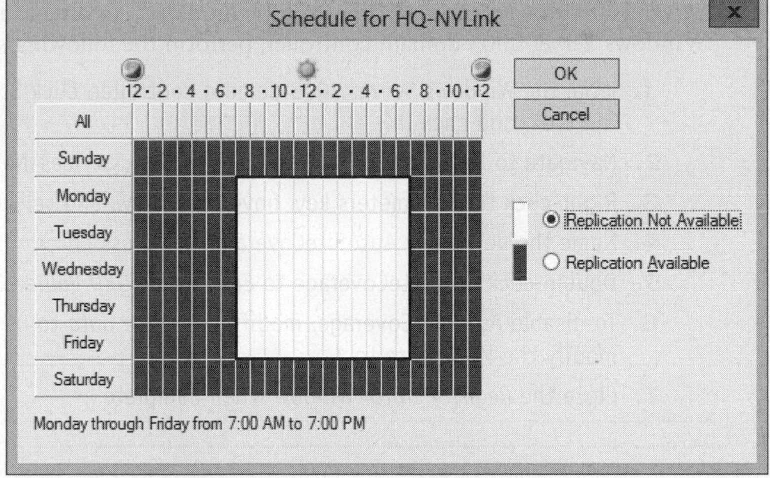

9. Click OK to save the changes.
10. Click OK to close the displayed window.

Managing Site Coverage

Not all environments require a domain controller at each site. In certain scenarios, you might allow sites to be automatically covered by a domain controller in an adjacent site.

CERTIFICATION READY
Manage site coverage.
Objective 5.3

AUTOMATIC SITE COVERAGE

Domain controllers in sites can take over for missing domain controllers in remote sites. If a site does not have a domain controller to authenticate clients against, depending on cost, domain controllers in the closest site will automatically register an SRV record in the client site to automatically cover the site for the missing domain controller. This allows clients to be able to contact the closest domain controller to access the resources needed.

The clients in the site that are automatically covered are still traversing the WAN to connect to the domain controller for authentication and resource access.

DISABLE AUTOMATIC SITE COVERAGE

Unfortunately, Windows Server 2003 domain controllers perform automatic site coverage in sites with Read-only Domain Controllers (RODCs) because they are unable to recognize that an RODC might be currently covering a site. If the closest site to an RODC contains only Windows Server 2003 domain controllers, there are a few options that are recommended.

- Download the RODC compatibility pack for the Windows Server 2003 domain controllers.
- Upgrade the domain controllers in the next closest site to at least Windows Server 2008.
- Modify the site costs to a site running only Windows Server 2008 domain controllers.
- Disable automatic site coverage on the Windows Server 2003 domain controllers, through the registry or Group Policy.

DISABLE AUTOMATIC SITE COVERAGE ON WINDOWS SERVER 2003

WARNING Always use caution when making changes in the registry and back up the registry before changes are made. Always fully understand the steps you perform before the steps are acted upon.

GET READY. Log on to a Windows Server 2003 domain controller as a user that is a member of the forest root domain Domain Admins or Enterprise Admins group of the Windows Server 2003 domain controller that will be modified. To disable automatic site coverage on a Windows Server 2003 domain controller, perform the following steps.

1. From the Windows Server 2003 domain controller, click Start, select Run, type in REGEDIT, and click OK.
2. Navigate to HKLM\SYSTEM\CurrentControlSet\Services\Netlogon\Parameters.
3. Right-click the Parameters key, hover over New, and select DWORD Value.
4. Name the new entry AutoSiteCoverage and press Enter.
5. Double-click AutoSiteCoverage to *Edit the DWORD Value*.
6. To disable AutoSiteCoverage, modify the *Value data* to 0. To enable AutoSiteCoverage, modify the *Value data* to 1.
7. Close the *Registry Editor* window when complete.

Managing Registration of SRV Records

Domain controller SRV records are a critical part of domain controller and client communications. All domain controllers register an SRV record for their clients to find them.

CERTIFICATION READY
Manage registration of SRV records.
Objective 5.3

After a member server is promoted to become a domain controller, it registers itself in DNS for advertisement so clients know how to find it. As you learned previously, clients ask the DNS for a list of all domain controllers and a list of domain controllers within its site for efficient authentication to occur. In DNS, the domain controller registers SRV records for the client to find. During this process, if AD DS recognizes that there are no domain controllers in another site, it will allow a domain controller to register its SRV records in the site, performing Automatic Site Coverage. During SRV registration, the _kerberos and _ldap SRV records are created and advertised at the following locations in the domain's zone: _msdcs/dc/_Sites/Sitename/_tcp and _msdcs/dc/_tcp.

NETLOGON SERVICE

The NETLOGON service running on a domain controller is the service that requests and issues that the registration request of the SRV records to DNS. In versions previous to Windows Server 2008, you were required to run *netdiag/fix* to re-register SRV records on a domain controller. On servers running Windows Server 2008, Windows Server 2008 R2, Windows Server 2012, and Windows Server 2012 R2, the SRV records and _msdcs zone records can be reregistered by stopping then starting the NETLOGON service on the domain controller. A reboot will also perform a reregistration of SRV records, but will cause unneeded downtime.

NETLOGON.DNS

When a domain controller registers its SRV records in DNS, it creates a copy of those records and stores them locally in the NETLOGON.DNS file. The NETLOGON.DNS file located within the `%systemroot%\System32\config\` can be viewed in Notepad.exe. The NETLOGON.DNS provides critical information when troubleshooting SRV record registration on a domain controller. If removed or renamed, the NETLOGON.DNS will be restored with existing records for the DNS server at the next reboot or next NETLOGON service stop and start command on the domain controller.

Moving Domain Controllers between Sites

Moving a domain controller to a different site is a simple task once your environment is ready for the change to occur.

CERTIFICATION READY
Move domain controllers between sites.
Objective 5.3

During domain controller promotion, you are prompted to assign the domain controller to a site. If you do not choose the site for the domain controller to be added to during promotion, it will assign itself to a site based on the IP address it has at the time of promotion. If it is one of the first domain controllers added to a forest, the domain controllers will be placed into the Default-First-Site-Name site until the site, subnet, and site link topology are in place. Once the site topology is in place, the domain controllers can be moved to the appropriate sites and replicate properly with one another. The Default-First-Site-Name site can be renamed to match the naming standard for its current location or it can be removed if it is not part of the new topology.

Depending on the roles installed on a domain controller that will be moved to a different site, you need to do some planning and prepare to make some network adapter, DNS server, and environment changes.

PREPARING THE DOMAIN CONTROLLER, DNS, AND ENVIRONMENT

Before moving the domain controller to a new site, review the following steps:

1. Assign the new IP, subnet, gateway, preferred DNS, alternate DNS, and WINS (if still in use) addresses to the domain controller. After completing this task, verify that all host (A), host (AAAA), and name server (NS) records have updated automatically in DNS.
2. If the server is or will be a DNS server, modify the client and server environment to match the upcoming change.
3. Update any DNS delegations the domain controller is a part of by updating, from the parent domain, the Name Servers tab of the delegated zone.
4. If the server is configured to be a forwarder for any other DNS server, modify the Forwarders tab on the DNS server that is forwarding the queries to the domain controller's new IP address.
5. Verify sites and subnets are configured correctly for the new site. The new site needs to contain the IP range and subnet of the domain controller's new IP address.
6. If the domain controller had previously been manually configured to be a preferred bridgehead server, remove the manual configuration from the domain controller and any others before moving it to the new site. It is best practice to allow AD DS to dynamically assign bridgehead servers. If you choose to not follow best practice, ensure a bridgehead server has been assigned or still exists in each site.
7. Move the domain controller to the new site.
8. Verify that the domain controller SRV records have been registered to reflect the new site.

USING WINDOWS POWERSHELL

You can move a domain controller to a new site using the following cmdlet:

```
Get-ADDomainController DCName | Move-ADDirectoryServer -Site SiteName
```

MOVE A DOMAIN CONTROLLER TO A NEW SITE

GET READY. Log on to a domain controller as a user who is a member of one of the following groups: forest root domain Domain Admins, Enterprise Admins, or delegated equivalent security group. To move a domain controller to a new site, perform the following steps:

1. Click Start, and click the Active Directory Sites and Services shortcut. This displays the *Active Directory Sites and Services* tool.
2. If needed, expand the Sites container.
3. Expand the site name where the server is located.
4. Expand Servers.
5. Right-click the server object that will be moved to the new site.
6. Select Move....
7. Choose the site name that will contain the server.
8. Click OK.
9. Expand the site that the server has just been moved to and confirm that the server has moved.
10. Expand the server object, and verify that the *NTDS Settings* object exists.
11. Close the *Active Directory Sites and Services* tool.

SKILL SUMMARY

IN THIS LESSON YOU LEARNED:

- Clients separated by physical locations are grouped through the creation of sites and subnets.
- Multiple sites are linked together to perform Intersite replication between domain controllers spread across multiple physical locations.
- Domain controllers can register their records in remote sites when a domain controller is not present in that site.
- When Read-Only Domain Controllers (RODCs) are the only domain controllers in a site and the next closest site contains only Windows 2003 domain controllers, Automatic Site Coverage can be disabled. This prevents the Windows Server 2003 domain controllers from automatically registering their SRV records in the RODCs site.
- Domain controller SRV records can be reregistered by restarting the NETLOGON service. A copy of the records that are registered are saved locally to the domain controller's NETLOGON.dns file.
- Domain controllers can be easily moved between sites, once careful planning and strategies are in place to ensure clients can connect to the domain controller once moved to its destination site.

Knowledge Assessment

Multiple Choice

Select the correct answer for each of the following questions.

1. You have recently installed a domain controller, but your clients are unable to authenticate against it. You notice the SRV records for the domain controller have not been populated in DNS. What will you do to reregister the SRV records in DNS?
   a. Modify NETLOGON.DNS
   b. Restart the NETLOGON service
   c. Restart the DNS Server service
   d. Modify NETLOGON.LOG

2. Clients at a remote site are complaining that it takes an unacceptable amount of time to log in to their computers when they come in every morning. You check the logs of the domain controllers and notice that the clients are authenticating with a domain controller at the headquarters office and not with the domain controller at the remote office. You verify that the domain controller at the remote office is configured and registering SRV records in DNS correctly. What must be done to ensure all clients in the remote site authenticate with the domain controller in the remote site?
   a. Create a new organizational unit and move the computers into it
   b. Require all users to log in with their e-mail address for the username
   c. Delete the NETLOGON.DNS file on the remote site domain controller
   d. Create a subnet in the Active Directory Sites and Services tool

3. You have installed a Read-Only Domain Controller (RODC) at a remote location. After looking through the logs, you notice that the Windows Server 2003 servers have automatically covered the remote site. What is the next step you need to take?
   a. Modify the SearchFlags attribute
   b. Open REGEDIT on the Windows Server 2003 domain controllers
   c. Install the Microsoft Assessment and Planning Toolkit
   d. Restart the NETLOGON service of the RODC

4. You have recently had a physical domain controller fail during a routine maintenance reboot. The drives have failed and you cannot purchase new drives. Luckily you have recently implemented a Hyper-V solution. Instead of restoring it from backup, you brought online a new virtual domain controller running Windows Server 2012 R2. Once the new server is back up and replicating with other partners within its site, you notice no replication is taking place between sites. Why has replication stopped between sites?
   a. The failed domain controller was a manually configured bridgehead server
   b. The second site is not compatible with Windows Server 2012 R2
   c. The site link needs to be reregistered
   d. The Default-First-Site-Name still exists

5. You have recently brought a new site online. During your planning stages, you set up two new domain controllers for the new site and you are ready to move them. What tool will you use to move the domain controllers to the remote site?
   a. Active Directory Domains and Trusts
   b. Active Directory Users and Computers
   c. Active Directory Sites and Services
   d. Active Directory Administrative Center

6. You are working in an environment that has a non-Windows DNS server resolving all client requests. You are unable to use DNS Manager to view what records your Windows Server 2012 R2 server has registered with DNS. Where can you view the SRV records that the domain controller has created?
   a. NETLOGON.DNS
   b. DNS Manager
   c. HOSTS
   d. NETLOGON.LOG

7. You have recently purchased a new building. There is not a secure location to put a domain controller, but there will be 800 end users requiring authentication. The WAN link between sites is as reliable as you would like. What will be your solution to authenticate the users?
   a. Create a new site and allow Automatic Site Coverage to handle authentication
   b. Copy the netlogon.dns file to all client computers
   c. Create a new site and install RODCs
   d. Choose five user computers to install Windows Server 2012 R2 with the AD DS role running in the background

8. By default, which of the following values represents the site link cost?
   a. 10
   b. 50
   c. 100
   d. 500

9. While monitoring replication traffic, you notice that replication traffic between two sites is traversing three site links instead of going directly site to site. The Bridge All Site Links option is enabled.
   a. Check the replication schedule
   b. Check the site link costs
   c. Configure a dedicated bridgehead server
   d. Disable Automatic Site Coverage

10. You receive a warning in the event logs of your domain controllers recommending you view the `%SystemRoot%\debug\netlogon.log` file. When you open the log file, you notice it is full of entries stating NO_CLIENT_SITE. What should you do first to stop these entries from populating in the log file? Your environment has no remote offices.
    a. Delete netlogon.log
    b. Restart the NETLOGON service
    c. Create a subnet
    d. Create a site

Best Answer

Choose the letter that corresponds to the best answer. More than one answer choice may achieve the goal. Select the BEST answer.

1. What do you do to reregister SRV records as soon as possible?
   a. Reboot the domain controller
   b. Run `repadmin /syncall /APed` from an elevated command prompt
   c. Open DNS and manually put them in
   d. Restart the NETLOGON service

2. Intersite replication occurs between what two domain controllers?
   a. bridgehead servers
   b. Infrastructure Master FSMO role holders
   c. domain-naming masters
   d. primary and secondary

3. You must create 100 site links based on a list provided to you in a text file. What is the fastest way to perform this action?
   a. Hire an assistant
   b. Use Windows PowerShell
   c. Use the Active Directory Sites and Services tool
   d. Create one site, right-click, and select copy

4. Replication is not occurring between sites when a domain controller is not accessible. Each site has five domain controllers. What is configured incorrectly?
   a. site costs
   b. subnets
   c. preferred bridgehead servers
   d. SRV registration

5. During the Intersite replication process, replication occurs over what links?
   a. most configured bandwidth
   b. most replicated
   c. least cost
   d. most linked

Matching and Identification

1. Match the description with the appropriate term. Not all items will be used and items can be used more than once.
   _______ a) Intersite replication occurs between these two servers
   _______ b) Replication occurs on the link with the lowest of this
   _______ c) When replication occurs
   _______ d) How often replication occurs
   _______ e) Clients and servers are grouped together using this
   1. replication interval
   2. replication schedule
   3. cost
   4. bridgeheads
   5. subnet
   6. site

2. Match the description with the appropriate term. Not all items will be used and items can be used more than once.
   _______ a) Connects two branch offices together by passing links to the hub site
   _______ b) All replication occurs through the hub site
   _______ c) Replicates all domain controller partitions between sites
   _______ d) Domain controller registers SRV records in another site
   _______ e) Connects two sites together
   1. automatic site coverage
   2. site link bridge
   3. SMTP Transport
   4. site link
   5. Hub-and-Spoke Topology
   6. IP transport

3. Identify the tools that can be used to create AD DS sites and subnets. (Select all that apply.)
   _______ Active Directory Domains and Trusts
   _______ Active Directory Users and Computers
   _______ DHCP
   _______ Windows PowerShell
   _______ dssite.msc
   _______ Active Directory Sites and Services

4. Identify the group membership required to modify enterprise-wide sites, site links, and subnets.
   _______ delegated equivalent security group
   _______ Domain Administrators
   _______ forest root domain Domain Administrators
   _______ Enterprise Administrators
   _______ DNS Administrators
   _______ RODC Administrators

Build a List

1. List the steps to add a site to an IP site link.
   _______ Right-click Subnets, and select New Subnet
   _______ Select the Intersite Transport SMTP folder
   _______ Select the site, and click Add
   _______ Open Active Directory Sites and Services
   _______ Right-click the site link, and select Properties
   _______ Select the Intersite Transport IP folder
   _______ Right-click the site, and select Properties

■ Business Case Scenarios

Scenario 16-1: Configuring Replication between New Sites

You are the Enterprise Administrator for a new worldwide company headquartered in South Dakota. You currently have one site link, DEFAULTIPSITELINK, in AD DS. Over the past month, three new offices have opened up: one in Montana, one in New Zealand, and the last in Spain. Each new site has three domain controllers. Replication between sites is not happening efficiently and when your support teams attempt to connect to Active Directory Users and Computers, they are rarely connecting to their local domain controller. What steps must you take to resolve the support team's issues?

Scenario 16-2: Planning for Private IP Addressing

You are the Enterprise Administrator for a large forest with 20 domains. A Network administrator for one of the domains has recently contacted you with a list of private IP addresses he would like added to the site. When you connect to AD DS, you notice those IPs already exist and are tied to an entirely separate site and you cannot add that range to the requested site. What must be done to approach this situation?

LESSON 17

Managing Active Directory and SYSVOL Replication

70-412 EXAM OBJECTIVE

Objective 5.4 – Manage Active Directory and SYSVOL replication. This objective may include but is not limited to: Configure replication to Read-Only Domain Controllers (RODCs); configure Password Replication Policy (PRP) for RODCs; monitor and manage replication; upgrade SYSVOL replication to Distributed File System Replication (DFSR).

Lesson Heading	Exam Objective
Managing Active Directory Replication	
Understanding Intrasite Replication	
Understanding Intersite Replication	
Controlling Active Directory Replication	
Configuring Read-Only Domain Controllers	Configure replication to Read-Only Domain Controllers (RODCs) Configure Password Replication Policy (PRP) for RODCs
Monitoring Replication	Monitor and manage replication
Upgrading SYSVOL Replication to Distributed File System Replication (DFSR)	Upgrade SYSVOL replication to Distributed File System Replication (DFSR)

KEY TERMS

change notification
Filtered Attribute Sets
non-urgent replication
password change replication
Password Prepopulation
Password Replication Policy (PRP)
replication conflicts
store-and-forward replication
unidirectional replication
urgent replication

Managing Active Directory Replication

THE BOTTOM LINE

Active Directory replication is a critical piece of every Active Directory Domain Services (AD DS) environment. By replicating all naming contexts or directory partitions of AD DS, all domain controllers throughout the enterprise keep one another up-to-date with all changes, ranging from schema updates to modifying items as simple group membership. Having accurate and up-to-date directory partitions allows enterprise operations to run smoothly.

AD DS replication occurs between two or more domain controllers, a source domain controller, and a replica domain controller. The replication process does the following:

- Replicates new changes/updates
- Replicates updates of directory objects
- Ensures all directory updates are transferred to a replica partner
- Keeps all directory partitions up to date
- Keeps all domain controllers synchronized
- Replicates contents of the SYSVOL folder

Through the replication process, the domain controllers keep each other informed about changes happening with objects and partitions connected to the domain controller. Put simply, a change is made on a domain controller and is automatically replicated to a replica domain controller.

Replication occurs between domain controllers within a site, intrasite replication, or between domain controllers in separate sites, intersite replication. Each process ensures correct information is relayed to replica domain controllers as fast and as efficiently as possible.

Understanding Intrasite Replication

Intrasite replication occurs using ***change notification*** between domain controllers located within that site. Change notification is a notification given by source domain controllers within a site, to their replica domain controllers notifying them it has new changes that can be replicated. Intrasite replication is considered Notify-Pull replication, which means that the source domain controller notifies a replica, and then the replica requests the changes.

Taking advantage of localized high-speed local area networks, Intrasite replication allows changes to occur as soon as possible. Intrasite replication utilizes Remote Procedure Call over Internet Protocol (RPC over IP) connectivity, Kerberos authentication, and data encryption allowing efficient and secured data transfer between domain controllers. Unlike intersite replication, where replication data is compressed, all replication data within a site is not compressed. Intrasite replication topology is generated by the Knowledge Consistency Checker (KCC).

The KCC on each domain controller creates a bidirectional connection between the source domain controller and the replica domain controller. It ensures no more than three hops are taken to get directory updates to replica domain controllers. To circumvent more than three hops happening between a source domain controller and a replica domain controller, the KCC creates a shortcut connection and makes a connection with the replica domain controller across the ring to increase the speed of replication.

When handling the naming contexts (such as directory partitions), the KCC creates a separate replication topology for the schema, configuration, domain, and application partitions to ensure replica domain controllers have all changes required as soon as possible. The KCC continually checks the topology and dynamically makes needed changes based on the availability of the domain controllers and other factors within the topology.

To further enhance replication within a site, domain controllers use the Store-and-Forward mechanism to replicate changes to other domain controllers within the site. ***Store-and-forward replication*** allows the replica domain controller to store the updates it has received from the source domain controller and issue or forward a change notification to other replica domain controllers. This mechanism allows faster replication so the source domain controller does not have to contact every domain controller in the domain to replicate the latest update.

The following process illustrates the intrasite replication process:

1. A directory change occurs on the source domain controller.
2. The source domain controller recognizes the change has been made and waits fifteen seconds before issuing a change notification.
3. The source domain controller contacts the closest replica domain controller notifying the replica of its latest update.
4. The replica domain controller receives the change notification from the source domain controller.
5. The replica domain controller requests the updates from the source domain controller.
6. The source domain controller initiates the replication operation to the replica domain controller.
7. The replica domain controller pulls the latest replica.

If there are multiple replica domain controllers in the site, the source domain controller will wait three seconds after issuing the first change notification before sending a change notification to the next domain controller. By waiting three seconds for each change notification, the domain controller can efficiently answer and forward the replication operations to requesting replica domain controllers without being overloaded with replication requests at the same time. To ensure additional efficiency, once a domain controller has received the directory update, it will not ask or attempt replication back to the source until a new update is required.

Urgent replication allows for critical directory information to be delivered to replica domain controllers without waiting the normal, non-urgent, fifteen-second and three-second subsequent intervals. For instance, if a user's account locks out on a domain controller, that domain controller urgently replicates the lockout to the primary domain controller emulator (PDC emulator). The PDC emulator domain controller then urgently replicates the lockout to all other domain controllers. Examples of directory updates that are urgently replicated include account lockouts, changes in account lockout policies, changes in the domain password policy, and changes of a domain controller account password.

Non-urgent replication is all other replication that does not include account lockouts, account/password policies, and domain controller accounts. Non-urgent replication occurs through normal change notification replication operations. For instance, if a computer object is created on a domain controller, it will take about 15 seconds to replicate to the next closest domain controller through the automatic process.

Password change replication allows domain controllers to reference one domain controller in the event a password has been changed on one domain controller, and the change has not yet replicated throughout the enterprise. Do not confuse password change replication with Password Replication Policies (PRPs). Although it might seem it would be covered by Urgent Replication, password changes are replicated through the use of non-urgent replication. When a user changes his or her password, that password change is immediately sent to the PDC emulator. The PDC emulator then initiates a non-urgent replication with its replica domain controllers. If a user attempts to log in to a domain controller and the domain controller has not yet received the password change for the user, the domain controller that the user is authenticating against checks with the PDC emulator to see whether it knows the user's latest password. If the PDC emulator has the latest password, it authenticates the user and replicates the new password to the domain controller that the user is attempting authenticating against. If a domain controller changes a user's password and cannot contact the PDC emulator, the password change will be included in the next non-urgent replication cycle.

Replication conflicts occur when objects are modified by users in an environment. It is possible that the same object might be modified by two different users at the same time. At this occurrence, the domain controller receiving the update first compares the version of the change and accepts only the latest version. In the event that both versions are identical, the domain controller will accept the newest update based on the object's version and timestamp. The latest revision always wins in a replication conflict.

Understanding Intersite Replication

As discussed in Lesson 16, "Configuring Sites," intersite replication is replication between domain controllers in different sites across a Wide Area Network (WAN). Intersite replication is considered request-pull replication, meaning the replica bridgehead server in one site requests the changes from the source bridgehead server.

Intersite replication occurs between domain controllers residing in separate physical locations within the AD DS topology. Site topology is created by the KCC and the Intersite Topology Generator, and replication occurs between each site's assigned bridgehead servers. Intersite replication is a cost-based replication, allowing replication to occur across the least expensive link. Using scheduling, configured replication intervals, and costs, site links are optimized to provide the fastest and cheapest replication possible between two sites. Intersite replication traffic can occur over RPC over IP or Simple Mail Transfer Protocol (SMTP).

Unlike intrasite replication, change notification, by default, is not used to notify domain controllers in other sites about changes. Replication between sites depends on replication intervals, costs, and schedules. Though change notification between sites is not enabled by default, it can be enabled.

To learn more about advanced replication and configuration, visit Microsoft's TechNet website.

Controlling Active Directory Replication

As an administrator of an enterprise, there will be instances where replication needs to happen at your discretion (for example, when troubleshooting connectivity between domain controllers or forcing replication of partitions and/or objects between multiple domain controllers before normal replication occurs).

Through the use of REPADMIN, Windows PowerShell, and the Active Directory Sites and Services tool, you can control when replication happens, and whether you need it to happen within a site or across the enterprise.

USING THE REPADMIN COMMAND TO CONTROL ACTIVE DIRECTORY REPLICATION

From a command prompt window on a domain controller, you can control replication between domain controllers by using REPADMIN.exe. Before running REPADMIN.EXE across a multisite or multidomain environment, verify you have the proper access to each subdomain, domain tree, and replication partners that will participate in the replication process. Failure to have the required privileges prevents you from forcing replication across the enterprise. The following commands and switches allow for replication within a site or throughout the enterprise:

- **REPADMIN.EXE:** Used to monitor, troubleshoot, and diagnose replication within a forest, domain, or replication partners.
- **REPADMIN.EXE /SyncAll:** Often used with a variety of switches. Synchronization can be forced between adjacent partners, within a site, or across the enterprise. Any combination of the following switches can be used with the SyncAll switch; for example, `REPADMIN /SyncAll /A /P /e /d` is also accepted if formatted as `REPADMIN / SyncAll /APed`.
- **REPADMIN /SyncAll /a:** Running with the /a switch aborts the synchronization if any server that will be part of the synchronization process is down or unreachable.
- **REPADMIN /SyncAll /A:** Running with the /A switch synchronizes all directory partitions held on the server where you are synchronizing from.
- **REPADMIN /SyncAll /d:** Running with the /d switch identifies the replication partners with their distinguished names for.
- **REPADMIN /SyncAll /e:** Running with the /e switch synchronizes across the enterprise topology. Not using the /e switch synchronization occurs only within the site that the domain controller running REPADMIN is located.
- **REPADMIN /SyncAll /h:** Running with the /h switch returns Help.
- **REPADMIN /SyncAll /i:** Running with the /i switch repeats the synchronization indefinitely.
- **REPADMIN /SyncAll /I:** Running with the /I switch runs the REPADMIN /ShowRepl command on each replication pair. By using this switch, it will not perform a synchronization.
- **REPADMIN /SyncAll /j:** Running with the /j switch synchronizes the domain controller with its adjacent replication partners.
- **REPADMIN /SyncAll /p:** Running with the /p switch pauses after each synchronization result is returned.
- **REPADMIN /SyncAll /P:** Running with the /P switch pushes all updates outward to replication partners from the domain controller where the command is run.
- **REPADMIN /SyncAll /q:** Running with the /q switch allows syncall to run in Quiet mode.
- **REPADMIN /SyncAll /Q:** Running with the /Q switch allows syncall to be run in Very Quiet mode. Doing so returns only fatal error messages found during the synchronization process.
- **REPADMIN /SyncAll /s:** Running with the /s switch does not synchronize.
- **REPADMIN /SyncAll /S:** Running the /S switch skips checking each server for a response and continues synchronization.
- **REPADMIN.EXE /KCC:** Using the KCC switch forces the KCC to reexamine the AD DS topology. After significant changes have been made to the domain, forest, or if you recently upgraded your domain controllers from Windows Server 2008 or before, to Windows Server 2012 R2, running the `REPADMIN.EXE /KCC` command optimizes the topology using the latest benefits provided in the latest server operating systems.

- **`REPADMIN.EXE /Replicate`:** Using the /Replicate switch forces replication of a specified directory partition between specified source and destination domain controller. For instance, to force replication of the domain partition between SourceDC and DestinationDC, run the following command:

  `REPADMIN /Replicate SourceDC DestinationDC DC5adatum,DC5local`

- **`REPADMIN.EXE /ReplSingleObj`:** Using the /ReplSingleObj forces replication of a single object, using its Distinguished Name, between a source domain controller and destination domain controller. For instance, to force replication of User1 between SourceDC and DestinationDC in the adatum.local domain, run the following command:

  `REPADMIN /ReplSingleObj DestinationDC SourceDC CN5User1,CN5Users, DC5adatum,DC5local`

USING THE ACTIVE DIRECTORY MODULE WITH WINDOWS POWERSHELL TO CONTROL ACTIVE DIRECTORY REPLICATION

The Active Directory module for Windows PowerShell has seen significant improvements in relation to managing replication connections and monitoring replication within an AD DS topology; the ability to force replication across domain controllers and sites is still limited.

`Sync-ADObject: Using Sync-ADObject -object "distinguishedName" -Source "SourceDCName" -Destination "DestinationDCName"` helps prevent overloading WAN links when a single object needs to be immediately replicated between the source and destination domain controllers.

USING THE ACTIVE DIRECTORY SITES AND SERVICES TOOL TO CONTROL ACTIVE DIRECTORY REPLICATION

By using the AD DS tool as a domain administrator or enterprise administrator, you are able to force replication between two domain controllers. Simply expand the site containing the domain controllers, expand the domain controller, select *NTDS Settings*, and right-click on the domain controller you with to replicate to and select *Replicate Now*.

You can also use the AD DS tool to check the replication topology between domain controllers in a site. This can be done by expanding the Site and Domain Controller objects, right-clicking on *NTDS Settings,* hovering over *All Tasks,* and selecting *Check Replication Topology*. This performs the same check that happens when issuing the REPADMIN /KCC command from command prompt.

MANAGE ACTIVE DIRECTORY REPLICATION USING REPADMIN

GET READY. To force replication of all directory partitions, push the synchronization throughout the enterprise, and return domain controller names as Distinguished Names using one REPADMIN command, perform the following steps:

1. From the lower left corner of the Windows Server 2012 R2 taskbar, right-click Start and select Command Prompt. The *Administrator: Command Prompt* window appears.
2. From the *Administrator: Command Prompt* window, enter the `REPADMIN /SyncAll /APed` command.
3. View the results and search for errors. If errors exist, take action to resolve the errors.
4. Continue to run `REPADMIN /SyncAll /APed` until no errors exist.
5. Close the *Administrator: Command Prompt* window.

Configuring Read-Only Domain Controllers

Read-only domain controllers (RODCs) are used in environments where there is a need for a domain controller in a branch office that does not have a secured physical environment. They are also used where there is a risk of theft, or even rarely, where there is an application that requires installation on a domain controller that users must log in to at the terminal or with terminal services.

When planning for a new branch office or remote site, take into consideration the use of an RODC as a form of security if a secure datacenter is not available. Although placing an RODC in a site that contains writable Windows Server 2008 domain controllers provides limited security benefits, it can be used for those business applications requiring access to a domain controller and prevents changes from being made to the overall directory. RODCs should be used only for branch office security considerations, unless there are absolute requirements within an environment.

CONFIGURING REPLICATION TO A READ-ONLY DOMAIN CONTROLLER

CERTIFICATION READY
Configure replication to Read-Only Domain Controllers (RODCs).
Objective 5.4

As the name "read-only domain controller" implies, its involvement with AD DS is truly read-only. ***Unidirectional replication*** means replication occurs in only one direction, from a writeable domain controller to the read-only domain controller. Read-only domain controllers can only pull the domain partition from a writable Windows Server 2008 or higher domain controller; however, the application and global catalog partitions can be pulled from a domain controller running Windows Server 2003 or higher. Other replica domain controllers within the domain or site are unable to use an RODC as a source domain controller.

In order for an RODC to act as a replica server, there must be a writeable domain controller within the same domain as the RODC. In addition, the writable domain controller in the next closest site must be running Windows Server 2008 or higher. If the next closest site contains only a Windows Server 2003 server, the RODC will traverse site link bridges to reach the closest, writable, Windows Server 2008 domain controller. If the Bridge All Site Links option is disabled and the hub site contains only Windows Server 2003 domain controllers, a Site Link Bridge must be created to allow the RODC to connect to a writable Windows Server 2008 domain controller.

This need to connect to a writable Windows Server 2008 domain controller is required because the Password Replication Policy (PRP) applied to the RODC can be configured and enforced only from a writable Windows Server 2008 domain controller.

RODCs replicate AD DS partitions and Distributed File System Replication (DFSR) of the SYSVOL folder unidirectional. Other DFSR shares, not part of the AD DS process, located on the RODC replicate bidirectional with its configured replication partners.

Implementing ***Filtered Attribute Sets*** allows administrators the ability to mark attributes as "Confidential" when being replicated to RODCs. Attributes marked as confidential and that are part of the Filtered Attribute Set will not be replicated to an RODC. This provides additional security if there are attributes configured in the schema that contain information that can cause a security breach if a domain controller is stolen or compromised (for example, passwords, Social Security numbers, and Encryption Keys).

If there are plans to implement a Filtered Attribute Set, you must raise the Forest Functional Level to at least Windows Server 2008. Although configuring the Filtered Attribute Set does not require a Forest Functional Level of Windows Server 2008, it is highly recommended, because malicious users can take advantage of attribute replication from Windows Server 2003 domain controllers. Windows Server 2003 domain controllers permit requested changes to be replicated, whether configured as confidential or not.

To configure the Filtered Attribute Set, the configuration of the attribute must be done on a Windows Server 2008, Windows Server 2012, or Windows Server 2012 R2 domain controller that holds the Schema Master FSMO role. The Filtered Attribute Set and Confidential options are configured by modifying the attribute that you intend to not be replicated. From ADSI Edit, connect to the schema, and within the properties of the confidential attribute, modify its *searchFlags* attribute. To turn on the Read-Only Filtered Attribute Set, configure the 10th bit to be 0x200, and then turn on the Confidential bit by configuring the 7th bit to 0x080. Or simply add 640 to the existing decimal configuration of the attributes searchFlags attribute.

CONFIGURE FILTERED ATTRIBUTE SETS

GET READY. To configure Filtered Attribute Sets, perform the following steps:

1. Click Start and open ADSI Edit.
2. At the top of *ADSI Edit* window, click Action and select Connect to… The *Connection Settings* window opens.
3. From the *Select a well-known Naming Context:* selection, select Schema. From the *Select or type a domain or server:* selection, choose the domain controller running the Schema Master role, and click OK.
4. From the *ADSI Edit* window, expand Schema, and select the CN=SCHEMA, CN=Configuration,DC=YourDomain,DC=YourDomainSuffix container.
5. From the list of attributes, find and double-click on CN=Employee-ID. The *CN=Employee-ID Properties* window appears.
6. Scroll down, find, and double-click on searchFlags. The *Integer Attribute Editor* window appears.
7. Record its current value, add 640 to the value, enter the sum of the values in the *Value* text box, and click OK.
8. The new searchFlags value from the *CN=Employee-ID Properties* window should now read and/or contain the following value *0x280 = (CONFIDENTIAL|RODC_FILTERED)* as shown in Figure 17-1. The Employee-ID value is no longer replicated to the RODC.

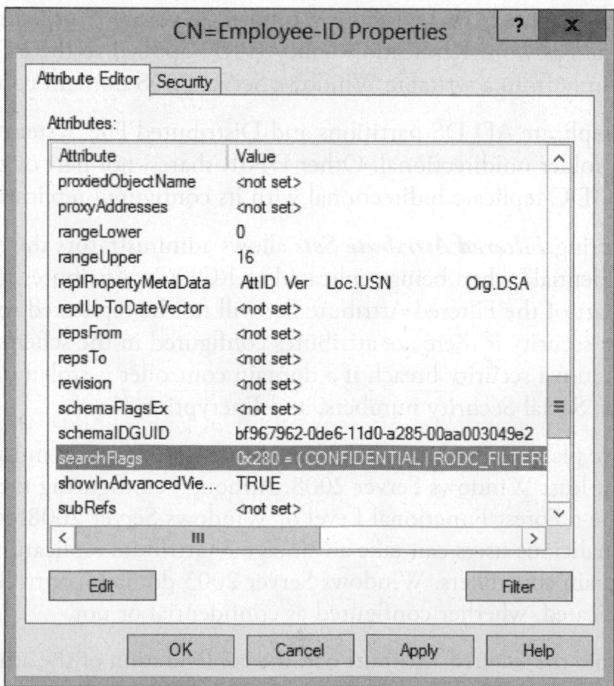

Figure 17-1

Modifying the Confidential RODC filtered attribute

9. Click Cancel to discard your changes or click OK to save your changes. Close the *CN=Employee-ID Properties* window.
10. Close the *ADSI Edit* window.

CONFIGURING PASSWORD REPLICATION POLICY FOR RODCS

CERTIFICATION READY
Configure Password Replication Policy (PRP) for RODCs.
Objective 5.4

To provide authentication of users and computers at a branch office that utilizes an RODC, the RODC must know and store the password of that user or computer. Otherwise, users and computers will traverse the WAN to authenticate to the next closest writable domain controller causing unneeded latency and WAN usage during the logon process. Because RODCs run the risk of theft or compromise at remote locations, not all users within a domain will need their credentials stored at the remote location. The same goes for privileged users, including domain administrators and enterprise administrators. If an RODC is stolen and compromised, all user accounts that have authenticated against the RODC, and have had their passwords cached, will need their passwords changed because their account has been compromised and the business is at risk. This is why user accounts, such as domain administrators and enterprise administrators, should never be cached and remotely access through terminal services or authenticate against an RODC at the site. To give a user or group elevated permissions to the RODC, configure the user or group under the Managed By tab of the RODCs computer account.

As a safeguard, to prevent unwanted users from logging into or authenticating against an RODC, all users except for those that are members of the Allowed RODC Password Replication Group will be allowed to authenticate to the RODC. The Allowed RODC Password Replication Group, by default, allows members to authenticate to the RODC. Keep in mind, the user or group that you configured under the Managed By tab are not, by default, allowed to log on or authenticate against the RODC unless they are members of the Allowed RODC Password Replication Group. As an additional option, to prevent users from authenticating against the RODC, add the users or user group to the Denied RODC Password Replication Group.

By modifying the ***Password Replication Policy (PRP)*** of the RODC within the Active Directory Users and Computers tool, you can *allow* or *deny* passwords to be cached for users.

When adding users to the Allowed RODC Password Replication Group, do not forget that computers have passwords as well. You must also add the users' computers that will be at the remote site to the Allowed RODC Password Replication Group. This eliminates authentication problems if the WAN link fails and computers attempt to authenticate. This concept of the PRP allows credentials to be cached on the RODC.

Password Prepopulation is the ability for a domain controller to store user credentials before a user logs into the RODC. Password Prepopulation allows user credentials to be pushed to the RODC before those users attempt log on to the RODC. Benefits of Password Prepopulation include the following:

- Initial logons are faster, since the authentication process won't have to traverse the WAN to the closest, writable, Windows 2008 or later, domain controller.
- The ability to prepare an RODC before shipment to the remote site if no WAN link is available when the RODC is brought online.

In order for Password Prepopulation to cache passwords, the users and computers must have their accounts configured to have their passwords replicated, or have been added to the Allowed RODC Password Replication Group.

READ-ONLY DOMAIN CONTROLLER SECURITY

In the event of an RODC theft or compromise, the user passwords need to be changed immediately at the hub site. To meet this immediate need, the fastest way to force all users, who have authenticated or who have their credentials cached on that RODC, simply delete the RODC object from the Active Directory Users and Computers tool. When you initiate the deletion of the RODC, you are prompted and given the option to reset all users passwords, reset all computer passwords, and export a list of compromised accounts.

Upon deletion, all passwords that have been cached will be reset to a random password. Users that had their user account passwords cached need to reset their password or contact the helpdesk to reset their passwords. All computers that have had their passwords reset will need to be rejoined to the domain.

CONFIGURE PASSWORD REPLICATION POLICIES ON AN RODC

GET READY. To create a staged RODC computer account and configure generic user and computer account credentials for password replication, perform the following steps. Once completed, you remove the staged read-only domain computer account and force all users with passwords replicated to be reset.

1. Click Start, and click Active Directory Users and Computers to open the *Active Directory Users and Computers* tool.
2. From the *Computers* container, precreate a generic computer account.
3. From the *Users* container, precreate a Generic User account.
4. Right-click on the Domain Controllers OU and select Pre-create Read-only Domain Controller Account. The *Active Directory Domain Services Installation Wizard* opens. Click Next.
5. On the *Network Credentials* window, authenticate with a domain administrator user account, and click Next.
6. On the *Specify the Computer Name* window, enter the computer name for the Staged RODC, and click Next.
7. On the *Select a Site* window, select a site for the new domain controller, and click Next.
8. On the *Additional Domain Controller Options* window, verify that DNS Server and Global catalog are selected, and click Next.
9. On the *Delegation of RODC Installation and Administration* window, click Next. You will not select a user or group in this exercise.
10. On the *Summary* window, review the selections and click Next.
11. On the *Completing the Active Directory Domain Services Installation Wizard* window, click Finish.
12. From the *Active Directory Users and Computers* tool, select the Domain Controllers OU.
13. Within the *Domain Controllers* OU, double-click on the RODCServerName you just created. The *RODCServerName Properties* window appears.
14. From the *RODCServerName Properties* window, select the Password Replication Policy tab. Notice the Allowed and Denied users, computers, and groups listed.
15. From the list, double-click Allowed RODC Password Replication Group. The *Allowed RODC Password Replication Group Properties* window appears.
16. Click on the Members tab. Within the *Members* tab, click Add. The *Select Users, Contacts Computers, Service Accounts* window appears.

17. Click Object Types.... In the *Object Types* window, check the Computers check box and click OK. You are returned to the *Select Users, Contacts Computers, Service Accounts* window.
18. Enter the object names of the precreated computer and user accounts you created in Steps 2 and 3. Click Check Names verifying the names resolve correctly, and click OK.
19. Verify that the user and computer are listed in the *Members* tab, and click OK.
20. From the *RODCServerName properties* window, click Advanced. The *Advanced Password Replication Policy for RODCServerName* window appears.
21. From the *Advanced Password Replication Policy for RODCServerName* window, click the Prepopulate Passwords... button. The *Select Users and Computers* window appears.
22. Enter the object names of the precreated computer and user accounts you created in Steps 2 and 3. Click Check Names verifying the names resolve correctly, and click OK. The *Prepopulate Passwords* window appears. Verify that you want to send the current account passwords to the RODC, and click Yes.
23. Because you cannot prepopulate account credentials on a Pre-staged RODC, you receive an error indicating you are unable to reach the RODC. In an environment with a live RODC, it succeeds and the accounts are listed within the *Policy Usage* tab of the *Advanced Password Replication Policy for RODCServerName* window. Click OK to close the error. This returns you to the *Advanced Password Replication Policy for RODCServerName* window. Click Close, to close the open window.
24. At the *RODCServerName Properties* window, click OK.
25. Within the *Domain Controllers* OU, right-click on the precreated RODC RODCServerName, and select Delete. You are prompted to verify you want to delete the Computer account. Click Yes, and the *Deleting Domain Controller* window appears.
26. Review the options available when deleting the RODC, and provide a path and file name in the Location: text box (see Figure 17-2). Click Delete. The *Delete Domain Controller* window appears warning you that you are about to reset all user account passwords that have been cached and all metadata for the domain controller will be removed. Click OK. If the RODC is a global catalog, you will be asked again if you are sure you want to delete it. Click Yes.

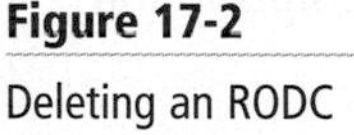

Figure 17-2

Deleting an RODC

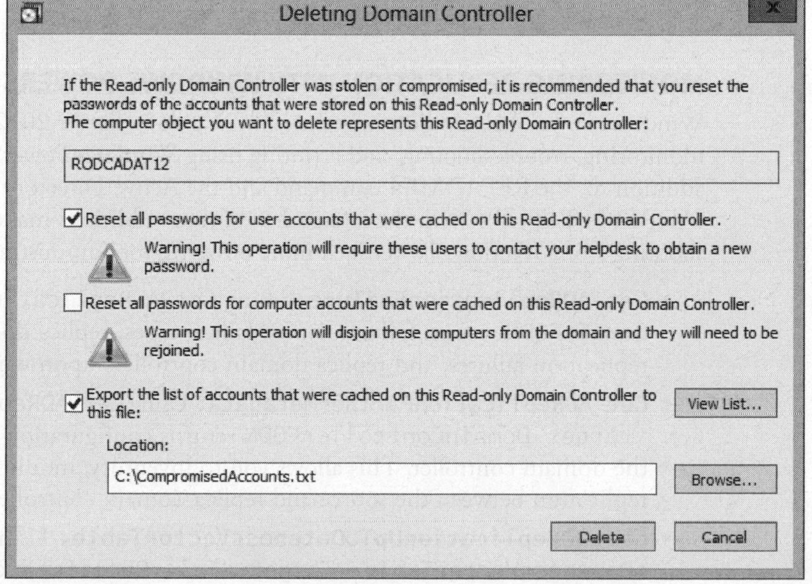

27. The pre-staged RODC has been removed, and any user and computer account passwords that have been cached on the domain controller have been reset to random values.
28. Once complete, close the *Active Directory Users and Computers* tool.

Monitoring Replication

Monitoring replication allows you to troubleshoot and narrow down problems between domain controllers when replication is not working properly. Monitoring replication in your enterprise allows you to ensure all domains within the enterprise are receiving updates to all directory partitions, keeping users and directory data fully accessible.

MONITORING REPLICATION WITH REPADMIN

CERTIFICATION READY
Monitor and manage replication.
Objective 5.4

By using REPADMIN.EXE, Windows PowerShell, and/or the Active Directory Replication Status tool (ADREPLSTATUS), you can monitor your environment for failures and take action to put a resolution in place. Use the following commands to monitor replication:

- **`REPADMIN.EXE /ReplSummary:`** This command also can be run as `REPADMIN /ReplSum`. It examines all inbound and outbound replication between domain controllers and returns a replication summary of the forest or specified domain controllers. After contacting and inventorying the domain controllers, it will then populate with a summary of failures and deltas (new changes) returned during its examination.
- **`REPADMIN.EXE /ShowRepl:`** Categorized by directory partitions, this command returns the replication status of all inbound connections from source domain controllers to the domain controller it is run from.
- **`REPADMIN.EXE /ShowRepl /RepsTo:`** Displays a summary of all outbound replication connections to replica domain controllers using the domain controller the command is run from as the source domain controller.
- **`REPADMIN.EXE /Queue:`** Displays the current inbound connections that are queued for replication. To view the active inbound replication queue of a domain controller from that domain controller, run `REPADMIN /Queue DCName`.
- **`REPADMIN.EXE /FailCache:`** Displays link and connection failure attempts found by the KCC.

MONITORING REPLICATION WITH WINDOWS POWERSHELL

Windows PowerShell cmdlets introduced in Windows Server 2012 allow for advanced monitoring, troubleshooting, and scripting using Windows PowerShell in the place of, or in addition to, the REPADMIN command and the Active Directory Replication Status Tool (ADREPLSTATUS). With the latest releases, these additions make monitoring and troubleshooting from Windows PowerShell more powerful for administrators.

- **`Get-ADReplicationFailure:`** Using `Get-ADReplicationFailure -target DomainFQDN` returns failure counts, failure types, replica domain controllers, most recent replication failures, and replica domain controllers upon which replication failed.
- **`Get-ADReplicationPartnerMetadata:`** Using `Get-ADReplicationPartnerMetadata -target DomainControllerFQDN` returns configuration data and replication state of the domain controller. This allows you to inventory, monitor, and troubleshoot replication between the source and replica domain controller.
- **`Get-ADReplicationUpToDatenessVectorTable:`** Using `Get-ADReplicationUpToDatenessVectorTable -Target "FullyQualifiedDomainName" -Scope Domain *` queries all replication partners' AD DS partitions in the domain returning listings of last replication successes, partitions, replica server, and UsnFilter.

MONITORING REPLICATION WITH ACTIVE DIRECTORY REPLICATION STATUS TOOL (ADREPLSTATUS)

Released by Microsoft in 2012, the Active Directory Replication Status Tool (ADREPLSTATUS) allows for much simpler and straightforward monitoring and troubleshooting, taking the results returned and placing them into an easy-to-use application. Using existing tools and commands such as REPADMIN.EXE, the Active Directory Replication Status Tool (ADREPLSTATUS) identifies, prioritizes, and assists in resolving replication errors on specified domain controllers, a domain, or the entire forest. The Active Directory Replication Status Tool auto-discovers domain controllers, gathers replication summaries, returns the results in a filterable, sortable list, and links directly to TechNet, providing direct access and faster turnaround time to resolve replication errors.

Compatible with operating systems including Server 2003/XP and later, you can download the latest version of the Active Directory Replication Status Tool (ADREPLSTATUS) from the Microsoft Download Center.

Before installation, ensure you have installed the required versions of .NET Framework the Active Directory Replication Status Tool (ADREPLSTATUS) might require (.NET Framework 3.5.1 and .NET Framework 4.0).

MONITOR ACTIVE DIRECTORY REPLICATION USING THE ACTIVE DIRECTORY REPLICATION STATUS TOOL (ADREPLSTATUS)

GET READY. To use the Active Directory Replication Status Tool, perform the following steps:

1. If not already installed, download and install the .NET Framework versions required for your operating system.
2. Download and install the Active Directory Replication Status Tool from the *Microsoft Download Center*.
3. On the Desktop of the client the tool is installed on, double-click AD Replication Status Tool.
4. Examine the contents of the *Home* tab and the *Configuration/Scope Settings*.
5. Select Forest from the *Configuration/Scope Settings*, and click Refresh Replication Status.
6. Once completed, if not already displayed, click the Replication Status Viewer tab and review the results.
7. After you review the *Replication Status Viewer* tab, select the Replication Error Guide tab and examine the *Error Code, Message,* and *TechNet Article Link* columns.
8. If errors are shown, click the Error Code listed in the *Replication Error Guide*.
9. Follow the direction provided by the displayed TechNet Article, and make the required changes.
10. After changes are made, run Refresh Replication Status from the *AD Replication Status Tool*.
11. Continue troubleshooting and resolving errors until there are no longer errors reported.
12. Close the *AD Replication Status Tool* when completed.

Upgrading SYSVOL Replication to Distributed File System Replication (DFSR)

Many environments started off as an Active Directory environment running Windows Server 2003 or earlier, prior to the addition of Windows Server 2008, Windows Server 2012, and Windows Server 2012 R2. The replication process of recently upgraded domain's SYSVOL folders might still be configured to use the File Replication Services (FRS). The SYSVOL folder on each domain controller contains a copy of logon scripts and Group Policies, and it is a repository for public access files used by domain controllers.

CERTIFICATION READY
Upgrade SYSVOL replication to Distributed File System Replication (DFSR).
Objective 5.4

If you recently upgraded your domain servers to Windows Server 2012 R2, it will be beneficial to migrate your SYSVOL folder replication from FRS to DFSR to take advantage of multimaster replication, scheduling, easier administration, and all other benefits of Distributed File System Replication concepts.

With Windows Server 2012 R2, upgrading to DFSR provides more reliable and easier to support replication solutions. It also provides improved integration with environments that contain RODCs.

UNDERSTANDING THE FRS TO DFSR MIGRATION PROCESS

To upgrade from FRS to DFSR, the Domain Functional Level must be Windows Server 2008 or higher. This means that all domain controllers in the domain must be at least Windows Server 2008 or higher. If there are existing Windows Server 2003 domain controllers in the environment, they will need to be upgraded or removed in accordance with best practices to allow the Domain Functional Level to be raised. So plan and prepare accordingly before the migration.

GLOBAL STATES

There are four Global States of an FRS to DFSR upgrade. Each one allows all domain controllers to balance and prepare for the next state.

- **Start (State 0):** Live AD DS SYSVOL replication between domain controllers is performed using FRS. DFSR is not being performed. FRS replication occurs with the SYSVOL folder.
- **Prepared (State 1):** Live AD DS SYSVOL replication between domain controllers is performed using FRS. A separate behind-the-scenes SYSVOL replication using DFSR is performed on the domain controllers in parallel with the live replication. FRS replication occurs with the SYSVOL folder. DSFR occurs with the SYSVOL_DFSR folder.
- **Redirected (State 2):** Live AD DS SYSVOL replication between domain controllers is performed using DFSR. A separate behind-the-scenes SYSVOL replication using FRS is performed on the domain controllers in parallel with the live replication. DFSR occurs with the SYSVOL_DFSR folder. FRS replication occurs with the SYSVOL folder.
- **Eliminated (State 3):** All Live AD DS SYSVOL replication between domain controllers is performed using DFSR. FRS SYSVOL replication is removed, including the SYSVOL folder and its contents, if it was not open during the elimination operation. DFSR occurs with the SYSVOL_DFSR folder.

You must understand the migration states and what replication types, FRS or DFSR, are replicating at each state of the migration. Thoroughly test and verify that each state is operating as designed throughout the migration process. Having a full understanding of the process and what steps are being performed reduces the risk of errors and your ability to rollback. You must also perform the action on each state in order. Do not attempt to skip any states. Doing so might leave your environment in a failed state. Practice and test the migration in a lab environment before performing the full migration in a production environment.

PREPARING THE DOMAIN FOR MIGRATION

Before migrating FRS to DFSR, you must plan and understand the process from beginning to end. Follow the steps below to prepare for the migration.

1. Before beginning your migration, download and understand the *SYSVOL Replication Migration Guide: FRS to DFS Replication Guide* from the Microsoft Download Center.
2. Upgrade and/or remove, by using best practices, all domain controllers running Windows Server 2003. Your domain must have only domain controllers running Windows Server 2008, Windows Server 2012, and/or Windows Server 2012 R2.
3. Ensure all domain controllers are online and accessible with one another.
4. Raise the Domain Functional Level to Windows Server 2008, Windows Server 2008 R2, Windows Server 2012, or Windows Server 2012 R2.
5. Verify that the replication is working as designed. Download the *Ultrasound Monitoring and Troubleshooting Tool for File Replication Services* from the Microsoft Download Center to verify the health of the current FRS environment.
6. Take any action to resolve replication problems reported by Ultrasound that might exist. If replication problems did exist and have since been resolved, allow replication to fully complete, ensuring domain controllers have the same data within their SYSVOL folders.
7. Back up the SYSVOL folder.
8. Verify on the PDC emulator that the DFSR service is running and Start Type is set to *Automatic*.
9. If the SYSVOL folder is open on any domain controller, close the window. Failure to do so locks the SYSVOL folder as in use, and it will not be deleted during the Eliminated state.
10. Run the migration process from the domain controller that is operating the PDC emulator FSMO role.

Once the migration process is complete and all domain controllers are upgraded and are using DFSR, you can use the DFSRDIAG command from an elevated command prompt to troubleshoot and diagnose problems.

UPGRADE SYSVOL REPLICATION TO DFSR

GET READY. To migrate SYSVOL from FSR to DFSR, perform the following steps:

1. Download, review, and fully understand the *SYSVOL Replication Migration Guide: FRS to DFS Replication Guide*.
2. Verify that your domain meets all prerequisites and replication is working. If open on any domain controllers, close all windows displaying *SYSVOL* or *NETLOGON*.
3. Log on to the domain controller that holds the PDC emulator role.
4. From the lower left corner of the *Windows Server 2012 R2* taskbar, right-click the Start menu and select Command Prompt. The *Administrator: Command Prompt* window appears.
5. Migrate all domain controllers to the Prepared state by issuing the following command:

```
dfsrmig /SetGlobalState 1
```

6. Verify that all domain controllers have migrated successfully to the Global state (Prepared), by issuing the following command:

```
dfsrmig /GetMigrationState
```

7. Once all domain controllers are in the Prepared state, migrate all domain controllers to the Redirected state by issuing the following command:

   `dfsrmig /SetGlobalState 2`

8. Verify all domain controllers have migrated successfully to the Global state (Redirected), by issuing the following command:

   `dfsrmig /GetMigrationState`

9. Verify replication is working properly by running the following command:

   `REPADMIN /ReplSum`

10. Back up the system state of all domain controllers.
11. Once you have verified all domain controllers are in the Redirected state and replication is working between all domain controllers, migrate all domain controllers to the Eliminated state by issuing the following command. This is *not* reversible and might take some time to complete:

    `dfsrmig /SetGlobalState 3`

12. Verify all domain controllers have migrated successfully to the Global state (Eliminated), by issuing the following command:

    `dfsrmig /GetMigrationState`

13. Verify the SYSVOL folder no longer exists.
14. Verify the current DFSR Global state is Eliminated and has succeeded, by issuing the following command:

    `dfsrmig /GetGlobalState`

15. Verify that the SYSVOL and NETLOGON shares continue to exist on all domain controllers and point to their corresponding folder located within *C:\Windows\SYSVOL_DFSR\sysvol* by logging into each domain controller and running the following command from *Command Prompt:*

    `net share`

16. Navigate to the *C:\Windows* directory and verify that the *SYSVOL* directory no longer exists.
17. If you are no longer using FRS on your domain controllers, it might be uninstalled.
18. When the installation is complete, click Close.

SKILL SUMMARY

IN THIS LESSON YOU LEARNED:

- Intrasite replication uses change notification when replicating to replica domain controllers within the same site.
- Filtered Attribute Sets can be configured to prevent attributes, considered confidential, from being replicated to Read-Only Domain Controllers (RODCs).
- User and computer passwords can be allowed or prevented from being cached on RODCs.
- The REPADMIN.EXE command can be used to troubleshoot and monitor Active Directory replication.
- The Windows PowerShell cmdlet Get-ADReplication* can be used to troubleshoot and monitor Active Directory replication.

- The Active Directory Replication Status Tool (ADREPLSTATUS) can be used to troubleshoot and monitor Active Directory replication.
- The SYSVOL folder replication process can be migrated from the File Replication Service to Distributed File Service Replication.

■ Knowledge Assessment

Multiple Choice

Select the correct answer for each of the following questions.

1. Which of the following commands, run from command prompt, allows you to monitor, troubleshoot, and force replication on Windows Server 2012 R2?
   a. REPLMON
   b. NETSH
   c. REPLSUM
   d. REPADMIN

2. Which of the following replication topologies, by default, uses change notification?
   a. Knowledge Consistency Checker (KCC)
   b. Intersite Topology Generator
   c. Intrasite Replication
   d. Intersite Replication

3. Which of the following Forest Functional Levels is the minimum requirement to securely implement Filtered Attribute Sets?
   a. Windows Server 2003
   b. Windows Server 2008
   c. Windows Server 2008 R2
   d. Windows Server 2012 R2

4. You have configured a user group on the Managed by tab of an RODC. You receive a call from a member of the group indicating he is not able to log in to the RODC at the remote location when the WAN link goes down. What do you need to do?
   a. Add the group to the Domain Admins Group
   b. Add the group to the Enterprise Admins Group
   c. Add the group to the Allowed RODC Password Replication Group
   d. Add the group to the Authenticated Users Group

5. When replicating a single object between domain controllers, what will you use to specify the object name?
   a. Distinguished Name (DN)
   b. Relative Distinguished Name (RDN)
   c. Security Account Manager ID (SAM ID)
   d. Common Name (CN)

6. Which of the following allows passwords to be cached on an RODC before users log in to the RODC?
   a. Change the user's password on the PDC emulator
   b. Disable and then re-enable the user account
   c. Allow Password Replication and configure "User must change password at next logon"
   d. Allow Password Replication and Password Prepopulation

7. Before upgrading your SYSVOL replication from FRS to DFSR, the Domain Functional Level must be at least what version?
   a. Windows Server 2003
   b. Windows Server 2008
   c. Windows Server 2008 R2
   d. Windows Server 2012 R2

8. What Global state of FRS to DFSR migration allows for rollback? (Choose all that apply.)
   a. State 0
   b. State 1
   c. State 2
   d. State 3

9. After performing an FRS to DFSR upgrade, what will the SYSVOL share be named?
   a. It will no longer exist.
   b. DFSR_SYSVOL
   c. SYSVOL
   d. SYSVOL_DFSR

10. What downloadable tool provides immediate access to related TechNet articles to assist in the resolution of common replication errors?
   a. ADREPLSTATUS
   b. Ultrasound
   c. REPADMIN
   d. Bing

Best Answer

1. Which cmdlet would you use to force replicate a single active directory object?
   a. `REPADMIN.EXE /ReplSingleObj`
   b. repadmin.exe /syncall /APed
   c. Sync-ADReplicationObject
   d. Sync-ADObject

2. What is the fastest way to reset 1000 user and computer passwords that have been cached on a stolen read-only domain controller?
   a. Delete the RODC
   b. Highlight all objects, right click, and select Reset Password
   c. Delete and recreate all user and computer objects
   d. Direct users to Forefront Identity Manager 2010 SP1 webpage

3. What command would you issue to verify your DFSR migration is in the "Eliminated" state and has succeeded?
   a. dfsrmig /GetGlobalState
   b. REPLMON.EXE
   c. REPADMIN /ReplSum
   d. dfsrmig /GetMigrationState

4. What attribute must be changed to mark an attribute as confidential and RODC Filtered?
   a. confidentialFlags
   b. secureRepl
   c. searchWindow
   d. searchFlags

5. Change notification is enabled by default in which of the following topologies?
   a. Intersite
   b. Intrasite
   c. Active Directory Domain Services
   d. Read-only domain controller

Matching and Identification

1. Identify the REPADMIN /SyncAll switches used to push replication across the enterprise, traversing between all sites, and synchronizing all partitions.
   _______ a) Push replication
   _______ b) All partitions
   _______ c) Enterprise wide
   _______ d) Resolve all names to Distinguished Name
   1. /d
   2. /a
   3. /e
   4. /P
   5. /p
   6. /A

2. Identify the tools and indicate how they can be used to monitor and manage replication.
   _______ a) Graphical User Interface (GUI) replication monitoring
   _______ b) Run from command prompt
   _______ c) Run from Windows PowerShell
   _______ d) Run from Active Directory Sites and Services
   1. Replicate Now
   2. REPADMIN.exe
   3. Sync-ADObject
   4. Set-ADObjectReplicate
   5. REPLMON
   6. Active Directory Replication Status Tool

3. Identify the command to force reexamination of the AD DS topology
   _______ REPADMIN /ReplSum
   _______ REPADMIN /ShowRepl
   _______ REPADMIN /SyncAll
   _______ REPADMIN /KCC
   _______ REPADMIN /XMN
   _______ REPADMIN /Scan

4. Identify the objects that should have their passwords cached on RODCs. Not all items will be used.
   _______ Group members
   _______ All users
   _______ Domain adminstrators
   _______ All computers
   _______ Only users and computers in the remote office
   _______ RODC administrators

Build a List

1. List the steps to migrate the SYSVOL folder from FRS to DFSR
   _______ dfsrmig /SetGlobalState 4
   _______ dfsrmig /SetGlobalState 2
   _______ dfsrmig /SetGlobalState 1
   _______ dfsrmig /SetGlobalState Status
   _______ dfsrmig /SetGlobalState 3
   _______ dfsrmig /SetGlobalState 0

Business Case Scenarios

Scenario 17-1: Forcing Replication

You are an enterprise administrator for a multisite, multidomain forest. You have recently made significant changes to the schema-naming context, and you must synchronize all domain controllers throughout the enterprise as soon as possible without waiting for Intersite replication to take place. What can you do to replicate the changes as soon as possible?

Scenario 17-2: Handling a Stolen Remote Site

You are the enterprise administrator for a multidomain, multisite forest. A remote site that held 30 desktops and 2 RODCs has been a victim of theft. All computers and servers have been stolen from the site. You have been notified within hours of the theft and are asked to reset all user account passwords, reset all computer accounts, and provide a list of all user accounts that have had their passwords potentially compromised. What steps must you take to perform the requested actions and to generate a report?

Scenario 17-3: Upgrading SYSVOL to DFSR

You are a domain administrator for a single forest, single domain. Your enterprise administrator has tasked you with planning and preparing the domain for an upgrade to DFSR for SYSVOL replication. Your environment contains two Windows Server 2003 domain controllers and two Windows Server 2012 R2 domain controllers. What steps must you take to prepare the domain for the upgrade?

LESSON 18

Implementing Active Directory Federation Services

70-412 EXAM OBJECTIVE

Objective 6.1 – Implement Active Directory Federation Services (AD FS). This objective may include but is not limited to: Install AD FS; implement claims-based authentication including relying party trusts; configure authentication policies; configure Workplace Join; configure multi-factor authentication.

LESSON HEADING	EXAM OBJECTIVE
Understanding Active Directory Federation Services	
Implementing AD FS	
Installing AD FS	Install AD FS
Creating a Standalone Federation Server	
Implementing Claims-Based Authentication	Implement claims-based authentication including relying party trusts
Implementing Relying Party Trusts	Implement claims-based authentication including relying party trusts
Configuring Claims Provider Trust Rules	
Configuring Authentication Policies	Configure authentication policies
Configuring Multi-Factor Authentication	Configure multi-factor authentication
Configuring Workplace Join	Configure Workplace Join
Testing Active Directory Federation	

KEY TERMS

account organizations
Active Directory Federation Services (AD FS)
attribute store
authentication policy
claim rules
claims
claims provider trust
claims providers
Device Registration Service
federated trust relationship
federation server
federation server proxy
multi-factor authentication (MFA)
relying parties
relying party trust
resource organizations
single sign-on (SSO)
Workplace Join

Understanding Active Directory Federation Services

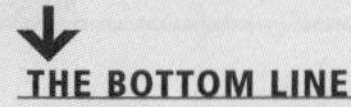
THE BOTTOM LINE

Active Directory Federation Services (AD FS) role allows administrators to configure ***Single Sign-On (SSO)*** for web-based applications across a single organization or multiple organizations without requiring users to remember multiple usernames and passwords. This enables you to configure Internet-facing business-to-business (B2B) applications between organizations. For example, a user from contoso.com can use contoso.com credentials to access a web-based application that is hosted by adatum.com.

Traditionally, if users from one organization/domain need to access a website provided by another organization/domain, you can do it one of two ways:

- For the web application, depending on the web application, create web or domain accounts for the user and have the user log in with the second account. Unfortunately, this does not give a single sign-on solution.
- Create a virtual private network (VPN) between the two organizations and establish a trust relationship between the two Active Directory domains. Although this gives a single sign-on solution, it is difficult to set up and maintain.

AD FS-enabled applications are claims based, which allows a much more scalable authentication model for Internet-facing applications. Therefore, AD FS is an identity access solution that allows any browser-based clients to access a website with a single login to one or more protected Internet-facing applications, even when the user accounts and applications are on different networks and exist within different organizations via a federated trust relationship.

An AD FS configuration consists of two types of organizations:

- ***Resource organizations:*** Organizations that own the resources or data that are accessible from the AD FS-enabled application, similar to a trusting domain in a traditional Windows trust relationship.
- ***Account organizations:*** Organizations that contain the user accounts that access the resources controlled by resource organizations.

Federation can be used within a single organization. Therefore, the single organization is the resource organization and the account organization.

Of course, to establish an identity federation partnership, both partners agree to create a ***federated trust relationship***. Each partner defines what resources are accessible to the other organization, and how access to the resources is enabled. User identities and their associated credentials are stored, owned, and managed by the organization where the user is located.

As you recall from lesson 6, claims based access control uses a trusted identity provider to provide authentication. The trusted identity provider issues a token to the user, which is then presented to the application or service as proof of identity. In other words, with claims-based authentication, users can authenticate to the Active Directory that is located within their organization, and be granted a claim based on that authentication. The claim is then presented to an application that is running in a different organization.

The organization that accepts the claim and has the application the user is trying to access will require key information in the claim (for example, an e-mail address or User Principal Name (UPN) to identify the user, and group membership to specify the access allowed within the application by the user).

To keep the claims secure, all communications occur over HTTPS. Of course, both organizations need to agree on the format for exchanging claims. To simplify this process, a set of specifications identified as web services have been identified, which can be used when implementing AD FS.

Web services are based on Extensible Markup Language (XML), Simple Object Access Protocol (SOAP), Web Services Description Language (WSDL), and Universal Discovery Description and Integration (UDDI). It also uses Security Assertion Markup Language (SAML), which is an XML-based standard for exchanging claims between an identity provider and a service or application provider. The communication between federation servers is based around an XML document that stores the X.509 certificate for token-signing, and the SAML 1.1 or 2.0 token.

AD FS uses the following components:

- ***Federation server:*** The server that issues, manages, and validates requests involving identity claims. A federations server is needed in each participating forest.
- ***Federation server proxy:*** An optional component that is usually deployed in a perimeter network such as DMZ that can receive externally and forward the packets to the internal federation server. In the Windows Server 2012, the Federation server proxy is installed as a AD FS role. In Windows Server 2012, the Federation server proxy is replaced by the Remote Access role service called Web Application Proxy.
- ***Claims:*** A statement made by a trusted entity about an object, such as a user, that includes key information identifying the user.
- ***Claim rules:*** Rules that determine what makes up a valid claim and how claims are processed by the federation servers.
- ***Attribute store:*** A database, such as AD DS, that is used to look up claim values.
- ***Claims providers:*** The server that issues claims and authenticates users.
- ***Relying parties:*** The application or web service that accepts claims from the claims provider. The relying party server must have the Microsoft Windows Identity Foundation installed, or use the AD FS 1.0 claims-aware agent.
- ***Claims provider trust:*** Configuration data that specifies which client may request claims from a claims provider and subsequently submits them to a relying party.
- ***Relying party trust:*** Configuration data that is used to provide claims about a user or client to a relying party.

In the simplest scenario, an organization may deploy a federation server to be used with its own web applications. If the web application is running on Windows and is part of the same domain as the users who are accessing the web application, you can bypass the federation server and grant access directly to the Active Directory users. However, in more complicated scenarios, an organization might require AD FS:

- The application is not running on Windows or does not support AD DS authentication.
- The Windows server is not part of the domain and requires SAML or web services for authentication or authorization.
- A larger organization that consists of multiple domains or multiple forests, and the organization has multiple identities.
- Users from outside the organization need access to internal servers and are not part of the domain.

When a single organization uses AD FS, you need only one federation server (not including what might be needed for high-availability). If the network with the federation server is completely isolated, you need a second server to act as a federation proxy server. For AD FS to provide SSO for a single organization, the following would happen:

1. The client computer accesses a web-based application on a web server by sending an HTTPS request.
2. When the web server receives the request and identifies that the client computer does not have a claim, the web server redirects the client computer to the Federation Service Proxy, if a proxy is being used. If not, it will forward the request to the federation server.

3. If the AD FS is using a proxy, the client computer sends an HTTPS request to the Federation Service Proxy. Depending on the configuration and setup, the Federation Service Proxy might use the current Windows login (Integrated Windows authentication) or prompt for a login.
4. If the AD FS is using the proxy, the Federation Service Proxy passes on the request and the credentials to the federation server.
5. The federation server uses AD DS to authenticate the user.
6. If authentication is successful, the federation server collects AD DS information about the user and generates the user's claims.
7. The claim is put into a security token, which is passed back to the client computer.
8. The client presents the token to the web server and uses the claims to access to the application.

■ Implementing AD FS

Before you implement AD FS, you need to plan your implementation. You should also create a test environment so that you can foresee the potential problems.

First, you should make sure that the client and servers can communicate with the necessary computers, which includes:

- The client must be able to communicate with the web application, the resource federation server (or federation server proxy), and the account federation server (or federation proxy) using HTTPS.
- If you are using federation server proxy, you must be able to communicate with the federation servers in the same organization using HTTPS.
- The internal clients must be able to communicate with the organization's federation servers.
- The client federation server must be able to communicate with the client domain controllers for authentication.

The domain controllers must be running a minimum of Windows Server 2003 with SP1. The federation servers must be joined to the AD DS domain.

AD FS supports the following attribute stores:

- Active Directory Application Mode (ADAM) in Windows Server 2003
- Active Directory Lightweight Directory Services (AD LDS) in Windows Server 2008, Windows Server 2008 R2, Windows Server 2012, and Windows Server 2012 R2
- Microsoft SQL Server 2008 (all editions)
- Microsoft SQL Server 2008 R2
- Microsoft SQL Server 2012
- A custom attribute store

AD FS requires DNS names for internal federation servers to which they connect, and the web application that they are trying to use. If the user is an external user, he or she also needs to resolve the name of the internal federation server through the proxy server.

When installing the AD FS server role, you then configure the server as either a federation server or federation server proxy. After installing the federation server role, you can configure the server as a claims provider, a relying party, or both. The claims provider provides the users signed tokens that contain claims, whereas the relying party receives the security tokens from a trusted claims provider. The relying party accepts and validates the claim, and then issues new security tokens that the web server can use to provide appropriate access to the application.

Installing AD FS

Installing the Active Directory Federation Services role and creating the federation server is a simple process using Server Manager. To configure the federation server, you will need a SSL certificate.

CERTIFICATION READY
Install AD FS.
Objective 6.1

With Windows Server 2012, the Active Directory Federation Services role includes the Federation Service, AD FS 1.1 Web Agents, and Federation Service Proxy. With Windows Server 2012 R2, AD FS only includes the Federation Service. If you need a reverse proxy, you will instead install the Remote Access role, specifically the Web Application Proxy role service.

TAKE NOTE*
The Web Application Proxy configuration is stored on the AD FS servers in your organization. However, the Web Application Proxy is covered in the 70-411 exam.

INSTALL THE ACTIVE DIRECTORY FEDERATION SERVICES

GET READY. To install the Active Directory Federation Services, perform the following steps:

1. On *Server01*, click the Server Manager button on the task bar to open the *Server Manager*.
2. At the top of *Server Manager*, click Manage and click Add Roles and Features. The *Add Roles and Feature Wizard* opens.
3. On the *Before you begin* page, click Next.
4. Select Role-based or feature-based installation and then click Next.
5. Select Active Directory Federation Services and click Next.
6. On the *Select features* page, click Next.
7. On the *Active Directory Federation Services (AD FS)* page, click Next.
8. On the *Confirm installation selections* page, click Install.
9. When the installation is complete, leave the installation screen open for the next exercise.

Creating a Standalone Federation Server

You can configure Active Directory Federation Services as either a standalone server or as part of a server farm. You would use a standalone server when you want to evaluate AD FS or you want to use it for a small production environment. If you need high availability or load-balancing, you will create an AD FS farm.

Before you create the standalone federation server, you will need to have a managed service account, which will be used to run the federation services. You will also need an SSL digital certificate. If you need to import the digital certificate, you will import the certificate from a .pfx file, which will include the public and private key.

CREATE A STANDALONE FEDERATION SERVER

GET READY. To create a standalone federation server, perform the following steps:

1. On *Server01*, using the Server Manager, click Configure the federation service on this server.
2. In the *Active Directory Federation Services Configuration Wizard*, on the *Welcome page*, the Create the first federation server in a federation server farm is already selected. Click Next.
3. On the *Connect* to *AD DS* page, click Next.
4. On the *Specify Service Properties* page, select the certificate for the federation server. If a certificate is not available, you will need to import a certificate from a .pfx file using the Import button.
5. In the *Federation Service Name* box, type the name of the Federation Service (such as Contoso Corporation), as shown in Figure 18-1. Click Next.

Figure 18-1
Specifying the service properties

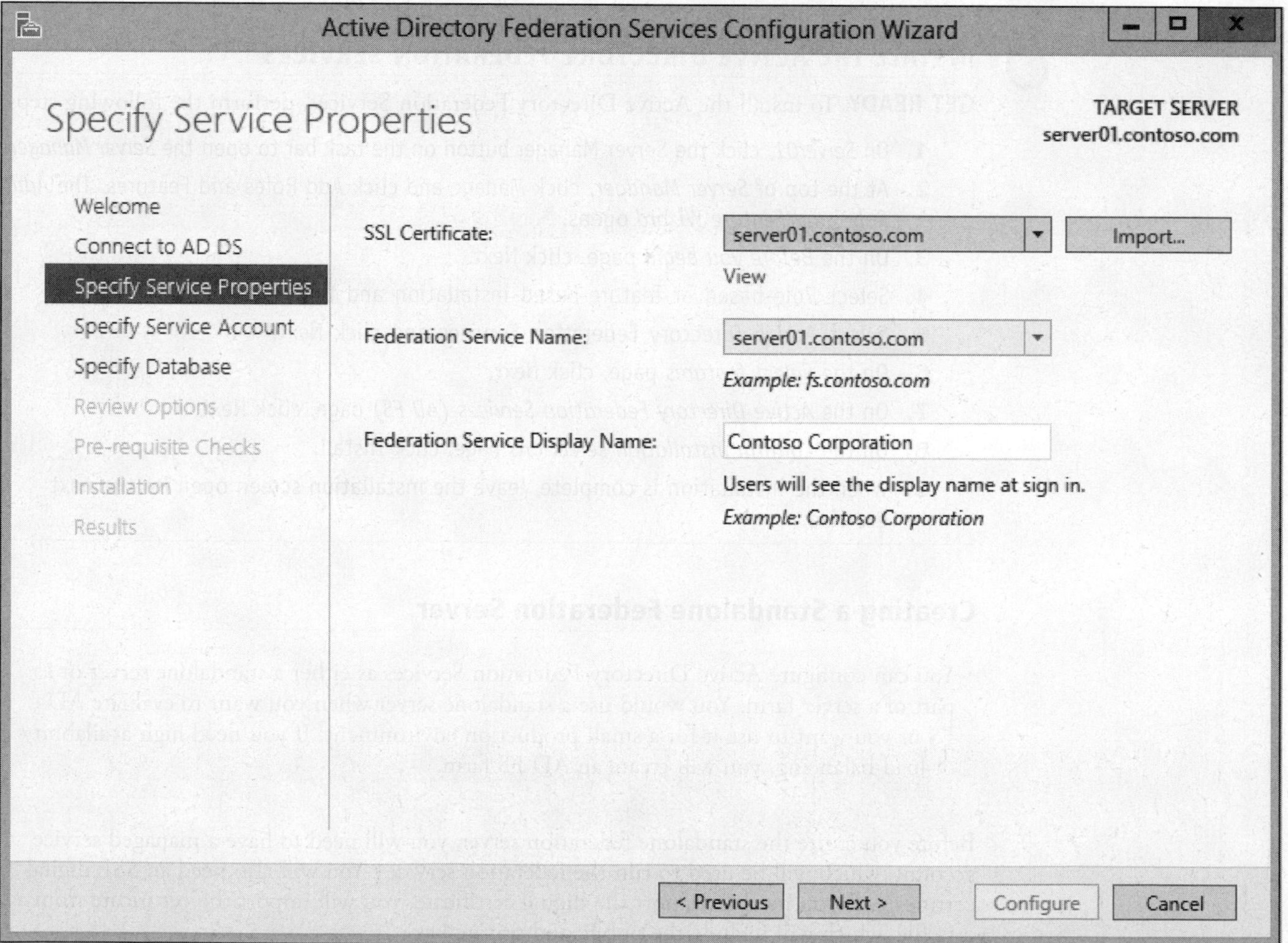

6. On the *Specify Service* Account page, select the Use an existing domain user account or group Managed Service Account option and then click Select. In the *Select User or Service Account* dialog box, in the *Enter the object name to select* text box, type the name of a service account (such as *adfs*) and then click OK.
7. Back on the *Specify Service Account* page, in the *Account Password* text box, type in the password for the *adfs* service account and then click Next.
8. On the Specify Configuration Database page, Create a database on this server using *Windows Internal Database is already* selected. Click Next.
9. On the *Review* Options page, click Next.
10. On the *Pre-requisite Checks* page, click Configure.

After the federation server is created, you will manage the Federation Service by using the AF FS console (as shown in Figure 18-2) or by using Windows PowerShell. In both methods, you can manage certificates within AD FS and you can create and manage Claims Provider Trusts, Relying Party Trusts, Attribute Stores, and Authentication Policies.

Figure 18-2

Accessing the AD FS console

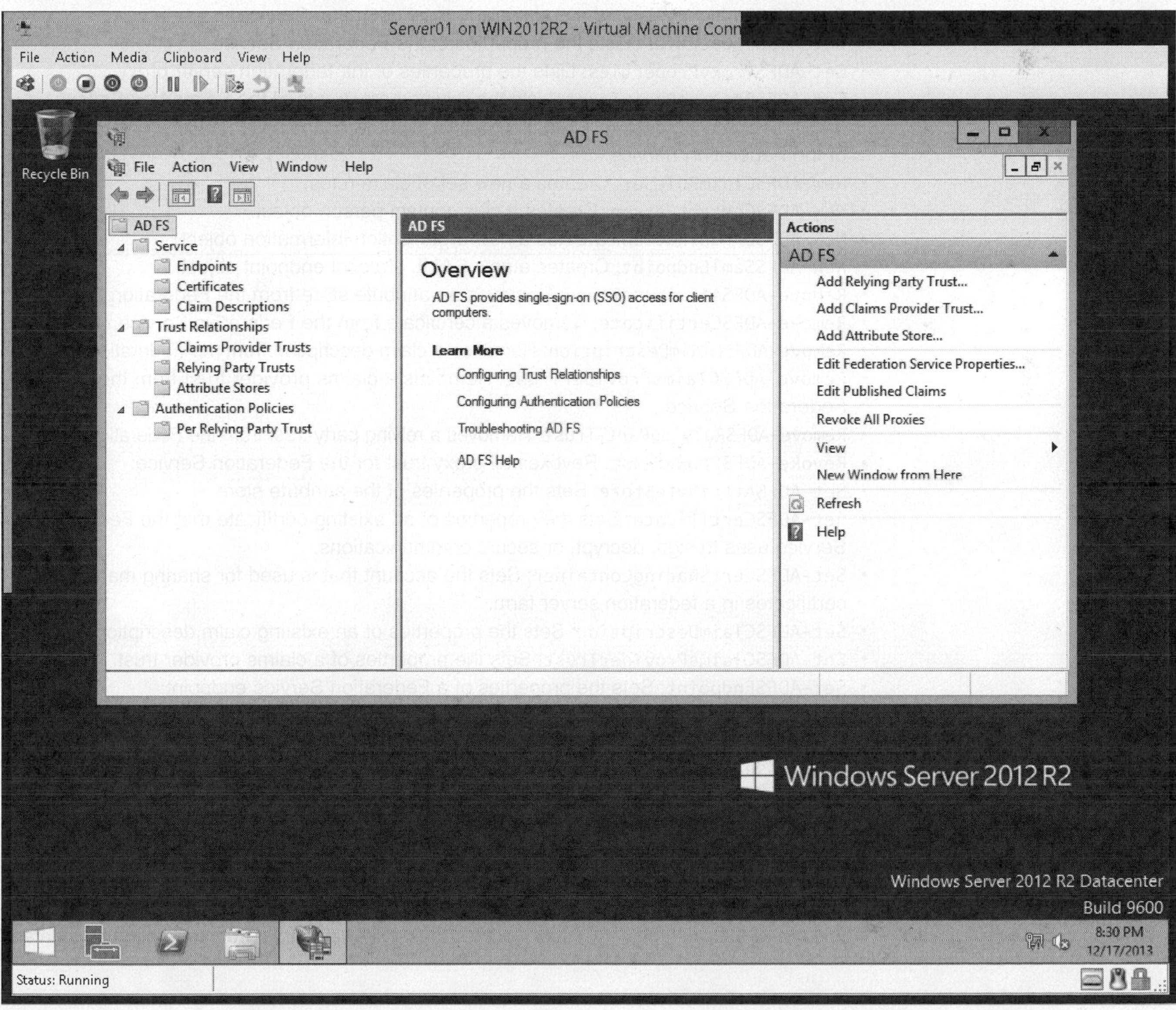

USING WINDOWS POWERSHELL

You can manage AD FS using Windows PowerShell by using the following cmdlets:

- `Add-ADFSAttributeStore`: Adds an attribute store to the Federation Service.
- `Add-ADFSCertificate`: Adds a new certificate to the Federation Service for signing, decrypting, or securing communications.
- `Add-ADFSClaimDescription`: Adds a claim description to the Federation Service.
- `Add-ADFSClaimsProviderTrust`: Adds a new claims provider trust to the Federation Service.
- `Add-ADFSRelyingPartyTrust`: Adds a new relying party trust to the Federation Service.
- `Disable-ADFSClaimsProviderTrust`: Disables a claims provider trust in the Federation Service.
- `Disable-ADFSEndpoint`: Disables an endpoint of the Federation Service.
- `Disable-ADFSRelyingPartyTrust`: Disables a relying party trust of the Federation Service.
- `Enable-ADFSClaimsProviderTrust`: Enables a claims provider trust in the Federation Service.
- `Enable-ADFSEndpoint`: Enables an endpoint in the Federation Service.
- `Enable-ADFSRelyingPartyTrust`: Enables a relying party trust of the Federation Service.
- `Get-ADFSAttributeStore`: Lists the attribute stores of the Federation Service.
- `Get-ADFSCertificate`: Lists the certificates that are in the Federation Service.
- `Get-ADFSClaimDescription`: Lists claim descriptions that are in the Federation Service.
- `Get-ADFSClaimsProviderTrust`: Lists the claims provider trusts in the Federation Service.
- `Get-ADFSEndpoint`: Lists the endpoints in the Federation Service.
- `Get-ADFSProperties`: Lists the properties of the Federation Service.
- `Get-ADFSProxyProperties`: Lists the properties of the federation server proxy.
- `Get-ADFSRelyingPartyTrust`: Lists the relying party trusts of the Federation Service.
- `Get-ADFSSyncProperties`: Lists the configuration database synchronization properties of the Federation Service.
- `New-ADFSClaimRuleSet`: Creates a new set of claim rules.
- `New-ADFSContactPerson`: Creates a new contact person object.
- `New-ADFSOrganization`: Creates a new organization information object.
- `New-ADFSSamlEndpoint`: Creates a new SAML protocol endpoint object.
- `Remove-ADFSAttributeStore`: Removes an attribute store from the Federation Service.
- `Remove-ADFSCertificate`: Removes a certificate from the Federation Service.
- `Remove-ADFSClaimDescription`: Removes a claim description from the Federation Service.
- `Remove-ADFSClaimsProviderTrust`: Removes a claims provider trust from the Federation Service.
- `Remove-ADFSRelyingPartyTrust`: Removes a relying party trust from the Federation Service.
- `Revoke-ADFSProxyTrust`: Revokes all proxy trust for the Federation Service.
- `Set-ADFSAttributeStore`: Sets the properties of the attribute store.
- `Set-ADFSCertificate`: Sets the properties of an existing certificate that the Federation Service uses to sign, decrypt, or secure communications.
- `Set-ADFSCertSharingContainer`: Sets the account that is used for sharing managed certificates in a federation server farm.
- `Set-ADFSClaimDescription`: Sets the properties of an existing claim description.
- `Set-ADFSClaimsProviderTrust`: Sets the properties of a claims provider trust.
- `Set-ADFSEndpoint`: Sets the properties of a Federation Service endpoint.
- `Set-ADFSProperties`: Sets the properties of the Federation Service.
- `Set-ADFSProxyProperties`: Sets the properties of the federation server proxy.
- `Set-ADFSRelyingPartyTrust`: Sets the properties of a relying party trust.
- `Set-ADFSSyncProperties`: Sets the properties of the database synchronization engine for the federation server farm.
- `Update-ADFSCertificate`: Updates the certificates of the Federation Service.
- `Update-ADFSClaimsProviderTrust`: Updates the claims provider trust from federation metadata.
- `Update-ADFSRelyingPartyTrust`: Updates the relying party trust from federation metadata.

Implementing Claims-Based Authentication

To implement claims-based authentication in a lab environment, you would use three servers. The RWDC01 acts as the domain controller. Server01 is the federation server, and Server02 is the application that will use the claims.

CERTIFICATION READY
Implement claims-based authentication including relying party trusts.
Objective 6.1

To install and configure AD FS for a single organization, you need to perform the following steps:

1. Install the AD FS server role.
2. Create and configure a server authentication certificate in IIS.
3. Create a standalone federation server.
4. Install and configure Windows Identity Foundation (WIF) and a sample application.
5. Create and configure the WIF application pool.
6. Configure the WIF sample application to trust incoming claims.
7. Configure AD FS to send claims to the application.
8. Configure the claim rule for the sample application.
9. Test access to the application.

Normally as a server administrator, you only deploy the application; you do not create the application. So for the test environment, you install the Windows Identity Foundation SDK 4.0, which can be found on the Microsoft website. To install the Windows Identity Foundation SDK 4.0, you need to install .NET Framework 3.5 and the Windows Identity Foundation 3.5, which is not included with Windows Server 2012 or Windows Server 2012 R2.

INSTALL THE WINDOWS IDENTITY FOUNDATION SDK 4.0

GET READY. To install the Windows Identity Foundation SDK 4.0, perform the following steps:

1. On *Server02*, click the Server Manager button on the task bar to open the *Server Manager*.
2. At the top of *Server Manager*, click Manage and click Add Roles and Features. The *Add Roles and Feature Wizard* opens.
3. On the *Before you begin* page, click Next.
4. Select Role-based or feature-based installation and then click Next.
5. On the *Select server roles* page, click Next.
6. On the *Select features* page, expand .Net Framework 3.5 Features, and click to select the .NET Framework 3.5 (includes .NET 2.0 and 3.0).
7. Click to select the Windows Identity Foundation 3.5. Click Next.
8. On the *Confirm installation selections* page, click Install.
9. When the installation is complete, click Close.
10. To install the *Windows Identity Foundation SDK*, double-click the WindowsIdentityFoundation-SDK-4.0.msi.
11. When the *Windows Identity Foundation SDK 4.0 Setup Wizard* starts, click Next.
12. On the *End-User License Agreement* page, click to select the I accept the terms in the License Agreement option. Click Next.
13. On the *Destination Folder* page, click Next.
14. On the *Ready to install Windows Identity Foundation SDK 40* page, click Install.

15. When the installation is complete, click Finish.
16. Close the Welcome to the Microsoft Windows Identity Foundation window.

The Windows Identity Foundation SDK 4.0 includes a sample WIF application. After you install the sample WIF application, you need to configure the application. Lastly, you need to create an application pool for the application.

CREATE AND CONFIGURE A SAMPLE WIF APPLICATION

GET READY. To create and configure a Sample WIF application, perform the following steps:

1. Using *Server Manager*, open the Tools menu, and click Internet Information Services (IIS) Manager.
2. When the *Internet Information Services (IIS) Manager* console opens, click Create Self-Signed Certificate.
3. On the *Specify Friendly Name* page, in the *Specify a friendly name for the certificate* text box, type Server02.contoso.com. Click OK.
4. In the left pane, expand Sites and click the Default Web Site.
5. Under Actions, click Bindings.
6. When the *Site Bindings* page opens, click Add.
7. When the *Add Site Binding* dialog box opens, change the *Type* to https. Then under *SSL certificate*, select the server02, contoso.com, and click OK.
8. Click Close to close the *Site Bindings* dialog box.
9. On the task bar, click the folder to open Windows Explorer and navigate to the `C:\Program Files (x86)\Windows Identity Foundation SDK\v4.0\Samples\Quick Start\Using Managed STS` folder.
10. Double-click setup.bat. When the application has been created, click OK.
11. Close the command prompt window and the Windows Explorer window.
12. Click the Start menu button, click the down arrow to show all programs, and click Windows Identity Foundation Federation Utility.
13. When the *Federation Utility Wizard* opens, in the *Application configuration location* text box, type the following:

    `C:\Program Files (x86)\Windows Identity Foundation SDK\v4.0\Samples\Quick Start\Using Managed STS\ClaimsAwareWebAppwithManagedSTS\web.config`
14. In *Application URI*, type `https://server02.contoso.com/ClaimsAwareWebAppWithManagedSTS` to indicate the path to the sample application that will trust the incoming claims from the federation server. Click Next to continue.
15. On the *Security Token Service* page, select Use an existing STS, type `https://server01.contoso.com/FederationMetadata/2007-06/FederationMetadata.xml` for the *STS WS-Federation metadata document location* text box, and then click Next to continue.
16. When you get a warning because you are using a self-signed certificate, click Yes.
17. On the *STS signing certificate chain validation error*, with Disabled certificate chain validation already selected, click Next.
18. On the *Security token encryption* page, select No encryption, and then click Next.
19. On the *Offered claims* page, review the claims that will be offered by the federation server, and then click Next.
20. On the *Summary* page, click Finish.
21. When you have successfully configured the application, click OK.

22. Using the *Server Manager*, open the Tools menu, and click Internet Information Services (IIS) Manager.
23. When the *Internet Information Services (IIS) Manager* console opens, click Application Pools. Figure 18-3 shows the Application Pools.

Figure 18-3
Viewing IIS Application Pools

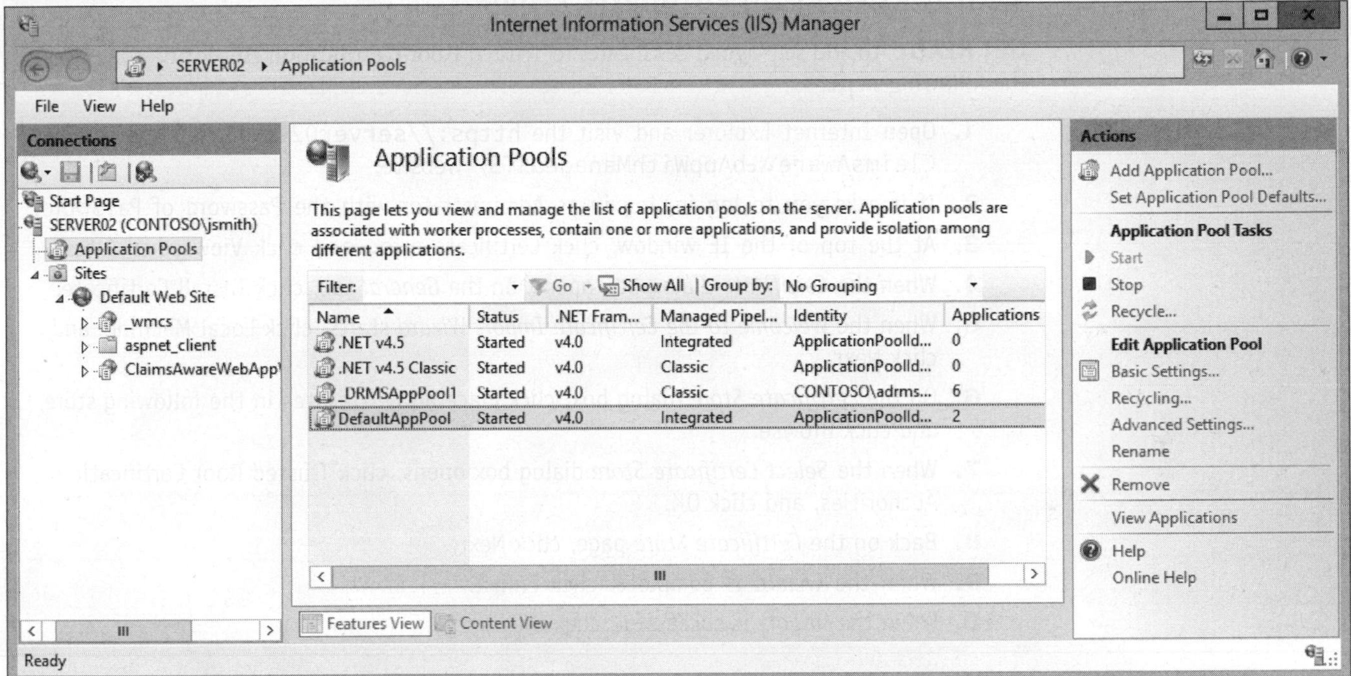

24. In the *Actions* pane, click Add Application Pool.
25. When the *Add Application Pool* dialog box opens, in the *Name* text box, type WIFSamples and click OK.
26. Click WIFSamples, and click Advanced Settings.
27. In the *Advanced Settings* dialog box, expand Process Model.
28. Change the *Load User Profile* setting from False to True.
29. Click OK to close the *Advanced Settings* dialog box.
30. In the left pane, expand Sites, expand Default Web Site, and click ClaimsAwareWebAppWithManagedSTS.
31. In the *Actions* pane, click Basic Settings.
32. When the *Edit Application* dialog box opens, click Select.
33. When the *Select Application Pool* dialog box opens, change the *Application pool* to WIFSamples and click OK.
34. Click OK to close the *Edit Application* dialog box.

In a test environment, it is common to use self-signed digital certificates. When you use self-signed certificates, you get warnings when accessing websites using self-signed certificates. To avoid the errors, and to allow the application using WIF to function properly, you need to add the websites digital certificate into the local computer Trusted Root Certification Authorities store.

ADD SELF-SIGNED CERTIFICATES TO TRUSTED ROOT CERTIFICATION AUTHORITY STORE

GET READY. To add self-signed certificates to Trusted Root Certification Authority store, perform the following steps:

1. Open Internet Explorer and visit the `https://server02.contoso.com/ClaimsAwareWebAppWithManagedSTS/` website.
2. If it asks you to log in, log in as Administrator with the Password of Pa$$word.
3. At the top of the IE window, click Certificate error, and click View certificates.
4. When the *Certificate* dialog box opens, on the *General* tab, click Install Certificate.
5. When the *Welcome to the Certificate Import Wizard* starts, click Local Machine, and click Next.
6. On the *Certificate Store* dialog box, click Place all certificates in the following store, and click Browse.
7. When the *Select Certificate Store* dialog box opens, click Trusted Root Certification Authorities, and click OK.
8. Back on the *Certificate Store* page, click Next.
9. When the wizard is complete, click Finish.
10. When the import is successful, click OK.

Implementing Relying Party Trusts

A relying party trust identifies the relying party so that the federation server knows which applications can use AD FS. It also defines the claim rules, from the claims provider. The relying party is defined on the federation server.

CERTIFICATION READY
Implement claims-based authentication including relying party trusts.
Objective 6.1

In a single organization that uses AD FS, the relying party trust defines how the AD FS server interfaces with the applications. When you configure the relying party trust, you specify the URL of the internal application, and configure settings such as whether the application supports SAML 2.0 or whether it requires AD FS 1.0 tokens, the SSL certificate and URL used by the web server, and the issuance authorization rules for the application. If you are configuring a Business-to-Business Federation, you need to create additional relying party trusts for each federated organization.

When configuring a relying party trust, you have three options (see Figure 18-4):

Figure 18-4

Configuring a relying party trust

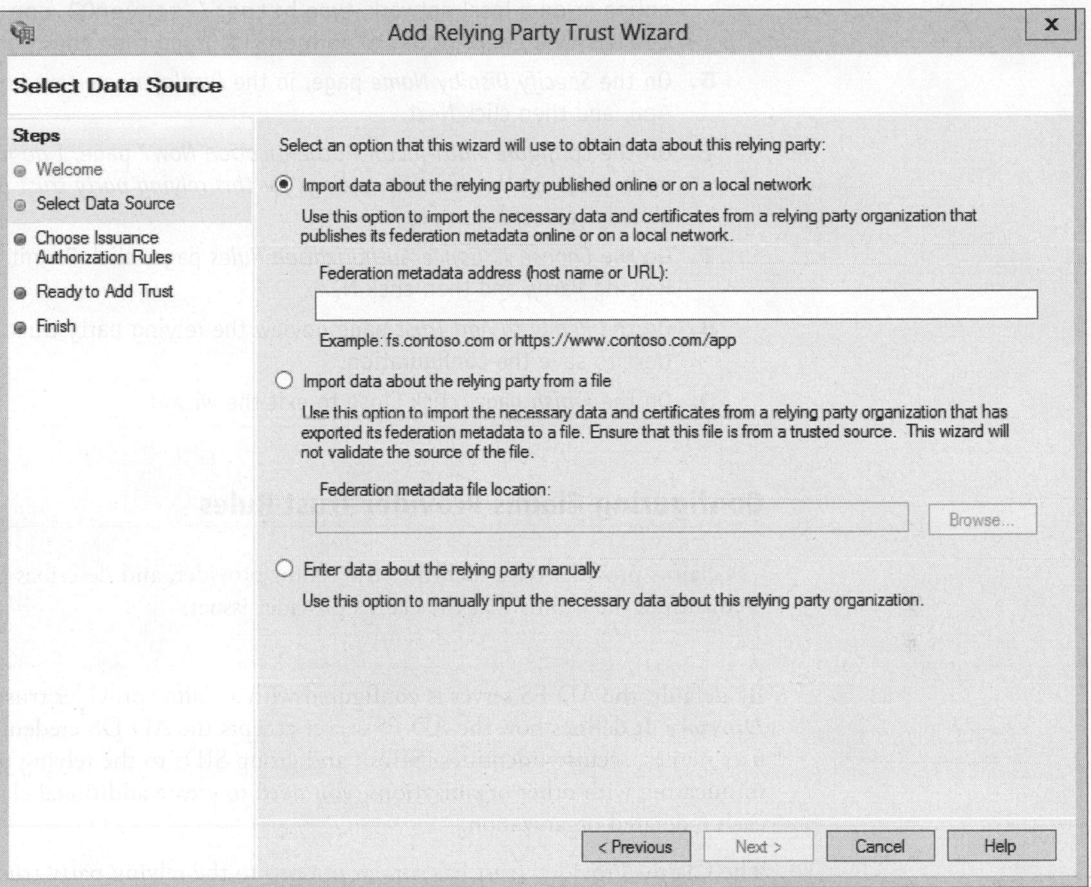

- **Import data about the relying party through the federation metadata:** If the AD FS federation server or federation proxy server is accessible through the network from your AD FS federation server, you can enter the host name or URL for the partner federation server. The AD FS connects to the AD FS federation server to download the federation metadata, which includes all the information that is required to configure the relying party trust. The trust also downloads the SSL certificate that the partner federation server uses.
- **Import data about the relying party from a file:** If the partner federation server is not directly accessible from the federation server, you can export the configuration information to a file, which you can then upload. The configuration file includes the configuration information for the partner organization and the SSL certificate that the partner federation server uses.
- **Manually configure the claims provider trust:** Allows you to manually configure all of the settings for the claims to provide trust.

IMPLEMENT RELYING PARTY TRUSTS

GET READY. To implement relying party trusts, perform the following steps:

1. In the *AD FS Management* console, click AD FS, expand Trust Relationships, and click Relying Party Trusts.
2. Right-click Relying Party Trusts, and click Add Relying Party Trust.

3. When the *Add Relying Party Trust Wizard* opens, click Start.
4. On the *Select Data Source* page, click Import data about the relying party published online or on a local network, type `https://server02.contoso.com/ClaimsAwareWebAppWithManagedSTS/`, and then click Next.
5. On the *Specify Display Name* page, in the *Display name* text box, type WIF Sample App, and then click Next.
6. On the *Configure Multi-factor Authentication Now?* page, *I do not want to configure multi-factor authentication settings for this relying party trust at this time* option is already selected. Click Next.
7. On the *Choose Issuance Authorization Rules* page, click Permit all users to access this Relying Party, and then click Next.
8. On the *Ready to Add Trust* page, review the relying party trust settings, and then click Next to save the configuration.
9. On the *Finish* page, click Close to exit the wizard.

Configuring Claims Provider Trust Rules

A claims provider trust identifies the claims provider, and describes how the relying party consumes the claims that the claims provider issues.

By default, the AD FS server is configured with a claims provider trust named *Active Directory*. It defines how the AD FS server accepts the AD DS credentials, including which user names, security identifies (SIDs), and group SIDs to the relying party. If you are communicating with other organizations, you need to create additional claims provider trusts for each federated organization.

The Claims Provider Trust has similar options to the relying party trusts. The options include:

- Import data about the claims provider through the federation metadata.
- Import data about the claims provider from a file.
- Manually configure the claims provider trust.

CONFIGURE THE ACTIVE DIRECTORY CLAIMS PROVIDER TRUST

GET READY. To configure the Active Directory Claims Provider Trust, perform the following steps:

1. In the *AD FS* console, expand Claims Provider Trusts.
2. In the middle pane, right-click Active Directory, and then click Edit Claim Rules. The *Edit Claims Rules for Active Directory* dialog box opens (see Figure 18-5).

Figure 18-5

Viewing the current claim rules

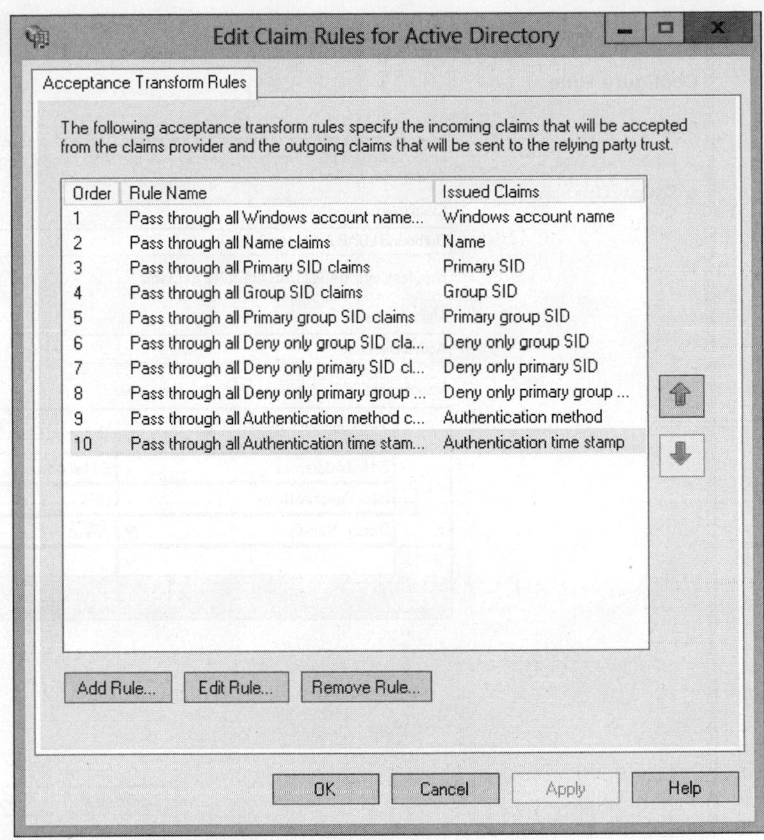

3. In the *Edit Claims Rules for Active Directory* window, on the *Acceptance Transform Rules* tab, click Add Rule.
4. When the *Add Transform Claim Rule Wizard* starts, in the *Select Rule Template* page, under *Claim rule template*, select Send LDAP Attributes as Claims, and then click Next.
5. On the *Configure Rule* page, in the *Claim rule* name box, type Outbound LDAP Attributes Rule.
6. In the *Attribute Store* drop-down list, select Active Directory.
7. In the *Mapping of LDAP attributes to outgoing claim types* section, select the following values for the *LDAP Attribute* and the *Outgoing Claim Type* (see Figure 18-6):
   - E-Mail-Addresses = E-Mail Address
   - User-Principal-Name = UPN
   - Display-Name = Name

Figure 18-6

Mapping LDAP attributes to outgoing claims

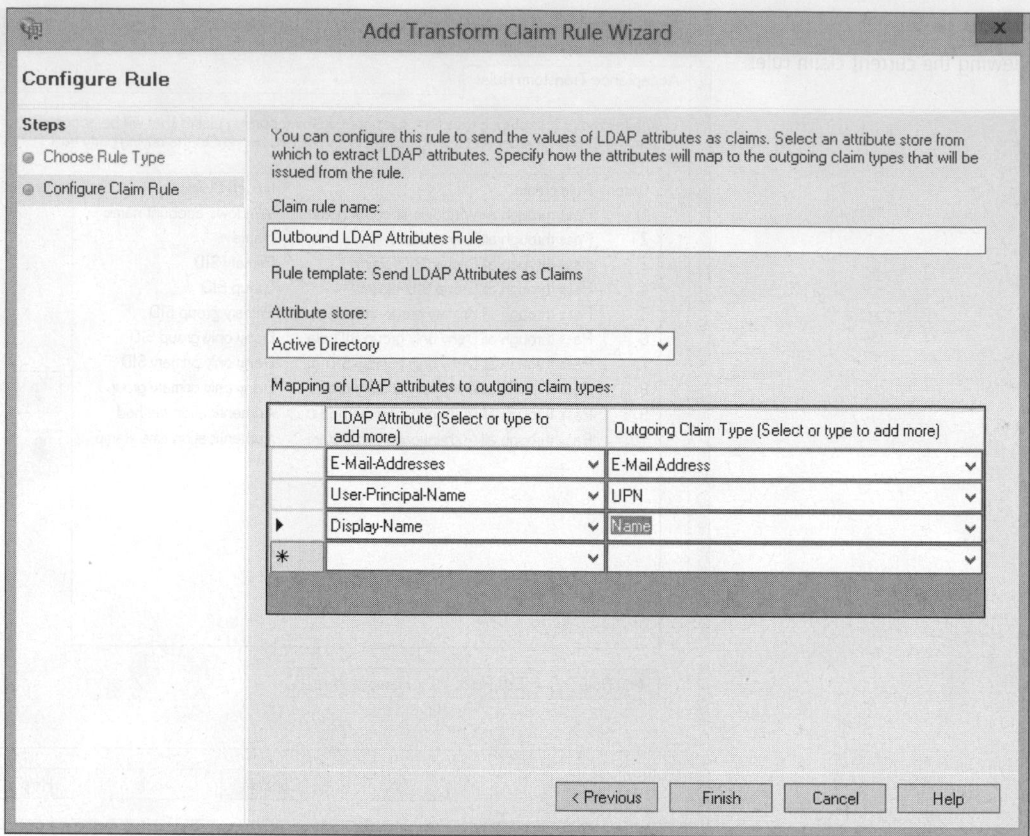

8. Click Finish, and then click OK.

Configuring Authentication Policies

Starting in Windows Server 2012, you can use authentication policies with AD FS to give you more control on who can use an AD FS application or service.

CERTIFICATION READY
Configure authentication policies.
Objective 6.1

In Windows Server 2012 R2, AD FS can be accessed with authentication policies and multi-factor authentication (including using user, device, location, and authentication data). The ***authentication policy*** specifies the type of authentication globally for applications and services that are secured by AD FS or for a particular application per relying party trust.

CONFIGURE A GLOBAL AUTHENTICATION POLICY

GET READY. To configure a global authentication policy, perform the following steps:

1. Using *Server Manager*, click Tools > AD FS Management.

2. In the *AD FS* console, click Authentication Policies, as shown in Figure 18-7.

Figure 18-7

Accessing the Authentication Policies node

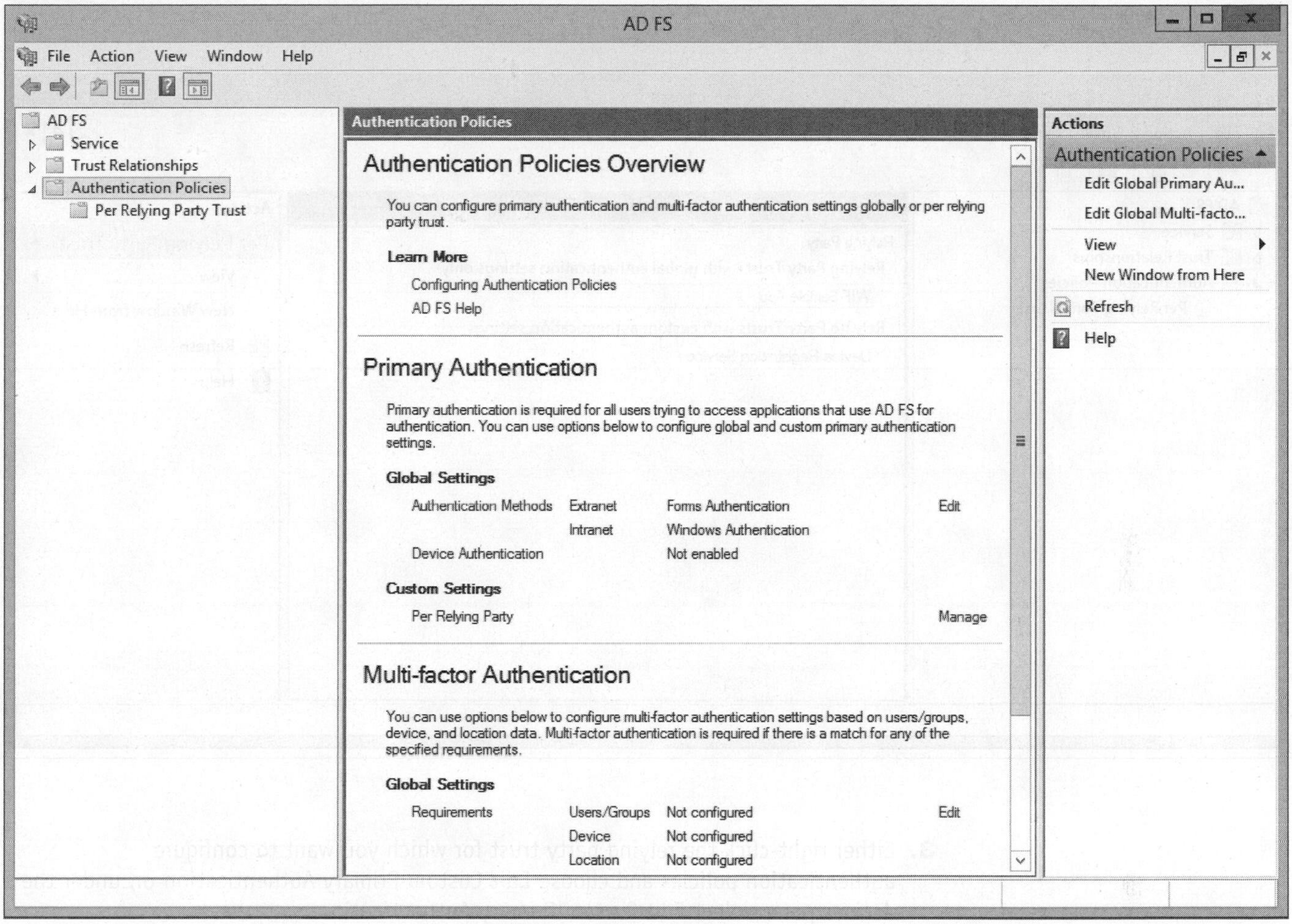

3. In the *Primary Authentication* section, click Edit. You can also right-click Authentication Policies and choose Edit Global Primary Authentication or, under the *Actions* pane, select Edit Global Primary Authentication.
4. In the *Edit Global Authentication Policy* dialog box, on the *Primary* tab, you can configure the following settings:
   - Authentication methods to be used for primary authentication including *Forms Authentication* and *Certificate Authentication* for *Extranet*, and *Forms Authentication*, *Certificate Authentication*, and *Windows Authentication* for *Intranet*.
   - Enable Device authentication via the *Enable device authentication* check box.
5. To close the *Edit Global Authentication Policy* dialog box, click OK.

CONFIGURE PRIMARY AUTHENTICATION PER RELYING PARTY TRUST

GET READY. To configure primary authentication per relying party trust, perform the following steps:

1. Using *Server Manager*, click Tools > AD FS Management.

2. In the *AD FS* console, click Authentication Policies\Per Relying Party Trust (as shown in Figure 18-8), and then click the relying party trust for which you want to configure authentication policies.

Figure 18-8

Accessing the Authentication Policies node

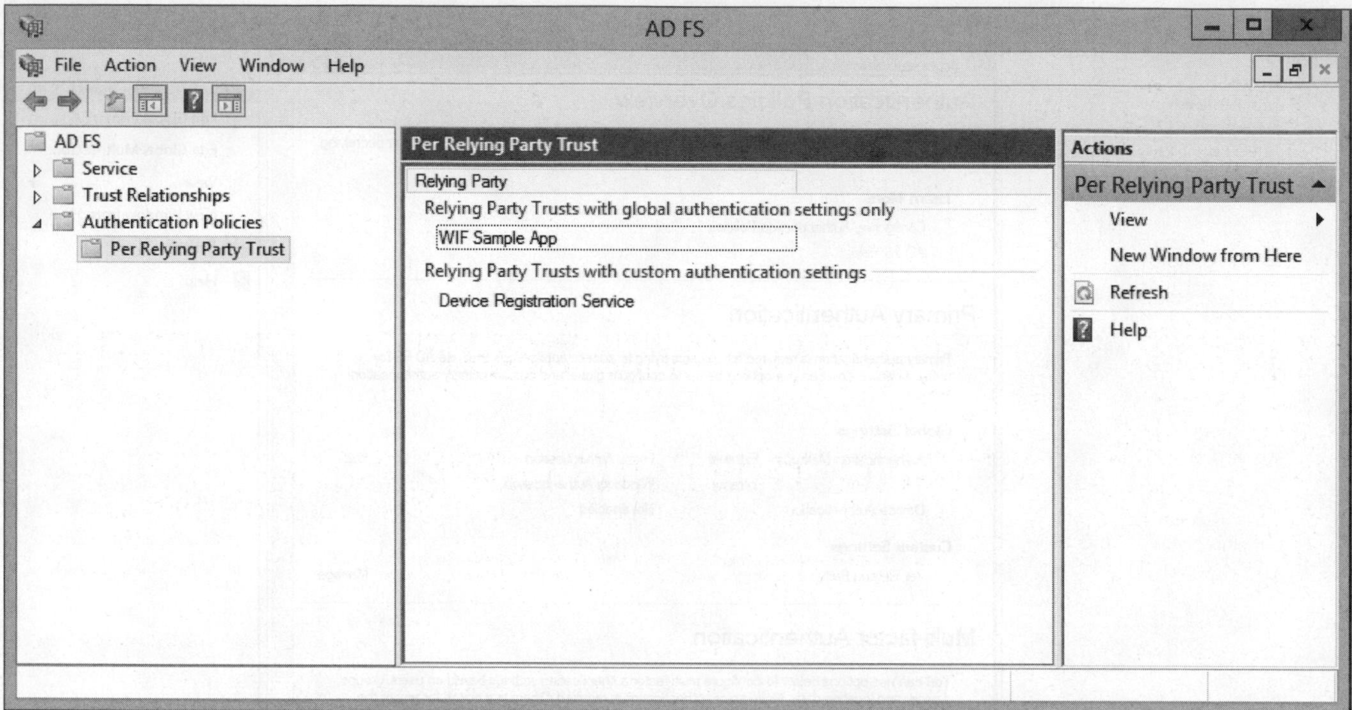

3. Either right-click the relying party trust for which you want to configure authentication policies and choose Edit Custom Primary Authentication or, under the *Actions* pane, select Edit Custom Primary Authentication.
4. In the Edit Authentication Policy dialog box, you can select or deselect the Users are required to provide credentials each time at sign in check box.
5. Click OK to close the *Edit Authentication Policy* dialog box.

Configuring Multi-Factor Authentication

With Windows Server 2012 R2, AD FS access control is enhanced with ***multi-factor authentication (MFA)***, including user, group, device, location, and authentication data. Windows Server 2012 R2 includes new claim types, such as client application, device operating system type, device operating system version, public key, thumbprint, inside corporate network, and password expiration time.

CERTIFICATION READY
Configure multi-factor authentication.
Objective 6.1

Using multifactor access control with AD FS in Windows Server 2012 R2 has the following benefits:

- Allows for flexible authorization policies that allow you to permit or deny access based on user, device, network location, and authentication state.
- Allows creating issuance authorization rules for relying party applications.
- Provides a rich UI experience for the common multifactor access control scenarios.

- Provides rich claims language and Windows PowerShell support for advanced multifactor access control scenarios.
- Allows you to use custom 'Access Denied' messages.

CONFIGURE GLOBAL MULTI-FACTOR AUTHENTICATION

GET READY. To configure global multi-factor authentication, perform the following steps:

1. Using *Server Manager*, click Tools > AD FS Management.
2. In the *AD FS* console, click the Authentication Policies node.
3. In the *Multi-factor Authentication* section (as shown in Figure 18-9), click Edit. You can also right-click Authentication Policies and choose Edit Global Multi-factor Authentication or, under the *Actions* pane, select Edit Global Multi-factor Authentication.

Figure 18-9

Accessing the Multi-factor Authentication settings

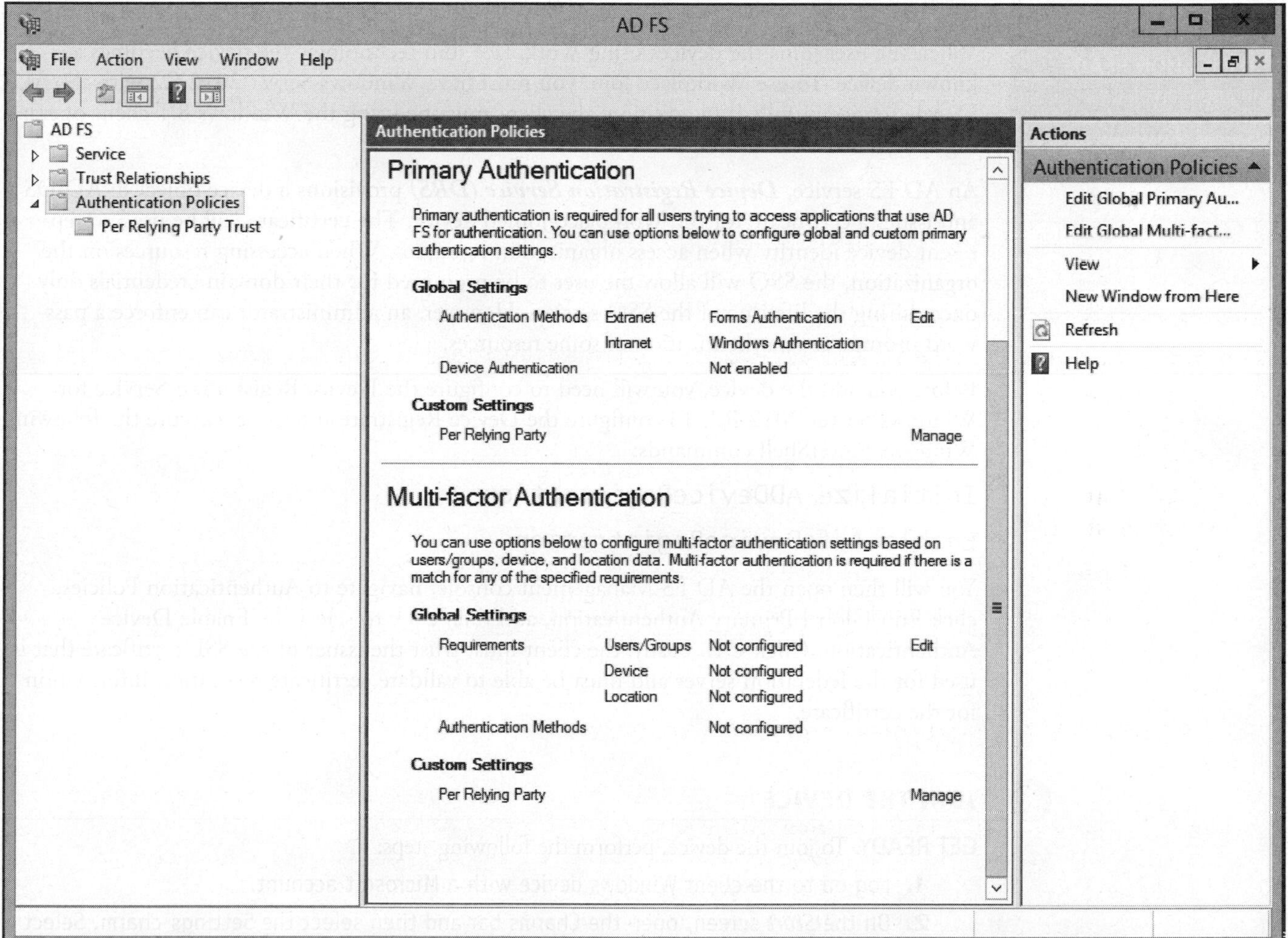

4. In the *Edit Global Authentication Policy* dialog box, under the *Multi-factor* tab, you can configure the following settings as part of the global multi-factor authentication policy:
   - If Multi-factor Authentication is required for the specified user and groups.
   - If MFA is required for unregistered or registered devices.

- If MFA is required for Extranet or Intranet.
- Which additional authentication method can be used with MFA, such as Certificate Authentication.

5. Click OK to close the *Edit Global Authentication Policy* dialog box.

Configuring Workplace Join

As users are using multiple computers and devices to access email and other business related applications and services, and as users use their personal devices—particularly if the organization uses a Bring Your Own Device (BYOD) policy)—you need to let users with non-company devices access the company resources while maintaining security. With ***Workplace Join*** technology, users can join their devices to the organization network without joining the device to the Active Directory domain. You can then manage access based on a wide range of attributes.

CERTIFICATION READY
Configure Workplace Join.
Objective 6.1

When the user joins the devices using Workplace Join technology, the device becomes a known device. To use Workplace Join, you must have Windows Server 2012 R2 with the AD FS role service installed. In addition, the client must be using the Windows 8.1 client operating system or iOS-based devices (such as an iPad).

An AD FS service, ***Device Registration Service (DRS)*** provisions a device object in AD DS and issues a certificate for the Workplace-Joined device. The certificate will be used to represent device identity when access organization resources. When accessing resources on the organization, the SSO will allow the user to be prompted for their domain credentials only once during the lifetime of the SSO session. However, an administrator can enforce a password prompt or reauthentication of some resources.

Before you add the device, you will need to configure the Device Registration Service for Windows Server 2012 R2. To configure the Device Registration Service, execute the following Windows PowerShell commands:

```
Initialize-ADDeviceRegistration

Enable-AdfsDeviceRegistration
```

You will then open the AD FS Management console, navigate to Authentication Policies, click Edit Global Primary Authentication, and then click to select the Enable Device Authentication. Click OK. Lastly, the client must trust the issuer of the SSL certificate that is used for the federation server and must be able to validate certificate revocation information for the certificate.

JOIN THE DEVICE

GET READY. To join the device, perform the following steps:

1. Log on to the client Windows device with a Microsoft account.
2. On the *Start* screen, open the Charms bar and then select the Settings charm. Select Change PC Settings.
3. On the *PC Settings* page, select Network and then click Workplace.
4. In the *Enter your UserID to get workplace access or turn on device management* dialog box, type the user name (such as JSmith@contoso.com) and then click Join.
5. When prompted for credentials, type the username and the associated password. Click OK. You should now see the message: This device has joined your workplace network.

Testing Active Directory Federation

After everything is all set up, you then need to test Active Directory Federation to make sure it is functioning properly.

When troubleshooting AD FS problems, you should check the following:

- Look at the Event Viewer and/or AD FS events for errors.
- Make sure that AD FS is installed and running.
- Make sure that you have network connectivity to the AD FS servers from the clients and, if you are using proxy, the AD FS proxy server.
- Make sure that DNS is resolving correctly to the AD FS servers.
- Verify that IIS is running properly, that the proper SSL certificates are bounded properly, and that the proper ports are used.
- Make sure that the certificates are configured properly, that the certificates have not expired or been revoked, and that the certificates have a trusted chain to the root CA. If you are connected to a partner AD FS, verify the same on the partner sites.
- Verify that the federation service can connect to the AD FS configuration database. Make sure you have the correct connection string if you are not using AD LDS or SQL databases. You can view the AD FS configuration database connection string with the following Windows PowerShell command:

```
Get-WmiObject -class SecurityTokenService
-namespace root/ADFS | select-object
ConfigurationDatabaseConnectionString
```

- Make sure the AD FS configuration database is operational.
- Verify that the AD FS service user account has permission to access the configuration store.
- Verify that the application pool is configuration.
- Verify that the metadata endpoints are accessible, such as `https:// <hostname>/FederationMetadata/2007-06/FederationMetadata.xml`

SKILL SUMMARY

IN THIS LESSON YOU LEARNED:

- Active Directory Federation Services (AD FS) role allows administrators to configure Single Sign-On (SSO) for Web-based applications across a single organization or multiple organizations without requiring users to remember multiple usernames and passwords.
- Claims are statements that are made by a trusted entity about an object, such as a user, that includes key information identifying the user.
- Installing the Active Directory Federation Services role and creating the AD FS server is a simple process when using Server Manager. When you select the AD FS role services, you install the Federation Server or the Federation Service Proxy.
- A relying party trust identifies the relying party so that the federation server knows which applications can use AD FS. It also defines the claim rules, from the claims provider.

- A claims provider trust identifies the claims provider, and describes how the relying party consumes the claims that the claims provider issues.
- By default, the AD FS server is configured with a claims provider trust named *Active Directory*.
- AD FS users an attribute store to look up claim values. Although AD DS is already configured, by default, as an attribute store, you can configure a database or another directory such as Active Directory Lightweight Directory Services (AD LDS).
- The Federation Service Proxy is used for the federation server of two organizations to securely communicate over the Internet using port 443. The proxy server is located in the perimeter network.
- In Windows Server 2012 R2, AD FS can be accessed with authentication policies and multi-factor authentication (including using user, device, location, and authentication data).
- With Workplace Join technology, users can join personal devices to the organization network without joining the device to the Active Directory domain.

■ Knowledge Assessment

Multiple Choice

Select the correct answer for each of the following questions.

1. What allows a single sign-on when deploying an application for another organization on your network?
   a. Active Directory Domain Services (AD DS)
   b. Active Directory Rights Management Services (AD RMS)
   c. Active Directory Lightweight Directory Services (AD LDS)
   d. Active Directory Federation Services (AD FS)

2. What is a statement made by a trusted entity for a user that includes key information to identity the user?
   a. store
   b. delegated party
   c. proxy
   d. claims

3. What is the application that accepts claims from a claim provider?
   a. claims provider
   b. relying party
   c. attribute store
   d. federation server proxy

4. What is the server that issues claims and authenticates users?
   a. claims provider
   b. relying party
   c. attribute store
   d. federation server proxy

5. What is a database that stores user information?
   a. claims provider
   b. relying party
   c. attribute store
   d. federation server proxy
6. What is used to identify the relying party so that it knows the application can use AD FS?
   a. relying party trust
   b. attribute trust
   c. claim provider trust
   d. claim rule
7. In AD FS, which claim provider is used by default?
   a. Active Directory
   b. AD LDS
   c. SQL database
   d. Oracle database
8. You have a domain called *contoso.com*. You install Active Directory Federation Services (AD FS) role on Server01. Contoso.com is defined as an account store. You have a partner company that has a web-based application that uses AD FS authentication. What do you need to configure on Server01 to allow contoso.com users to be authenticated by the partner company?
   a. a new application
   b. a resource partner
   c. an account partner
   d. an organization claim
9. You have a domain called *contoso.com*. You install Active Directory Federation Services (AD FS) role on Server01. You have an application called *App1* to use AD FS authentication. You want to install a second AD FS server that the App1 can use. What do you need to do on Server02?
   a. add an attribute store
   b. create a relying party trust
   c. create a claims provider trust
   d. create a relying provider trust
10. You deploy Active Directory Federation Services (AD FS) Federation Service Proxy on a server, Server01. What do you need to configure the Windows Firewall on Server01 to allow the users to access AD FS?
    a. 83
    b. 135
    c. 443
    d. 489
11. In Windows Server 2012 R2, which role replaced the Federation Service Proxy?
    a. Remote Access Proxy
    b. AD FS Proxy
    c. Reverse Proxy
    d. Web Application Proxy
12. In Windows Server 2012 R2, which of the following is used to specify which authentication can be used with devices connected within the intranet?
    a. authentication policy
    b. MFA policy
    c. relay policy
    d. Workplace Join policy

13. Which technology allows you users to connect personal devices to the organization resources? (Choose two answers)
    a. authentication policy
    b. multi-factor authentication
    c. Workplace Join
    d. Web Application Proxy
14. Which type of devices can you connect using Workplace Join? (Choose all that apply.)
    a. Windows 8.0 devices
    b. Windows 8.1 devices
    c. Android devices
    d. iOS-based devices
15. When installing and configuring AD FS on Windows Server 2012 R2, which version of Microsoft SQL can you use to run for AD FS? (Choose all that apply.)
    a. Microsoft SQL Server 2005
    b. Microsoft SQL Server 2008
    c. Microsoft SQL Server 2008 R2
    d. Microsoft SQL Server 2012

Build a List

1. Identify the steps to deploy AD FS for a single organization by placing the number of the step in the appropriate space. Not all steps will be used.
   _______ Configure claim rules
   _______ Create and configure a server authentication certificate
   _______ Configure AD FS to send claims to the application
   _______ Install the AD FS Server role
   _______ Configure an ADFS proxy
   _______ Test the application
   _______ Install and configure the application
   _______ Install .NET Framework 4.0
2. Identify the steps used when a client within an organization needs to use SSO for another application, also within the same organization by placing the number of the step in the appropriate space.
   _____ The federation uses AD DS to authenticate the user
   _____ Claim is put in, security token is sent back to the client computer
   _____ The client presents the token to the web server and uses the claims to access the application
   _____ Web server redirects to federation service
   _____ Client accesses application
   _____ If authentication is successful, the federation server collects AD DS information and generates the user's claims
3. Identify the steps to use Workplace Join in Windows Server 2012 R2 AD FS by placing the number of the step in the appropriate space. Not all answers will be used.
   _____ Execute the Windows PowerShell Initialize-ADDeviceRegistration cmdlet
   _____ Enable Device Authentication using an authentication policy
   _____ Install the digital certificate using a .pfx file
   _____ Execute the Windows PowerShell start-DeviceRegistrationService cmdlet
   _____ Execute the Windows PowerShell Enable-AdfsDeviceRegistration cmdlet
   _____ Enable Device Authentication using the DeviceRegistrationService console

Choose an Option

1. You are an administrator for the Contoso.com domain. You are setting up Active Directory Federation Services (AD FS), which will be used with your litware.com partner organization. You need to provide the file containing the federation metadata. Which node would you click to identify the location of the federation metadata? Refer to Figure 18-10.

Figure 18-10

Selecting the correct node

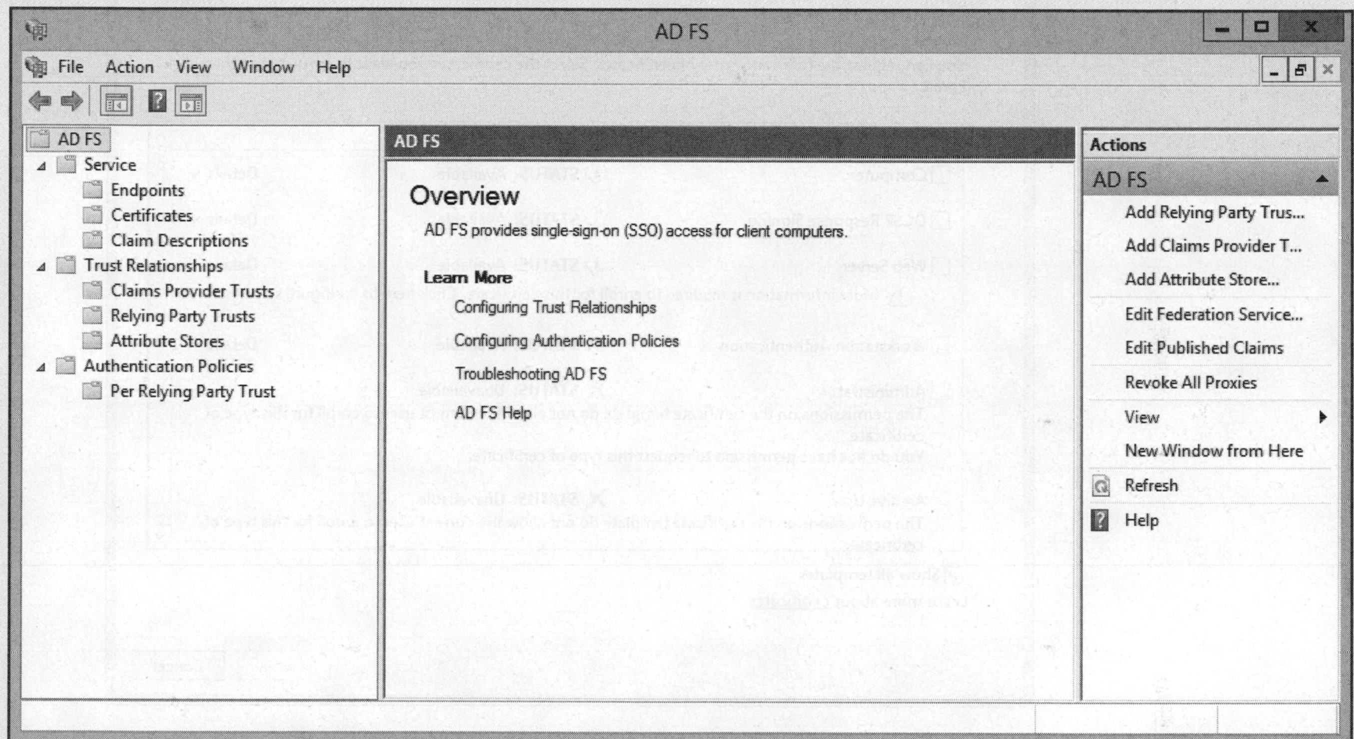

2. You are an administrator for the Contoso.com domain. You need to request a certificate to be used with the AD FS website. Which type of certificate do you want to deploy from the Certificate Authority? Refer to Figure 18-11.

Figure 18-11
Selecting a certificate type

■ Business Case Scenarios

Scenario 18-1: Creating a Federation Partnership

You are an administrator for the Contoso Corporation. You are partnering with Litware.com, which will order products from the Contoso Corporation. Therefore, you need to deploy an application that the users of Litware can access over the Internet. What should you do?

Scenario 18-2: Managing BYOD Devices

Your company has just implemented a BYOD policy where users can user their own smartphones and tablets at work. Therefore, these devices will need to be able to access a variety of AD FS application and services as well as other internal resources. What must you do to allow those devices to connect to your organization securely?

LESSON 19

Installing and Configuring Active Directory Certificate Services (AD CS)

70-412 EXAM OBJECTIVE

Objective 6.2 – Install and configure Active Directory Certificate Services (AD CS). This objective may include but is not limited to: Install an Enterprise Certificate Authority (CA); configure certificate revocation lists (CRL) distribution points; install and configure Online Responder; implement administrative role separation; configure CA backup and recovery.

Lesson Heading	Exam Objective
Understanding the Active Directory Certificate Services	
Installing an Enterprise Certificate Authority	Install an Enterprise Certificate Authority (CA)
Configuring AIA and CRL Distribution Points	Configure CRL distribution points
Installing and Configuring Online Responder	Install and configure Online Responder
Implementing Administrative Role Separation	Implement administrative role separation
Configuring CA Backup and Recovery	Configure CA backup and recovery

KEY TERMS

Active Directory Certificate Services (AD CS)
asymmetric encryption
auditors
Authority Information Access (AIA) extension
backup operators
CA administrator
CA Web Enrollment
certificate authority (CA)
Certificate Authority Policy Web Service
Certificate Enrollment Web Service
certificate manager
certification practice statement (CPS)
Certificate Revocation List (CRL)
CRL distribution point (CDP) extension
delta CRLs
digital certificate
enterprise CA
Network Device Enrollment Service
Online Certificate Status Protocol (OSCP)
Online Responder
public key infrastructure (PKI)
registration authority (RA)
root CA
standalone CA
subordinate CA

Understanding the Active Directory Certificate Services

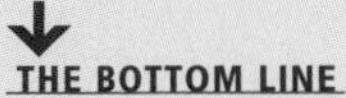

THE BOTTOM LINE

Active Directory Certificate Services (AD CS) is a server role that allows you to issue and manage digital certificates as part of a public key infrastructure. ***Public key infrastructure (PKI)*** is a system consisting of hardware, software, policies, and procedures that create, manage, distribute, use, store, and revoke digital certificates. PKI consists of certification authorities (CAs) and registration authorities that verify and authenticate the validity of each entity that is involved in an electronic transaction through the use of public key cryptography. Within the PKI, the ***certificate authority (CA)*** binds a public key with respective user identities and issues digital certificates containing the public key.

Asymmetric encryption, also known as *public key cryptography*, uses two mathematically related keys for encryption. One key is used to encrypt the data, whereas the second key is used to decrypt it. Unlike symmetric key algorithms, this method does not require a secure initial exchange of one or more secret keys to both sender and receiver. Instead, you can make the public key known to anyone and use the other key to encrypt or decrypt the data. The public key can be sent to someone or can be published within a digital certificate through a CA. For example, say you want a partner to send you data. To begin the asymmetric encryption process, you send your partner your public key. Your partner then encrypts the data with the key and sends you the encrypted message. You next use your private key to decrypt the message. If the public key falls into someone else's hands, that person still can not decrypt the message because you need the private key to decrypt a message that has been encrypted with the public key.

A ***digital certificate*** is an electronic document that contains an identity, such as a user or organization name, along with a corresponding public key. Because a digital certificate is used to prove a person's or computer's identity, it can also be used for authentication. A digital certificate is similar to a driver's license or passport because it contains a user's photograph and thumbprint so that there is no doubt of the user's identity.

The benefits of the PKI include:

- **Confidentiality:** The PKI allows you to encrypt data is that is stored or transmitted.
- **Integrity:** A digital signature identifies whether the data is modified while the data is transmitted.
- **Authenticity:** A message digest is digitally signed using the sender's private key. Because the digest can be decrypted only with the sender's corresponding public key, it proves that the message can come only from the sending user (non-repudiation).

For the PKI system to work, the CA must be trusted. Typically within an organization, you can install a CA on Windows server, and it would be trusted within your organization. If you require a CA that is trusted outside your organization, you have to use a trusted third-party CA, such as VeriSign or Entrust. Established commercial CAs charge to issue certificates that will automatically be trusted by most web browsers (see Figure 19-1).

The ***registration authority (RA)***, which might or might not be the same server as the CA, is used to distribute keys, accept registrations for the CA, and validate identities. The RA does not distribute digital certificates—instead, the CA does.

Installing an Enterprise Certificate Authority

The CA is a Windows Server 2012 or Windows Server 2012 R2 server role that verifies the identity of the certificate requestors; issues certificates to requesting users, computers, and services; and manages certificate revocation.

Figure 19-1

Showing trusted CAs in Internet Explorer

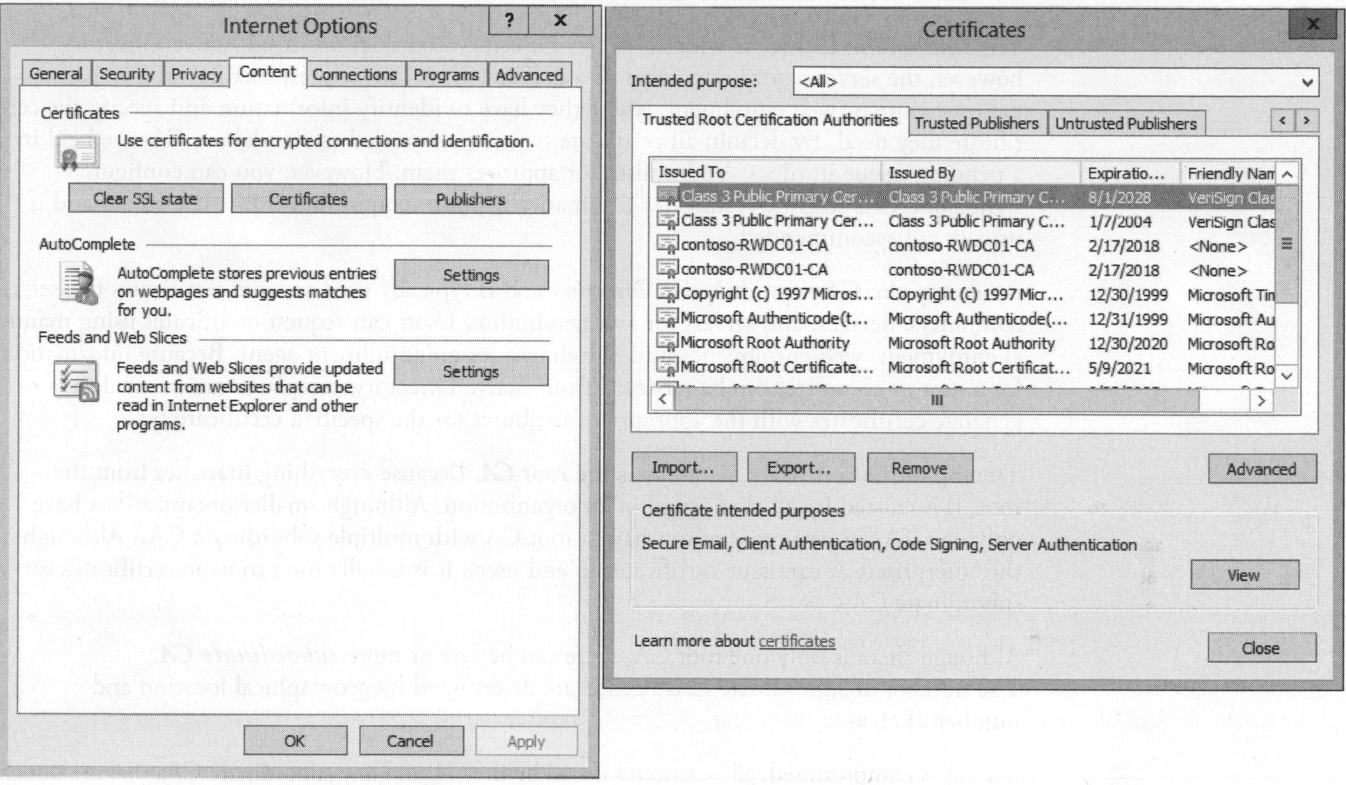

CERTIFICATION READY
Install an Enterprise Certificate Authority (CA).
Objective 6.2

Depending on your needs, you can install AD CS on multiple Windows servers to create an infrastructure of CAs. The first CA is known as the *root CA*, which establishes the PKI in the network and provides the highest point in the whole structure.

Each of the components that make up the PKI are deployed as role services of the AD CS server role. Each role service is responsible for a specific portion of the certificate infrastructure, while working together to form a complete solution.

Role services of the AD CS role include:

- **CA:** The component that issues certificates to users, computers, and services and manages certificate validity.
- ***CA Web Enrollment:*** The component that provides a method to issue and renew certificates for users, computers, and devices that are not joined to the domain, are not connected directly to the network, or are for users of non-Windows operating systems.
- ***Online Responder:*** The component that configures and manages Online Certificate Status Protocol (OCSP), which is used to validate and revoke certificates.
- ***Network Device Enrollment Service:*** The component that can be used to assign certificates to routers, switches, and other network devices.
- ***Certificate Enrollment Web Service:*** The component that allows computers to connect to a CA using a web browser to request, renew, and install issued certificates; retrieve CRLs; download a root certificate; and enroll over the Internet or across forests.
- ***Certificate Authority Policy Web Service:*** The component that is enables users to obtain certificate enrollment policy information.

When you install a CA, you have the following choices:

- Standalone CA or Enterprise CA
- Root CA or Subordinate CA

The ***standalone CA*** works without Active Directory and does not need Active Directory, however, the server can be a member of a domain. Users can request certificates using a manual procedure or web enrollment, where they have to identify information and specify the certificate they need. By default, all certificate requests submitted to standalone CAs are held in a pending queue until a CA administrator approves them. However, you can configure standalone CAs to issue certificates automatically upon request, but this is less secure and is usually not recommended.

An ***enterprise CA*** requires Active Directory and is typically used to issue certificates to users, computers, devices, and servers for an organization. Users can request certificates using manual enrollment, web enrollment, auto-enrollment, or an enrollment agent. Because information for a user or computer can be retrieved from Active Directory, templates can be used to generate certificates with the appropriate attributes for the specified certificate type.

The top of the certificate hierarchy is the ***root CA***. Because everything branches from the root, it is trusted by all clients within an organization. Although smaller organizations have only one CA, larger organizations have a root CA with multiple subordinate CAs. Although the enterprise CA can issue certificates to end users, it is usually used to issue certificates to subordinate CAs.

Although there is only one root CA, there can be one or more ***subordinate CA***. The number of subordinate CAs needed are determined by geographical location and number of clients.

If a CA is compromised, all certificates issued by the CA and any subordinate CAs that are under the compromised CA (and corresponding issued certificates) are also considered compromised.

To maximize the security of the root CA, the root CA can be disconnected from the network, and subordinate CAs are used to issue certificates to other subordinate CAs or to end users. If you are using a three-tiered hierarchy with root CA, intermediate CAs, and issuing CAs, you can disconnect the root CAs and intermediate CAs.

To install the Active Directory Certificate Services Server role, you need to be logged in as an enterprise administrator.

INSTALL THE ACTIVE DIRECTORY CERTIFICATE SERVICES SERVER ROLE

GET READY. To install and configure the Active Directory Certificate Services Server Role, perform the following steps:

1. In the *Server Manager* console, click Add roles and features.
2. When the *Add Roles and Features Wizard* opens, click Next.
3. On the *Select installation type* page, click Next.
4. On the *Select destination server* page, click Next.
5. On the *Select server roles* page, select Active Directory Certificate Services. When the *Add Roles and Features Wizard* window appears, click Add Features, and then click Next.
6. On the *Select features* page, click Next.
7. On the *Active Directory Certificate Services* page, click Next.

8. On the *Select role services* page (refer to Figure 19-1), ensure that Certification Authority is selected, and then click Next.
9. On the *Confirm installation selections* page, click Install.
10. On the *Installation progress* page, after installation is successful, click Configure Active Directory Certificate Services on the destination server.
11. On the *Credentials* page, click Next.
12. On the *Select role services to configure* page, click Certification Authority and click Next.
13. On the *Setup Type* page, select Enterprise CA or Standalone CA, and then click Next.
14. On the *CA Type* page, ensure that Root CA is selected, and then click Next.
15. On the *Private Key* page, ensure that Create a new private key is selected, and then click Next.
16. On the *Cryptography for CA* page, keep the default selections for Cryptographic Service Provider (CSP) and Hash Algorithm. For better security, change the *Key length* to 4096, and then click Next.
17. On the *CA Name* page (see Figure 19-2), click Next.

Figure 19-2

Specifying the name of the CA

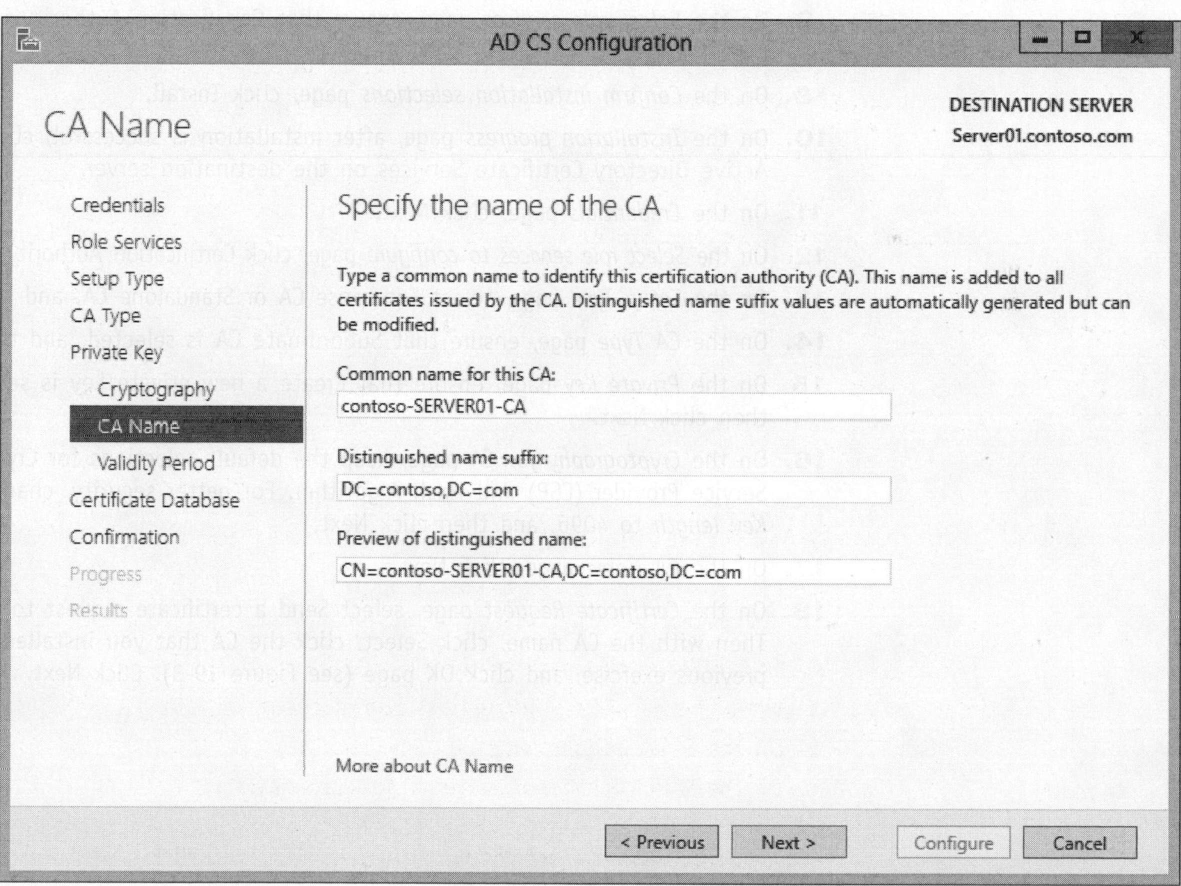

18. On the *Validity Period* page, the default is 5 years. Click Next.
19. The *CA Database* page displays where the certificate database will be stored. Click Next.
20. On the *Confirmation* page, click Configure.
21. On the *Results* page, click Close.

INSTALL SUBORDINATE CERTIFICATE SERVICES SERVER ROLE

GET READY. To install and configure the Active Directory Certificate Services Server Role, perform the following steps:

1. In the *Server Manager* console, click Add roles and features.
2. When the *Add Roles and Features Wizard* opens, click Next.
3. On the *Select installation type* page, click Next.
4. On the *Select destination server* page, click Next.
5. On the *Select server roles* page, select Active Directory Certificate Services. When the *Add Roles and Features Wizard* window appears, click Add Features, and then click Next.
6. On the *Select features* page, click Next.
7. On the *Active Directory Certificate Services* page, click Next.
8. On the *Select role services* page, ensure that Certification Authority is selected, and then click Next.
9. On the *Confirm installation selections* page, click Install.
10. On the *Installation progress* page, after installation is successful, click Configure Active Directory Certificate Services on the destination server.
11. On the *Credentials* page, click Next.
12. On the *Select role services to configure* page, click Certification Authority and click Next.
13. On the *Setup Type* page, select Enterprise CA or Standalone CA, and then click Next.
14. On the *CA Type* page, ensure that Subordinate CA is selected, and then click Next.
15. On the *Private Key* page, ensure that Create a new private key is selected, and then click Next.
16. On the *Cryptography for CA* page, keep the default selections for Cryptographic Service Provider (CSP) and Hash Algorithm. For better security, change the *Key length* to 4096, and then click Next.
17. On the *CA Name* page, click Next.
18. On the *Certificate Request* page, select Send a certificate request to a parent CA. Then with the CA name, click Select, click the CA that you installed in the previous exercise, and click OK page (see Figure 19-3). Click Next.

Figure 19-3

Requesting a certificate from a parent CA

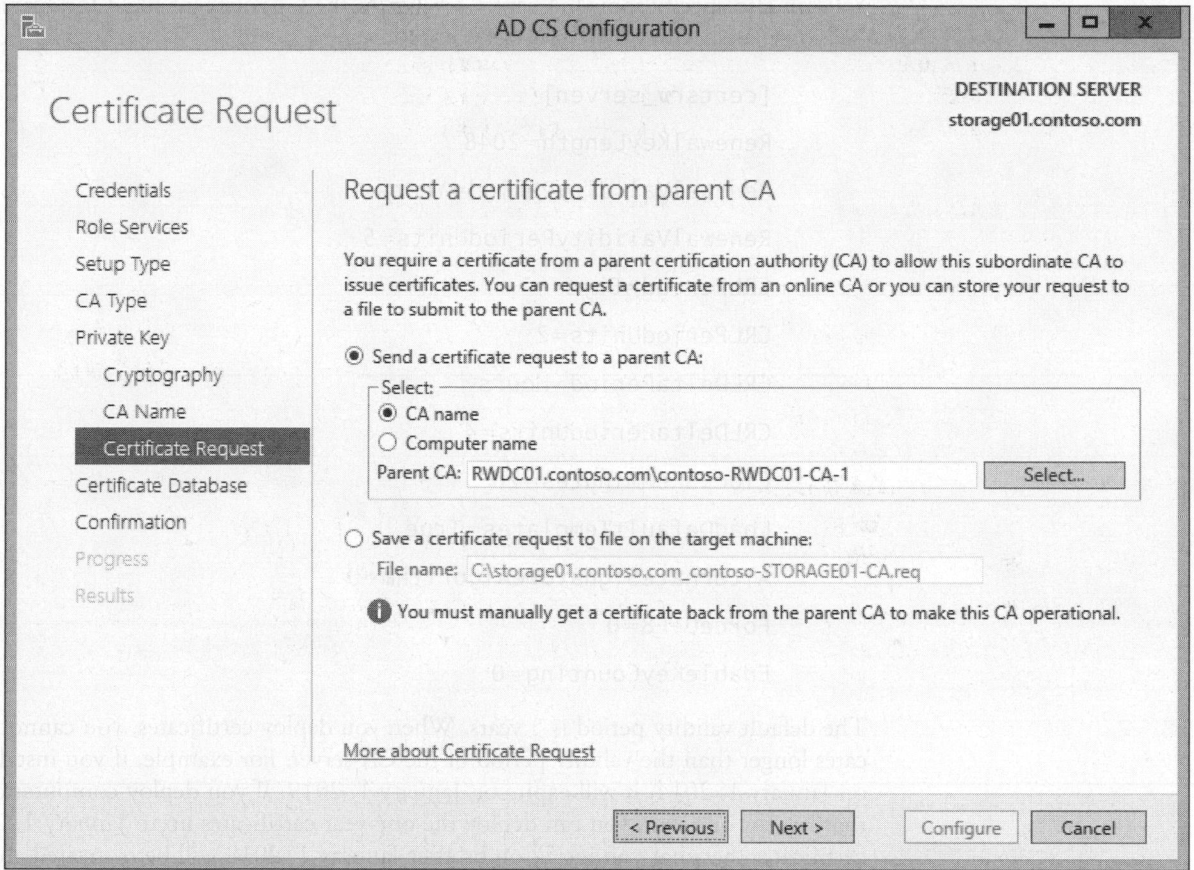

19. The *CA Database* page displays where the certificate database will be stored. Click Next.
20. On the *Confirmation* page, click Configure.
21. On the *Results* page, click Close.

To deploy CAs with predefined values or parameters during installation, you can use the CAPolicy.ini file. The CAPolicy.inf file is a text file that contains the settings that are used when installing the AD CS role or renewing the CA certificate. To use the CAPolicyl.inf file, you must copy the file into the %systemroot% folder, which is most likely the C:\Windows folder, before you install the AD CS or renew the CA certificate.

Each CAPolicy.inf file is divided into sections and has a simple structure, which can be described as follows:

- A section is an area in the .inf file that contains a logical group of keys. A section always appears in brackets in the .inf file.
- A key is the parameter that is to the left of the equal (=) sign.
- A value is the parameter that is to the right of the equal sign.

For example, to specify Authority Information Access point in the CAPolicy.inf file, you use following syntax:

```
[AuthorityInformationAccess]
URL=http://pki.contoso.com/CertData /contosoCA.crt
```

You can also specify some CA server settings in the CAPolicy.inf file. One example of the section that specifies these settings is as follows:

```
[certsrv_server]
RenewalKeyLength=2048
RenewalValidityPeriod=Years
RenewalValidityPeriodUnits=5
CRLPeriod=Days
CRLPeriodUnits=2
CRLDeltaPeriod=Hours
CRLDeltaPeriodUnits=4
ClockSkewMinutes=20
LoadDefaultTemplates=True
AlternateSignatureAlgorithm=0
ForceUTF8=0
EnableKeyCounting=0
```

The default validity period is 5 years. When you deploy certificates, you cannot deploy certificates longer than the validity period of the CA server. For example, if you install a CA server on January 1, 2014, it will expire on January 1, 2019. If you deploy computer certificates that last for one year, you can deploy the one-year certificates up to January 1, 2018. Any certificates that that you install on or after January 1, 2018 will be truncated and expire on January 1, 2019. Therefore, you want to update the certificate before January 1, 2018, so that you can assign computer certificates that are valid for an entire year.

RENEW A CA DIGITAL CERTIFICATE

GET READY. To renew a CA digital certificate, perform the following steps:

1. Using *Server Manager*, open the Tools menu and click Certification Authority.
2. When the *Certification Authority* opens, right-click the CA server, click All Tasks, and click Renew CA Certificate.
3. When it states that the AD CS cannot be running during this option and if you want to stop AD CS now, click Yes.
4. When the *Renew CA Certificate* dialog box opens, click OK.

If you have an enterprise CA, the domain computers will automatically receive a copy of the enterprise CA certificate in the Certificates (Computer)\Trusted Root Certification Authorities\Certificates folder so that the client computer automatically trusts the enterprise CA and the certificates that come from the CA.

To trust a CA including local standalone CAs, you need to manually add the CA certificate to the Trusted Root Certification Authorities\Certificates folder or you can use Group Policies to add the certificates. To use group policies, you need to export the CA certificate to a file and then use Group Policy Management console to create or modify a Group Policy Object (GPO).

EXPORT THE CA CERTIFICATE

GET READY. To export the CA certificate, perform the following steps:

1. Using *Server Manager*, open the Tools menu, and click Certification Authority.
2. When the *Certification Authority* console opens, right-click the CA, and click Properties.
3. When the *Properties* dialog box opens (see Figure 19-4), click View Certificate.

Figure 19-4
Opening a certificate

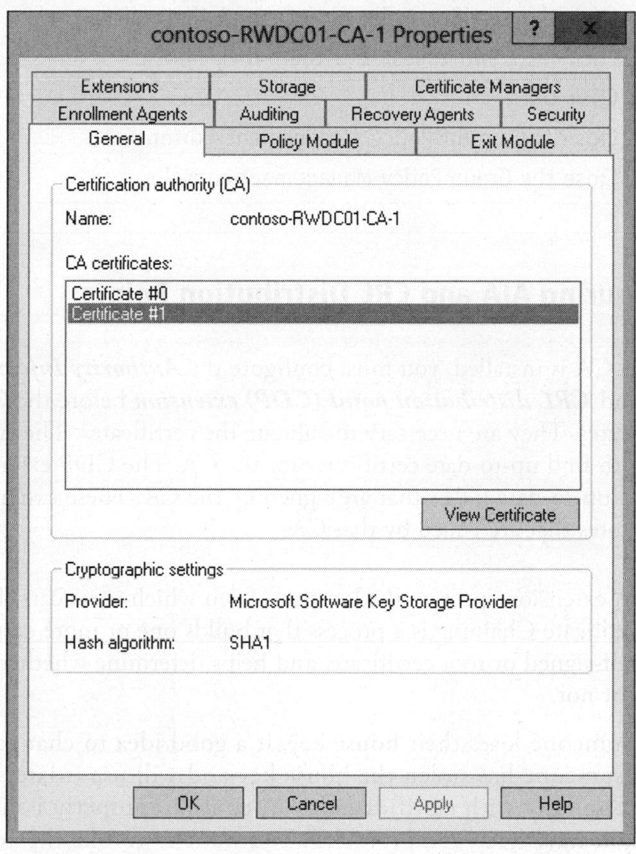

4. When the *Certificate* dialog box opens, click the Details tab.
5. Click Copy to File.
6. When the *Certificate Export Wizard* opens, click Next.
7. On the *Export File Format* page click Next.
8. In the *File to Export* page, type the path and name of the certificate file (the file name extension is .cer). For example, the path and file name could be *C:\CARoot.cer*. Click Next.
9. When the wizard is complete, click Finish.

 PUBLISH THE ROOT CA CERTIFICATE THROUGH GROUP POLICIES

GET READY. To publish the root CA certificate using a GPO, perform the following steps:

1. Using *Server Manager*, click Tools and click Group Policy Management.
2. When the Group Policy Management console opens, expand Forest, expand Domains, expand the domain, right-click Default Domain Policy, and then click Edit.

3. In the *Computer Configuration* node, expand Policies, expand Windows Settings, expand Security Settings, expand Public Key Policies, right-click Trusted Root Certification Authorities, and then click Import.
4. Click Next.
5. On the *File to Import* page, click Browse.
6. In the *file name* text box, type the path where the certificate file is located, and then press Enter.
7. Click the certificate file (*.cer), and then click Open.
8. Click Next two times, and then click Finish.
9. Click OK.
10. Close the Group Policy Management Editor.
11. Close the Group Policy Management console.

Configuring AIA and CRL Distribution Points

After a CA is installed, you must configure the ***Authority Information Access (AIA) extension*** and ***CRL distribution point (CDP) extension*** before the CA issues any certificates. They are necessary to validate the certificates. The AIA extension specifies where to find up-to-date certificates for the CA. The CDP extension specifies where to find up-to-date CRLs that are signed by the CA. These extensions apply to all certificates that are issued by that CA.

CERTIFICATION READY
Configure CRL distribution points.
Objective 6.2

The AIA extension specifies the locations from which users can obtain the certificate for this CA. Certificate Chaining is a process that builds one or more certificate paths, which trace to the self-signed or root certificate, and helps determine whether a digital certificate can be trusted or not.

When someone loses their house key, it a good idea to change the locks on the door in case someone has stolen the house key and will use it later to illegally enter the house. Similarly with certificates, a CA could improperly issue a certificate or a private key might have been compromised. You want to revoke the certificate so that the keys will no longer be valid and used in the future. In addition, after a set period of time, certificates expire.

Certificate Revocation List (CRL) is a digitally signed list issued by a CA that contains a list of certificates issued by the CA that have been revoked. The list includes all individual revoked certificates including the serial number of the certificate, the date that the certificate was revoked, and the revocation reason.

The application uses a CDP to check the CRL for a revoked certificate. The CDP is a certificate extension that indicates where the certificate revocation list for a CA can be retrieved.

The AIA and CDP extensions can be published to Active Directory, web servers including FTP servers, and file servers. For computers that are not members of Active Directory, you should place the CA certificate and CRL on web servers by using the HTTP protocol.

CONFIGURE CERTIFIED REVOCATION LIST (CRL) DISTRIBUTION

GET READY. To configure Certified Revocation List (CRL) Distribution, perform the following steps:

1. Using *Server Manager*, open the Tools menu and click Certification Authority.
2. When the *Certification Authority* console opens, right-click Revoked Certificates, and then click Properties.
3. In the *Revoked Certificates Properties* window, set the *CRL publication interval* to 1 Day and the Delta CRL *Publication interval* to 1 hour, and then click OK.
4. Right-click the CA, and click Properties.
5. Click the Extensions tab. Figure 19-5 shows the default CRL distribution points.

Figure 19-5

Specifying the CRL distribution points

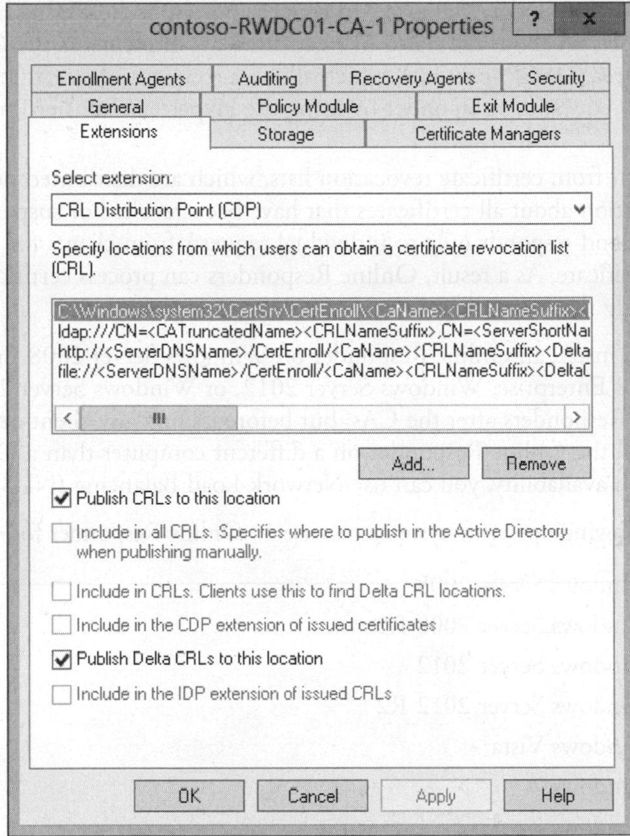

6. To add additional CRL points, click Add.
7. In the *Add Location* dialog box, you can type the location in the *Location* text box. As shown by the example, you can insert variables by choosing the variable and clicking the Insert button.
8. Click OK to close the *Add Location* dialog box.
9. Click OK to close the *Properties* dialog box.
10. Close *Certification Authority* console.

Because CRLs can become large, depending on the number of certificates issued and revoked by a CA, you can also publish smaller, interim CRLs called *delta CRLs*. ***Delta CRLs*** contain only the certificates revoked since the last regular CRL was published. This allows clients to retrieve the smaller delta CRL and more quickly build a complete list of revoked certificates. The use of delta CRLs also allows revocation data to be published more frequently because the size of the delta CRL usually does not require as much time to transfer as a full CRL.

A ***certification practice statement (CPS)*** is a policy that is defined by the issuing organization's responsibilities when issuing the certificates including identifying the organization issuing the certificates, what the certificates will be used for the process used when assigning the certificates, how the certificates are revoked, and how the certificates are protected. The CPS should be available publically to internal and external users.

Installing and Configuring Online Responder

An Online Responder is a trusted server that runs the Online Responder service and Online Responder Web proxy to receive and respond to individual client requests for information about the status of a certificate. It implements the ***Online Certificate Status Protocol (OSCP)*** protocol, which allows a recipient of a certificate to submit a certificate status request to a responder by using the Hypertext Transfer Protocol (HTTP).

CERTIFICATION READY
Install and configure Online Responder.
Objective 6.2

Different from certificate revocation lists, which are distributed periodically and contain information about all certificates that have been revoked or suspended, an Online Responder receives and responds only to individual requests from clients for information about the status of a certificate. As a result, Online Responders can process certificate status requests more efficiently than can CRLs.

You can install an Online Responder on Windows Server 2008 Enterprise, Windows Server 2008 R2 Enterprise, Windows Server 2012, or Windows Server 2012 R2. You should install Online Responders after the CAs, but before issuing any client certificates. It is recommended to install the Online Responder on a different computer than a CA. If you need scalability and high availability, you can use Network Load Balancing (NLB).

The following operating systems can use an Online Responder for validation of certificate status:

- Windows Server 2008
- Windows Server 2008 R2
- Windows Server 2012
- Windows Server 2012 R2
- Windows Vista
- Windows 7
- Windows 8
- Windows 8.1

For the clients to use the Online Responder, you must configure the CAs to include the URL of the Online Responder in the AIA extension of issued certificates. The OCSP client uses this URL to validate the certificate status. You must also issue the OCSP Response Signing certificate template, so that the Online Responder can also enroll that certificate.

When you configure a CA to support the Online Responder service, IIS will be installed on the computer when you install the Online Responder role. You will then have to configure an OCSP Response Signing certificate template on the CA and auto-enrollment must be used to issue the OCSP Response Signing certificate to the computer. Lastly, you need to include the URL for the Online Responder in the AIA extension of certificates issued by the CA.

INSTALL THE ONLINE RESPONDER ROLE

GET READY. To install the Online Responder Role, perform the following steps:

1. Using *Server Manager*, open the Manage menu and click Add roles and features.
2. When the *Add Roles and Feature Wizard* opens, click Next.
3. On *the Select installation type* page, click Next.
4. On the *Select destination* page, click Next.
5. On the *Select server roles* page, expand Active Directory Certificate Services (Installed), and then select Online Responder. When it asks to add features, click Add Features. Click Next.
6. On the *Select Features* page, click Next.
7. On the *Confirm installation selections* page, click Install.
8. When the message displays that the installation succeeded, click Configure Active Directory Certificate Services on the destination server.
9. When the *AD CS Configuration Wizard* opens, click Next.
10. On the *Role Services* page, click to select Online Responder, and then click Next.
11. Click Configure.
12. Click Close two times.
13. Using *Server Manager*, open the Certification Authority console.
14. In the *Certification Authority* console, right-click the CA, and then click Properties.
15. When the *Properties* dialog box opens, click Authority Information Access (AIA), and then click Add.
16. When the *Add Location* dialog box opens, type http://<servername>/ocsp (if the server is called *rwdc01*, you would type http://rwdc01/ocsp), and then click OK.
17. Click to select the Include in the AIA extension of issued certificates check box.
18. Click to select the Include in the online certificate status protocol (OCSP) extension check box, and then click OK.
19. When it asks you to restart AD CS, click Yes.
20. In the *certsrv* console, expand CA, right-click the Certificate Templates folder, and then click Manage.
21. In the *Certificate Templates* console, double-click the OCSP Response Signing template.
22. In the *OCSP Response Signing Properties* dialog box, click the Security tab. Under *Permissions for Authenticated Users*, select the Allow check box for Autoenroll (see Figure 19-6), and then click OK.

Figure 19-6

Specifying the OCSP Response Signing permissions

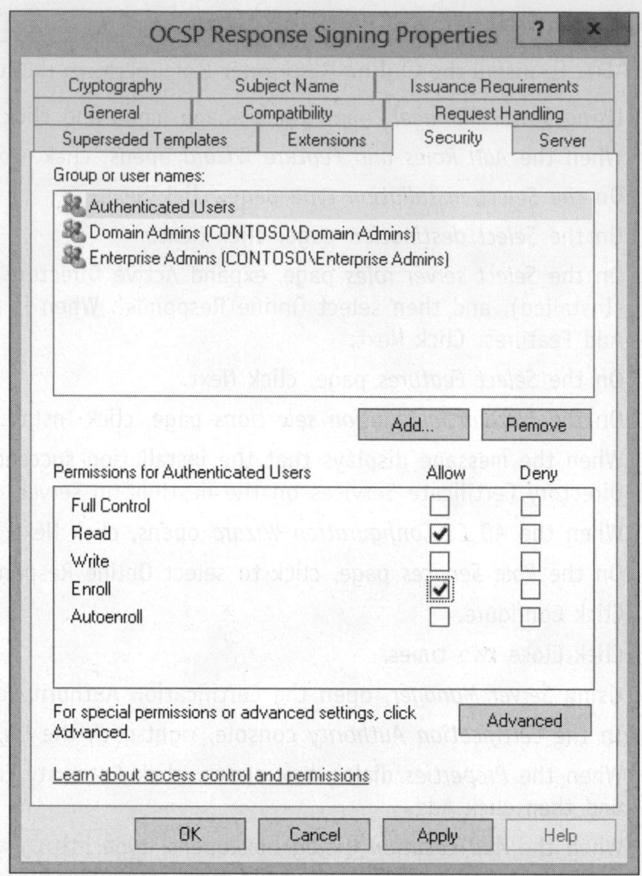

23. Close the Certificate Templates console.
24. In the *Certification Authority* console, right-click the Certificate Templates folder, point to New, and then click Certificate Template to Issue.
25. In the *Enable Certificate Templates* dialog box, select the OCSP Response Signing template, and then click OK.
26. Using *Server Manager*, click Tools, and then click Online Responder Management.
27. When the *ocsp* console opens (see Figure 19-7), right-click Revocation Configuration, and then click Add Revocation Configuration.

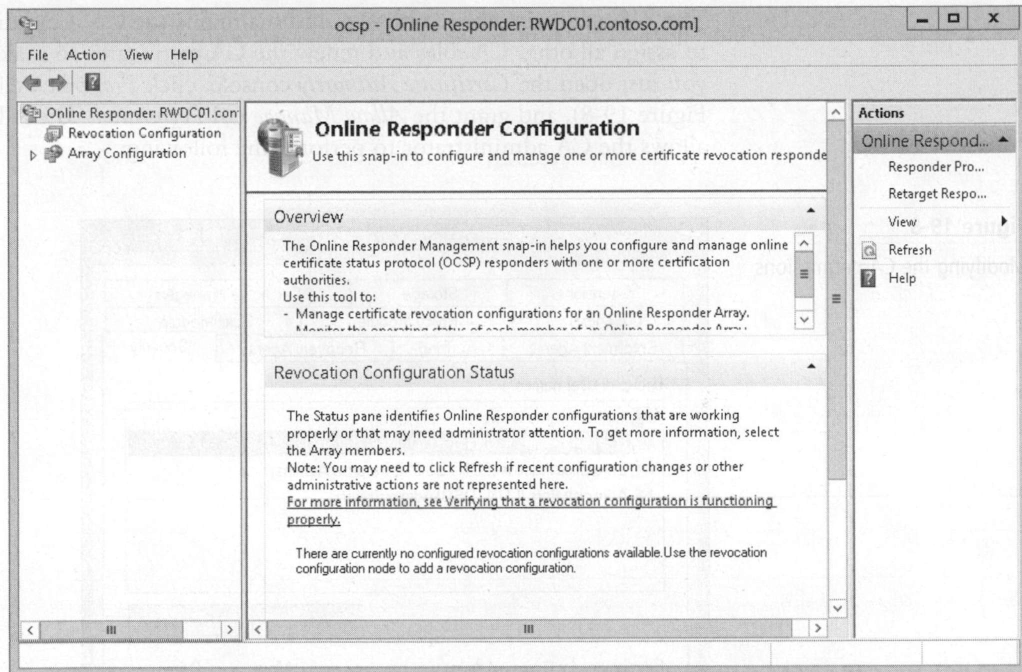

Figure 19-7

Viewing the Online Responder Configuration console

28. When the *Add Revocation Configuration Wizard* starts, click Next.
29. On the *Name the Revocation Configuration* page, in the *Name* text box, type Contoso CA Online Responder, and then click Next.
30. On the *Select CA Certificate Location* page, *Select a certificate for an Existing enterprise CA option* is already selected. Click Next.
31. On the *Choose CA Certificate* page, click Browse, click the certificate for the CA, and click OK. Then click Next.
32. On the *Select Signing Certificate* page, verify that Automatically select a signing certificate and Auto-Enroll for an OCSP signing certificate are both selected, and then click Next.
33. On the *Revocation Provider* page, click Finish.
34. Close the ocsp console.

Implementing Administrative Role Separation

Because certificates and CAs are important security tools used for a company, you need to consider using separation of duties to maintain the security of PKI infrastructure. You can use role-based administration to organize CA administrators into separate, predefined CA roles, each with his or her own set of tasks.

CERTIFICATION READY
Implement administrative role separation.
Objective 6.2

All CA roles are assigned and modified by members of local Administrators, Enterprise Admins, or Domain Admins. On enterprise CAs, local administrators, enterprise administrators, and domain administrators are CA administrators by default. If a standalone CA is installed on a server that is joined to an Active Directory domain, domain administrators are also CA administrators.

The ***CA administrator*** configures and maintains the CA. CA administrators have the ability to assign all other CA roles and renew the CA certificate. To make a user a CA Administrator, you just open the *Certificate Authority* console, click *Properties*, click the *Security* tab (see Figure 19-8), and grant the *Allow Manage CA Permission*. The Allow Manage CA permission allows the CA administrator to perform the following:

Figure 19-8

Modifying the CA permissions

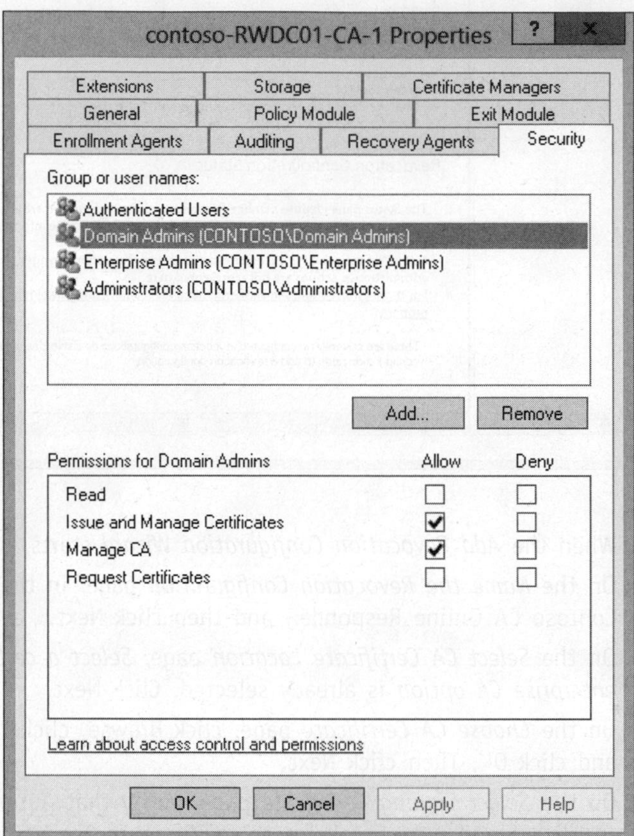

- Configure policy and exit modules.
- Start and stop the AD Certificate Services service.
- Configure AD CS roles and CA extensions.
- Define key recovery agents.
- Configure certificate manager restrictions.
- Delete one or more records in the CA database.
- Modify Certificate Revocation List (CRL) publication schedules.
- Read records and configuration information in the CA database.

The ***certificate manager*** issues and manages certificates, and approves certificate enrollment and revocation requests. To make a user a Certificate Manager, you just have to grant the Allow Issue and Manage Certificates, which grants the following:

- Perform bulk deletions in the CA database.
- Issue, approve, deny, revoke, reactivate, and renew certificates.
- Recover archived keys.
- Read records and configuration information in the CA database.

The ***backup operator*** backs up and restores files and directories. Backup Operators, which are assigned using Active Directory Users and Computers or Computer Management, can perform the following:

- Back up and restore the system state, including CA information.
- Start and stop the AD CS service.
- Possess the system backup user right.
- Read records and configuration information in the CA database.

By default, the local administrator holds the system backup user rights.

Auditors manage and read security logs on a computer running the AD CS role. Because they have the system audit user right, they can perform the following:

- Configure audit parameters.
- Read audit logs.
- Possess the system audit user right.
- Read records and configuration information in the CA database.

By default, the local administrator holds the system audit user rights. In addition to audit events, the computer must also be configured for auditing of object access using a group policy.

ENABLE CA EVENT AUDITING

GET READY. To enable CA event auditing, perform the following steps:

1. Using *Server Manager*, open the Certification Authority console.
2. Right-click the CA and click Properties.
3. Click the Auditing tab.
4. On the *Auditing* tab (see Figure 19-9), click the events that you want audit.
5. Right-click the CA, click All Tasks, and click Stop Service.
6. Right-click the CA, click All Tasks, and click Start Service.
7. Close the certsrv console.

Figure 19-9

Specifying CA audit event

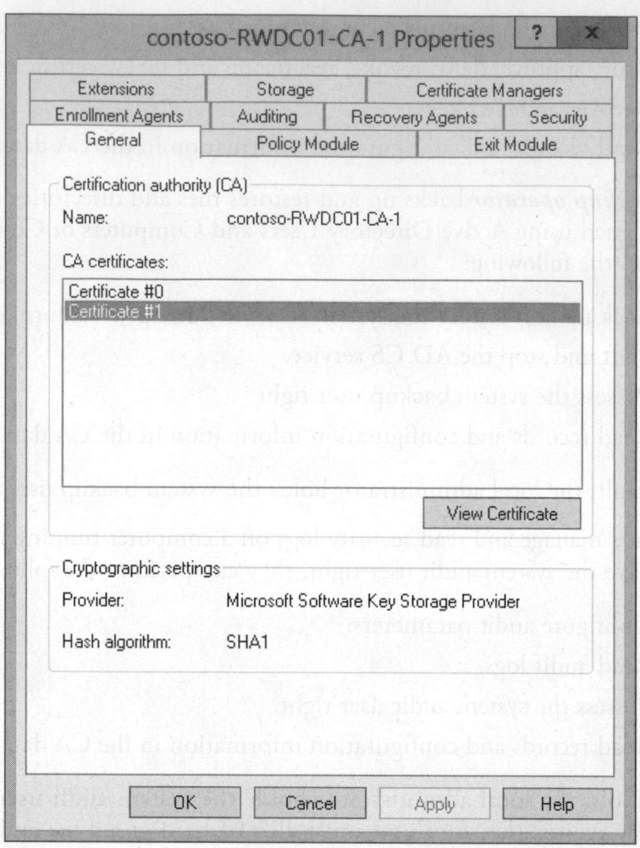

Configuring CA Backup and Recovery

By now, you should understand the importance of backups. If you lose your CA, you could lose your entire PKI infrastructure, which will stop users from logging on using a VPN tunnel, or accessing encrypted e-mails and files. Therefore, you need to know how to back up and restore the CA so that you can quickly bring the CA up after a disaster.

CERTIFICATION READY
Configure CA backup and recovery.
Objective 6.2

You can back up the entire server by backing up all files and the system state using Windows Server Backup. However, you can back up a CA without having to back up the entire server on which the CA is installed. You just need to back up the private and public key for the CA and the certificate database (including the certificate database logs). To perform a backup or restore, you must be a CA administrator or a member of the Backup Operators group, or equivalent.

BACK UP A CA USING THE CERTIFICATION AUTHORITY SNAP-IN

GET READY. To back up a CA using the Certification Authority snap-in, perform the following steps:

1. Using *Server Manager*, open the Certification Authority console.
2. In the console tree, right-click the name of the CA, click All Tasks, and click Back up CA.
3. When the *Certification Authority Backup Wizard* starts, click Next.
4. On the *Items to Back Up* page, click to select Private key and CA certificate and Certificate database and certificate database log options.
5. In the *Back up to this location* text box, type in the path to a folder. Click Next.

6. On the *Select a Password* page, type a password in the *Password* and *Confirm password* text boxes to help secure the private key. Click Next.
7. When the wizard is complete, click Finish.

You can also use the certutil to perform a backup. The syntax for the command is:

```
certutil -backup <BackupDirectory>
```

In addition to the CA, you should also back up the Internet Information Services (IIS) metabase. If a damaged or missing IIS metabase is not restored, IIS will fail to start and result in Certificate Services web pages failing to load. You can use the IIS snap-in to back up the IIS metabase, or you can back up the system state. An alternative method is to recreate the IIS metabase and then use the certutil.exe -vroot command at a command line to reconfigure the IIS server to support the CA web pages.

SKILL SUMMARY

IN THIS LESSON YOU LEARNED:

- Active Directory Certificate Services (AD CS) is a server role that allows you to issue and manage digital certificates as part of a public key infrastructure.
- Public key infrastructure (PKI) is a system consisting of hardware, software, policies, and procedures that create, manage, distribute, use, store, and revoke digital certificates.
- Within the PKI, the certificate authority (CA) binds a public key with respective user identities and issues digital certificates containing the public key.
- A digital certificate is an electronic document that contains an identity, such as a user or organization name, along with a corresponding public key. Because a digital certificate is used to prove a person's identity, it can also be used for authentication.
- The standalone CA works without Active Directory and does not need Active Directory. Users can request certificates using a manual procedure or web enrollment, where they have to identify information and specify the certificate they need.
- An enterprise CA requires Active Directory and is typically used to issue certificates to users, computers, devices, and servers for an organization.
- Certificate Revocation List (CRL) is a digitally signed list issued by a CA that contains a list of certificates issued by the CA that have been revoked.
- An Online Responder is a trusted server that runs the Online Responder service and Online Responder Web proxy to receive and respond to individual client requests for information about the status of a certificate.
- You can back up a CA without having to back up the entire server on which the CA is installed. You just need to back up the private and public key for the CA and the certificate database (including the certificate database logs).

Knowledge Assessment

Multiple Choice

Select the correct answer for each of the following questions.

1. What kind of system are you creating when you install a certificate authority (CA) on a domain controller?
   a. JIF
   b. SMB
   c. CIF
   d. PKI
2. Which of the following role services allows you to validate and revoke certificates?
   a. Certificate Authority Policy Web Service
   b. CA Web Enrollment
   c. Online Responder
   d. Network Device Enrollment Service
3. What is required to install an enterprise CA?
   a. Active Directory
   b. multiple CAs
   c. Online Responder
   d. IIS
4. Which of the following can be used to check the validity of a digital certificate? (Choose two answers.)
   a. Online Responder
   b. CAPolicy
   c. NDES
   d. CRL
5. You have two servers called *Server01* and *Server02*, which are running Windows Server 2012 R2. You configured Server01 as an enterprise root CA. You install the Online Responder role service on Server02. What do you need to do so that Server01 uses the Online Responder on Server02?
   a. Configure the CRL Distribution Point extension
   b. Configure the Authority Information Access (AIA) extension
   c. Add the Online Responder to Server01 and point to Server02
   d. Import the enterprise root CA certificate and install on Server02
6. You have an Active Directory domain. You install Active Directory Certificate Services (AD CS) role on a standalone server. However, when you install the AD CS role as an enterprise CA, the Enterprise CA option is not available. What should you do?
   a. Add the DNS server role
   b. Add the AD LDS role
   c. Join the server to the domain
   d. Load the AD CS Proxy role
7. You installed AD CS and configured it as a standalone CA. You need a fellow administrator to audit changes to the CA configuration settings and the CA security settings. What two things must be done to enable the auditing? (Choose two answers.)
   a. Configure auditing in the Certification Authority snap-in
   b. Enable auditing of the %SYSTEM32%\CertSrv folder
   c. Enable auditing of the System and Application Logs
   d. Enable the Audit object access settings in the Local Security Policy for the AD CS server

8. You have a two-tier PKI consisting of an offline root CA and an online issuing CA. The Enterprise CA is running Windows Server 2012 R2. You need to ensure the CA can hand out new certificates. What should you do?
   a. With the root CA running and connected, renew the CRL on the issuing CA. Copy the CRL to the CertEnroll folder on the issuing CA.
   b. With the root CA running and connected, renew the CRL on the root CA. Copy the CRL to the CertEnroll folder on the issuing CA.
   c. Import the root CA certificate to the Trusted Root CA to the issuing CA.
   d. With the root CA running, create a shortcut to the CertEnroll folder on the root CA.
9. You have installed an Enterprise Root CA on Server01. You need to ensure that the ITManagers group is authorized to revoke the certificate on Server01. What should you do?
   a. Assign the Allow Issue and Manage Certificates permission
   b. Assign the Allow Manage CA permission
   c. Assign the Allow Request Certificates permission
   d. Assign the Allow Read permission
10. You have an enterprise CA and an ITManagers group that you want to allow to publish new certificate revocation lists but not allow to revoke certificates. What should you do?
    a. Assign the Manage CA permissions to the ITManagers group
    b. Assign the Issue and Manage Certificates permission to the ITManagers group
    c. Add the ITManagers group to the local administrators of the server running the enterprise CA
    d. Add the ITManagers to the CRL List group
11. You are an administrator for the Contoso Corporation, which has a Windows Server 2012 R2 Active Directory domain. You need to install an Enterprise Root Certificate Authority (CA) that also provides highly available revoke certificate information. What should you do?
    a. Implement an Online Certificate Protocol (OCSP) responder by using an IIS server
    b. Implement an Online Certificate Protocol (OCSP) responder by using Network Load Balancing
    c. Implement an Online Certificate Protocol (OCSP) responder by using a proxy server
    d. Implement a CRL responder by using a UNC and a URL
12. You deployed an enterprise root CA on your Active Directory domain. You create a global security group called *CertAdmins*. You need to ensure that the CertAdmins can issue, approve, and revoke certificates. What should you do?
    a. Run the certsrv –add CertAdmins command
    b. Place the CertAdmins group to the CA Admins group
    c. Add the CertAdmins group to the domain admins group
    d. Assign the Certificate Manager role to the CertAdmins group
13. You have a two-tier PKI consisting of an offline root CA and an online issuing CA. The Enterprise CA is running Windows Server 2012 R2. You need to ensure the CA can hand out new certificates. What should you do?
    a. With the root CA running and connected, renew the CRL on the issuing CA. Copy the CRL to the CertEnroll folder on the issuing CA.
    b. With the root CA running and connected, renew the CRL on the root CA. Copy the CRL to the CertEnroll folder on the issuing CA.
    c. Import the root CA certificate to the Trusted Root CA to the issuing CA.
    d. With the root CA running, create a shortcut to the CertEnroll folder on the root CA.

14. You are installing an Enterprise CA on a new member server that is part of the domain. However when you run the Add Roles Wizard, the enterprise CA is disabled. What is the problem?
   a. You do not have the proper SRV records in DNS
   b. You are not using the Data Center Edition of Windows Server 2012 R2
   c. You are not logged on as an enterprise admin
   d. You need to run the certsrv -enable command first

15. You have an enterprise CA. What do you need to minimize the amount of network bandwidth required to validate a certificate?
   a. Configure an LDAP publishing point for the CRL
   b. Configure an OCSP responder
   c. Modify the settings of the delta CRL
   d. Modify the OCSP delta

Matching and Identification

1. Identify the role that can perform the following tasks:
   _______ a) Configure policy and exit modules
   _______ b) Back up CA database
   _______ c) Start the Certificate Services service
   _______ d) Modify CRL publication schedules
   _______ e) Recover archived keys
   _______ f) Issue certificates
   _______ g) Read audit logs
   1. CA Administrator
   2. Certificate Manager
   3. Backup Operator
   4. Auditor

2. Which of the following is a CA role?
   _______ Certification Authority
   _______ Certificate Enrollment Web Service
   _______ Certificate Authority Policy Web Service
   _______ Certificate Generator
   _______ Online Responder
   _______ Encryption Checker
   _______ CA Web enrollment

Build a List

1. Identify the steps, in order, to install and configure the Online Responder by placing the number of the step in the appropriate space. Not all steps will be used.
   _______ Add Revocation configuration
   _______ Configure the AD CS Services on the server
   _______ Import the Enterprise CA certificate
   _______ Configure CRL extensions
   _______ Configure AIA extensions
   _______ Install the Active Directory CS Online Responder role
   _______ Deploy an OCSP Response Signing template
   _______ Deploy an OCSP Membership template

2. Identify the steps, in order, to install and configure a CRL. Not all steps will be used.
   _______ Configure CRL extensions
   _______ Configure AIA extensions
   _______ Modify the CRL publication interval and Delta CRL publication interval
   _______ Deploy the CRL certificate
   _______ Click the Extensions tab
   _______ In Certification Authority, right-click Managed Certificates
   _______ In Certification Authority, right-click Revoked Certificates

Choose an Option

1. Which tab would you use to define the CRL location when configuring the CA? Refer to Figure 19-10.

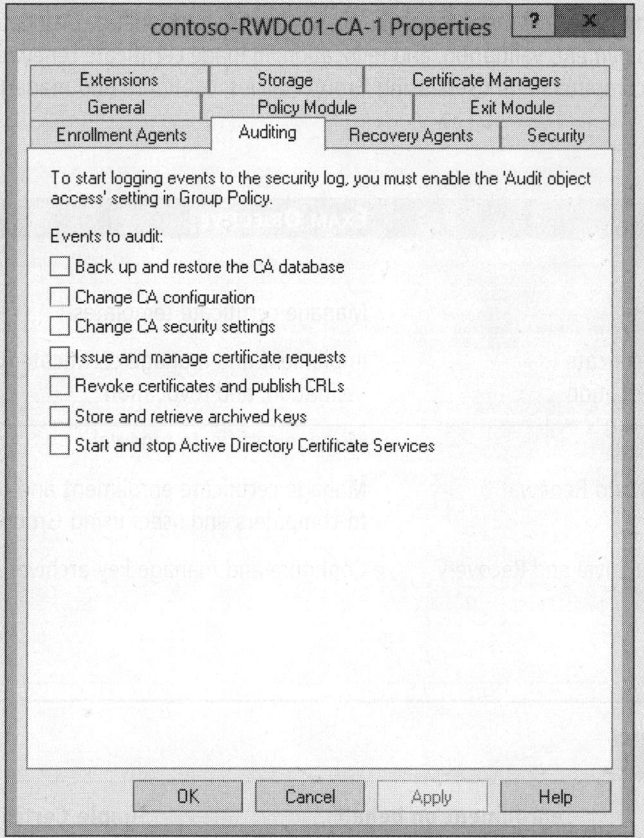

Figure 19-10
Defining the CRL location

Business Case Scenarios

Scenario 19-1: Securing a Two-Tier PKI

You want to deploy multiple CA servers to form a PKI consisting of several CA servers that will deploy certificates to the users and computers. How would you configure the servers to form the PKI and what steps would you use to secure the PKI?

Scenario 19-2: Backing Up a CA

You have just installed an Enterprise CA. What are the three ways that you can back up the CA so that it can be restored if the server fails in the future?

Managing Certificates

70-412 EXAM OBJECTIVE

Objective 6.3 – Manage certificates. This objective may include but is not limited to: Manage certificate templates; implement and manage certificate deployment, validation, and revocation; manage certificate renewal; manage certificate enrollment and renewal to computers and users using Group Policies; configure and manage key archival and recovery.

Lesson Heading	Exam Objective
Managing Digital Certificates	
Managing Certificate Templates	Manage certificate templates
Implementing and Managing Certificate Deployment, Validation, and Revocation	Implement and manage certificate deployment, validation, and revocation
Managing Certificate Renewal	Manage certificate renewal
Managing Certificate Enrollment and Renewal Using Group Policies	Manage certificate enrollment and renewal to computers and users using Group Policies
Configuring and Managing Key Archival and Recovery	Configure and manage key archival and recovery

KEY TERMS

autoenrollment
CA Web enrollment
certificate chain
certificate templates
Credential Roaming
digital certificate
enrollment agent
enrollment on behalf
Key Recovery Agents (KRA)
manual enrollment
Network Device Enrollment Service (NDES)
restricted enrollment agent
Simple Certificate Enrollment Protocol (SCEP)
X.509 version 3

Managing Digital Certificates

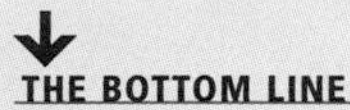

A ***digital certificate*** is similar to an electronic identification card used to certify the online identify of individuals, organizations, and computers. It contains a person's or an organization's name, a serial number, an expiration date, a copy of the certificate holder's public key (used for encrypting messages and creating digital signatures), and the digital signature of the Certification Authority (CA) that assigned the certificate so that recipients can verify that the certificate is real.

The most common digital certificate is the ***X.509 version 3***. The X.509 version 3 standard specifies the format for the public key certificate, certificate revocation lists, attribute certificates, and a certificate path validation algorithm (see Figure 20-1).

Figure 20-1

Viewing a digital certificate

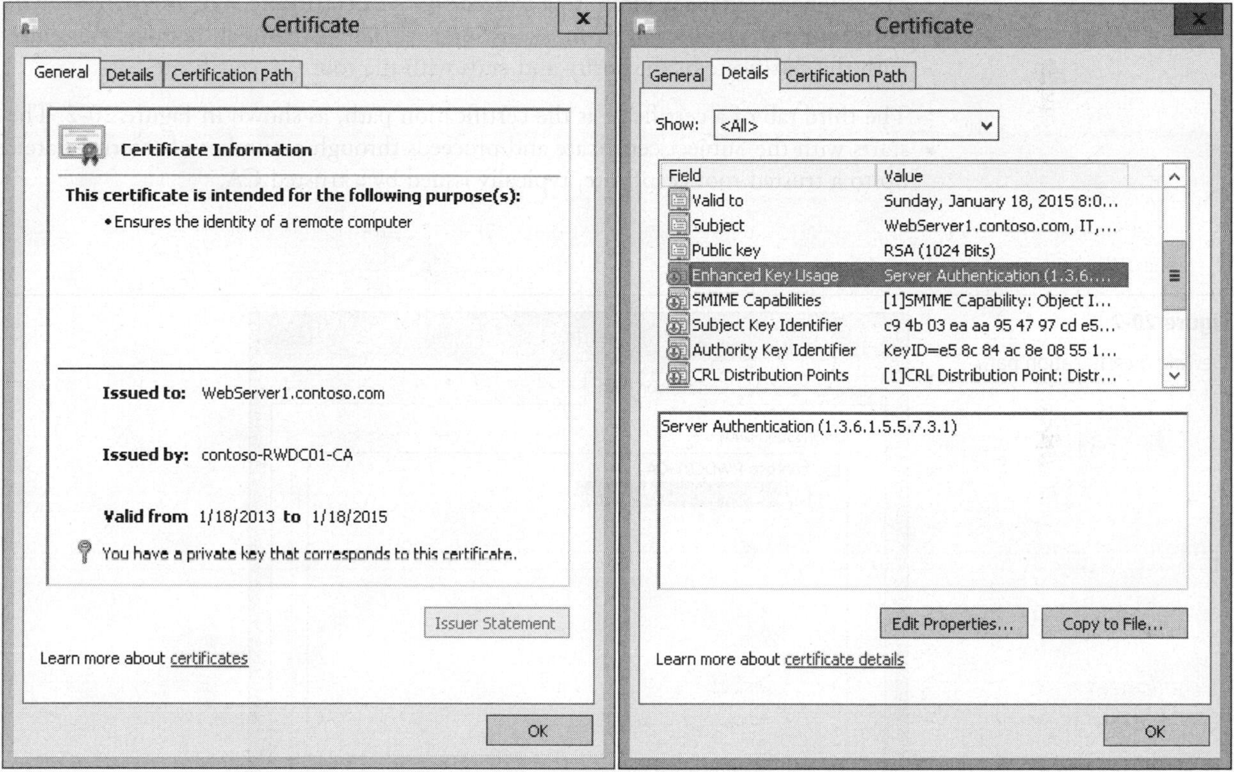

The X.509 digital certificate includes the following fields:

- **Version:** Version of the certificate format, such as version 3.
- **Certificate Serial Number:** The unique serial number that is assigned by the issuing CA. Based on the serial number, the CA maintains an audit history for each certificate so that certificates can be traced, including when the certificate has been revoked.

- **Certificate Algorithm Identifier:** The public key cryptography and message digest algorithms that are used by the issuing CA to digitally sign the certificate.
- **Issuer:** The name of the issuing CA.
- **Validity Period including the valid-from and valid-to dates:** The certificate's start and expiration dates.
- **Subject:** The person, entity, or owner identified in the certificate.
- **Subject Public-Key Information:** The public key and a list of the public key cryptography algorithms.
- **Key-usage:** Purpose of the public key such as encipherment, signature, certificate signing, and so on).
- **Certification Authority's digital signature:** The CA's digital signature that is used to verify it came from the issuer.

There are only so many root CA certificates that are assigned to commercial third-party organizations. Therefore, when you acquire a digital certificate from a third-party organization, you might need to use a certificate chain to obtain the root CA certificate so that it can be trusted. In addition, you might need to install an intermediate digital certificate that links the assigned digital certificate to a trusted root CA certificate. The ***certificate chain***, also known as the certification path, is a list of certificates used to authenticate an entity. It begins with the certificate of the entity and ends with the root CA certificate.

The third tab of a certificate is the certification path, as shown in Figure 20-2. The path starts with the Subject certificate and proceeds through a number of intermediate certificates up to a trusted root certificate, typically issued by a trusted CA.

Figure 20-2
Viewing a certification path

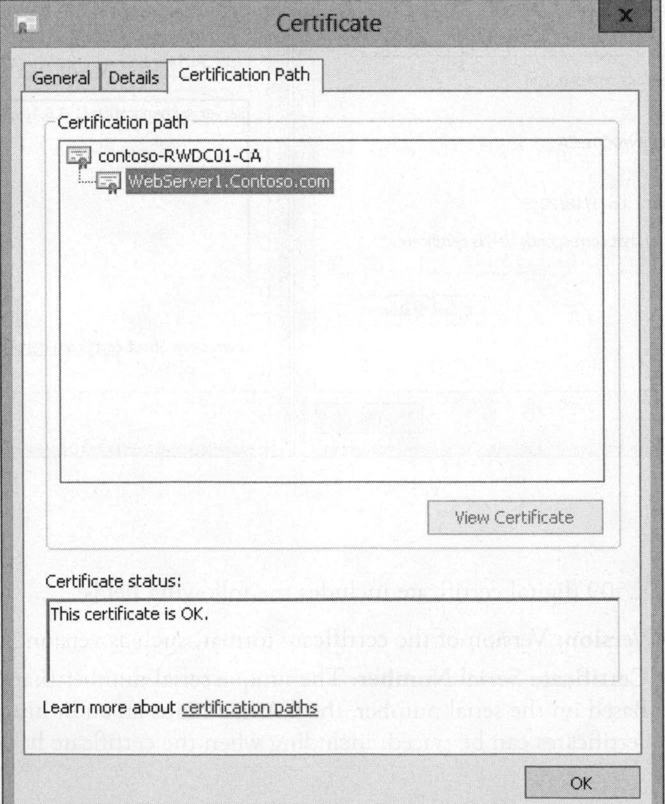

On a local computer running Windows, the certificates are stored in a certificate store. Using the Certificates MMC snap-in, you can display the certificate store for a user, a computer, or a service according to the purpose for which the certificates were issued or by using their logical storage categories. Certificates are then organized into the following folders:

- **Personal:** Certificates associated with public keys to which you have access. These are the certificates that have been issued to the user, the computer, or service that you are viewing.
- **Trusted Root Certification Authorities:** Implicitly trusted CAs, including all of the certificates in the third-party root CAs, store plus root certificates from your organization and Microsoft.
- **Enterprise Trust:** A container for certificate trust lists including self-signed root certificates from other organizations.
- **Intermediate Certification Authorities:** Certificates issued to subordinate CAs.
- **Trusted People:** Certificates issued to people or end entities that are explicitly trusted. Most often these are self-signed certificates or certificates explicitly trusted in an application such as Microsoft Outlook.
- **Other People:** Certificates issued to people or end entities that are implicitly trusted. These certificates must be part of a trusted certification hierarchy. Most often these are cached certificates for services such as Encrypting File System, where certificates are used for creating authorization for decrypting an encrypted file.
- **Trusted Publishers:** Certificates from CAs that are trusted by Software Restriction policies.
- **Third-Party Root Certification Authorities:** Trusted root certificates from CAs other than Microsoft and your organization.
- **Certificate Enrollment Requests:** Pending or rejected certificate requests.
- **Active Directory User Object:** Certificates associated with your user object and published in Active Directory.

Windows can also publish certificates to Active Directory. Publishing a certificate in Active Directory enables all users or computers with adequate permissions to retrieve the certificate as needed.

ACCESS A CERTIFICATE STORE

GET READY. To access a certificate store, perform the following steps:

1. Click the Start menu, type mmc.exe, and press the Enter key.
2. When the console opens, click File > Add/Remove snap-in.
3. When the *Add or Remove Snap-ins* dialog box opens, double-click Certificates.
4. On the Certificates snap-in dialog box, click one of the following:
   My user account
   Service account
   Computer account
5. If you pick *My user*, click Finish. If you pick *My Computer*, click Next, choose Local computer, and then click Finish. If you pick *Service Account*, click Local computer, click Next, click a service account to manage, and then click Finish.
6. In the *Add or Remove Snap-ins* dialog box, click OK. The certificate store opens (see Figure 20-3).

Figure 20-3
Viewing a certificate store

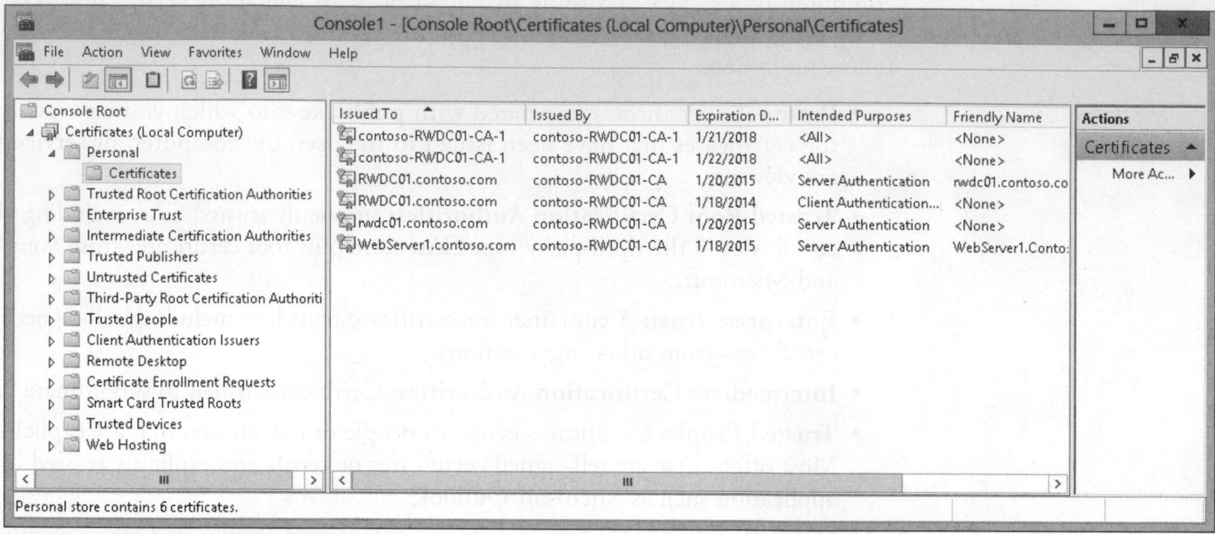

Digital certificates can be imported and exported via electronic files. Four common formats are as follows:

- **Personal Information Exchange (PKCS #12):** The Personal Information Exchange format (PFX, also called PKCS #12) supports secure storage of certificates, private keys, and all certificates in a certification path. The PKCS #12 format is the only file format that can be used to export a certificate and its private key. It usually has a .pfx or .p12 filename extension.
- **Cryptographic Message Syntax Standard (PKCS #7):** The PKCS #7 format supports storage of certificates and all certificates in a certification path. It usually has a .p7b or .p7c filename extension.
- **DER-encoded binary X.509:** The Distinguished Encoding Rules (DER) format supports storage of a single certificate. This format does not support storage of the private key or certification path. It usually has a .cer, .crt, or .der filename extension.
- **Base64-encoded X.509:** The Base64 format supports storage of a single certificate. This format does not support storage of the private key or certification path.

EXPORT A DIGITAL CERTIFICATE

GET READY. To export a digital certificate, perform the following steps:

1. Using the *certificate snap-in*, right-click the certificate that you want to export, click All Tasks, and click Export.
2. When the *Certificate Export Wizard* starts, click Next.
3. In the *Export Private key* page, if the private key is available and you want to export the private and public key, click Yes, export the private key. If you want to export only the public key, click No, do not export the private key. Click Next.
4. In the *Export file format* page, click the format that you want to export to. You can also select options to delete the private key upon successful export. Click Next.
5. If you selected to export the private key, on the *Security* page, click to select Password. Then type a password in the *Password* box if you want to associate a password with the exported certificate. Retype the password in the *Confirm password* box. Click Next.

6. In the *File to Export* page, type a filename in the *Export to* box or click the Browse button to navigate to the name of a file in which to store the certificate for exporting.
7. When the format is complete, click Finish.
8. When the export is successful, click OK.

IMPORT A DIGITAL CERTIFICATE

GET READY. To import a digital certificate, perform the following steps:

1. Using *File Explorer*, navigate to the location of the digital certificate.
2. Double-click the digital certificate.
3. When the *Certificate Import Wizard* opens, click either Current User or Local Machine.
4. On the *File to Import* page, click Next.
5. On the *Private key protection* page, type the password, and then click Next.
6. On the *Certificate Store* page, click Automatically select the certificate store based on the type of certificate. Click Next.
7. When the wizard is complete, click Finish.
8. When the import is successful, click OK.

After you import a certificate, you should use the Certificates MMC to verify that the certificate is stored in the correct location.

Managing Certificate Templates

Certificate templates are used to simplify the task of administering a CA by allowing an administrator to identify, modify, and issue certificates that have been preconfigured for selected tasks. The Certificate Templates snap-in enables you to view and modify the properties for each certificate template, and copy and modify certificate templates.

CERTIFICATION READY
Manage certificate templates.
Objective 6.3

Certificate templates are an integral part of the enterprise CA. They are used to establish a set of rules and format for certificate enrollment that are applied to incoming certificate requests. Certificate templates also give instructions to the client to create and submit a valid certificate request.

Certificates based on a certificate template can be issued only by an enterprise CA. The templates are stored in Active Directory Domain Services (AD DS) for use by every CA in the forest. This allows the CA to always have access to the current standard template and ensures consistent application of the certificate policy across the forest.

When accessing the Certificate Templates console, there are several preconfigured certificate templates that act as a starting point to use certificate templates. However, most organizations will need to customize the built-in templates by copying the current templates and creating new certificates based on the copied certificate. Some of these templates (as seen in Figure 20-4) include:

- **Basic EFS (Template Version 1):** Used by Encrypting File System (EFS) to encrypt data.
- **Computer Template Version 1:** Allows a computer to authenticate itself to the network.
- **EFS Recovery Agent (Template Version 1):** Allows the subject to decrypt files that were previously encrypted with EFS.

- **IPSEC (Template Version 1):** Used by IPsec to digitally sign, encrypt, and decrypt network communication when the subject name is supplied to the request.
- **Smartcard Logon (Template Version 1):** Allows the holder to authenticate using a smart card.
- **User (Template Version 1):** Used by users for email, EFS, and client authentication.
- **Web Server (Template Version 1):** Proves the identity of a Web server.

Figure 20-4

Viewing the Certificate Template console

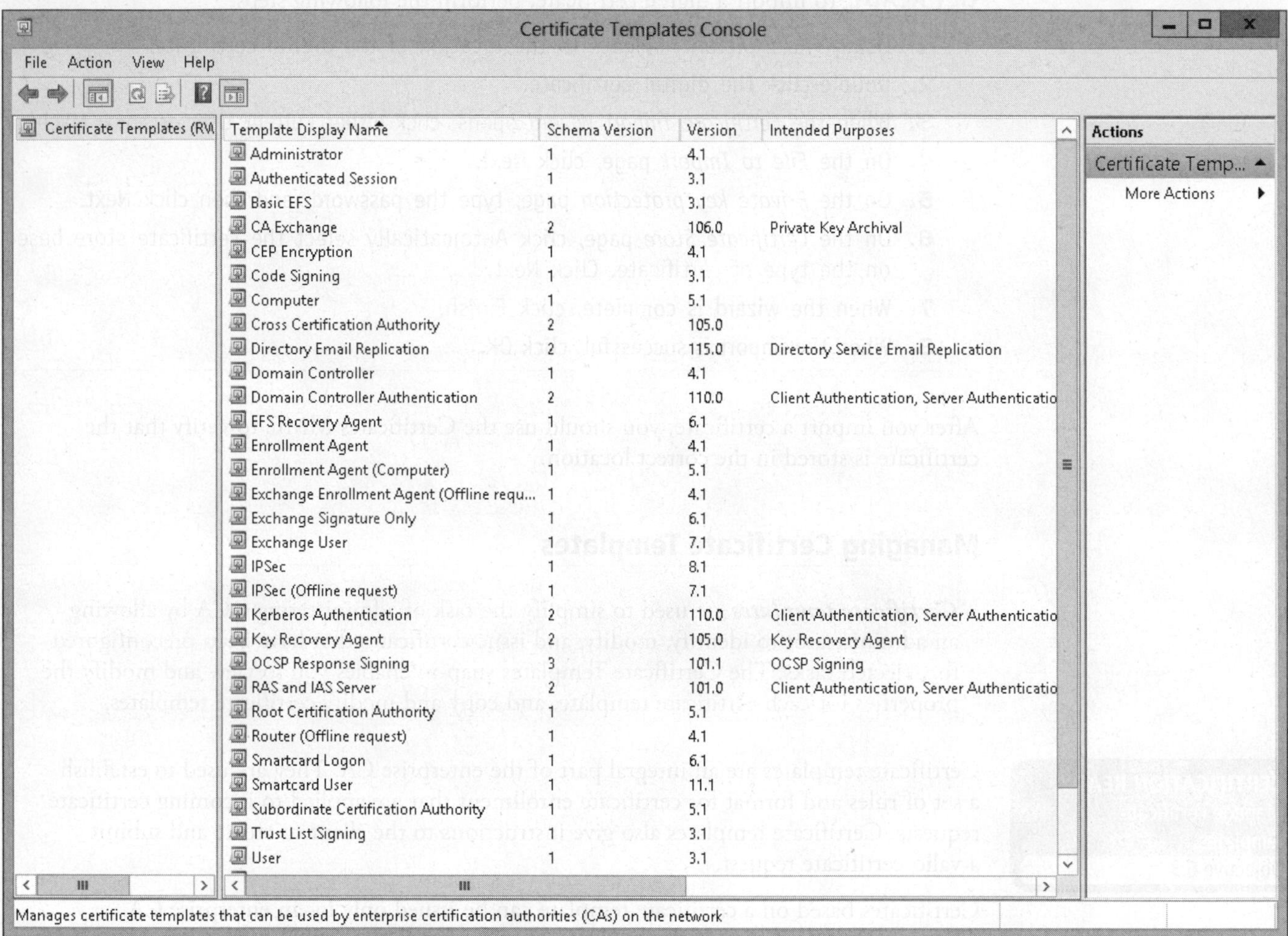

Some certificates have a single purpose, whereas others have multiple purposes. A single-purpose certificate serves a single purpose, such as allowing users to log on with a smart card. Organizations utilize single-purpose certificates in cases where the certificate configuration differs from other certificates that are being deployed. A multi-purpose certificate serves more than one purpose (often unrelated) at the same time. Some templates (such as the User template) serve multiple purposes by default, but organizations often modify templates to serve additional purposes, so that users and computers have to enroll only once for a certificate.

Active Directory Certificate Services (AD CS) provides four schema versions of certificate templates:

- **Version 1 certificate templates:** Support general certificate needs and provide compatibility with clients and issuing CAs running Windows 2000 operating systems or later. Version 1 templates are installed by default during CA setup and cannot be deleted. The only property that can be modified on a version 1 template is the set of assigned permissions that control access to the template.

- **Version 2 certificate templates:** Introduced in Windows Server 2003. These certificates can be configured by an administrator to control the way certificates are requested, issued, and used. Version 2 templates provide support for certificate autoenrollment.
- **Version 3 certificate templates:** Introduced with Windows Server 2008. They support Suite B cryptographic algorithms. Suite B was created by the U.S. National Security Agency to specify cryptographic algorithms that must be used by U.S. government agencies to secure confidential information.
- **Version 4 certificate templates:** Introduced with Windows Server 2012, version 4 certificate templates allow administrators to separate what features are supported by which operating system version by adding a Compatibility tab to the certificate template Properties tab. Version 4 certificate templates also support both Cryptographic Service Providers (CSPs) and Key Storage Providers (KSPs). They can also be configured to require renewal with a same key.

Assuming that you use the corresponding version of Windows, you can upgrade the certificate template to a higher version.

When you access the properties of a certificate template, you have the following tabs:

- **General:** Specifies the template display name and template name. It allows you to modify the validity period and the renewal period and if the certificate is published in Active Directory.
- **Compatibility:** Used to specify the earliest operating system that can use a certificate.
- **Request Handling:** Specifies the purpose of the digital certificates and gives some control on the certificates that are made with this template.
- **Superseded Templates:** Specifies which certificate template that the current template will replace.
- **Extensions:** Specifies the application policies, basic constraints, issuance policies, and key usage.
- **Security:** Specifies you can access and use a certificate template.
- **Server:** Allows an administrator not to store certificates, requests, or revocation information in the CA database.
- **Cryptography:** Specifies the minimum key size and which providers can be used.
- **Subject Name:** Specifies what Subject name is used in the certificate.
- **Issuance Requirements:** Specifies if a certificate has to be approved, the number of authorized signatures, and what is required for reenrollment.

To configure certificate template permissions, you need to define the Discretionary Access Control List (DACL) for each certificate template in the Security tab (see Figure 20-5). The permissions that are assigned to a certificate template define which users or groups can read, modify, enroll, or autoenroll for that certificate template.

The permissions for a certificate template include:

- **Full Control:** Allows a security principal to modify all attributes of a certificate template, which includes permissions for the certificate template.
- **Read:** Allows a user or computer to view the certificate template when enrolling for certificates. The Read permission is also required by the certificate server to find the certificate templates in AD DS.

- **Write:** Allows a user or computer to modify the attributes of a certificate template, including permissions for the certificate template.
- **Enroll:** Allows a user or computer to enroll for a certificate based on the certificate template. However, to enroll for a certificate, you must also have Read permissions for the certificate template.
- **Autoenroll:** Allows a user or computer to receive a certificate through the autoenrollment process. However, the Autoenroll permission requires the user or computer to also have both Read and Enroll permissions for a certificate template. This permission will not show for templates based on schema version 1.

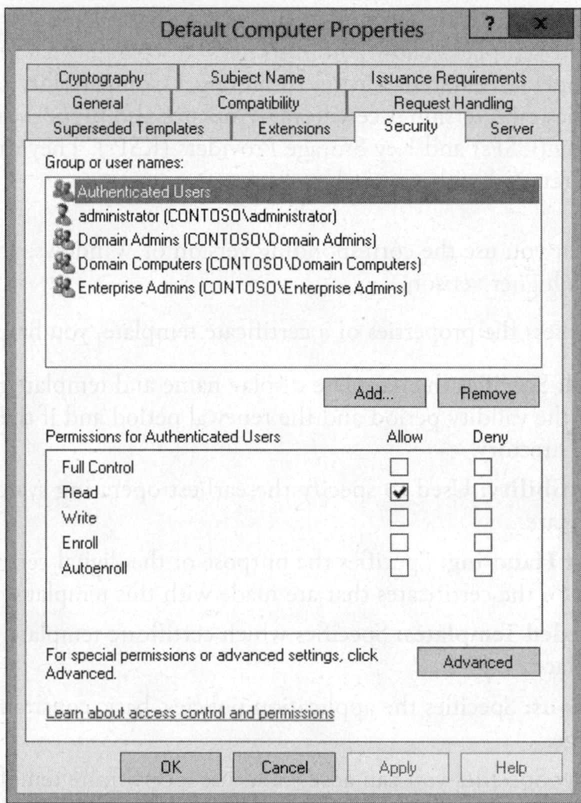

Figure 20-5

Modifying permissions for a certificate template

Similar to assigning NTFS or share permissions, it is best to assign the certificate template permissions to a global or universal group. It is also a best practice to keep the Read permission allocated to the Authenticated Users group to view the certificate templates in Active Directory and it allows a CA that runs under the System context of a computer account to view the certificate templates when assigning certificates.

CREATE A NEW USER CERTIFICATE TEMPLATE

GET READY. To create a new User Certificate Template, perform the following steps:

1. Using Server Manager, open the *Certification Authority* console.
2. Expand certificate authority, right-click Certificate Templates, and then select Manage.
3. When the *Certificate Templates* console opens, right-click the User template, and then click Duplicate Template.
4. Click the General tab.
5. Modify the Validity period for the certificate.
6. In the *Template display name* field, type Corporate User Certificate.

7. Click the Subject Name tab.
8. Clear the Include e-mail name in the subject name and the E-mail name check boxes.
9. Click the Extension tab.
10. Click Application Policies, and then click Edit.
11. When the *Edit Application Policies Extension* dialog box opens, click Add.
12. When the *Add Application Policy* dialog box opens, click Smart Card Logon, and then click OK two times.
13. Click the Superseded Templates tab.
14. Click Add. Click the User template, and then click OK.
15. Click OK to close the *Properties of New Template* dialog box.
16. Close the *Certification Template* console and *Certification Authority* console.

By default, only a handful of digital certificates are available to users and computers. To make other certificate templates available so that users or computers can request a certificate, you use the CA. You can then use the Certificates console to request a certificate.

CONFIGURE THE TEMPLATE SO IT CAN BE ISSUED

GET READY. To configure the template so it can be issued, perform the following steps:

1. Using Server Manager, open Certification Authority.
2. Right-click Certificate Templates, click New, and then click Certificate Template to Issue.
3. In the *Enable Certificate Templates* window, select the template that you want to make available, and click OK.
4. Close *Certification Authority*.

Implementing and Managing Certificate Deployment, Validation, and Revocation

In Windows 8/8.1 and, Windows Server 2012, and Windows Server 2012 R2 you can use multiple methods to enroll user and computer certificates. If you have hundreds, or even thousands, of users, you should use autoenrollment so that you can automatically deploy certificates to those users or computers.

CERTIFICATION READY
Implement and manage certificate deployment, validation, and revocation.
Objective 6.3

The available methods for a user or computer to enroll for a certificate include:

- Manual enrollment
- CA Web enrollment
- Enrollment on behalf (enrollment agent)
- Autoenrollment

USING MANUAL ENROLLMENT

When you use ***manual enrollment***, you create a private key and certificate request is generated on a device such as a web service or a computer. The request is sent to the CA to generate the certificate. The certificate is sent back to the device for installation. You typically use manual enrollment when the device does not support autoenrollment, you do not want to wait for autoenrollment to be applied, or the certificate is not available through autoenrollment.

REQUEST A CERTIFICATE USING MANUAL ENROLLMENT

GET READY. To request a certificate using manual enrollment, perform the following steps:

1. Click the Start menu, type mmc.exe, and press the Enter key.
2. When the console opens, click File > Add/Remove snap-in.
3. When the *Add or Remove Snap-ins* dialog box opens, double-click Certificates.
4. On the *Certificates snap-in* dialog box, click My user account. Click Finish.
5. Expand the Certificates-Current User, expand Personal, and click Certificates.
6. Right-click the Certificates folder, click All Tasks, and click Request NewCertificate.
7. When the *Certificate Enrollment wizard* starts, click Next.
8. On the *Certificate Enrollment Policy* page, *Active Directory Enrollment Policy* is already selected. Click Next.
9. Click to select Corporate User Certificate and then click Enroll.
10. After the certificate has been installed, click Finish.

USING CA WEB ENROLLMENT

The ***CA Web enrollment*** uses a website on a CA to obtain certificates. The website uses Internet Information Server (IIS), and the AD CS web enrollment role has been installed and configured. The URL to make a request is `https://<servername>/certsrv`. Similar to the manual enrollment, CA Web enrollment is used on devices that do not support autoenrollment, or you do not want to wait for autoenrollment to be applied.

REQUEST A CERTIFICATE USING WEB ENROLLMENT

GET READY. To request a certificate using web enrollment, perform the following steps:

1. Open Internet Explorer and open the following URL:
   `https://<servername>/certsrv`
   For example, if the CA is RWDC01, you would open `http://rwdc01/certsrv`.
2. Click Request a certificate.
3. On the *Request a Certificate* page, click Advanced certificate request.
4. On the *Advanced Certificate Request*, click Create and submit a request to this CA. If you are asked to allow a web site to perform digital certificate operation on your behalf, click Yes.
5. On the *Advanced Certificate Request* page (as shown in Figure 20-6), specify the certificate template that you want to use. Click Submit. If you are asked to allow a web site to perform digital certificate operation on your behalf, click Yes.

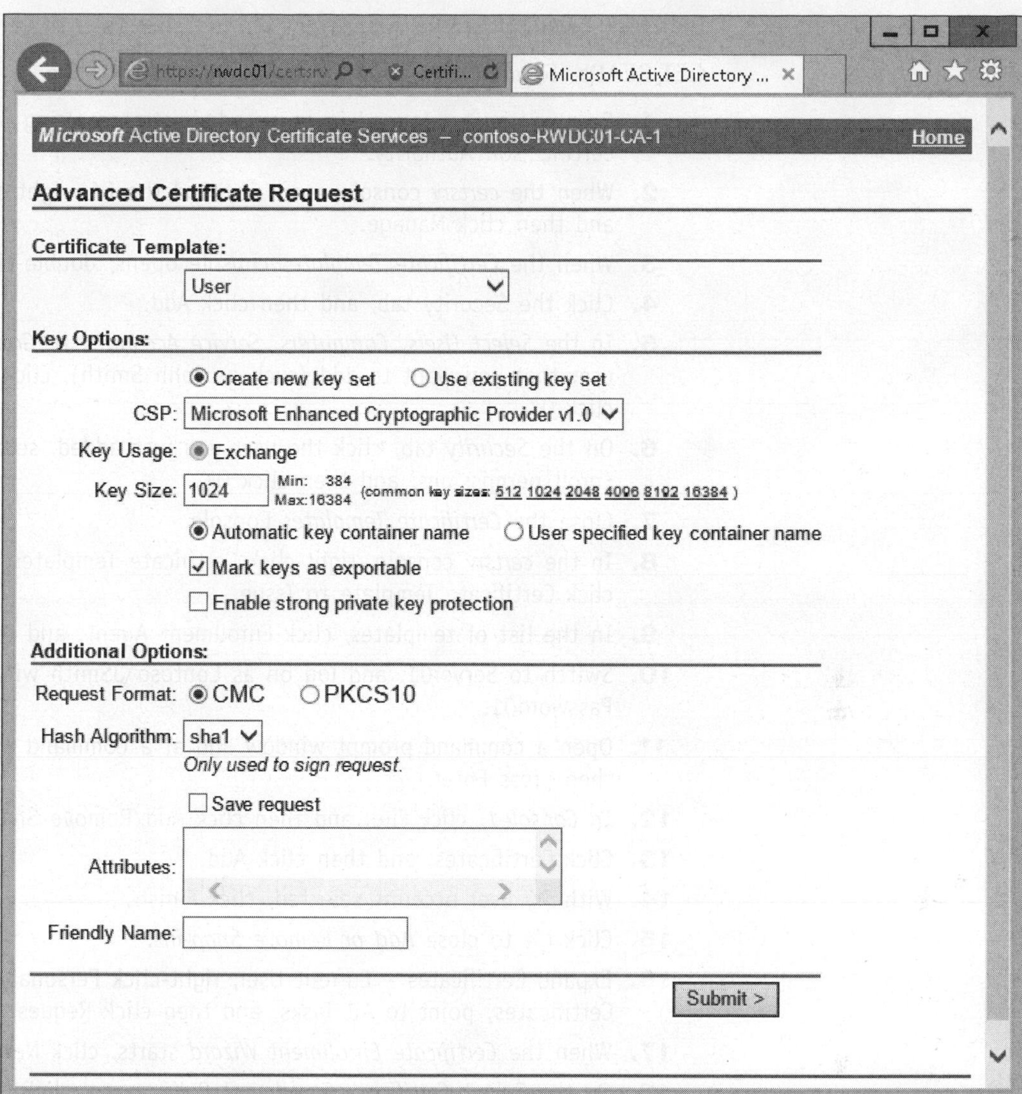

Figure 20-6

Specifying the certificate template to use when using web enrollment

6. On the *Certificate issued* page, click Install this certificate.
7. When the certificate has been installed, close *Internet Explorer*.

ENROLLING USING ENROLLMENT AGENTS

When you use ***enrollment on behalf (enrollment agent)***, the CA administrator creates an enrollment agent account for the user. The user with enrollment agent rights can then enroll for certificates on behalf of other users such as when the administrator needs to preload logon certificates of new employees' smart cards. The ***restricted enrollment agent*** allows you to limit the permissions for users (usually administrators and help desk personnel) who are designated as enrollment agents, and to enroll for smart card certificates on behalf of other users.

ENABLE ENROLLMENT AGENTS

GET READY. To enable enrollment agents, perform the following steps:

1. Be sure you are logged in as an administrator. Using Server Manager, open Certification Authority.
2. When the *certsrv* console opens, expand the CA, right-click Certificate Templates, and then click Manage.
3. When the *Certificate Templates* console opens, double-click Enrollment Agent.
4. Click the Security tab, and then click Add.
5. In the *Select Users, Computers, Service Accounts, or Groups* window, type the user that you want to add (such as John Smith), click Check Names, and then click OK.
6. On the *Security* tab, click the user you just added, select Allow for Read and Enroll permissions, and then click OK.
7. Close the *Certificate Templates* Console.
8. In the *certsrv* console, right-click Certificate Templates, point to New, and then click Certificate Template to Issue.
9. In the list of templates, click Enrollment Agent, and then click OK.
10. Switch to Server01, and log on as Contoso\JSmith with the password Password01.
11. Open a command prompt window and at a command prompt, type mmc.exe, and then press Enter.
12. In *Console1*, click File, and then click Add/Remove Snap-in.
13. Click Certificates, and then click Add.
14. With My user account selected, click Finish.
15. Click OK to close *Add or Remove Snap-ins*.
16. Expand Certificates – Current User, right-click Personal, click Certificates, right-click Certificates, point to All Tasks, and then click Request New Certificate.
17. When the *Certificate Enrollment Wizard* starts, click Next.
18. On the Select *Certificate Enrollment Policy* page, click Next.
19. On the *Request Certificates* page, select Enrollment Agent, and then click Enroll.
20. When the certificate is installed, click Finish.
21. Go back to the CA server.
22. In the *Certification Authority* console, right-click the CA, and then click Properties.
23. Click the Enrollment Agents tab (see Figure 20-7).

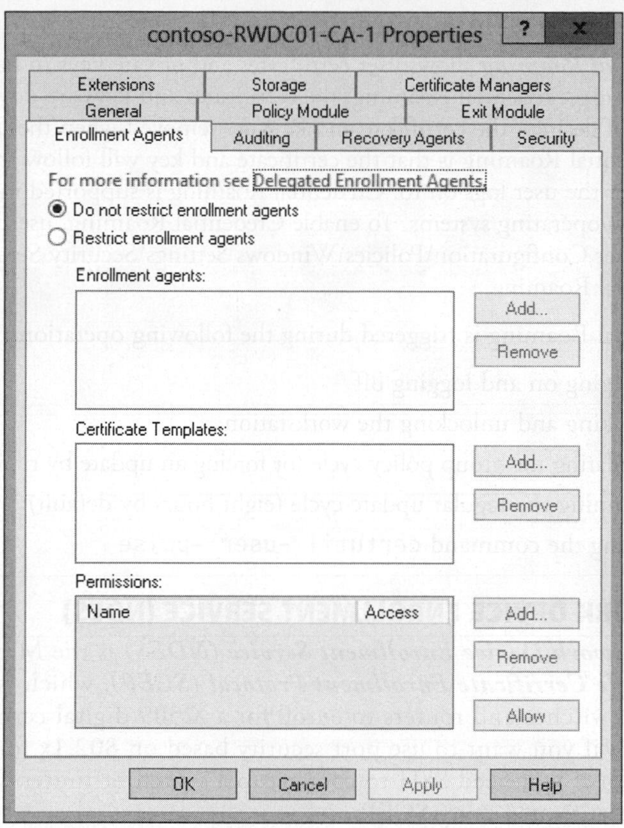

Figure 20-7
Specifying enrollment agents

24. Click Restrict enrollment agents.
25. When a warning states that restrictions on delegated enrollment agents can be enforced only on Windows Server 2008 CAs or later, click OK.
26. In the *Enrollment agents* section, click Add.
27. In the *Select User, Computer or Group* field, type JSmith, click Check Names, and then click OK.
28. Click Everyone, and then click Remove.
29. In the *certificate templates* section, click Add.
30. In the list of templates, click Corporate User Certificate, and then click OK.
31. In the *Certificate Templates* section, click <All>, and then click Remove.
32. In the *Permission* section, click Add.
33. In the *Select User, Computer or Group* field, type the name of the group that you want to restrict enrollment agents, click Check Names, and then click OK.
34. In the *Permission* section, click Everyone, and then click Remove.
35. Click OK to close the *Properties* dialog box.

USING AUTOENROLLMENT

Most certificates will be assigned through ***autoenrollment***, which are deployed using group policies, specifically the *Computer Configuration\Policies\Windows Settings\Security Settings\Public Key Policies\Certificate Services Client – Auto-Enrollment* and *User Configuration\Policies\Windows Settings\Security Settings\Public Key Policies\Certificate Services Client – Auto-Enrollment.* However, autoenrollment can be applied only to enterprise CA (not standalone CA), and you have to deploy schema template version 2 or higher. In addition, the user needs Read, Enroll, and Autoenroll permissions for the certificate to deployed. Certificates installed with Autoenroll are shown later in the lesson.

USING CREDENTIAL ROAMING

Credential Roaming allows user certificates and private keys to be stored in Active Directory. When using Credential Roaming, the certificates and keys are downloaded when a user logs on, and if desired, the certificate and keys are removed when the user logs off. The advantage of Credential Roaming is that the certificate and key will follow the user no matter which computer the user logs on to. Credential Roaming is supported in Windows 7 and newer Windows operating systems. To enable Credential Roaming, use the following settings in a GPO User Configuration\Policies\Windows Settings\Security Settings\Public Key Policies\Credential Roaming.

Credential Roaming is triggered during the following operations:

- Logging on and logging off
- Locking and unlocking the workstation
- Updating the group policy cycle (or forcing an update by typing the `gpupdate` command)
- Running the regular update cycle (eight hours by default)
- Using the command `certutil -user -pulse`

NETWORK DEVICE ENROLLMENT SERVICE (NDES)

The ***Network Device Enrollment Service (NDES)*** is the Microsoft implementation of ***Simple Certificate Enrollment Protocol (SCEP)***, which is used for network devices such as switches and routers to enroll for a X.509 digital certificate from a CA. For example, if you want to use port security based on 802.1x for your switches and access points, or if you need SSH to connect to a switch or router, you can use NDES to install certificates using SCEP.

CONFIGURE THE NETWORK DEVICE ENROLLMENT SERVICE

GET READY. To configure the Network Device Enrollment Service, perform the following steps:

1. On the server that will perform Network Device Enrollment, using Server Manager, open Computer Management.
2. Expand Local Users and Groups, and then click Groups.
3. Double-click the IIS_IUSRS built-in group.
4. Click Add, type the domain name of the account that will be the registration authority, and then click OK.
5. Close *Computer Management*.
6. On the server where you want to install the Network Device Enrollment Service, open Server Manager.
7. Open the Manage menu and click Add Roles and Features.
8. When the *Add Roles and Features Wizard* starts, click Next.
9. On the *Select installation type* page, click Next.
10. On the *Select destination server*, click Next.
11. Click to select Active Directory Domain Services. When it asks to add a feature, click Add Features. Back at the Select server roles, click Next.
12. On the *Select features* page, click Next.
13. On the *Active Directory Certificate Services* page, click Next.
14. On the select *role services* page, click to select Network Device Enrollment Service. When it asks you to add features, click Add Features.
15. Deselect the Certification Authority. Click Next.
16. On the *Web Server Role (IIS)* page, click Next.
17. On the *Select role services* page, click Next.

18. On the *Confirm installation selections* page, click Install.
19. When the installation is complete, click Close.
20. Using the Server Manager, click the Red box with the white flag, and click Configure Active Directory Certificates on the destination server.
21. On the *Credentials* page, click Change. Then type the user name and password for the account that the Network Device Enrollment Service will use to authorize certificate requests. Click OK, and then click Next.
22. On the *Role Services* page, click Network Device Enrollment Service, and then click to select the Network Device Enrollment Service. Click Next.
23. On the *Specify service account* page, click Select, specify the member of the domain that you added to the local IIS_IUSRS group and click Next.
24. On the *CA for NDES* page, if this computer does not host a CA, click Computer name. Then click Select, type in the name of the CA in the *Target CA* text box, and then click OK. Click Next.
25. On the *Specify Registry Authority Information* page, type the name of the registration authority in the *RA* name box. Under *Country/region*, select the country/region you are in, and then click Next.
26. On the *Configure Cryptography* page, accept the default values for the signature and encryption keys, and click Next.
27. On the *Confirmation* page, click Install.
28. When the installation is complete, click Close.

Managing Certificate Renewal

Every certificate has a validity period and a finite life. At the end of the validity period, the certificate is no longer considered acceptable, and the certificate will have to be renewed. Of course, it is always best to renew the certificate before the certificate actually expires.

CERTIFICATION READY
Manage certificate renewal.
Objective 6.3

You can renew certificates in much the same way as you request certificates. For example, you can use the Certificates console to renew a certificate or you can configure the GPO that assigned the certificate to automatically renew the certificate.

When you renew the certificate, you can renew with different keys or with the same keys. You can use the same key if the key is long enough and the key has not been in use too long where it could be cracked using trial and error.

RENEW A CERTIFICATE USING THE CERTIFICATES CONSOLE

GET READY. To renew a certificate using the Certificates console, perform the following steps:

1. Click the Start menu, type mmc.exe, and press the Enter key.
2. When the console opens, click File > Add/Remove snap-in.
3. When the *Add or Remove Snap-ins* dialog box opens, double-click Certificates.
4. On the Certificates snap-in dialog box, click My user account. Click Finish.
5. Expand the Certificates-Current User, expand Personal, and click Certificates.
6. If you want to use the new key, click All Tasks, and click Renew Certificate with new Key. If you want to use the same key, click All Tasks, Advanced Operations, and click Renew This Certificate with the Same key.
7. When the *Certificate Enrollment wizard* opens, click Next.
8. On the *Request Certificates* page, click Enroll.
9. When the certificate is installed, click Finish.

Managing Certificate Enrollment and Renewal Using Group Policies

As mentioned previously, you can use a group policy object (GPO) to perform autoenrollment of certificates and the renewal of certificates. Remember that autoenrollment can be used only to enterprise CA, and when you have been deploying schema template version 2 or higher. In addition, the user needs Enroll and Autoenroll permissions for the certificate to be deployed.

CERTIFICATION READY
Manage certificate enrollment and renewal to computers and users using Group Policies.
Objective 6.3

You can use the Default Domain Policy to install certificates for users and computers. However, for more control, you can use a new GPO. For example, with a different GPO, you can assign to specific OUs and use filtering.

INSTALL A USER CERTIFICATE USING AUTOENROLL

GET READY. To install a user certificate using autoenroll, perform the following steps:

TAKE NOTE*
If you want to install a computer certificate, you will navigate to Computer Configuration\Policies\Windows Settings\Security Settings\Public Key Policies\.

1. Using Server Manager, open Group Policy Management.
2. Expand Forest: Contoso.com, expand Domains, expand Contoso.com, right-click Default Domain Policy, and then click Edit.
3. When the *Group Policy Management Editor* opens, expand User Configuration, expand Policies, expand Windows Settings, expand Security Settings, and then click to highlight Public Key Policies.
4. In the right pane, double-click Certificate Services Client – Auto-Enrollment.
5. In the *Configuration Model* drop-down list box, click Enabled, as shown in Figure 20-8.

Figure 20-8
Configuring the Auto-Enrollment Policy

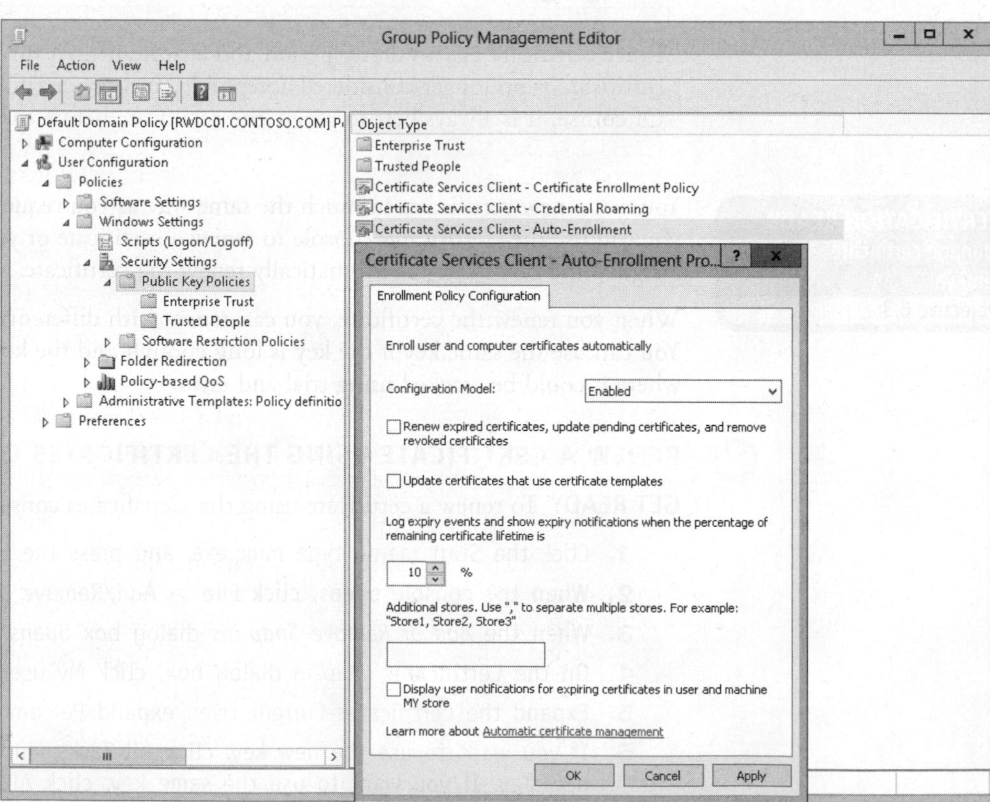

6. Click to select the Renew expired certificates, update pending certificates, and remove revoked certificates option.

7. Click to select the Update certificates that use certificate templates option.
8. Click OK to close the *Properties* dialog box.
9. In the right pane, double-click the Certificate Services Client – Certificate Enrollment Policy object.
10. On the *Enrollment Policy* tab, set the *Configuration Model* to Enabled, and ensure that the certificate enrollment policy list displays the *Active Directory Enrollment Policy*.
11. Click OK to close the dialog box.
12. Close the *Group Policy Management Editor* and *Group Policy Management* console.

By default, group policy is applied when you restart computers, or at logon for users. In addition, group policies are refreshed every 90 minutes for domain members. If a certificate requires user interaction to complete the request, a pop-up window appears approximately 60 seconds after the user logs on. However, most certificates are installed without the user knowing enrollment is taking place. If you don't want to wait for the certificate to be applied, you can execute the `gpupdate /force` to refresh group policies.

Configuring and Managing Key Archival and Recovery

Because certificates often provide keys to the kingdom, you do not want to lose the keys. Therefore, you need to provide key archival and recovery when needed. To recover lost keys, you use a key archival and recovery agent. You can also use automatic or manual key archival and key recovery methods to ensure that you can gain access to data in the event that your keys are lost. It should also be emphasized that when restoring a key, the process does not provide data recovery. The restored key provides the ability to read a restored file but you need to use another mechanism to actually back up the encrypted data, such as Windows Server Backup.

CERTIFICATION READY
Configure and manage key archival and recovery.
Objective 6.3

The CSP encrypts a private key and stores the encrypted private key on the local profile and registry. If you lose a key, if the user profile gets deleted or corrupted, the operating system is reinstalled, the hard drive is rebuilt, the disk becomes corrupted, or the computer is stolen, you will also lose the encrypted private key.

To recover private keys, you need to archive (or back them up). Then you you use a ***Key Recovery Agent (KRA)***, which is a designated user who is able to retrieve the original certificate, private key, and public key that was used to encrypt the data, from the CA database. Similar to setting up an EFS recovery agent, you can apply a key archival in a version 2 certificate template, which then makes the CA store the subject's private key in the CA database as certificates are requested. Then during the key recovery process, the KRA retrieves the encrypted file that contains the certificate and private key from the CA database, and returns the certificate and private key to the user.

When you have a configured CA to issue a KRA certificate, any user with Read and Enroll permission on the KRA certificate template can enroll and become a KRA. As a result, Domain Admins and Enterprise Admins receive permission by default. Of course, you should assign the KRA certificate to trusted users only. The KRA's recovery key is securely stored and the keys are in a separate physical secure location.

To perform key archival, you must perform the following:

1. Configure the KRA certificate template.
2. Configure Certificate Managers.
3. Enable KRA.
4. Configure user templates.

CONFIGURE THE KRA CERTIFICATE TEMPLATE

GET READY. To configure the KRA certificate template, perform the following steps:

1. Using the Server Manager, open Certification Authority.
2. In the Certification Authority console, expand the CA node, right-click the Certificates Templates folder, and then click Manage.
3. In the Details pane, right-click the Key Recovery Agent certificate, and then click Properties.
4. In the *Key Recovery Agent Properties* dialog box, click the Issuance Requirements tab.
5. Clear the CA certificate manager approval check box.
6. Close the *Certificate Templates* console.
7. In the *Certification Authority* console, right-click Certificate Templates, click New, and then click Certificate Template to Issue.
8. In the *Enable Certificate Templates* dialog box, select the Key Recovery Agent template, and then click OK.

CONFIGURE CERTIFICATE MANAGERS

GET READY. To configure the certificate managers, perform the following steps:

1. Click the Start menu, type mmc.exe, and press the Enter key.
2. When the console opens, click File > Add/Remove Snap-in.
3. In the *Add or Remove Snap-ins* dialog box, click Certificates, and then click Add.
4. In the *Certificates snap-in* dialog box, click My user account, click Finish, and then click OK.
5. Expand the Certificates - Current User node, right-click Personal, click All Tasks, and then click Request New Certificate.
6. When the *Certificate Enrollment Wizard* opens, click Next.
7. On the *Select Certificate Enrollment Policy* page, click Next.
8. On the *Request Certificates* page, select the Key Recovery Agent check box. Click Enroll, and then click Finish.
9. Close the console.

ENABLE KRA

GET READY. To enable KRA, perform the following steps:

1. If the Certification Authority console is not open, open Certification Authority.
2. Right-click the CA, and click Properties.
3. In the CA *Properties* dialog box, click the Recovery Agents tab, and then select Archive the key (as shown in Figure 20-9).

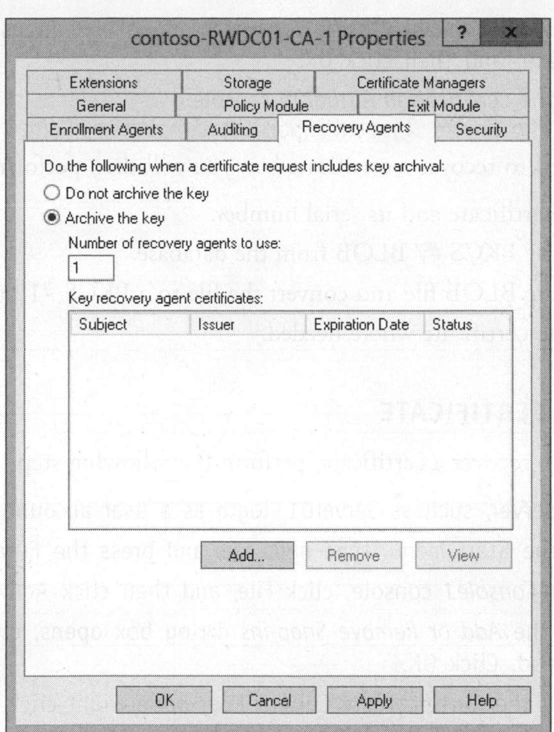

Figure 20-9

Configuring recovery agents

4. Under *Key recovery agent certificates*, click Add.
5. In the *Key Recovery Agent Selection* dialog box, click the certificate that is for *Key Recovery Agent purpose* (as verified by using the *Click here to view certificate properties* option). It will most likely be last on the list. Then click OK two times.
6. When prompted to restart the CA, click Yes.

CONFIGURE THE USER TEMPLATES

GET READY. To configure the user template, perform the following steps:

1. If the *Certification Authority* console is not open, using the Server Manager, open Certification Authority.
2. Right-click the Certificates Templates folder, and then click Manage.
3. In the *Certificate Templates* console, right-click the User certificate, and then click Duplicate Template.
4. In the *Properties of New Template* dialog box, on the General tab, in the *Template display name* box, type Archive User.
5. On the Request Handling tab, select the Archive subject's encryption private key check box. When it says that there are no certification authorities currently issuing certificates based on this template, click OK.
6. Click the Subject Name tab, clear the E-mail name and Include e-mail name in subject name check boxes, and then click OK.
7. Close the Certificate Templates console.
8. In the *Certification Authority* console, right-click the Certificates Templates folder, click New, and then click Certificate Template to Issue.

9. When the *Enable Certificate Templates* dialog box opens, click the Archive User template, and then click OK.
10. Close the *Certification Authority* console.

When you need to recover a certificate key, you will then perform the following:

1. Find the certificate and its serial number.
2. Retrieve the PKCS #7 BLOB from the database.
3. Retrieve the BLOB file and convert the file to a PKCS #12 (.pfx).
4. Import the certificate where needed.

RECOVER A CERTIFICATE

GET READY. To recover a certificate, perform the following steps:

1. On a server, such as Server01, login as a user account such as JSmith.
2. Click the Start menu, type mmc.exe, and press the Enter key.
3. In the *Console1* console, click File, and then click Add/Remove Snap-in.
4. When the *Add or Remove Snap-ins* dialog box opens, click Certificates, and then click Add. Click OK.
5. Expand the Certificates - Current User node, right-click Personal, click All Tasks, and then click Request New Certificate.
6. When the *Certificate Enrollment Wizard* opens, click Next.
7. Click Next.
8. On the *Request Certificate* page, click to select the Archive User check box, click Enroll, and then click Finish.
9. In the *Personal\Certificates* folder, delete the new certificate that you just added that is based on the Archive User certificate template.
10. Go to the CA server and open the *Certification Authority* console.
11. Expand the CA and click Issued Certificates.
12. In the details pane, double-click a certificate with the name and with the *Certificate Template name of Archive User.*
13. In the *Certificate* dialog box, click the Details tab.
14. Highlight the serial number, right-click the highlighted serial number, and copy the serial number to the Clipboard by pressing Ctrl+C.
15. Open Windows PowerShell console from task bar.
16. In the Windows PowerShell console window that appears, type the following command (where <serial number> is the serial number that you copied), and then press Enter:

    ```
    certutil -getkey <serial number> c:\outputblob
    ```

    If you paste the serial number from Notepad, remove spaces between numbers.
17. To convert the outputblob file into a pfx file, execute the following command:

    ```
    Certutil -recoverkey c:\outputblob c:\ jsmith.pfx
    ```
18. When prompted for a password, type Password01 in the *password*, and *confirm the password* text boxes.
19. Close the *Windows PowerShell* window.

The pfx file is the certificate file that contains the public and private keys. It can be copied to whatever computer the user is using and the certificate can be imported for the user.

SKILL SUMMARY

IN THIS LESSON YOU LEARNED:

- A digital certificate is similar to an electronic identification card used to certify the online identify of individuals, organizations, and computers.
- The digital certificate contains a person's or organization's name, a serial number, an expiration date, a copy of the certificate holder's public key (used for encrypting messages and creating digital signatures), and the digital signature of the certificate authority (CA) that assigned the certificate so that recipients can verify that the certificate is real.
- Certificate templates are used to simplify the task of administering a CA by allowing an administrator to identify, modify, and issue certificates that have been preconfigured for selected tasks.
- Active Directory Certificate Services (AD CS) provides four schema versions of certificate templates.
- To support autoenrollment, you need to use the Version 2 certificate template schema version or higher.
- To configure certificate template permissions, you need to define the Discretionary Access Control List (DACL) for each certificate template in the Security tab.
- The available methods for a user or computer to enroll for a certificate include: manual enrollment, CA Web enrollment, enrollment on behalf (enrollment agent), and autoenrollment.
- The CA Web enrollment uses a website on a CA to obtain certificates. The website uses Internet Information Server (IIS) and the AD CS web enrollment role has been installed and configured.
- When you use Enrollment on behalf (enrollment Agent), the CA administrator creates an enrollment agent account for the user. The user with enrollment agent rights can then enroll certificates on behalf of other users such as when the administrator needs to preload logon certificates of new employees' smart cards.
- Most certificates will be assigned through autoenrollment, which are deployed using group policies.
- Credential Roaming allows user certificates and private keys to be stored in Active Directory.
- The Network Device Enrollment Service (NDES) is the Microsoft implementation of Simple Certificate Enrollment Protocol (SCEP), which is used for network devices such as switches and routers to enroll for an X.509 digital certificate from a CA.
- Every certificate has a validity period and a finite life. At the end of the validity period, the certificate is no longer considered acceptable, and the certificate has to be renewed. Of course, it is always best to renew the certificate before the certificate actually expires.
- To recover private keys, you need to archive them (or back them up). Then you use Key Recovery Agents (KRAs), which are designated users who are able to retrieve the original certificate, private key, and public key that were used to encrypt the data from the CA database.

Knowledge Assessment

Multiple Choice

Select the correct answer for each of the following questions.

1. You are replacing a web server and you need to retrieve the digital certificate used for your website so that you can import it to the new web server. What format should you export the certificate to?
   a. Base-64 encoded X.509 (.cer)
   b. Cryptographic Message Syntax Standard PKCS #7 (.p7b)
   c. DER encoded binary X.509 (.cer)
   d. Personal Information Exchange PKCS #12 (.pfx)

2. You have an enterprise certification authority for your company. You need to issue a certificate to all users for email security, client authentication, and Encrypting File System (EFS). What two actions do you need to perform to complete?
   a. Duplicate the User certificate template, and then publish the template
   b. Modify the properties of the User certificate template and publish the template
   c. Using a group policy, configure the Certificate Services Client – Autoenrollment settings
   d. Using group policies, configure the Certificate Services Client – Certificate Enrollment Policy settings

3. You have an enterprise certification authority for your company. Which console do you need to use to ensure that all members of the Sales group can enroll in the Sales certificate?
   a. Certification Authority
   b. Certificate Templates
   c. Authorization Manager
   d. Active Directory Administrative Center

4. Which of the following is the minimum schema version for certificates that is required for autoenrollment?
   a. v1
   b. v2
   c. v3
   d. v4

5. Which of the following are ways you can deploy certificates? (Choose all that apply.)
   a. manual enrollment
   b. blackbox copy
   c. autoenrollment
   d. web enrollment

6. Which of the following is the default URL for the CA Web enrollment?
   a. https://<servername>/enroll
   b. https://<servername>/certenroll
   c. https://<servername>/certsrv
   d. https://<servername>/webcert

7. Which of the following limits who can enroll a certificate on behalf of other users?
   a. Limiting ACL
   b. ACL templates
   c. Enrollment templates
   d. Restricted Enrollment Agent

8. Which mechanism is used to automatically deploy certificates to users and computers?
a. Login scripts
b. Credential Roaming
c. DHCP server
d. Group policies

9. What is used to recover certificate keys?
a. Key Recovery Agents
b. Enrollment agent
c. NDES
d. Trusted publisher

10. Which of the following is the most common digital certificate format used?
a. X.500 version 1
b. X.509 version 3
c. X400 version 2
d. X.601

Best Answer

Circle the letter that corresponds to the best answer.

1. You have an enterprise root certification authority. You need to grant the ITManager group to manage only Basic EFS certificates. Therefore, you grant the ITManager group the Issue and Manage Certificates permission on the CA. What three tasks do you need to complete the group's access? (Choose three answers.)
a. Add the Basic EFS certificate template for the ITManager group
b. Make sure that the ITManager group is not assigned to other certificate templates
c. Enable the Restrict Enrollment Agent
d. Enable the Restrict Enrollment option on the CA

2. You have an enterprise root certification authority. You have configured a certificate template called CorpCert for autoenrollment. However, the certificate is not being issued to any client computers and you do not see any autoenrollment errors in the logs. What should you do next?
a. Modify a GPO to deploy certificates
b. Upgrade the CA server to Windows Server 2012 R2
c. Restart the Certificate Services
d. Install the CA web enrollment

3. You have an enterprise certification authority. You need to ensure that the encryption keys for e-mail certificates can be recovered from the CA. What do you need to do to support key archival?
a. Run the `certutil.exe -recoverkey`
b. Modify the AIA distribution point
c. Assign the EFS recovery agent
d. Issue the Key Recovery Agent certificate template

4. You have an enterprise root certification authority. You have three key recovery agent certificates issued and the CA is configured to use two recovery agents. What do you need to do to ensure that all of the recovery agent certificates are used to recover all new private keys?
a. Add a third recovery agent to the Default Domain Policy
b. Modify the values in the *Number of recovery agents to use* box
c. Revoke the current key recovery agent and issue three new certificates
d. Assign the *Issue and Manage* certificates permission to the three users

5. Which option would you use so that the certificate and private keys are stored in Active Directory?
   a. Configure a Key Recovery Agent
   b. Click the Auto-archive option
   c. Install the Certificate Archive console
   d. In a GPO, use Credential Roaming

Matching and Identification

1. Match the correct description with the appropriate field used in an X.409 digital certificate.
   _______ a) The public key
   _______ b) Digital signature
   _______ c) Name of issuing CA
   _______ d) Describes purpose of the public key
   _______ e) Person, entity, or owner identified in certificate
   1. Subject
   2. Verifies that a certificate came from the issuer
   3. Subject Public-Key Information
   4. Issuer
   5. Key usage
2. Match the correct description with the correct certificate store.
   _______ a) Personal
   _______ b) Trusted Root Certification Authority
   _______ c) Trusted People
   _______ d) Enterprise Trust
   _______ e) Intermediate Certification Authorities
   1. Certificates issued to subordinate certification authorities.
   2. Certificates issued to people that are implicitly trusted.
   3. Implicitly specified trusted CAs.
   4. Used to store trusting self-signed root certificates from other organizations.
   5. Certificates have been granted to the computer.

Build a List

1. What are the four steps that you must complete to perform key archival?
   _______ Configure user templates
   _______ Configure Certificate Managers
   _______ Install a CA Archival server
   _______ Enable KRA
   _______ Run the `certutil -Enableachival` command
   _______ Configure the KRA certificate template
   _______ Choose the PFX format in the certificate template
2. Identify the steps to deploy a certificate using autoenrollment.
   _______ Enable the Certificate Services Client – Auto-Enrollment
   _______ Publish the certificate template
   _______ Configure the certificate template
   _______ Open a GPO using the Group Policy Management console
   _______ Place the certificate template in a centrally located shared folder
   _______ Copy a certificate template
   _______ Specify the administrators for the template

Choose an Option

1. See Figure 20-10. In the Permissions for Domain Users section, which permission or permissions are needed for autoenrollment?

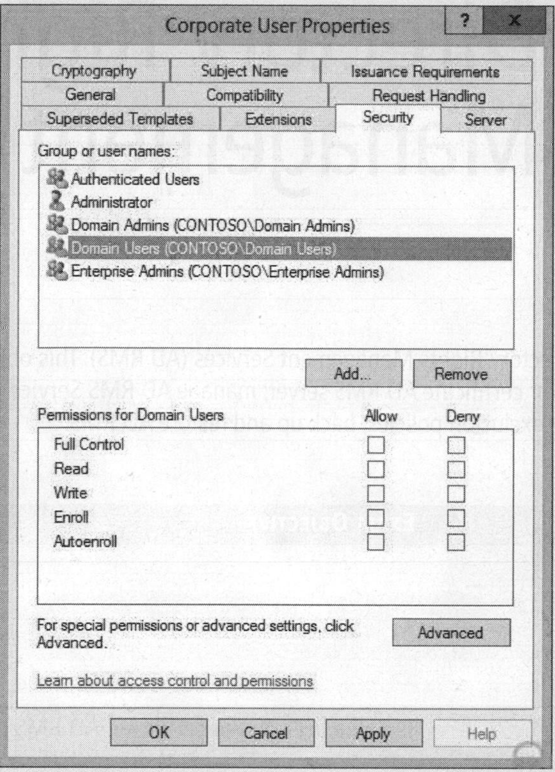

Figure 20-10
Configuring permissions

Business Case Scenarios

Scenario 20-1: Deploying Digital Certificates

You are an administrator for the Contoso Corporation. You want to implement a VPN that requires all users who want to connect to the corporation using a VPN client to have the IPsec digital certificate. Therefore, you want to deploy the digital certificate to all users in your corporation. What do you need to do to make this happen?

Scenario 20-2: Recovering a Digital Certificate

You are an administrator for the Contoso Corporation. Because the certificates are an essential part of the security infrastructure, you need to ensure that all certificates can be recovered if a system needs to be replaced or if a certificate becomes lost. What do you need to do?

Installing and Configuring Active Directory Rights Management Services

70-412 EXAM OBJECTIVE

Objective 6.4 – Install and configure Active Directory Rights Management Services (AD RMS). This objective may include but is not limited to: Install a licensing or certificate AD RMS server; manage AD RMS Service Connection Point (SCP); manage RMS templates; configure exclusion policies; back up and restore AD RMS.

LESSON HEADING	EXAM OBJECTIVE
Understanding Active Directory Rights Management	
Understanding the Rights Management Processes	
Installing a Licensing or Certificate AD RMS Server	Install a licensing or certificate AD RMS server
Managing AD RMS Service Connection Point	Manage AD RMS Service Connection Point (SCP)
Managing AD RMS Client Deployment	
Supporting Mobile Devices	
Managing RMS Templates	Manage RMS templates
Configuring Exclusion Policies	Configure exclusion policies
Backing Up and Restoring AD RMS	Back up and restore AD RMS

KEY TERMS

Active Directory Federation Services (AD FS) RACs
Active Directory Rights Management Services (AD RMS)
AD RMS client
AD RMS Enabled Applications
AD RMS Machine Certificate
AD RMS root certification cluster
AD RMS Server
Client Licensor Certificate
End Use License
exclusion policies
licensing-only cluster
permissions
publishing license (PL)
rights
rights account certificate (RAC)
rights policy templates
server licensor certificate (SLC)
service connection point (SCP)
Temporary Rights Account Certificate
Windows Live ID RAC

■ Understanding Active Directory Rights Management

THE BOTTOM LINE

Active Directory Rights Management Services (AD RMS) is technology used to provide an extra level of security to documents such as email and Microsoft Office documents by using encryption to limit who can access a document or web page and what can be done with a document or web page. For example, you can limit if a document or web page can be printed, copied, edited, forwarded, or deleted. RMS helps contain confidential information so that it stays within the organization and helps limit who can access the data.

Basic security mechanisms included with Windows are rights and permissions. ***Rights*** specify what a user or group can do on a system. For example, backup operators can back up files even if the user or group does not have permissions to the file or folder. Rights also define who can shut down or reboot a computer, who can logon to a computer, and so on. Rights are defined using Group Policy Objects (GPOs).

Permissions specify what a user or group can do with an object. For example, NTFS permissions are used to specify who can access and read a file, who can modify a file, who can delete a file, and who can manage the file.

However while rights and permissions are powerful tools, they do have their limitations. For example, anyone who can access and read a file protected with NTFS can copy the file to a USB drive or other storage device, email the file, or print the file, allowing a user to easily steal or copy confidential information.

AD RMS is an information protection technology is used to minimize unauthorized transmission of data or data leakage, specifically with Microsoft products and operating systems including Microsoft Exchange, Microsoft SharePoint, and the Microsoft Office suite.

To control who can access a file or email, AD RMS encrypts the file or email. To read the file, the user will need the encryption key to decrypt the file, which is stored in the AD RMS server. As a user opens or accesses the file, he or she will automatically retrieve the key from the AD RMS server and open the file. Since Microsoft products are AD RMS aware, they also help limit what you can do with a document as specified with the rights assigned using rights management.

If someone copies the file to a USB storage device and takes it offsite or emails it to someone else, whoever opens the file needs to access the AD RMS to retrieve the keys. If the person cannot access the rights management server (for whatever reason) or is not authorized to access the file, he or she will not get the key and will not be able to open and read its content.

Understanding the Rights Management Processes

After the AD RMS server is installed and configured and the clients are configured to use the AD RMS server, when accessing secure documents, the decryption of a document occurs transparently. In addition, when using applications that are aware of AD RMS, it is quite easy to secure a document or email.

The AD RMS infrastructure has the following components:

- ***AD RMS Server:*** A Windows server that is a member of an Active Directory Domain Services (AD DS) domain. When you install AD RMS servers, the location of the server is published to AD DS to a location known as the service connection point. Because RMS can be an important component when securing documents, AD RMS might deploy AD RMS with high availability using clustering.
- ***AD RMS client:*** Computers with the AD RMS client. Windows Vista, Windows 7, Windows 8, Windows Server 2008, Windows Server 2008 R2, Windows Server 2012, and Windows Server 2012 R2 operating systems have the client built-in. The client for Windows XP, Windows Server 2003, and Windows Server 2003 R2 can be downloaded and installed. Computers that are members of the domain query AD DS for the service connection point to determine the location of AD RMS services.
- ***AD RMS Enabled Applications:*** An application that allows users to create and consume AD RMS-protected content. Examples of AD RMS clients include Microsoft Word, Microsoft Excel, and Microsoft Outlook.
- ***AD RMS root certification cluster:*** The first AD RMS server that you deploy in a forest. It manages all licensing and certification traffic for the domain in which it is installed. The configuration information is installed in a Microsoft SQL database. AD RMS root certification clusters are typically found in large branch offices to distribute licenses that are used in content consumption and publishing.
- ***Licensing-only cluster:*** An optional component that is not part of the root cluster. However, it relies on the root cluster for certification and other services. It provides both publishing licenses and use licenses to users. It is typically used when supporting unique right management requirements of a department or when supporting rights management of external business partners.

TAKE NOTE* The AD RMS root certification is not a fail-over or NLB cluster, and should not be confused with one. However, the AD RMS cluster can be used to to provide high availability and load balancing to ensure that the service is always available.

For AD RMS to operate, it uses various certificates and licenses to encrypt and limit access to the files or emails including the following:

- ***Server licensor certificate (SLC):*** A certificate that contains the public key that encrypts the content key in a publishing license. It allows the AD RMS server to extract the content key and issue end use licenses (EULs) against the publishing key. It is generated when you create the AD RMS cluster. It allows the AD RMS cluster to issue SLCs to other servers in the cluster, rights account certificates to clients, client licensor certificates, publishing licensing, use licenses; and to deploy rights policy templates. It has a validity of 250 years. Since it is one of the core components, it is important to back up the SLCs on a regular basis.
- ***AD RMS Machine Certificate:*** Used to identify a trusted computer or device. It is also used to encrypt the rights account certificate private key and decrypt the rights account certificates.

- ***Rights account certificate (RAC):*** A RAC is issued the first time a user attempts to access AD RMS-protected content, which is used to identify a specific user. RACs can be issued only to users in AD DS whose user accounts have email addresses that are associated with them. The default validity time for a RAC is 365 days.
- ***Temporary Rights Account Certificate:*** Issued to users who are accessing AD RMS-protected content from a computer that is not a member of the same or trusted forest as the AD RMS cluster. A temporary RAC has a validity time of 15 minutes.
- ***Active Directory Federation Services (AD FS) RACs:*** Issued to federated users. They have a validity of seven days.
- ***Windows Live ID RAC:*** Used with a Microsoft account, formerly called a Windows Live Account. Windows Live ID RACs used on private computers have a validity of six months. Windows Live ID RACs on public computers are valid until the user logs off.
- ***Client Licensor Certificate:*** Allows a user to publish AD RMS-protected content when the client computer is not connected to the same network as the AD RMS cluster. The client licensor certificate public key encrypts the symmetric content key and includes it in the publishing license that it issues. The client licensor certificate private key signs any publishing licenses that are issued when the client is not connected to the AD RMS cluster. Since the client licensor certificates are tied to a specific user's RAC, if another user who does not have a RAC attempts to publish AD RMS-protected content from the same client, they will not be able to until the client is connected to the AD RMS cluster so that the user can get a RAC.
- ***Publishing license (PL):*** Determines the rights that apply to AD RMS-protected content. It contains the content key, which is encrypted using the public key of the licensing service. It also contains the URL and the digital signature of the AD RMS server.
- ***End Use License:*** Required to consume AD RMS-protected content. The AD RMS server issues one EUL per user per document. EULs are cached by default.

The following shows how a document is protected and accessed using AD RMS:

1. When an author configures rights protection for information the first time, he or she receives a client licensor certificate from the AD RMS server.
2. When the author defines a collection of usage rights and usage of the file, the application encrypts the file with a symmetric key.
3. This symmetric key is encrypted to the public key of the AD RMS server that is used by the author.
4. When a recipient opens the file using an AD RMS application or browser, if the recipient does not have an account certificate on the current host, one will be issued to the user.
5. When the user has the account certificate, the application or browser transmits a request to the author's AD RMS server for a Use License.
6. The AD RMS server determines whether the recipient is authorized. If the recipient is authorized, the AD RMS server issues a Use License.
7. The AD RMS server decrypts the symmetric key that was encrypted in step 3, using its private key.
8. The AD RMS server re-encrypts the symmetric key using the recipient's public key and adds the encrypted session key to the Use License.

If an application or browser does not support AD RMS, the user will not be able to open RMS-protected content.

Installing a Licensing or Certificate AD RMS Server

An AD RMS deployment consists of one or more servers known as a cluster. Additional servers can be added for scalability if you use a dedicated SQL server. When you deploy AD RMS in a single forest, you will have a single AD RMS cluster. If you have multiple forests, each forest will have its own AD RMS root cluster. Only one root cluster can exist in an AD DS forest.

CERTIFICATION READY
Install a licensing or certificate AD RMS server.
Objective 6.4

Alhough you can use the Windows Internal Database for a test environment, you should use a dedicated SQL server, particularly if you need to have more than one server. You should not deploy AD RMS on a domain controller. If you do, the service account that AD RMS uses must be a member of the Domain Admins group.

CREATE AD RMS SERVICE ACCOUNTS AND GROUP AND CREATE A DNS CNAME FOR AD RMS

GET READY. To create an AD RMS service account and group and to create a DNS CNAME for an AD RMS server, perform the following steps:

1. On a domain controller, using Server Manager, click Tools > Active Directory Administrative Center.
2. On the *Active Directory Administrative Center*, right-click Contoso (local), click New, and then click Organizational Unit.
3. When the *Create Organizational Unit* dialog box opens, type Service Accounts in the *Name* text box, and click OK.
4. Right-click the Service Accounts OU, click New, and then click User.
5. When the *Create User* dialog box opens, enter the following:

   First name: ADRMS_SVC

   User UPN logon: ADRMS_SVC

   Password: Password01

   Password options: Other password options

   Password never expires: Enabled

   User cannot change password: Enabled
6. Click OK to close the *Create User* dialog box.
7. Right-click Users organization unit, click New, and then click Group.
8. When the *Create Group* dialog box opens, type the following:

   Group name: RMS Users

   E-mail: RMSUsers@Contoso.com
9. Click Members.
10. Click Add. Type John Smith and click OK.
11. Click OK to close the *Create Group* dialog box.
12. Close Active Directory Administrative Center.
13. Using Server Manager, click Tools > DNS.
14. In *DNS Manager*, expand the DNS server Forward Lookup Zones and click contoso.com.
15. Right-click the contoso.com domain and click New Alias (CNAME).
16. In the *New Resource Record* dialog box, enter the following:

    Alias name: ADRMS

    Fully qualified domain name (FQDN) for target host: server02.contoso.com
17. Click OK to close the *New Resource Record* dialog box.
18. Close *DNS Manager*.

INSTALL AD RMS

GET READY. To install AD RMS, perform the following steps:

1. On Server02, using Server Manager, click Manage, and then click Add Roles and Features.
2. When the *Add Roles and Features Wizard* opens, click Next.
3. On the *Select installation type* page, click Next.
4. On the *Select destination server* page, click Next.
5. Click to select Active Directory Rights Management Services. When you are asked to add features, click Add Features.
6. Back at the *Select server roles* page, click Next.
7. At the *Select features* page, click Next.
8. On the *Active Directory Rights Management Services* page, click Next.
9. When the *Role Services* page appears, if Active Directory Rights Management Server is already selected, click Next.
10. On the *Confirm installation selections* page, click Install.
11. When the installation is complete, click Close.
12. Using Server Manager, click the AD RMS node.
13. At the top of the *Servers* section, next to *Configuration required for Active Directory Rights Management Services at SERVER02* (as shown in Figure 21-1), click More.

Figure 21-1

Viewing the AD RMS node in Server Manager

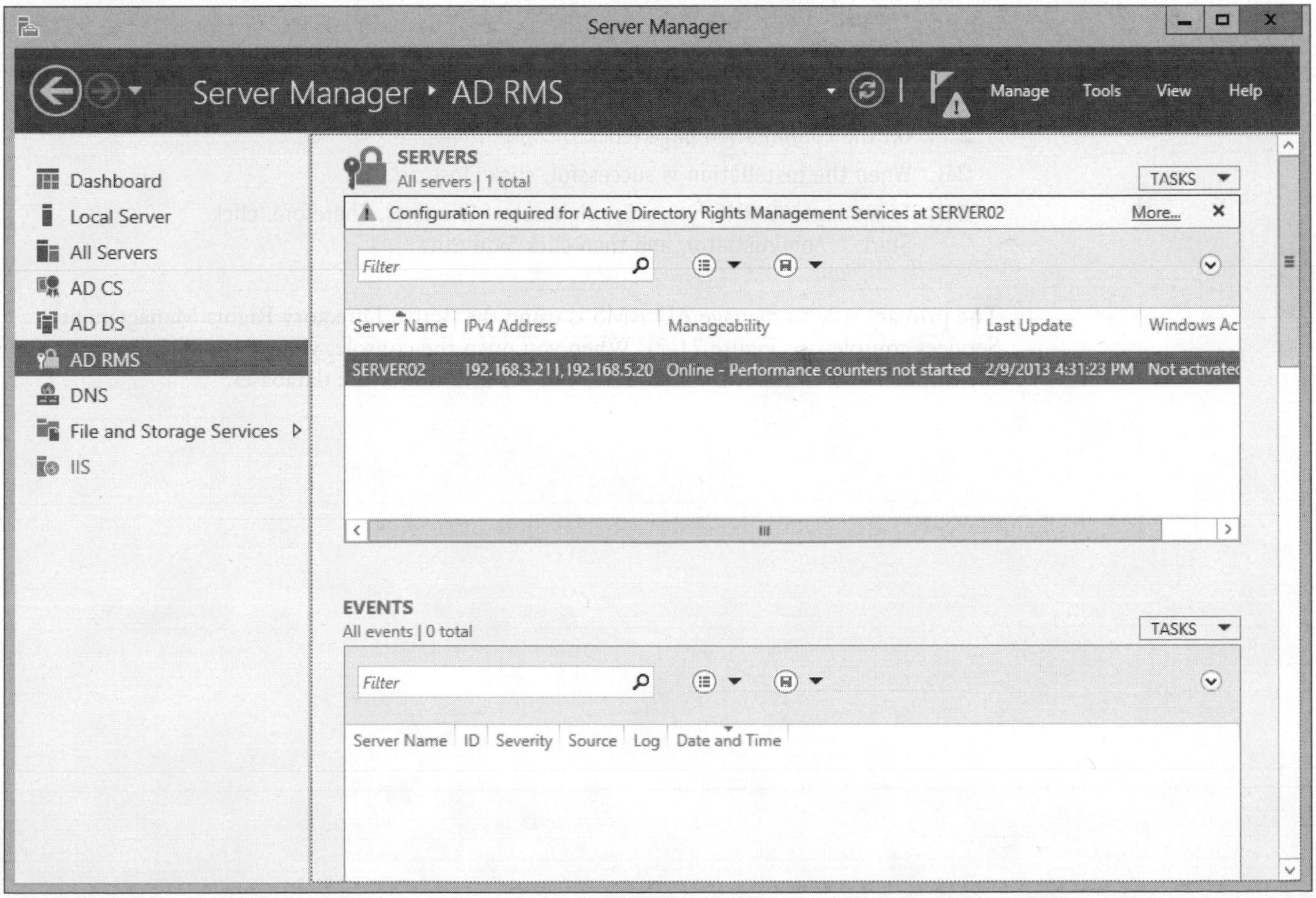

14. When the *All Servers Task Details* dialog box page opens, click Perform additional configuration.
15. When the *AD RMS Configuration wizard* starts, click Next.
16. On the *AD RMS Cluster* page, if Create a new AD RMS root cluster is already selected, click Next.
17. On the *Configuration Database Server* page, click Use Windows Internal Database on this server. Click Next.
18. On the *Server Account* page, click Specify.
19. In the *Windows Security* dialog box, enter the following details, click OK, and then click Next:
    - **Username:** ADRMS_SVC
    - **Password:** Pa$$w0rd
20. On the *Cryptographic Mode* page, click Cryptographic Mode 2, and then click Next.
21. On the *Cluster Key Storage* page, click Use AD RMS centrally managed key storage, and then click Next.
22. On the *Cluster Key Password* page, enter the password Password01 in the *Password* and *Confirm Password* dialog box, and then click Next.
23. On the *Cluster Web Site* page, verify that Default Web Site is selected, and then click Next.
24. On the *Cluster Address* page, provide the following information, and then click Next:
    - **Connection Type:** Use an unencrypted connection (http://)
    - **Fully Qualified Domain Name:** adrms.contoso.com
    - **Port:** 80
25. On the *Licensor Certificate* page, type Contoso AD RMS, and then click Next.
26. On the *SCP Registration* page, click Register the SCP now, and then click Next.
27. On the *Confirmation* page, click Install.
28. When the installation is successful, click Close.
29. To manage AD RMS, you must sign out of Windows. Therefore, click Start > Administrator, and then click Sign Out.

The primary tool to manage AD RMS is using the Active Directory Rights Management Services console (see Figure 21-2). When you open the console, you can see the cluster name, the intranet and extranet cluster URLs, and the location of the databases.

Figure 21-2

Looking at the Active Directory Rights Management Services console

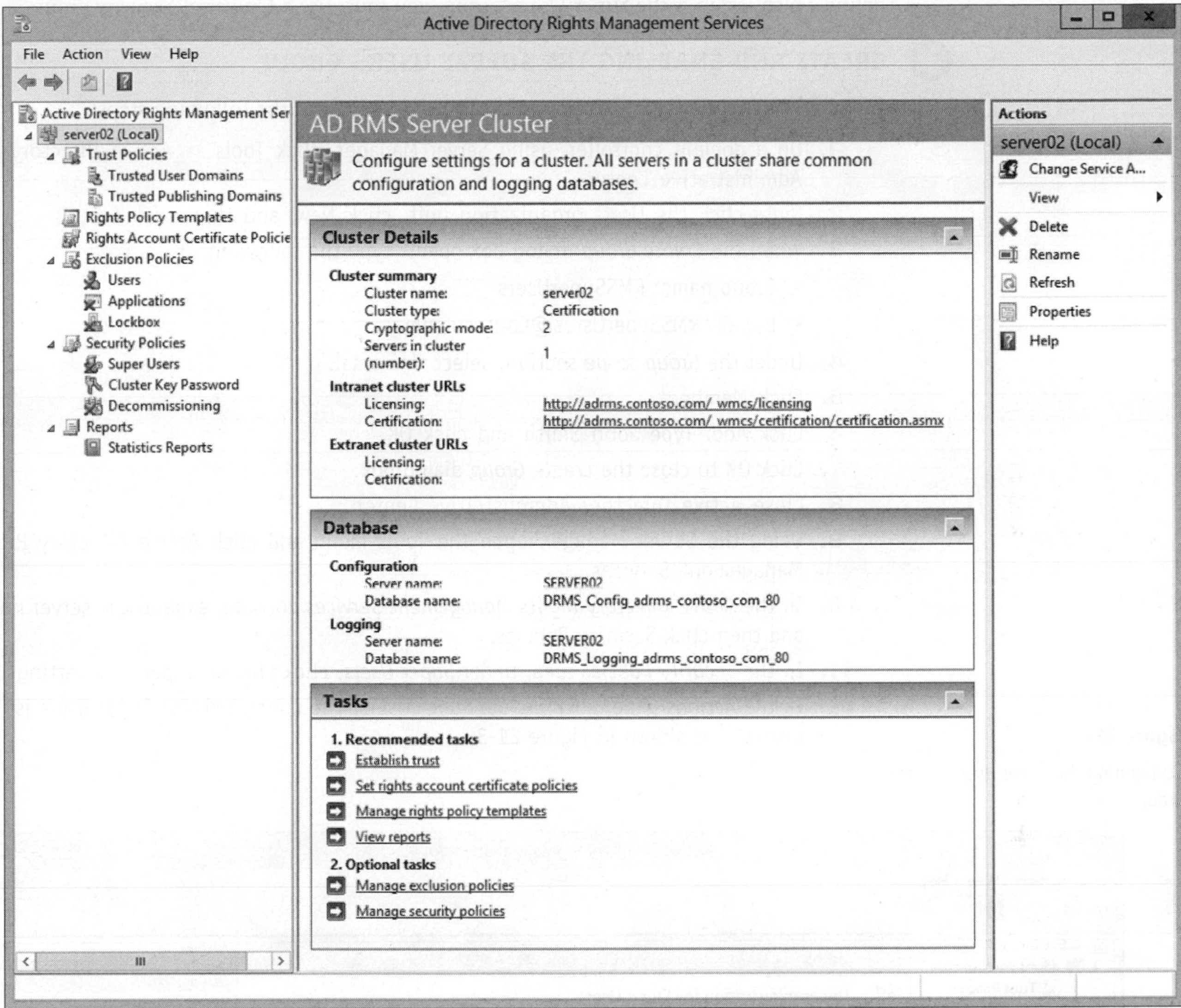

When AD RMS is deployed, the following administration groups are created:

- **AD RMS Enterprise Administrators:** Have access to all features in the AD RMS console. During installation of AD RMS, the installing user account is automatically added to this group.
- **AD RMS Template Administrators:** Can only access rights policy template administration features in the AD RMS console.
- **AD RMS Auditors:** Access the reports feature in the AD RMS console.
- **AD RMS Service Group:** Act as the AD RMS service account. During the installation of AD RMS, the user account designated as the service account is automatically added to this group.

To change the AD RMS service account or the cluster key password, you need to be a member of the AD RMS Enterprise Administrators group, and a member of the local administrators group on the server.

Another important group, which is separated from the administration groups, is the super users group. By default, the group is disabled and undefined. Members of the super users group are granted owner use licenses when they request a user license from the AD RMS cluster. It allows the members to decrypt all AD RMS-protected content published by the cluster. When you define which group is the Super Users Group, you must use a Universal Security group.

CREATE AND ENABLING THE SUPERS USERS GROUP

GET READY. To configure the Super Users Group, perform the following steps:

1. On a domain controller, using Server Manager, click Tools > Active Directory Administrative Center.
2. Right-click the Users organization unit, click New, and then click Group.
3. When the *Create Group* dialog box opens, type the following:
   - Group name: RMSSuperUsers
   - E-mail: RMSSuperUsers@Contoso.com
4. Under the *Group scope* section, select Universal.
5. Click Members.
6. Click Add. Type John Smith and click OK.
7. Click OK to close the *Create Group* dialog box.
8. Close Active Directory Administrative Center.
9. Using the Server Manager, open the Tools menu and click Active Directory Rights Management Services.
10. In the *Active Directory Rights Management Services* console, expand the server node, and then click Security Policies.
11. In the *Security Policies* area, under *Super Users*, click Change super user settings.
12. In the *Actions* pane, click Enable Super Users. The console shows Super users is enabled, as shown in Figure 21-3.

Figure 21-3

Configuring the super user group

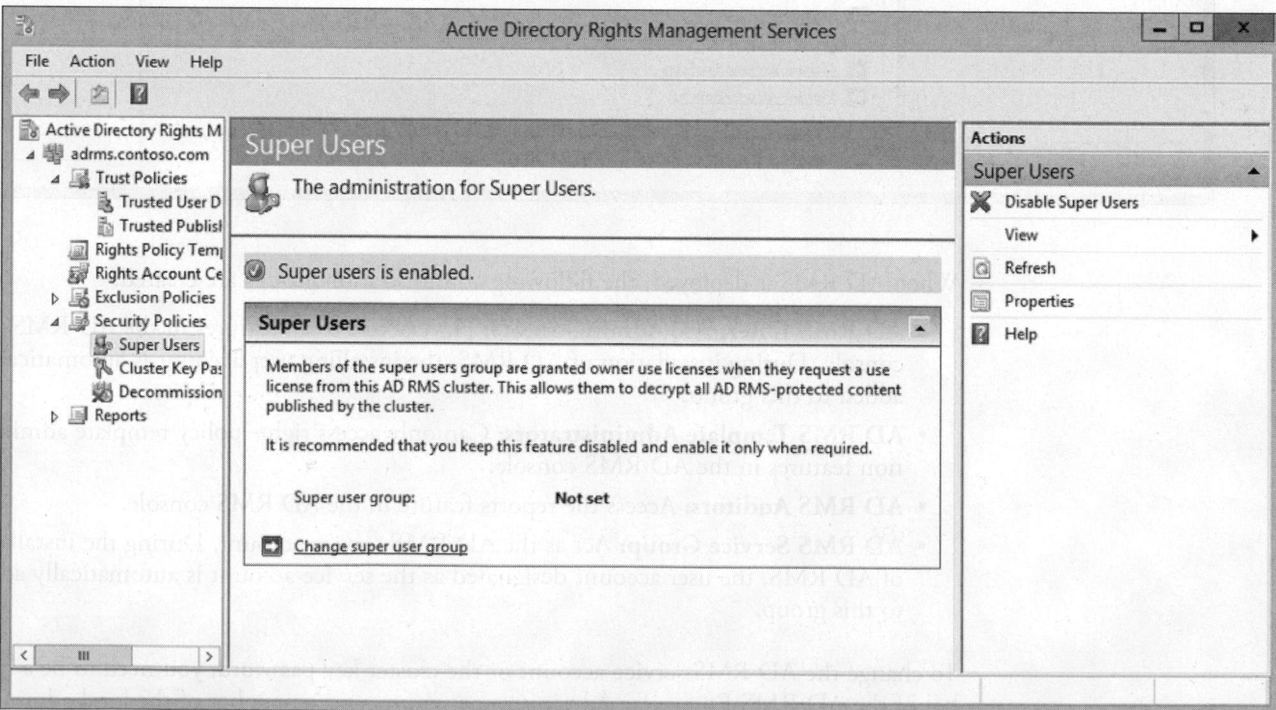

13. In the *Super* Users area, click Change super user group.
14. In the Super Users dialog box, in the *Super user group* text box, type RMS_Superusers@contoso.com, and then click OK.
15. When done, click OK to close the Properties dialog box.

If you wish to use Kerberos authentication with AD RMS, you will first need to be a member of the AD RMS Enterprise Administrators group and the Enterprise Admins group. You will then have to perform the following:

- Set the Internet Information Services (IIS) useAppPoolCredentials variable to True
- Set the Service Principal Names (SPN) value for the AD RMS service account

CONFIGURE AD RMS TO SUPPORT KERBEROS

GET READY. To configure AD RMS to support Kerberos, perform the following steps:

1. Open an elevated command prompt window.
2. Navigate to %windir%\system32\inetsrv.
3. Execute the following command:
```
appcmd.exe set config -section:system.
webServer/security/authentication/ windowsAuthentication
-useAppPoolCredentials:true
```
4. Execute the following command:
```
setspn -a HTTP/<ServerName>
<ServiceAccountDomain>\<ServiceAccount>
```
where <ServerName> is the name of the server, <ServiceAccountDomain> is the name of the domain containing the AD RMS service account, and <ServiceAccount> is the name of the AD RMS service account.
5. Execute the following command:
```
setspn -a HTTP/<ServerFQDN>
<ServiceAccountDomain>\<ServiceAccount>
```
where <ServerFQDN> is the fully qualified domain name (FQDN) of the server.
6. Execute the following command:
```
setspn -a HTTP/<ClusterName>
<ServiceAccountDomain>\<ServiceAccount>
```
where <ClusterName> is the name of the AD RMS cluster.
7. Execute the following command:
```
setspn -a HTTP/<ClusterFQDN>
<ServiceAccountDomain>\<ServiceAccount>
```
where <ClusterFQDN> is the fully qualified domain name (FQDN) of the cluster.
8. Close the command prompt.

Managing AD RMS Service Connection Point

The Active Directory Rights Management Services (AD RMS) ***service connection point (SCP)*** is an object in Active Directory that holds the web address of the AD RMS certification cluster. It was defined during the installation of AD RMS. AD RMS-enabled applications use the SCP to find the AD RMS service.

CERTIFICATION READY
Manage AD RMS Service Connection Point (SCP).
Objective 6.4

Only one SCP for AD RMS can exist in your Active Directory forest. An SCP can be viewed using ADSI Edit or LDP. To view the SCP, connect to the configuration container in ADSI Edit and navigate the following nodes:

```
CN=Configuration [server name], CN=Services,
CN=RightsManagementServices, CN=SCP
```

The Certification links show in the Cluster Details of the Active Directory Rights Management Services console.

If you need to remove a previous SCP so that you can install a new AD RMS, you can remove an SCP by using the ADScpRegister.exe tool included in the RMS Administration Toolkit, which can be downloaded using the Microsoft Download Center's website. You can also use ASDI Edit.

To register the SCP, you must be a member of the local AD RMS Enterprise Administrators group and the Active Directory Domain Services (AD DS) Enterprise Admins group.

CHANGE THE SCP

GET READY. To change the SCP, perform the following steps:

1. Using the Server Manager, click Tools > Active Directory Rights Management Services.
2. When the *Active Directory Rights Management Services* console opens, right-click the server, and then click Properties.
3. When the *Properties* dialog box open, click the SCP tab.
4. On the *SCP* tab (see Figure 21-4), click to select the Change SCP option.

Figure 21-4
Changing SCP

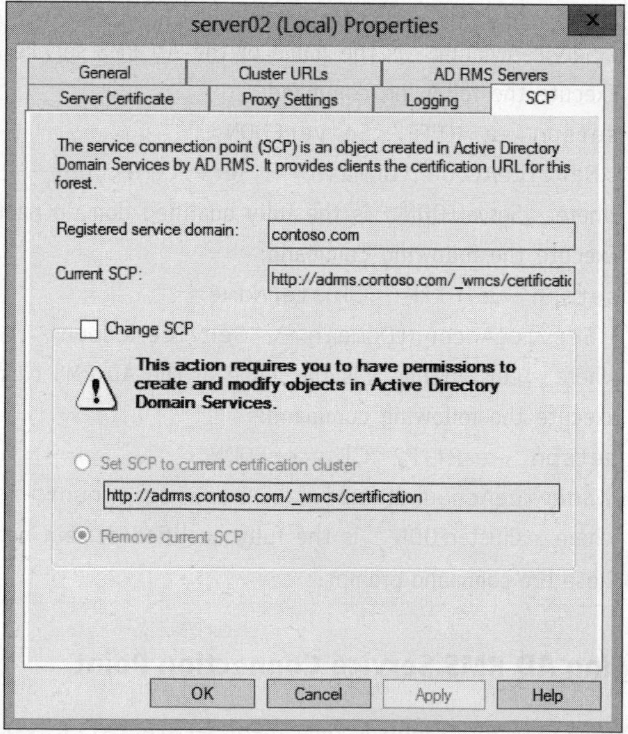

5. Click to select the Set SCP to current certification cluster, and type the new URL.
6. Click OK to close the *Properties* dialog box.

AD DS clients automatically get the SCP from Active Directory. If you have a client computer that is not part of the Active Directory forest, you must use registry keys to point to the AD RMS cluster. These registry keys are created in:

```
HKEY_Local_Machine\Software\Microsoft\MSDRM\ServiceLocation\Activation
```

The Activation key is a string, which would have the value of:

```
http(s)://<your_cluster>/wmcs/certification
```

Managing AD RMS Client Deployment

For clients to use AD RMS, the clients must be running the AD RMS client.

Windows Vista, Windows 7, Windows 8, Windows Server 2008, Windows Server 2008 R2, Windows Server 2012, and Windows Server 2012 R2 include the AD RMS client. These clients do not need additional configuration when part of the forest hosts AD RMS. The AD RMS client software is available from Microsoft.com for Windows XP, Windows Server 2003, Windows Server 2003 R2, and MAC OS X.

Besides having the AD RMS client software, you also need an AD RMS compatible applications, such as Microsoft Office 2003, 2007, 2010, or 2013. Figure 21-5 shows Microsoft

Figure 21-5

Restricting a Microsoft Word document

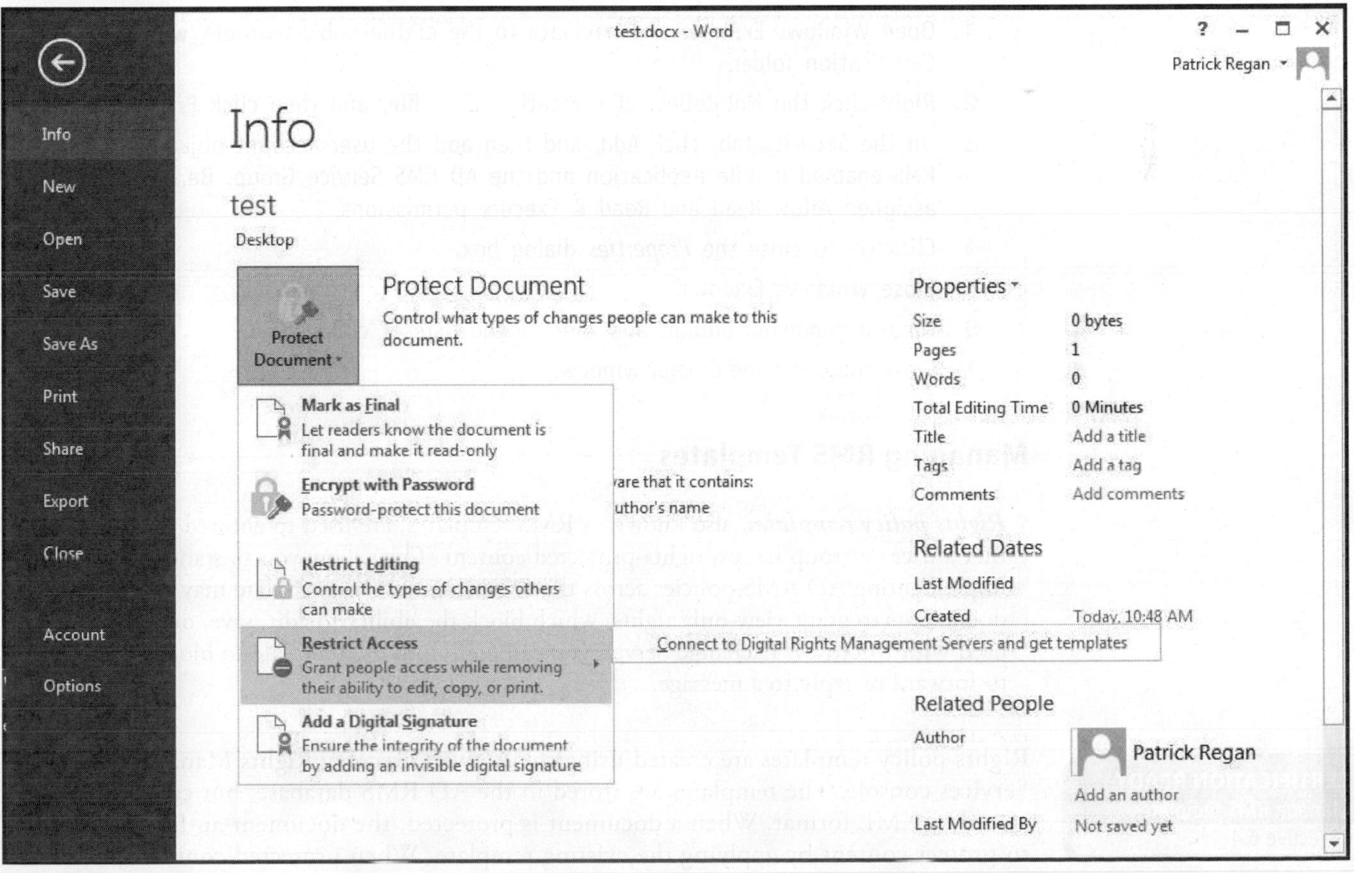

Word 2012 restricting editing by using AD RMS. In addition, Microsoft XPS viewer and Windows Internet Explorer are also able to view AD RMS-protected content. Server applications that support AD RMS include the following:

- Microsoft Exchange Server 2007
- Exchange Server 2010
- Exchange Server 2013
- Microsoft Office SharePoint Server 2007
- SharePoint Server 2010
- SharePoint Server 2013

Supporting Mobile Devices

AD RMS can provide rights account certificates and use licenses to AD RMS-enabled applications and devices running Windows mobile operating systems such as Windows Mobile 6 and above.

In a default AD RMS installation, mobile devices cannot obtain certificates and licenses for their users. However, you can enable mobile devices by configuring the DACLs of the MobileDeviceCertification.asmx file.

ENABLE AND CONFIGURE FEDERATED IDENTITY SUPPORT SETTINGS

GET READY. To enable and configure Federated Identity Support Settings, perform the following steps:

1. Open Windows Explorer and navigate to the c:\Inetpub\wwwroot_wmcs\Certification folder.
2. Right-click the MobileDeviceCertification.asmx file, and then click Properties.
3. On the Security tab, click Add, and then add the user account object of the AD RMS-enabled mobile application and the AD RMS Service Group. Be sure both are assigned Allow Read and Read & Execute permissions.
4. Click OK to close the *Properties* dialog box.
5. Close Windows Explorer.
6. Open a command prompt and execute the iisreset command.
7. Close the *command prompt* window.

Managing RMS Templates

Rights policy templates, also known as RMS templates, are used to enforce the rights that a user or group has on rights-protected content. They allow you to standardize the implementing AD RMS policies across the organization. One template may be used on documents to grant view-only rights, which block the ability to edit, save, or print. If used with Microsoft Exchange Server, you can configure the template to block the ability to forward or reply to a message.

CERTIFICATION READY
Manage RMS templates.
Objective 6.4

Rights policy templates are created using the Active Directory Rights Management Services console. The templates are stored in the AD RMS database, but can also be stored in XML format. When a document is protected, the document author can choose to protect content by applying the existing template. When protected content is accessed, the AD RMS-aware application checks with AD RMS to verify that it has the most recent version of the template.

AD RMS templates support the following rights:

- **Full Control:** Gives a user full control over an AD RMS–protected document including the ability to give other people access to the document.
- **View:** Gives a user the ability to view an AD RMS–protected document.
- **Edit:** Allows a user to modify an AD RMS–protected document.
- **Save:** Allows a user to use the Save function with an AD RMS–protected document.
- **Export (Save as):** Allows a user to use the Save As function with an AD RMS–protected document.
- **Print:** Allows an AD RMS–protected document to be printed.
- **Forward:** Used with Exchange Server, allows the recipient of an AD RMS–protected message to forward that message.
- **Reply:** Used with Exchange Server, allows the recipient of an AD RMS–protected message to reply to that message.
- **Reply All:** Used with Exchange Server, allows the recipient of an AD RMS–protected message to use the Reply All function to reply to that message.
- **Extract:** Allows the user to copy data from the file. If this right is not granted, the user cannot copy data from the file.
- **Allow Macros:** Allow the user to utilize macros.
- **View Rights:** Allow the user to view assigned rights.
- **Edit Rights:** Allow the user to modify the assigned rights.

Different from NTFS permissions, AD RMS rights can only be granted and cannot be explicitly denied. If a user has not been assigned rights to the document or email, users will automatically be denied to the document or email.

AD RMS templates can also be used to configure documents with the following properties:

- **Content expiration:** Determines when the content expires. The options are Never, Expires on a particular date, or Expires after a set number of days.
- **Use license expiration:** Determines the time interval in which the use license expires. When the use license expires, a new one needs to be acquired.
- **Enable users to view protected content using a browser add-on:** Allows content to be viewed using a browser add-on, which allows a user to not have an AD RMS–aware application to access a document.
- **Require a new use license each time content is consumed:** This option also disables client-side caching, which means that the document cannot be accessed when the computer is offline.
- **Revocation policies:** Allows the use of a revocation list so that you can revoke rights to consume content after the rights have been granted. By default, the revocation list is checked once every 24 hours.

CREATE A DISTRIBUTED RIGHTS POLICY TEMPLATE

GET READY. To create a distributed rights policy template, perform the following steps:

1. Using the Server Manager, open the Active Directory Rights Management Services console.
2. Expand the cluster, and click Rights Policy Templates.

3. In the *Actions* pane, click Create Distributed Rights Policy Template.
4. When the *Create Distributed Rights Policy Template Wizard* starts, click Add.
5. On the *Add New Template Identification Information* page, enter the following information, and then click Add:
    - **Language:** English (United States)
    - **Name:** Read-only template
    - **Description:** Read only access. No copy or print
6. Click Next.
7. On the *Add User Rights* page (see Figure 21-6), click Add.

Figure 21-6

Adding user rights to a rights policy template

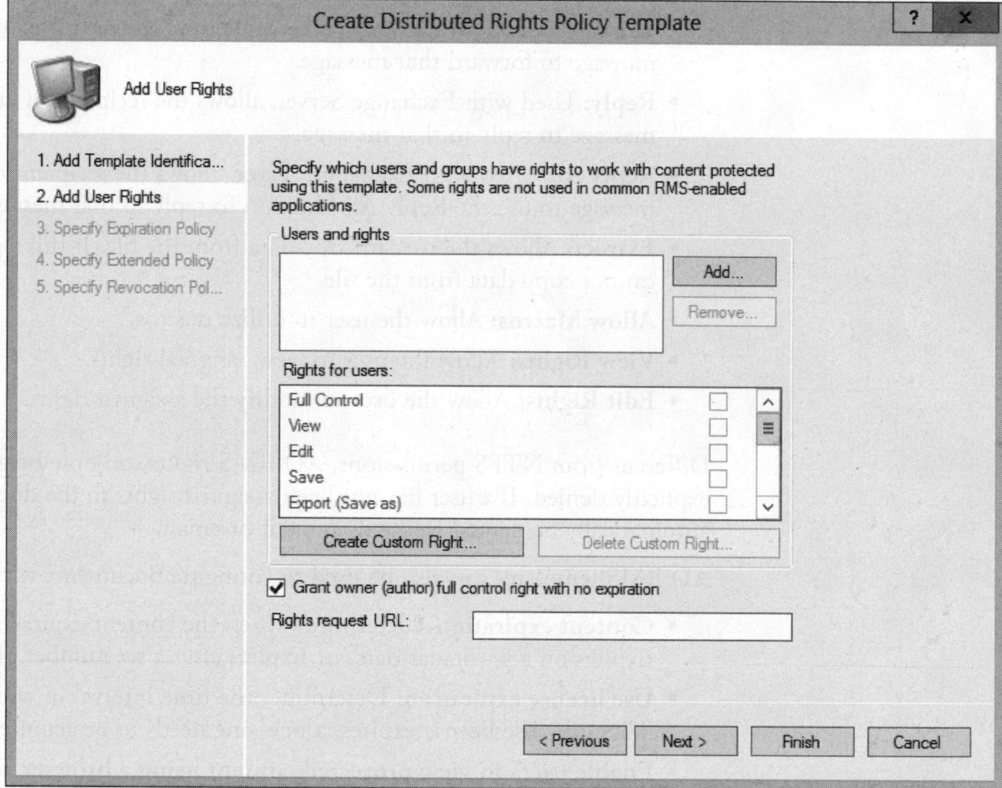

8. On the Add User or Group dialog box, enter managers@contoso.com, and then click OK.
9. When *managers@contoso.com* is selected, under the *Rights* section, click the View right. The Grant owner (author) full control right with no expiration is selected. Click Next.
10. On the *Specify Expiration Policy* page, choose the following settings and then click Next:
    - Content Expiration: Expires after the following duration (days): 7
    - Use license expiration: Expires after the following duration (days): 7
11. On the *Specify Extended Policy* page, click Require a new use license every time content is consumed (disable client-side caching), and then click Next.
12. On the *Specify Revocation Policy* page, click Finish.

After an AD RMS policy template is applied to a document, when the template is updated, the protected documents using the template are also modified. Template changes occur when the EUL is acquired. If EULs are configured not to expire and the user who is accessing the document already has a license, then the user may not receive the updated template.

It is recommended that you do not delete templates. If you do delete a template, any document that uses the template will become inaccessible to everyone except the members of the super users group. Instead, it is recommended to archive templates.

You can view the rights associated with a template by selecting the template in the Active Directory Rights Management Services console, and then in the Actions menu, clicking *View Rights Summary*.

In some instances, you may have a need for users to access RMS-protected content when the user is offline and not have access to the RMS server. You can configure computers to acquire and store published rights policy templates automatically, so that they are available offline. To enable this feature, computers must run the following Windows operating systems:

- Windows Vista SP1 or newer
- Windows 7
- Windows 8
- Windows Server 2008
- Windows Server 2008 R2
- Windows Server 2012
- Windows Server 2012 R2

Next, you need to configure a local copy of the available rights policy templates. To accomplish this, you need to perform the following:

1. In Task Scheduler, enable the AD RMS Rights Policy Template Management (Automated) Scheduled Task.
2. Edit the following registry key:
   `HKEY_CURRENT_USER\Software\Microsoft\Office\12.0\Common\DRM to %LocalAppData%\Microsoft\DRM\Templates`
3. Create a shared folder to store the templates.
4. Open the Active Directory Rights Management Services console, right-click the *Rights Policy Templates* node, and then click *Properties* to specify the location of the shared folder to which the templates will be published.

As the scheduled task executes, the AD RMS client polls the AD RMS cluster for new templates and updates the existing templates.

Configuring Exclusion Policies

Exclusion policies allow you to specify which user accounts, client software, and applications are automatically denied access to AD RMS. They also allow you to specify a minimum version of the AD RMS client software.

CERTIFICATION READY
Configure exclusion policies.
Objective 6.4

The User Exclusion policy allows you to configure AD RMS so that specific user accounts cannot obtain Use Licenses. User Exclusion is disabled by default. After you enable User Exclusion, you can specify the RACs based on the user's email address (Active Directory Domain Services accounts) or public key strings (for external users).

WARNING The Application Exclusion can be circumvented by renaming the executable file.

Application Exclusion allows you to block specific applications, such as Office PowerPoint, from creating or consuming AD RMS–protected content. Application Exclusion is disabled by default. After enabling application exclusion information, you can add an exclusion, where you specify the name of the executable file and the minimum and maximum version of the executable.

The Lockbox Exclusion allows you to exclude older AD RMS clients. Lockbox version exclusion is disabled by default. After you have enabled Lockbox version exclusion, you must specify the minimum lockbox version that can be used with the AD RMS cluster.

ENABLE AND CONFIGURE APPLICATION EXCLUSION

GET READY. To enable and configure application exclusion, perform the following steps:

1. Using the Server Manager, open the Active Directory Rights Management Services console.
2. Expand the cluster, and click Exclusion Policies node.
3. Click Manage application exclusion list.
4. In the *Actions* pane, click Enable Application Exclusion.
5. In the *Actions* pane, click Exclude Application.
6. In the *Exclude Application* dialog box, enter the following information, and then click Finish:
   - Application File name: Powerpnt.exe
   - Minimum version: 14.0.0.0
   - Maximum version: 16.0.0.0
7. To close the Exclude Application dialog box, click Finish.

Backing Up and Restoring AD RMS

As with any recovery from a disaster, the best method of recovery for AD RMS is to have a back up of the AD RMS environment from which you can restore. If the RMS server and any remote database servers are a virtual machine, you can back up VMs using Windows Backup with Hyper-V. If not, you will have to back up all related machines using Windows Backup, including the system state and all databases.

CERTIFICATION READY
Back up and restore AD RMS.
Objective 6.4

In a worst-case scenario, if you have recreate the entire AD RMS system from scratch, you will need to back up the following three databases from the database server:

- **Configuration database:** Stores, shares, and retrieves all configuration data and other data that the service needs to manage account certification, licensing, and publishing services for a whole cluster.
- **Directory services database:** Contains information about users, identifiers (such as e-mail addresses), security ID (SID), group membership, and alternate identifiers.
- **Logging database:** The historical data about client activity and license acquisition.

To back up these databases, you can use Windows Backup (as explained in the 70-411 course) or you can use SQL Server Management Studio. If you lose the SQL server, you will just have to restore or rebuild the computer with the same name, install or restore the SQL server software, and then restore the AD RMS databases.

If you have to recreate a new AD RMS cluster, you will need to first delete the existing Service Connection Point from Active Directory using the Active Directory Sites and Services, specifically the Services\RightsManagementServices\SCP node. You will then install a new database server or provision a database server that will host the new AD RMS database. You can then install the new AD RMS cluster with the same AD RMS URL that points to the new AD RMS database. If necessary, you will finish by restoring the SQL databases from backup.

The AD RMS protected content will not typically be found on the AD RMS server. For all intents and purposes, you should regularly back up those folders that contain AD RMS protected content for any other account that can open and read the files. If the content is missing, you can restore the files from backup. In some situations, you might need to use a super user to back up protected individual files or emails within Microsoft SharePoint or Exchange.

SKILL SUMMARY

IN THIS LESSON YOU LEARNED:

- Active Directory Rights Management Services (AD RMS) is technology used to provide an extra level of security to documents such as email, Microsoft Office documents, and web pages by using encryption to limit who can access a document or web page and what can be done with a document or web page.
- After the AD RMS server is installed and configured and the clients are configured to use the AD RMS server, when accessing secure documents, the decryption of a document occurs transparently.
- The primary tool to manage AD RMS is using the Active Directory Rights Management Services console (as shown in Figure 21-2). When you open the console, you can see the cluster name, the intranet and extranet cluster URLs, and the location of the databases.
- Members of the super users group are granted owner use licenses when they request a user license from the AD RMS cluster. It allows the members to decrypt all AD RMS-protected content published by the cluster.
- The Active Directory Rights Management Services (AD RMS) Service Connection Point (SCP) is an object in Active Directory that holds the web address of the AD RMS certification cluster. It was defined during the installation of AD RMS. AD RMS-enabled applications use the SCP to find the AD RMS service.
- For clients to use AD RMS, they must run the AD RMS client.
- Windows Vista, Windows 7, and Windows 8, Windows Server 2008, Windows Server 2008 R2, Windows Server 2012, and Windows Server 2012 R2 include the AD RMS client.
- Rights policy templates, also known as RMS templates, are used to enforce the rights that a user or group has on rights-protected content. They allow you to standardize the implementation of AD RMS policies across the organization.
- Exclusion policies allow you to specify accounts, client software, and applications to be denied access to AD RMS. It also allows you to specify a minimum version of the AD RMS client software.
- The best method to restore a failed AD RMS system is to back up the AD RMS systems, including the system state, all AD RMS databases, and the AD RMS protected content.

Knowledge Assessment

Multiple Choice

Select the correct answer for each of the following questions.

1. What do you need to configure to grant licenses to another forest within your organization?
   a. trusted publishing domain
   b. trusted user domains
   c. federation trust
   d. email server
2. By default, which group is the Super Users?
   a. Domain admins
   b. Enterprise admins
   c. RMS Admins
   d. It is disabled and not defined
3. What is the default validity time for RAC?
   a. 7 days
   b. 30 days
   c. 365 days
   d. 90 days
4. Which certificate contains the public key that encrypts the content key in a publishing license?
   a. AD RMS machine certificate
   b. Client licensor certificate
   c. RAC
   d. SLC
5. In addition to the AD RMS root cluster, what is needed before you can create the AD RMS root cluster?
   a. Failover cluster feature
   b. Network load balancing feature
   c. Microsoft SQL Server 2008
   d. File Sharing Services role
6. Which two actions are needed to configure AD RMS to use Kerberos? (Choose two answers.)
   a. Configure the app pool used for the IIS application to a domain admin accountt
   b. Register a service principal name (SPN) for AD RMS
   c. Register a service connection point (SCP) for AD RMS
   d. Configure the useAppPoolCredentials attribute in IIS
7. You are responsible for the Active Directory Rights Management Services cluster for your organization. You use several policy templates that are updated frequently. You need to ensure that users can receive the updated policy templates. What should you do? (Choose two answers.)
   a. Modify the registry on the AD RMS servers
   b. Modify the registry on the client computers
   c. Enable the AD RMS Rights Policy Template Management Scheduled task
   d. Configure the AD RMS Push utility
8. You change the password for the service account that is used by AD RMS. Which console should you use to configure AD RMS to use the new password?
   a. Active Directory Rights Management Services
   b. Active Directory Sites and Services
   c. Active Directory Users and Computers
   d. Services

9. You want a fellow administrator to modify the service connection point (SCP) for the AD RMS. She is a member of the AD RMS Enterprise Administrators group. What other group must be a member so that she can perform her assigned tasks?
    a. AD RMS Super Users
    b. AD RMS Auditors
    c. Schema admins
    d. Domain admins
    e. Enterprise admins
10. You have Windows XP, Windows 7, and Windows 8 clients on your network. You have two domain controllers running Windows Server 2012 R2, and the file server runs Windows Server 2008 R2. What do you need to do so that all users can access the content-protected documents?
    a. Update the Windows XP to Windows 7 or Windows 8
    b. Make sure Windows XP has the latest service pack and install the RMS client on the XP machines
    c. Migrate the AD RMS to a domain controller
    d. Install the RMS client on the Windows XP and Windows 7 computers
11. You have deployed Active Directory Rights Management Services (AD RMS). You have clients running Windows 7 and Windows 8. You discover that some users cannot use AD RMS to protect their documents. What do you need to do to fix this problem?
    a. Configure an email account for each user
    b. Add the AD RMS Admin account in the local administrators group on each client computer
    c. Reinstall the Active Directory domain in user computers
    d. Change the domain functional level to Windows Server 2008 R2
12. Last year, you had a junior administrator who was installing and configuring an Active Directory Rights Management server. Although he removed the server, you still get an error message indicating that an existing AD RMS service connection point (SCP) was found. How do you remove the existing AD RMS SCP?
    a. Use Active Directory Sites and Services
    b. Use Active Directory Users and Computers
    c. Use ADSI Edit
    d. Use the Certificate Authority
13. How many databases are used by an AD RMS system?
    a. 1
    b. 2
    c. 3
    d. 4
14. What is the first action you should perform before you reinstall a new AD RMS cluster that previously failed?
    a. Restore the databases
    b. Restore the system state
    c. Restore the AD RMS program folder
    d. Delete the SCP from Active Directory
15. Which database stores the users that have been granted access to AD RMS protected documents?
    a. Logging database
    b. Directory service database
    c. ADSI database
    d. Configuration database

Matching and Identification

1. Match the following certificates and licenses.
   _______ **a)** Client Licensor Certificate
   _______ **b)** rights account certificate
   _______ **c)** End User License
   _______ **d)** Publishing License
   _______ **e)** server licensor certificate
   _______ **f)** AD RMS machine certificate
   1. Determines the rights that apply to AD RMS-protected content
   2. Issued the first time a user attempts to access AD RMS-protected content and is used to identify a specific user
   3. Used to identity a trusted computer or device
   4. Contains the public key that encrypts the content key in a publishing license
   5. Required to consume AD RMS-protected content
   6. Allows a user to publish AD RMS-protected content when the client is not connected to the same network as the AD RMS cluster

Build a List

1. Identify the steps in order of how a document is protected using AD RMS by placing the number of the step in the appropriate space. Not all steps will be used.
   _____ The author defines the usage rights and usage of the file
   _____ The symmetric key is encrypted to the public key of the AD RMS that is used by the author
   _____ The AD RMS decrypts the symmetric key
   _____ The application encrypts the file with a symmetric key
   _____ First time users get a client licensor certificate from the AD RMS server
   _____ NTFS rights are regenerated
2. Identify the steps in order used to access content-protected documents by placing the number of the step in the appropriate space. Not all steps will be used.
   _____ User opens the file-protected document
   _____ User is granted EFS rights
   _____ AD RMS server decrypts the symmetric key
   _____ First time users get a client licensor certificate from the AD RMS server
   _____ First time users have an account certificate issued
   _____ AD RMS server re-encrypts the symmetric key using the recipients public key and adds the encrypted session key to the Use License
   _____ If the user is authorized, the AD RMS issues a Use License
3. Identify the four basic steps in order when configuring a local copy of the available policy templates. Not all steps will be used.
   _____ Create a shared folder to store the templates
   _____ Specify the NTFS permissions to Everyone Allow Full Control
   _____ Edit the DRM registry key
   _____ Configure an exclusion policy
   _____ Enable the AD RMS Rights Policy Template Management Scheduled task
   _____ Open the properties of the Rights Policy Templates and specify the location of the shared folder

Choose an Option

1. See Figure 21-7. Under Active Directory Rights Management Services at the left, which node would you access to enable and configure the AD RMS Super Users?

Figure 21-7

Enabling and configuring AD RMS Super Users

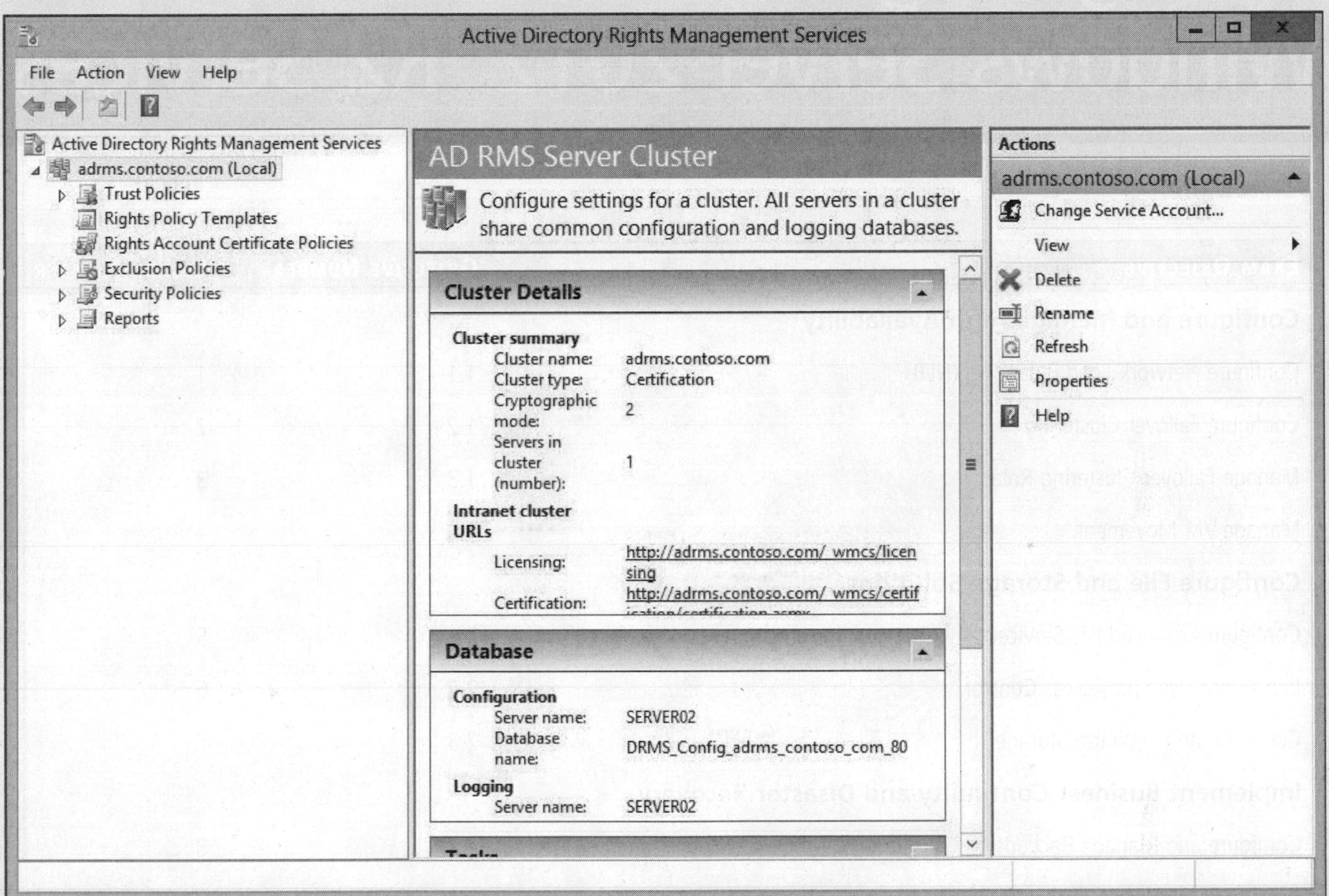

■ Business Case Scenarios

Scenario 21-1: Protecting Confidential Information

You are the administrator for the Contoso Corporation. The Contoso Corporation has some design documents that must not fall into the hands of competitors. You want to ensure that the documents cannot be forwarded to anyone outside of the company. What should you do?

Scenario 21-2: Recovering AD RMS

You are the administrator for the Contoso Corporation. Your AD RMS server crashed. You have a back up of the databases, but you do not have a back up of the AD RMS server. What should you do to restore everything back to the way it was?

Appendix A
Exam 70-412 Configuring Advanced Windows Server 2012 R2 Services

Exam Objective	Objective Number	Lesson Number
Configure and Manage High Availability		
Configure Network Load Balancing (NLB)	1.1	1
Configure Failover Clustering	1.2	2
Manage Failover Clustering Roles	1.3	3
Manage VM Movement	1.4	4
Configure File and Storage Solutions		
Configure Advanced File Services	2.1	5
Implement Dynamic Access Control	2.2	6
Configure and Optimize Storage	2.3	7
Implement Business Continuity and Disaster Recovery		
Configure and Manage Backups	3.1	8
Recover Servers	3.2	9
Configure Site-Level Fault Tolerance	3.3	10
Configure Network Services		
Implement an Advanced Dynamic Host Configuration Protocol (DHCP) Solution	4.1	11
Implement an Advanced DNS Solution	4.2	12
Deploy and Manage IP Address Management (iPAM)	4.3	13
Configure the Active Directory Infrastructure		
Configuring a Forest or a Domain	5.1	14
Configure Trusts	5.2	15
Configure Sites	5.3	16
Manage Active Directory and SYSVOL Replication	5.4	17

(continued)

Exam Objective	Objective Number	Lesson Number
Configure Identity and Access Solutions		
Implement Active Directory Federation Services (AD FS)	6.1	18
Install and Configure Active Directory Certificate Services (AD CS)	6.2	19
Manage Certificates	6.3	20
Install and Configure Active Directory Rights Management Services (AD RMS)	6.4	21

Index

Note: Page numbers followed by 'f' and 't' indicates figure and table respectively.

B

D

P

Q

R

S

W

X

Z